STUDIES ON VOLTAIRE AND
THE EIGHTEENTH CENTURY

239

General editor

PROFESSOR H. T. MASON

Department of French
University of Bristol
Bristol BS8 1TE

C. P. COURTNEY

A guide to the published works
of Benjamin Constant

THE VOLTAIRE FOUNDATION

AT THE TAYLOR INSTITUTION, OXFORD

1985

ISSN 0435-2866

ISBN 0 7294 0330 0

Printed in England at The Alden Press, Oxford

Contents

Introduction

THIS guide is arranged in two parts. The first part is a checklist in which I have attempted to record all editions of Constant's writings published in his lifetime and from his death in 1830 to the present day. The term 'edition' has been interpreted broadly to include collections of correspondence and, for the sake of completeness, I have listed separate letters published in monographs and periodicals. I have also listed Constant's contributions to newspapers and periodicals, though research on this important topic is far from complete. The second part is a chronology of works by Constant published (or prepared for the press) in his lifetime.

The checklist

The arrangement of the checklist is similar to that of my *Bibliography of editions of the writings of Benjamin Constant to 1833* (London 1981), items being listed chronologically within each section and each series of entries, with translations being placed together to follow editions in the original French. For editions published up to 1833 I offer an abridgment of the descriptions given in the *Bibliography* and the information recorded normally includes titles (adapted to lower-case transcription), format, pagination, imprints of both publisher and printer and selected locations, usually one English, one French and one Swiss library where possible. For editions published after 1833 I give a simpler description, omitting printers' imprints and references to format, except for *Adolphe*, where the size of each edition is given in centimetres. For these later editions I likewise give selected locations (except for items which are still in print or readily available) and, whenever possible, reviews. Smaller selections of Constant's works which contain *Adolphe* (often along with *Le Cahier rouge* and *Cécile*) are listed in the section devoted to *Adolphe*, and cross-references from the other sections are provided where this seems appropriate. However, exhaustive cross-references are not given to works in the various collections listed in section E of the bibliography, where individual items can be located by consulting the index. The checklist is based, as far as possible, on personal inspection of the items listed, and, where this has proved impossible, I have relied on photocopies and information supplied by librarians or, as a last resort, on such works of reference as national bibliographies and the *Index translationum*. Where a location is given it can be assumed that I have seen the edition in question myself or received a description of it from a reliable authority.

The reader requiring fuller information on items published up to 1833 should consult the *Bibliography of editions*, which includes full bibliographical descriptions, discussion of dates of publication, details of printers' declarations and (where available) references to contemporary reviews.

The chronology

This provisional account lists works published in Constant's lifetime by date of publication, except for speeches, which are listed by the date on which they were delivered. Posthumous works and works no longer extant are listed, as far as possible, by date of composition. The date of publication of works published in France after 1810 is normally given from the records of the Archives de la librairie (Archives nationales); it should be noted that when two dates of *dépôt légal* are given, the first is the 'date de l'expédition' and the second the 'date de l'arrivée'. While the list excludes any detailed account of Constant's manuscripts, it has seemed useful to include the *Œuvres manuscrites* of 1810, most of which have now been published, as well as the early manuscripts (1774-1794) and a few other items described by Rudler. Among printed material the chronology excludes volumes of miscellaneous parliamentary oratory, except when Constant's name is on the title page. Also excluded are contemporary newspaper reports of Constant's speeches, which, for convenience, are cited from the *Archives parlementaires*.

While the present guide offers a fuller record of Constant's published writings than any of the existing bibliographies of his works, it would be surprising if there were not many items (particularly translations and articles in periodicals) that have eluded my enquiry. Information which might contribute to a list of addenda and corrigenda will be gratefully received and acknowledged.

Christ's College   C.P.C.
Cambridge

Acknowledgements

IN preparing this guide I have been fortunate in receiving help from many sources. I am grateful for advice and information to Professor Alison Fairlie, Professor L. R. Lewitter, Mr George Gömöri, Dr Roger Paulin, Dr Paul Ries, Dr Geoffrey Walker and Mr Joachim Whaley of the University of Cambridge; Mr J. C. T. Oates, Mr A. G. Parker, Mr Geoffrey Roper, Mr E. P. Tyrrell, Mrs C. J. Whitford, Miss E. L. Moffatt, Mrs Valerie Hall, Mr A. K. Dalby and Mr David Lowe of the Cambridge University Library; Miss Elizabeth Falconer and Mr Timothy Penton of the Modern and Medieval Languages Libraries; Mr Giles Barber and Mr David Gilson of the Taylor Institution Library; and Dr Dennis Wood of the University of Birmingham. Among librarians who kindly answered my bibliographical queries and helped in other ways, I wish to thank Mlle Annie Angremy, Bibliothèque nationale, Paris; Dr Leonard N. Beck, Curator of Special Collections, Library of Congress; M. G. Bouchard, Conservateur-adjoint, Bibliothèque municipale, Montpellier; M. P. Boussel, Conservateur en chef, Bibliothèque historique de la ville de Paris; Dr Müjgan Cunbur, Librarian of the Millî Kütüphane, Ankara; Mme Yvonne Fernillot, Bibliothèque de la Sorbonne; Dr Branko Hanž, Associate Director, Nacionalna i sveučilišna Bibloteka, Zagreb; Dr István Márffy, Fövárosi Szabó Ervin Könyvtár, Budapest; Mrs Libby Kahane, Jewish National and University Library, Jerusalem; Mgr Mirosława Kocięcka, Biblioteka Narodowa, Warsaw; Dr Åke Lilliestam, Kungliga Biblioteket, Stockholm; Mr Roberto Liter, Biblioteca Nacional, Madrid; M. M. Lordereau, Bibliothèque municipale, Besançon; Mr Y. Morita, National Diet Library, Tokyo; M. M. Nortier, Centre national des échanges (Bibliothèque nationale, Paris); Dr György Pajkossy, Országos Széchényi Könyvtár, Budapest; Miss Katharine F. Pantzer, Houghton Library, Harvard University; Mrs Yordanka Parvanova, Deputy Director, Cyril and Methodius National Library, Sofia; Miss A. Phillips, Librarian of Newnham College, Cambridge; Dr Åse Reymann, Kongelige Bibliotek, Copenhagen; Mrs Ann M. Seemann, Schaffer Library, Union College, Schenectady; Mrs Maria Alzira Proença Simões, Biblioteca Nacional, Lisbon; Dr John L. Sharpe III, Curator of Rare Books, William R. Perkins Library, Duke University; Mrs Florence E. Blakely and Mrs Janet L. Thomason of the same library; Dr W. Sperisen, Director, Zentralbibliothek, Lucerne; Dr Magda Strebl, Österreichische Nationalbibliothek, Vienna; Dr K. Thomsen, Universitetsbiblioteket, Oslo; Mr N. R. Thorpe, Glasgow University Library; M. Chr. Viredaz, Institut Benjamin Constant, Lausanne; and Miss Marjorie G. Wynne, Yale University Library. I am particularly grateful to Dr E. L. Nemirovsky, Director of the Department of Rare Books in the State Lenin Library, Moscow, and to Mrs E. I. Yatsunok of the same library, who (with Mr Tyrrell kindly acting as intermediary) supplied information given in the checklist on the early Russian translations of *Adolphe*. I am grateful to Maître Claude Raymond (Lausanne) who kindly placed his private collection of rare Constant items at my disposal, and to M. Paul Delbouille of the University of

Liège, for supplying information based on his extraordinary collection of editions of *Adolphe*. To the many librarians who replied anonymously to my queries I am likewise extremely grateful. The secondary sources to which I am indebted are listed at the end of the checklist. Those of Cordié, Delbouille, Harpaz, Hofmann and Lowe have been particularly useful. Material from my *Bibliography of editions* is reproduced by kind permission of the publisher, the Modern Humanities Research Association. For financial assistance which enabled me to visit a large number of libraries I am grateful to the French government, the British Academy, the University of Cambridge and Christ's College. Finally, for the physical preparation of the guide I am indebted to Dr J. L. Dawson and his staff (particularly Mrs Monique Johnson and Ven. S. K. Yeshe Zangmo), of the Literary and Linguistic Computing Centre, Faculty of Modern and Medieval Languages, University of Cambridge.

Abbreviations

Library symbols

Note: the symbols used for American libraries are those of the *National Union Catalog*.

A   Universiteitsbibliotheek, Amsterdam
ADS   Archives départementales de la Sarthe, Le Mans
AN   Archives nationales, Paris
Ankara   Millî Kütüphane, Ankara
AR   Bibliothèque de l'Arsenal, Paris
B   Schweizerische Landesbibliothek, Bern
BAN   Bibliothèque de l'Assemblée nationale, Paris
BCU   Bibliothèque cantonale et universitaire, Lausanne
Bes   Bibliothèque municipale, Besançon
BI   Bibliothèque de l'Institut, Paris
BL   British Library, London
BN   Bibliothèque nationale, Paris
Bp   Országos Széchényi Könyvtár, Budapest
BpFS   Fővárosi Szabó Ervin Könyvtár, Budapest
BPL   Bibliothèque des Pasteurs, Lausanne
BPU   Bibliothèque publique et universitaire, Geneva
BR   Bibliothèque royale Albert 1er, Brussels
Bs   Öffentliche Bibliothek der Universität, Basel
Buch   Biblioteca Academiei Republicii Socialiste România, Bucharest
Bx   Bibliothèque municipale, Bordeaux
C   Cambridge University Library
Ca   Bibliothèque municipale, Cahors
CKB   Kongelige Bibliotek, Copenhagen
CN   Newnham College Library, Cambridge
CtY   Yale University
CU   University of California, Berkeley
DLC   Library of Congress
E   Edinburgh University Library
G   Niedersächsische Staats- und Universitätsbibliothek, Göttingen
GL   Glasgow University Library
Graz   Universitätsbibliothek, Graz
H   Koninklijke Bibliotheek, The Hague
Hels   Helsinki University Library
ICRL   Center for Research Libraries, Chicago
J   The Jewish National and University Library, Jerusalem
L   Bibliotheek der Rijksuniversiteit, Leyden
Lisbon   Biblioteca nacional, Lisbon
LU   Zentralbibliothek, Lucerne

M   Universitätsbibliothek, Marburg
Mar   Deutsches Literaturarchiv, Schiller-Nationalmuseum, Marbach a. Neckar
MB   Boston Public Library
MBN   Biblioteca nacional, Madrid
MiU   University of Michigan, Ann Arbor
MH   Harvard University
MnU   University of Minnesota
Mp   Bibliothèque municipale, Montpellier
MU   University of Massachusetts
MWelC   Wellesley College, Wellesley
N   Bibliothèque publique de la Ville, Neuchâtel
NcD   Duke University
NcU   University of North Carolina
NIC   Cornell University, Ithaca
NLH   Niedersächsische Landesbibliothek, Hanover
NmLcU   Thomas Brannigan Memorial Library, Las Cruces
NN   New York Public Library
NSchU   Union College, Schenectady
O   Bodleian Library, Oxford
OrPS   Portland State Library
Oslo   Universitetsbiblioteket, Oslo
OT   Taylor Institution Library, Oxford
OU   Ohio State University, Columbus
PPL   Library Company of Philadelphia
Prague   Státní Knihovna, Prague
S   Kungliga Biblioteket, Stockholm
SG   Bibliothèque Sainte-Geneviève, Paris
SLL   State Lenin Library, Moscow
Sofia   Cyril and Methodius National Library, Sofia
Sor   Bibliothèque de la Sorbonne, Paris
St   Bibliothèque nationale et universitaire, Strasbourg
T   Universitätsbibliothek, Tübingen
Tokyo   The National Diet Library, Tokyo
U   Bibliotheek der Rijksuniversiteit, Utrecht
V   Österreichische Nationalbibliothek, Vienna
VA   Victoria and Albert Museum, London
VP   Bibliothèque historique de la Ville de Paris
W   Herzog-August Bibliothek, Wolfenbüttel
Ww   Biblioteka Narodowa, Warsaw
Zagreb   Nacionalna i sveučilišna Biblioteka, Zagreb

Periodicals

ABC   *Annales Benjamin Constant*
AUS   *Annales Universitatis Saraviensis*

CBC   *Cahiers Benjamin Constant*
EHR   *English historical review*
FL   *Le Figaro littéraire*
FQ   *French quarterly*
FR   *French review*
FS   *French studies*
FSB   *French studies bulletin*
GF   *Gazette de France*
GL   *Gazette de Lausanne*
IL   *L'Information littéraire*
ICC   *Intermédiaire des chercheurs et des curieux*
JD   *Journal des débats*
JG   *Journal de Genève*
MF   *Mercure de France*
MLJ   *Modern language journal*
MLR   *Modern language review*
NL   *Les Nouvelles littéraires*
NRF   *Nouvelle revue française*
QL   *La Quinzaine littéraire*
RDM   *Revue des deux mondes*
RF   *Romanische Forschungen*
RHLF   *Revue d'histoire littéraire de la France*
RHV   *Revue historique vaudoise*
RLC   *Revue de littérature comparée*
RLMC   *Rivista di Letterature moderne e comparate*
RLV   *Revue des langues vivantes*
RP   *Revue de Paris*
RR   *Romanic review*
RSH   *Revue des sciences humaines*
SF   *Studi francesi*
TLS   *Times literary supplement*
TR   *La Table ronde*
ZFSL   *Zeitschrift für französische Sprache und Literatur*

Short-title references

Archives parlementaires.   J. Mavidal & E. Laurent, *Archives parlementaires. Deuxième série (1800 à 1860)*. Paris: Paul Dupont, 1862-1895. 92 vols.
C.   C. P. Courtney, *A bibliography of editions of the writings of Benjamin Constant to 1833*. London: Modern Humanities Research Association, 1981.
C. Suppl.   C. P. Courtney, *A bibliography ...: a supplement*. Cambridge: privately printed, 1984; second edition, revised, 1985.
Caddeo.   Rinaldo Caddeo, *Le Edizioni di Capolago, storia e critica*. Milano: Bompiani, 1934.
Catálogo general.   *Catálogo general de la Librería española e hispanoamericana*. Madrid,

Barcelona 1932-1951, 5 vols; *Catálogo general de la Librería española*. Madrid 1957-1965, 4 vols.

Cordié.   Carlo Cordié, 'Contributo bibliografico sul gruppo di Coppet', *Annali della Scuola Normale Superiore di Pisa. Lettere, storia e filosofia*, Ser. 2, 32 (1964), pp.257-350; 'Secundo contributo', *Annali* ... 36 (1967), pp.103-35; 'Terzo contributo', *Annali* ... 38 (1969), pp.129-48; 'Quarto contributo', *Annali* ... *Classe di lettere e filosofia*, Ser. 3, 1 (1971), pp.439-53; 'Quinto contributo', *Annali* ... 6 (1976), pp.1017-50.

Coulmann.   Jean-Jacques Coulmann, *Réminiscences*. Paris: Michel Lévy frères, 1862-1869. 3 vols.

De Jong.   Dirk de Jong, *Het vrije boek in onvrije tijd. Bibliografie van illegale en clandestiene bellettrie*. Leiden: Sijthoff, 1958.

Fromm.   Hans Fromm, *Bibliographie deutscher Übersetzungen aus dem Französischen, 1700-1948*. Baden-Baden: Kunst und Wissenschaft, 1950-1953. 6 vols.

Harpaz (1972).   Benjamin Constant, *Recueil d'articles: Le Mercure, La Minerve et La Renommée*; introduction, notes et commentaires par Ephraïm Harpaz. Genève: Droz, 1972. 2 vols.

Harpaz (1978).   Benjamin Constant, *Recueil d'articles, 1795-1817*; introduction, notes et commentaires par Ephraïm Harpaz. Genève: Droz, 1978.

Harpaz (1981).   Benjamin Constant, *Recueil d'articles, 1820-1824*; introduction, notes et commentaires par Ephraïm Harpaz. Genève: Droz, 1981.

Hasselrot.   Benjamin Constant, *Lettres à Bernadotte: sources et origine de l'Esprit de conquête et de l'usurpation*, publiées par Bengt Hasselrot. Genève: Droz, Lille: Giard, 1952.

Heinsius.   W. Heinsius, *Allgemeines Bücher-Lexicon*. Leipzig, 1793-1894. 19 vols.

Hidalgo.   Dionisio Hidalgo, *Diccionario general de bibliografía española*, Madrid: Escuelas Pías, 1862-1872. 5 vols.

Index translationum.   *Index translationum; Répertoire international des traductions: international bibliography of translations*. Paris: UNESCO, 1932- [in progress].

Jasinski.   Béatrice W. Jasinski, *L'Engagement de Benjamin Constant: amour et politique (1794-1796)*. Paris: Minard, 1971.

Kayser.   C. G. Kayser, *Index locupletissimus librorum* ... *Vollständiges Bücher-Lexicon*. Leipzig, 1834-1910. 36 vols.

Laboulaye.   *Cours de politique constitutionnelle*, par Benjamin Constant, avec une introduction et des notes par M. Edouard Laboulaye. Paris: Guillemin, 1861. 2 vols; deuxième édition, 1872.

Lorenz.   Otto Lorenz, *Catalogue général de la Librairie française*. Paris: Lorenz, etc., 1867-1945. 34 vols.

Palau y Dulcet.   Antonio Palau y Dulcet, *Manual del librero hispano-americano*. Barcelona, 1923- [in progress].

Pléiade.   Benjamin Constant, *Œuvres*, texte présenté et annoté par Alfred Roulin [et Charles Roth]. Paris: Gallimard, 1957. (Bibliothèque de la Pléiade 123).

Pozzo di Borgo (1964).   *Ecrits et discours politiques* par Benjamin Constant. Présentation, notes et commentaires par O. Pozzo di Borgo. [Paris]: J.-J. Pauvert, 1964. 2 vols.

Pozzo di Borgo (1965).   Benjamin Constant, *Choix de textes politiques*. Présentation et notes par O. Pozzo di Borgo. [Paris]: J.-J. Pauvert, 1965.

Quérard.　J.-M. Quérard, *La France littéraire*. Paris: Didot, 1827-1864. 12 vols.

Roulin & Roth.　Benjamin Constant, *Journaux intimes*, édition intégrale des manuscrits autographes publiée par Alfred Roulin et Charles Roth. Paris: Gallimard, 1952.

Rudler, *Bibliographie*.　Gustave Rudler, *Bibliographie critique des œuvres de Benjamin Constant*. Paris: Armand Colin, 1909.

Rudler, *Jeunesse*.　Gustave Rudler, *La Jeunesse de Benjamin Constant*. Paris: Armand Colin, 1909.

Simoni.　Anna E. C. Simoni, *Publish and be free: a catalogue of clandestine books printed in the Netherlands 1940-1945 in the British Library*. The Hague: Nijhoff, 1975.

Staël, *Correspondance*.　Madame [A.-L.-G] de Staël[-Holstein], *Correspondance générale*, texte établi et présenté par Béatrice W. Jasinski. Paris: J.-J. Pauvert, 1962- [in progress].

Summary of checklist

A Separate works

[1805-1807], 1980
Lettres de d'Arsillé fils, de Sophie Durfé et autres [1787-1788], 1981
A Sa Majesté l'Empereur Napoléon, [1815], 1982
Pièces relatives à mes différends avec Madame de Constant, née de
Cramm, [1793], 1982

B Speeches and official papers
Corps législatif: Conseil des Cinq-cents

B1   Aux citoyens représentans du peuple, 9 thermidor an IV [27 juillet 1796]

Tribunat: Speeches

B2   Discours ... Séance du 15 nivôse an 8 [5 janvier 1800]
B3   Opinion ... Séance du 12 pluviôse an 8 [1ᵉʳ février 1800]
B4   Opinion ... Séance du 15 ventôse an 8 [6 mars 1800]
B5   Discours ... Séance du 17 ventôse an 8 [8 mars 1800]
B6   Opinion ... Séance du 27 ventôse an 8 [18 mars 1800]
B7   Opinion ... Séance du 29 ventôse an 8 [20 mars 1800]
B8   Discours ... Séance du 3 messidor an 8 [22 juin 1800]
B9   Opinion ... Séance du 2 pluviôse an 9 [22 janvier 1801]
B10   Opinion ... Séance du 5 pluviôse an 9 [25 janvier 1801]
B11   Opinion ... Séance du 28 ventôse an 9 [19 mars 1801]
B12   Opinion ... Séance du 4 nivôse an 10 [25 décembre 1801]
B13   Seconde Opinion ... Séance du 7 nivôse an 10 [28 décembre 1801]

Chambre des Députés: Speeches and papers

B14   Opinion ... Séance du 14 avril 1819
B15   Amendemens ... Séance du [16 avril 1819]
B16   Opinion ... Séance du 14 mai 1819
B17   Opinion ... Séance du [17 mai 1819]
B18   Opinion ... Séance du 8 juin 1819
B19   Opinion ... Séance du 15 juin 1819
B20   Opinion ... Séance du 16 juin 1819
B21   Opinion ... Séance du 21 juin 1819
B22   Opinion ... Séance du 28 juin 1819
B23   Développemens ... [Séance du 14 janvier 1820]
B24   Opinion ... Séance du [7 mars 1820]
B25   Opinion ... Séance du [13 mars 1820]
B26   Rapport ... Séance du 20 mars 1820
B27   Opinion ... Séance du 23 mars 1820
B28   Opinion ... Séance du 5 avril 1820
B29   Opinion ... Séance du 15 avril 1820
B30   Opinion ... Séance du 18 avril 1820
B31   Opinion ... Séance du 28 avril 1820
B32   Discours prononcé ... dans le comité secret du 3 mai 1820
B33   Opinion ... Séance du 23 mai 1820

B34 Second discours ... Séance du 3 juin 1820
B35 Eclaircissemens sur quelques faits ... 25 décembre 1820
B36 Discours prononcés dans le comité secret du 31 janvier 1821
B37 Opinion ... Séance du 19 février 1821
B38 Opinions ... Séances du 6, 14 avril 1821
B39 Opinion ... Séance du 27 juin 1821
B40 Opinion ... Séance du 22 décembre 1821
B41 Opinion ... Séance du 11 janvier 1822
B42 Opinion ... Séance du 31 janvier 1822
B43 Opinion ... Séance du 4 février 1822
B44 Opinion ... Séance du 9 février 1822
B45 Discours ... Séance du 13 mars 1822
B46 Opinion ... Séance du 3 avril 1822
B47 Opinion ... Séance du 6 août 1822
B48 Extraits des minutes du greffe du Tribunal de première instance, 9 novembre 1822
B49 Consultation pour M. Benjamin Constant, mai 1824
B50 Discours ... Séance du 8 juin 1824
B51 Discours ... Séance du 28 juin 1824
B52 Opinion ... Séance du 8 juillet 1824
B53 Opinion improvisée ... Séance du 14 juillet 1824
B54 Opinion ... Séance du 16 juillet 1824
B55 Opinion ... Séance du 22 juillet 1824
B56 Discours ... Séance du 23 février 1825
B57 Opinion ... Séance du 7 avril 1825
B58 Opinion ... Séance du 28 avril 1825
B59 Opinion ... Séance du 10 mai 1825
B60 Discours ... Séance du 20 mars 1826
B61 Discours ... Séance du 24 avril 1826
B62 Discours ... Séance du 17 mai 1826
B63 Opinion ... Séance du 13 février 1827
B64 Développemens ... Session du 13 mars 1828
B65 Développemens ... Séance du 7 mai 1828
B66 Opinion ... Séance du 18 mars 1829
B67 Développemens ... Séance du 13 septembre 1830

C Contributions to collective works and to works by other writers

C1 Biographie universelle, 1811-1813
C2 Mémoires sur la vie de Necker, 1818 [=1817]
C3 Alphonse et Mathilde, 1819
C4 Lettres sur la situation de la France, 1820
C5 Pascaline, 1821
C6 Chefs-d'œuvre des Théâtres étrangers, 1822-1823
C7 Mélanges politiques et historiques, 1829
C8 Paris, ou le livre des Cent-et-un, 1832
C9 Des circonstances actuelles, 1906

Checklist of the published works
of Benjamin Constant

A Separate works

A1 Translation from Gillies

A1/1 1787 Essai sur les mœurs des tems héroïques de la Grèce, tiré de l'Histoire grecque de M. Gillies. A Londres; et se trouve à Paris, chez Lejay ... 1787. 8° pp.35.
Translation of chapter 2 of the following work: John Gillies, *The History of Ancient Greece*, 2 vols, London: A. Strahan and T. Cadell, 1786. For attribution of the translation to B. Constant see Rudler, *Bibliographie*, pp.44-46.
Copies: B, BN. (C.1a).

A2 De la force du gouvernement actuel de la France

A2/1 1796 De la force du gouvernement actuel de la France et de la nécessité de s'y rallier. Par Benjamin Constant, 1796. 8° pp.111, Errata [p.112].
Published in Switzerland by J. Mourer, Lausanne. Reprinted in *Le Moniteur*, 1-9 May 1796.
Copies: BCU, BL, BN. (C.2a).

A2/2 1796 De la force du gouvernement actuel de la France ... 1796. 8° pp.111.
Reprint and, in part, a reissue of the preceding item with text corrected.
Copies: BCU, BL, BN. (C.2b).

A2/3 1796 De la force du gouvernememt [*sic*] actuel de la France ... A Besançon, de l'imprimerie de J. F. Couche. IVᵉ année de la république. 8° pp.IV, [5]-45.
Copy: Bes. (C.2c).

A2/4 1797 De la force du gouvernement actuel de la France ... Strasbourg: Levrault, 1797.
Copy not located. Cited by Heinsius and Quérard. (C.2d).

Another edition: Cordié, 1944 (E4/3).

Translations

A2/t1 1796 Ueber die Kraft der gegenwärtigen Regierung Frankreichs und über die Nothwendigkeit, sich an sie anzuschließen; von Benjamin Constant.
Klio. Eine Monatschrift für die französische Zeitgeschichte, Leipzig, im Verlag der Peter Philipp Wolffischen Buchhandlung, Bd. II (1796), 5.Heft, 106-134; 6.Heft, 137-204. Translation by [Paul Usteri].

Copies: Kraus reprints in BL, C. (C.2e).

A2/t2 1796   Benjamin Constant. Von der Stärke der gegenwärtigen Regierung Frankreichs und von der Nothwendigkeit sich derselben anzuschliessen.
Frankreich im Jahr 1796. Aus den Briefen Deutscher Männer in Paris, Altona [Lübeck: Niemann], 1796, Bd. II, St. 7, 211-244; St. 8, 291-324.
Copies: C, St. (C.2f).

A2/t3 1797   Observations on the Strength of the present Government of France and upon the necessity of rallying round it. Translated from the French of Benjamin Constant, by James Losh. Bath, printed by R. Cruttwell, for G. G. and J. Robinson ... London, MDCCXCVII. 8° pp.iv, 100.
Preface (dated: 'Bath, Jan. 26th 1797') and notes by the translator.
Copies: DLC, H, O, VA. (C.2g).

A3 Des réactions politiques

A3/1 1797   Des réactions politiques. Par Benjamin Constant. An V. 8° pp.vii, 110.
Preface dated: 'Hérivaux, ce 10 Germinal, an V' [30 March 1797]. Published probably by Mourer et Pinparé, Paris.
Copies: BCU, BL, BN. (C.3a).

A3/2 1797   Des réactions politiques ... Seconde édition, augmentée de l'examen des effets de la terreur. An V. 8° pp.xlvii, 110.
Text of addition dated 10 prairial an 5 [29 May 1797]. Published probably by Mourer et Pinparé, Paris.
Copies: B, BCU, BI. (C.3b).

Other editions: *Cours de politique* 1819 (E1/1(3)), *Cours de politique* 1820 (E1/2(3)), Laboulaye 1861 (E1/5a), Laboulaye 1872 (E1/5b), Cordié 1944 (E4/3), Pozzo di Borgo 1964 (E4/6).

Translations

A3/t1 1797   Von den politischen Gegenwirkungen. Von Benjamin Constant.
Frankreich im Jahr 1797. Aus den Briefen Deutscher Männer in Paris, Altona [Lübeck: Niemann], 1797, Bd. II, St. 5, 3-27; St. 6, 99-127; St. 7, 200-213; St. 8, 291-298.
Copies: C, St. (C.3c).

A3/t2 1799   Van Wederwerkingen in den Staat. (Politieke Réactien.) Naar het Fransch door J.G.H. Hahn. In de Haag, by Izaac van Cleff. Jaar V, 1799. 8° pp.xxxii, 131.
Translator's preface dated: 'In de Haag den 30 van Lentemaand [March], Jaar V'.

Copies: H, L. (C.3d).

A3/t3 1844 Benjamín Constant. Tratado de las reacciones políticas. Barcelona, 1844. pp.80.
(Palau y Dulcet).

A3/t4 1845 A politicai ellenhatások. Irta Constant Benjamin. Fordította Halimbai Sándor. Pesten, 1845. Nyomatott Trattner-Károlyi Betüivel. (Rózsa Kálmán és neje). pp.60.
Halimbai Sándor is a pseudonym for Perlaky Sándor.
Copy: Bp.

A3/t5 1950 Benjamin Constant. Le reazioni politiche. Gli effetti del Terrore. A cura di Franco Calandra. Traduzione di Manrico Fiore. Napoli: Edizioni scientifiche italiane, 1950. (Biblioteca storica, fondata da Adolfo Omodeo, diretta da Luigi Russo). pp.126.
'Prefazione' by Franco Calandra, pp.5-12; 'Nota del traduttore', p.13.
Copies: B, BCU, BL. (Cordié 214).

A4 Des effets de la terreur

A4/1 1797 Des effets de la terreur. Par Benjamin Constant. [Paris, Mourer et Pinparé], An V. 8° pp.44.
Reprinted from item A3/2.
Copies: BCU, BL, BN. (C.4a).

A4/2 1948 Benjamin Constant. Des effets de la terreur. Introduction de Daniel Simond. Lausanne: Editions des Terreaux, [1948]. pp.59.
Review: B. Croce, *Quaderni della critica*, 19-20 (September 1951), pp.191-192.
Copies: B, BCU, BL, BN.

Other editions: Laboulaye 1861 (E1/5a), Laboulaye 1872 (E1/5b), Cordié 1944 (E4/3), Pozzo di Borgo 1964 (E4/6). See also item A3/2 above.

Translation

A4/t1 1797 Ueber die Wirkungen des Schrekens. Von Benjamin Constant.
Frankreich im Jahr 1797. Aus den Briefen Deutscher Männer in Paris, Altona [Lübeck: Niemann], 1797, Bd. III, St. 9, 3-24.
Copies: C, St. (C.4b).

A5 Speech of 16 September 1797 to the Cercle constitutionnel

A5/1 1797 Discours prononcé au Cercle constitutionnel, pour la plantation de l'arbre de la liberté, le 30 fructidor an 5 [16 September 1797]. Par Benjamin Constant. 8° pp.27. Impr. Lemaire, [Paris].

Copies: BCU, BL, BN. (C.5a).

A5/2 1797   Extrait du discours de Benjamin Constant, prononcé le 30 fructidor, au Cercle constitutionnel. f° p.1. Impr. Lemaire, [Paris].
Copy: BN. (C.5b).

Other editions: Cordié 1944 (E4/3), Pozzo di Borgo 1964 (E4/6).

A6 Speech of 27 February 1798 to the Cercle constitutionnel

A6/1 1798   Discours prononcé au Cercle constitutionnel, le 9 ventôse an VI [27 February 1798], par Benjamin Constant. 8° pp.23. Impr. Veuve Galletti, [Paris].
Reprinted in *Le Moniteur*, 11-12 March 1798.
Copies: BL, BN, VP. (C.6a).

A6/2 1798   Discours prononcé au Cercle constitutionnel, le 9 ventôse an VI, par Benjamin Constant. Le Directoire exécutif, adoptant tous les principes contenus dans ce Discours, en a ordonné l'impression de plusieurs milliers d'exemplaires. Sur l'imprimé de Paris, à Marseille, de l'imprimerie de Bertrand et Compagnie. 8° pp.23.
Copy: MH. (C. Suppl. Add. 1).

Translation

A6/t1 1798   Rede, gehalten im Cercle constitutionnel am 9ten Ventose im 6ten Jahre, von Benjamin Constant.
Frankreich im Jahr 1798. Aus den Briefen Deutscher Männer in Paris, Altona [Lübeck: Niemann], 1798, Bd. I, St. 4, 291-315.
Copies: C, St.

A7 A ses collègues de l'assemblée électorale

A7/1 1798   Benjamin Constant à ses collègues de l'assemblée électorale du département de Seine et Oise. 8° pp.14, 14.
Text dated at end: 'Versailles, le 21 germinal, an 6 de la république' [10 April 1798]. This edition exists in two states: one as described above, the second with a four-page 'Note essentielle à la *page* 8, *lig*. 4 et 5' inserted between the two gatherings.
Copies: [1] BN; [2] BL, OT. (C.7a).

A8 Des suites de la contre-révolution de 1660 en Angleterre

A8/1 1799   Des suites de la contre-révolution de 1660 en Angleterre. Par Benjamin Constant. A Paris ... chez F. Buisson ... An VII. 8° pp.x, [11]-94.
Copies: BCU, BL, BN. (C.8a).

A8/2 1799   Des suites de la contre-révolution ... Seconde édition ... An VII.
Reissue of the preceding item; text corrected and in part reset.
Copies: B, G. (C.8b).

Other editions: *Cours de politique* 1819 (E1/1(3)), *Cours de politique* 1820 (E1/2(3)).

A9   Wallstein

A9/1 1809   Wallstein, tragédie en cinq actes et en vers, précédée de quelques
réflexions sur le théâtre allemand, et suivie de notes historiques, par Benjamin
Constant de Rebecque. A Genève, chez J. J. Paschoud ... 1809. 8° pp.lii, 214,
[1].
Title page exists in two states, one as described above, the other with imprint:
A Paris, chez J.J. Paschoud ... A Genève, chez le même libraire, 1809.
Copies: [1] BCU, BN, OT; [2] BCU, BL, BN. (C.9a).

1849   See item A18/11 (Adolphe ... Paris: Garnier, 1849).

A9/2 1965   Wallstein, tragédie en cinq actes et en vers de Benjamin Constant.
Edition critique publiée avec de nombreuses variantes et des documents inédits
par Jean-René Derré. Paris: Les Belles Lettres, 1965. (Bibliothèque de la Faculté
des Lettres de Lyon, 10). pp.[iv], 262.
Reviews: A. Monchoux, *RLC*, XL (1966), 481-484. Lilian R. Furst, *Romanistisches
Jahrbuch*, XVII (1966), 218-219. Frank Paul Bowman, *MLR*, LXII (1967), 343.
Gerhard Göbel, *Archiv für das Studium der neueren Sprachen und Literaturen*, CCIV
(1967), 317-319. Patrice Thompson, *RHLF*, LXVII (1967), 158-159. Pierre
Deguise, *RR*, LVIII (1967), 224-225. Walter Mönch, *ZFSL*, LXXVII (1967),
289-295. Alison Fairlie, *FS*, XXI (1967), 253-255.

A10   De l'esprit de conquête et de l'usurpation

A10/1 1814   De l'esprit de conquête et de l'usurpation, dans leurs rapports
avec la civilisation européenne. Par Benjamin de Constant-Rebecque ... 1814.
8° pp.[I]-[II], [i]-[ii], [III]-VIII, 209, [1].
Published by Hahn, Hanover, 30 January 1814.
Copies: BCU, BN, OT. (C.10a).

A10/2 1814   De l'esprit de conquête et de l'usurpation ... A Londres: de
l'imprimerie de W. Clowes ... et se trouve chez J. Murray ... 1814. 8° pp.xii, 208.
Copy: NcD. (C.10b).

A10/3 1814   De l'esprit de conquête et de l'usurpation ... Troisième édition,
revue et augmentée. Paris, chez Le Normant ... H. Nicolle ... M.DCCC.XIV. 8°
pp.viii, 199.
Copies: BCU, BL, BN. (C.10c).

A10/4 1814   De l'esprit de conquête et de l'usurpation ... Quatrième édition,

revue et augmentée. Paris, chez H. Nicolle ... Le Normant ... M.DCCCXIV. 8°
pp.viii, 234.
Copies: BCU, BN. (C.10d).

1839   See item A18/9 (Adolphe ... Paris: Charpentier, 1839).

1843   See item A18/9 (reprint of Adolphe ... Paris: Charpentier, 1839).

1845   See item A18/9 (reprint of Adolphe ... Paris: Charpentier, 1839).

1907   See item A18/30 (Adolphe ... Paris: J. Guillequin, [1907]).

A10/5 1910   Benjamin Constant et la paix. Réédition de l'esprit de conquête
(d'après la 3ᵉ édition publiée à Paris chez Le Normand et chez H. Nicolle, en
1814). Précédée d'une introduction de M. d'Estournelles de Constant, Sénateur
de la Sarthe. Paris: Delagrave, 1910. (*Conciliation internationale. Bulletin*, 1910,
n° 2). pp.72. Frontispiece (portrait).
Two issues: one as given above, the other with imprint of Gustave Ficker, Paris,
n.d.
Copies: A, BN, BPU.

1912   See items A18/33 (Adolphe ... Londres: Dent, 1912) and A18/34 (Adolphe ... Paris: Garnier, [1912]).

1913   See item A18/30 (reprint of Adolphe ... Paris: J. Guillequin [1907]).

1914   See item A18/40 (Adolphe ... Paris: Larousse, [1914]).

A10/6 1918   Benjamin Constant. L'esprit de conquête. Avant-propos de M.
Albert Thomas. Paris: Bernard Grasset, 1918. (*Le Fait de la semaine*, 6ᵉ année,
n° 16, 20 avril 1918). pp.62.
Copies: B, BCU, VP.

1919   See item A18/34 (reprint of Adolphe ... Paris: Garnier, [1912]).

1920   See item A18/34 (reprint of Adolphe ... Paris: Garnier, [1912]).

1923   See item A18/40 (reprint of Adolphe ... Paris: Larousse, [1914]).

1924   See item A18/34 (reprint of Adolphe ... Paris: Garnier, [1912]).

1931   See item A18/34 (reprint of Adolphe ... Paris: Garnier, [1912]).

1935   See item A18/65 (Adolphe ... Paris: Simon, [1935]).

A10/7 1942   Benjamin Constant. De l'esprit de conquête. Neuchâtel: Aux
Ides et Calendes, 1942. pp.162.
Copies: B, BCU, BL, BN.

A10/8 1943   Benjamin Constant. De l'esprit de conquête ... Photographic reproduction of the preceding item, distributed in Italy by the Casa editrice Chiantore, 1943. (Cordié 199).

A10/9 1944   De l'esprit de conquête, par Benjamin Constant. Buenos Aires: Lettres françaises, Editions Sur, [1944]. (La Porte étroite, 1). pp.74.

'Avertissement', p.7, by R[oger] C[aillois].

Copies: A, BN.

A10/10 1947   Benjamin Constant. De l'esprit de conquête, 1813. [Texte établi par M.-Th. Génin sur l'édition originale de 1814]. Paris: Librairie de Médicis, [1947]. (Le Jardin du Luxembourg, 1). pp.68. Colophon.

Review: René Lalou, *NL*, 15 mai 1947, p.3.

Copies: B, BL, SG.

1957   See item A18/103 (Adolphe ... [Paris]: Mazenod, [1957]).

A10/11 1980   Benjamin Constant. De l'esprit de conquête et de l'usurpation. Texte de la première édition (1814). Présentation d'Ephraïm Harpaz. Paris-Genève: Ressources, [1980]. (Collection Ressources, 79). pp.15, 208.

A10/12 1980   Benjamin Constant. De l'esprit de conquête. Préface de Denis de Rougemont. [Lausanne]: Pierre-Marcel Favre, 1980. pp.93.

Includes 'Chronologie' by Norbert Furrer.

Other editions: Laboulaye 1861 (E1/5a), Laboulaye 1872 (E1/5b), Pléiade 1957, 1964, 1979 (E4/5), Gauchet 1980 (E4/11).

Translations

A10/t1 1814   Ueber den Eroberungsgeist und die Usurpation, im Verhältniß zur europäischen Bildung, von Benjamin de Constant-Rebecque ... Aus dem Französischen übersetzt von J. J. Stolz, Professor. Hannover, bei den Gebrüdern Hahn, 1814. 8° pp.xvi, 204.

'Vorbericht des Uebersetzers' signed at end: 'Bremen am Ende des März 1814. Stolz'.

Copies: T, W. (Fromm 5706; C.10e).

A10/t2 1815   Om Eröfrings-Systemet och om Usurpationen uti deras samband med odlingen i Europa; af Benjamin de Constant-Rebecque ... Stockholm, tryckt hos A. Gadelius, 1815. 8° pp.225.

Translation by Lars Augustin Mannerheim.

Copies: MnU, S. (C.10f).

A10/t3 1941   Prophecy from the Past. Benjamin Constant on conquest and usurpation, edited and translated by Helen Byrne Lippmann. New York: Reynal and Hitchcock, [1941]. pp.122.

Reviews: Emmanuel Chapman, *Commonweal*, 11 April 1941, p.626. *Nation*, 29 November 1941, p.547.

Copies: BL, DLC.

A10/t4 1942   Benjamin Constant. Über die Gewalt. Vom Geist der Eroberung und von der Anmaßung der Macht. Aus dem Französischen übertragen und herausgegeben von Hans Zbinden. Bern: Herbert Lang & Cie, [1942]. pp.XLIII, 218. Facsimile. Bibliography.
Note on verso of title page: 'Übertragung nach der ersten Auflage (Januar 1814). Mit den Nachträgen der vierten Auflage'.
Copies: AR, B, BCU. (Fromm 5707).

A10/t5 1944   Benjamin Constant. Conquista e usurpazione. Prefazione di Franco Venturi. Traduzione di Carlo Botti. Torino: Giulio Einaudi, 1944. (Universale Einaudi, 51). pp.197. Bibliography.
Copy: B. (Cordié 206).
Reprinted: 1983 (Nuova Universale Einaudi, 184), pp.XVI, 187.

A10/t6 1945   B. Constant. I conquistatori e la libertà, a cura di Enrico Lecci. Milano: M. A. Denti, [1945]. (Saggi, 5). pp.XIX, 149.
Includes: *Dello spirito di conquista*, pp.1-109; *Della libertà degli antichi comparata a quella dei moderni*, pp.111-149.
Copy: B. (Cordié 208).

A10/t7 1945   Constant. Dello spirito di conquista, a cura di Salvatore Annino. Venezia: Miuccio, [1945]. (Lo Zodiaco, Orizzonti vecchi e nuovi, 2). pp.164.
(Cordié 209).

A10/t8 1945   Benjamin Constant. Lo spirito di conquista, seguíto da La libertà degli antichi e la libertà dei moderni. Traduzione di Umberto Ortolani, introduzione di Guido Calogero. Roma: Atlantica, 1945. (Saggi, a cura di Umberto Ortolani, 3). pp.XXXII, 118. Bibliography.
Copy: B. (Cordié 210).

A10/t9 1945   Benjamin Constant. Lo spirito di conquista. Con introduzione di Alessandro Visconti. Milano: Ambrosiana, [1945]. (Piccola biblioteca di cultura politica, Serie 1ª: Problemi generali, 2). pp.92.
Copy: B. (Cordié 211).

A10/t10 1946   Benjamin Constant. Über den Geist der Eroberer. Übersetzung von Josef Ziwutschka. Wien: Amandus-Edition, 1946. (Schriftenreihe Symposium, 2). pp.28.
'Nachwort' by Josef Ziwutschka, pp.25-28.
Copies: B, BCU. (Fromm 5709).

A10/t11 1946   Benjamin Constant. Der Geist der Usurpation. Übersetzung von Josef Ziwutschka. Wien: Amandus-Edition, 1946. (Schriftenreihe Symposium, 3). pp.40.
'Nachwort' by Josef Ziwutschka, pp.37-40.

Copies: B, BCU. (Fromm 5710).

A10/t12 1947   Benjamin Constant. Vom Geist der Eroberung. Aus dem Französischen neu übertragen von Hans H. Haußer. Heidelberg: Adolf Rausch, [1947]. (Kultursoziologische Reihe/Geschichtsphilosophische Dokumente. Herausgegeben von Kurt Rossmann. (Wie lebt und denkt man in anderen Ländern? 4). pp.84.
'Vorwort des Übersetzers' dated Oktober 1947, pp.5-16; 'Nachwort', pp.82-83.
Copies: B, T. (Fromm 5711).

A10/t13 1948   Benjamin Constant. Über die Gewalt. Vom Geist der Eroberung und von der Anmaßung der Macht. Aus dem Französischen übertragen und herausgegeben von Hans Zbinden. Stuttgart: Reclam, 1948. (Reclams Universal-Bibliothek 7618-7620). pp.xxxviii, 182. Facsimiles. Bibliography.
Copy: B. (Fromm 5708).

A10/t14 1961   Benjamin Constant. Dello spirito di conquista e dell'usurpazione nei loro rapporti con la civiltà europea. Traduzione di Augusto Donaudy. [Milano]: Rizzoli, [1961]. (Biblioteca Universale Rizzoli, 1722-1723). pp.200.
Copy: B. (Cordié 227).

1983   See item A10/t5 (reprint of Conquista ... Torino: Einaudi, 1944).

A11   Réflexions sur les constitutions et les garanties

A11/1 1814   Réflexions sur les constitutions, la distribution des pouvoirs, et les garanties, dans une monarchie constitutionnelle. Par Benjamin de Constant. Paris, H. Nicolle ... Gide, fils ... M.DCCC.XIV. 8° pp.xvi, 168. Impr. Hocquet, [Paris].
Preface dated: 'Paris, ce 24 Mai 1814'.
Copies: BCU, BL, BN. (C.11a).

Other editions: *Cours de politique* 1817 (E1/1(1)), *Cours de politique* 1820 (E1/2(1)), Laboulaye 1861 (E1/5a), Laboulaye 1872 (E1/5b).

Translations

A11/t1 1814   Betrachtungen über Constitutionen, über die Vertheilung der Gewalten, und die Bürgschaften in einer constitutionnellen Monarchie, von Benjamin de Constant. Aus dem Französischen übersetzt von J. J. Stolz. Bremen, gedruckt bei Johann Georg Heyse, 1814. 8° pp.[iv], xiv, [2], 119.
Copy: LU. (Fromm 5717; C.11b).

A11/t2 1836   Benjamin Constant. Betrachtungen über die Verfassungen und Garantieen, herausgegeben am 24. Mai 1814, mit einem Entwurf einer Verfassungsurkunde. Von F. J. Buß. Freiburg: Wagner, 1836.
Translation by Franz Josef Ritter von Buß. (Fromm 5718).

A12 De la liberté des brochures

A12/1 1814   De la liberté des brochures, des pamphlets et des journaux, considérée sous le rapport de l'intérêt du gouvernement; par Benjamin de Constant. De l'imprimerie de A. Belin. A Paris, chez H. Nicolle ... 1814. 8° pp.[ii], 48.
Copies: BCU, BL, BN. (C.12a).

A12/2 1814   De la liberté ... Seconde édition, revue et considérablement augmentée ... 1814. 8° pp.[ii], 75.
Copies: BN, BPU, OT. (C.12b).

Other editions: *Cours de politique* 1817 (E1/1(1)), *Cours de politique* 1820 (E1/2(1)), Laboulaye 1861 (E1/5a), Laboulaye 1872 (E1/5b), Pléiade 1957, 1964, 1979 (E4/5).

Translation

A12/t1 1815   On the Liberty of the Press; or an Enquiry how far Government may safely allow the publication of political pamphlets, essays, and periodical works. By M. B. H. de Constant. Translated from the French exclusively for the Pamphleteer, 1815.
The Pamphleteer, London: A. J. Valpy, VI (1815), 205-238.
Copies: BL, BN. (C.12c).

A13 Observations

A13/1 1814   Observations sur le discours prononcé par S.E. le Ministre de l'Intérieur en faveur du projet de loi sur la liberté de la presse, par M. Benjamin de Constant. De l'imprimerie de Mame frères. A Paris, chez H. Nicolle ... 1814. 8° pp.[ii], 51.
Copies: BCU, BL, BN. (C.13a).

A13/2 1814   Observations ... Seconde édition, revue et corrigée ... 1814. 8° pp.[ii], 51.
Copies: BCU, BN, OT. (C.13b).

Other editions: *Cours de politique* 1818 (E1/1(2)), *Cours de politique* 1820 (E1/2(2)), Laboulaye 1861 (E1/5a), Laboulaye 1872 (E1/5b), Pléiade 1957, 1964, 1979 (E4/5).

A14 De la responsabilité des ministres

A14/1 1815   De la responsabilité des ministres; par M. Benjamin de Constant. De l'imprimerie de A. Belin. Paris, H. Nicolle ... M.DCCC.XV. 8° pp.[ii], 100.
Copies: BCU, BL, C. (C.14a).

Other editions: *Cours de politique* 1818 (E1/1(2)), *Cours de politique* 1820 (E1/2(2)),

Laboulaye 1861 (E1/5a), Laboulaye 1872 (E1/5b).

Translations

A14/t1 1815   On the Responsibility of Ministers. By M. Benjamin de Constant. Paris, printed; London, reprinted, 1815.
The Pamphleteer, London: A. J. Valpy, V, n° 10 (May 1815), 299-330, 315*-329*.
Copies: BL, BN. (C.14b).

A14/t2 1831   Über Verantwortlichkeit der Minister von Benjamin de Constant. Aus dem Französischen übersetzt von D. G. v. Ekendahl. Neustadt a.d. Orla, bei Johann Karl Gottfried Wagner, 1831. 8° pp.iv, 56.
Copies: DLC, NLH, St, W. (Fromm 5713; C.14c).

A15 Le transfuge Benjamin de Constant

A15/1 1815   Le transfuge Benjamin de Constant, au peuple français. Extrait du Journal des débats du 19 mars 1815. 4° pp.2.
An unauthorised reprint of Constant's article of 19 March 1815, followed by *Extrait du Moniteur du 22 avril 1815. – Paris le 21 avril* (nomination of Constant Conseiller d'Etat by decree of 20 April 1815).
Copy: BN. (C.15a).

A16 Note sur les droits de cité

A16/1 [1815]   Note sur les droits de cité appartenant à la famille Constant de Rebecque. Par Benjamin Constant. 8° pp.4.
Copy: BCU. (C.16a).

A16/2 [1815]   Note sur les droits de cité ... 8° pp.4.
Reprint of the preceding item with *Nota* added to p.4.
Copy: Mp. (C.16b).

A16/3 [1817]   Note sur les droits de cité appartenant à la famille de Constant-Rebecque, par Benjamin de Constant. 8° pp.4.
Text revised and expanded.
Copies: BCU, BN. (C.16c).

A17 Principes de politique

A17/1 1815   Principes de politique, applicables à tous les gouvernemens représentatifs et particulièrement à la constitution actuelle de la France; par M. Benjamin Constant ... Paris, chez Alexis Eymery ... De l'imprimerie de Hocquet ... Mai 1815. 8° pp.xii, [13]-324.
Copies: BCU, BL, BN. (C.17a).

Other editions: Laboulaye 1861 (E1/5a), Laboulaye 1872 (E1/5b), Pléiade 1957, 1964, 1979 (E4/5), Gauchet 1980 (E4/11).

Translations

A17/t1 1848   Principii di politica costituzionale del signor Beniamino Costant. Palermo: Tipografia e Libreria del sig. Antonio Muratori, 1848. 8° pp.viii, 92. (Cordié 175).

A17/t2 1890-1891   Benjamín Constant. Principios de política aplicables a todos los gobiernos representativos. Traducción y prólogo de Antonio Zozaya. Madrid: Imp. José Rodríguez, 1890-1891. 2 vols. (Bibl. Económica Filosófica). (Palau y Dulcet).

A17/t3 1965   Benjamin Constant. Introduzione e Traduzione di Umberto Cerroni. Roma: Samonà e Savelli, 1965. (Testi della democrazia moderna e del socialismo. Parte prima. La democrazia politica, 6). pp.[iv], 266.
Includes *Principî di politica*, pp.59-240; *Discorso sulla libertà degli antichi paragonata a quella dei moderni*, pp.241-266.
Review: Carlo Cordié, *SF*, IX (1965), 563-564.
Copy: BCU. (Cordié 337).

A17/t4 1970   Benjamin Constant. Principi di politica a cura di Umberto Cerroni. [Roma]: Editori riuniti, [1970]. pp.244.
Includes same works as preceding item: *Principi*, pp.47-216; *Discorso*, pp.219-239. (Cordié 339).

A17/t5 1970   Benjamín Constant. Principios de política. Traducción del francés por Josefa Hernández Alfonso. Introducción de José Alvarez Junco. Madrid: Aguilar, 1970. (Iniciación política). pp.xxxv, 180.
Copy: BPU.

A18 Adolphe

A18/1 1816   Adolphe; anecdote trouvée dans les papiers d'un inconnu, et publiée par M. Benjamin de Constant. Londres: chez Colburn ... Paris: chez Tröttel et Wurtz, 1816. 12° pp.vii, 228. Impr. Schulze et Dean, [London].
Copies: BL, MH, OT. (C.18a).

A18/2 1816   Adolphe, anecdote trouvée dans les papiers d'un inconnu ... Paris, chez Treuttel et Würtz ... Londres, chez H. Colburn ... 1816. 12° pp.vii, 228. Imprint of Crapelet, [Paris], on p.228. At foot of p.[ii]: 'Les formalités d'usage requises ont été observées; nous poursuivrons le contrefacteur. Treuttel et Würtz.'.
This edition exists in two states, one as described above, the other with p.[ii] blank, lacking imprint on p.228 and with the title page as follows: Adolphe ...

Londres, chez H. Colburn ... Paris, chez Treuttel et Würtz ... 1816.
Copies: [1] BCU, BI, BN, BPU, Bx, CN, W; [2] A, B, BN, G. (C.18b).

A18/3 1816   Adolphe; anecdote trouvée dans les papiers d'un inconnu ...
Seconde édition. Revue, corrigée et augmentée. Londres: chez Colburn ... Paris:
chez Treuttel et Würtz, 1816. 12° pp.[i]-xii, [iii]-vii, [1]-228. Impr. Schulze et
Dean.
Reissue of item A18/1 with new preliminaries and addition of 'Préface de la
seconde édition'.
Copies: BCU, BN, E, GL. (C.18c).

A18/4 1816   Adolphe, Anecdote trouvée dans les papiers d'un inconnu, et
publiée par M. Benjamin de Constant.
Le Nouvelliste français ... rédigé par Henri et Richard. Pesth: chez Conrade
Adolphe Hartleben. Tome X, livr. xiv (31 July 1816), 104-124; livr. xv (15
August 1816), 180-214; livr. xvi (31 August 1816), 241-276. Impr. Antoine
Straus, Vienne.
Copies: BN, BPU. (C.18d).

A18/5 1817   Adolphe, histoire trouvée dans les papiers d'un inconnu, et
publiée par M. Benjamin de Constant. A Vienne, de l'imprimerie de Schrämbl ...
1817. 8° pp.167.
Copy: V. (C.18e).

A18/6 1824   Adolphe, anecdote trouvée dans les papiers d'un inconnu, et
publiée par M. Benjamin Constant. Troisième édition. Paris, Brissot-Thivars ...
1824. 12° pp.xvii, 239. Impr. Lachevardière fils, [Paris].
In two states, with different settings for title pages and preliminaries. See F.-C.
Lonchamp, 'Un "état" inconnu de la troisième édition d'*Adolphe* de Benjamin
Constant', *BB*, 1937, 295-301.
Copies: BCU, BN, C. (C.18f).

A18/7 1828   Adolphe, anecdote trouvée dans les papiers d'un inconnu. Qua-
trième édition. Paris, chez Dauthereau ... 1828. 32° pp.xiv, [15]-308. Impr.
Firmin Didot, [Paris].
Copies: BCU, BN, OT, PPL. (C.18g).

A18/8 1830   Adolphe, anecdote trouvée dans les papiers d'un inconnu et
publiée par M. Benjamin Constant. Cinquième édition. Bruxelles, Louis Hauman et compagnie ... 1830. 12° pp.xv, 198.
Copy: BR. (C.18h).

A18/9 1839   Adolphe. Anecdote trouvée dans les papiers d'un inconnu, par
Benjamin Constant. Nouvelle édition, suivie des ouvrages du même écrivain:
Quelques Réflexions sur le Théâtre Allemand et sur la tragédie de Wallstein,
et de l'Esprit de Conquête et de l'Usurpation. Paris: Charpentier, 1839. 18 cm.
pp.xiv, 15-387.

Includes 'Essai sur *Adolphe*' by Gustave Planche, pp.371-387.
Copies: AR, B, BCU, BN.
Reprinted: 1843. *Copy*: BCU. 1845, pp.389. *Copies*: BCU, BN, OT.

1843   See item A18/9 (reprint of Adolphe ... Paris: Charpentier, 1839).

1845   See item A18/9 (reprint of Adolphe ... Paris: Charpentier, 1839).

A18/10 1847   Adolphe, anecdote trouvée dans les papiers d'un inconnu, par
M. Benjamin Constant. *Revue des feuilletons*, VII (avril-mai 1847), 158-202. Illus.
Edition described by F.-C. Lonchamp, '*Adolphe* "illustré" en 1847!', *BB* (1953),
176-183.
Copies: BCU, BN.

A18/11 1849   Adolphe. Anecdote trouvée dans les papiers d'un inconnu. Par
Benjamin Constant. Nouvelle édition suivie de la tragédie de Wallstein. Paris:
Garnier frères, 1849. (Bibliothèque Cazin). 15 cm. pp.[iv], 252.
Copies: AR, BCU, BN.

A18/12 1849   Adolphe. Par Benjamin Constant. Jeannot et Colin, com. en 3
a. par Florian. [Paris]: J. Bry aîné, 1849. (Les Veillées littéraires illustrées.
Choix de romans, nouvelles, poésies, pièces de théâtre, etc., etc. Par les meilleurs
écrivains anciens et modernes. Deux cents dessins par Edouard Frère. Gravés
sur bois par Rouget). 31 cm. pp.24. Illus.
Adolphe, pp.1-17.
Copies: A, BN, BPU.

A18/13 1853   Adolphe. Anecdote trouvée dans les papiers d'un inconnu,
par Benjamin Constant. Nouvelle édition suivie des Réflexions sur le théâtre
allemand du même auteur et précédée d'un essai sur Adolphe, par Gustave
Planche. Paris: Charpentier, 1853. 19 cm. pp.273.
Copies: BN, SG.
Reprinted: 1857. *Copy*: BN. 1860 ('1858' on paper cover). *Copy*: BN. 1864. *Copy*:
BN. 1868 ('1864' on paper cover). *Copies*: BN, BPU. 1875. *Copies*: BN, C. 1889.
Copies: BL, BN, VP.
See also item A18/27 below (Adolphe ... Paris: Charpentier, Fasquelle, 1903).

A18/14 1855   Benjamin Constant. Adolphe, Paris: Martinon, 1855. (Les Romans miniatures). Illustrations par G. Roux. pp.122.
(*Bibliographie de la France*, 3 mars 1855).

1857   See item A18/13 (reprint of Adolphe ... Paris: Charpentier, 1853).

1860   See item A18/13 (reprint of Adolphe ... Paris: Charpentier, 1853).

1864   See item A18/13 (reprint of Adolphe ... Paris: Charpentier, 1853).

A18/15 1867   Adolphe. Anecdote trouvée dans les papiers d'un inconnu par

Benjamin Constant. Nouvelle édition. Suivie de la Lettre sur Julie et des Réflexions sur le théâtre allemand du même auteur. Avec un avant-propos de M. Sainte-Beuve. Paris: Michel Lévy frères, 1867. (Collection Michel Lévy). 18 cm. pp.[iv], VIII, 275.

Copies: B, BCU, BN. See also item A18/19 below (Adolphe ... Paris: Calmann Lévy, 1884).

1868   See item A18/13 (reprint of Adolphe ... Paris: Charpentier, 1853).

1875   See item A18/13 (reprint of Adolphe ... Paris: Charpentier, 1853).

A18/16 1877   Adolphe, par Benjamin Constant. Préface de A. J. Pons. Paris: Jules Claye, A. Quantin, successeur, 1877 (Edition G. Decaux). 20 cm. pp.228. Frontispiece (portrait), illus. Bibliography.

Includes 3 portraits by Régamy. Facsimile of autograph letter dated 'ce 22 May' from Constant to an unidentified correspondent. Statement on p.[3]: '2me volume de la Collection stéréotypée imprimée à un petit nombre d'exemplaires'. Includes *Lettre sur Julie*. Introduction, 'Les femmes d'Adolphe', pp.9-44, includes selections from Constant's letters to Isabelle de Charrière and others.

Copies: NN, OT.

A18/17 1878   Benjamin Constant. Adolphe. Préface de A. J. Pons. Eaux-fortes de Fr. Régamey. Variantes et bibliographie. Paris: A. Quantin, 1878. (Petite bibliothèque de luxe, 2). 20 cm. pp.228. Frontispiece (portrait), illus. Bibliography.

Reissue of the preceding item.

Copies: AR, B, BCU, BL, BN.

A18/18 1879   Benjamin Constant. Adolphe. Précédé d'une préface par M. de Lescure. Paris: Librairie des Bibliophiles, M DCCC LXXIX. (Collection des petits chefs-d'œuvre). 17.5 cm. pp.[iv], XIX, 146.

Copies: BCU, BL, BN.

A18/19 1884   Adolphe. Anecdote trouvée dans les papiers d'un inconnu par Benjamin Constant. Nouvelle édition. Suivie de la lettre sur Julie et des Réflexions sur le théâtre allemand du même auteur. Avec un avant-propos de M. Sainte-Beuve. Paris: Calmann Lévy, 1884. 18 cm. pp.[iv], VII, 275.

Reprint of item A18/15 (Michel Lévy frères, 1867).

Copies: AR, BPU. Reprinted: 1893. *Copy*: O. 1897. *Copy*: MWelC.

1889   See also item A18/13 (reprint of Adolphe ... Paris: Charpentier, 1853).

A18/20 1889   Benjamin Constant. Adolphe. Portrait gravé par Courboin d'après Desmarais. Préface par Paul Bourget. Paris: L. Conquet, 1889. 18 cm. pp.[iv], xv, 201. Frontispiece (portrait).

300 numbered copies printed.

Copies: B, BL, BN.

A18/21 1889 Œuvres de Benjamin Constant. Adolphe. Notice par A. France. Paris: Alphonse Lemerre, M DCCC LXXXIX. (Petite bibliothèque littéraire). 19 cm. pp.[iv], xv, 183. Frontispiece (portrait by A. Mongin d'après Devéria). *Copies*: B, BCU, BL, BN.

A18/22 1889 Benjamin Constant. Adolphe, suivi des Aventures du Chevalier de Warwick. [Paris]: E. Dentu, 1889. (Bibliothèque des chefs-d'œuvre français & étrangers, 39). 17.5 cm. pp.[iv], xvii, 293.
'Notice sur Adolphe', pp.i-xvii; *Adolphe*, pp.1-158; *Aventures du faux chevalier de Warwick* [by Louis d'Aunay], pp.159-293.
Copies: BN, OT. Reprinted: 1897.

A18/23 1890 Benjamin Constant. Adolphe. Paris: C. Marpon & E. Flammarion, [1890]. (Auteurs célèbres, 163). 15.5 cm. pp.[iv], 210.
Copies: AR, B, BN.

A18/24 1892 Benjamin Constant. Adolphe. Paris: Librairie illustrée, 1892. (Chefs-d'œuvre du siècle illustrés, 7). 16 cm. pp.96. Illus.
'L'auteur d'*Adolphe*', by H. Duclos, pp.95-96.
Copies: AR, BN.

1893 See also item A18/19 (reprint of Adolphe … Paris: Calmann Lévy, 1884).

A18/25 1893 Adolphe. Benjamin Constant. Nouvelle édition. Paris: H. Geffroy, 1893. (Collection Roy. Petite bibliothèque omnibus illustrée. Série classique, 7). 15 cm. pp.[iii], 187. Illus.
Includes *Lettre sur Julie*, pp.165-187.
Copies: AR, BN, C.

1897 See items A18/19 (reprint of Adolphe … Paris: Calmann Lévy, 1884) and A18/22 (reprint of Adolphe … Paris: Dentu, 1889).

A18/26 1901 [=1902] Benjamin-Constant. Adolphe. Anecdote trouvée dans les papiers d'un inconnu. Préface de Paul Hervieu. Cinquante eaux-fortes par G. Jeanniot. Paris: [Jeanniot], 1901 [=1902]. 27 cm. pp.ix, 167.
Colophon: 'Achevé d'imprimer: à Paris. Pour le texte, sur la presse à bras de G. Jeanniot le 10 juin 1902. Emile Fequet, compositeur-pressier. Pour les eaux-fortes, sur les presses de Wittmann le 15 septembre 1902'.
151 numbered copies printed, including 20 'tirés spécialement sur vélin d'Arches pour la société des XX'.
Copies: BCU, BN.

A18/27 1903 Benjamin Constant. Adolphe. Anecdote trouvée dans les papiers d'un inconnu. Nouvelle édition, suivie des Réflexions sur le théâtre allemand du même auteur et précédée d'une note sur Adolphe par Gustave Planche. Paris: Bibliothèque Charpentier, Eugène Fasquelle, 1903. 19 cm. pp.273.
Reprint of Charpentier edition (item A18/13).

Copies: B, BCU.

A18/28 1905 Benjamin Constant. Adolphe. Préface de Paul Bourget. London: J. M. Dent & Co.; New York: G. P. Putnam's Sons, 1905. (Les Classiques français, publiés sous la direction de M. Daniel S. O'Connor). 16.5 cm. pp.xviii, 184. Frontispiece (portrait of Benjamin Constant the painter). Bibliography.
Copies: BL, BN.

A18/29 1907 Adolphe. Anecdote trouvée dans les papiers d'un inconnu et publiée par M. Benjamin de Constant. Paris: Louis Conard, 1907. (Cinq confessions d'amour, [5]). 22 cm. pp.xi, 194. Frontispiece.
225 numbered copies printed.
Copy: BCU.

A18/30 1907 Benjamin Constant. Adolphe et choix de discours. Paris: La Renaissance du livre, J. Guillequin & Cie, [1907]. (Tous les chefs-d'œuvre de la littérature française). 17.5 cm. pp.157.
Includes 'Avertissement des éditeurs', pp.7-8; 'Benjamin Constant' pp.9-14; Speeches of 7 March 1820 (*Sur la loi d'exception contre la liberté individuelle*, pp.95-106), 29 April 1826 (*Sur une pétition des écoles relativement au droit d'aînesse*, pp.107-110), and 13 February 1827 (*Sur le projet de loi relatif à la police de la presse*, pp.111-124); and *De l'esprit de conquête*, pp.127-155.
Copies: B, BN. Reprinted: [1913]. See also item A18/33.

A18/31 1911 Benjamin Constant. Adolphe. Lausanne: Payot et Cie, [1911]. (Les 100 chefs d'œuvre qu'il faut lire, 46). 16 cm. pp.126.
Editor's introduction, p.6.
Copies: B, BPU.

A18/32 1911 Benjamin Constant. Adolphe. Paris: Nilsson, [1911]. (Les 100 chefs-d'œuvre qu'il faut lire). 17 cm. pp.126.
Separate issue of the preceding item.
Copy: BCU.

A18/33 1912 Benjamin Constant. Adolphe, et choix de discours. Londres: J.M. Dent & Sons, Ltd; Paris: Ed. Mignot, [1912]. (Tous les chefs-d'œuvre de la littérature française, 88). 17 cm. pp.157.
Reissue of item A18/30. *Copies*: BL, O.

A18/34 1912 Adolphe. Anecdote trouvée dans les papiers d'un inconnu. Par Benjamin Constant. Nouvelle édition suivie de la Lettre sur Julie, des Réflexions sur le théâtre allemand, de l'Esprit de conquête et de l'usurpation dans leurs rapports avec la civilisation européenne et de notes du même auteur avec une introduction de M. Sainte-Beuve Paris: Garnier frères, [1912]. (Classiques Garnier). pp.xv, 326.
Reprinted: [1919] (Collection 'Sélecta'), [1920], [1924], [1931]. In the 1924

reprint 'et de notes ...' is dropped; in the 1931 reprint the title stops at 'européenne'.

1913   See also item A18/30 (reprint of Adolphe ... Paris: Guillequin, [1907]).

A18/35 1913   Benjamin Constant. Adolphe. Anecdote trouvée dans les papiers d'un inconnu, avec un portrait de l'auteur gravé sur bois par P.-E. Vibert. Paris: Georges Crès et Cie., MCMXIII. (Les maîtres du livre, 23). 19 cm. pp.[viii], 248. Frontispiece (portrait).

Colophon: 'Ce livre, le vingt-troisième de la collection des Maîtres du livre, a été établi par Ad. van Bever ... Le présent ouvrage a été achevé d'imprimer par Protat frères, à Macon, le 25 mars MCMXIII. Les ornements typographiques ont été dessinés et gravés sur bois par P.-E. Vibert.'

1371 numbered copies printed.

Appendice, pp.237-243, includes two letters from Sismondi to the Countess of Albany, 9 September and 14 October 1816.

Copies: B, BN, BPU.

A18/36 1913   Benjamin Constant. Adolphe. Illustrations en couleurs par Serge de Solomko. Paris: A. Ferroud, 1913. (Petite Bibliothèque Andréa). 19 cm. pp.[iv], 213. Frontispiece, illus.

1013 numbered copies printed.

Copies: BCU, BN.

A18/37 1913   Benjamin Constant. Adolphe. Paris: Ferreyrol, [1913]. (La petite bibliothèque). 17 cm. pp.179.

650 numbered copies printed.

Copies: BCU, BN.

A18/38 1914   Benjamin Constant. Adolphe. Introduction par Paul Bourget. Paris: Georges Crès et Cie; Londres: J. M. Dent & Sons Ltd, [1914]. (Collection Gallia, publiée sous la direction de Charles Sarolea, XV). 17 cm. pp.xix, 180. Portrait.

Includes *Lettre sur Julie*, pp.157-180.

Copies: BCU, BL, BPU.

A18/39 1914   Benjamin Constant. Adolphe. Introduction par Paul Bourget. Paris: J. M. Dent et fils; Londres et Toronto: J. M. Dent & Sons Limited; New York: E. P. Dutton & Co., [1914]. (Collection Gallia, XV). 16.5 cm. pp.xix, 180. Frontispiece (portrait).

Separate issue of the preceding item.

Copies: BCU, BL, BN.

A18/40 1914   Benjamin Constant. Adolphe, et Œuvres choisies. Notice et annotations par Maurice Allem. Paris: Bibliothèque Larousse, [1914]. 19.5 cm. pp.247. Two portraits (including frontispiece). Bibliography.

Includes *Lettre sur Julie*, pp.115-126; *Réflexions sur le théâtre allemand*, pp.127-157; *De l'esprit de conquête et de l'usurpation* (extracts), pp.211-240; and selections from other works.

Copy: BN. Reprinted: 1923. *Copy*: BN.

A18/41 1918   Adolphe, par Benjamin Constant. Edited with an introduction, notes and vocabulary by William Morton Dey. New York: Oxford University Press, 1918. (Oxford French Series by American Scholars. General Editor: Raymond Weeks, Ph.D.). 18 cm. pp.xxii, 164. Frontispiece (portrait). Bibliography.

Copies: BL, O. Reprinted: 1920.

1919   See also item A18/34 (reprint of Adolphe ... Paris: Garnier, [1912]).

A18/42 1919   Benjamin Constant. Adolphe. Edition historique et critique, par Gustave Rudler. Manchester: Imprimerie de l'Université, 1919. (Modern Language Texts. French series: modern section). 19 cm. pp.lxxxvi, xxi, 168. Frontispiece (portrait), facsimiles. Bibliography.

Reviews: Alexis François, *La Semaine littéraire*, 31 janvier 1920, pp.50-52. Pierre Souday, *Le Temps*, 16 septembre 1920, p.3. Fernand Baldensperger, *Revue critique d'histoire et de littérature*, LXXXVII (1920), 328-330. Emile Henriot, *La Minerve française*, 1er juillet 1920, 559-571. Daniel Mornet, *RHLF*, XLIII (1936), 133-134.

Copies: B, BL, BN. Another issue: Paris: E. Champion, 1920. Also issued in 1920 by Manchester University Press in an edition of 100 numbered copies. *Copy*: BL.

1920   See also items A18/34 (reprint of Adolphe ... Paris: Garnier, [1912]), A18/41 (reprint of Adolphe ... New York: Oxford University Press, 1918) and A18/42 (separate issue of Adolphe ... Manchester, 1919).

A18/43 1920   Benjamin Constant. Adolphe, précédé du Cahier rouge. Préface de Robert de Traz, bois de H. Bischoff. Genève: Georg & Cie; Paris: G. Crès & Cie, 1920. (Collection helvétique, 4). 19 cm. pp.xxix, 267. Frontispiece (portrait). Colophon.

1660 numbered copies printed.

Copies: B, BCU, BPU.

A18/44 1921   Benjamin Constant. Adolphe, publié avec des documents et une étude sur Adolphe et la vie de B. Constant par Pierre Kohler. Lausanne: Editions Spes, 1921. 19 cm. pp.iv, 272. Frontispiece (portrait), illus.

In two states: (1) as above; (2) pp.iv, 268 and without illustrations. Includes extract from *Lettre sur Julie* and selection of Constant's letters.

Copies: [1] B, BL, OT; [2] BCU.

A18/45 1921   Benjamin Constant. Adolphe, anecdote trouvée dans les papiers d'un inconnu, suivi des Réflexions sur le théâtre allemand, d'extraits du Journal intime et de la Lettre sur Julie, avec une notice de Sainte-Beuve. Berlin: Internationale Bibliothek, G.M.B.H., 1921. (Bibliothèque française, publiée sous la direction de M. Max Fuchs, xv). 17.5 cm. pp.[iv], xvi, 182. Bibliography. *Copies*: BPU, Mar.

A18/46 1922   Adolphe. Anecdote trouvée dans les papiers d'un inconnu, et publiée par Benjamin Constant. [Amersfoort]: Palladium, 1922. pp.32.

Text incomplete. Proofs printed by G. J. van Amerongen (Typogr. Jan van Krimpen) for the Paris Exhibition, 1925.

Copy: A.

1923   See also item A18/40 (reprint of Adolphe ... Paris: Larousse, [1914]).

A18/47 1923   Benjamin Constant. Adolphe, roman, suivi des Réflexions sur la tragédie. Illustrations de Gaude Roza. Paris: Eugène Figuière, [1923]. (Bibliothèque Figuière). 16 cm. pp.173. Illus.

Introduction, pp.5-12, by Sainte-Beuve.

Copy: BN.

A18/48 1923   Benjamin Constant. Adolphe. Anecdote trouvée dans les papiers d'un inconnu. Paris: H. Piazza, MCMXXIII. (Le Livre français, 3). 24 cm. pp.xxvii, 124. Colophon. Bibliography.

Preface by Edmond Pilon.

Copies: BCU, BN, BPU.

A18/49 1923   Benjamin Constant. Adolphe. Anecdote trouvée dans les papiers d'un inconnu. Paris: Albin Michel, [1923]. (Collection des dames, 9). 12 cm. pp.136.

Copy: BN.

1924   See item A18/34 (reprint of Adolphe ... Paris: Garnier, [1912]).

A18/50 1926   Benjamin Constant. Adolphe. Paris: F. Rouff, 1926. (Nouvelle collection nationale, 54). 2 cols, pp.46. Illus.

Copy: BN.

A18/51 1928   Benjamin Constant. Adolphe. Portrait à l'eau-forte par Paul Baudier, d'après Lamotte. Paris: André Plicque et Cie, 1928. 20cm. pp.150. Frontispiece (portrait).

950 numbered copies printed.

Copy: BN.

A18/52 1928   Adolphe, par Benjamin Constant. Paris: A la Cité des livres, M DCCCC XXVIII. 20 cm. pp.[iv], 191. Colophon.

1040 numbered copies printed. Colophon: 'Ce livre a été achevé d'imprimer sur les presses du maître imprimeur Coulouma, à Argenteuil, H. Barthélemy étant

directeur, le vingt février mil neuf cent vingt-huit.'
Copies: BN, BCU, OT.

A18/53 1928   Le Roman sentimental. Paul et Virginie, Adolphe, Graziella. Paris: Aristide Quillet, MCMXXVIII. (Classiques Quillet, publiés sous la direction de Raoul Mortier). 17.5 cm. pp.356. Portraits.
Adolphe: pp.125-228, with Introduction by Paul Bourget.
Copies: BN, BPU.

A18/54 1929   Benjamin Constant. Adolphe, suivi de lettres choisies de Benjamin Constant. Préface d'André Thérive. Paris: Payot, M CM XXIX. (Collection prose et vers). 19 cm. pp.xvi, 285. Pen drawings. Bibliography.
Adolphe, pp.1-123; *Lettres choisies, 1776-1816*, pp.125-276.
Copies: AR, BCU, BN.
Review: Emile Magne, *MF*, 15 novembre 1929, pp.167-168.

A18/55 1929   Benjamin Constant. Adolphe. Illustrations en couleurs de Daniel-Girard. Paris: Editions Maurice Glomeau, 1929. 20 cm. pp.ix, 126. Illus. 1000 numbered copies printed.
Copies: B, BCU, BN, C.

A18/56 1929   Benjamin Constant. Adolphe. Texte établi et présenté par Jacques Bompard. Paris: Fernand Roches, 1929. (Œuvres complètes de Benjamin Constant. Les Textes français. Collection des Universités de France, publiée sous les auspices de l'Association Guillame Budé). 21 cm. pp.lxxiii, 129. Bibliography.
Reviews: Emile Magne, *MF*, 15 novembre 1929, pp.167-168. Wolfgang Wurzbach, *ZFSL*, LV (1931), 109-110.
Copies: B, BCU, BN, CN. Reprinted: Paris: Les Belles Lettres, 1946, 1948.

A18/57 1930   Benjamin Constant. Adolphe. [Aquarelles de Ro Keezer]. Paris: Editions Nilsson, [1930]. (Collection Emeraude). 23 cm. pp.174.
Includes *Lettre sur Julie*, pp.155-174.
Copies: AR, B, BN.

A18/58 1930   Benjamin Constant. Adolphe. Anecdote trouvée dans les papiers d'un inconnu et publiée par Benjamin Constant. Illustrée de gravures au burin de Pierre Gandon. Paris: Société d'Edition 'Le Livre', M.CM.XXX. 24 cm. pp.v, 213. Illus.
530 numbered copies printed.
Copies: B, BCU, BN.

A18/59 1930   Benjamin Constant. Adolphe. Anecdote trouvée dans les papiers d'un inconnu. Nouvelle édition précédée d'une notice sur 'Adolphe' par Gustave Planche, et d'une étude sur Benjamin Constant par Pierre Mortier. Paris: Bibliothèque-Charpentier; Fasquelle éditeurs, 1930. 19 cm. pp.xviii, 212.

Copies: B, BL, BN.

1931   See item A18/34 (reprint of Adolphe ... Paris: Garnier, [1912]).

A18/60 1931   Benjamin Constant. Adolphe. Anecdote trouvée dans les papiers d'un inconnu, précédée d'une étude sur Adolphe par Gustave Planche. Préface de Paul Bourget. Paris: Plon, [1931]. (Bibliothèque reliée Plon, 91). 17 cm. pp.251.
Copies: B, BCU, BN.

A18/61 1931   Benjamin Constant. Adolphe. Le Cahier rouge. [Aquarelles de Maurice Berty]. Paris: Editions Nilsson, [1931]. (La Bibliothèque précieuse). 18 cm. pp.252. Illus.
Copies: B, BN. See also item A18/66 below (Adolphe ... Paris: Gründ, 193[6]).

A18/62 1931   Adolphe. Le Cahier Rouge. Paris: R. Hilsum, [1931]. (Génie de la France. Œuvres de Benjamin Constant). 18 cm. pp.171.
'Texte conforme à la dernière édition du vivant de l'auteur' [Paris, 1828, item A18/7]. Editor's introduction, pp.7-8.
Copies: B, BN.

A18/63 1932   Benjamin Constant. Adolphe. Anecdote trouvée dans les papiers d'un inconnu. Préface pour 'Adolphe' par Edmond Pilon. Paris: Fernand Nathan, 1932. 19 cm. pp.xxv, 102.
Copy: BN.

A18/64 1933   Adolphe. Anecdote trouvée dans les papiers d'un inconnu et publiée par Benjamin Constant. Liège: Les Editions du Balancier, MCMXXXIII. 21 cm. pp.129. Colophon.
Colophon: 'Le texte de cette édition fut établi par Jean Jacob et Arsène Soreil. Le tirage, achevé le 20 avril 1933 sur les presses de Joh. Enschedé en Zonen, à Haarlem, pour les Editions du Balancier, à Liège, est limitée à 150 exemplaires sur vergé de Hollande Pannekoek numérotés de 1 à 150 et 10 exemplaires hors commerce, sur le même papier numérotés de 1 à x'.
Copies: B, BCU, BN, BR. Reprinted: 1937.

A18/65 1935   Benjamin Constant. Adolphe. Paris: R. Simon, [1935]. 18 cm. pp.251.
Editor's introduction (unsigned), pp.5-14. Includes *De l'esprit de conquête et de l'usurpation*, pp.119-251.
Copy: BCU.

A18/66 1935 [=1936]   Benjamin Constant. Adolphe. Le Cahier rouge. Paris: Gründ, 1935 [=1936]. (La Bibliothèque précieuse). 18.5 cm. pp.253.
Reprint of item A18/61 (Adolphe ... Paris: Editions Nilsson, [1931]).

Copies: BCU, BN.

A18/67 1936 Benjamin Constant. Adolphe. Introduction d'Edmond Pilon. Illustrations en couleurs de Paul-Emile Bécat. Paris: L'Edition d'Art H. Piazza, 1936. (Contes de France et d'ailleurs). 19 cm. pp.xix, 205. Illus. Bibliography. *Copies*: B, BN.

A18/68 1936 Benjamin Constant. Adolphe, roman, avec une notice biographique, une notice historique et littéraire, des notes explicatives, des jugements, un questionnaire sur le roman et des sujets de devoirs, par Emmanuel Beau de Loménie. Paris: Larousse, [1936]. (Classiques Larousse publiés sous la direction de Félix Guirand). 17 cm. pp.96. Frontispiece (portrait). Frequently reprinted.

1937 See item A18/64 (reprint of Adolphe ... Liège: Editions du Balancier, 1933).

A18/69 1940 [=1941] Adolphe. Anecdote trouvée dans les papiers d'un inconnu et publiée par M. Benjamin de Constant. Paris: La Compagnie typographique, M.CM.XL [=1941]. 23 cm. pp.xix, 155. Bibliography. Colophon: 'Achevé d'imprimer le 24 octobre 1941 sur les presses de A. A. M. Stols à Maestricht pour la Compagnie typographique. Le tirage, exécuté sur vélin pur chiffon des papeteries G. H. Bührmann, a été limité à 88 exemplaires.' Reprint of first Paris edition (item A18/2 above) with preface of second edition and variants from the 1824 edition. See below, item A18/72. *Copies*: A, BPU, BN. (De Jong 154; Simoni C6).

A18/70 1941 Benjamin Constant. Adolphe, édité par Gustave Rudler. Manchester University Press, [1941]. (French Classics. General editor: Eugène Vinaver). 18.5 cm. pp.xxiv, 103. Reprinted: 1950, 1956, 1961, 1971, 1979.

A18/71 1941 Benjamin Constant. Adolphe. Bruxelles: Société anonyme belge d'édition, [1941]. (Ma lecture, 14). pp.69. *Copy*: BR.

A18/72 1942 [=1941] Adolphe. Anecdote trouvée dans les papiers d'un inconnu et publiée par M. Benjamin de Constant. [Maestricht]: Editions académiques Panthéon, [A. A. M. Stols], 1942. 23 cm. pp.xix, 156. Bibliography. Justification du tirage: 'Cette nouvelle édition d'Adolphe a été achevée d'imprimer le 27 octobre 1941 sur les presses de l'imprimerie Boosten & Stols à Maestricht. Le tirage à [sic] été limité à 220 exemplaires sur papier de Hollande Bührmann, numérotés de 1 à 220.' This is a reissue of item A18/69. *Copies*: B, BCU, BL. (De Jong 155; Simoni C6).

A18/73 1942 Adolphe, anecdote trouvée dans les papiers d'un inconnu et publiée par Benjamin Constant. Eaux-fortes originales d'Emilien Dufour. Paris:

La Tradition, [1942]. 24 cm. pp.137. Colophon.

750 copies printed.

Colophon: 'Réalisée par Paul Durupt, cette édition a été achevée d'imprimer le 15 juin 1942 sur les presses de l'imprimerie Dumoulin, H. Barthélemy directeur. Les eaux-fortes d'Emilien Dufour ont été tirées sur les presses à bras des éditeurs, Léon Aubert contremaître.'

Copy: BN.

A18/74 1942   Adolphe par Benjamin Constant. Précéde d'une introduction par Arnold de Kerchove. Bruxelles: Editions Libris, [1942]. (Collection Erasme). pp.xii, 166.

Copy: BR.

A18/75 1944   Benjamin Constant. Adolphe a cura di Carlo Cordié. Milano: Leonardo, 1944. (Minerva: testi-saggi manuali, 7). pp.134. Illus. Bibliography.

500 numbered copies printed.

Copy: BCU. (Cordié 202).

A18/76 1944   Benjamin Constant. Adolphe. Milano: Leonardo, [1944]. (Dafne Capolavori d'ogni letteratura, 2). 17 cm. pp.126.

200 numbered copies printed. Introduction by Carlo Cordié pp.5-9.

Copy: BCU. (Cordié 203).

A18/77 1944   Benjamin Constant. Adolphe. Bruxelles: Editions de l'Etoile, [1944]. (Je chante clair, 21). pp.157.

Introduction by Sainte-Beuve.

Copy: BR.

A18/78 1944   Adolphe, par Benjamin Constant. Illustrations de Ferdinand Fargeot. Paris: La Bonne Compagnie, MCMXLIV. 22.5 cm. pp.192.

1000 copies printed.

Copy: BN.

A18/79 1945   Benjamin Constant. Adolphe. Eaux-fortes de Jean Traynier. [Edition préparée par Maurice Malingue et André Jardot]. Monaco: Les Documents d'art, [1945]. 28 cm. pp.IV, 153. Illus.

995 numbered copies printed.

Copies: B, BN.

A18/80 1945   Benjamin Constant. Adolphe. Le Cahier rouge. Londres: Editions Penguin, 1945. 19 cm. pp.viii, 121.

'Texte conforme à la dernière édition du vivant de l'auteur (Paris, Dauthereau, 1828)'.

Copies: BCU, BL.

A18/81 1945   Benjamin Constant. Journal intime, précédé du Cahier rouge et d'Adolphe. Etablissement du texte, introduction et notes par Jean Mistler.

Monaco: Editions du Rocher, 1945. (Grands et petits chefs-d'œuvre). 22 cm.
pp.XXXVII, 437.

Reviews: Alain Girard, *Critique*, I, n°s 3-4 (août-septembre 1946), 250-258, 'Destin
de Benjamin Constant'. Jacques Lethève, *Paru*, n° 21 (août 1946), 59-60. Robert
de Traz, *JG*, 30 avril 1946, p.1. Dorette Berthoud, *JG*, 4-5 mai 1946, p.3. René
Lalou, *NL*, 14 mars 1946, p.3. Michel Robida, *Gazette des lettres*, 16 mars 1946,
p.3. Carlo Cordié, *Annali della Scuola normale superiore di Pisa: lettere, storia e filosofia*,
XVIII (1949), 231-248.

Copies: B, BL, BN. Seconde édition, revue et corrigée, [1946]; 'd'Adolphe' on
title page replaced by: 'de Adolphe'.

A18/82 1945   Benjamin Constant. Adolphe. Illustrations de Marcel Chapuis.
Monaco: L'Intercontinentale d'Edition, [1945]. (Les Romans romantiques).
23.5 cm. pp.86.

950 numbered copies printed.

Copy: B.

1946   See also items A18/56 (reprint of Adolphe ... Paris: Roches, 1929), A18/81
(reprint of Journal intime ... Adolphe ... Monte-Carlo: Editions du Rocher,
1945).

A18/83 1946   Benjamin Constant. Adolphe, presenté par Fernand Perdriel.
Lyon: IAC, [1946]. (Les Chefs-d'œuvre français). 11 cm. pp.XLVI, 123.

Published by l'Imprimerie artistique en couleurs, Lyon.

Copies: B, BN.

A18/84 1946   Benjamin Constant. Adolphe. Neuf hors-texte en couleurs de
Jacques Roubille. Paris: Editions du Panthéon, MCMXLVI. (Collection Pas-
tels). 19 cm. pp.182. Illus.

2500 numbered copies printed.

Copies: B, BN.

A18/85 1946   Benjamin Constant. Adolphe, édité par Fernand Baldensperger.
Paris: Droz, 1946. (Textes littéraires français). 19 cm. pp.XXXII, 118. Bibliography.

Review: Jules Dechamps, *FS*, I (1947), 270-272. Reprinted: (Genève) 1950,
pp.XXXII, 123.

A18/86 1946   Benjamin Constant. Adolphe. Monaco: Bibliothèque mondiale,
[1946]. (Les documents d'art). 19 cm. pp.161.

Copy: BN.

A18/87 1946   Benjamin Constant. Adolphe. Lithographies de P. Noury.
Monte-Carlo: Editions du livre, 1946. (Grandes œuvres littéraires).

Copy: private collection.

A18/88 1947   Benjamin Constant. Adolphe. Dessins de René Auberjonois.

[Lausanne]: Mermod, [1947]. (Les Amoureuses, 2). 17 cm. pp.148. Frontispiece (portrait), illus.
Copies: B, BCU, BN.

A18/89 1947   Benjamin Constant. Adolphe. [Rio de Janeiro:] Americ=Edit.; [Paris: Presses universitaires de France], [1947]. (La France de toujours). 19 cm. pp.233.
Introduction by Sainte-Beuve.
Copies: AR, BCU, BN.

1948   See also item A18/56 (reprint of Adolphe ... Paris: Roches, 1929).

A18/90 1948   Adolphe, anecdote trouvée dans les papiers d'un inconnu et publiée par M. Benjamin de Constant. La Haye & Paris: A. A. M. Stols, 1948. 19 cm. pp.XVII, 143, [5].
Justification du tirage: 'Achevé d'imprimer à Maestricht (Pays-Bas) le 30 juin 1948 sur les presses de l'Imprimerie Boosten & Stols. Le tirage de cette nouvelle édition est limité à 1000 exemplaires sur papier pur fil'.
Copies: B, BCU, BN.

A18/91 1948   Benjamin Constant. Adolphe. Texte présenté par René-Louis Doyon. Paris: René Rasmussen, [1948]. (Collection Reflets). 17.5 cm. pp.189. Frontispiece (pen drawing).
Copies: BCU, BN.

A18/92 1948   Benjamin Constant. Adolphe. Roman. Illustrations de P.-W. Giraudié. Paris: Gründ, [1948]. (Collection Gründ illustrée. Série Coquelicot, 40). 17 cm. pp.157.
Copy: BN.

A18/93 1948   Adolphe. Par Benjamin Constant. Pointes-sèches de Hermine David. Paris: Fernand Hazan, [1948]. 23 cm. pp.127.
389 numbered copies printed.
Copies: B, BN, BR.

A18/94 1949   Benjamin Constant. Adolphe. Genève: Pierre Cailler, [1949]. (Les Trésors de la littérature française, Collection dirigée par Edmond Jaloux, 44). 20 cm. pp.110.
Reprint of fourth (Paris) edition, item A18/7.
Copies: B, BCU, BPU.

1950   See also items A18/70 (reprint of Adolphe ... Manchester University Press, 1941) and A18/85 (reprint of Adolphe ... Paris: Droz, 1946).

A18/95 1950   Adolphe. Anecdote trouvée dans les papiers d'un inconnu et publiée par Benjamin Constant. Illustrée de pointes sèches de Michel Ciry.

Lausanne: Henri Kaeser, 1950. (Editions du Grand-Chêne, Lausanne). 21 cm. pp.227.

275 numbered copies printed.

Copies: B, BCU, BR.

A18/96 1952 Adolphe, par Benjamin Constant. Introduction de Alfred Roulin. [Paris]: Le Club français du livre, M.C.M.L.I.I. (Le Club français du livre. Classiques, 29). 22 cm. pp.[viii], 153. Illus.

Copies: B, BCU, BN.

Reprinted: 1961 (see below, item A18/111).

A18/97 1953 Benjamin Constant. Adolphe et le Cahier rouge. Introduction de Dominique Aury. Lausanne: Guilde du Livre, 1953. (Collection des classiques français, 19). 15 cm. pp.234.

Copies: B, BCU, BPU.

Reprinted: 1962.

A18/98 1953 Benjamin Constant. Adolphe. Préface et notes d'Henry Muller. [Paris]: Delmas, [1953]. 17 cm. pp.xix, 101.

Copies: B, BCU, BN.

A18/99 1953 Benjamin Constant. Adolphe, suivi du Cahier rouge. Préface de Gérard Baüer. Burin original de Pierre Gandon. [Monte-Carlo]: A. Sauret, [1953]. (Grand prix des meilleurs romans du XIXe siècle, 1). 22.5 cm. pp.248. Frontispiece (portrait). Colophon.

Copy: BCU. Also issued with imprint: Paris, Imprimerie nationale, [1953]. *Copy*: BN.

A18/100 1953 Benjamin Constant par André Ferré. *Adolphe* par Jean Mistler. *Adolphe* par Benjamin Constant ... Benjamin Constant, esprit de transition et de raison, par Henri Clouard. Paris: Editions de la Bibliothèque mondiale, 1953. (*Bibliothèque mondiale*, n° 10, 15 juin 1953). 17.5 cm. pp.[iv], 96, [8].

Copy: BN. Reissued [1953?] with title page as follows: Benjamin Constant. Adolphe. Précédé de : Benjamin Constant par André Ferré. Adolphe par Jean Mistler et suivi de: Benjamin Constant, Esprit de Transition et de Raison par Henri Clouard. Le Livre mondial. 18.5 cm. pp.[iv], 96. Frontispiece (portrait). *Copy*: BCU.

A18/101 1955 Benjamin Constant. Adolphe. Anecdote trouvée dans les papiers d'un inconnu. Texte établi, avec introduction, bibliographie, variantes, notes et, en appendice, des extraits de la correspondance de Benjamin Constant avec Anna Lindsay, Lettre sur Julie, De Madame de Staël et de ses ouvrages, par Jacques-Henry Bornecque. Paris: Garnier frères, [1955]. (Classiques Garnier). 18.5 cm. pp.cxxi, 332. Bibliography.

Reviews: R. Coiplet, *Le Monde*, 31 décembre 1955, p.7. Pierre Reboul, *RSH*, LXXXII (1956), 245-249. Carlo Pellegrini, *RLMC*, IX (1956), 76. Pierre

Deguise, *FR*, XXX (1956-57), 241-242. H. Weinrich, *Archiv für das Studium der neueren Sprachen*, CXCV (1958), 77-78.

Reprinted (with illustrations): [1960], etc. Revised edition: 1968 (Edition revue et augmentée d'un itinéraire biographique de B. Constant).

A18/102 1955 Benjamin Constant. Adolphe. Avec un commentaire par Eurialo de Michelis. Roma: Angelo Signorelli, 1955. .(Scrittori francesi, Collezione diretta dal prof. P.P. Trompeo dell' Università di Roma). 19 cm. pp.116. Facsimile.

Copies: B, BCU. (Cordié 225). Second edition, revised, pp.135, 1970. *Copy*: B.

1956 See item A18/70 (reprint of Adolphe ... Manchester University Press, 1941).

1957 See also item E4/5 (Œuvres, Paris: Bibliothèque de la Pléiade, 1957).

A18/103 1957 Le Romantisme. Benjamin Constant. Adolphe. Lettre sur Julie. De l'Esprit de conquête. [Paris]: Lucien Mazenod, [1957]. (Les Ecrivains célèbres, Œuvres, 1). 24.5 cm. pp.230. Illus., facsimiles.

Postface by Raymond Queneau ('Sur Adolphe et la vie de Benjamin Constant'), pp.211-222. Includes facsimile of letter from Constant to Jouy, Bains de Tivoli, ce 31 Aoust 1830, from Fonds Lacroix, Bibliothèque de l'Arsenal.

Copies: AR, B, BN.

Review: René Le Grand Roy, *CBC*, sér. I, n° 4 (1967), 163.

A18/104 1957 Benjamin Constant. Adolphe, suivi de Cécile. Préface de Marcel Arland. Paris: Le Livre de poche, [1957]. 16.5 cm. pp.181.

Frequently reprinted: 1958, 1961, etc. Reprinted in 1967 with Postface ('La vie et l'œuvre de Benjamin Constant') by Geneviève Bulli, pp.183-192.

A18/105 1957 Benjamin Constant. Adolphe, suivi du Cahier Rouge. Introduction d'Henriette Guex-Rolle. Lausanne: Editions Rencontre, [1957]. 18 cm. pp.307.

Copies: BCU, BN. Reprinted: 1968, pp.253. *Copies*: BCU, BN.

A18/106 1957 Benjamin Constant. Le Cahier rouge. Adolphe. [Paris]: Hachette, [1957]. (Collection du Flambeau). 18 cm. pp.221.

Includes *Lettre sur Julie*, *Journaux intimes* (extracts), and notes by Victor Bernard. Introductions by Jean Mistler and Victor Bernard.

Copies: BCU, BN.

1958 See item A18/104 (reprint of Adolphe ... [Paris]: Le Livre de poche, [1957]).

A18/107 1959 Benjamin Constant. Adolphe. [Le Cahier rouge]. Paris: Robert Laffont, [1959]. (Collection des cent chefs-d'œuvre de la langue française, 16). 18 cm. pp.247. Illus.

Reprint of 1824 edition of *Adolphe* (item A18/6) and 1907 edition of *Le Cahier rouge* (item A68/1).
Copies: BN, BR.

A18/108 1959   Benjamin Constant. Adolphe. Le Cahier rouge. [Bruxelles]: J. L. Kellinckx, 1959. (A travers le temps, 6). pp.190. Illus. [Maquette et dessin original du peintre Collet].
1000 copies printed.
Copy: BR.

A18/109 1959   Benjamin Constant. Adolphe. [Liège: G. Thone]; [Paris]: Le Club du livre sélectionné, [1959]. pp.173.
Copy: BR.

1960   See also item A18/101 (Adolphe ... Paris: Garnier, 1955).

1961   See also items A18/70 (reprint of Adolphe ... Manchester University Press, 1941) and A18/104 (reprint of Adolphe ... [Paris]: Le Livre de poche, [1957]).

A18/110 1961   Mme de La Fayette, Bernardin de Saint-Pierre, Benjamin Constant, Xavier de Maistre, Le Roman sentimental. Paris: Quillet, 1961. (Collection encyclopédique des classiques Quillet, 2e série, 3). pp.461. Illus.

A18/111 1961   Benjamin Constant. Adolphe. Introduction de Alfred Roulin. [Paris]: Le Club français du livre, 1961. 20.5 cm. pp.170.
Reprint of item A18/96 without illustrations and without reference to a collection.
Copies: AR, BN.

1962   See also item A18/97 (reprint of Adolphe ... Lausanne: Guilde du Livre, 1953).

A18/112 1963   Benjamin Constant. Adolphe. Le Cahier rouge. Paris: Charpentier, [1963]. (Ouvrages de poche, 15).
Copy: private collection.

A18/113 1963   Benjamin Constant. Adolphe. Con un'appendice di testi e documenti a cura di Carlo Cordié. Napoli: Edizioni scientifiche italiane, 1963. (Collana di letterature moderne, 19). pp.307. Bibliography.
Includes the *Lettre sur Julie*.
(Cordié 229).
Reviews: Olga Ragusa, *RR*, LVI (1965), 224-225. Paul Delbouille, *RLV*, XXXII (1966), 431-432. P. Ciureanu, *SF*, IX (1965), 167-168. Béatrice Le Gall, *RHLF*, LXVI (1966), 183-184. Alison Fairlic, *MLR*, LXI (1966), 519-520.

A18/114 1963   Le Cahier rouge, Cécile, Adolphe, par Benjamin Constant. [La trilogie romanesque présentée par Henri Thomas avec une iconographie

illustrant le caractère autobiographique de l'œuvre et un dictionnaire des personnages par René Le Grand Roy des *Cahiers Benjamin Constant*]. [Paris]: Club des Libraires de France, 1963. (Livres de toujours, 72). 20 cm. pp.[16], [viii], VIII, 266, [9]. Illus, facsimiles.
Copies: AR, BN.

1964   See also item E4/5 (Œuvres, Paris, Bibliothèque de la Pléiade, 1957, reprint, 1964).

A18/115 1964   Benjamin Constant. Adolphe. Le Cahier rouge. Journal intime (1804-1809). Paris: Nelson, 1964. (Collection Nelson, 453). 15.5 cm. pp.349.
Copy: B. Also issued as Nelson de luxe, 1965.

1965   See item A18/115 (Adolphe ... Paris: Nelson, 1964: reissued as Nelson de luxe, 1965).

A18/116 1965   Benjamin Constant. Adolphe. Chronologie et introduction par Antoine Adam. Paris: Garnier-Flammarion, 1965. (Texte intégral, 80). 18 cm. pp.185.
Frequently reprinted.

A18/117 1966   Benjamin Constant. Adolphe suivi de Le Cahier rouge et Amélie et Germaine. [Paris]: Le Trésor des Lettres françaises, [1966]. 21 cm. pp.235. Frontispiece (portrait).
'Avant-propos' (unsigned), pp.9-14. Reprint of 1824 edition (item A18/6).
Copies: BCU, BN. Reprinted: 1973. *Copy*: BCU.

A18/118 1966   Benjamin Constant. Adolphe. Introduction d'Alfred Roulin. [Paris]: Le Club français du livre, MCMLXVI. (Collection Privilège, 17). 13 cm. pp.XLVI, 242.
Copies: BCU, BN.

A18/119 1966   Benjamin Constant. Adolphe. Lavis originaux de Géa Augsbourg. Lausanne: Imprimerie La Concorde, 1966. (Collection du Renard, 3). 21 cm. pp.113.
500 numbered copies printed.
Copies: B, BCU.

1967   See item A18/104 (reprint of Adolphe ... Paris: Le Livre de poche, [1957]).

A18/120 1967   François-René de Chateaubriand, René; Benjamin Constant, Adolphe; A. de Lamartine, Graziella. Paris: S.E.C.A., 1967. (Les grands romans classiques français). 16.5 cm. pp.299.
Adolphe: pp.47-147.
Copy: BN. Reprinted: 1974 (see item A18/126).

1968   See also items A18/101 (revised edition of Adolphe ... Paris: Garnier,

1955) and A18/105 (reprint of Adolphe ... Lausanne: Editions Rencontre, [1957]).

A18/121 1968 Benjamin Constant. Adolphe, suivi de Cécile. Kapellen-Anvers: Walter Beckers, 1968. (Collection "Club"). 21.5 cm. pp.209.
Copies: B, BN.

A18/122 1968 Benjamin Constant. Adolphe. Anecdote trouvée dans les papiers d'un inconnu. Edited by W. Andrew Oliver. London, [etc.]: Macmillan; New York: St Martin's Press, 1968. (Macmillan's Modern Language Texts). pp.lii, 153. Bibliography. Includes selections from *Cécile*.
Reviews: Alison Fairlie, *FS*, XXIII (1969), 187-188. Helen H. S. Hogue, *MLJ*, LIII (1969), 518-519.

A18/123 1969 Benjamin Constant. Adolphe. Illustrations originales de Philippe Poncet de la Grave. Genève: Editions Edito-Service, 1969; distribué par le Cercle du bibliophile. 12 cm. pp.122. Frontispiece (portrait), illus.
Reprint of 1828 edition (item A18/7).
Copies: B, BN, BPU.

1970 See item A18/102 (second edition of Adolphe ... Roma: Signorelli, 1955).

1971 See item A18/70 (reprint of Adolphe ... Manchester University Press, 1941).

A18/124 1972 Benjamin Constant. Adolphe, suivi du Cahier rouge et de Poèmes inédits. Edition de Jean Mistler. [Paris]: Le Livre de poche, [1972]. (Le livre de poche, 360). 16.5 cm. pp.XXXVIII, 279.
Includes *Fragments du carnet disparu* pp.231-238 (see item A64/1-3), *Mémoires sur la Révolution*, pp.239-259 (see item A65/1) and two poems: *La Prière* and *Chant des ombres*, pp.263-271 (see items A74/9a-b).
Review: Carlo Cordié *SF*, XVII (1973), 370.

1973 See also item A18/117 (reprint of Adolphe ... [Paris]: Le Trésor des Lettres françaises, [1966]).

A18/125 1973 Benjamin Constant. Adolphe. Le Cahier rouge. Cécile. Préface de Marcel Arland. Edition établie et annotée par Alfred Roulin. [Paris]: Gallimard, [1973]. (Folio, 514). 18 cm. pp.310.
Frequently reprinted.

A18/126 1974 François-René de Chateaubriand, René; Benjamin Constant, Adolphe; A. de Lamartine, Graziella. [Neuilly-sur-Seine: Editions de St Clair, 1974]. 16.5 cm. pp.299. Illus.
Adolphe: pp.45-147. Two issues, one as described above, the other 18 cm. Reprint of item A18/120. Reprinted: 1980 (item A18/129).

Copies: BN, BPU.

A18/127 1977   Benjamin Constant. Adolphe. Anecdote trouvée dans les papiers d'un inconnu. Texte établi avec une introduction, une bibliographie, des notices, des notes et les variantes des deux manuscrits et des premières éditions par Paul Delbouille. Paris: Les Belles Lettres, 1977. (Les Textes français. Collection des universités de France publiée sous le patronage de l'Association Guillaume Budé). 19.5 cm. pp.300.
Review: Kurt Kloocke, *ZFSL*, LXXXIX (1979), 88-92.

1979   See also items A18/70 (reprint of Adolphe ... Manchester University Press, 1941) and E4/5 (reprint of Œuvres, Paris: Bibliothèque de la Pléiade, 1957).

A18/128 1979   Benjamin Constant. Adolphe, suivi de Cécile, Kahnthout-Anvers: Beckers, 1979. (Collection Les Amours célèbres). 24.5 cm. pp.148.

A18/129 1980   François-René de Chateaubriand, René, Benjamin Constant, Adolphe, Lamartine, Graziella. Préface de Maurice Toesca. [Genève]: Editions Famot, 1980. 20.5 cm. pp.VI, 7-299. Frontispiece.
Reprint of item A18/126.

A18/130 1982   Benjamin Constant. Adolphe. Préface de Bernard Frank. Paris: Nouvelles Editions Rupture, 1982. 20.5 cm. pp.170.
Reprint of item A18/17.

A18/131 1983   Benjamin Constant. Adolphe. [Genève: Editions de l'Eventail, 1983]. 20 cm. pp.147. Illus.

Translations

A18/t1 1816   Adolphe: An Anecdote found among the papers of an unknown person, and published by M. Benjamin de Constant ... London: printed for H. Colburn ... 1816. 12° pp.xvi, 222. Impr. Schulze & Dean, [London].
Translation by Alexander Walker. *Copies*: BL, BN, C, E. (C.18i).

A18/t1a 1816   Adolph. (Auszugsweise nach dem Französichen des Benjamin de Constant.) *Morgenblatt für gebildete Stände*. Tübingen: J. G. Cotta, Jahrgang 1816, n°s 199-203 (19-23 August), 205-208 (26-29 August), 210 (31 August), 211 (2 September), 213-217 (4-7, 9 September).
Copy: BN. (C. Suppl. Add. 3).

A18/t2 1817   Adolphe: An Anecdote found among the papers of an unknown person and published by M. Benjamin de Constant. Philadelphia: published by M. Carey and Son, 1817. 12° pp.xvi, [17]-238. Impr. G. Phillips, Carlisle, Pa.
Reprint of item A18/t1.
Copy: DLC. (C.18j).

A18/t3 1817 Adolf. Eine Erzählung, aus den gefundenen Papieren eines Unbekannten. Herausgegeben von Benjamin von Constant. Aus dem Französischen. Pesth 1817, bey K. A. Hartleben. 12° pp.[iv], VI, [7]-183. Frontispiece.

Copies: CtY, G. (Fromm 5697; C.18k).

A18/t4 1818 Adol'f i Eleonora, ili opasnost' lyubovnykh svyazey. Istinnoe proisshestvie. Naydeno v bumagakh odnago neizvestnago, i izdano v svêt Benzhamenom Konstanom. Perevod s frantsuzskago. Orel, v gub. tip. 1818. [Adolf and Eleonora, or the perils of amorous ties. A true event. Found in the papers of an unknown person. A translation from the French. Orel: at the Provincial Press, 1818]. pp.IX, [10]-212.

Translator anonymous.

Copy: SLL. (C.18l).

A18/t5 1826 Adolf. Af Benjamin Constant. Oversat af J. J. Østrup. Kjøbenhavn: 1826. Trykt paa Bog- og Papiirhandler C. Steens Forlag hos S. A. Nissen. 8° pp.[ii], 142.

Copy: CKB. (C.18m).

A18/t6 1828 [= 1827] Adolfo, anécdota hallada en los papeles de un desconocido, y publicada por Benjamín de Constant. Traducción castellana. Paris: Imprenta de A. Belin ... 1828. 18° pp.[iv], 212.

Copy: BN. (C.18n).

A18/t7 1831 Adol'f. (Povêst', rasskazannaya Benzhamenom Konstanom). [Adolphe. (A tale, related by Benjamin Constant)]. *Moskovsky telegraf*, 1831, Part 37, n° 1, 49-75; n° 2, 203-266; n° 3, 321-359; n° 4, 460-499.

Translation by N. A. Polevoy. See Paul Léon, 'Une analyse russe d'*Adolphe*', *The French Quarterly*, IX (1927), 265-272.

Copy: SLL. (C.18o).

A18/t8 1831 'Adol'f'. Roman Benzhamen-Konstana. Sanktpeterburg. V tipografii Departamenta narodnago prosvêshcheniya, 1831. Pechatano s dozvoleniya tsensora Nikity Butyrskago. 12° pp.xxiv, 222.

Translation by P. A. Vyazemsky, with dedication to Pushkin. See Paul Léon, article cited in the preceding item.

Copy: SLL. (C.18p). Reprinted in 1886 (see below A18/t15).

A18/t9 1835 Adolfo. Aneddoto trovato nelle carte d'un incognito e pubblicato dal signor Beniamino Constant. Prima traduzione italiana. Livorno: Tipografia Vignozzi, 1835. (Nuova Collezione di scelti romanzi, 27). pp.170.

(Cordié 171). Cordié suggests the translator may be Carlo Bini.

A18/t10 1839 Benjamin Constant. Adolph. Novelle. Nach dem Französischen von H. Künzel. Frankfurt am M.: Sauerländer, 1839.

(Fromm 5698).

A18/t11 1845   Benjamín Constant. Adolfo. Traducción del francés por P. Vidal. Anécdota, precedida de un ensayo analítico por Gustavo Planche. Barcelona: Imp. de Miguel Borrás, 1845. pp.147.
(Palau y Dulcet).

A18/t12 1854   Adolfo. Por Benjamín Constant. Madrid: Folletín de 'Las Novedades'. Impr. del Semanario de la Ilustración, 1854. pp.34. Illus.
(Hidalgo; Palau y Dulcet).

A18/t13 1858   Adolf. Roman istoric găsit în hîrtiile unui necunoscut. Tradus din limba franceză de Elena Drăghici. Jaşii, 1858. pp.122.
Copy: Buch.

A18/t14 1877   Benjamin Constant. Adolphe 1816. In: Cd. Busken Huet, *Oude Romans*, Amsterdam: G.L. Funke, 1877, II, 154-248.
Reprinted: Cd. Busken Huet, *Litterarische Fantasien en Kritieken*, Haarlem: H.D. Tjeenk Willinck, XX, 1888, 154-250.

A18/t15 1886   Adol'f. Roman. Benzhamen-Konstana. S.-Peterburg: Tipografiya M. M. Stasyulevicha, 1886.
Polnoe sobranie sochineniy Knyazya P.A. Vyazemskago, Tom X, 1853-1878 gg. Izdanie Grafa S. D. Sheremeteva. S.-Peterburg: Tipografiya M. M. Stasyulevicha, 1886.
Reprint of A18/t8.

A18/t16 1886   Adolf. Egy ismeretlen iratai közt talált történet. Irta Constant Benjamin. Francziából fordította és bevezetéssel ellátta Dr Béri Moravcsik Gyula. Budapest: Franklin-Társulat, 1886. (Olcsó Könyvtár. Szerkeszti Gyulai Pál, 530-531). 15 cm. pp.148.
Copies: B, BL, Bp.

1888   See item A18/t14 (reprint of Adolphe ... Haarlem: Tjeenk Willinck, 1877).

A18/t17 1890   Adolfo. Romanzo di Beniamino Constant. Con prefazione di C.A. Sainte-Beuve. Napoli: E. Pietrocola, 1890. (Piccola Collezione Amena, diretta da C. Petitti e O. Fava. Seconda serie, 19). pp.190.
Translator anonymous. (Cordié 180).

A18/t18 1892   Benjamín Constant. Adolfo. Trad. del francés por P. Vidal. Salamanca, 1892.
(Palau y Dulcet).

A18/t19 1893   Benjamín Constant. Adolfo. Madrid, 1893. pp.144.
(Palau y Dulcet).

A18/t20 1894   Benjamin Constant. Adolphe, oversat, med en inledning af

Hjalmar Christensen. Kristiania: H. Aschehoug & Co., 1894. 14 cm. pp.xxxi, 164.

Copies: CKB, Oslo.

A18/t21 1898　Adolphe. Roman von Benjamin Constant. Deutsch von Josef Ettlinger. Halle a.d. S.: Otto Hendel, [1898]. (Bibliothek der Gesamtliteratur des In- und Auslandes, 1197-1199). 18 cm. pp.151.

Copy: OT. (Fromm 5699).

A18/t22 1898　Adolf. Roman. Manuscris găsit între hîrtiile unui necunoscut. Traducere de B. Marian. Craiova: Ralian şi Ignat Samitca, [1898]. (Biblioteca romanelor celebre. Colecţia Samitca). pp.192.

Copy: Buch.

A18/t23 1903　Benjamin Constant. Adolf. Román. Přeložil R. Traub. V Praze: Nákladem J. Otty, 1903. (Světová knihovna sv. 305-306). 15 cm. pp.115.

Copy: Prague.

A18/t24 1903　Adolfo. Aneddoto trovato tra le carte d'un manoscritto [*sic*] di Beniamino Constant. Traduzione di Aristide Polastri. Milano: Società Editrice Sonzogno, 1903. (Biblioteca romantica economica, Seconda Serie, 305). pp.268.

Includes preface by Sainte-Beuve and essay on *Adolphe* by G. Planche.

Copy: B. (Cordié 182).

A18/t25 1903　Beniamino Constant. Adolfo. Romanzo. Milano: Fratelli Treves, 1903. (Biblioteca amena ad una lira il volume, 15 dicembre 1903, 658). 19 cm. pp.[iv], xii, 230.

Translator anonymous.

Copies: B, BN. (Cordié 183). Reprinted in the same year with, after the date: Secondo migliaio. *Copy*: B. (Cordié 183A).

A18/t26 1903　Benzhamen Konstan. Adolf. Psikhologicheski roman. Prêvede ot originala Iv. D. Stoynov. Sofiya: Izdanie na sp. 'Biblioteka', 1903. 20 cm. pp.100.

Copy: Sofia.

A18/t27 1907　Benjamin Constant. Trofast Kærlighed eller Ellénore og Adolf, [Copenhagen, 1907]. 14 cm. pp.xxxi, 164.

Copy: CKB.

A18/t28 1910　Benjamin Constant. Adolf. Aus den Papieren eines Unbekannten. Übersetzt und eingeleitet von Otto Flake. München und Leipzig: Georg Müller, 1910. 18.5 cm. pp.[iv], 152.

1500 numbered copies printed.

Copies: B, BPU, Mar. (Fromm 5700).

A18/t29 1911　Benjamin Constant. Adolph, een kleine roman, vertaald en

ingeleid door Cd. Busken Huet. Amsterdam: Wereldbibliotheek, [1911]. (Maatschappij voor goede en goedkoope lectuur). 18 cm. pp.116.
Copies: B, BCU.

A18/t30 1912   Benjamín Constant. Adolfo. Novela. Traducción de R. Leval. Barcelona: Antonio López, 1912. 20 cm. pp.256.
(*Catálogo general*, 17.891).

A18/t31 1912   Benjamín Constant. Adolfo. Novela. Traducción de R. Leval. Paris: L. Michaud, [1912]. (Autores selectos).
Copy: MH.

A18/t32 1912   Benjamin Constant. Adolf. Pròleg i traducció d'Augustí Esclasans. Barcelona-Badalona: Proa, [1912]. (Biblioteca A tot vent).
(*Catálogo general*, 17.891). Reprinted: 1928, 1982.

A18/t33 1913   Benjamin Constant. Pribeagul, tradus de Scarlat Georgescu. Bucureşti: Cartea românească, [1913]. (Biblioteca 'Minerva', 133-133a). 15 cm. pp.91.
Copies: Buch, Sofia.

A18/t34 1914   B. Constant. Adolfo. Firenze: Quattrini, 1914. (Biblioteca Amena Quattrini, 64). pp.149.

Translator anonymous. (Cordié 186). Reprinted: 1928, see below, item A18/t56.

A18/t35 1917   Benjamin Constant. Adolphe. Übersetzung von Otto Hauser. Weimar: Duncker, 1917. (Aus fremden Gärten, 51-52). pp.XII, 94.

(Fromm 5701).

A18/t36 1917   Constant. Adolfo. Versione italiana di L. Mazzucchetti. Milano: Istituto Editoriale Italiano, [1917]. (Raccolta di breviari intellettuali, 56). pp.252.
Introduction by Paul Bourget.
Copy: B. (Cordié 187).

A18/t37 1917   Benjamin Constant. Adolf. Przełożył Boy, Kraków: G. Gebethner i Spółka; Warszawa: Gebethner i Wolff; Poznań: Księgarnia M. Niemierkiewicza, 1917. (Bibljoteka Boya. T. 15). 18.5 cm. pp.XXI, 133.
Copies: BN, Ww. Second edition revised: 1922. pp.147. *Copy*: Ww.

A18/t38 1918   Benjamín Constant. Adolfo. Prólogo y traducción de Vicente Clavel. Barcelona: Cervantes, 1918. (Biblioteca Serie Apassionata). pp.139.
(*Catálogo general*, 17.891).

A18/t39 1919   Benjamin Constant. Adolf. Übertragen von Elisabeth Schellenberg. Leipzig: Insel, [1919]. (Insel-Bücherei, 284). 18 cm. pp.79.
Includes 'Nachwort' by the translator, p.79.

Copies: BCU, BL, BN. (Fromm 5702).

A18/t40 1919   Benjamín Constant. Adolfo. Viuda de P. Pérez. Madrid: Saturnino Calleja, 1919. (Colección Fémina, 5). pp.199.
(*Catálogo general*, 17.891).

A18/t41 1919   Benjamín Constant. Adolfo. Traducción de Antonio Espino. Madrid: Calpe, [1919]. (Colección Universal, 945).
(*Catálogo general*, 17.891). Reprinted: 1924.
Copy: MBN.

A18/t42 1919   Benjamín Constant. Adolfo, novela. Traducción de Manuel Abril. Madrid: [Biblioteca Estrella], 1919. (Colección Fémina, 5). 14.5 cm. pp.199.
Copy: DLC.

A18/t43 1920   Benjamin Constant. Adolphe. Fordította Zolnai Béla. Budapest: Az Athenaeum irodalmi és nyomdai R.-T. Kiadása, 1920. 15 cm. pp.160.
Copy: Bp.

A18/t44 1920   Benjamin   Constant.   Adolphe.   Erään   tuntemattoman papereista löydetty tarina. Suomentanut L. Onerva. Kustannusosakeyhtiö Kirja. Helsinki: Karlsson & Jantunen, Kirjapaino, 1920. 18.5 cm. pp.128.
Two issues, both dated 1920.
Copies: Hels.

A18/t45 1921   Benzhamen Konstan. Adolf. Prêvede ot frenski Georgi D. Yurukov. Sofiya: Mozaika ot znameniti savrêmenni romani, [1921]. 20 cm. pp.76.
Copy: Sofia.

1922   See also item A18/t37 (second edition of Adolf ... Kraków, 1917).

A18/t46 1922   Adolf de Benjamin Constant. Tradus din franţuzeşte de T. Teodorescu-Branişte. Bucureşti: Cultura natională, [1922]. 18 cm. pp.132.
Copies: Buch, Sofia.

A18/t47 1923   Beniamino Constant. Adolfo. Traduzione di Massimo Bontempelli. Milano: Casa Editrice Milano, 1923. (Serie verde, 2). pp.205.
(Cordié 188).

A18/t48 1923   Beniamino Constant. Adolfo. Traduzione di Massimo Bontempelli. Milano: Casa Editrice Imperia Milano, [1923]. (Fiore di ogni letteratura, 9). pp.205.
Reissue of the preceding item. (Cordié 188A).

A18/t49 1923   Beniamino Constant. Adolfo. Traduzione di Massimo Bontempelli. Milano: Bietti, [1923]. pp.205.

Reissue of item A18/t47. (Cordié 189).
Copy: CU.

A18/t50 1923   Benjamin Constant. Adolfo. Lettera su Giulia (Mme Talma). Il racconto di Guilietta (Mme Récamier). Versione, notizia introduttiva e bibliografia di Maria Ortiz. Firenze: G. C. Sansoni, 1923. (Biblioteca sansoniana straniera, diretta da Guido Manacorda, 25). 16 cm. pp.cxxviii, 144. Bibliography.
Copies: B, BPU. (Cordié 190). Reprinted: 1949. *Copy*: B.

1924   See also item A18/t41 (reprint of Adolfo ... Madrid: Calpe, [1919]).

A18/t51 1924   Adolphe. A narrative found among the papers of an unknown person and edited by M. Benjamin de Constant, translated by Paul Hookham, introduction by Gustave Rudler. London: A. M. Philpot, Ltd., 1924. 19 cm. pp.183. Frontispiece (portrait).
500 copies printed.
Copies: BL, C, OT.

A18/t52 1924   Benjamin Constant. Adolf. Roman. Manuscris găsit între hârtiile unui necunoscut cu o prefaţă de Anatole France. Traducere de B. Marian. Ediţia III-a. Bucureşti: Editura librăriei 'Universala' Alcalay et Cie., 1924. (Biblioteca pentru toţi). 15 cm. pp.160.
Preface by Anatole France, pp.2-15.
Copy: B. Reprinted: 1936.

A18/t53 1924   Benjamin Constant. Adolf. Tradus de Paul Ionescu. Bucureşti, n.d. [*ca.* 1924]. (Bibliotheca 'Lumina', 119). pp.vi, 135.
Copy: Buch.

A18/t54 1925   Adolphe, by Benjamin Constant. Translated by J. Lewis May. London: Stanley Paul & Co. Ltd; Philadelphia: David McKay Company, [1925]. (The International Library). 17.5 cm. pp.153. Frontispiece.
Copies: BL, O, OT.

A18/t55 1925   Adolphe; a narrative found among the papers of an unknown person and edited by M. Benjamin de Constant, translated by Paul Hookham, with an introduction by Henry K. Marks. New York: A. A. Knopf, [1925]. (Borzoi Pocket Books). 17.5 cm. pp.[iv], 173.
Copies: DLC, O.

1928   See also item A18/t32 (reprint of Adolf ... Barcelona-Badalona, [1912]).

A18/t56 1928   Beniamino Constant. Adolfo. Firenze: Attilio Quattrini, [1928]. (Il romanzo universale, 51). pp.142.

Translator anonymous. Reprint of item A18/t34 (1914), with *Prefazione* [to the third edition] omitted. (Cordié 192).

A18/t57 1929 Benjamin Constant. Adolphe ved Knud Engel. København: Woel, 1929. 20.5 cm. pp.136.
Copies: BL, CKL.

A18/t58 1929 Benjamín Constant. Adolfo. Madrid: Revista literaria, 1929. pp.23.
(Palau y Dulcet).

A18/t59 1930 Adolfo di B. Constant. M.CM.XXX. [Bruxelles: Edizioni Psiche, 1930]. (I grandi romantici, 2). 18 cm. pp.xxii, 181. Illus. Bibliography.
Printed by the Società Tipografica, Bari. 333 numbered copies printed. Translated by Francesco Carbonara. Introduction by the translator.
Copies: B, BL, BR, SG. (Cordié 193).

A18/t60 1930 Benjamin Constant. Adolphe. *Zabavna biblioteka*, Serie XV, vol. 485. Zagreb: Naklada Zaklade tiskare Narodnih novina, 1930, pp.140-228.
Croat translation by Ivo Hergešić, preceded by translation of Goethe's *Werther*. Introduction by the translator: 'Werther i Adolphe', pp.3-11. *Copy*: Zagreb.

A18/t61 1930 Benjamin Constant. Adolf. Warszawa: Bibljoteka Boya, 1930. (Arcydzieła Literatury Francuskiej). pp.100
New edition of A18/t37 with introduction by Tadeusz Żeleński (Boy).
Copy: Ww. Reprinted: Warszawa: Wiedza, 1948. pp.141. *Copy*: Ww. [Warszawa]: Państwowy Instytut Wydawniczy, [1957]. pp.116. *Copies*: B, Ww.

A18/t62 1932 Beniamino Constant. Adolfo. Romanzo. Traduzione di Francesco Flora. Milano-Roma: Treves-Treccani-Tumminelli, MCMXXXII-X. (Nuova biblioteca amena, 24). pp.222.
Includes *Il Quaderno rosso (La mia vita (1767-1787))*, pp.137-222.
Copy: BN. (Cordié 194).

A18/t63 1932 Shatobrian, F.O., René; Konstan, B., Adol'f. Moskva: Zhurn.-gaz. ob"ed., 1932. (Istoriya molodogo cheloveka XIX stoletiya. Ser. romanov. – Pod red. M. Gor'kogo, V. Vinogradova). 22 cm. pp.144. Illus.
Adolphe: pp.77-144.
Copies: BN, SLL.

A18/t64 1933 Adolphe, an autobiographical novel, by Benjamin Constant, with an introduction by Sainte-Beuve. Translated by W. Lalor Barrett. New York: L. MacVeagh, Dial Press Inc., 1933. 19.5 cm. pp.xiv, 128.
Reviews: *Commonweal*, 22 February 1933, p.476. *New York Times*, 21 May 1933, p.8.
Copy: B.

A18/t65 1933 Benjamin Constant. Adolphe-Diario. A cura di Giulia Gerace. Torino: Unione Tipografico-Editrice Torinese, 1933-XI. (Collana di traduzioni: I grandi scrittori stranieri, diretta da Arturo Farinelli). 19 cm. pp.165. Portrait. Includes extracts from the *Journal*. (Cordié 196). Reprinted: 1941, 1944, 1951, 1956. (Cordié 198, 204, 319, 303).

A18/t66 1934 Benjamin Constant. Adolphe. [Japanese translation by Kasho Shinjo]. Tokyo: Shunyodo, 1934. (Sekai meisaku bunko, 172).
Copy: Tokyo.

A18/t67 1935 Benjamin Constant. Adolphe. [Japanese translation by Yukio Otsuka]. Tokyo: Iwanami Shoten, 1935. (Iwanami bunko). pp.133.
Copy: Tokyo. Reprinted: Tokyo: Tancho Shobo, 1948. pp.160. *Copy*: Tokyo. Revised edition: Tokyo: Iwanami Shoten, 1965. pp.147. *Copy*: Tokyo.

A18/t68 1935 Benjamin Konstan. Adolf. Çeviren: A. Kâmi Akyüz. Bastıran ve Yayan Ibrahim Hilmi. Hilmi Kitapevi. İstanbul: Matbaai Ebüzziya, 1935. 18.5 cm. pp.133.
Copy: Ankara.

1936 See item A18/t52 (reprint of Adolf, Bucureşti: Alcalay).

A18/t69 1937 Benjamin Constant. Adolfo. Romance. Tradução de Campos Lima. Lisboa: Guimarães & Cª, [1937]. (Os livros imortais). 19 cm. pp.160.
Copy: Lisbon.

1941 See A18/t65 (reprint of Adolphe-Diario, Torino, 1933).

A18/t70 1942 Benjamín Constant. Adolfo. Traducción de Fernando Gutiérrez. Barcelona: Gráficas Marco, Edit. Apolo, 1942. 20 cm. pp.95.
Copy: MBN.

A18/t71 1942 Benjamín Constant. Adolfo. Traducción de J. Z. Barragán. Barcelona: Maucci, 1942. 16 cm. pp.122.
Copy: MBN.

A18/t72 1943 Benjamín Constant. Adolfo. Traducción de Luis Valle. Buenos Aires: Editorial Nova, 1943. (Serie romántica). 21 cm. pp.148. Portrait.
Copy: DLC.

A18/t73 1943 A szerelem kalandjai. [Budapest]: Franklin-Társulat Kiadása, [1943]. 20 cm. pp.315.
On pp.251-315, Benjamin Constant: Adolphe ... Fordította Bóka László, a bevezetést Cs. Szabó László írta. Also includes *La Princesse de Clèves* and *Manon Lescaut*.
Copy: Bp.;

1944 See also item A18/t65 (reprint of Adolphe-Diario, Torino, 1933).

A18/t74 1944   Benjamin Constant. Adolf, uit het Fransch vertaald door Hendrik van Tichelen, met houtsneden van Luc de Jaegher. Hoogstraten: Moderne Uitgeverij, [1944]. 19 cm. pp.142. Illus.
Copies: B, BR.

A18/t75 1944   Benjamin Constant. Adolph. Roman. [Deutsch von Werner Johannes Guggenheim]. Zürich: Pegasus, 1944. (Vom Dauernden in der Zeit, 4). 18.5 cm. pp.178.
Copies: B, BCU. (Fromm 5703).

A18/t76 1944   Constant. Adolfo. Traduzione di Enrico Emanuelli. [Roma]: Colombo, [1944]. (Labirinto d'Amore, 2). 18.5 cm. pp.199. Bibliography.
Introduction by the translator, pp.5-29.
Copy: B. (Cordié 201).

A18/t77 1944   Benjamin Constant. Adolphe. Roman. Efterskrift av Carl Ivar Sandström. [Stockholm]: Natur och Kultur, [1944]. 20.5cm pp.151. Frontispiece (portrait). Översättningen är utförd av Carl Ivar Sandström.
Copy: S. See below, item A18/t102.

A18/t77a 1944   Benjamín Constant. Adolfo. Introducción de Paul Bourget; traducción de Antonio Sánchez Barbudo. México: Editorial Leyenda, 1944. (Obras maestras de la literatura amorosa). 23 cm. pp.170.
Copy: NmLcU.

A18/t78 1945   Benjamin Constant. Povestea dragostei (Adolf). Tradus de Pen. Rozopol. Bucureşti: Enciclopedia Fotografică, 1945. (Colecţia pentru toţi). pp.96.
Copy: Buch.

A18/t79 1946   Benjamin Constant. Adolphe. Oversættelse ved Karen Nyrop Christensen. [Ill. af Ulla Lindstrøm]. [Copenhagen]: Carit Andersen, 1946. (Karatserien, 12). pp.167. Illus.
Copy: CKB.

A18/t80 1947   Benjamin Constant. Adolphe. (Übertr. und Vorwort von Josef Ziwutschka. Illustr. von Arnulf Neuwirth). Wien: Amandus-Ed., [1947]. pp.127. Illus.
(Fromm 5704).

A18/t81 1947   Benjamín Constant. Adolfo. Traducción directa del francés por José Barrio Olivares. Texto íntegro. (3a ed.) Buenos Aires: Editorial Sopena Argentina, [1947]. (Colección Universo). 23 cm. pp.126.
Copy: B.

A18/t81a 1947   Benjamin Constant. Adolfo; tradução e prefácio de Ary de Mesquita. Rio de Janeiro: I. Pongetti, 1947. 19 cm. pp.155.

Copy: OrPS.

1948   See also items A18/t61 (Adolf ... Warszawa, 1930) and A18/t67 (reprint of Adolphe ... Tokyo, 1935).

A18/t82 1948   Adolphe and The Red Note-Book by Benjamin Constant. With an introduction by Harold Nicolson. London: Hamish Hamilton, [1948]. (The Novel Library). 17 cm. pp.xxxii, 152.
Adolphe translated by Carl Wildman; Le *Cahier rouge* translated by Norman Cameron. See below, items A18/t83, A18/t99-101
Review: *TLS*, 22 January 1949, p.53, 'The classical manner'.

A18/t83 1948   Benjamin Constant. Adolphe and The Red Note-Book. New York: Pantheon Books, [1948]. 18 cm. pp.xxxii, 152.
Adolphe translated by Carl Wildman; *Le Cahier rouge* translated by Norman Cameron. Another issue of the preceding item. See below items A18/t99-101.

A18/t84 1948   Benjamin Constant. Adolphe. [Japanese translation by Kenichiro Hayashi]. Tokyo: Sekai Bungakusha (Kyoto), 1948. pp.201.
Copy: Tokyo.

A18/t84a 1948   Benjamin Constant. Kharīf al-ḥubb. Taʿrīb Shams al-Dīn al-Ghuriyānī. Cairo: Maṭbaʿat Rīwāyāt al-Jayb, 1948. (Rīwāyāt al-Jayb, 589). pp.98. [The autumn of love. Rendered in Arabic by Shams al-Dīn al-Ghuriyānī. Cairo: Pocket Novel Press, 1948. (Pocket Novels, 589)].   \
(Manṣūr, *Dalīl al-Maṭbūʿāt al-Miṣrīya 1940-1956*, item 8019).

1949   See also item A18/t50 (reprint of Adolfo ... Firenze: Sansoni, 1923).

A18/t85 1949   Benjamin Constant. Adolphe. Geschichte einer Leidenschaft. Roman. [Aus dem Französischen übertragen von Luise Roth-Schlenk]. Bühl/Baden: Roland-Verlag, 1949. 19 cm. pp.155.
Includes postface, 'Henri Benjamin Constant', by 'D.U.', pp.153-155.
Copies: B, BN, T.

A18/t86 1950   Benjamín Constant. Adolfo. [Traducción del francés por Antonio Espina]. Buenos Aires-México: Espasa-Calpe Argentina, [1950]. (Colección Austral, 938). 18 cm. pp.146.
Copy: OU. Segunda edición: 1950. *Copy*: B.

1951   See also item A18/t65 (reprint of Adolfo-Diario ... Torino, 1933).

A18/t87 1951   Benjamin Constant. Een kleine roman, vertaald door Cd. Busken Huet. Amsterdam, Antwerpen: Wereldbibliotheek. Tweede druk, 1951. (De Wereldboog, 7). 18.5 cm. pp.124.
'Naschschrift' [by Cd. Busken Huet], dated February 1876, pp.105-124.
Copies: B, BCU, BR.

A18/t88 1951 Murry, John Middleton. The Conquest of Death. London, New York: Peter Nevill, 1951. 21 cm. pp.306.

Includes translation of *Adolphe*, pp.11-121.

Copies: BL, BN.

Reviews: Martin Turnell, *The Observer*, 21 October 1951, 'Constant and Mr Murry'. *TLS*, 28 December 1951, p.833, 'Of love and death'. P. Henderson, *Britain Today*, n° 192, April 1952, p.46, 'Mr Murry and Adolphe'.

A18/t89 1953 Benjamin Constant. Adolphe ... s'aghapo. [Translated by] P. Vovolinis. Athinae: Kerameus, 1953. pp.128.

(*Bulletin analytique de bibliographie hellénique*, XIV (1953), 304 (item 1247); *Index translationum*, VI, 8296).

A18/t90 1953 Benjamin Constant. Adolfo. Il quaderno rosso-Cecilia, Amelia e Germana, Lettere intorno a Giulia. [Traduzione di Piero Bianconi]. Milano: Rizzoli, [1953]. (Biblioteca Universale Rizzoli, 549-551). 16 cm. pp.245.

Copy: B. (Cordié 218).

A18/t91 1953 Benjamin Constant. Adolphe. Anegdota nadjena medju papirima nekoga neznanca. [S francuskoga preveo Ivo Hergešić]. Zagreb: [Zora], 1953. (Mala Biblioteka, 151). 17 cm. pp.121.

Postface by Ivo Hergešić.

Copies: B, Zagreb.

A18/t92 1953 Benžamen Konstan. Adolf. Priča nadjena medju hartijama jednog nepoznatog čoveka. [Preveo Nikola Trajković. Red.: Raško Dimitrijević]. Beograd: Novo pokolenje, 1953. (Mala Knjiga, 5). 17 cm. pp.116.

Copy: B.

A18/t93 1954 Benjamin Constant. Adolphe / Cécile. Amsterdam: L. J. Veen; Brussel: D. A. P. Reinaert, 1954. (Amstel literaire paperbacks, Reinaert literaire paperbacks). pp.156.

Adolphe translated by Busken Huet; *Cécile* by Dr C. Serrurier.

Copies: A, BR. Reprinted: 1967. *Copy*: B.

A18/t94 1954 Benjamin Constant. Adolphe. [Japanese translation by Kasho Shinjo]. Tokyo: Shinchosha, 1954. (Shincho bunko). pp.121.

Copy: Tokyo.

1956 See also item A18/t65 (reprint of Adolphe-Diario, Torino, 1933).

A18/t95 1956 Benjamin Constant. Adolphe. [Deutsch von Margrit Voigt und Reinhard Kilbel. Mit einem Nachwort von Karl Blasche]. Leipzig: Dieterich, 1956. (Sammlung Dieterich, 193). 17 cm. pp.135.

Copies: B, BCU. Reprinted: 1965.

1957 See also item A18/t61 (Adolf ... Warszawa, 1930).

A18/t96 1957 Benjamin Constant. Adolf. Praha: Státní Nakladatelství Krásné Literatury, Hudby a Umění, 1957. (Světová četba sv. 136). 17 cm. pp.138. Translation by Josef Pospíšil.
Copy: Prague.

A18/t97 1958 Benjamin Constant. Adolphe. Regény. [Fordította és az utószót írta Bóka László. A fordítást átdolgozta és a jegyzeteket írta Bartócz Ilona]. [Budapest]: Európa, 1958. (Világirodalmi kiskönyvtár). 18 cm. pp.97.
Postface by László Bóka, pp.87-97.
Copies: B, Bp, BpFS.

A18/t98 1958 Benjamin Constant. Ǎ Tu Êrh Fu. Pê Yün. Taipei: Hsin Hsing Book Co., [1958]. pp.128.
(*Index translationum*, XI, 5841).

A18/t99 1959 Adolphe and The Red Note-Book, by Benjamin Constant. With an introduction by Harold Nicolson. Indianapolis: Bobbs-Merrill, [1959]. 21 cm. pp.252.
Adolphe translated by Carl Wildman; *Le Cahier rouge* by Norman Cameron. Reprint of item A18/t82.

A18/t100 1959 Adolphe and The Red Note-Book, by Benjamin Constant. With an introduction by Harold Nicolson. London: Hamish Hamilton, 1959. 19.5 cm. pp.252.
Adolphe translated by Carl Wildman; *Le Cahier rouge* by Norman Cameron. Reprint of item A18/t82.
Review: V. S. Pritchett, *New Statesman*, 30 May 1959, pp.763-764, 'The Tyrant of Coppet'.

A18/t101 1959 Benjamin Constant. Adolphe and The Red Notebook. With an introduction by Harold Nicolson. [New York]: New American Library, [1959]. (A Signet Classic). 18 cm. pp.xxvi, 160.
Adolphe translated by Carl Wildman; *Le Cahier rouge* by Norman Cameron. Reprint of item A18/t82.

A18/t102 1959 Benjamin Constant. Adolphe. [Till svenska och med efterskrift av Carl Ivar Sandström]. Stockholm: Natur och Kultur, [1959]. (Levande Litteratur). 17.5 cm. pp.134.
Reprint of item A18/t77.
Copies: B, S.

A18/t103 1959 Benjamin Constant. Adolphe. Samih Tiryakioğlu. İstanbul: Varlık Yayınevi, 1959. pp.79.
(*Index translationum*, XI, 23746).

A18/t104 1959 Benzhamen Konstan. Adol'f. A. S. Kulisher. Moskva: Goslitizdat, 1959. pp.159.

(*Index translationum*, XII, 25962).

A18/t105 1960 Benjamin Constant. Adolphe. Ingeleid door G. H. M. van Huet; vertaald door L. J. Plemp van Duiveland. Amsterdam/Antwerpen: Contact, [1960]. (De Onsterfelijken). 19.5 cm. pp.ix, 142.
Copies: B, BR. Reprinted: 1962, 1967.

A18/t106 1960 Benjamin Constant. Adolphe. [Japanese translation by Takeshi Takemura]. Tokyo: Kadokawa Shoten, 1960. (Kadokawa bunko). pp.120.
Copy: Tokyo.

A18/t107 1960 Benjamin Constant. Adolphe. [Japanese translation by Isamu Kurita]. Tokyo: Tozai Gogatsusha, 1960. (*France Bungaku Zenshu*, vol. 13, pp.115-200).
Copy: Tokyo.

A18/t108 1961 Benjamin Constant. Adolphe. [Vert. uit het Frans door Jacoba van Velde]. Utrecht: Bruna, [1961]. (Zwarte beertjes, 406). 17.5 cm. pp.156.

A18/t109 1961 Longo ..., Dafnis y Cloe. Abate Prévost, Historia de Manón Lescaut y el Caballero des Grieux. Goethe, Werther. Benjamín Constant, Adolfo. Barcelona: Exito, 1961. (Grandes novelas de la literatura universal, 2). 20 cm. pp.xii, 440.
Copy: MBN.

1962   See also item A18/t105 (reprint of Adolphe ... Amsterdam/Antwerpen: Contact, [1960]).

A18/t110 1962 Benjamin Constant. Adolphe. Roman. Aus dem Französischen übertragen von Werner Johannes Guggenheim. München: Goldmann, 1962. (Goldmanns gelbe Taschenbücher, 854). pp.162.

A18/t111 1963 Benjamin Constant. Adolphe-Diario, a cura di Stefano de Simone, Nuova edizione. Torino: Unione Tipografico-Editrice Torinese, 1963. (Collana di traduzioni: I grandi scrittori stranieri, fondata da Arturo Farinelli, diretta da Giovanni Vittorio Amoretti). pp.207. Portrait. Bibliography.
(Cordié 320).

A18/t112 1963 Benjamin Constant. Adolphe. Cécile. Zwei Romane. (Aus dem Französischen übertragen von Max Hölzer und Hanno Helbling.) [Frankfurt am Main]: Insel-Verlag, 1963. (Insel Bücherei, 776). 18 cm. pp.151.
Copies: B, BL.

A18/t113 1963 Benjamin Constant. L'Adolfo. L. G. Tenconi. Milano: Leda, 1963. pp.188.
(*Index translationum*, XVII, 17540).

A18/t114 1964 Benjamin Constant. Adolphe. Translated with an introduc-

tion by L. W. Tancock. [London]: Penguin Books, [1964]. (The Penguin Classics edited by E. V. Rieu). 18 cm. pp.125.
Copies: BL, BN. Reprinted: 1980.

A18/t115 1964   Benžamen Konstan. Adolf. Sesila. Nikola Trajković & Cveta Kotevska. Beograd: Rad, 1964. pp.151.
(*Index translationum*, XIX, 37501).

A18/t116 1964   Benjamin Constant. Adolphe. În romineşte de Tudor Teodorescu-Branişte. Prefaţă de Şerban Cioculescu. Bucureşti: Editura pentru literatură universală, 1964. 17 cm. pp.159.
Copy: B.

A18/t117 1964   Benjamin Constant. Adolphe. [Japanese translation by Toyota Ichihara]. Tokyo: Chikuma Shobo, 1964. (*Sekai Bungaku Taikei*, vol. 91, pp.271-312).
Copy: Tokyo. Reprinted: *Sekai Bungaku Zenshu*, vol. 68 (1969), pp.5-68. *Copy*: Tokyo. Also reprinted in *Chikuma Sekai Bungaku Taikei*, [1969?] vol. 86, pp.69-110. *Copy*: Tokyo.

1965   See also item A18/t67 (revised edition of Adolphe ... Tokyo, 1935) and A18/t95 (reprint of Adolphe ... Leipzig: Dieterich, 1956).

1967   See also item A18/t93 (reprint of Adolphe ... Amsterdam-Brussel, 1954) and A18/t105 (reprint of Adolphe ... Amsterdam/Antwerp: Contact, [1960]).

A18/t118 1968   Benjamin Constant. Adolphe. Oreste Del Buono. Milano: 1968. pp.177.
(*Index translationum*, XXII, 20452).

A18/t119 1968   Benjamin Constant. Adolfo. Cecília. Prefácio de Marcel Arland. Lisboa: Portugália, [1968]. (Os Romances universais, 41). 21 cm. pp.276.
Translation by Maria José Marinho.
Copy: Lisbon.

1969   See also item A18/t117 (reprints of Adolphe ... Tokyo, 1964).

A18/t120 1969   Benjamin Constant. Adolphe. Cécile. L. J. Plemp van Duiveland & Johan Fredric. Amsterdam: Contact, 1969. pp.215. Illus.

A18/t121 1969   Benjamin Constant. Adolphe. [Japanese translation by Fumihiko Takita]. Tokyo: Chuo Koronsha, 1969. (*Sekai no Bungaku Shinshu*, vol. 3, pp.169-254).
Copy: Tokyo.

1970   See item E4/t7 (Werke ... Berlin, Bd. I, 1970).

A18/t122 1970   Adolphe by Benjamin Constant. Ada Zemah. Tel-Aviv: Dvir, 1970. 18 cm. pp.107.

Copy: J.

A18/t123 1973 Benjamin Constant. Adolphe. Çeviren: Samih Tiryakioğlu. Istanbul: Hayat Neşriyat Anonim Şirketi, 1973. (Altın Kalem Klasik Romanlar yöneten Vahdet Gültekin. Fransız Edebiyatı, 16). 19.5 cm. pp.235. Illus.
Copy: Ankara.

A18/t124 1973 Doamna de La Fayette, Principesa de Clèves. Benjamin Constant, Adolf. Bucureşti: Editura 'Eminescu', 1973. (Colecţia Romanul de dragoşte, 63).
Copy: Buch.

A18/t125 1975 Benjamin Constant. Adolphe. [Japanese translation by Motoo Ando]. Tokyo: Shueisha, 1975. (*Sekai Bungaku Zenshu*, vol. 8, pp.371-432).
Copy: Tokyo.

A18/t126 1977 Benjamin Constant. Adolphe. Cécile. Il Quaderno rosso. [Traduzione del francese di Lisa Tullio]. [Milano]: Curcio, 1977. (I classici della narrativa. Collana diretta da Libero Bigiaretti). 21 cm. pp.197.
Copy: B.

A18/t127 1978 Benjamin Constant. Adolphe, [tr. George Pape]. Wijnigem: Het Spectrum, 1978. (Prisma Klassieken, 9). pp.112.

A18/t128 1979 Jacques Cazotte, A szerelmes ördög; Benjamin Constant, Adolphe. Budapest: Szépirodalmi Könyvkiadó, [1979]. [Fordította Bóka László, az utószó Réz Pál munkája]. (Olcsó Könyvtár). 18 cm. pp.177.
Adolphe, pp.91-177, preceded by translation by Pál Réz of *Le diable amoureux*.
Copy: Bp.

A18/t129 1979 Benjamin Constant. Adolphe, a cura di Teresa Cremisi. Milano: Garzanti, 1979. (I grandi libri, 227). pp.136. Frontispiece (portrait).

1980 See item A18/t114 (reprint of Adolphe ... [London]: Penguin books, 1964).

1982 See item A18/t32 (reprint of Adolphe ... Barcelon-Badalona: Proa, [1912]).

A18/t130 1982 Benjamin Constant. Adolphe. Erzählung aus den gefundenen Papieren eines Unbekannten. München: Winkler, 1982. 19.5 cm. pp.151. Frontispiece, illus. Bibliography.
Reprint of item A18/t3, überarbeitet und herausgegeben von Kurt Kloocke.

A19 De la doctrine politique

A19/1 1816 De la doctrine politique, qui peut réunir les partis en France, par M. Benjamin de Constant. A Paris, chez Delaunay ... Décembre 1816. 8° pp.43. Impr. Fain, [Paris].

Copies: BCU, BL, BN. (C.19a).

A19/2 1817   De la doctrine ... Seconde édition, revue et corrigée ... Janvier 1817. 8° pp.43. Impr. Fain, [Paris].
Copies: BCU, BN, C. (C.19b).

Other editions: *Cours de politique* 1818 (E1/1(2)), *Cours de politique* 1820 (E1/2(2)), Laboulaye 1861 (E1/5a), Laboulaye 1872 (E1/5b), Pozzo di Borgo 1964 (E4/6).

Translation

A19/t1 1817   On the Political Doctrine calculated to unite parties in France; by Benjamin de Constant. Translated by Thomas Elde Darby, under the inspection of the Author. London: Ridgways ... 1817. 8° pp.[ii], 42. Impr. W. Flint, London.
Copy: BL. (C.19c).

A20 Considérations sur le projet de loi relatif aux élections

A20/1 1817   Considérations sur le projet de loi relatif aux élections, adopté par la Chambre des députés; par M. B. de Constant. (Extrait du *Mercure de France* du 18 Janvier.) Paris, chez Delaunay ... 1817. 8° pp.28. Impr. Dubray, [Paris].
Copies: BCU, BL, O. (C.20a).

A21 Tableau politique du royaume des Pays-Bas

A21/1 1817   Tableau politique du royaume des Pays-Bas. Par Benjamin de Constant. A Paris [=Brussels], chez les marchands de nouveautés, 1817. 8° pp.24.
Reprinted from *MF*, April 1817, pp.131-139 and May 1817, pp.278-285.
Copies: A, BR, C, NN, T. (C.21a).

A22 Questions sur la législation actuelle de la presse en France

A22/1 1817   Questions sur la législation actuelle de la presse en France, et sur la doctrine du ministère public, relativement à la saisie des écrits, et à la responsabilité des auteurs et imprimeurs, par M. Benjamin de Constant ... A Paris, chez les marchands de nouveautés, 1817. 8° pp.[iii], 101. Impr. Renaudière, [Paris].
Copies: BCU, BL, BN. (C.22a).

A22/2 1817   Questions ... Seconde édition; A Paris, chez Delaunay ... et chez les marchands de nouveautés, 1817. 8° pp.[iii], 101.
Reissue of the preceding item; text corrected.
Copies: BCU, BN, OT. (C.22b).

Other editions: *Cours de politique* 1818 (E1/1(2)), *Cours de politique* (E1/2(2)), Laboulaye 1861 (E1/5a), Laboulaye (E1/5b).

A23 Des élections prochaines

A23/1 1817 Des élections prochaines, par M. Benjamin de Constant. A Paris, chez Plancher ... Delaunay ... et Hubert, 1817. 8° pp.[iv], 64. Impr. Renaudière, [Paris].
Copies: BCU, BL, BN. (C.23a).

A23/2 1817 Des élections prochaines, par M. Benjamin de Constant. Edition entièrement conforme à celle de Paris. Bruxelles, de l'imprimerie de J. Maubach ... M.DCCC.XVII. 8° pp.56.
Copy: BR. (C.23b).

Other editions: *Cours de politique* 1819 (E1/1(3)), *Cours de politique* 1820 (E1/2(3)), Laboulaye 1861 (E1/5a), Laboulaye 1872 (E1/5b).

A24 Entretien d'un électeur avec lui-même

A24/1 1817 Entretien d'un élécteur avec lui-même. A Paris. Chez Plancher ... Delaunay, 1817. 8° pp.20. Impr. Doublet, [Paris].
Copies: BCU, BL, BN. (C.24a).

A24/2 1818 Entretien ... recueilli et publié par M. Benjamin-Constant, éligible. A Paris, chez Plancher ... 1818. 8° pp.21. Impr. Madame Jeunehomme-Crémière, [Paris].
Copy: BN. (C.24b).

A24/3 1818 Entretien ... A Paris, chez Plancher ... 1818. 8° pp.21. Impr. Madame Jeunehomme-Crémière, [Paris].
Another issue, with title page in different state. *Copy*: MH. (C.24c).

Other editions: *Cours de politique* 1919 (E1/1(3)), *Cours de politique* 1820 (E1/2(3)), Laboulaye 1861 (E1/5a), Laboulaye 1872 (E1/5b), Pozzo di Borgo 1965 (E4/7).

Translation

A24/t1 1820 Pensieri sugli ultimi avvenimenti, seguiti dal Ragionamento di un elettore con se stesso. Pubblicati da V. Balsamo. Lecce il 15 luglio 1820. 8° pp.51.
Includes, pp.27-40, *Ragionamento di un elettore con se stesso di B. Constant. Traduzione italiana con note ed aggiunte*; pp.41-44, *Addizioni del traduttore. -- Sui Deputati*; pp.45-51, *Sulla Camera de' Pari*. (Cordié 336; C.24d).

A25 Notes sur quelques articles de journaux

A25/1 1817   Notes sur quelques articles de journaux; par M. Benjamin de Constant ... Paris, Plancher ... Delaunay ... 1817. 8° pp.34. Impr. Madame Jeunehomme-Crémière, [Paris].
Copies: BCU, BL, BN. (C.25a).

A26 Seconde réponse

A26/1 [1817]   Seconde réponse de Benjamin Constant. 8° pp.7. Impr. Porthmann, [Paris].
End of text signed: 'Benjamin Constant'.
Copies: BCU, BL, BN. (C.26a).

Other editions: *Cours de politique* 1819 (E1/1(3)), *Cours de politique* 1820 (E1/2(3)).

A27 Annales de la session de 1817 à 1818

A27/1 1817-1818   Annales de la session de 1817 à 1818. Paris: Béchet [livraisons 1-5]; Bruxelles: Le Charlier [livraison 4], 1817-1818. 8° pp.iii, 327.
By Benjamin Constant (livr. 1 and 5), J. P. Pagès (livr. 2) and Saint-Aubin (livr. 3 and 4). Livr. 5 contains Constant's *Du Discours de M. de Marchangy, avocat du Roi, devant le tribunal de police correctionnelle, dans la cause de M. Fiévée*, pp.291-327. *Copies*: BCU, BL, BN. (C.27a).

1829   See item E4/1 (*Œuvres diverses*, 1829).

Other editions and selections: *Cours de politique* 1820 (E1/1(4)), *Cours de politique* 1833 (E1/2(4)), Laboulaye 1861 (E1/5a), Laboulaye 1872 (E1/5b).

A28 Lettre à M. Odillon-Barrot sur l'affaire de W. Regnault

A28/1 1818   Lettre à M. Odillon Barrot, avocat en la cour de cassation, par M. Benjamin Constant, sur l'affaire de Wilfrid Regnault, condamné à mort. Paris. De l'imprimerie de Renaudière ... Se vend: chez Plancher ... et chez Delaunay ... 1818. 8° pp.[i], 49.
Title page exists in three states, two as described above, with different spacing of type, the third as follows: Lettre à M. Odillon-Barrot, avocat à la cour royale, sur le procès de Wilfrid Regnault ... Paris. De l'imprimerie de Renaudière ... 1818. (Names of Plancher and Delaunay not on title page).
Copies: [1] BCU, BL, BN; [2] C; [3] Bx, C. (C.28a).

Other editions: *Cours de politique* 1819 (E1/1(3)), *Cours de politique* 1820 (E1/2(3)), Laboulaye 1861 (E1/5a), Laboulaye 1872 (E1/5b), Bourgeois 1979 (E4/10).

A29 Seconde lettre à M. Odillon-Barrot

A29/1 1818   2me lettre à M. Odillon-Barrot, avocat en la cour de cassation, par M. Benjamin Constant, sur le procès de Wilfrid Regnault, condamné à mort. Avec un plan figuré du lieu où s'est commis l'assassinat. A Paris, chez Béchet ... Plancher ... Delaunay ... 1818. 8° pp.[iv], 96. Impr. C.-F. Patris, [Paris].
Copies: BCU, BN, C. (C.29a).

Other editions: *Cours de politique* 1819 (E1/1(3)), *Cours de politique* 1820 (E1/2(3)), Bourgeois 1979 (E4/10).

A30 De l'appel en calomnie de M. le marquis de Blosseville

A30/1 1818   De l'appel en calomnie de M. le marquis de Blosseville, contre Wilfrid-Regnault; par M. Benjamin Constant ... Paris, chez Béchet ... Juillet 1818. 8° pp.[i], 27. Impr. J.-L. Chanson, [Paris].
Copies: BN, Bx, C. (C.30a).

Other editions: *Cours de politique* 1819 (E1/1(3)), *Cours de politique* 1820 (E1/2(3)), Bourgeois 1979 (E4/10).

A31 Lettres à M. Charles Durand

A31/1 1818   Lettres à M. Charles Durand, avocat, en réponse aux questions contenues dans la troisième partie de son ouvrage, intitulée: Marseille, Nîmes et ses environs, en 1815. Par M. Benjamin Constant. A Paris, chez Béchet ... 1818. 8° pp.49. Impr. J.-L. Chanson, [Paris].
Originally published in *La Minerve française*, III, 2 (14-17 August 1818) and III, 4 (29-31 August 1818). Here revised and enlarged.
Copies: BL, BN, BPU. (C.31a).

Other editions: *Cours de politique* 1819 (E1/1(3)), *Cours de politique* 1820 (E1/2(3)), Laboulaye 1861 (E1/5a), Laboulaye 1872 (E1/5b).

A32 Des élections de 1818

A32/1 1818   Des élections de 1818, par M. Benjamin Constant. A Paris, chez Béchet ... 1818. 8° pp.82. Impr. J.-L. Chanson, [Paris].
Copies: BCU, BL, BN. (C.32a).

1829   See item E4/1 (Œuvres diverses, 1829).

Other editions: *Cours de politique* 1819 (E1/1(3)), *Cours de politique* 1820 (E1/2(3)), Laboulaye 1861 (E1/5a), Laboulaye 1872 (E1/5b).

A33 Lettre à M. Odillon-Barrot sur le procès de Lainé

A33/1 1818 Lettre de M. Benjamin Constant, à Monsieur Odillon Barrot, sur le procès de Lainé, serrurier, entraîné au crime de fausse monnaie, par un agent de la gendarmerie, et condamné à mort. Paris, chez Béchet ... 1818. 4°
pp.[i], 10. Impr. Dubray, [Paris].
End of text dated: 'Paris, 1er octobre 1818'.
Copy: AN. (C.33a).

Other editions: *Cours de politique* 1819 (E1/1(3)), *Cours de politique* 1820 (E1/2(3)).

A34 A Messieurs les électeurs de Paris, 23 October 1818

A34/1 1818 A Messieurs les électeurs de Paris. 4° pp.3. Impr. Renaudière, [Paris].
End of text signed: 'Benjamin Constant. Paris, le 23 octobre 1818'.
Copy: BL. (C.34a).

A35 A Messieurs les électeurs de Paris, 29 October 1818

A35/1 1818 Benjamin Constant. A Messieurs les électeurs de Paris. 8° pp.2.
End of text signed: 'Benjamin Constant. Paris, le 29 octobre 1818'.
Copies: BCU (uncorrected proof), BN. (C.35a).

A35/2 1818 Benjamin Constant. A Messieurs les électeurs de Paris. 8° pp.2.
End of text signed as in preceding item with variant 'ce 29'.
Copy: Mp. (C.35b).

A36 Eloge de Sir Samuel Romilly

A36/1 1819 Eloge de Sir Samuel Romilly, prononcé à l'Athénée royal de Paris, le 26 décembre 1818, par M. Benjamin Constant ... A Paris, chez F. Béchet aîné ... et à Bruxelles, chez Lecharlier, Demat ... 1819. 8° pp.[iv] 74. Impr. J.-L. Chanson, [Paris].
Copies: BCU, BN, OT. (C.36a).

1829 See item E4/1 (Œuvres diverses, 1829).

A36/2 1867 Bennet, William Heath. Select biographical sketches from the Note-Books of a Law Reporter. London: George Routledge and Sons, 1867. pp.xiv, 218, xlvii.
On pp.44-55: extracts from an unpublished manuscript of the 'second edition' of the *Eloge* in the Library of Lincoln's Inn, London.
Copies: BL, C.

Other editions: *Cours de politique* 1820 (E1/1(4)), *Cours de politique* 1833 (E1/2(4)).

Translations

A36/t1 1819   An Eulogium on Sir Samuel Romilly, pronounced at the Royal Athenæum of Paris, on the 26th of December 1818, by M. Benjamin Constant. Edited by Sir T. C. Morgan ... London: Printed for Henry Colburn ... 8° pp.xvi, 78.
Translator's preface dated at end: 'Paris, Jan 20th, 1819' and signed: 'T.C.M.'
Copies: ICRL, NN, VA. (C.36b).

A36/t2 1867   Bennet, William Heath. Select biographical sketches from the Note-Books of a Law Reporter. London: George Routledge and Sons, 1867. pp.xiv, 218, xlvii.
On pp.iii-xi (Appendix): *Translation of an Address* or *Eloge, pronounced before the Athénée Royal in Paris, by M. Benjamin Constant on the 26th December, 1818.*
Copies: BL, C.

A37 De la proposition de changer la loi des élections

A37/1 1819   De la proposition de changer la loi des élections. Par M. Benjamin Constant. A Paris, chez Poulet ... 1819. 8° pp.8. Impr. Poulet.
Copies: B, BL, BN. (C.37a).

A37/2 1819   De la proposition ... A Paris, chez J. B. Poulet ... A la librairie constitutionnelle, de Brissot Thivars ... 1819. 8° pp.8.
Copy: Ca. (C.37b).

Other editions: *Cours de politique* 1820 (E1/1(4)), *Cours de politique* 1833 (E1/2(4)).

A38 [Première] Lettre à Messieurs les habitans de la Sarthe

A38/1 1819   Lettre à Messieurs les habitans du département de la Sarthe. 8° pp.11. Impr. Fain, [Paris].
Incipit: 'Appelé par vos suffrages ...' Text signed at end: 'Benjamin Constant'. Reprinted from *La Minerve française*, V, 9, 1-2 April 1819, pp.447-455.
Copies: ADS, BN. (C.38a).

Other editions: *Cours de politique* 1820 (E1/1(4)), *Cours de politique* 1833 (E1/2(4)), Laboulaye 1861 (E1/5a), Laboulaye 1872 (E1/5b).

A39 [Deuxième] Lettre à Messieurs les habitans de la Sarthe

A39/1 1819   Lettre à Messieurs les habitans de la Sarthe. 8° pp.15. Impr. Fain, [Paris].
Incipit: 'Au moment où ...' End of text signed: 'Benjamin Constant'. Reprinted from *La Minerve française*, VII, 13, 30 October-2 November 1819, pp.577-590.
Copies: BN, O, OT. (C.39a).

Other editions: *Cours de politique* 1820 (E1/1(4)), *Cours de politique* 1833 (E1/2(4)), Laboulaye 1861 (E1/5a), Laboulaye 1872 (E1/5b).

A40 De l'état de la France

A40/1 1819 De l'état de la France et des bruits qui circulent. Par M. Benjamin Constant, député de la Sarthe. A Paris, chez Brissot-Thivars ... Béchet aîné ... 1819. 8° pp.16. Impr. Plassan, [Paris].
Extracts published in *La Renommée*, n° 149, 11 novembre 1819, pp.587-588.
Copies: BCU, BN, C. (C.40a).

A41 Aux auteurs de *La Renommée*

A41/1 1820 Aux auteurs de *La Renommée*. 8° pp.4. Impr. Plassan, [Paris].
Signed at end: 'Benjamin Constant. (Extrait de la *Renommée* du 20 [=21] janvier.)'.
Copy: BN. (C.41a).

A42 Mémoires sur les Cent Jours

A42/1 1820 Mémoires sur les Cent Jours, en forme de lettres; par M. Benjamin Constant. Première partie. A Paris, chez Béchet aîné ... et à Rouen, chez Béchet fils ... 1820. 8° pp.[iii], 182. Impr. Mme Ve Courcier, [Paris].
Originally published in *La Minerve française*, September-November 1819.
Copies: BCU, BL, BN. (C.42a).

A42/2 1822 Mémoires sur les Cent Jours, en forme de lettres, avec des notes et documens inédits; par M. Benjamin Constant. A Paris, chez Béchet aîné ... et à Rouen, chez Béchet ... 1822. 8° pp.[iii], 182. Impr. Huzard-Courcier, [Paris].
Reissue of the preceding item with new preliminaries.
Copy: N. (C.42b).

A42/3 1822 Mémoires sur les Cent Jours, en forme de lettres, avec des notes et documens inédits; par M. Benjamin Constant. Deuxième et dernière partie. A Paris, chez Béchet aîné ... et à Rouen, chez Béchet ... 1822. 8° pp.[iv], 196. Impr. Huzard-Courcier, [Paris].
Originally published in *La Minerve française*, November 1819-March 1820.
Copies: BCU, BL, BN. (C.42c).

1829 See item E4/1 (Œuvres diverses, 1829).

A42/4 1829 Mémoires sur les Cent Jours, en forme de lettres, avec des notes et documens inédits; par M. Benjamin Constant. Nouvelle édition, augmentée d'une Introduction. Paris. Pichon et Didier ... 1829. 8° pp.xxx, 182, 196. Impr. Huzard Courcier, [Paris]. Frontispiece (portrait of B. Constant député, with inscription: 'Imp. Lith. de Melle Formentin, r. des Sts Pères 10').

This 'nouvelle édition' is a reissue of editions A42/1 and A42/3, with a new introduction and the following pages reset: Vol. I, pp.[1]-2; pp.181-182; Vol. II, pp.[1]-2; pp.193-196.

Copies: BCU, BL, BN. (C.42d).

A42/5 1961 Mémoires sur les Cent-Jours par Benjamin Constant. Préface, notes et commentaires de O. Pozzo di Borgo. [Paris]: Jean-Jacques Pauvert, 1961. pp.LII, 284. Portrait, facsimile.

Includes Constant's *Mémoire apologétique* of 21 July 1815, pp.223-229. See item A74/1.

Review: Leo Neppi Modona, *SF*, VI (1962), 165.

Translation

A42/t1 1944 Memorie sui Cento giorni di Benjamin Constant. A cura di Enrico Emanuelli. Milano: Gentile, [1944]. (La Ruota, libri di varia umanità, 1). pp.221. Bibliography.

Copy: B. (Cordié 205). Reprinted: 1945. *Copies*: B, BCU.

A43 Troisième Lettre à MM. les habitans de la Sarthe

A43/1 1820 Troisième lettre à MM. les habitans du département de la Sarthe. (Extrait de la 112e livraison de La Minerve française.) 8° pp.8. Impr. Plassan, [Paris].

Text signed at end: 'Benjamin Constant. Paris, le 21 mars 1820'. Reprinted from *La Minerve française*, IX (8), 22-24 March 1820.

Copies: BL, BN, C. (C.43a).

Other editions: Laboulaye 1861 (E1/5a), Laboulaye 1872 (E1/5b).

A44 Des motifs qui ont dicté le nouveau projet de la loi sur les élections

A44/1 1820 Des motifs qui ont dicté le nouveau projet de loi sur les élections; par M. Benjamin Constant ... A Paris, chez Béchet aîné ... et chez les marchands de nouveautés. Mai M.DCCC.XX. 8° pp.v, 76. Impr. Plassan, [Paris].

Copies: BL, BN, C. (C.44a).

1829 See item E4/1 (Œuvres diverses, 1829).

Other editions: Laboulaye 1861 (E1/5a), Laboulaye 1872 (E1/5b).

A45 Pièces relatives à la saisie de lettres et de papiers

A45/1 1820 Pièces relatives à la saisie de lettres et de papiers dans le domicile de MM. Goyet et Pasquier, l'un juge et l'autre agréé au tribunal de commerce du Mans, avec quelques réflexions sur la direction de la police générale. Par M. Benjamin Constant ... Paris, chez les marchands de nouveautés. 1820. 8° pp.51. Impr. Plassan, [Paris].

The edition is in two states, one as described above (imprint of Plassan on p.2), the other without printer's imprint.

Copies: [1] AR, BN; [2] VP. (C.45a).

A46 De la dissolution de la Chambre des Députés

A46/1 1820   De la dissolution de la Chambre des Députés, et des résultats que cette dissolution peut avoir pour la nation, le gouvernement et le ministère; par M. Benjamin Constant ... A Paris, chez Béchet aîné ... et à Rouen, chez Béchet fils ... 1820. 8° pp.[iv], 67. Impr. Huzard-Courcier, [Paris].
Copies: BCU, BL, BN. (C.46a).

A46/2 1820   De la dissolution ... Deuxième édition, revue et corrigée ... 1820. 8° pp.[iv], 67. Impr. Huzard-Courcier, [Paris].
Copies: BN, OT. (C.46b).

Translation

A46/t1 1821   On the Dissolution of the Chamber of Deputies, and on the possible consequence of this dissolution to the nation, the government, and the ministry ... Translated exclusively for the Pamphleteer. Paris, 1820 – London, 1821.
The Pamphleteer, London: A.J. Valpy, XVIII (1821), 97-128.
Copies: BL, BN. (C.46c).

A47 Lettre à Monsieur le marquis de Latour-Maubourg

A47/1 1820   Lettre à M. le marquis de Latour-Maubourg, ministre de la guerre, sur ce qui s'est passé à Saumur les 7 et 8 octobre 1820; par M. Benjamin Constant ... A Paris, chez Béchet aîné ... et à Rouen, chez Béchet fils ... 1820. 8° pp.22. Impr. Huzard-Courcier, [Paris].
Copies: BCU, BN, OT. (C.47a).

A47/2 1820   Lettre ... Seconde édition ... 1820. 8° pp.22. Impr. Huzard-Courcier, [Paris].
Copies: ADS, BN, VP. (C.47b).

A47/3 1820   Lettre ... Troisième édition, augmentée d'une réponse aux articles du Moniteur, et à un pamphlet du 2ᵉ adjoint du maire de Saumur sur les mêmes évènemens. A Paris, chez Béchet aîné ... et à Rouen, chez Béchet fils ... 1820. 8° pp.56. Impr. Huzard-Courcier, [Paris].
Copies: BN, OT, VP. (C.47c).

A47/4 1820   Réponses aux articles du Moniteur et à un pamphlet du 2ᵉ adjoint

du maire de Saumur, sur ce qui s'est passé dans cette ville les 7 et 8 octobre 1820; par M. Benjamin Constant ... Pour faire suite à sa lettre à M. le marquis de Latour-Maubourg, sur ces évènemens. A Paris, chez Béchet aîné ...et à Rouen chez Béchet fils ... 1820. 8° pp.[ii], 23-56. Impr. Huzard-Courcier, [Paris].
Copies: BN, BR. (C.47d).

A47/5 1959   Lettre à Monsieur le marquis de Latour-Maubourg, 1820, *Cahiers des saisons*, n° 17 (été 1959), 152-160.

A48 Lettre à Monsieur Goyet

A48/1 1820   Lettre à Monsieur Goyet, électeur de la Sarthe, par M. Benjamin-Constant, député. 8° pp.10. Impr. Renaudin, Le Mans.
Text signed at end: 'Benjamin Constant. Paris, ce 6 novembre 1820.'
Copy: BN. (C.48a).

A49 Du triomphe inévitable et prochain des principes constitutionnels en Prusse

A49/1 1821   Du triomphe inévitable et prochain des principes constitutionnels en Prusse, d'après un ouvrage imprimé, traduit de l'allemand de M. Koreff, conseiller intime de régence, par M.****; avec un avant-propos et des notes de M. Benjamin-Constant ... Paris, chez tous les marchands de nouveautés. Mars 1821. 8° pp.xvi, 86. Impr. P. Didot l'aîné, [Paris].
A translation of [J. F. Benzenberg], 'Carl August Fürst von Hardenberg', *Zeitgenossen*, Bd VI, 2 (1821), 5-76, which Constant thought mistakenly was by J. F. Koreff.
Copies: BCU, BL, BN. (C.49a).

Translation

A49/t1 1844   Preußen, der Beamtenstaat, in seiner politischen Entwickelung und seinen sociäl-ökonomischen Zuständen. Dargestellt durch Benjamin Constant und Samuel Laing. Bearbeitet von Adolph Heller. Mannheim. Verlag von Friedrich Bassermann, 1844. pp.xvi, 165.
Includes: Der Sieg der Constitution in Preußen als unausbleiblich und nach bevorstehend dargestellt in der Vertheidigung eines ehemaligen Staatsministers. Mit einem Vorwort und Anmerkungen von Benjamin Constant (In Auszuge).
Copy: BL. (Fromm 5719).

A50 Commentaire sur l'ouvrage de Filangieri

Commentaire sur l'ouvrage de Filangieri: Prospectus.
The Prospectus is described as follows in *Bibliographie de la France*, 16 Septembre 1820: Œuvres de Filangieri; traduites de l'italien. Nouvelle édition accompagnée

de notes par M. Benjamin Constant, et de l'*Eloge de Filangieri* par M. Salfi. Six volumes in-8° imprimés par M. P. Didot aîné. (Prospectus.) In-8° d'un quart de feuille. Imp. de P. Didot, à Paris. – A Paris, chez P. Dufart. Les six volumes paraîtront en trois livraisons; la première en décembre, les autres de deux en deux mois. Prix de chaque livraison pour les souscripteurs ... 12-0.

A50/1 1822   Commentaire sur l'ouvrage de Filangieri par M. Benjamin Constant. A Paris, chez P. Dufart ... M.DCCCXXII. 8° pp.[iii], 111. Impr. P. Didot l'aîné, [Paris].
Copies: BCU, BL, BN. (C.50a(1)).

A50/2 1824   Commentaire sur l'ouvrage de Filangieri par M. Benjamin Constant. Deuxième partie. A Paris, chez P. Dufart ... M.DCCCXXIV. 8° pp.[v], 303. Impr. Jules Didot aîné, [Paris].
Copies: BCU, BL, BN. (C.50a(2)).

A50/3 1840   Œuvres de G. Filangieri, traduites de l'italien. Nouvelle édition, accompagnée d'un commentaire par Benjamin Constant et de l'éloge de Filangieri, par M. Salfi. Paris: J. P. Aillaud, 1840, 3 vols.
Commentaire ... par Benjamin Constant, III, 187-410.
Copies: BI, BN, BPU.

Translations

A50/t1 1825   Comentario sobre la ciencia de la legislación de Filangieri, Por M. B. Constant; traducido al castellano por D. J.C. Pages, Intérprete real. Tomo Primero [Segundo]. Paris ... F. Rosa y compª ...y en Bruselas ... 1825. 12° 2 vols. pp.[iii], 362 + [iii], 328. Vol. I: impr. Moreau, [Paris]; vol. II: impr. E. Pochard, [Paris].
Copies: BN, DLC, NcU. (C.50b).

A50/t2 1826   Commentario alla scienza della legislazione di G. Filangieri scritto dal signor Beniamino Constant. Prima traduzione italiana. Italia, [Lugano], 1826. 8° pp.[i], 403.
Copies: BPU, MB. (Cordié 168; C.50c).

A50/t3 1828   Comento sulla scienza della legislazione di G. Filangieri scritto dal signor Beniamino Constant. Prima traduzione italiana. Seconda edizione. Italia, [Lugano], 1828. 8° pp.403.
Copies: B, MH, PPL. (Cordié 169; C.50d).

A50/t4 1833   Comento sulla scienza della legislazione di G. Filangieri scritto dal signor Beniamino Constant. Prima traduzione italiana. Terza edizione. Capolago: Tipografia e Libreria Elvetica, 1833. 8° pp.352.
Copies: B, BL, BPU. (Caddeo, 122; Cordié 170; C.50e).

A50/t5 1836   Ciencia de la legislación, por G. Filangieri, ilustrada con comen-

tarios por Benjamín Constant. Tercera edición, revista, corregida y aumentada. Paris: Librería Americana, 3 vols., 1836. Impr. Moquet y comp, [Paris].
Copy: BN.

A50/t6 1838   Comento sulla scienza della legislazione di G. Filangeri [*sic*] scritto dal signor Beniamino Constant. Prima traduzione italiana. Quarta edizione. Capolago: Tipografia e Libreria Elvetica, 1838. pp.352.
Copies: BCU, Bs. (Caddeo, 123; Cordié 173).

A50/t7 1841   La Scienza della legislazione e gli opuscoli scelti di Gaetano Filangieri. Brusselles: Tipografia della Società belgica, 1841. (Scelta collezione di autori classici italiani e stranieri, in versi ed in prosa, vols II-III). 2 vols, pp.730 + 649.
Includes (II, 429-649): *Comento sulla Scienza della legislazione di G. Filangieri scritto da Beniamino Constant. Prima traduzione italiana.* (Cordié 174).

A50/t8 1855-1856   La Scienza della legislazione e gli opuscoli scelti di Gaetano Filangieri, col commento intorno alla medesima di Beniamino Constant, arricchita di note illustrative. Milano: Borroni e Scotti, 1855-1856. (Biblioteca scelta del Foro criminale italiano, diretta dall'avvocato Giuseppe Toccagni, 7). 2 vols, pp.LI, 736 + 690.
Includes: *Comento sulla Scienza della legislazione di Beniamino Constant*, I, 9-53; 145-182; 353-444; II, 137-171; 447-454; 515-549.
Copy: BL. (Cordié 177).

A51   A Messieurs les électeurs du premier arrondissement

A51/1 1822   A Messieurs les électeurs du premier arrondissement du département de la Seine 4° p.1.
Text signed at end: 'Benjamin Constant, député de la Sarthe, Rue d'Anjou, n. 17' and dated: 'Ce 28 janvier 1822'.
Copies: AN, BCU (Co 4054). (C.51a).

A51/2 1906   A Messieurs les électeurs ...
Reprint of the preceding item in Victor Glachant, *Benjamin Constant sous l'œil du guet*, Paris: Plon-Nourrit, 1906, pp.327-329.

A52   Lettre adressée à M. le rédacteur du *Courrier français*

A52/1 1822   Lettre adressée à M. le rédacteur du Courrier français. 8° pp.4. Impr. Constant-Chantpie, [Paris].
Text signed at end: 'Benjamin Constant'. Published in *Le Courrier français*, n° 129, 9 mai 1822, pp.1-2.
Copy: BN. (C.52a).

A53 Lettre à M. le procureur-général de la cour royale de Poitiers

A53/1 1822   Lettre à Monsieur le procureur-général de la cour royale de Poitiers, par M. Benjamin-Constant. Paris, chez les marchands de nouveautés. Imprimerie de Constant-Chantpie ... 1822. 8° pp.24.
Text signed at end: 'Benjamin Constant, député de la Sarthe. Paris, septembre 1822'.
Copies: B, BN, BPU. (C.53a).

A53/2 1822   Lettre à Monsieur le procureur-général ... 1822. 8° pp.24.
Reprint of the preceding item with wider spacing between lines and plain swelled rule (instead of ornamental swelled rule) on title page. Text corrected.
Copies: C, N. (C.53b).

A53/3 1822   Lettre ... Deuxième édition. Bruxelles, imprimerie de Voglet ... se trouve chez Lecharlier ... Lacrosse ... Remy ... Wahlen ... 1822. 8° pp.[ii], 18.
Copies: BR, L. (C.53c).

A54 Avis aux électeurs de la seconde série

A54/1 [1822]   Avis aux électeurs de la seconde série. 8° p.[1]. Impr. Constant-Chantpie, [Paris].
Copy: BN. (C.54a).

A55 A MM. les électeurs du département de la Sarthe

A55/1 [1822]   A MM. les électeurs du département de la Sarthe. 8° pp.3. Impr. Constant-Chantpie, [Paris].
Text signed at end: 'Benjamin Constant'.
Copy: BN. (C.55a).

A56 Seconde lettre à MM. les électeurs de la Sarthe

A56/1 1822   Seconde lettre de M. Benjamin Constant à Messieurs les électeurs de la Sarthe. 8° pp.7. Impr. Constant-Chantpie, [Paris].
Text signed at end: 'Benjamin Constant' and dated 'Paris, ce 3 novembre 1822'.
Copy: BN. (C.56a).

A57 Note sur la plainte en diffamation

A57/1 [1822]   Note sur la plainte en diffamation, adressée à Messieurs les conseillers, membres de la cour de cassation, contre M. Mangin, procureur-général près la Cour royale de Poitiers. 8° pp.10. Impr. Constant-Chantpie, [Paris].
Text signed at end: 'Benjamin Constant'.

Copy: BN. (C.57a).

A58 De la religion

De la religion: Prospectus.

Juillet 1823. De la religion, considérée dans sa source, ses formes et ses développements. Par M. Benjamin Constant. Prospectus. 8° pp.4. Impr. Firmin Didot.
[Paris].

The work, as announced here, was to appear in six parts (livraisons) and form
three octavo volumes, each of 400 pages. The parts were to appear monthly, from
15 October 1823. Subscriptions received by Bossange frères (Paris), Ponthieu
(Paris), the author, and Martin Bossange (London).

Copy: BCU. (C.58).

A58/1 1824-1831 (1) De la religion, considérée dans sa source, ses formes et
ses développements. Par M. Benjamin Constant ... Tome premier. Paris, Bossange père, Bossange frères, Treuttel et Wurtz, Rey et Gravier, Renouard,
Ponthieu, 1824, 8° pp.XLIV, 370. Impr. Firmin Didot, [Paris].

(2) De la religion ... Tome II. Paris, chez Béchet aîné ... 1825. 8° pp.x, 496.
Impr. Firmin Didot, [Paris].

In two states, one without cancels, the other with cancels (pp.89-90, 97-98, 251-
252, 293-294).

(3) De la religion ... Tome III. Paris, chez Béchet aîné ... 1827. 8° pp.[iii], 478.
Impr. Firmin Didot, [Paris].

(4) De la religion ... Tome quatrième. Paris, chez Pichon et Didier ... 1831. 8°
pp.[iii], vi, 515. Impr. Amb. Firmin Didot, [Paris].

(5) De la religion ... Tome cinquième. Paris, chez Pichon et Didier ... 1831. 8°
pp.[iii], 459, iv. Impr. Amb. Firmin Didot, [Paris].

Copies: BL, BN, BPU. (C.58a).

A58/2 1824-1833 De la religion, considérée dans sa source, ses formes et ses
développements. Par M. Benjamin Constant ... Tome premier. Bruxelles, P. J.
de Mat, imprimeur-libraire de l'Académie, 1824. 8° pp.[iii], XXIII, 159, 120.
Tome II ... 1825. 8° pp.[iii], III, 362. Tome III ... 1825 [=1827]. 8° pp.[iii], 370.
Tome IV ... Vᵉ P. J. de Mat ... 1833. 8° pp.[iii], [iv], 393. Tome V ... Bruxelles,
P. J. de Mat ... 1834. 8° pp.[iii], 355.

Unauthorised reprint of item A58/1.

Copies: BR, C, H, L, U. (C.58b).

A58/3 1824-1827 De la religion, considérée dans sa source, ses formes et
ses développements. Par Benjamin Constant ... Tome premier. Bruxelles. H.
Tarlier ... P.-J. Voglet ... 1824. 18° pp.xxx, [31]-424. Impr. P.-J. Voglet, [Brus-
sels]. Tome second ... 1825. 18° pp.[iii], iv, 523. Tome troisième ... 1827. 18°
pp.[iii], 531.

Authorised reprint of item A58/1 (1-3).

Copies: A, AR, Bs. (C.58c).

A58/4 1826   (1) De la religion, considérée dans sa source, ses formes et ses développements. Par M. Benjamin Constant ... Deuxième édition. Tome premier. Paris, A. Leroux et C. Chantpie, éditeurs. Béchet aîné, libraire ... 1826. 8° pp.XL, 352. Impr. Firmin Didot, [Paris].
Reprint of item A58/1(1).
Copies: B, BCU, BL. (C.58d).

A58/5 1830   (1) De la religion, considérée dans sa source, ses formes et ses développements. Par M. Benjamin Constant ... Tome premier. Paris, chez Pichon et Didier ... 1830. 8° pp.XL, 352. Imprint Amb. Firmin Didot, [Paris] on p.[II].
Reissue of item A58/4(1) with new preliminaries.
(2) De la religion ... Tome deuxième ... 1830. 8° pp.x, 498. Impr. Amb. Firmin Didot, [Paris].
Reprint of item A58/1(2).
(3) De la religion ... Tome troisième ... 1830. 8° pp.[iii], 478. Impr. Amb. Firmin Didot, [Paris] on p.[ii].
Reissue of item A58/1(3) with new preliminaries.
Copies: (vols I-III): BPL, C, L, O. (C.58e).

A58/6 1971   Benjamin Constant. De la religion considérée dans sa source, ses formes et ses développements. Livre premier, suivi d'extraits des autres livres. Postface et notes de Pierre Deguise. [Lausanne]: Bibliothèque romande, [1971]. pp.274.

Another edition: Pléiade 1957, 1964, 1979: selection (E4/5).

Translation

A58/t1 1824-1829   Die Religion, nach ihrer Quelle, ihren Gestalten und ihren Entwickelungen. Von Benjamin Constant. Mit Vorwissen des Verfassers aus dem Französischen übersetzt, und mit einigen Anmerkungen. Deutsch herausgegeben von Dr. Philipp August Petri, Prediger zu Lüethorst im Königreiche Hannover ... Erster Band. Berlin, bei G. Reimer. 1824. [Zweiter Band ... 1827. Dritter Band ... 1829]. 8° pp.XVI, XXXII, 414 + vi, 536 + [ii], 528. Impr. (Bd I), J. J. Feysel, Einbeck; (Bd II), Heinrich Ehlers.
Copies: M, St, T. (Fromm 5712; C.58f).

A59 Christianisme

A59/1 1825   Extrait de l'Encyclopédie moderne. Christianisme. Par M. Benjamin Constant. 8° pp.25. Impr. Moreau, [Paris].
Reprinted in *Le Globe*, 7-12 mai 1825.
Copy: BN. (C.59a).

A59/2 1825   Extrait ... par. [*sic*] M. Benjamin-Constant. 8° pp.25. Impr. Moreau, [Paris].

Reprint of the preceding item, with longer publisher's announcement and text revised.

Copy: BN. (C.59b).

A59/3 1895   J. B. Dupuis. Abrégé de l'origine de tous les cultes ... suivi du Christianisme par Benjamin Constant. Avec une notice et des notes critiques par B. Saint-Marc. Paris: Garnier, [1895]. pp.IX, 412.

On pp.388-410: Le Christianisme. Causes humaines qui, indépendemment de sa source divine, ont concouru à son établissement, par Benjamin Constant.

Copies: BN, BPU.

Translations

A59/t1 1827   Religion und Philosophie in Frankreich, eine Folge von Abhandlungen, aus dem Französischen übersetzt und herausgegeben von F. W. Carové, Dr. der Philosophie und Licencié en droit. Erster Band. Göttingen, bei Vandenhoeck und Ruprecht, 1827. 8° pp.LI, 156.

On pp.1-14: Ueber die Einführung des Christenthums, von Benjamin-Constant. (Globe Nro. 104-106, 1825.) This is a translation from a reprint in *Le Globe* (7 May 1825, pp.521-523; 10 May 1825, pp.530-531; 12 May 1825, pp.533-535) of item A59/1.

Copies: BL, T. (Fromm 5714: C.59c).

A59/t2 185-?   On the human causes which have concurred toward the establishment of Christianity. Translated from the French of Benjamin Constant, by William Maccall. [Glasgow: J. Robertson, 185-?]. pp.16. (Tracts for the times, 4).

Copy: BL.

A60 Appel aux nations chrétiennes en faveur des Grecs

A60/1 1825   Appel aux nations chrétiennes en faveur des Grecs, rédigé par M. Benjamin Constant; et adopté par le Comité des Grecs de la Société de la morale chrétienne ... Se vend au profit des Grecs. A Paris, chez tous les marchands de nouveautés; chez Treuttel et Würtz ... et à l'agence du comité ... 1825. 8° pp.16. Impr. Crapelet, [Paris].

Copies: BN, OT. (C.60a).

A60/2 1825   Appel ... 1825. 8° pp.16. Impr. Crapelet, [Paris].

Reprint of the preceding item, with fuller information about the Société de la morale chrétienne and additional names of members, given on pp.[3] and [4]. The editions can be distinguished by the devices on the title pages: in item A60/1 this is a cross, 20 x 10 mm. and sunrise; in the present item it is a cross, 5×3 mm., in centre of sunburst.

Copies: AR, BN, BPU. (C.60b).

A60/3 1954   Carlo Cordié. Ideali e figure d'Europa. Pisa: Nistri-Lischi, 1954. (Saggi di varia umanità, collana diretta da Francesco Flora, 7).
Includes: Benjamin Constant: *Appel aux nations chrétiennes en faveur des Grecs*, pp.320-327. (Cordié 224).

Translations

A60/t1 1825   Beroep op de Christen Natien, ten gunste der Grieken; door Benjamin Constant. Goedgekeurd door het grieksch comité van de Maatschappij der christelijke zedeleer. Uit het Fransch vertaald. Te 's Gravenhage, bij S. de Visser. MDCCCXXV. 8° pp.16.
Copy: BR. (C.60c).

A60/t2 1825   Appell till de Christna Folken för Grekerna. Uppå anmodan af Sällskapet för den Christna Moralen författad af Benjamin Constant, Sällskapets Ledamot. Öfversättning. Stockholm, tryckt hos Fr. B. Nestius, 1825. 8° pp.15.
Copy: S. (C.60d).

A61 Coup d'œil sur la tendance générale des esprits

A61/1 1825   Coup-d'œil sur la tendance générale des esprits dans le dix-neuvième siècle; extrait du discours prononcé par M. Benjamin Constant, dans la séance d'ouverture de l'Athénée royal de Paris, le 3 décembre 1825. 8° pp.15. Impr. Rignoux, [Paris].
Extract from the *Revue encyclopédique*, 84ᵉ Cah. T. XXVIII, seconde série, décembre 1825.
Copy: BN. (C.61a).

A62 Religion

A62/1 1826   Encyclopédie progressive. Religion. 8° pp.23.
Signed: 'Mai 1826. Benjamin-Constant'. Offprint from the *Encyclopédie progressive*, published in Paris, au bureau de l'Encyclopédie progressive, impr. J. Pinard, [Paris].
Copy: BN. (C.62a).

A63 Du polythéisme romain

A63/1 1833   Du polythéisme romain, considéré dans ses rapports avec la philosophie grecque et la religion chrétienne; ouvrage posthume de Benjamin Constant; précédé d'une introduction de M. J. Matter, Inspecteur général de l'Université de France. Paris: Béchet aîné, 1833. 8° 2 vols, pp.[iii], LIX, 284 + [iii], 384. Impr. Mᵐᵉ Vᵉ Poussin, [Paris].
Vol. II is in two states; one as described above, the other with imprint of Edouard Bautruche. [Paris].

Copies: [1] BCU, BL, BN. [2] Private collection. (C.63a).

A63/2 1842   Du Polythéisme romain ... Paris: Béchet aîné, 1842. 2 vols.
Reissue of the preceding item with new preliminaries.
Copy: BCU.

A64 Carnet

A64/1 1852   Sainte-Beuve, C.-A. Derniers portraits littéraires. Paris: Didier,
1852, pp.535.
On pp.272-276: 'Note', including text of Constant's *Carnet* for 1814-1820.

A64/2 1881   Sainte-Beuve, C.-A. Causeries du lundi, Portraits de femmes et
Portraits littéraires. Table générale et analytique, par Ch. Pierrot. Paris: Garnier
frères, 1881, pp.iii, 448.
On pp.35-37: 'Notes et remarques', including text of *Carnet* for 1767-1814.

1957   See item E4/5 (Œuvres, Paris ... Bibliothèque de la Pléiade, 1957).

A64/3 1963   Deguise, Pierre. 'Le Carnet de Benjamin Constant: fragments
inédits', *RP*, août, 1963, pp.91-106.
Complete text of the *Carnet* from the Louvenjoul manuscript.
Review: P. Ciureanu, *SF*, VIII (1964), 168.

1964   See item E4/5 (reprint of Œuvres, Paris ... Bibliothèque de la Pléiade,
1957).

1972   See item A18/124 (Adolphe ... [Paris]: Le Livre de poche, [1972]).

1979   See item E4/5 (reprint of Œuvres, Paris ... Bibliothèque de la Pléiade,
1957).

A65 Mémoires inédits

A65/1 1869   Mémoires inédits de B. Constant.
Coulmann, Jean-Jacques, *Réminiscences*, Paris: Michel Lévy, 1862-1869, III, 44-
56.

1972   See item A18/124 (Adolphe ... [Paris]: Le Livre de poche, [1972]).

A66 Journaux intimes

A66/1 1887   'Le Journal intime de Benjamin Constant', *Revue internationale*,
XIII (1887), 81-110, 209-239, 423-450, 622-642, 762-777, 934-947.
Introduction, pp.81-91, by Adrien de Constant. Includes, in introduction, letter
to Constant from François de Neufchâteau, [14 April 1798]; see below, item F6.

Reviews: Jean Bourdeau, *JD*, 20, 30 janvier, 23 février, 12 mars, 7 avril 1887. Anatole France, *Le Temps*, 27 février 1887.

A66/2 1895   Journal intime de Benjamin Constant et lettres à sa famille et à ses amis, précédés d'une introduction par D. Melegari. Paris: Paul Ollendorff, 1895. pp.LXXI, 447. Portraits, facsimile. Bibliography.

Reviews and notices: Henri Lapauze, *Le Gaulois*, 3 décembre 1894. D. Melegari, *Le Figaro*, 5 décembre 1894. E. Lautier, *Le Temps*, 20 décembre 1894. E. Rod, *JD*, 21 décembre 1894. Léon-A. Daudet, *Nouvelle Revue*, 1er janvier 1895. René Doumic, *RDM*, 15 janvier 1895, 457-468. [A. Laugel], *The Nation* (New York), LX (1895), 47-48. P. Monceaux, *Revue bleue*, 26 janvier 1895. G. Renard, *Petite république*, 16 avril 1895; *Critique de combat*, 3e série 1897, 87-94. J. Ettlinger, *Allgemeine Zeitung* (Munich), Beilage, 116-117, 20-21 May 1895, pp.1-5; 5-6. Anon., *The Saturday Review* (London), LXXX, 31 August 1895. 267-268. Anon., *Blackwood's Edinburgh Magazine*, CLVIII (1895), 341-350. R. Mahrenholtz, *Literaturblatt für germanische und romanische Philologie*, 1896, pp.275-277.

Reprinted: Paris: Albin Michel, [1928]. Paris: Stock, 1931.

A66/3 1915   Rudler, Gustave. 'Le vrai "Journal intime" de Benjamin Constant', *Revue des études napoléoniennes*, VII (1915), 73-123.

Text of Monamy-Valin manuscript (copy: 19 October 1814-19 July 1815). Also published as an offprint, paginated [1]-53.

1921   See item A18/45 (Adolphe ... Berlin: Internationale Bibliothek, 1921).

1928   See also item A66/2 (reprint of Journal ... Paris: Ollendorff, 1895).

A66/4 1928   Benjamin Constant. Journal intime. Nouvelle édition avec des éclaircissements biographiques, des notes et une préface de Paul Rival Paris: Stock, Delamain et Boutelleau, 1928. (Lettres, mémoires, chroniques, 2). pp.XXXVIII, 227.

Review: Marcel Arland, *NRF*, XXXI, n° 182 (1928), 724-729.

1931   See also item A66/2 (reprint of Journal ... Paris: Ollendorff, 1895).

A66/5 1945   Benjamin Constant. Journal intime, précédé du Cahier rouge et d'Adolphe. Etablissement du texte, introduction et notes par Jean Mistler. Monaco: Editions du Rocher, 1945. (Grands et petits chefs-d'œuvre). pp.XXXVII, 437.

For reviews see above, item A18/81.

Seconde édition, revue et corrigée, 1946.

1946   See preceding item and item A18/81 (Journal intime ... Adolphe ... Monaco: Editions du Rocher, seconde édition, revue et corrigée, 1946).

A66/6 1947   Chapelan, Maurice. Anthologie du journal intime. Témoins d'eux-mêmes. Avec introductions et notes. Paris: R. Laffont, 1947. pp.643.

Benjamin Constant: pp.127-181.

A66/7 1951-1952 Amélie et Germaine par Benjamin Constant avec une introduction d'Alfred Roulin, *Les Cahiers de la Pléiade*, XIII (automne 1951-printemps 1952), pp.179-204.

A66/8 1952 Roulin, Alfred. 'Un journal inédit de Benjamin Constant: Amélie et Germaine', *Gazette de Lausanne*, 21-22 juin 1952, pp.1, 13.
Extracts from the following item.

A66/9 1952 Benjamin Constant. Journaux intimes; édition intégrale des manuscrits autographes publiée pour la première fois avec un index et des notes par Alfred Roulin et Charles Roth. Paris: Gallimard, 1952. (La Connaisance de soi). pp.574. Facsimiles.
Reprinted: 1961 and in item E4/5. *Reviews*: Jean Mistler, *RP*, octobre 1952, 133-135. Hans Naef, *Neue Schweizer Rundschau*, XX, n° 8, December 1952- Januar 1953, pp.475-478. M. Saillet, *MF*, CCCXVII (1953), 166-167. Pierre Reboul, *AUS*, philosophie-lettres, II (1953), 138-142. Pierre Kohler, *Erasmus*, VI (1953), 523-529. Samuel S. de Sacy, *MF*, CCCXVII (1953), 166-167. Bernard de Fallois, *Nouvelle NRF*, n° 1 (janvier 1953), 151-155. René Lalou, *Preuves*, 2ᵉ année, n° 21, (novembre 1952), 67-69. René Ternois, *L'Education nationale*, n° 16, 7 mai 1953, pp.8-9.

1957 See items E4/5 (Œuvres, Bibliothèque de la Pléiade, 1957) and A18/106 (Adolphe ... [Paris]: Hachette, [1957]).

1961 See item A66/9 (reprint of Journaux intimes ... Paris: Gallimard, 1952).

1964 See items A18/115 (Adolphe ... Paris: Nelson, 1964) and E4/5 (reprint of Œuvres, Bibliothèque de la Pléiade, 1957).

1965 See item A18/115 (Adolphe ... Paris: Nelson de luxe, 1965).

1966 See item A18/117 (Adolphe ... [Paris]: Le Trésor des Lettres françaises, [1966]).

1973 See item A18/117 (reprint of Adolphe ... [Paris]: Le Trésor des Lettres françaises, [1966]).

1979 See item E4/5 (reprint of Œuvres, Bibliothèque de la Pléiade, 1957).

Translations

A66/t1 1919 Benjamin Constant. Reise durch die deutsche Kultur. Ein französisches Tagebuch. Herausgegeben von Fritz Schwarz. Potsdam: Gustav Kiepenheuer, 1919. pp.235. Portraits, facsimiles.
Includes 'Benjamin Constant (1767-1830)', pp.206-214; 'C.A. Böttiger über Benjamin Constant' [from Böttiger manuscripts, Dresden], pp.221-224; 'Drei

Briefe Benjamin Constants an der Frau von Krüdener' [originally published in *JG*, 9 March 1908], pp.225-229.
Copies: B, BPU, T. (Fromm 5715).

A66/t2 1923   Benjamin Constant. Giornale intimo, a cura di G. Gallavresi. Milano: Facchi, [1923]. (Collezione di memorie, diretta da G. Gallavresi, 4). pp.189.
Includes translation of *Le Cahier rouge*, pp.13-85. *Copy*: B. (Cordié 191).

1933   See item A18/t65 (Adolphe-Diario ... Torino, 1933).

1941   See item A18/t65 (reprint of Adolphe-Diario ... Torino, 1933).

1943   See item A68/t2 (Il quaderno rosso ... Milano: Bompiani, 1943).

1944   See item A18/t65 (reprint of Adolphe-Diario ... Torino, 1933).

1951   See item A18/t65 (reprint of Adolphe-Diario ... Torino, 1933).

A66/t3 1951   B. Constant. Dalla Rivoluzione a Napoleone. Giornale e lettere intime (1779-1816). Roma: Capriotti, [1951]. (Documenti, 12). pp.277.
Includes *Giornale intimo* [extracts], pp.23-180; lettere di B. Constant alla signora di Chandieu [Mme de Nassau], pp.181-235; lettere ... alla signora de Charrière, pp.236-277.
Copy: B. (Cordié 216).

1953   See item A18/t90 (Adolfo ... Milano: Rizzoli, [1953]).

1956   See item A18/t65 (reprint of Adolphe-Diario ... Torino, 1933).

1963   See item A18/t111 (Adolphe-Diario ... Torino, 1963).

A66/t4 1969   Benjamin Constant. Diari. A cura di Paolo Serini. Torino: G. Einaudi, 1969. (Nuova Universale Einaudi, 100). pp.xv, 844.
Preface by Guido Neri. Includes *Il Quaderno rosso*, pp.3-60.
Copies: B, BCU.

1970   See item E4/t7 (Werke, Bd. II, Berlin, 1970).

1977   See item A18/t126 (Adolphe ... [Milano]: Curcio, 1977).

A66t/5 1980   Benjamin Constant. Dzienniki Poufne. Przełożyła Joanna Guze. Warszawa: Czytelnik, 1980. pp.658.
Copy: BCU.

A67 Le Siège de Soissons

A67/1 1890-1892   'Le Siège de Soissons. Epopée anti-napoléonienne de Benjamin Constant. Publiée pour la première fois, d'après le manuscrit de Poligny, par Victor Waille', *Bulletin de la Société d'agriculture, sciences & arts de Poligny (Jura)*, XXXI (1890), 231-249, 273-288, 311-319, 335-351; XXXII (1891), 29-32, 33-45, 87-91, 106-118, 149-160, 216-224, 255-256, 286-288; XXXIII (1892), 13-25, 62-64, 92-96, 123-128, 155-160.

Preceded by: Waille, Victor, 'Un poème inédit de Benjamin Constant', XXXI (1890), 193-211; followed by: 'Appendice. Les clefs', XXXIII (1892), 161-164.
Copy: BN.

A67/2 1892   Le Siège de Soissons, épopée anti-napoléonienne de Benjamin Constant, interprétée et publiée pour la première fois par Victor Waille. Poligny: Imprimerie Gustave Cottez, 1892. pp.[iv] 179.

Reprint of the preceding item.
Copies: BI, BN, BPU.

A67/3 1971   Hogue, Helen Hope Shallcross. Benjamin Constant's *Florestan ou le Siège de Soissons, poème*. A critical edition with introduction and notes. Ph.D, 1971, Ann Arbor, Michigan: Xerox University Microfilms, 1976. (Thesis, Columbia University, 1971). pp.578. Bibliography.

Summary: *Dissertation Abstracts International*, XXXII, n° 7, (January 1972), 4002A.

1972   See item A74/9b ('Chant des Ombres', in Adolphe ... [Paris]: Le Livre de poche, [1972]).

A68 Le Cahier rouge

A68/1 1907   'Le *Cahier rouge* de Benjamin Constant', [publié par Adrien Constant de Rebecque], *RDM*, 1er janvier 1907, 67-81; 15 janvier 1907, 241-272.

Reviews: André Chaumeix, *JD*, 6 septembre 1907, 451-452. W. Küchler, *Allgemeine Frankfurter Zeitung*, 2 July 1907. Gustave Lanson, *Revue universitaire*, 15 février 1908.

A68/2 1907   Le 'Cahier rouge' de Benjamin Constant, publié par L. Constant de Rebecque. Paris: Calmann-Lévy, [1907]. pp.[iv], ii, 129. Frontispiece (portrait).

Appendices include selections from Constant's early correspondence.
Copies: BL, BN.

1920   See item A18/43 (Adolphe ... Genève: Georg; Paris: Crès, 1920).

A68/3 1928   Le Cahier rouge de Benjamin Constant, publié par L. Constant de Rebecque. Paris: Stock, Delamain et Boutelleau, [1928]. (A la promenade, 1). pp.VIII, 126.

Copies: BCU, BL, BN.

Review: Marcel Arland, *NRF*, XXXI (1928), 724-729.

1931   See items A18/61 (Adolphe ... Paris: Nilsson, [1931]) and A18/62 (Adolphe .... Paris: Hilsum, [1931]).

1936   See item A18/66 (Adolphe ... Paris: Gründ, [1936]).

1945   See items A18/80 (Adolphe ... Londres: Penguin, 1945), A18/81 (Journal intime ... Monaco: Editions du Rocher, [1945]).

A68/4 1945   Benjamin Constant. Le Cahier rouge. Ma Vie. Amsterdam: A.A. Balkema, 1945. pp.84. Frontispiece (bust: 'S. Hartz sculp. 1942'). Colophon. 350 copies printed.
Copies: A, B, BCU. (De Jong 156; Simoni C7).

1946   See also item A18/81 (reprint of Journal intime ... Monaco: Editions du Rocher, [1945]).

A68/5 1946   Benjamin Constant. Le Cahier rouge. Genève: Editions du Verbe, [1946]. (Collection: 10 chefs-d'œuvre classiques, [5]). pp.105.
Copies: B, BPU.

A68/6 1949   Benjamin Constant. Le Cahier rouge. Genève: Pierre Cailler, [1949]. (Les Trésors de la littérature française, 47). pp.68.
Copies: B, BCU, C.

1953   See items A18/97 (Adolphe ... Lausanne: Guilde du livre, 1953) and A18/99 (Adolphe ... [Monte Carlo]: Sauret, [1953]).

1957   See items A18/105 (Adolphe ... Lausanne: Rencontre, [1957]), A18/106 (Le Cahier rouge, Adolphe ... [Paris]: Hachette, [1957]) and E4/5 (Œuvres, Paris: Bibliothèque de la Pléiade, 1957).

1959   See items A18/107 (Adolphe ... Paris: Laffont, [1959]) and A18/108 (Adolphe ... [Bruxelles]: Kellinckx, 1959).

1962   See item A18/97 (reprint of Adolphe ... Lausanne: Guilde du livre, 1953).

1963   See items A18/112 (Adolphe ... Paris: Charpentier, 1963) and A18/114 (Le Cahier rouge, Cécile, Adolphe ... [Paris]: Club des libraires de France, 1963).

1964   See items A18/115 (Adolphe ... Paris: Nelson, 1964) and E4/5 (reprint of Œuvres, Paris: Bibliothèque de la Pléiade, 1957).

1965   See item A18/115 (Adolphe ... 1964, reissued as Nelson de luxe).

1966   See item A18/117 (Adolphe ... [Paris]: Le Trésor des Lettres françaises, [1966]).

1968   See item A18/105 (reprint of Adolphe ... Lausanne: Editions Rencontre ... 1957).

1972   See item A18/124 (Adolphe ... [Paris]: Le Livre de poche, [1972]).

1973   See items A18/117 (Adolphe ... [Paris]: Le Trésor des Lettres françaises, [1966]) and A18/125 (Adolphe ... Paris: Gallimard, 1973).

1979   See item E4/5 (reprint of Œuvres, Paris: Bibliothèque de la Pléiade, 1957).

Translations

1923   See item A66/t2 (Gionale intimo ... Milano, [1923]).

1932   See item A18/t62 (Adolpho ... Milano-Roma, 1932).

A68/t1 1932   Benjamin Constant. Czerwony kajet. [Przełożył i wstępem opatrzył Tadeusz Żeleński (Boy)]. Warszawa: Bibljoteka Boya, [1932]. (Bibljoteka Boya. Arcydzieła Literatury Francuskiej). pp.110.
Includes translation of letters from Constant to Isabelle de Charrière, 1787-1790, pp.69-100.
Copies: B, Ww.

A68/t2 1943   Il quaderno rosso di Benjamin Constant. A cura di Enrico Emanuelli. Milano: Bompiani, [1943]. (Corona, Collezione universale Bompiani, 28). pp.160.
Includes *Ritratto di Giulia* and extracts from *Journaux intimes*.
Copy: DLC. (Cordié 200).

1948   See items A18/t82 (Adolphe ... London: Hamish Hamilton, [1948] and A18/t83 (Adolphe ... New York: Pantheon Books, [1948]).

A68/t3 1949   Benjamin Constant. Kırmızı Defter (Le Cahier Rouge). Bu eseri Sona Tatlıcan dilimize çevirmiştir. İstanbul: Millî Eğitim Basımevi, 1949. (Dünya Edebiyatından Tercümeler. Fransız Klâsikleri, 169). pp.[6], 72.
Translation by Sona Tatlıcan. Introduction by İsmet İnönü, p.5.
Copies: Ankara, T.

1953   See item A18/t90 (Adolfo ... Milano: Rizzoli, [1953]).

1959   See items A18/t99 (Adolphe ... Indianapolis: Bobbs-Merrill, 1959), A18/t100, (Adolphe ... London: Hamish Hamilton, 1959) and A18/t101 (Adolphe ... New York: New American Library, 1959).

1969   See item A66/t4 (Diari ... Torino: Einaudi, 1969).

1970   See item E4/t7 (Werke, Bd. I, Berlin 1970).

1977   See item A18/t126 (Adolphe ... [Milano]: Curcio, 1977).

A69 Les Chevaliers

A69/1 1927   Benjamin Constant. Les Chevaliers. Avant-propos de G. Rudler. Paris: Simon Kra, 1927. pp.77. Frontispiece (facsimile).
Copies: BL, BN.
Review: F. Montel, *Le Figaro*, 5 novembre 1927.

A70 Cécile

A70/1 1951   Benjamin Constant. Cécile, présenté et annoté par Alfred Roulin. Paris: Gallimard, 1951. pp.155. 18.5 cm. Facsimiles. Colophon.
Reprinted several times in the same year.
Reviews: Emile Henriot, *Le Monde*, 20 juin 1951, p.7. Colette Audry, *Les Temps modernes*, n° 69, juillet 1951, pp.183-184. H. Guillemin, *JG*, 29-30 décembre 1951, pp.3-4. M. Levaillant, *RHLF*, LII, (1952), 81-85. Alain Girard, *RHLF*, LII, (1952), 93-96. Pierre Reboul, *AUS*, philosophie-lettres, II (1953), 138-142. E. Briquet, *GL*, 23-24 février 1952 p.12. P. Bénichou, *Critique*, VIII, n° 67, décembre 1952, 1027-1046. Carlo Pellegrini, *RLMC*, II (1951), 335-343. G. Charlier, *Revue belge de philologie et d'histoire*, XXX (1952), 572. Pierre Kohler, *Erasmus*, V (1952), 93-98. *TLS*, 31 August 1951, p.545, 'Unfinished narrative'. Ernst Howald, *Neue Zürcher Zeitung*, 8 März 1952, pp.9-10.
Copies: BCU, BL, BN.

A70/2 1953   Cécile, par Benjamin Constant. Présenté et annoté par Alfred Roulin. Paris: Le Club du meilleur livre, 1953. pp.XVI, 192.
Copy: BN.

1957   See items A18/104 (Adolphe ... [Paris]: Le Livre de poche, [1957]) and E4/5 (Œuvres, Paris: Bibliothèque de la Pléiade, 1957).

1958   See item A18/104 (reprint of Adolphe ... [Paris]: Le Livre de poche, [1957]).

1961   See item A18/104 (reprint of Adolphe ... [Paris]: Le Livre de poche, [1957]).

1963   See item A18/114 (Le Cahier rouge ... [Paris]: Club des Libraires de France, 1963).

1964   See item E4/5 (reprint of Œuvres, Paris: Bibliothèque de la Pléiade, 1957).

A70/3 1964   Benjamin Constant. Cécile, présenté et annoté par Alfred Roulin. Eaux-fortes originales de Bernard Gantner. [Paris]: les Bibliophiles comtois, [1964]. pp.133, [134-135]. Illus. Colophon.
160 numbered copies printed.
Copy: BN.

1967   See item A18/104 (reprint of Adolphe ... [Paris]: Le Livre de poche, [1957]).

1968   See items A18/121 (Adolphe ... Kapellen-Anvers: Beckers, 1968) and A18/122 (Adolphe ... London: Macmillan, 1968).

1973   See item A18/125 (Adolphe ... Paris: Gallimard, 1973).

1979   See items A18/128 (Adolphe ... Kahnthout-Anvers: Beckers, 1979) and E4/5 (reprint of Œuvres, Paris: Bibliothèque de la Pléiade, 1957).

Translations

A70/t1 1951   Cécile. [Japanese translation]. Tokyo: L. Prou, [1951?].
Copy: BCU.

A70/t2 1952   Benjamin Constant. Cécile. Edited and annotated by Alfred Roulin. Translated by Norman Cameron. London: J. Lehmann, [1952]. pp.125.
Copies: BCU, BL

1953   See also item A18/t90 (Adolfo ... Milano: Rizzoli, [1953]).

A70/t3 1953   Benjamin Constant. Cécile. [Japanese translation by Keisaku Kubota]. Tokyo: Shinchosha, 1953. pp.138.
Copy: Tokyo.

A70/t4 1953   Benjamin Constant. Cecile. Edited and annotated by Alfred Roulin. Translated by Norman Cameron. Norfolk, Conn.: James Laughlin [1953]. (A New Directions Book). pp.xx, 125.
Reviews: *New Statesman*, 22 November 1952, p.608. *New York Times*, 5 July 1953, p.4. *New York Herald Tribune Book Review*, 30 August 1953, p.6.

A70/t5 1953   Benjamín Constant. Cecilia. [Traducción de Silvina Bullrich. Prólogo de José A. Oría. Introducción y notas de Alfredo Roulin]. Buenos Aires: Emecé, 1953. pp.150. Illus., facsimile.
Copy: BCU.

1954   See also item A18/t93 (Adolphe/Cécile, Amsterdam: Veen; Brussel: Reinaert, 1954).

A70/t6 1954   Benjamin Constant. Cecile. Met een woord vooraf door Dr Victor E. van Vriesland. Amsterdam-Antwerpen: Wereldbibliotheek, [1954]. (Wereldboog, 41). pp.86. [Translation by Cornelia Serrurier. Notes by Alfred Roulin].
Copies: B, BCU, BR. Reprinted in the same year and in 1957. *Copy* (1957): BR.

A70/t7 1955   Benjamin Constant. Cécile. Roman. Herausgegeben von Alfred Roulin. [Übersetzt von Hanno Helbling]. Zurich, Stuttgart: Fretz und Wasmuth, 1955. pp.136.

Copies: B, BCU.

1957   See item A70/t6 (reprint of Cécile ... Amsterdam, [1954]).

1963   See item A18/t112 (Adolphe ... Frankfurt am Main: Insel Verlag, 1963).

1964   See item A18/t115 (Adolf ... Beograd: Rad, 1964).

1967   See item A18/t93 (reprint of Adolphe ... Amsterdam: Veen; Brussel: Reinaert, [1954]).

1968   See item A18/t119 (Adolfo ... Lisboa: Portugália, [1968]).

1969   See item A18/t120 (Adolphe ... Amsterdam: Contact, 1969).

1970   See item E4/t7 (Werke, Bd. I, Berlin, 1970).

1977   See item A18/t126 (Adolphe ... [Milano]: Curcio, 1977).

A71 L'Esprit des religions

A71/1 1970   Benjamin Constant. Deux chapitres inédits de L'Esprit des religions (1803-1804). Des rapports de la morale avec les croyances religieuses et De l'intervention de l'autorité dans ce qui a rapport à la religion. Publiés avec une introduction et des notes par Patrice Thompson. Neuchâtel: Faculté des Lettres; Genève: Droz, 1970. (Université de Neuchâtel: Recueil de travaux publiés par la Faculté des Lettres, 33e fascicule). pp.250. Bibliography.

Reviews: Olivier Pozzo di Borgo, *RHLF*, LXXIII (1973), 903-906. Albert Kies, *Revue belge de philologie et d'histoire*, LII (1974), 215. H. Bernard-Maître, *Revue de Synthèse*, LXXXIV (1973), 400-401.

A72 Translation of Godwin

A72/1 1972   Benjamin Constant. De la justice politique. Traduction inédite de l'ouvrage de William Godwin: *Enquiry concerning Political Justice and its Influence on General Virtue and Happiness*, éditée par Burton R. Pollin. Québec: Les Presses de l'Université Laval, 1972. (Droit et science politique, Collection dirigée par Jean-Charles Bonenfant, 5). pp.[iv] 393.

Includes the following works in appendices: *De Godwin, de ses principes, et de son ouvrage sur la justice politique* (Appendix A); *Fragmens d'un essai sur la perfectibilité humaine* (Appendix B); *De Godwin, et de son ouvrage sur la justice politique* (Appendix C).

Reviews: Patrice Thompson, *RHLF*, LXXIV (1974), 514-515. Alison Fairlie, *FS*, XXVIII (1974), 85-86. Duane Koenig, *FR*, XLVII (1974), 850-851. Norman King, *MLR*, LXX (1975), 906.

A73 Principes de politique (1806)

A73/1 1980   Benjamin Constant. *Principes de politique applicables à tous les gouvernements. Texte établi d'après les manuscrits de Lausanne et de Paris avec une introduction et des notes par Etienne Hofmann.* Genève: Droz, 1980. (Travaux d'histoire éthico-politique, 34), pp.690.

A74 Miscellaneous works and inédits

In this section are listed various *inédits* published mainly in books and articles on Constant.

A74/1 1835   Mémoire de M. Benjamin de Constant.
Text signed: 'Paris, 21 juillet 1815. Signé: Benjamin de Constant'.
[Réal, P.-F.], *Indiscrétions 1780-1830. Souvenirs anecdotiques et politiques tirés du portefeuille d'un fonctionnaire de l'Empire,* mis en ordre par Musnier-Desclozeaux, Paris: Dufey, 1835, II, 152-172.
Reprinted: Carlo Cordié, 'L'originario memoriale del Constant sui Cento giorni', *Paideia,* V (1950), 298-305; Cordié *Ideali e figure d'Europa,* Pisa: Nistri-Lischi, 1954, pp.234-248; Pozzo di Borgo, *Mémoires sur les Cent-Jours,* 1961, item A42/5, pp.223-229.

A74/2 1882 [=1881]   Idées sur la Conservation du royaume de Naples au roi Joachim Ier, [septembre 1814].
[Lenormant, A.], *Lettres de Benjamin Constant à Madame Récamier,* Paris: Calmann Lévy, 1882 [=1881], pp.351-354. (Item F4, below). Reprinted in item F16.

A74/3 1906   Speech of 13 November 1797 to the Administration municipale, canton de Luzarches.
Tambour, Ernest, 'Benjamin Constant à Luzarches', *Revue de l'histoire de Versailles et de Seine-et-Oise,* 1906, pp.169-172. Also in Tambour, *Benjamin Constant à Luzarches,* Versailles: L. Bernard, 1906. Published from Archives de Seine-et-Oise.

A74/4 1909   Juvenilia
The following early writings are published in Rudler, *La Jeunesse de Benjamin Constant,* 1909 (item F163 below) and described in the same author's *Bibliographie critique des œuvres de Benjamin Constant* (item F164 below). The page references given below are to *La Jeunesse.*
Prière au créateur du monde [1774-1775], p.88.
Sur l'homme juste [1774-1775], p.88.
Dialogue. Frugalité et Bombance [1775-1776], p.89.
Didon, fragment de tragédie [1777], pp.90-94.
Pastorale [1779], pp.94-95.
Bouts rimés, by Benjamin, Rosalie de Constant and Mlle Gallatin [1779], p.96.
Bouts rimés [1779], p.96.

Des mortels voïez la chimère [1779], pp.91-92.
Le dévouement de Décius [1779], pp.92-94.

A74/5 1933   Prayer. [September-October 1815].
Lavedan, Henri, *Avant l'oubli, I. Un enfant rêveur*, Paris: Plon, 1933, I, 46-51.
Also published by the same author in *La Petite Illustration*, n° 624, Roman n°
290, 29 avril 1933, pp.17-18. Reprinted: Maurice Levaillant, *Chateaubriand,
Madame Récamier et les Mémoires d'Outre-Tombe*, Paris: Delagrave, 1936, pp.308-
309; Levaillant, *Les Amours de Benjamin Constant*, Paris: Hachette, 1958, pp.224-
225; Henri Gouhier, *Benjamin Constant*, n.p.: Desclée de Brouwer, 1967 (Les
écrivains devant Dieu, 15), pp.124-125.

A74/6 1935   Political writings for Bernadotte, 1813-1814.

A74/6a 1935   Benjamin Constant – 'Projet corrigé'.
Scott, Franklin D. 'Benjamin Constant's "Projet" for France in 1814', *Journal of
modern history*, VII (1935), 41-48 (text of *Projet* on pp.44-48). Reprinted by
Hasselrot, below.

A74/6b 1952   Hasselrot, Bengt. Benjamin Constant. Lettres à Bernadotte.
Sources et origine de l'Esprit de conquête et de l'usurpation publiées par Bengt
Hasselrot. Genève: Droz; Lille: Giard, 1952. [Item F12, below].
Includes the following works by Constant published from Swedish archives:
1. Mémoire sur les communications à établir avec l'intérieur de la France,
[November 1813], pp.3-6.
2. Commentaire sur la réponse faite par Buonaparté, [14] novembre 1813, pp.7-
14. (Published in *L'Ambigu*, 20 February 1814).
3. Projet corrigé, [4-5 February 1814], pp.14-21.
4. Notes instructives, 22 mars 1814, pp.21-24.

A74/7 1967   Pensées inédites.
Le Monde (des livres), 4 octobre 1967.

A74/8 1968   Esquisse d'un essai sur la littérature du 18ᵉ siècle. Texte établi
par Simone Balayé.
Europe, n° 467 (mars 1968), pp.18-21. Printed to follow 'Constant et les lumières'
by Roland Mortier. Reprinted in: Mortier, *Clartés et ombres du siècle des lumières:
études sur le XVIIIᵉ siècle littéraire*, Genève: Droz, 1969, pp.154-156. Written in July
1807.

A74/9 1968   La Prière and other poems.

A74/9a 1968   Mistler, Jean. 'Benjamin Constant, prophète du libéralisme',
Les Annales. Conferencia, nouvelle série, n° 208 (février 1968), 2-16.
Includes 'La Prière', pp.6-7; see the following item. Also includes extracts of
Polycrate tyran de Samos (tragedy) and of letters from Constant to Charlotte de
Constant.

A74/9b 1972   Benjamin Constant. Adolphe, suivi du Cahier rouge et de

Poèmes inédits. Edition de Jean Mistler. [Paris]: Le Livre de poche, [1972]. [Item A18/124 above]. On pp.263-271: text of *La Prière* and *Chant des Ombres*, the latter from *Le Siège de Soissons* (item A67). Also included in the preface is a previously unpublished poem, *Il feindra la tristesse*, pp.XXXVII-XXXVIII.

A74/10 1980   Fragmens d'un essai sur la littérature dans ses rapports avec la liberté [1805-1807].

Kloocke, Kurt, 'Une étude littéraire inachevée de Benjamin Constant: les Fragmens d'un essai sur la littérature dans ses rapports avec la liberté', *ABC*, n° 1 (1980), 180-200. Text of *Fragmens*: pp.173-200.

A74/11 1981   Lettres de d'Arsillé fils, de Sophie Durfé et autres [1787-1788].

Isabelle de Charrière/Belle de Zuylen, *Romans, contes et nouvelles, II, 1798-1806*, texte établi et annoté par Patrice Thompson et Dennis M. Wood avec la collaboration de C. P. Courtney et M. Gilot, Amsterdam: van Oorschot, 1981, pp.651-678. (Vol. IX of Isabelle de Charrière/ Belle de Zuylen, *Œuvres complètes*, Amsterdam: van Oorschot, 1979-1984).

Apparently written by Benjamin Constant and Isabelle de Charrière in collaboration. See introduction and notes to the edition and the following articles by Dennis Wood: 'Benjamin Constant's first novel?' *TLS*, 6 February 1981, p.151; 'Rediscovering Constant'; *FSB*, special members' issue (autumn 1981), pp.2-3; 'A Constant *inédit*', *FSB*, n° 1 (winter 1981/82), pp.3-5; 'Isabelle de Charrière et Benjamin Constant: à propos d'une découverte récente', *Studies on Voltaire and the eighteenth century*, CCXV (1982), 273-279; 'Isabelle de Charrière et Benjamin Constant: problématique d'une collaboration, *ABC*, n° 4 (1984), pp.17-30.

A74/12 1982   A Sa Majesté l'Empereur Napoléon.

Harpaz, Ephraïm. 'Une lettre inconnue de Benjamin Constant à Napoléon (30 avril 1815)', *Revue de la Bibliothèque nationale*, n° 3, mars 1982, pp.27-34. The edition, *A Sa Majesté l'Empereur Napoléon*, 8° pp.10, is signed at end: 'Benj. Constant'. Printed, but apparently not published. Only one copy (apparently a proof) has been preserved (BN, Fonds Monamy). (C. Suppl. Add. 2).

A74/13 1982   Pièces relatives à mes différends avec Madame de Constant née de Cramm.

Kloocke, Kurt. 'Benjamin Constant et Minna von Cramm: documents inédits', *ABC*, n° 2 (1982), pp.81-109.

B Speeches (Tribunat and Chambre des députés) and official papers

B1/1 1796 Corps législatif. Conseil des Cinq-Cents. Aux Citoyens représentans du peuple composant le Conseil des Cinq-Cents. Séance du 9 thermidor, an IV [27 July 1796]. 8° pp.6. Imprimerie nationale, thermidor l'an IV.

Text signed at end: 'Benjamin-Constant Rebecque'. Reprinted in *Le Républicain français*, 11 thermidor an IV (29 July 1796) and in *Le Moniteur*, 14 thermidor an IV (1 August 1796).

Copies: AN, BL, BN. (C.64a).

Translation

B1/t1 1796 Bittschrift von Benjamin Constant Rebecque an den Rath der Fünfhundert (in der Sitzung vom 26sten July vorgelesen).

Frankreich im Jahr 1796. Aus den Briefen Deutscher Männer in Paris. Altona [Lübeck: Niemannn]. Bd. I (1796); 8. St., 363-367.

Copies: C, St. (C.64b).

B2 1800 Tribunat. Discours prononcé par Benjamin Constant, sur le projet concernant la formation de la loi, proposé au Corps législatif par le gouvernement le 12 nivôse an 8. Séance du 15 nivose an 8 [5 January 1800]. 8° pp.18. Imprimerie nationale, nivôse an 8.

Copies: BCU, BL, BN. (C.65a).

Another edition: Pozzo di Borgo 1964 (E4/6).

B3 1800 Tribunat. Opinion de Benjamin-Constant, sur le mode à adopter pour prendre en considération les pétitions adressées au Tribunat. Séance du 12 Pluviose an 8 [1 February 1800]. 8° pp.18. Imprimerie nationale, pluviôse an 8.

Copies: BCU, BL, BN. (C.66a).

B4 1800 Tribunat. Opinion de Benjamin Constant, sur le projet de loi qui met à la disposition du gouvernement les citoyens qui ont atteint leur vingtième année au premier vendémiaire an 8. Séance du 15 ventôse an 8 [6 March 1800]. 8° pp.18. Imprimerie nationale, ventôse an 8.

Copies: BL, BN. (C.67a).

B5 1800 Discours prononcé par Benjamin Constant, l'un des orateurs du Tribunat, sur le projet de loi tendant à mettre à la disposition du gouvernement les citoyens qui ont atteint l'âge de 20 ans. Séance du 17 ventôse an 8 [8 March 1800]. 8° pp.8. Impr. Baudouin, [Paris].

Copies: BN, MH, MnU. (C.68a).

B6 1800 Tribunat. Opinion de Benjamin Constant, sur le projet de loi relatif

aux rentes foncières. Séance du 27 ventose an 8 [18 March 1800]. 8° pp.10.
Imprimerie nationale, ventôse an 8.
Copies: BCU, BL, BN. (C.69a).

B7 1800   Tribunat. Opinion de Benjamin Constant, sur le projet de loi relatif
à la faculté de tester. Séance du 29 ventose an 8 [20 March 1800]. 8° pp.12.
Imprimerie nationale, germinal an 8.
Copies: BCU, BL, BN. (C.70a).

B8 1800   Tribunat. Discours de Benjamin Constant, sur les victoires de l'armée
d'Italie. Séance du 3 Messidor an 8 [22 Juin 1800]. 8° pp.3. Imprimerie
nationale, messidor an 8.
Copies: BL, BN. (C.71a).

Translation

B8/t1 1800   Sitzung des Tribunats vom 3ten Messidor.
Frankreich im Jahr 1800. Aus den Briefen Deutscher Männer in Paris. Altona [Lübeck:
Niemann]. Bd. II (1800), 7 St., 195-213.
Copies: C, St.

B9 1801   Tribunat. Opinion de Benjamin Constant, sur le projet de loi concernant la réduction des justices de paix. Séance du 2 Pluviose an 9 [22 January
1801]. 8° pp.12. Imprimerie nationale, pluviôse an 9.
Copies: BL, BN. (C.72a).

B10 1801   Tribunat. Opinion de Benjamin Constant, sur le projet de loi
concernant l'établissement de tribunaux criminels spéciaux. Séance du 5 Pluviose an 9 [25 January 1801]. 8° pp.38. Imprimerie nationale, pluviôse an 9.
Copies: BL, BN. (C.73a).

Another edition: Pozzo di Borgo 1964 (E4/6).

B11 1801   Tribunat. Opinion de Benjamin Constant, sur le projet de loi relatif
à la dette publique et aux domaines nationaux. Séance du 28 Ventose an 9 [19
March 1801]. 8° pp.38. Imprimerie nationale, germinal an 9.
Copy: BN. (C.74a).

B12 1801   Tribunat. Opinion de Benjamin Constant, sur le projet de loi relatif
aux actes de l'état civil. Séance du 4 Nivose an 10 [25 December 1801]. 8° pp.23.
Imprimerie nationale, frimaire an 10.
Copies: BL, BN. (C.75a).

B13 1801   Tribunat. Seconde opinion de Benjamin Constant, sur le projet de
loi relatif aux actes de l'état civil. Séance du 7 nivose an 10 [28 December 1801].
8° pp.19. Imprimerie nationale, nivôse an 10.

Copies: BL, BN. (C.76a).

B14 1819   Chambre des Députés. Opinion de M. Benjamin Constant, député du département de la Sarthe, sur le projet de loi relatif à la répression des délits de la presse. Prononcée dans la séance du 14 avril 1819. 8° pp.38. Impr. Hacquart, [Paris].
Copies: BL, BN. (C.77a). *Discours* (1827-1828), I, 1-27.

Other editions: *Cours de politique* 1820 (E1/1(4)), *Cours de politique* 1833 (E1/2(4)).

B15 1819   Chambre des Députés. Amendemens de M. Benjamin Constant, sur le projet de loi relatif à la répression des délits de la presse. 8° pp.3. Impr. Hacquart, [Paris]. (Impressions ordonnées. Session de 1818: vol. I, n° 43 [16 April 1819]).
Copies: BL, BN. (C.78a). *Discours* (1827-1828), I, 28-31.

B16 1819   Chambre des Députés. Opinion de M. Benjamin Constant, député du département de la Sarthe, sur le projet de loi relatif à la fixation des budgets des années 1815, 1816, 1817 et 1818. Prononcée dans la séance du 14 mai 1819. 8° pp.22. Impr. Hacquart, [Paris]. (Impressions ordonnées. Session de 1818, vol. II, n° 67*bis*).
Copies: BL, BN. (C.79a). *Discours* (1827-1828), I, 88-102.

B17 1819   Chambre des Députés. Opinion de M. Benjamin Constant, sur la pétition tendant à demander le rappel des bannis. Paris: Brissot-Thivars, 1819. 8° pp.11. (Discours et opinions imprimés sans ordre. Session de 1818, n° 43 [Séance du 17 mai 1819; opinion non prononcée]).
Copies: AN, BN. (C.80a). *Discours* (1827-1828), I, 139-151.

B18 1819   Chambre des Députés. Opinion de M. Benjamin Constant, député de la Sarthe, sur le budget des dépenses à ordonnancer par le Ministre des Finances, pour l'exercice 1819. Séance du 8 juin 1819. 8° pp.41. Impr. Hacquart, [Paris]. (Impressions ordonnées. Session de 1818, vol. III, n° 113).
Copies: BL, BN. (C.81a). *Discours* (1827-1828), I, 111-136.

B19 1819   Chambre des Députés. Opinion de M. Benjamin Constant, député de la Sarthe, sur les douanes. Séance du 15 juin 1819. 8° pp.18. Impr. Hacquart, [Paris]. (Impressions ordonnées. Session de 1818, vol. IV, n° 143).
Copies BL, BN. (C.82a).

B20 1819   Chambre des Députés. Opinion de M. Benjamin Constant, député de la Sarthe, sur l'administration des contributions indirectes. Prononcée dans la séance du 16 juin 1819. 8° pp.23. Impr. Hacquart, [Paris]. (Impressions ordonnées. Session de 1818, vol. IV, n° 146).
Copies: BL, BN. (C.83a).

B21 1819   Chambre des Députés. Opinion de M. Benjamin Constant, député de la Sarthe, sur les pensions. Prononcée dans la séance du 21 juin 1819. 8°

pp.20. Impr. Hacquart, [Paris]. (Impressions ordonnées. Session de 1818, vol. IV, n° 164).

Copies: BL, BN. (C.84a).

B22 1819   Chambre des Députés. Opinion de M. Benjamin Constant, député de la Sarthe, sur le titre IV du projet de loi des voies et moyens de 1819. Séance du 28 juin 1819. 8° pp.24. Impr. Hacquart, [Paris]. (Impressions ordonnées. Session de 1818, vol. IV, n° 185).

Copies: BL, BN. (C.85a).

B23 1820   Chambre des Députés. Développemens de la proposition de M. Benjamin-Constant, député de la Sarthe, tendant à améliorer le mode de scrutin et les articles 15, 22 et 33 du règlement. 8° pp.8. Impr. Hacquart, [Paris]. (Impressions ordonnées. Session de 1819, vol. I, n° 19 [Séance du 14 janvier 1820]).

Copies: BL, BN. (C.86a). *Discours* (1827-1828), I, 164-172.

B24 1820   Chambre des Députés. Opinion de M. Benjamin Constant, député de la Sarthe, sur le projet de loi relatif à la suspension de la liberté individuelle. [7 March 1820]. 8° pp.14. Impr. Plassan, [Paris]. (Discours et opinions imprimés sans ordre. Session de 1819).

Copy: BN. (C.87a). *Discours* (1827-1828), I, 188-205.

Another edition: Pléiade 1957, 1964, 1979 (E4/5). See also items A18/30 (Adolphe ... Paris: Guillequin, [1907]) and A18/33 (Adolphe ... Londres: Dent; Paris: Mignot, [1912]).

B25 1820   Chambre des Députés. Opinion de M. Benjamin Constant, député de la Sarthe, sur le projet de loi relatif à la suspension de la liberté individuelle. Séance du 13 mars 1820. 8° pp.14. Impr. Plassan, [Paris]. (Discours et opinions imprimés sans ordre. Session de 1819).

Copy: BN. (C.88a). *Discours* (1827-1828), I, 212-223.

B26 1820   Chambre des Députés. Rapport fait au nom de la commission centrale, par M. Benjamin Constant, député de la Sarthe; sur la proposition tendant à améliorer les articles 15, 22 et 33 du règlement. Séance du 20 mars 1820. 8° pp.8. Impr. Hacquart, [Paris]. (Impressions ordonnées. Session de 1819, vol. I, n° 24).

Copies: BL, BN. (C.89a). *Discours* (1827-1828), I, 229-232.

B27 1820   Chambre des Députés. Opinion de M. Benjamin Constant, député de la Sarthe, sur le projet de loi relatif à la censure des journaux. Séance du 23 mars 1820. 8° pp.14. Impr. Plassan, [Paris]. (Discours et opinions imprimés sans ordre. Session de 1819).

Copy: BN. (C.90a). *Discours* (1827-1828), I, 232-248.

Another edition: Pléiade 1957, 1964, 1979 (E4/5).

B28 1820   Chambre des Députés. Opinion de M. Benjamin Constant, député

de la Sarthe, sur le projet de loi relatif au règlement définitif des comptes antérieurs à l'exercice 1819. Séance du 5 avril 1820. 8° pp.23. Impr. Hacquart, [Paris]. (Impressions ordonnées. Session de 1819, vol. II, n° 32).
Copies: BL, BN. (C.91a). *Discours* (1827-1828), I, 280-295.

B29 1820   Chambre des Députés. Opinion de M. Benjamin Constant, député de la Sarthe, sur les amendemens proposés à l'art. 8 du second projet de loi relatif aux comptes arriérés. Séance du 15 avril 1820. 8° pp.15. Impr. Hacquart, [Paris]. (Impression ordonnées. Session de 1819, vol. II, n° 57).
Copies: BL, BN. (C.92a). *Discours* (1827-1828), I, 296-305.

B30 1820   Chambre des Députés. Opinion de M. Benjamin Constant, député de la Sarthe, sur le deuxième projet de loi relatif aux comptes arriérés. Séance du 18 avril 1820. 8° pp.10. Impr. Hacquart, [Paris]. (Impressions ordonnées. Session de 1819, vol. III, n° 79).
Copies: BL, BN. (C.93a).

B31 1820   Chambre des Députés. Opinion de M. Benjamin Constant, député de la Sarthe, sur trois pétitions relatives au renvoi de M. Decazes. Séance du 28 avril 1820. 8° pp.8. Impr. Plassan, [Paris].
Copy: BN. (C.94a). *Discours* (1827-1828), I, 310-318.

B32 1820   Discours prononcé par M. Benjamin Constant, député de la Sarthe, dans le comité secret du 3 mai (1), à l'occasion de la proposition d'adresse, faite à la Chambre des députés par M. Manuel. 8° pp.17. Impr. Plassan, [Paris]. (Discours et opinions imprimés sans ordre. Session de 1819).
Copies: BL, BN. (C.95a). *Discours* (1827-1828), I, 318-331.

B33/1 1820   Opinion de M. Benjamin-Constant, député de la Sarthe, sur le projet de loi relatif aux élections; prononcée dans la séance du 23 mai 1820. (Extrait du *Moniteur* du 25 mai 1820.) 8° pp.19. Impr. Mme veuve Agasse, [Paris].
Copies: ADS, BN. (C.96a). *Discours* (1827-1828), I, 336-365.

B33/2 1820   Discours prononcé par M. Benjamin Constant, à la Chambre des députés, sur la loi des élections. 8° pp.11. Impr. L. Barnel, Grenoble.
Copy: BL. (C.96b).

B34/1 1820   Opinion de M. Benjamin-Constant, député de la Sarthe, sur l'article premier du projet de loi relatif aux élections; prononcée dans la séance du 3 juin 1820. (Extrait du *Moniteur* du 4 juin 1820). 8° pp.8. Impr. Mme Ve Agasse, [Paris].
Copy: BL. (C.97a). *Discours* (1827-1828), I, 372-384.

B34/2 1820   Second discours prononcé par M. Benjamin Constant, à la Chambre des députés, sur la loi des élections, dans la séance du 3 juin 1820. 8° pp.8. Impr. L. Barnel, Grenoble.
Copy: BN. (C.97b).

B35 1820   Eclaircissemens sur quelques faits, adressés à MM. les membres de la Chambre des députés, par M. Benjamin Constant, l'un d'entr'eux. 4° pp.8. Impr. Moreau, [Paris].

Text signed at end: 'Benjamin Constant. Paris, ce 25 Décembre 1820'.

Copies: C, Ca. (C.98a).

B36 1821   Discours prononcés dans le Comité secret du 31 janvier 1821, par MM. Manuel, le Général Sébastiani, Chauvelin, Camille Jordan, B. Constant, le Comte Alexandre de Lameth, le Général Foy, Stanislas de Girardin, le Général Demarçay, Casimir Perier. A Paris, à la librairie constitutionnelle, chez Brissot-Thivars ... 1821. 8° pp.[iv], 54. Impr. P. Dupont, [Paris].

Constant's speeches: pp.34-35; 50-51.

Copies: BCU, BN. (C.99a).

B37 1821   Chambre des Députés. Opinion de M. Benjamin Constant, député de la Sarthe, sur l'amendement proposé par M. Bertin de Vaux au projet de loi relatif au remboursement du premier cinquième des reconnaissances de liquidation. Séance du 19 février 1821. 8° pp.23. Impr. Hacquart, [Paris]. (Impressions ordonnées. Session de 1820, vol. I, n° 43).

Copies: BL, BN. (C.100a). *Discours* (1827-1828), I, 429-444.

B38 1821   Opinions de M. Benjamin Constant, sur l'interdiction de la parole, par suite du rappel à l'ordre et à la question, dans les séances des 6 et 14 avril, avec un avertissement et des notes de l'auteur ... A Paris, chez Kleffer ... Moreau ... Mongie ... Béchet aîné ... Delaunai, Pélicier et Ponthieu ... Mai 1821. 8° pp.41. Impr. Moreau, [Paris].

Copies: BN, SG. (C.101a). *Discours* (1827-1828), I, 445-480.

B39 1821   Opinion prononcée dans la séance du 27 juin 1821, par M. Benjamin Constant député de la Sarthe. Paris, de l'Imprimerie de Constant-Chantpie ... 1821. 8° pp.8. [*Sur la traite des nègres*].

Copy: BN. (C.102a). *Discours* (1827-1828), I, 548-560.

Another edition: Pléiade 1957, 1964, 1979 (E4/5).

B40 1821   Opinion de M. Benjamin Constant, député de la Sarthe. Prononcée dans la séance du 22 décembre 1821. 8° pp.4. Impr. Constant-Chantpie, [Paris]. [*Modification au règlement*].

Copies: BL, BN. (C.103a).

B41 1822   Opinion de M. Benjamin Constant, député de la Sarthe, prononcée à la séance du 11 janvier 1822. 8° pp.3. Impr. Constant-Chantpie, [Paris]. [*Sur une petition relative à la censure*].

Copy: BN. (C.104a). *Discours* (1827-1828), II, 1-5.

B42 1822   Opinion de M. Benjamin Constant, député de la Sarthe, dans la discussion sur le projet de loi relatif à la presse, prononcée dans la séance du 31

janvier 1822. 8° pp.8. Impr. Constant-Chantpie, [Paris].
Copies: BL, BN. (C.105a). *Discours* (1827-1828), II, 29-40.

B43 1822   Opinion de M. Benjamin Constant, député de la Sarthe, dans la discussion sur le projet de loi relatif au jury, prononcée dans la séance du 4 février 1822. 8° pp.6. Impr. Constant-Chantpie, [Paris].
Copies: BL, BN. (C.106a).

B44 1822   Opinion de M. Benjamin Constant, député de la Sarthe, sur le projet de loi relatif à la police des journaux, prononcée dans la séance du 9 février 1822. 8° pp.8. Impr. Constant-Chantpie, [Paris].
Copies: BL, BN. (C.107a). *Discours* (1827-1828), II, 56-72.

B45/1 1822   Discours de M. Benjamin Constant, député de la Sarthe, sur la loi relative aux finances. A Paris, à la Librairie Nationale ... chez Plancher ... 1822. 8° pp.12. On p.[3] caption title ' ... Prononcée dans la séance du 13 mars 1822'. Impr. Constant-Chantpie, [Paris].
Copy: BN. (C.108a). *Discours* (1827-1828), II, 108-131.

B45/2 1822   Discours de M. Benjamin Constant, député de la Sarthe, sur la loi relative aux finances, prononcé dans la séance du 13 mars 1822. 8° pp.16. Impr. Constant-Chantpie, [Paris].
Copy: BN. (C.108b).

B46 1822   Chambre des Députés. Opinion de M. Benjamin-Constant, député de la Sarthe, sur le chapitre XI du budget du Ministère de la marine. Imprimée par ordre de la Chambre. Séance du 3 avril 1822. 8° pp.8. Impr. Hacquart, [Paris]. (Impressions ordonnées. Session de 1821, vol. III, n° 166).
Copies: BL, BN. (C.109a). *Discours* (1827-1828), II, 137-144.

Another edition: Pléiade 1957, 1964, 1979 (E4/5).

B47 1822   Chambre des Députés. Session de 1822. Opinion de M. Benjamin-Constant, député de la Sarthe, sur l'amendement de M. Dequeux Saint-Hilaire, tendant à obtenir une réduction proportionnelle sur les traitemens. Imprimée par ordre de la Chambre. Séance du 6 août 1822. 8° pp.4. Impr. Hacquart, [Paris]. (Impressions ordonnées. Session de 1822, vol. IV, n° 259).
Copies: BL, BN. (C.110a). *Discours* (1827-1828), II, 190-196.

B48 1822   Extrait des minutes du Greffe du Tribunal de première instance du département de la Seine, séant au Palais de Justice, à Paris. 8° pp.3. Impr. Constant-Chantpie, [Paris].
Text dated 9 November 1822.
Copy: BN. (C.111a).

B49 1824   Consultation pour M. Benjamin Constant. 8° pp.24. Impr. Gaultier-Laguionie, [Paris].

Text dated 4-10 April 1824 (p.20), 10 April 1824 (p.21), and 10 May 1824 (p.22); p.23 written by Constant in the first person. Distributed by Constant to members of the Chambre des députés.

Copies: BCU, BN. (C.112a).

B50 1824   Discours de M. Benjamin-Constant, député de la Seine, dans la discussion du projet de loi de la septennalité; prononcé dans la séance du 8 juin 1824. (Extrait du *Moniteur* du 10 juin 1824). 8° pp.22. Impr. Mme veuve Agasse, [Paris].

Copies: BL, BN. (C.113a). *Discours* (1827-1828), II, 243-273.

B51 1824   Discours de M. Benjamin-Constant, député de la Seine, dans la discussion du projet de loi relatif aux crédits supplémentaires pour l'exercice 1823, prononcé dans la séance du 28 juin 1824. (Extrait du *Moniteur* du 29 juin 1824). 8° pp.6. Impr. Mme veuve Agasse, [Paris].

Copies: BL, BN. (C.114a).

B52 1824   Chambre des Députés. Session de 1824. Opinion de M. Benjamin-Constant, député de la Seine, sur le budget de 1825. Séance du 8 juillet 1824. 8° pp.18. Impr. Hacquart, [Paris]. (Impressions ordonnées. Session de 1824, vol. III, n° 225).

Copies: BL, BN. (C.115a). *Discours* (1827-1828), II, 274-289.

B53 1824   Chambre des Députés. Session de 1824. Opinion improvisée de M. Benjamin- Constant, député du département de la Seine, à l'occasion du chapitre V du budget du Ministère de l'intérieur (Haras). Imprimée par ordre de la Chambre. Séance du 14 juillet 1824. 8° pp.6. Impr. Hacquart, [Paris]. (Impressions ordonnées. Session de 1824, vol. IV, n° 276).

Copies: BL, BN. (C.116a).

B54 1824   Chambre des Députés. Session de 1824. Opinion de M. Benjamin-Constant, député de la Seine, sur le chapitre X du budget du Ministère de la guerre (frais de justice militaire). Séance du 16 juillet 1824. 8° pp.7. Impr. Hacquart, [Paris]. (Impressions ordonnées. Session de 1824, vol. IV, n° 308).

Copies: BL, BN. (C.117a).

B55 1824   Chambre des Députés. Session de 1824. Opinion de M. Benjamin-Constant, député de la Seine, sur l'article du budget des recettes relatif aux jeux de la ville de Paris. Imprimée par ordre de la Chambre. Séance du 22 juillet 1824. 8° pp.4. Impr. Hacquart, [Paris]. (Impressions ordonnées. Session de 1824, vol. IV, n° 365).

Copies: BL, BN. (C.118a).

B56 1825   Discours de M. Benjamin Constant, député de la Seine, sur le projet de loi d'indemnités; prononcé dans la séance du 23 février 1825. (Extrait du *Moniteur*). 8° pp.26. Impr. Firmin Didot, [Paris]. (Discours et opinions imprimés sans ordre. Session de 1825).

Copies: BL, BN. (C.119a). *Discours* (1827-1828), II, 309-330.

Other editions: Pozzo di Borgo 1964 (E4/6), Pozzo di Borgo 1965 (E4/7).

B57 1825   Chambre des Députés. Opinion de M. Benjamin Constant, député de la Seine, sur la loi relative au sacrilége. Séance du 7 avril 1825. 8° pp.24. Impr. Antoine Béraud, [Paris].
Copy: BN. (C.120a). *Discours* (1827-1828), II, 347-365.

B58 1825   Chambre des Députés. Session 1825. Opinion de M. Benjamin Constant, député de la Seine, sur le projet de loi portant réglement des crédits et des dépenses de l'exercice 1823. Imprimée par ordre de la Chambre. Séance du 28 avril 1825. 8° pp.15. Imprimerie royale, mai 1825. (Impressions ordonnées. Session de 1825, vol. III, n° 138).
Copies: BL, BN. (C.121a). *Discours* (1827-1828), II, 366-382.

B59 1825   Chambre des Députés. Session 1825. Opinion de M. Benjamin Constant, député de la Seine, sur la discussion des articles du projet de loi relatif au budget de 1826. Imprimée par ordre de la Chambre. Séance du 10 mai 1825. 8° pp.10. Imprimerie royale, mai 1825. (Impressions ordonnées. Session de 1825, vol. IV, n° 191).
Copies: BL, BN. (C.122a).

B60 1826   Discours de M. Benjamin-Constant, député de la Seine, dans la dicussion des articles du projet de loi sur l'indemnité à accorder aux colons de Saint-Domingue: prononcé dans la séance du 20 mars 1826. (Extrait du *Moniteur* du 21 mars 1826). 8° pp.12. Impr. Mme veuve Agasse, [Paris].
Copy: BN. (C.123a). *Discours* (1827-1828), II, 387-400.

B61 1826   Discours de M. Benjamin-Constant, député de la Seine, dans la discussion du projet de loi concernant le réglement définitif du budget de 1824; prononcé dans la séance du 24 avril 1826. (Extrait du *Moniteur* du 26 avril 1826). 8° pp.16. Impr. Mme veuve Agasse, [Paris].
Copy: BN. (C.124a). *Discours* (1827-1828), II, 408-425.

B62 1826   Discours prononcé par M. Benjamin Constant, député de la Seine, dans la discussion générale du budget de 1827. Séance du 17 mai 1826. Paris. Chez l'Huillier ... M.DCCC.XXVI. 16° pp.30. Impr. J. Tastu, [Paris].
Copy: BN. (C.125a). *Discours* (1827-1828), II, 462-474.

B63 1827   Opinion de M. Benjamin Constant, député de la Seine, sur le projet de loi relatif à la police de la presse. Séance du 13 février 1827. 8° pp.24. Impr. A. Henry, [Paris].
Copies: B, BN. (C.126a). *Discours* (1827-1828), II, 538-557.

Other editions: Laboulaye 1861 (E1/5a), Laboulaye 1872 (E1/5b), Pléiade 1957, 1964, 1979 (E4/5). See also items A18/30 (Adolphe ... Paris: Guillequin, [1907]) and A18/33 (Adolphe ... Londres: Dent; Paris: Mignot, [1912]).

B64 1828   Chambre des Députés. Session 1828. Développemens de la proposition de M. Benjamin-Constant, député du Bas-Rhin, tendante à supplier le Roi de proposer une loi qui abroge l'article 4 de la loi du 17 mars 1822 sur la censure facultative. Imprimé par ordre de la Chambre. Séance du 13 mars 1828. 8° pp.8. Imprimerie royale, mars 1828. (Impressions ordonnées. Session de 1828, n° 4).
Copies: BCU, BL, BN. (C.127a).

B65 1828   Chambre des Députés. Session 1828. Développement de la proposition de M. Benjamin Constant, député du Bas-Rhin, tendant à ce que les noms des députés qui n'auront pas répondu à l'appel, ni au réappel, sans être absens par congé ou pour cause de maladie, soient inscrits au procès-verbal. Imprimé par ordre de la Chambre. Séance du 7 mai 1828. 8° pp.8. Imprimerie royale, mai 1828. (Impressions ordonnées. Session de 1828, n° 44).
Copies: BL, BN. (C.128a).

B66 1829   Chambre des Députés. Session de 1829. Opinion de M. Benjamin Constant, député du Bas-Rhin, sur le projet de loi relatif à la fabrication et à la vente exclusive du tabac. Séance du 18 mars 1829. 8° pp.54. Impr. A. Henry, [Paris].
Copy: St. (C.129a).

B67 1830   Chambre des Députés. Session 1830. Développemens de la proposition de M. Benjamin Constant, sur la libre profession d'imprimeur et de libraire. Séance du 13 septembre 1830. 8° pp.7. Imprimerie royale, septembre 1830. (Impressions ordonnées. Session de 1830, vol. I, n° 38).
Copies: BL, BN. (C.130a).

C Contributions to collective works and to works of other writers

C1 Biographie universelle

C1/1 1811-1813 (1) Biographie universelle, ancienne et moderne, ou histoire, par ordre alphabétique, de la vie publique et privée de tous les hommes qui se sont fait remarquer par leurs écrits, leurs actions, leurs talents, leurs vertus ou leurs crimes. Ouvrage entièrement neuf, rédigé par une société de gens de lettres et de savants ... Tome premier. A Paris, chez Michaud frères, imprim.-libraires ... 1811.

Articles by Constant:

Adolphe de Nassau, pp.232-233
Agnès d'Autriche, pp.297-299
Albert Ier, pp.400-405
Albert II, pp.405-407
Albert III, pp.407-408
Albert IV, pp.408-409
Albert V, pp.409-413

(2) Biographie universelle ... Tome deuxième ... 1811

Arnoul, pp.522-523

(6) Biographie universelle ... Tome sixième ... 1812

Brunswick, Ferdinand, duc de, pp.149-150

(8) Biographie universelle ... Tome huitième ... 1813

Charles III, dit le Gros, pp.160-161
Charles IV, pp.161-166

(9) Biographie universelle ... Tome neuvième ... 1813

Conrad Ier, pp.428-429
Constant de Rebecque (David) -- Constant de Rebecque (Samuel), pp.464-465.

Note: Constant's contributions to the *Biographie universelle* have been listed and published by Carlo Cordié: 'La collaborazione di Benjamin Constant alla *Biographie universelle*', *Atti della Accademia delle Scienze di Torino, Classe di scienze morali, storiche e filologiche*, CI (1966-1967), 411-457. Reprinted by Harpaz, item E4/9. (C. Appendix B1a).

C1/2 1843-1852 Biographie universelle ... nouvelle édition. Paris: A. Thoisnier Desplaces, vols I-IX, 1843-1852.
Reprint of the preceding item.

Translations

C1/t1 1822-1823 Biografia universale antica e moderna ossia storia per alfabeto della vita pubblica e privata di tutte le persone che si distinsero per opere,

azioni, talenti, virtù e delitti. Opera affatto nuova compilata in Francia da una
società di dotti ed ora per la prima volta recata in italiano con aggiunte e
correzioni. Volume I. Venezia: Presso Gio. Battista Missiaglia, 1822. Dalla
Tipografia di Alvisopoli.

Articles by Constant:

(1) Adolfo di Nassau, pp.234-236

Agnese, pp.296-297

Alberto I, pp.417-423

Alberto II, pp.423-425

Alberto III, pp.425-426

Alberto IV, pp.426-427

Alberto V, pp.427-430

(3) Biografia universale ... Volume III ... 1822

Arnolfo, pp.292-293

(8) Biografia universale ... Volume VIII ... 1823

Brunswick, Ferdinando, duca di, pp.185-187

(10) Biografia universale ... Volume X ... 1823

Carlo III, pp.33-34
Carlo IV, pp.34-39

(13) Biografia universale ... Volume XIII ... 1823

Constant de Rebecque (Davide) – Constant de Rebecque (Samuele), pp.108-
109
Corrado I, pp.276-277

(Cordié 299-302; C. Appendix B1b).

C1/t2 1840-1842 Dizionario biografico universale ... vol. I. Firenze: David
Passigli, 1840; vol. II, 1842.

Reprint of the preceding item. (Cordié 347-348).

C2 Mémoires sur la vie de Necker

C2/1 181[7] Mémoires sur la vie privée de mon père, par Mme la baronne
de Staël-Holstein. Suivis des Mélanges de M. Necker. Paris; Londres: Colburn,
1818. 8° pp.xvi, 373. Impr. Cox et Baylis, [London].

Introduction by Benjamin Constant: 'Notice sur Mme de Staël Holstein. Extrait
du *Mercure de France*', pp.iii-xii. Originally published in *MF*, 26 juillet 1817,
pp.175-180; reprinted in *Mélanges* (1829), pp.163-210.
Copies: BL, BN. (C. Suppl. Add. 6).

Translation

C2/t1 181[7] Memoirs of the Private Life of my father ... to which are added
Miscellanies by M. Necker. London: Colburn, 1818. 8° pp.xvi, 416. Impr. J.
Gillet, London.

Introduction: pp.iii-xii.
Copies: BL, C. (C. Suppl. Add. 7).

C3 Alphonse et Mathilde

C3/1 1819   Alphonse et Mathilde; par Madame L. D'E****. Paris: Brissot-Thivars, 1819. 12° 2 vols. pp.[iv], 251 + [iv], 196. Impr. P. F. Dupont.

Note: It can be inferred from Constant's unpublished correspondence with his half-sister, Louise d'Estournelles, that he was responsible not only for finding a publisher for her novels, but also for seeing them through the press and making stylistic revisions.

Copy: BN. (C. Appendix C1).

C4 Lettres sur la situation de la France

C4/1 1820   Lettres sur la situation de la France. Prix: 2 f. 25 c. Paris. De l'imprimerie de Plassan, rue de Vaugirard, N° 15. Avril 1820. (Libraire de Lacretelle aîné, et Comp^ie., rue Dauphine, n° 20). 8° pp.[ii], 72.

On pp.5-11: 'Lettre à M. Lacretelle aîné, sur les attaques autorisées par les ministres, dans les journaux censurés, contre les individus et les grands corps de l'état', dated '5 avril 1820' and signed 'Benjamin Constant'.

Copy: C. (C. Appendix B2).

C5 Pascaline

C5/1 1821   Pascaline; par Mme L. D'E**, auteur d'Alphonse et Mathilde. Paris: Ch. Villet, 1821. Impr. Denugon. 12° 2 vols. pp.[iv], 269 + [iv], 259.

See note to item C3/1.

Copy: BN. (C. Appendix C2).

C6 [Dubious contribution]

C6/1 1822-1823   Chefs-d'œuvre des théâtres étrangers, allemand, anglais, danois, espagnol, hollandais, italien, polonais, portugais, russe, suédois. Traduit en français par MM. Aignan, Andrieux, membres de l'Académie française; le baron de Barante, Benjamin Constant, Chatelain, Cohen, Denis, Esménard, Guizard, Guizot, Labeaumelle, Malte-Brun, Merville, Charles Nodier, Pichot, Rémusat, le comte de Saint-Aulaire, le baron de Staël, Trognon, Villemain, membre de l'Académie française. Paris: Ladvocat, 25 vols, 1822-1823.

Note: An announcement in vol. II (1822) refers to the forthcoming vol. IV containing 'œuvres de Müllner, Werner et Grillparzer, traduit[es] par MM. Benjamin-Constant, le comte de Sainte-Aulaire et Michel Berr'. The plays of Müllner and Werner are in vol. VI (1823), with introductions by Michel Berr and Charles de Rémusat, with no mention of Constant. None of the later volumes appears to include contributions by Constant.

Copies: BN, BPU. (C. Appendix B3).

C7 [Dubious contribution]

C7/1 1829   Mélanges politiques et historiques relatifs aux événemens contemporains, par MM. Benjamin-Constant, Ganilh, de Pradt, et autres publicistes célèbres. Paris, à la librairie américaine, 1829. 8° 3 vols. Imprint of A. Barbier.

Note: These three volumes are made up of publishers' remainders of miscellaneous pamphlets, with original title pages removed. Contents vary from copy to copy. None of the copies inspected contains works by Constant.

Copies (BN has preliminaries only): AR, BCU, BPU, Bx, C (2 copies), VP. (C. Appendix B4).

C8 Portraits et souvenirs contemporains

C8/1 1832   Paris, ou le livre des Cent-et-un. Tome septième. A Paris, chez Ladvocat ... MDCCCXXXII. Impr. Firmin Didot frères. [Vol. 7 of 15 vols published 1831-1834].

On pp.143-171: Portraits et souvenirs contemporains, par Benjamin Constant; suivis d'une lettre de Jefferson, président des Etats-Unis, à Madame de Staël: Note de l'éditeur, pp.145-146; L'Abbé Sièyes, pp.147-150; M. de Talleyrand, pp.151-154; Mme Récamier, La Harpe, Mme de Staël et M. Necker, pp.155-164.

Copy: BN. (C. Appendix B5a).

C8/2 1832   Paris, ou le livre des Cent-et-un. Seconde édition. Tome septième. A Paris, chez Ladvocat ... MDCCCXXXII. [Vol. 7 of 15 vols published 1832-1834].

Reprint of the preceding item.

Copy: BN. (C. Appendix B5b).

C8/3 1832   Paris, ou le livre des Cent-et-un. VIII, Stuttgart, Au bureau des nouveautés de la littérature française, 1832. [Vol. VIII of 12 vols published 1831-1833; vols I-IV: Stuttgart, chez Charles Hoffmann].

On pp.49-63: Portraits et souvenirs par Benjamin Constant. Reprint of item C8/1.

Copy: T. (C. Appendix B5c).

C8/4 1849   Chateaubriand, François-René de. Mémoires d'Outre-Tombe. Paris: E. et V. Penaud frères, 1849-1851. 12 vols.

Troisième partie, Livre VII, chap. 3 includes extracts from 'portraits' of Mme Récamier, La Harpe, Lucien Bonaparte and Mme de Staël.

C8/5 1849   Colet, Louise. *La Presse*, 3-5 juillet 1849.

Contents similar to item C8/1 plus additions and with 'portrait' of Lucien Bonaparte.

C8/6 1864   Lettres de Benjamin Constant à Mme Récamier avec introduction

et épilogue par Mme Louise Colet. Paris: E. Dentu, 1864. (Item F1).
Includes, pp.xi-xxiii, 'portraits' of Mme Récamier, Mme de Staël and Necker.

C8/7 1882 [=1881]   Lettres de Benjamin Constant à Mme Récamier, 1807-1830, publiées par l'auteur des Souvenirs de Mme Récamier [Amélie Lenormant]. Paris: Calmann Lévy, 1882 [=1881]. (Item F4).
Includes, pp.337-350, 'portraits' of Mme Récamier, Madame de Staël, La Harpe and Lucien Bonaparte.

C8/8 1904   Herriot, Edouard. Mme Récamier et ses amis d'après de nombreux documents inédits. Paris: Plon-Nourrit, 1904. 2 vols.
Includes, pp.67-73, 'portrait' of Adrien de Montmorency.

1957   See also item E4/5 (Œuvres, Paris: Bibliothèque de la Pléiade, Paris 1957).

C8/9 1957   Levaillant, Maurice. 'Benjamin Constant et Madame Récamier', *RP*, 64e année, septembre 1957, 41-62.
Includes, pp.46-62, 'Les Mémoires de Juliette par Benjamin Constant'. See the following item. See also the earlier work by the same author: *Chateaubriand, Madame Récamier et les Mémoires d'Outre-Tombe*, Paris: Delagrave, 1936, Quatrième partie, chap. 6 and notes (fragments of the *Mémoires* and bibliographical discussion).

C8/10 1958   'Les Mémoires de Juliette par Benjamin Constant', in: Maurice Levaillant, *Les Amours de Benjamin Constant. Lettres et documents, avec un opuscule inédit*, Paris: Hachette, 1958, pp.167-190.
Includes: 1. Enfance et jeunesse; 2. Monsieur de La Harpe; 3. Madame de Staël; 4. Lucien Buonaparte; 5. Adrien de Montmorency; 6. Voyage en Angleterre; 7. Bernadotte et Moreau; 8. Un homme ... Published from Lenormant archives. Bibliographical discussion and notes, pp.263-269.

1964   See item E4/5 (reprint of Œuvres, Paris: Bibliothèque de la Pléiade, 1957).

1979   See item E4/5 (reprint of Œuvres, Paris: Bibliothèque de la Pléiade, 1957).

Translations

C8/t1 1835   'L'abbate Siéyes', *Il Gondoliere, Giornale di scienze, lettere, arti, mode e teatri*, [Venezia], 14 Agosto 1835, Anno Terzo, N. 65, p.259. col. II.
(Cordié 172).

C8/t2 1923   Benjamin Constant. Lettera su Giulia (Mme Talma); Il racconta di Giulietta (Mme Récamier). Versione di Maria Ortiz. Firenze: Sansoni, 1923. pp.cxxviii, 144.

C9 Des circonstances actuelles of Germaine de Staël-Holstein

Constant's contributions to the posthumously published *Des circonstances actuelles* of A.-G.-L. de Staël-Holstein has been studied in the following works: Edouard Herriot, *Un ouvrage inédit de Madame de Staël*, Paris: Plon-Nourrit, 1904, pp.67-76 ('De la collaboration de Benjamin Constant à l'ouvrage'); Lucia Omacini, 'Benjamin Constant, correcteur de Madame de Staël', *Cahiers staëliens*, n° 25, 2me semestre 1978, pp.5-23. See also introductions to the editions listed below.

C9/1 1906 Baronne de Staël. Des Circonstances actuelles qui peuvent terminer la Révolution et des principes qui doivent fonder la République en France. Ouvrage inédit publié pour la première fois avec une Introduction et des notes par John Viénot. Paris: Fischbacher, 1906. pp.c, 352.

C9/2 1979 Madame de Staël. Des Circonstances actuelles qui peuvent terminer la Révolution et des principes qui doivent fonder la République en France. Edition critique par Lucia Omacini. Paris-Genève: Droz, 1979. (Textes littéraires français). pp.LXXXVIII, 477.

D Contributions to periodicals and newspapers

The present list is provisional; it has not been possible to make an exhaustive search in all the periodicals and newspapers to which Constant may have contributed or in which translations of his work may have appeared. Besides, the fact that he did not always sign his contributions makes it impossible to compile a definitive list. It is known, for example, that he wrote articles for *Le Temps* in 1829 and 1830, but no article in that journal carries his signature. Fortunately, in the case of *Le Courrier français* a contemporary marked file (presumably an official record) has been preserved in the Bibliothèque nationale. Most of the items in this section, up to 1824, have been published by M. Ephraïm Harpaz and in each case I give a reference to the relevant *Recueil d'articles* (1972, 1978 and 1981). However, I have not included articles which are ascribed to Constant on insufficient grounds and I have drawn on the records of dépôt légal in the Archives de la librairie (Archives nationales) in order to give the correct dates of publication of the separate issues of *La Minerve française*; where two dates are given the first is the 'date de l'expéditon' and the second the 'date de l'arrivée'.

1795

D1 'Lettre à un Député à la Convention', *Nouvelles politiques nationales et étrangères*, n° 276, 6 messidor an III, 24 juin 1795, pp.1101-1102.
Continued in the following item.

D2 'Seconde lettre à un député', *Nouvelles politiques nationales et étrangères*, n° 277, 7 messidor an III, 25 juin 1795, pp.1106-1107.
Continued in the following item.

D3 'Troisième lettre à un député', *Nouvelles politiques nationales et étrangères*, n° 278, 8 messidor an III, 26 juin 1795, pp.1110-1112.
Unsigned. For attribution to Constant see Coulmann (1869), III, 54. Jasinski (1971), pp.110-125; Harpaz (1978), pp.15-24.

D4 'A Charles His, rédacteur du Républicain français', *Le Républicain français*, 6 thermidor an III, 24 juillet 1795.
Signed: 'B.C.' Jasinski (1971), pp.134-141; Harpaz (1978), pp.25-29.

D5 Discours de Jean-Baptiste Louvet à la Convention, 3-4 fructidor an III, 20-21 août 1795, *Le Moniteur universel*, 9 fructidor an III, 26 août 1795.
For attribution to Constant see Coulmann (1869), III, 55-56. Jasinski (1971), pp.146-150, 285-290.

1796

D6 'De la force du gouvernement actuel de la France', *La Sentinelle*, 11-15 floréal an IV, 30 avril-4 mai 1796.
Extracts of item A2/1.

D7 'De la force du gouvernement actuel de la France', *Le Moniteur universel*, 12-20 floréal an IV, 1-9 mai 1796.
Reprint of item A2/1.

D8 'Aux citoyens représentans du peuple composant le Conseil des Cinq-Cents', *Le Républicain français*, 11 thermidor an IV, 29 juillet 1796.
Reprint of item B1/1.

D9 'Aux Citoyens représentans du peuple composant le Conseil des Cinq-Cents', *Le Moniteur universel*, 14 thermidor an IV, 1er août 1796.
Reprint of item B1/1.

D10 'De la restitution des droits politiques aux descendans des religionnaires fugitifs', *Le Moniteur universel*, 9 fructidor an IV, 26 août 1796.
Signed: 'Benjamin Constant.' Jasinski (1971), pp.251-257; Harpaz (1978), pp.38-41.

D11 'Ueber die Kraft der gegenwärtigen Regierung Frankreichs und über die Nothwendigkeit, sich an sie anzuschließen', *Klio. Eine Monatschrift für die französische Zeitgeschichte*, 1796, Bd. II, 5. Heft, 106-134; 6. Heft, 137-204.
Published by 10 October 1796 (Staël, *Correspondance générale*, III (2), 255). C.2e. *Checklist* A2/t1.

D12 '*De l'influence des passions sur le bonheur des individus et des nations*, par Madame de Staël', *Le Moniteur universel*, 5 brumaire an V, 26 octobre 1796.
Unsigned. Harpaz (1978), pp.42-47. For attribution to Constant see Staël, *Correspondance générale*, III (2), 270, note 1.

D13 'Von der Stärke der gegenwärtigen Regierung Frankreichs und von der Nothwendigkeit sich derselben anzuschliessen', *Frankreich im Jahr 1796*, 1796, Bd. II, 7. St., 211-244, 8. St., 291-324.
C.2f. *Checklist* A2/t2.

D14 'Bittschrift von Benjamin Constant Rebecque an den Rath der Fünfhundert', *Frankreich im Jahr 1796*, 1796 Bd. II, 8. St., 363-367.
C.64b. *Checklist* B1/t1.

1797

D15 'Des réactions politiques', *La Sentinelle*, 16-22 germinal an V, 5-11 avril 1797.
Extracts of item A3/1.

D15a [Obituary notice on J.-B. Louvet], *La Sentinelle*, 11 fructidor an V, 28 août 1797.
Béatrice W. Jasinski, *Annales Benjamin Constant*, n° 3 (1983), pp.112-113.

D16 'Discours prononcé au Cercle constitutionnel ... le 30 fructidor', *Echo des cercles patriotiques*, n° 14, [21 septembre 1797].
Extracts (continued below).

D16a 'Discours prononcé au Cercle constitutionnel ... le 30 fructidor', *La Sentinelle*, 12 vendémiaire an VI, 3 octobre 1797.
Extract of item A5/1.

D17 'Discours prononcé au Cercle constitutionnel ... le 30 fructidor', *Echo des cercles patriotiques*, n° 15, [16 octobre 1797].Extracts of item A5/1.

D18 'Von den politischen Gegenwirkungen', *Frankreich im Jahr 1797*, 1797, Bd. II, 5. St., 3-27; 6. St., 99-127; 7. St., 200-213; 8. St., 291-298.
C.3c. *Checklist* A3/t1.

D19 'Ueber die Wirkungen des Schreckens', *Frankreich im Jahr 1797*, 1797, Bd. III, 9. St., 3-24.
C.4b. *Checklist* A4/t1.

1798

D20 'Discours prononcé au Cercle constitutionnel, le 9 ventôse an VI', *Le Moniteur universel*, 21-22 ventôse an VI, 11-12 mars 1798.
Reprint of item A6/1.

D21 'Au citoyen G ...', *Le Républicain*, n° 2, 2 floréal an VI, [21 avril 1798].
Letter, dated 'Hérivaux, 15 germinal, an VI' [4 April 1798]. Cited by Eugène Asse, 'Benjamin Constant et le Directoire', *Revue de la Révolution*, XVI (1889), 107-108.

1799

D21a [Obituary notice on Baudin], *Journal de Paris*, 25 vendémiaire an VIII, 17 octobre 1799.
Béatrice W. Jasinski, *Annales Benjamin Constant*, n° 3 (1983), pp.116-118.

D21b [Obituary notice on Baudin], *Le Rédacteur*, 26 vendémiaire an VIII, 18 octobre 1799.
Béatrice W. Jasinski, *Annales Benjamin Constant*, n° 3 (1983), pp.116-118.

D22 'Ueber den jungverstorbenen Rapräsentanten Baudin. Von Benjamin Constant', *Frankreich im Jahr 1799*, 1799, Bd. III, 11. St., 195-197.
Obituary notice on Pierre-Charles-Louis Baudin (1748-14 October 1799).

D23 'Weder die Folgen der Gegenrevolution 1660 in England. Von Benjamin Constant. (In Auszuge)', *Frankreich im Jahr 1799*, 1799, Bd. II, 8. St., 291-297.

1800

D24 '*De la littérature considérée dans ses rapports avec les institutions sociales*: par madame de Staël de Holstein', *Le Publiciste*, 6 prairial an VIII, 26 mai 1800.
Continued in the following article.

D25 '*De la littérature* ... par madame de Staël de Holstein, Second extrait', *Le Publiciste*, 11 prairial an VIII, 31 mai 1800.
Unsigned. Harpaz (1978), pp.48-56. For attribution to Constant see Harpaz (1978), p.51, note 1.

D26 'Sitzung des Tribunats vom 3ten Messidor', *Frankreich im Jahr 1800*, 1800, Bd. II, 7. St., 195-213.
Checklist B8/t1.

D27 'Extrait d'une lettre de Genève', *Le Citoyen français*, 30 vendémiaire an IX, 22 octobre 1800.
Unsigned. Obituary of Samuel de Constant (1729-1800). Harpaz (1978). pp.57-58. For summary of evidence concerning Constant's authorship (based on letters to Rosalie de Constant) see Harpaz (1978), p.58, note 2.

D27a [Samuel de Constant], *Le Journal de Paris*, 1er brumaire an IX, 23 octobre 1800.
Abridgement of the obituary of Samuel de Constant.

D27b [Samuel de Constant], *Le Publiciste*, 2 brumaire an IX, 24 octobre 1800.
Abridgement of the obituary of Samuel de Constant.

1803

D28 [Review of *Delphine* by Germaine de Staël], *Le Citoyen français*, 16 janvier 1803.
Unsigned. For attribution to Constant see S. Balayé, 'A propos de Benjamin Constant lecteur de *Corinne*', *Cahiers staëliens*, nos 26-27 (1979), 117-120. Harpaz (1978), pp.59-62.

1805

D29 [Article for a newspaper, *ca.* 25 February 1805]. Not identified.
For reference to this article see Constant's *Journal* of 25 February 1805: 'Composé un petit article en réponse à celui du *Journal de Paris* contre les *Œuvres posthumes* ... voici ma réponse' (followed by text).

D29a [Article on German literature for *Le Publiciste*, *ca.* 2 March 1805]. Not identified.
For reference to this article see Constant's *Journal* of 28 February-2 March 1805.

D30 'Dialogue entre deux hommes d'autrefois sur des hommes d'aujourd'hui', *Le Publiciste*, 16 avril 1805.

Unsigned. Harpaz (1978), pp.63-65. For attribution to Constant see *Journal*, 11-25 April 1805 and Harpaz (1978), p.65, note 2.

D31 'Aux auteurs du Publiciste', *Le Publiciste*, 26 mai 1805.
Article on *Les Templiers* of Fr.-J.-M. Raynouard. Unsigned. Harpaz (1978), pp.66-68. For attribution to Constant see *Journal*, 22 May 1805 and Harpaz (1978), p.67, note 1.

D32 *'Essai sur les causes de la supériorité des Grecs dans les arts d'imagination*; par M. Leulliette', *Le Publiciste*, 17 juin 1805, pp.3-4.
Continued in the following item.

D33 *'Essai sur les causes de la supériorité des Grecs dans les arts d'imagination.* Deuxième et dernier extrait', *Le Publiciste*, 3 juillet 1805, pp.3-4.
Unsigned. Harpaz (1978), pp.69-74. For attribution to Constant see *Journal abrégé*, 12 June 1805 and Harpaz (1978), p.70, note 1.

1807

D34 [Article for a newspaper, *ca.* 16 February 1807]. Not identified.
For reference to this article see Constant's *Journal* of 3, 7, 8, 9 and 16 February 1807. On 16 February he writes, 'Mon article est inséré, voyons-en l'effet. Il n'en fera peut-être pas'.

D35 'Observations sur un article du *Journal de l'Empire* du 21 février 1807'.
Harpaz (1978), pp.78-81; here first published from *Œuvres manuscrites* of 1810 (BN, N.a.fr. 14362).

D36 *'Corinne ou l'Italie*, par Mme de Staël Holstein. Premier extrait', *Le Publiciste*, 12 mai 1807.
Continued in the following item.

D37 *'Corinne ou l'Italie.* Second extrait', *Le Publiciste*, 14 mai 1807.
Continued in the following item.

D38 *'Corinne ou l'Italie.* Troisième et dernier extrait', *Le Publiciste*, 16 mai 1807.
Three articles signed 'D.D.' Harpaz (1978), pp.84-94. For attribution to Constant, see *Journal*, 9 and 12 May 1807 and Harpaz, p.87, note 1, with references to the manuscript (*Œuvres manuscrites* of 1810, BN, N.a.fr. 14362). Reprinted in *Mélanges* (1829).

1809

D39 *'Lettres & Pensées du maréchal Prince de Ligne*, publiées par Mme la baronne de Staël-Holstein', *Le Publiciste*, 25 février 1809, pp.3-4.
Continued in the following item.

D40 *'Lettres & Pensées du maréchal Prince de Ligne.* Deuxième et dernier extrait', *Le Publiciste*, 2 mars 1809, pp.3-4.

Harpaz (1978), pp.95-100. For attribution to Constant see Robert de Luppé, *Madame de Staël et J.-B.-A. Suard, Correspondance inédite (1786-1817)*, Genève: Droz, 1970, p.103.

1813

D41 'Lettre de Mr. Constant aux Rédacteurs', *Bibliothèque britannique*, LII (1813), 266-267.
Letter dated 'Genève, le 6 février 1813' and signed 'Constant'. On a work falsely attributed to Maria Edgeworth by the *Journal de l'Empire*. See *Benjamin Constant* a cura di Carlo Cordié, Milano: Hoepli, 1946, p.98. Probably not by Benjamin, but by his cousin Charles de Constant.

1814

D42 'Sur la réponse faite par Buonaparté à la députation du Sénat, le [14] novembre 1813', *L'Ambigu*, 20 février 1814.
Hasselrot (1952), pp.7-14; Harpaz (1978), pp.137-140. *Checklist* A74/6b.

D43 'Au Rédacteur', *Journal des débats*, 18 avril 1814.
Signed: 'Benjamin de Constant'. Concerning the statement made in the same journal, on 16 April, that Constant was 'secrétaire intime de S.A.R. le prince royal de Suède', Harpaz (1978), p.141.

D44 'Des révolutions de 1660 et de 1688 en Angleterre, et de celle de 1814 en France', *Journal des débats*, 21 avril 1814.
Signed: 'Benjamin de Constant'. Harpaz (1978), pp.142-143.

D45 'Au Rédacteur', *Journal des débats*, 4 août 1814.
Signed: 'Benjamin de Constant'. On the freedom of the press. Harpaz (1978), pp.144-145.

D45a [Article for a newspaper, *ca.* 10 August 1814]. Not identified.
'Travaillé à une réponse à la *Gazette de France*' (*Journal*, 10 August 1814).

D45b [Article for a newspaper, *ca.* 27 September 1814]. Not identified.
'Faisons un bon article sur Monlosier pour laisser une grande impression de talent, et partons' (*Journal*, 27 September 1814).

D46 [Reply to the *Journal des débats*, *ca.* 29 December 1814]. Not identified.
On 29 December 1814 Constant wrote in his *Journal*, 'Infâme article du *Journal des Débats*. Envoyé une réponse. L'imprimera-t-on?'

1815

D47 *Incipit*: 'Nous avons été opprimés pendant douze années par un seul homme', *Journal de Paris*, 11 mars 1815.
Signed: 'Benjamin Constant'. Defence of the Bourbon régime against Napoleon. Harpaz (1978), pp.146-148.

D48   *Incipit*: 'Les représentans de la nation ont porté au pied du trône l'expression de leur dévouement', *Journal des débats*, 19 mars 1815.
Signed: 'Benjamin de Constant'. Same topic as preceding item and violent attack on Napoleon. Harpaz (1978), pp.149-152.

D49   'Observations sur une déclaration du Congrès de Vienne', *Journal de Paris*, 4 avril 1815.
Unsigned. Harpaz (1978), pp.153-156. For attribution to Constant see Harpaz, p.155, note 1.

D50   'Comparaison de l'ordonnance de réformation de Louis XVIII avec la constitution proposée à la France le 22 avril 1815', *Journal des débats*, 1er mai 1815.
Unsigned. Harpaz (1978), pp.187-191. For possible attribution to Constant see Harpaz, p.190, note 1.

D51   'On the Responsibility of Ministers', *The Pamphleteer*, V, n° 10 (May 1815), 299-330, 315*-329*.
C.14b. *Checklist* A14/t1.

D52   'Sur les discours écrits', [June 1815]. Not extant.
On 14 June 1815 Constant wrote in his *Journal*, 'Fait un article sur les discours écrits'.

D53   [Article for *L'Indépendant*, July 1815]. Not identified.
On 28 July 1815 Constant wrote in his *Journal*, 'Fait un article pour l'*Indépendant*'.

D54   [Article for *L'Indépendant*, August 1815]. Not identified.
On 1 August 1815 Constant wrote in his *Journal*, 'Fait un article pour l'*Indépendant*'.

D55   'Au Rédacteur'. *Incipit*: 'Je réfléchissais hier aux circonstances dans lesquelles se trouvent la France et l'Europe', *L'Indépendant*, 4 août 1815.
See the following item.

D56   'Au Rédacteur'. *Incipit*: 'Puisque vous avez jugé ma lettre d'avant-hier digne d'être insérée', *L'Indépendant*, 6 août 1815.
Signed: 'J.R.' Harpaz (1978), pp.206-213. For attribution to Constant see Harpaz, p.209, note 1.

D57   [Article for the *Journal des arts*, September 1815]. Not identified.
'Fait un article pour le nouveau *Journal des arts*' (*Journal*, 8 September 1815).

D58   [Article for *Le Courrier*, September 1815]. Not identified.
'Fait un article pour le *Courrier*' (*Journal*, 9 September 1815).

D59   [Articles for the *Journal* [*des arts*], September 1815.] Not identified.

'Petits articles pour le Journal' (*Journal*, 12 September 1815).

D60 'Sur les assemblées électorales, et les discours de leurs présidens', *Journal des Arts*, 15 septembre 1815.
See the following item.

D61 'Sur les assemblées électorales et sur les discours de leurs présidens. (Second article)', *Journal des arts*, 18 septembre 1815.
See the following item.

D62 'Sur les assemblées électorales et sur les discours de leurs présidens. (Troisième et dernier article)', *Journal des arts*, 21 septembre 1815.
Unsigned. Harpaz (1978), pp.228-239. For attribution to Constant see Harpaz, p.230, note 1.

D63 '*Des désordres actuels de la France et des moyens d'y remédier*, par M. le comte de Montlosier. (Premier article)', *Le Courrier*, 1ᵉʳ octobre 1815.
Continued below, item D67.

D64 [Article for the *Journal des arts*, October 1815]. Not identified.
'Fait un petit article pour le *Journal des arts*' (*Journal*, 1 October 1815).

D65 [Article for the *Journal des arts*, October 1815]. Not identified.
'Fait une profession de foi pour le *Journal des arts*' (*Journal*, 2 October 1815).

D66 *Incipit*: 'Le Journal Général nous attaque aujourd'hui', *Journal des arts*, 3 octobre 1815.
Unsigned. Harpaz (1978), pp.244-246. Defence of the Charte and the Bourbon régime. For attribution to Constant see Harpaz, p.245, note 1.

D67 '*Des désordres actuels de la France et des moyens d'y remédier*. (Second article)', *Le Courrier*, 18 octobre 1815.
Unsigned. Harpaz (1978), pp.240-243; 247-251. For attribution to Constant see Harpaz, p.243, note 1, and *Journal*, 13-20 October 1815.

D68 'La liberté politique, essentielle à la liberté civile. De la liberté en général', *Mercure de France*, n° 3, [19] octobre 1815.
Unsigned. Harpaz (1978), pp.254-59. For attribution to Constant see Harpaz, p.258, note 1.

D69 'On the Liberty of the Press', *The Pamphleteer*, VI (1815), 205-238.
C.12c. *Checklist* A12/t1.

1816

D70 'To the Editor', *Morning Chronicle*, 24 June 1816.
Letter signed 'B. de Constant' and dated 'June 23, 1816'. Concerning *Adolphe*. Gustave Rudler (ed)., *Adolphe*, Manchester University Press, 1919, p.157.

D71 [Summary of preceding item]. *Courrier de Londres*, 25 juin 1816.

D72 [Summary of same item]. *Journal des débats*, 30 juin 1816.

D73 'Adolphe, Anecdote trouvée dans les papiers d'un inconnu', *Le Nouvelliste français*, Pesth: Hartleben, tome X, livr. 14 (31 juillet 1816); livr. 15 (15 août 1816); livr. 16 (31 août 1816).
C.18d. *Checklist* A18/4.

D74 *Adolphe, Morgenblatt*, 1816, n°s 199-217 (19 August-9 September).
Checklist A18/t1a.

1817

D75 'Des Chambres, depuis leur convocation jusqu'au 31 décembre 1816', *Mercure de France*, I, 4 janvier 1817, pp.28-32.
Signed: 'B. de Constant'. Harpaz (1972), pp.10-14. Reprinted in *Cours de politique*, II (1818).

D76 'Des Chambres, depuis leur convocation jusqu'au 31 décembre 1816. (IIe article)', *Mercure de France*, I, 11 janvier 1817, pp.69-77.
Signed: 'B. de Constant'. Harpaz (1972), pp.15-23. Reprinted in *Cours de politique*, II (1818).

D77 'Tableau politique de l'Europe', *Mercure de France*, I, 18 janvier 1817, pp.104-113.
Signed: 'B. de Constant'. Harpaz (1972), pp.24-33.

D78 'Des Chambres. (IIIe article). Loi sur les élections', *Mercure de France*, I, 18 janvier 1817, pp.113-127.
Signed: 'B. de Constant'. Harpaz (1972), pp.34-48. Reprinted in item A20/1 and in *Cours de politique*, II (1818).

D79 'Des Chambres. (IVe article). Projet de loi relatif à la liberté individuelle', *Mercure de France*, I, 25 janvier 1817, pp.155-171.
Signed: 'B. de Constant'. Harpaz (1972), pp.49-65. Reprinted in *Cours de politique*, II (1818).

D80 'Des Chambres. (V^e article). Projet de loi sur la liberté de la Presse', *Mercure de France*, I, 1er février 1817, pp.203-215.
Signed: 'B. de Constant'. Harpaz (1972), pp.67-79. Reprinted in *Cours de politique*, II (1818).

D81 'Réponse à la lettre de M***, à M. B. de Constant, insérée dans le dernier numéro', *Mercure de France*, I, 1er février 1817, pp.215-221.
Signed: 'B. de Constant'. Harpaz (1972), pp.80-86.

D82 'Des Chambres. (VIe article). Projet de loi sur les Journaux', *Mercure de France*, I, 8 février 1817, pp.262-272.

Signed: 'B. de Constant'. Harpaz (1972), pp.87-97. Reprinted in *Cours de politique*, II (1818).

D83   'Des Chambres. (VIIe article). Projet de loi sur les Journaux', *Mercure de France*, I, 15 février 1817, pp.301-319.

Signed: 'B. de Constant'. Harpaz (1972), pp.98-116. Reprinted in *Cours de politique*, II (1818).

D84   'Tableau politique de l'Europe. (Deuxième article)', *Mercure de France*, I, 22 février 1817, pp.354-365.

Signed: 'B. de Constant'. Harpaz (1972), pp.117-128.

D85   'Des Chambres. Discussion sur le Budget', *Mercure de France*, I, 1er mars 1817, pp.401-415.

Signed: 'B. de Constant'. Harpaz (1972), pp.129-143. Reprinted in *Cours de politique*, II (1818).

D86   'Des Chambres. (Art. IX). Projet de loi sur le Budget, (Continuation)', *Mercure de France*, I, 8 mars 1817, pp.450-462.

Signed: 'B. de Constant'. Harpaz (1972), pp.144-156. Reprinted in *Cours de politique*, II (1818).

D87   'Des Chambres. (article X). Projet de loi sur le Budget. (Continuation)', *Mercure de France*, I, 15 mars 1817, pp.497-509.

Signed: 'B. de Constant'. Harpaz (1972), pp.157-169. Reprinted in *Cours de politique*, II (1818).

D88   'Des Chambres. (article XI). Continuation du budget', *Mercure de France*, I, 22 mars 1817, pp.547-555.

Signed: 'B. de Constant'. Harpaz (1972), pp.170-178. Reprinted in *Cours de politique*, II (1818).

D89   'Des Chambres. (XIIe article). Projet de loi sur le Budget. (Continuation)', *Mercure de France*, I, 29 mars 1817, pp.599-603.

Signed: 'B. de Constant'. Harpaz (1972), pp.179-183. Reprinted in *Cours de politique*, II (1818).

D90   'Lettre de M. Saint-Aubin, relativement à la dette publique de l'Angleterre', *Mercure de France*, II, 5 avril 1817, pp.33-44.

Text by Saint-Aubin; note, signed 'B.C', by Constant. Harpaz (1972), pp.184-195.

D91   'Des Chambres. (Article XIIIe). Continuation et fin du budget', *Mercure de France*, II, 12 avril 1817, pp.77-85.

Signed: 'B. de Constant'. Harpaz (1972), pp.196-204. Reprinted in *Cours de politique*, II (1818).

D92 'Tableau politique de l'Europe. (Article III)', *Mercure de France*, II, 19 avril 1817, pp.131-139.
Signed: 'B. de Constant'. Harpaz (1972), pp.205-213. Reprinted; see below, item D94.

D93 'De Godwin et de son ouvrage sur la justice politique', *Mercure de France*, II, 26 avril 1817, pp.161-173.
Signed: 'B. de Constant'. Harpaz (1972), pp.214-226. Reprinted in *Mélanges* (1829).

D94 'Tableau politique de l'Europe. (Art. IVe)', *Mercure de France*, II, 10 mai 1817, pp.278-285.
Signed: 'B. de Constant'. Reprinted as *Tableau politique du royaume des Pays-Bas*. Harpaz (1972), pp.227-234. C.21a. *Checklist* A21/1.

D95 'Pensées détachées', *Mercure de France*, II, 24 mai 1817, pp.346-352.
Signed: 'B. de Constant'. Harpaz (1972), pp.235-241. Reprinted in *Mélanges* (1829).

D96 'De Madame de Krudener', *Journal de Paris*, 30 mai 1817.
For attribution to Constant see Francis Ley, *Bernardin de Saint-Pierre, Madame de Staël, Chateaubriand, Benjamin Constant et Madame de Krüdener*, Paris, 1967, pp.256-257. Harpaz (1978), pp.260-261.

D97 '*Eloge de Saint-Jérôme*', *Mercure de France*, II, 31 mai 1817, pp.401-413.
Signed: 'B. de Constant'. Review of work by Gustave-François Fournier-Pescay. Harpaz (1972), pp.242-254.

D98 'Pensées détachées', *Mercure de France*, II, 14 juin 1817, pp.509-523.
Signed: 'B. de Constant'. Harpaz (1972), pp.255-269. Reprinted in *Mélanges* (1829).

D99 '*Théorie des Révolutions* ... [par Antoine-François-Claude Ferrand], (1er Article)', *Mercure de France*, II, 28 juin 1817, pp.581-591.
Signed: 'B. de Constant'. Harpaz (1972), pp.270-280.

D100 'Sur Madame de Staël', *Journal général de France*, 18 juillet 1817.
Harpaz (1978), pp.262-265. For attribution to Constant see S. Balayé, *Cahiers staëliens*, n° 9 (décembre 1969), pp.17-38.

D101 [Nécrologie: Germaine de Staël-Holstein], *Mercure de France*, III, 19 juillet 1817, pp.136-137.
Unsigned. Harpaz (1972), p.287. For attribution to Constant see Harpaz, p.1385, note 1.

D101a [Nécrologie: Germaine de Staël-Holstein], *Mercure de France*, III, 26 juillet 1817, pp.175-180.

Unsigned. Harpaz (1972), pp.282-287. Reprinted in item C2/1 and in *Mélanges* (1829).

D102   Letter dated 'Paris, 25 juillet 1817'. *Incipit*: 'J'ai lu hier, Monsieur, avec un sentiment tres penible, un article du journal relatif à madame de Staël', *Journal général de France*, 26 juillet 1817.
Harpaz (1978), p.266. For attribution to Constant see Balayé, article cited in item D100.

D103   '*Théorie des Révolutions*, (Deuxième Article)', *Mercure de France*, III, 16 août 1817, pp.307-313.
Signed: 'B. de Constant'. Harpaz (1972), pp.288-294. Reprinted in *Mélanges* (1829).

D104   'De la Littérature dans ses rapports avec la Liberté', *Mercure de France*, III, 13 septembre 1817, pp.485-495.
Signed: 'B. de Constant'. Harpaz (1972), pp.295-305. Reprinted in *Mélanges* (1829).

D104a   'Au Rédacteur', *Le Moniteur universel*, 18 septembre 1817, p.1030.
Letter dated 'Paris, 16 septembre 1817' and signed 'Benjamin Constant'.

D104b   Summary of letter from Constant, 21 September 1817, concerning the 'listes supplémentaires d'éligibles', *Le Moniteur universel*, 22 septembre 1817, p.1047.

D105   'De la Juridiction du gouvernement sur l'Education', *Mercure de France*, IV, 11 octobre 1817, pp.53-63.
Signed: 'B. de Constant'. Harpaz (1972), pp.306-316. Reprinted in *Mélanges* (1829).

D106   'De l'obéissance à la loi. Fragmens d'un chapitre extrait des additions inédites à la collection des ouvrages politiques de M. B. de Constant', *Mercure de France*, IV, 8 novembre 1817, pp.244-255.
Signed: 'B. de Constant'. Harpaz (1972), pp.317-328.

D107   'Du Théâtre français et du Théâtre étranger', *Mercure de France*, IV, 13 décembre 1817, pp.484-490.
Signed: 'B. de Constant'. Harpaz (1972), pp.329-335.

1818

D108   'Sur les provocations au crime pour le dénoncer', *La Minerve française*, I, cahier 2 [23-24 février 1818], pp.70-72.
Signed: 'B.C.' Harpaz (1972), pp.342-344.

D109   'D'une assertion de M. Bailleul dans sa brochure contre M. de Château-

briand', *La Minerve française*, I, cahier 4 [2-3 mars 1818], pp.165-169.
Signed: 'B.C.' Harpaz (1972), pp.345-349.

D110 'Encore un mot sur le procès de Wilfrid Regnault, ou Réflexions sur cette question: L'examen public des actes de l'autorité judiciaire est-il contraire à l'esprit de la charte, et blesse-t-il le respect dû aux tribunaux et à leurs sentences?', *La Minerve française*, I, cahier 6 [16-17 mars 1818], pp.261-273.
Signed: 'B.C.' Harpaz (1972), pp.350-362. Reprinted in *Cours de politique*, III (1819).

D111 'Des égards que, dans les circonstances présentes, les écrivains se doivent les uns aux autres', *La Minerve française*, I, cahier 9 [3-4 avril 1818], pp.413-420.
Signed: 'B.C.' Harpaz (1972), pp.363-370.

D112 'Introduction à l'*Histoire des Républiques italiennes*, par M. de Sismondi', *La Minerve française*, I, cahier 11 [17-20 avril 1818], pp.508-517.
Signed: 'B.C-T.' Harpaz (1972), pp.371-380.

D113 'Aperçus sur la marche et les révolutions de la philosophie à Rome. (Extrait d'un ouvrage inédit)', *La Minerve française*, I, cahier 13 [29 avril-1er mai 1818], pp.602-611.
Signed: 'B.C.' Harpaz (1972), 381-390. Reprinted in *Mélanges* (1829).

D114 'De l'Angleterre', *La Minerve française*, II, cahier 1 [6-7 mai 1818], pp.42-50.
Signed: 'B.C.' Harpaz (1972), pp.391-399. Reprinted in *Mélanges* (1829).

D115 'Aperçus sur la marche et les révolutions de la philosophie à Rome. (Extrait d'un ouvrage inédit). – Deuxième et dernier article', *La Minerve française*, II, cahier 2 [14-15 mai 1818], pp.71-77.
Signed: 'B.C.' Harpaz (1972). pp.400-406. Reprinted in *Mélanges* (1829).

D115a 'Au Rédacteur', *Le Moniteur universel*, 17 mai 1818, p.610.
Letter dated 'Paris, 15 mai 1818' and signed 'B. Constant'. On quotation by Malte-Brun from *Des réactions politiques*.

D116 '*Considérations sur les principaux événemens de la Révolution française*, ouvrage posthume de madame la baronne de Staël, publié par M. le duc de Broglie et M. le baron de Staël.', *La Minerve française*, II, cahier 3 [25-26 mai 1818], pp.105-110.
Signed: 'B.C.' Harpaz (1972), pp.407-412. Reprinted in *Mélanges* (1829).

D117 'Quelques réflexions sur la brochure de M. Aignan, *de l'Etat des Protestans en France*, et sur des critiques dirigées contre cette brochure', *La Minerve française* II, cahier 3 [25-26 mai 1818], pp.119-123.
Signed: 'B.C.' Harpaz (1972), pp.413-417.

D118 '*Antiquités romaines, ou Tableau des mœurs, usages et institutions des Romains,*

etc., traduites de l'anglais par Alexandre Adam, recteur de la grande école d'Edimbourg', *La Minerve française*, II, cahier 3 [25-26 mai 1818], pp.159-160.
Signed: 'B.C.' Harpaz (1972), pp.418-419.

D119 *'Compte rendu des événemens qui se sont passés à Lyon*, par M. Charrier Sainneville, ancien lieutenant de police à Lyon', *La Minerve française*, II, cahier 5 [4-5 juin 1818], pp.209-223.
Signed: 'B.C.' Harpaz (1972), pp.420-434. Reprinted in *Cours de politique*, III (1819).

D120 *'Compte rendu des événemens ·qui se sont passés à Lyon*, par M. Charrier-Sainneville, ancien lieutenant de police à Lyon, (Second article)', *La Minerve française*, II, cahier 6 [10-11 juin 1818], pp.265-279.
Signed: 'B.C.' Harpaz (1972), pp.435-449. Reprinted in *Cours de politique*, III (1819). See below, item D339.

D121 *'Considérations sur les principaux événemens de la Révolution française*, ouvrage posthume de madame la baronne de Staël, (Second article)', *La Minerve française*, II, cahier 7 [16-17 juin 1818], pp.316-325.
Signed: 'B.C.' Harpaz (1972), pp.450-459. Reprinted in *Mélanges* (1829).

D122 *'Le dernier cri d'un dépositaire de la charte, ou coup d'œil rapide sur l'état actuel des libertés nationales*; par J.-B. Mailhos, avocat à la cour royale de Paris', *La Minerve française*, II, cahier 7 [16-17 juin 1818], pp.325-326.
Signed: 'B.C.' Harpaz (1972), pp.460-461.

D123 'De la nécessité et des moyens de nous faire une juste idée des doctrines du ministère public, dans les causes relatives aux délits de la presse', *La Minerve française*, II, cahier 10 [11-13 juillet 1818], pp.474-480.
Signed: 'B.C.' Harpaz (1972), pp.462-468.

D124 *'Considérations sur les principaux événemens de la Révolution française*, ouvrage posthume de madame la baronne de Staël, (Troisième article)', *La Minerve française*, II, cahier 13 [28-29 juillet 1818], pp.601-610.
Signed: 'B.C.' Harpaz (1972), pp.469-478. Reprinted in *Mélanges* (1829).

D125 'Première lettre de M. Benjamin Constant à M. Charles Durand, avocat, en réponse aux questions contenues dans la troisième partie de son ouvrage, intitulé: *Marseille, Nîmes et ses environs, en 1815*', *La Minerve française*, III, cahier 2 [14-17 août 1818], pp.49-63.
Signed: 'Benjamin Constant'. Harpaz (1972), pp.479-93. Reprinted in *Lettres à M. Charles Durand* (1818). C.31a. *Checklist* A31/1.

D126 *'Précis historique, militaire et critique des batailles de Fleurus et de Waterloo ...*, par le maréchal-de-camp Berton', *La Minerve française*, III, cahier 3 [21-22 août 1818], pp.107-112.
Signed: 'B.C.' Harpaz (1972), pp.494-499.

D127 '*Question judiciaire*', *La Minerve française*, III, cahier 3 [21-22 août 1818], pp.118-121.
Signed: 'B.C.' Harpaz (1972), pp.500-503.

D128 'Seconde lettre de M. Benjamin Constant à M. Charles Durand, avocat, en réponse aux questions contenues dans la troisième partie de l'ouvrage intitulé: *Marseille, Nîmes et ses environs en 1815*', *La Minerve française*, III, cahier 4 [29-31 août 1818], pp.145-157.
Signed: 'Benjamin Constant'. Harpaz (1972), pp.504-516. Reprinted in *Lettres à M. Charles Durand* (1818). C.31a. *Checklist* A31/1.

D129 'Réflexions sur les pièces ci-dessus' [documents sur Charles Lainé: *Tribunaux: Département du Pas-de-Calais*], *La Minerve française*, III, cahier 5 [8-9 septembre 1818], pp.219-221.
Signed: 'B.C.' Harpaz (1972), pp.523-525.

D130 '*Revue de la session de 1817*; par le vicomte de Saint-Chamans', *La Minerve française*, III, cahier 7 [21-22 septembre 1818], pp.302-313.
Signed: 'B.C.' Harpaz (1972), pp.526-537.

D131 '*Eclaircissemens historiques en réponse aux calomnies dont les protestans du Gard sont l'objet, et Précis des agitations et des troubles de ce département, depuis 1790 jusqu'à nos jours*; par P.-J. Lauze de Perret, avocat à la cour royale de Nîmes', *La Minerve française*, III, cahier 7 [21-22 septembre 1818], p.314.
Signed: 'B.C.' Harpaz (1972), p.538.

D132 '*Coup d'œil sur les démêlés des cours de Bavière et de Bade ...*, par M. Bignon', *La Minerve française*, III, cahier 9 [2-3 octobre 1818], pp.385-391.
Signed: 'B.C.' Harpaz (1972), pp.539-545.

D133 [Letter from Gamot to the editors], *La Minerve française*, III, cahier 9 [2-3 octobre 1818], p.425.
Footnote signed: 'B.C.'

D134 '*Réponse à M. Benjamin Constant*, par M. Duvergier de Hauranne, député de la Seine-Inférieure', *La Minerve française*, III, cahier 11 [15-16 octobre 1818], pp.493-497.
Signed: 'B.C.' Harpaz (1972), pp.546-550.

D135 '*Lettre à M. Benjamin Constant sur l'ordonnance du 20 mai*, par M. Delapoterie, officier en non-activité, chevalier de la Légion d'Honneur', *La Minerve française*, III, cahier 11 [15-16 octobre 1818], pp.497-502.
Signed: 'B.C.' Harpaz (1972), pp.551-556.

D136 '*Rosaure, ou l'Arrêt du Destin*, traduit de l'allemand, d'Auguste Lafontaine; par madame la comtesse de M ....', *La Minerve française*, III, cahier 11 [15-16 octobre 1818], pp.503-504.

Signed: 'B.C.' Harpaz (1972), pp.557-558.

D137 [Les protestants de Vaucluse, de la Drôme et de la Lozère], *La Minerve française*, III, cahier 12 [21-22 octobre 1818], pp.542-544.
Signed: 'B.C.' Harpaz (1972), pp.559-561.

D138 'Pensées diverses sur les élections', *La Minerve française*, III, cahier 12 [21-22 octobre 1818], pp.544-552.
Signed: 'B.C.' Harpaz (1972), pp.562-570.

D139 'Sur les élections', *La Minerve française*, III, cahier 13 [26-27 octobre 1818], pp.610-615.
Signed: 'B.C.' Harpaz (1972), pp.571-576.

D140 'Des élections, du ministère, de l'esprit public et du parti libéral en France', *La Minerve française*, IV, cahier 1 [4-5 novembre 1818], pp.14-22.
Signed: 'Benjamin Constant'. Harpaz (1972), pp.577-585.

D141 [Sur la circulaire du Préfet de la Seine aux maires des communes rurales], *La Minerve française*, IV, cahier 2 [12-13 novembre 1818], pp.91-92.
Signed: 'B.C.' Harpaz (1972), pp.586-587.

D142 *'A M. le vicomte de Châteaubriant, pair de France, sur ses projets politiques et sur la situation actuelle des choses et des esprits*; par M. Azaïs', *La Minerve française*, IV, cahier 3 [19-20 novembre 1818], pp.97-104.
Signed: 'B.C.' Harpaz (1972), pp.588-95.

D143 'Affaire du sieur Raman [Roman de Lourmarin], condamné par le tribunal de police correctionnelle de Gap, pour avoir résisté à l'ordre de tapisser sa maison pendant la procession de la Fête-Dieu', *La Minerve française*, IV, cahier 4 [2-3 décembre 1818], pp.161-162.
Signed: 'B.C.' Harpaz (1972), pp.596-597.

D144 'D'un article de M. de Bonald contre M. Camille Jordan', *La Minerve française*, IV, cahier 5 [11-12 décembre 1818], pp.193-202.
Signed: 'B.C.' Harpaz (1972), pp.598-607.

D145 [Note sur l'affaire Lainé], *La Minerve française*, IV, cahier 5 [11-12 décembre 1818], pp.226-227.
Unsigned. Harpaz (1972), pp.608-609.

D146 *'Petit cours de jurisprudence littéraire, ou Répertoire de police correctionnelle, à l'usage des gens de lettres*; par M. Jouslin de La Salle. Tome premier, première et deuxième partie', *La Minerve française*, IV, cahier 5 [11-12 décembre 1818], p.228.
Signed: 'B.C.' Harpaz (1972), p.610.

D147 'Session des Chambres', *La Minerve française*, IV, cahier 6 [15-16 décembre 1818], pp.289-296.

Signed: 'B.C.' Harpaz (1972), pp.611-618. Reprinted in *Cours de politique*, IV (1820).

D148   *Incipit*: 'Le *Journal du commerce* a parlé déjà du dîner patriotique', *La Minerve française*, IV, cahier 7 [19-21 décembre 1818], pp.326-327.
Signed: 'B.C.'.

D149   'Session des Chambres', *La Minerve française*, IV, cahier 7 [19-21 décembre 1818], pp.327-330.
Signed: 'B.C.' Harpaz (1972), pp.619-622. Reprinted in *Cours de politique*, IV (1820).

D150   '*Charlemagne ou la Caroléide*; par M. Victor d'Arlincourt', *La Minerve française*, IV, cahier 8 [28-29 décembre 1818], pp.349-356.
Signed: 'B.C.' Harpaz (1972), pp.623-630.

D151   'Session des Chambres', *La Minerve française*, IV, cahier 8 [28-29 décembre 1818], pp.379-384.
Signed: 'B.C.' Harpaz (1972), pp.631-636. Reprinted in *Cours de politique*, IV (1820).

1819

D152   'Session des Chambres', *La Minerve française*, IV, cahier 9 [4-5 janvier 1819], pp.430-436.
Signed: 'B.C.' Harpaz (1972), pp.637-643. Reprinted in *Cours de politique*, IV (1820).

D153   'Session des Chambres', *La Minerve française*, IV, cahier 10 [8-9 janvier 1819], pp.477-486.
Signed: 'B.C.' Harpaz (1972), pp.644-653. Reprinted in *Cours de politique*, IV (1820).

D154   'Session des Chambres', *La Minerve française*, IV, cahier 11 [14-15 janvier 1819], pp.541-545
Signed: 'B.C.' Harpaz (1972), pp.654-658. Reprinted in *Cours de politique*, IV (1820).

D155   'Session des Chambres', *La Minerve française*, IV, cahier 12 [23-25 janvier 1819], pp.581-585.
Signed: 'B.C.' Harpaz (1972), pp.659-663. Reprinted in *Cours de politique*, IV (1820).

D156   'Session des Chambres', *La Minerve française*, IV, cahier 13 [28-29 janvier 1819], pp.631-637.
Signed: 'B.C.' Harpaz (1972), pp.664-670. Reprinted in *Cours de politique*, IV (1820).

D157 *'Lettre au général Gourgaud, sur la relation de la campagne de 1815, écrite à Sainte-Hélène*; par M. Marchand, ex-adjoint aux commissaires des guerres', *La Minerve française*, V, cahier 1 [5-6 février 1819], pp.12-13.
Signed: 'B.C.' Harpaz (1972), pp.671-672.

D158 'Session des Chambres', *La Minerve française*, V, cahier 1 [5-6 février 1819], pp.31-44.
Signed: 'B.C.' Harpaz (1972), pp.673-686. Reprinted in *Cours de politique*, IV (1820).

D159 'Session des Chambres', *La Minerve française*, V, cahier 2 [15-16 février 1819], pp.76-91.
Signed: 'B.C.' Harpaz (1972), pp.687-702. Reprinted in *Cours de politique*, IV (1820).

D160 'Session des Chambres', *La Minerve française*, V, cahier 3 [19-20 février 1819], pp.141-150.
Signed: 'B.C.' Harpaz (1972), pp.703-712. Reprinted in *Cours de politique*, IV (1820).

D161 'Session des Chambres', *La Minerve française*, V, cahier 4 [24-25 février 1819], pp.181-186.
Signed: 'B.C.' Harpaz (1972), pp.713-718. Reprinted in *Cours de politique*, IV (1820).

D162 'Session des Chambres', *La Minerve française*, V, cahier 5 [3-4 mars 1819], pp.242-257.
Signed: 'B.C.' Harpaz (1972), pp.719-734. Reprinted in *Cours de politique*, IV (1820).

D163 'Session des Chambres', *La Minerve française*, V, cahier 6 [9-10 mars 1819], pp.289-310.
Signed: 'B.C.' Harpaz (1972), pp.735-756. Reprinted in *Cours de politique*, IV (1820).

D164 'Session des Chambres', *La Minerve française*, V, cahier 7 [17-18 mars 1819], pp.337-347.
Signed: 'B.C.' Harpaz (1972), pp.757-767. Reprinted in *Cours de politique*, IV (1820).

D165 'Session des Chambres', *La Minerve française*, V, cahier 8 [25-26 mars 1819], pp.382-405.
Signed: 'B.C.' Harpaz (1972), pp.769-792. Reprinted in *Cours de politique*, IV (1820).

D166 'Lettre à MM. les habitans du département de la Sarthe', *La Minerve française*, V, cahier 9 [1-2 avril 1819], pp.447-455.

Signed: 'Benjamin Constant'. Harpaz (1972), pp.793-801. Reprinted as pamphlet. C38a. *Checklist* A38/1. Also reprinted in *Cours de politique*, IV (1820).

D167 [Pétition du commerce de Bordeaux en faveur de la loi des élections], *La Minerve française*, V, cahier 10 [9-10 avril 1819], pp.493-497.
Signed: 'B.C.' Harpaz (1972), pp.802-806.

D168 'D'un amendement proposé à la loi sur la liberté de la presse', *La Minerve française*, V, cahier 11 [16-17 avril 1819], pp.538-541.
Signed: 'B.C.' Harpaz (1972), pp.807-810.

D169 'De la religion et de la morale religieuse', *La Minerve française*, V, cahier 12 [21-22 avril 1819], pp.583-590.
Signed: 'B.C.' Harpaz (1972), pp.811-818.

D170 '*Constitutions de la nation française*; par M. le comte Lanjuinais. (Premier article)', *La Minerve française*, VI, cahier 1 [7-8 mai 1819], pp.5-12.
Signed: 'B.C.' Harpaz (1972), pp.819-826.

D171 '*Constitution de la nation française*, par M. le comte Lanjuinais. (Seconde article)', *La Minerve française*, VI, cahier 3 [22-24 mai 1819], pp.110-119.
Signed: 'B.C.' Harpaz (1972), pp.827-836.

D172 'De l'examen des emprunts de 16 et de 24 millions dans le budget de 1819, avec quelques observations sur l'ancien et le nouveau ministère', *La Minerve française*, VI, cahier 4 [28-29 mai 1819], pp.149-155.
Signed: 'Benjamin Constant'. Harpaz (1972), pp.837-843.

D173 'De la formation d'un nouveau ministère', *La Minerve française*, VI, cahier 6 [10-11 juin 1819], pp.245-251.
Signed: 'B.C.' Harpaz (1972), pp.844-850.

D174 'De l'état constitutionnel de la France', *La Renommée*, n° 1, 15 juin 1819, pp.2-4.
Signed: 'Benjamin-Constant'. Harpaz (1972), pp.1232-1237.

D175 '*Constitution de la nation française*, par M. le comte Lanjuinais. (Troisième et dernier article)', *La Minerve française*, VI, cahier 7 [18-19 juin 1819], pp.312-317.
Signed: 'B.C.' Harpaz (1972), pp.851-856.

D176 *Incipit*: 'Un des symptômes les plus satisfaisans qu'on puisse remarquer dans notre situation politique', *La Renommée*, n° 11, 25 juin 1819, p.41.
Signed: 'Benjamin Constant'. Harpaz (1972), pp.1237-1239.

D177 'Aux rédacteurs de la Renommée', *La Renommée*, n° 13, 27 juin 1819, p.49.

Signed: 'Benjamin-Constant'. Defence of the 'indépendants' against articles in *Le Courrier français*. Harpaz (1972), pp.1240-1242.

D178 'Aux rédacteurs de la Renommée', *La Renommée*, n° 17, 1ᵉʳ juillet 1819, p.65.
Signed: 'Benjamin Constant'. On the same topic as Constant's speech of 30 June. Harpaz (1972), pp.1243-1244.

D179 'Des rapports de la grande propriété avec nos institutions', *La Minerve française*, VI, cahier 9 [3-5 juillet 1819], pp.409-415.
Signed: 'B.C.' Harpaz (1972), pp.857-863. Reprinted in *Mélanges* (1829).

D180 'Aux rédacteurs de la Renommée', *La Renommée*, n° 21, 5 juillet 1819, pp.81-82.
Signed: 'Benjamin-Constant'. Reply to article in *Le Courrier français*. Harpaz (1972), pp.1245-1247.

D181 'Du ministère pendant la session qui vient de finir', *La Minerve française*, VI, cahier 11 [16-17 juillet 1819], pp.497-507.
Signed: 'B.C.' Harpaz (1972), pp.864-874.

D182 'Aux Auteurs de la Renommée', *La Renommée*, n° 32, 18 juillet 1819, pp.134-135.
Signed: 'Benjamin Constant'. Reply to *Journal des débats* concerning Constant's views on religion. Harpaz (1972), pp.1248-1250.

D183 'Aux Auteurs de la Renommée', *La Renommée*, n° 38, 22 juillet 1819, pp.149-150.
Signed: 'Benjamin Constant'. Reply to *Le Drapeau blanc* concerning coups d'état. Harpaz (1972), pp.1250-1252.

D184 '*Trois règnes de l'histoire d'Angleterre*; par M. Sauquaire-Souligné', *La Minerve française*, VI, cahier 12 [23-24 juillet 1819], pp.568-576.
Signed: 'B.C.' Harpaz (1972), pp.875-883.

D185 'Aux Auteurs de la Renommée', *La Renommée*, n° 41, 25 juillet 1819, pp.162-163.
Signed: 'Benjamin Constant'. Reply to various journals concerning monarchy and liberty. Harpaz (1972), pp.1252-1256.

D186 'De l'état de l'Europe sous le point de vue constitutionnel', *La Minerve française*, VI, cahier 13 [31 juillet-2 août 1819], pp.593-605.
Signed: 'B.C.' Harpaz (1972), pp.884-896. See below, item D192.

D187 'Aux Auteurs de la Renommée', *La Renommée*, n° 48, 1ᵉʳ août 1819, p.191.
Signed: 'Benjamin Constant'. Concerning electoral laws. Harpaz (1972), pp.1256-1259.

D188 'Aux Auteurs de la Renommée', *La Renommée*, n° 49, 2 août 1819, p.193.
Signed: 'Benjamin Constant'. Reply to an article by Chateaubriand in *Le Conservateur* concerning the Vendée. Harpaz (1972), pp.1259-1261.

D189 *'Recueil de discours prononcés au parlement d'Angleterre par J.-C. Fox et W. Pitt*, par MM. H …, de J[anvry] et de Jussieu', *La Minerve française*, VII, cahier 1 [6-7 août 1819], pp.6-13.
Signed: 'B.C.' Harpaz (1972), pp.897-904. Reprinted in *Mélanges* (1829).

D190 'Aux Auteurs de la Renommée', *La Renommée*, n° 56, 9 août 1819, pp.222-223.
Signed: 'Benjamin Constant'. Reply to an article in *Le Courrier français* concerning the responsibility of ministers. Harpaz (1972), pp.1262-1266.

D191 'Aux Auteurs de la Renommée', *La Renommée*, n° 57, 10 août 1819, p.227.
Signed: 'Benjamin Constant'. Reply to an article in *Le Courrier français* attacking the opposition. Harpaz (1972), pp.1266-1270.

D192 'De l'état de l'Europe sous le point de vue constitutionnel', *La Minerve française*, VII, cahier 2 [14-16 août 1819], pp.49-58.
Signed: 'B.C.' Harpaz (1972), pp.905-914.

D193 'De la traite des nègres au Sénégal', *La Minerve française*, VII, cahier 3 [18-23 août 1819], pp.113-124.
Signed: 'B.C.' Harpaz (1972), pp.915-926.

D194 'Aux Auteurs de la Renommée', *La Renommée*, n° 73, 27 août 1819, pp.287-288.
Signed: 'Benjamin Constant'. Reply to an article by Chateaubriand in *Le Conservateur* concerning the responsibility for political revolution in Europe. Harpaz (1972), pp.1270-1273.

D195 'Des accusateurs de la France', *La Minerve française*, VII, cahier 4 [28-30 août 1819], pp.154-160.
Signed: 'B.C.' Harpaz (1972), pp.927-933.

D196 'Lettres sur les Cent Jours. (Première lettre.)', *La Minerve française*, VII, cahier 5 [4-6 septembre 1819], pp.193-199.
Signed: 'B.C.' Harpaz (1972), 934-940. Reprinted in *Mémoires sur les Cent Jours* (1820).

D197 'Aux Auteurs de la Renommée', *La Renommée*, n° 82, 5 septembre 1819, p.322.
Signed: 'Benjamin Constant'. Reply to Chateaubriand concerning free elections. Harpaz (1972), pp.1274-1276.

D198 'Lettres sur les Cent Jours. (Seconde lettre.)', *La Minerve française*, VII,

cahier 6 [11-13 septembre 1819], pp.241-249. Reprinted in *Mémoires sur les Cent Jours* (1820).
Signed: 'B.C.' Harpaz (1972), pp.941-949.

D199 'Lettres sur les Cent Jours. (Troisième lettre.)', *La Minerve française*, VII, cahier 7 [18-20 septembre 1819], pp.292-303.
Signed: 'B.C.' Harpaz (1972), pp.950-961. Reprinted in *Mémoires sur les Cent Jours* (1820).

D200 'Aux Auteurs de la Renommée', *La Renommée*, n° 96, 19 septembre 1819, p.378.
Signed: 'Benjamin Constant'. Attack on the ultra-conservative opinions of the *Journal des débats*. Harpaz (1972), pp.1277-1279.

D201 'Aux Auteurs de la Renommée', *La Renommée*, n° 101, 24 septembre 1819, p.397.
Signed: 'Benjamin Constant'. Analysis of the Bourbon régime of 1815. Harpaz (1972), pp.1279-1281.

D202 'Lettres sur les Cent Jours. (Quatrième lettre.)', *La Minerve française*, VII, cahier 8 [25-27 septembre 1819], pp.337-347.
Signed: 'B.C.' Harpaz (1972), pp.962-972. Reprinted in *Mémoires sur les Cent Jours* (1820).

D203 'Lettres sur les Cent Jours. (Cinquième lettre.)', *La Minerve française*, VII, cahier 9 [2-4 octobre 1819], pp.385-394.
Signed: 'B.C.' Harpaz (1972), 973-982. Reprinted in *Mémoires sur les Cent Jours* (1820).

D204 'Aux Auteurs de la Renommée', *La Renommée*, n° 117, 10 octobre 1819, p.461.
Signed: 'Benjamin Constant'. Concerning the new administration and the Congrès de Carlsbad. Harpaz (1972), pp.1282-1284.

D205 'Lettres sur les Cent Jours. (Sixième lettre.)', *La Minerve française*, VII, cahier 10 [9-11 octobre 1819], pp.433-443.
Signed: 'B.C.' Harpaz (1972), pp.983-993. Reprinted in *Mémoires sur les Cent Jours* (1820).

D206 'Aux Auteurs de la Renommée', *La Renommée*, n° 121, 14 octobre 1819, p.477.
Signed: 'Benjamin Constant'. Reply to the *Journal des débats* concerning the freedom of the press. Harpaz (1972), pp.1285-1286.

D207 'Lettres sur les Cent Jours. (Septième lettre.)', *La Minerve française*, VII, cahier 11 [16-18 octobre 1819], pp.481-491.
Signed: 'B.C.' Harpaz (1972), pp.994-1004. Reprinted in *Mémoires sur les Cent Jours* (1820).

D208 'Aux Auteurs de la Renommée', *La Renommée*, n° 129, 22 octobre 1819, p.509.
Signed: 'Benjamin Constant'. Reply to *Le Drapeau blanc* concerning church property. Harpaz (1972), pp.1286-1288.

D209 'Lettres sur les Cent Jours. (Huitième lettre.)', *La Minerve française*, VII, cahier 12 [23-25 octobre 1819], pp.531-540.
Signed: 'B.C.' Harpaz (1972), pp.1005-1014. Reprinted in *Mémoires sur les Cent Jours* (1820).

D210 'Aux Auteurs de la Renommée', *La Renommée*, n° 135, 28 octobre 1819, p.533.
Signed: 'Benjamin Constant'. Reply to *Le Courrier français* concerning the Société des amis de la liberté de la presse. Harpaz (1972), pp.1288-1291.

D211 'Aux Auteurs de la Renommée', *La Renommée*, n° 137, 30 octobre 1819, p.541.
Signed: 'Benjamin Constant'. Same topic as the preceding item. Harpaz (1972), pp.1291-1293.

D212 'Lettre à MM. les habitans de la Sarthe', *La Minerve française*, VII, cahier 13 [30 octobre-2 novembre 1819], pp.577-590.
Signed: 'Benjamin Constant'. Harpaz (1972), pp.1015-1028. Reprinted as pamphlet, 1819. C.39a. *Checklist* A39/1. Also reprinted in *Cours de politique*, IV (1820).

D213 *Incipit*: 'La *Minerve* qui doit paraître demain contient une lettre de M. Benjamin Constant aux habitans de la Sarthe', *La Renommée*, n° 138, 31 octobre 1819, pp.545-546.
Extract of the letter. *Signed*: 'Benjamin Constant'. Harpaz (1972), pp.1293-1295.

D214 'Aux Auteurs de la Renommée', *La Renommée*, n° 143, 5 novembre 1819, pp.561-562.
Signed: 'Benjamin Constant'. On J.-M.-E.-F. Legraverend's *Observations sur le Jury en France* (Paris, 1819). Harpaz (1972), pp.1296-1299.

D215 'Lettres sur les Cent Jours. (Neuvième lettre.)', *La Minerve française*, VIII, cahier 1 [8-9 novembre 1819], pp.3-11.
Signed: 'B.C.' Harpaz (1972), pp.1029-1237. Reprinted in *Mémoires sur les Cent Jours* (1820).

D216 'Aux Auteurs de la Renommée', *La Renommée*, n° 148, 10 novembre 1819, p.581.
Signed: 'Benjamin Constant'. Reply to allegations which had been made in *La Quotidienne* that Constant had been in correspondence with Görres. Harpaz (1972), pp.1299-1300.

D217 'De l'état de la France et des rumeurs qui circulent', *La Renommée*, n°
149, 11 novembre 1819, pp.587-588.
Extracts from item A40/1. Harpaz (1972), pp.1300-1307.

D218 'Lettres sur les Cent Jours. (Dixième lettre.)', *La Minerve française*, VIII,
cahier 2 [14-15 novembre 1819], pp.49-59.
Signed: 'B.C.' Harpaz (1972), pp.1038-1048. Reprinted in *Mémoires sur les Cent
Jours* (1822).

D219 *Incipit*: 'Le *Courrier* d'hier reproche à la brochure de M. B. Constant de
contenir des idées à la portée de tout le monde', *La Renommée*, n° 157, 19
novembre 1819, p.617.
Unsigned. See item D217. Harpaz (1972), pp.1307-1308.

D220 'Napoléon et les 100 jours', *La Renommée*, n° 158, 20 novembre 1819,
p.621. ['Ce fragment fait partie de la 94ᵉ livraison de la *Minerve*, qui doit paraître
demain, 20 novembre'].
Unsigned. Harpaz (1972), pp.1308-1310.

D221 'Lettres sur les Cent Jours. (Onzième lettre.)', *La Minerve française*, VIII
cahier 3 [20-22 novembre 1819], pp.97-105.
Signed: 'B.C.' Harpaz (1972), pp.1049-1057. Reprinted in *Mémoires sur les Cent
Jours* (1822).

D222 'Aux Auteurs de la Renommée', *La Renommée*, n° 160, 22 novembre 1819,
pp.629-630.
Signed: 'Benjamin Constant'. On the new administration (Decazes). Harpaz
(1972), pp.1310-1316.

D223 'Aux Auteurs de la Renommée', *La Renommée*, n° 163, 25 novembre 1819,
p.641.
Signed: 'Benjamin Constant'. Reply to attack by the *Journal de Paris* on Constant's
article of 22 November. Harpaz (1972), pp.1316-1319.

D224 'De l'inviolabilité de la Charte', *La Minerve française*, VIII cahier 4 [26-
27 novembre 1819], pp.145-153.
Signed: 'B.C.' Harpaz (1972), pp.1058-1066.

D225 'Aux Auteurs de la Renommée', *La Renommée*, n° 167, 29 novembre 1819,
p.658.
Signed: 'Benjamin Constant'. Reply to *La Quotidienne* concerning subscriptions
for the Champ d'Asile and Wilfred Regnault. Harpaz (1972), pp.1319-1320.

D226 'Du projet de conférer aux Chambres le droit de s'épurer, et de quelques
autres projets de même nature', *La Minerve française*, VIII, cahier 5 [2-3 décembre
1819], pp.193-202.
Signed: 'B.C.' Harpaz (1972), pp.1067-1076.

D227 'Aux Auteurs de la Renommée', *La Renommée*, n° 171, 3 décembre 1819, p.672.
Signed: 'Benjamin Constant'. Disclaims letter to be published with his signature in the *Journal de Paris*. Harpaz (1972), p.1320.

D228 'Aux Auteurs de la Renommée', *La Renommée*, n° 172, 4 décembre 1819, p.675.
Signed: 'Benjamin Constant'. On the same topic as the preceding item. Harpaz (1972). pp.1320-1321.

D229 'Aux Auteurs de la Renommée', *La Renommée*, n° 179, 11 décembre 1819, p.703.
Signed: 'Benjamin Constant'. On the responsibility of ministers. Harpaz (1972), pp.1322-1323.

D230 'De la responsabilité des ministres dans la proposition des lois', *La Minerve française*, VIII, cahier 6 [11-13 décembre 1819], pp.241-251.
Signed: 'B.C.' Harpaz (1972), pp.1077-1087.

D231 'Aux Auteurs de la Renommée', *La Renommée*, n° 190, 22 décembre 1819, p.742.
Signed: 'Benjamin Constant'. On the freedom of the press. Harpaz (1972), pp.1323-1324.

D232 'De l'adresse au Roi', *La Minerve française*, VII, cahier 7 [22-23 décembre 1819], pp.289-295.
Signed: 'Benjamin Constant'. Harpaz (1972), pp.1088-1094.

D233 'Aux Auteurs de la Renommée', *La Renommée*, n° 194, 26 décembre 1819, pp.761-762.
Signed: 'Benjamin Constant'. On petitions. Harpaz (1972), pp.1324-1328.

D234 'Lettres sur les Cent Jours. (Douzième lettre.)', *La Minerve française*, VIII, cahier 8 [27-28 décembre 1819], pp.337-343.
Signed: 'B.C.' Harpaz (1972), 1095-1101. Reprinted in *Mémoires sur les Cent Jours* (1822).

D235 'Lettres sur les Cent Jours. (Treizième lettre.)', *La Minerve française*, VIII, cahier 9 [31 décembre 1819-3 janvier 1820], pp.385-396.
Signed: 'B.C.' Harpaz (1972), pp.1102-1113. Reprinted in *Mémoires sur les Cent Jours* (1822).

1820

D236 'Aux Auteurs de la Renommée', *La Renommée*, n° 201, 2 janvier 1820, p.784.
Signed: 'Benjamin Constant'. Reply to *Le Courrier français* concerning petitions. Harpaz (1972), pp.1328-1331.

D237 'Lettres sur les Cent Jours. (Quatorzième lettre.)', *La Minerve française*, VIII, cahier 10 [8-10 janvier 1820], pp.433-438.
Signed: 'B.C.' Harpaz (1972), pp.1114-1119. Reprinted in *Mémoires sur les Cent Jours* (1822).

D238 'Aux Auteurs de la Renommée', *La Renommée*, n° 210, 11 janvier 1820, p.821.
Signed: 'Benjamin Constant'. On the monarch and ministerial responsibility. Harpaz (1972), pp.1331-1333.

D239 'Aux Auteurs de la Renommée', *La Renommée*, n° 211, 12 janvier 1820, p.825.
Signed: 'Benjamin Constant'. Reply to the *Journal de Paris* concerning an alleged conspiracy involving Constant and Manuel. Harpaz (1972), pp.1333-1335.

D240 'Lettres sur les Cent Jours. (Quinzième lettre.)', *La Minerve française*, VIII, cahier 11 [15-17 janvier 1820], pp.481-488.
Signed: 'B.C.' Harpaz (1972), 1120-1127. Reprinted in *Mémoires sur les Cent Jours* (1822).

D241 'Aux Auteurs de la Renommée', *La Renommée*, n° 220, 21 janvier 1820, p.861.
Signed: 'Benjamin Constant'. Reply to the *Journal de Paris* concerning Constant's speech of 15 January. Harpaz (1972), pp.1335-1337. Reprinted as a pamphlet, *Checklist* A41/1.

D242 'Des aveux échappés aux ennemis de la loi des élections', *La Minerve française*, VIII, cahier 12 [22-24 janvier 1820], pp.529-543.
Signed: 'B.C.' Harpaz (1972), pp.1128-1142.

D243 'Aux Auteurs de la Renommée', *La Renommée*, n° 225, 26 janvier 1820, p.881.
Signed: 'Benjamin Constant'. Reply to Barante (speech of 18 March) concerning quotation from a speech by C. J. Fox. Harpaz (1972), pp.1337-1339.

D244 'Aux Auteurs de la Renommée', *La Renommée*, n° 227, 28 janvier 1820.
Signed: 'Benjamin Constant'. Concerning the views of ministerial newspapers on Spanish politics. Harpaz (1972), pp.1340-1341.

D245 'Lettres sur les Cent Jours (Seizième lettre.)', *La Minerve française*, VIII, cahier 13 [29-31 janvier 1820], pp.593-601.
Signed: 'B.C.' Harpaz (1972), pp.1143-1151. Reprinted in *Mémoires sur les Cent Jours* (1822).

D246 'Du plan de la faction contre-révolutionnaire', *La Minerve française*, IX, cahier 1 [5-7 février 1820], pp.3-11.
Signed: 'B.C.' Harpaz (1972), pp.1152-1160.

D247 'Aux Auteurs de la Renommée', *La Renommée*, n° 214, 14 février 1820, pp.955-956.
Signed: 'Benjamin Constant'. Concerning electoral reform. Harpaz (1972), pp.1342-1344.

D248 'De l'influence de la faction contre-révolutionnaire sur les projets de loi des ministres', *La Minerve française*, IX, cahier 2 [14-15 février 1820], pp.49-56.
Signed: 'B.C.' Harpaz (1972), pp.1161-1168.

D249 'Reflexions sur le moment présent', *La Minerve française*, IX, cahier 3 [19-21 février 1820], pp.97-103.
Signed: 'B.C.' Harpaz (1972), pp.1169-1175.

D250 'Aux Auteurs de la Renommée', *La Renommée*, n° 224, 24 février 1820, p.1003.
Signed: 'Benjamin Constant'. On the political consequences of the assassination of the Duc de Berry. Harpaz (1972), pp.1344-1346.

D251 'Du rétablissement de la censure des journaux', *La Minerve française*, IX, cahier 4 [27-28 février 1820], pp.133-143.
Signed: 'B.C.' Harpaz (1972), pp.1176-1186.

D252 'Lettres sur les Cent Jours. Dix-septième lettre', *La Minerve française*, IX, cahier 5 [3-4 mars 1820], pp.197-207.
Signed: 'B.C.' Harpaz (1972), pp.1187-1197.

D253 'Aux Auteurs de la Renommée', *La Renommée*, n° 233, 4 mars 1820, p.1045.
Signed: 'Benjamin Constant'. Reply to the *Journal des débats* concerning his conduct in the committee of 2 March. Harpaz (1972), pp.1347-1348.

D254 'De la contre-révolution et du ministère', *La Minerve française*, IX, cahier 6 [14 mars 1820], pp.229-237.
Signed: 'B.C.' Harpaz (1972), pp.1198-1206.

D255 'Symptômes du moment', *La Minerve française*, IX, cahier 7 [16-17 mars 1820], pp.285-291.
Signed: 'B.C.' Harpaz (1972), pp.1207-1213.

D256 'Troisième lettre à Messieurs les habitans du département de la Sarthe', *La Minerve française*, IX, cahier 8 [22-24 mars 1820], pp.333-339.
Signed: 'Benjamin Constant' and dated 'Paris, le 21 mars 1820'. Harpaz (1972), pp.1214-1220. Reprinted as pamphlet, 1820. C.43a. *Checklist* A43/1.

D257 'Conspiration des contre-révolutionnaires contre le trône et la vie du Roi d'Espagne', *La Minerve française*, IX, cahier 9 [29 mars 1820], pp.381-386.
Signed: 'B.C.' Harpaz (1972), pp.1221-1226.

D258 'Aux Auteurs de la Renommée', *La Renommée*, n° 259, 31 mars 1820, p.1049.
Signed: 'Benjamin Constant'. Concerning freedom of the press and the law of 30 March 1820, and announcement of a work in preparation: *De la charte constitution-nelle telle que le ministère de 1820 l'a faite*. Harpaz (1972), pp.1349-1350.

D259 'Aux Auteurs de la Renommée', *La Renommée*, n° 269, 9 avril 1820, p.1087.
Signed: 'Benjamin Constant'. Reply to the *Journal des débats* concerning electoral procedures. Harpaz (1972), pp.1350-1351.

D260 'Aux Auteurs de la Renommée', *La Renommée*, n° 298, 8 mai 1820, p.1202.
Dated: 'Paris, 6 mai 1820', and signed: 'Benjamin Constant'. Announcement that his work *De la Charte constitutionnelle* (see above, item D258) has been temporarily suspended. Harpaz (1972), pp.1351-1352.

D261 'Au Rédacteur', *Le Courrier français*, n°ˢ 337-338, 22-23 mai 1820, p.4.
Letter (undated), signed 'Benjamin Constant'. Reply to article in *Journal de Paris* of 21 May concerning the contents of Constant's *Des motifs qui ont dicté le nouveau projet de loi sur les élections*. Harpaz (1981), n° 1, pp.11-12.

D262 'A M. Kératry, membre de la Chambre des Députés et homme de lettres', *Le Courrier français*, n° 365, 19 juin 1820, p.3.
Letter dated '18 juin 1820' and signed 'B. Constant'. Article relating to Constant's contribution to the *Courrier français*. Harpaz (1981), n° 2, pp.13-14.

D263 'Au rédacteur', *Le Moniteur universel*, 30 juin 1820.
Signed: 'Benjamin Constant'. Reply to article in *Le Moniteur* of 29 June concerning Constant's speech of 27 June 1820 on the activities of the police in the Sarthe. Harpaz (1981), n° 3, pp.15-17.

D264 'A M. Kératry, député du Finistère', *Le Courrier français*, n° 378, 2 juillet 1820, p.2.
Letter (undated), signed 'Benjamin Constant'. Concerning measures taken by the authorities against liberal députés in June 1820. Harpaz (1981), n° 4, pp.18-19.

D265 'Au Rédacteur', *Le Courrier français*, n° 378, 2 juillet 1820, pp.2-3.
Letter (undated), signed 'Benjamin Constant'. Reply to report in *Le Moniteur* relating to police activity in Le Mans.

D266 'Au Rédacteur', *Le Courrier français*, n° 380, 4 juillet 1820, p.3.
Letter (undated), signed 'Benjamin Constant'. Concerning police activities in the Sarthe. Harpaz (1981), n° 5, pp.19-22.

D267 'Au Rédacteur', *Le Courrier français*, n° 382, 6 juillet 1820, pp.3-4.
Letter dated 'Paris, 5 juillet 1820' and signed 'Benjamin Constant'. Concerning

police activities in the Sarthe. Harpaz (1981), n° 6, p.23.

D268 'Au Rédacteur', *Le Courrier français*, n° 387, 11 juillet 1820, p.4.
Letter (undated), signed 'Benjamin Constant'. Concerning police activities in the Sarthe. Harpaz (1981), n° 7, p.24.

D269 'Au Rédacteur', *Le Courrier français*, n° 395, 19 juillet 1820, pp.2-3.
Letter (undated), signed 'Benjamin Constant'. Concerning police activities in the Sarthe. Harpaz (1981), n° 8, pp.25-26.

D270 'Au Rédacteur', *Le Courrier français*, n° 396, 20 juillet 1820, p.2.
Letter (undated), signed 'Benjamin Constant'. Defence of A.-T. Leseigneur against attacks in *La Quotidienne*, Harpaz (1981), n° 9, p.27.

D271 'Au Rédacteur' *Le Courrier français*, n° 436, 29 août 1820, p.2.
Letter dated 'Paris, le 28 août 1820' and signed 'Kératry, Benjamin Constant'. Concerning lack of impartiality in reporting in *Le Moniteur* with reference to activities of the authorities directed against liberal deputies on 3 June 1820. Harpaz (1981), n° 11, p.29.

D272 'Au Rédacteur', *Le Courrier français*, n° 439, 1ᵉʳ septembre 1820, p.3.
Letter dated 'Paris, 28 août 1820' and signed 'Kératry, Benjamin Constant'. Further development of the preceding article. Harpaz (1981), n° 12, pp.30-32.

D273 'A M. le Rédacteur', *Le Courrier français*, n° 486, 18 octobre 1820, p.2.
Letter dated 'La Grange, ce 16 octobre 1820' and signed 'Benjamin Constant'. Concerning public disorders at Saumur on 7-8 October 1820. Harpaz (1981), n° 13, p.33.

D274 'Au Rédacteur', *Le Courrier français*, n° 503, 4 novembre 1820, p.2.
Letter dated 'Paris, ce 3 novembre 1820' and signed 'Benjamin Contant'. Same topic as preceding article.

D275 'Au Rédacteur', *Le Courrier français*, n° 506, 7 novembre 1820, p.2.
Letter dated 'Paris, ce 6 novembre 1820' and signed 'Benjamin Constant'. Same topic as preceding article. Harpaz (1981), n° 15, pp.36-37.

D276 *Saggio di costituzione. Prima versione italiana corredata di note relative alla costituzion spagnuola*, issued in parts in *La Biblioteca costituzionale*, [Naples: L. Nobile, 1820].
C.131c. *Checklist* E1/t2.

1821

D277 *'Notice sur M. Necker*, par A. de Staël, son petit-fils. A Paris, chez Treuttel et Wurtz …', *Le Courrier français*, n° 2, 2 janvier 1821, pp.3-4.
('B. Const' in pen and ink in BN copy). Harpaz (1981), n° 16, pp.38-40.

D278 '*Sur la vie de Jacques II, roi d'Angleterre, écrite de sa propre main*', *Le Courrier français*, n° 5, 5 janvier 1821, pp.3-4.
('B. Const' in pen and ink in BN copy). Review of *Vie de Jacques II*, par J.S. Clarke, traduite de l'anglais par Jean Cohen, Paris, 1819. 4 vols. Harpaz (1981), n° 17, pp.41-43.

D279 'Au Rédacteur', *Le Constitutionnel*, n° 19, 19 janvier 1821.
Signed: 'Benjamin Constant.' Concerning the reporting of Constant's speech of 16 January (on the budget). Harpaz (1981), n° 18, p.44.

D280 'A M. le rédacteur', *Le Courrier français*, n° 52, 22 février 1821, p.4.
Letter dated 'Paris, le 21 février 1821' and signed 'Benjamin Constant'. Reply to allegation in *Gazette de France* of 21 February concerning the 'affaire du baril de poudre'. Harpaz (1981), n° 19, pp.45-46.

D281 '*Etat actuel de la Corse, caractère et mœurs de ses habitans*, par P. P. Pompei', *Le Courrier français*, n° 85, 27 mars 1821, p.4.
('B. Const' in pen and ink in BN copy). Harpaz (1981), n° 20, pp.47-48.

D282 'Au Rédacteur', *Le Courrier français*, n° 95, 6 avril 1821, p.3.
Letter dated 'Paris, 5 avril 1821' and signed 'Benjamin Constant'. Reply to attack in *Le Drapeau blanc* concerning *Du triomphe inévitable et prochain des principes constitutionnels en Prusse*. Harpaz (1981), n° 21, pp.49-50.

D283 'Au Rédacteur', *Le Courrier français*, n° 101, 12 avril 1821, p.4.
Letter dated 'Paris, ce 10 avril 1821' and signed 'Benjamin Constant'. Concerning the authorship of the German original of *Du triomphe inévitable*. Harpaz (1981), n° 22, p.51.

D284 'Au Rédacteur', *Le Courrier français*, n° 114, 26 avril 1821, p.4.
Letter dated 'Paris, 23 avril 1821' and signed 'Benjamin Constant'. Same topic as preceding article. Harpaz (1981), n° 23, p.52.

D285 '*Précis historique des principaux événemens politiques et militaires qui ont amené la Révolution d'Espagne*, par M. Louis Jullian', *Le Courrier français*, n° 116, 28 avril 1821, p.4.
('M. Benjamin Const' in pen and ink in BN copy). Harpaz (1981), n° 24, p.53.

D286 'Au Rédacteur', *Le Courrier français*, n° 118, 30 avril 1821, p.3.
Letter (undated), signed 'Benjamin Constant'. Concerning the authorship of the German original of *Du triomphe inévitable*. Harpaz (1981), n° 25 p.54.

D287 'Au Rédacteur', *Le Courrier français*, n° 119, 1ᵉʳ mai 1821, p.3.
Letter dated 'Paris ce 30 avril' and signed 'Benjamin Constant'. Same topic as the preceding article. Harpaz (1981), n° 26, p.55.

D288 'Au Rédacteur', *Le Courrier français*, n° 133, 16 mai 1821, p.4.

Letter (undated), signed 'Benjamin Constant'. Concerning inaccurate reporting of his speech of 14 May (pensions ecclésiastiques). Harpaz (1981), n° 27, p.56.

D289   'Au Rédacteur', *Le Courrier français*, n° 139, 22 mai 1821, p.4.
Letter (undated), signed 'Benjamin Constant'. Obituary notice on Camille Jordan (1771- 19 May 1821). Harpaz (1981), n° 28, pp.57-59.

D290   'Au Rédacteur', *Le Courrier français*, n° 141, 24 mai 1821, p.4.
Letter (undated), signed 'Benjamin Constant'. Concerning inaccurate reporting of his speech of 21 May. Harpaz (1981), n° 29, p.60.

D291   'Au Rédacteur', *Le Courrier français*, n° 173, 26 juin 1821, p.4.
Letter (undated), signed 'Benjamin Constant'. Concerning the authorship of the German original of *Du triomphe inévitable*. Harpaz (1981), n° 30, pp.61-62.

D292   'Au Rédacteur', *Le Courrier français*, n° 180, 3 juillet 1821, p.2.
Letter dated 'Paris le 1er juillet 1821' and signed 'Benjamin Constant'. Note on Constant's speech of 27 June 1821 on the slave trade. Harpaz (1981), n° 31, p.63.

D293   '*Pascaline*, par Madame L. d'E** auteur d'*Alphonse et Mathilde*', *Le Courrier français*, n° 208, 30 juillet 1821, p.4.
('B. Constant', in pen and ink in BN copy). Review of novel by Louise d'Estournelles. Harpaz (1981), n° 32, pp.64-65.

D294   'Au Rédacteur', *Le Courrier français*, n° 218, 9 août 1821, p.3.
Letter dated 'Paris ce 8 août 1821' and signed 'Benjamin Constant'. Reply to article in *La Quotidienne* on the Protestant Church. Harpaz (1981), n° 33, p.66.

D295   *Incipit*: 'La cour d'assises de Paris', *Le Courrier français*, n° 221, 12 août 1821, pp.2-3.
Signed: 'Benjamin Constant'. Defence of Cauchois-Lemaire. Harpaz (1981), n° 34, pp.67-69.

D296   '*Histoire de l'Assemblée constituante*; par M. Ch. Lacretelle', *Le Courrier français*, n° 230, 22 août 1821, pp.3-4.
('Benjamin Constant' in pen and ink in BN copy). Harpaz (1981), n° 35, pp.70-73. Continued below.

D297   '*Histoire de l'Assemblée constituante*, par M. Ch. Lacretelle', *Le Courrier français*, n° 238, 30 août 1821, pp.3-4.
('B. Constant' in pen and ink in BN copy). Harpaz (1981), n° 36, pp.74-77.

D298   '*Voyage aux Alpes et en Italie*, par M. Albert Montémont', *Le Courrier français*, n° 258, 21 septembre 1821, p.4.
('B. Constant' in pen and ink in BN copy). Harpaz (1981), n° 37, pp.78-79.

D299 'Histoire de la session de 1820, par J. Fiévée', Le Courrier français, n° 266, 29 septembre 1821, pp.2-3.

('B. Constant' in pen and ink in BN copy). Harpaz (1981), n° 38, pp.80-83.

D300 Incipit: 'Le Drapeau blanc prend occasion d'une brochure', Le Courrier français, n° 266, 29 septembre 1821, p.3.

('B. Constant' in pen and ink in BN copy). Reply to attack on civil liberties in Le Drapeau blanc. Harpaz (1981), n° 39, p.84.

D301 Incipit: 'Nous avons sous les yeux le journal du fameux Cobbet', Le Courrier français, n° 269, 2 octobre 1821, p.4.

('B. Constant' in pen and ink in BN copy). Discussion of article by William Cobbett in Cobbett's Weekly Political Register of 22 September 1821. Harpaz (1981), n° 40, pp.85-87.

D302 Incipit: 'Au moment où nous prenions la plume', Le Courrier français, n° 274, 7 octobre 1821, p.2.

('B. Constant' in pen and ink in BN copy). Concerning article in Le Moniteur on his review of Fiévée in Le Courrier français, of 29 September. Harpaz (1981), n° 41, pp.88-90.

D303 'A Monsieur le rédacteur', Le Courrier français, n° 288, 22 octobre 1821, pp.3-4.

('B. Constant' in pen and ink in BN copy). Reflexions on the French economy. Harpaz (1981), n° 42, pp.91-92.

D304 Incipit: 'Le Journal des Débats, en rapportant le jugement', Le Courrier français, n° 320, 24 novembre 1821, pp.2-3.

('B. Constant' in pen and ink in BN copy). Attack on praise given to the Quarterly review by the Journal des débats. Harpaz (1981), n° 43, pp.93-95.

D305 'On the Dissolution of the Chamber of Deputies, and on the possible consequence of this dissolution to the nation, the gouvernment, and the ministry', The Pamphleteer, XVIII (1821), 97-128. C.46c. Checklist A46/t1.

1822

D306 'Œuvres de Filangieri, traduites de l'italien, nouvelle édition, accompagnée d'un commentaire, par M. Benjamin Constant ...', Le Courrier français, n° 13, 13 janvier 1822, p.4.

('B. Constant' in pen and ink in BN copy). Harpaz (1981), n° 44, pp.96-98.

D307 'A M. le Rédacteur', Le Courrier français, n° 34, 3 février 1822, p.4.

Letter dated 'Paris, 2 février' and signed 'Benjamin Constant'. A note on his speech of 1 February. Harpaz (1981), n° 45, pp.99-100.

D308 'Au Rédacteur', Le Courrier français, n° 38, 7 février 1822, pp.3-4.

Letter, undated, signed 'Benjamin-Constant'. Concerning the Association constitutionnelle of J.-R.-P. Sarran. Harpaz (1981), n° 46, pp.101-104.

D309 'A M. le Rédacteur', *Le Courrier français*, n° 54, 23 février 1822, pp.1-2.
Letter, undated, signed 'Benjamin-Constant'. On the electoral laws. Harpaz (1981), n° 47, pp.105-108.

D310 'Au rédacteur', *Le Courrier français*, n° 65, 6 mars 1822, pp.1-2.
Letter dated 'Paris, 5 mars 1822' and signed 'Benjamin-Constant'. The costs of criminal justice. Harpaz (1981), n° 48, pp.109-112.

D311 'Au rédacteur', *Le Courrier français*, n° 77, 18 mars 1822, p.3.
Letter, undated, signed 'A.M.' ('B. Constant' in pen and ink in BN copy). Concerning the speech of Ch.-G. Etienne on 16 March (loi des finances). Harpaz (1981), n° 49, pp.113-114.

D312 *Incipit*: 'Le roi d'Espagne, à peine arrivé à Aranjuez', *Le Courrier français*, n° 83, 24 mars 1822, p.3.
('B. Constant' in pen and ink in BN copy). Concerning remarks in *La Quotidienne* occasioned by the reception the King of Spain by his *sujets fidèles*. Harpaz (1981), n° 50, p.115.

D313 *Incipit*: '*L'Etoile* réfute l'assertion d'un député', *Le Courrier français*, n° 84, 25 mars 1822, p.2.
('B. Constant' in pen and ink in BN copy). On an article in *L'Etoile* alleging plans made by foreign powers for France. Harpaz (1981), n° 51, pp.116-117.

D314 *Incipit*: 'On raconte qu'un soldat', *Le Courrier français*, n° 88, 29 mars 1822, p.6.
('B. Constant' in pen and ink in BN copy). Concerning report in *La Quotidienne* of arrest of Piedmontese exiles. Harpaz (1981), n° 52, p.118.

D315 'Au rédacteur', *Le Courrier français*, n° 91, 1er avril 1822, p.2.
Letter, undated, signed 'Benjamin-Constant'. Clarification of a motion made by Constant in the Chambre des Députés on 29 March. Harpaz (1981), n° 53, pp.119-120.

D316 *Incipit*: '*L'Etoile* d'hier, 30 mars', *Le Courrier français*, n° 91, 1er avril 1822, p.2.
('B. Constant' in pen and ink in BN copy). Concerning inaccurate reporting in *L'Etoile* of the liberals' attitude to Spanish refugees. Harpaz (1981), n° 54, p.121.

D317 *Incipit*: 'La *Gazette de France* attaque un député', *Le Courrier français*, n° 91, 1er avril 1822, pp.2-3.
('Benjamin Constant' in pen and ink in BN copy). Concerning elections. Harpaz (1981), n° 56, p.123.

D318 *Incipit*: 'La Quotidienne prétend', *Le Courrier français*, n° 91, 1er avril 1822, p.3.

('B. Constant' in pen and ink in BN copy). Reply to accusations by *La Quotidienne* against the opposition. Harpaz (1981), n° 55, p.122.

D319 *Incipit*: 'Les personnes qui connaissent les doctrines politiques que l'*Etoile professe*', *Le Courrier français*, n° 91, 1er avril 1822, p.4.

('B. Constant' in pen and ink in BN copy). Concerning the views of *L'Etoile* on legitimacy. Harpaz (1981), n° 57, pp.124-126.

D320 *Incipit*: 'A qui en veut donc le *Drapeau Blanc*', *Le Courrier français* n° 94, 4 avril 1822, p.1.

('B. Constant' in pen and ink in BN copy). Concerning the views of *Le Drapeau blanc* on the monarchy. Harpaz (1981), n° 58, p.127.

D321 'A M. le Rédacteur', *Le Courrier français*, n° 95, 5 avril 1822, p.3.

Letter, undated, signed 'Benjamin Constant'. Concerning inaccurate reporting of his speech of 30 March.

D322 *Incipit*: '"Le Drapeau Blanc" était hier plus naïf encore', *Le Courrier français*, n° 103, 13 avril 1822, p.1.

('B. Constant' in pen and ink in BN copy). Concerning the views of *Le Drapeau blanc* on the assassination of General Ramel. Harpaz (1981), n° 60, p.129.

D323 *Incipit*: '*Le Drapeau Blanc* rapporte qu'un membre des Cortès', *Le Courrier français*, n° 104, 14 avril 1822, p.1.

('B. Constant' in pen and ink in BN copy). Concerning the views of *Le Drapeau blanc* on Spanish politics. Harpaz (1981), n° 61, p.130.

D324 'Au rédacteur', *Le Courrier français*, n° 104, 14 avril 1822, p.4.

Letter dated 'Paris, ce 13 avril 1822' and signed 'Benjamin Constant'. Concerning Jacques Corbière and the falsification of electoral lists. Harpaz (1981), n° 62, pp.131-132.

D325 'Au rédacteur', *Le Courrier français*, n° 113, 23 avril 1822, pp.2-3.

Letter, undated, signed 'Benjamin Constant'. Concerning the abstention of the opposition from voting on 18-20 April. Harpaz (1981), n° 63, pp.133-135.

D326 '*Fastes civils de la France depuis l'ouverture de l'Assemblée des notables*, par MM. Dupont de l'Eure, Etienne, Manuel, Pagès, Tissot, Alex Goujon, Paris, 1822', *Le Courrier français*, n° 119, 29 avril 1822, pp.3-4.

Signed: 'Benjamin Constant'. Harpaz (1981), n° 64, pp.136-140.

D327 'Au Rédacteur', *Le Courrier français*, n° 125, 5 mai 1822, pp.2-3.

('B. Constant' in pen and ink in BN copy). Concerning the circular issued by the authorities on elections. Harpaz (1981), n° 65, pp.141-143.

D328   *Incipit*: '*Le Drapeau Blanc* consacre deux colonnes à prouver', *Le Courrier français*, n° 127, 7 mai 1822, pp.1-2.

('B. Constant' in pen and ink in BN copy). Concerning allegations by *Le Drapeau blanc* imputing arson in the Oise and Somme to liberals. Harpaz (1981), n° 66, pp.144-145.

D329   'Au rédacteur', *Le Courrier français*, n° 129, 9 mai 1822, pp.1-2.

Letter, undated, signed 'Benjamin Constant'. Concerning irregularities in elections. Harpaz (1981), n° 67, pp.146-147. Also published as a pamphlet, *Checklist* A52/1.

D330   *Incipit*: 'Sur les huit candidats', *Le Courrier français*, n° 133, 13 mai 1822, p.2.

('B. Constant' in pen and ink in BN copy). On the success of liberal candidates in the elections of May 1822. Harpaz (1981), n° 68, pp.147-150.

D331   *Incipit*: 'Portrait des électeurs payant 300 fr. (Extrait de la *Gazette de France* du 14 mai)', *Le Courrier français*, n° 136, 16 mai 1822, pp.4.

('B. Constant' in pen and ink in BN copy). Reply to an article in *Gazette de France*. Harpaz (1981), n° 69, pp.151-153.

D332   *Incipit*: 'Les journaux de l'aristocratie', *Le Courrier français*, n° 137, 17 mai 1822, p.3.

('B. Constant', in pen and ink in BN copy). Concerning the impartiality of presidents of electoral colleges. Harpaz (1981), n° 70, p.154.

D333   *Incipit*: 'Les élections de Paris sont terminées', *Le Courrier français*, n° 140, 20 mai 1822, pp.2-4.

('B. Constant' in pen and ink in BN copy). Concerning the success of liberal candidates in the elections of May 1822. Harpaz (1981), n° 71, pp.155-159.

D334   *Incipit*: 'Nous lisons aujourd'hui, dans le *Journal des Débats*', *Le Courrier français*, n° 146, 26 mai 1822, p.2.

('B. Constant' in pen and ink in BN copy). Reply to an article in *Journal des débats* concerning order and liberty. Harpaz (1981), n° 72, p.160.

D335   'Au Rédacteur', *Le Courrier français*, n° 150, 30 mai 1822, p.3.

('B. Constant' in pen and ink in BN copy). Reply to attack on the liberals in *La Quotidienne*. Harpaz (1981), n° 73, pp.161-162.

D336   *Incipit*: '*La Quotidienne* déclare aujourd'hui', *Le Courrier français*, n° 151, 31 mai 1822, pp.2-3.

('B. Constant' in pen and ink in BN copy). Reply to article in *La Quotidienne* demanding war with Spain. Harpaz (1981), n° 74, pp.163-164.

D337   'Au Rédacteur', *Le Courrier français*, n° 156, 5 juin 1822, p.3.

Letter, undated, signed 'Benjamin Constant'. Concerning reports in newspapers of the memorial service for Lallemand held on 3 June 1822 and followed by public disorders. Harpaz (1981), n° 75, pp.165-167.

D338 *Incipit*: 'Un journal s'étonnait hier', *Le Courrier français*, n° 186, 5 juillet 1822, p.2.
('B. Constant' in pen and ink in BN copy). Brief note on the views of *Le Drapeau blanc*. Harpaz (1981), n° 78, p.171.

D339 'Au rédacteur', *Le Courrier français*, n° 193, 12 juillet 1822, pp.2-3.
Letter, undated, signed 'Benjamin Constant'. Concerning security measures taken by the government (reprint, with some changes, of part of Constant's article of 10-11 June 1818 in *La Minerve française*: see above, item D120). Harpaz (1981), n° 79, pp.172-173.

D340 'Au Rédacteur', *Le Courrier français*, n° 258, 15 septembre 1822, p.4.
Letter dated 'Paris, le 15 septembre' and signed 'Benjamin Constant'. Reply to Carrère, sous-préfet of Saumur. Harpaz (1981) n° 81, pp.176-178.

D341 *'Théorie des Cortès, ou Histoire des grandes assemblées nationales des royaumes de Castille et de Léon ...*, par don Fr. Martinez Marina, traduit de l'espagnol par P.F.L. Fleury', *Le Courrier français*, n° 265, 22 septembre 1822, pp.3-4.
('B. Constant' in pen and ink in BN copy). Harpaz (1981), n° 86, pp.187-191.

D342 *Incipit*: '*De M. de Villèle*, tel est le titre', *Le Courrier français*, n° 279, 6 octobre 1822, pp.1-2.
('B. Constant' in pen and ink in BN copy). Review of Bertin de Veaux, *De M. de Villèle*, Paris, 1822. Harpaz (1981), n° 87, pp.192-194.

D343 *Incipit*: 'Dans un département qui doit renouveler', *Le Courrier français*, n° 294, 21 octobre 1822, pp.1-2.
('B. Constant' in pen and ink in BN copy). Concerning irregularities in provincial elections. Harpaz (1981), n° 90, pp.197-199.

D344 'Des droits des présidens dans les collèges électoraux', *Le Courrier français*, n° 295, 22 octobre 1822, p.2.
('B. Constant' in pen and ink in BN copy). Harpaz (1981), n° 91, pp.200-201.

D345 *Incipit*: 'On a beaucoup écrit sur la sainte-alliance', *Le Courrier français*, n° 301, 28 octobre 1822, pp.2-3.
('B. Constant' in pen and ink in BN copy). Review of J.-A. Mahul, *De la Sainte-alliance et du prochain congrès*, Paris, 1822. Harpaz (1981), n° 92, pp.202-205.

D346 *Incipit*: 'L'année 1822 a été remarquable', *Le Courrier français*, n° 353, 19 décembre 1822, p.3.
('B. Constant' in pen and ink in BN copy). On Karl-August von Hardenberg (died on 26 November 1822). Harpaz (1981), n° 103, pp.261-263.

D347   *Incipit*: 'Nous nous sommes arrêtés', *Le Courrier français*, n° 358, 24 décembre 1822, p.4.

('B. Constant' in pen and ink in BN copy). On Hardenberg. Harpaz (1981), n° 105, pp.268-270.

1823

D348   *Incipit*: 'Personne ne peut avoir oublié', *Le Courrier français*, n° 2, 2 janvier 1823, pp.3-4.

('B. Constant' in pen and ink in BN copy). On Hardenberg. Harpaz (1981), n° 108, pp.275-278.

D349   *Incipit*: 'Il y a des argumens de position', *Le Courrier français*, n° 27, 27 janvier 1823, p.2.

('B. Constant' in pen and ink in BN copy). Concerning the support of the right-wing press of war against Spain. Harpaz (1981), n° 110, pp.281-282.

D350   *Incipit*: '*La Quotidienne*' essayait hier le raisonnement', *Le Courrier français*, n° 71, 12 mars 1823, p.3.

('B. Constant' in pen and ink in BN copy). Concerning the exclusion of Manuel from the Chambre des députés. Harpaz (1981), n° 113, pp.309-310.

D351   'Au rédacteur', *Le Courrier français*, n° 74, 15 mars 1823, pp.2-3.

('B. Constant' in pen and ink in BN copy). On the same topic as preceding article. Harpaz (1981), n° 114, pp.311-313.

D352   *Incipit*: 'La *Gazette de France* s'épuise en raisonnement', *Le Courrier français*, n° 78, 19 mars 1823, p.2.

('B. Constant' in pen and ink in BN copy). Reply to the *Gazette de France* on passive obedience. Harpaz (1981), n° 115, pp.314-315.

D353   *Incipit*: 'Il y a des naïvetés précieuses', *Le Courrier français*, n° 153, 2 juin 1823, p.3.

('B. Constant' in pen and ink in BN copy). Note on an article in *Le Drapeau blanc* referring to reactions to foreign invasions. Harpaz (1981), n° 116, p.316.

D354   'Fragment d'un Catéchisme constitutionnel', *Le Courrier français*, n° 158, 7 juin 1823, p.4.

('B. Constant' in pen and ink in BN copy). Harpaz (1981), n° 117, 317-318.

D355   'Logique et arithmétique tirées de l'*Etoile* et du *Journal des débats*', *Le Courrier français*, n° 161, 10 juin 1823, p.3.

('B. Constant' in pen and ink in BN copy). Harpaz (1981), n° 118, p.319.

D356   *Incipit*: 'Des officiers de la 10ᵉ division', *Le Courrier français*, n° 163, 12 juin 1823, pp.3-4.

('B. Constant' in pen and ink in BN copy). On reporting of the war in Spain in

Le Drapeau blanc and *La Quotidienne*. Harpaz (1981), n° 119, p.320.

D357 'Prix de littérature et de politique', *Le Courrier français*, n° 195, 14 juillet 1823, pp.2-3.
('B. Constant' in pen and ink in BN copy). Ironic account of a competition for an essay on the advantages of absolutism and disadvantages of representative government. Harpaz (1981), n° 120, pp.321-323.

D358 *Incipit*: 'Hier *La Quotidienne* insultait M. le duc de Larochefoucault-Liancourt', *Le Courrier français*, n° 200, 19 juillet 1823, p.2.
('B. Constant' in pen and ink in BN copy). Reply to *La Quotidienne* and *Le Drapeau blanc*. Harpaz (1981), n° 121, p.324.

D359 *Incipit*: 'Des journaux français ont rapporté que Bessières a écrit', *Le Courrier français*, n° 201, 20 juillet 1823, p.3.
('B. Constant' in pen and ink in BN copy). Concerning arbitrary decisions taken by General Bessières in Spain. Harpaz (1981), n° 122, pp.325-326.

D360 *Incipit*: '*La Quotidienne* ne recule pas', *Le Courrier français*, n° 204, 23 juillet 1823, p.2.
('B. Constant' in pen and ink in BN copy). On the same topic as the preceding article. Harpaz (1981), n° 123, p.327.

D361 'A M. le Rédacteur', *Le Courrier français*, n° 258, 15 septembre 1823, p.2.
('B. Constant' in pen and ink in BN copy). Letter signed 'Un abonné'. Concerning the Spanish royalists. Harpaz (1981), n° 124, pp.328-330.

D362 *Incipit*: 'Balaam voulait maudire et il bénissait', *Le Courrier français*, n° 277, 4 octobre 1823, p.2.
('B. Constant' in pen and ink in BN copy). Concerning reporting of Spanish affaires in *L'Oriflamme* and other newspapers. Harpaz (1981), n° 125, p.331.

D363 *Incipit*: 'Depuis la loi du 29 juin 1820', *Le Courrier français*, n° 365, 31 décembre 1823, p.2.
Address to electors. Cited by Harpaz (1981), n° 127, pp.333-334.

1824

D364 'A M. le Rédacteur', *Le Courrier français*, n° 5, 5 janvier 1824, p.2.
('B. Constant' in pen and ink in BN copy). Concerning the laws on printing. Harpaz (1981), n° 128, pp.335-336.

D364a 'Assemblées représentatives', *Encyclopédie moderne, ou Dictionnaire abrégé des sciences, des belles-lettres et des arts*, III (1824).
Published *ca.* April 1824. *Signed*: 'Benjamin Constant'.

D365 'A M. le Rédacteur', *Le Constitutionnel*, 24 juin 1824. *Signed*: 'Benjamin Constant'.

On *De la religion* vol. I. Harpaz (1981), n° 131, pp.342-346.

D366   'A M. le Rédacteur', *Le Constitutionnel*, 2 juillet 1824. *Signed*: 'Benjamin Constant'.
Concerning Spanish politics. Harpaz (1981), n° 132, p.347.

D367   'M. B. Constant's Work on Religion. To the Director of the European Review', *European Review*, July 1824, pp.322-324.
Signed: 'Benjamin Constant'. Translation of the article published in the *Revue européenne*, August 1824 (see below).

D368   'De la religion, par M. Benjamin Constant', *Revue européenne*, août 1824, pp.306-308.
Signed: 'Benjamin Constant'. C.P. Courtney, *French Studies*, XXIX (1975), 144-146.

1825

D368a   Lettre au Président de la Chambre des députés, *Le Moniteur universel*, 1er janvier 1825, p.4.
Dated '29 décembre 1824' and signed 'Benjamin Constant'.

D369   *Extrait de l'Encyclopédie moderne. Christianisme*, par M. Benjamin Constant, [Paris]: impr. Moreau, [1825].
Dépôt légal: 26 April 1825. C.59a. *Checklist* A59/1.

D370   'Christianisme. Causes humaines qui, indépendamment de sa source divine, ont concouru à son établissement', *Le Globe*, n° 104, 7 mai 1825, pp.521-523.
The first of three articles; see below.

D371   'Christianisme ... Par M. Benjamin Constant. (IIᵉ article)', *Le Globe*, n° 105, 10 mai 1825, pp.530-531.
Continued below.

D372   'Christianisme ... Par M. Benjamin Constant (IIIᵉ et dernier article)', *Le Globe*, n° 106, 12 mai 1825, pp.533-535.
Reprinted from article in *L'Encyclopédie moderne*, 26 avril 1825. See C.59a. *Checklist* A59/1.

D373   'A M. le Rédacteur', *Le Courrier français*, n° 233, 21 août 1825, p.3.
('B. Constant' in pen and ink in BN copy). On customs and the book trade.

D374   *Extrait de l'Encyclopédie moderne. Christianisme*. Par. [*sic*] M. Benjamin-Constant, [Paris]: impr. Moreau, [1825].
Dépôt légal: 13 September 1825. C.59b. *Checklist* A59/2.

D375   'A M. le Rédacteur', *Le Courrier français*, n° 283, 10 octobre 1825, p.2.

Signed: 'Le cousin d'un des préposés réprimandés'. ('B. Constant' in pen and ink in BN copy). On the affaire Joly.

D375a *Incipit*: 'Nous trouvons dans un journal littéraire la lettre suivante [de Benjamin Constant]', *Journal du Commerce*, n° 2172, 7 décembre 1825, p.2.
Concerning a review in *Le Producteur* of Constant's lecture at the Athénée royal. See also the *Journal du Commerce*, n° 2175, 10 décembre 1825, p.2: reply by A. Cerclet, rédacteur général of *Le Producteur*.

D376 *Coup d'œil sur la tendance générale des esprits dans le dix-neuvième siècle; extrait du discours prononcé par M. Benjamin Constant, dans la séance d'ouverture de l'Athénée royal de Paris, le 3 décembre 1825*, [Paris]: impr. Rignoux, [1825]. (*Revue encyclopédique*, 84ᵉ cahier, T. XXVIII).
Dépôt légal: 23 December 1825. C.61a. *Checklist* A61/1.

1826

D377 'A M. le Rédacteur,' *Le Courrier français*, n° 58, 27 février 1826, pp.1-2.
Letter dated 'Paris, 26 février 1826' and signed 'Benjamin Constant'. Affair of the *Journal du Commerce*.

D377a *'L'Industrie et la morale considérées dans leur rapport avec la liberté*; par Charles-Barthélemi Dunoyer', *Revue encyclopédique*, XXIX (février 1826), 416-435.
Signed: 'B-n C.' Reprinted in *Mélanges* (1829).

D378 'A M. le rédacteur ', *Le Constitutionnel*, 22 mai 1826, p.2.
Letter dated 'Paris, 21 mai 1826' and signed 'Benjamin Constant'. On the consistency of his ideas on the freedom of the press from *Des réactions politiques* to the present.

D379 *Encyclopédie progressive. Religion*, [Paris]: impr. Pinard, [1826].
Signed: 'Benjamin Constant'. Offprint from the *Encyclopédie progressive*, 1ᵉʳᵉ livraison. Dépôt légal: 26 June 1826. C.62a. *Checklist* A62/1. Reprinted in *Mélanges* (1829).

D380 [Réponse aux électeurs], *Le Courrier français*, n° 195, 14 juillet 1826, pp.2-3.
Signed: 'Casimir Périer. Benjamin Constant'.

D381 *Incipit*: 'L'Etoile d'hier, 7 août', *Le Courrier français*, n° 220, 8 août 1826, p.2.
('B. Constant' in pen and ink in BN copy). Concerning reporting of Spanish affairs in *L'Etoile*.

D382 'De l'intervention de la France dans les affaires de Portugal', *Le Courrier français*, n° 233, 21 août 1826, p.2.

('B. Constant' in pen and ink in BN copy).

D383   'A Monsieur le Rédacteur', *Le Courrier français*, n° 258, 15 septembre 1826, p.2.
Signed: 'Benjamin Constant'. On protestantism.

1827

D383a   [A un étudiant de médecine], *L'Indépendant*, n° 220, 29 mai 1827, p.3.
Signed: 'Benjamin Constant'.

D384   'A M. le rédacteur', *Le Courrier français*, n° 181, 30 juin 1827, p.2.
Signed: 'Benjamin Constant'. Concerning the publication of unauthorised collections of his speeches.

D384a   Réponse de l'honorable M. Benjamin Constant au toast qui lui a été porté, au banquet qu'on lui a offert à son passage à Strasbourg, le 2 octobre dernier, *Courrier du Haut-Rhin*, 11 novembre 1827.

D384b   Discours, Colmar, 16 octobre 1827, *Courrier du Haut-Rhin*, 13 novembre 1827.

D385   Souscription. Recueil des discours de M. Benjamin Constant à la chambre des députés. *Le Courrier français*, n° 338, 4 décembre 1827, p.4.
See C.132. *Checklist* E2.

D386   'A M. le rédacteur', *Le Courrier français*, n° 338, 4 décembre 1827, p.3.
Signed: 'Benjamin Constant'. Concerning his success in the elections (Paris and Strasbourg).

1828

D387   'A M. le rédacteur', *Le Courrier français*, n° 175, 23 juin 1828, p.2.
Letter dated 'Paris, 22 juin 1828' and signed: 'Benjamin Constant'. On the petition of Corty (Wasselonne, Bas-Rhin).

D388   'A M. le Rédacteur', *Le Courrier français*, n° 200, 18 juillet 1828, p.2.
Dated 'Paris, 17 juillet 1828' and signed 'Benjamin Constant'. Concerning reporting in *Le Courrier français*, of the parlementary debate of 16 July.

D389   'Vote important dans la séance de ce jour', *Le Courrier français*, n° 211, 29 juillet 1828, p.1.
('Benjamin Constant' in pen and ink in BN copy). The article is headed: 'Paris, 28 Juillet'.

D390   'A M. le rédacteur', *Le Courrier français*, n° 224, 11 août 1828, p.2.
Letter dated 'Paris, le 9 août 1828' and signed 'Benjamin Constant'. Reply to the *Gazette de France* concerning his relations with *Le Courrier français*.

D391 'A M. le Rédacteur', *Le Courrier français*, n°s 361-362, 26-27 décembre 1828, pp.1-2.
Signed: 'Benjamin Constant'. Reply to an article in the *Journal des débats* and in defence of liberal principles.

D392 'A M. le Rédacteur', *Le Courrier français*, n° 366, 31 décembre 1828, pp.1-2.
Signed: 'Benjamin Constant'. On the constitutional crisis in France. Continued below, item D394.

D392a 'Une victoire sur la conscience. Fragment', *Annales romantiques*, 1827-1828, 1828, pp.209-210.
Extrait from preface to *Adolphe* (1824).

1829

D393 'A M. le Rédacteur', *Le Courrier français*, n° 1, 1er janvier 1829, pp.2-3.
Letter, undated, signed 'Benjamin Constant'. On Bolivar.

D394 'A M. le Rédacteur', *Le Courrier français*, n° 1, 1er janvier 1829, pp.3-4.
Signed: 'Benjamin Constant'. Continuation of article of 31 December.

D395 'A M. le Rédacteur', *Le Courrier français*, n° 5, 5 janvier 1829, pp.1-2.
Letter dated 'Paris, 4 janvier' and signed 'Benjamin Constant'. Defence of parliamentary government.

D396 'A M. le Rédacteur', *Le Courrier français* n° 11, 11 janvier 1829, p.2.
Letter dated 'Paris, 10 janvier 1829' and signed 'Benjamin Constant'. On the role of a free press, particularly newspapers.

D397 'A M. le Rédacteur', *Le Courrier français*, n° 15, 15 janvier 1829, pp.1-2.
Letter, dated 'Paris, 4 janvier 1829' and signed 'Benjamin Constant'. On Bolivar.

D398 'A M. le Rédacteur', *Le Courrier français*, n° 17, 17 janvier 1829, pp.2-3.
Letter, undated, signed 'Benjamin Constant'. On Bolivar.

D399 'A M. le Rédacteur', *Le Courrier français*, n° 20, 20 janvier 1829, pp.1-2.
Letter, dated 'Paris, 19 janvier' and signed 'Benjamin Constant'. On the decline of liberty in France.

D400 'Comment le ministère aura-t-il la majorité dans la Chambre des députés?', *Le Courrier français*, n° 27, 27 janvier 1829, pp.1-2.
('Benjamin Constant' in pen and ink in BN copy).

D401 'De la répartition des voix part dans la Chambre', *Le Courrier français*, n° 31, 31 janvier 1829, pp.1-2.
('Benjamin Constant' in pen and ink in BN copy).

D402 'A M. le Rédacteur', *Le Courrier français*, n° 33, 2 février 1829, p.2.
Letter, dated 'Paris, 1ᵉʳ février', unsigned. ('Benjamin Constant' in pen and ink in BN copy).

D403 'Réponse à la *Quotidienne* sur M. Daunou', *Le Courrier français*, n° 37, 6 février 1829, p.2.
('Bⁱⁿ Constant' in pen and ink in BN copy).

D404 'A M. Kératry, député de la Vendée', *Le Courrier français*, n° 39, 8 février 1829, p.3.
Letter, dated 'Paris ce 7 février 1829' and signed 'Benjamin Constant'. On Montbel and the *affaire* Béranger.

D405 'De *la Quotidienne* et du général Saldanha', *Le Courrier français*, n° 40, 9 février 1829, pp.1-2.
('Benjamin Constant' in pen and ink in BN copy).

D406 'A M. le Rédacteur', *Le Courrier français*, n° 46, 15 février 1829, p.3.
Letter, dated 'Paris, le 14 février 1829' and signed 'Benjamin Constant'. On Audry de Puiraveau.

D407 *Incipit*: 'Un correspondant de la *Gazette de France*', *Le Courrier français*, n° 54, 23 février 1829, pp.1-2.
('B. Constant' in pen and ink in BN copy). On Labbey de Pompierres' criticisms of the ministers.

D408 'De la prétendue scission dont les journaux parlent', *Le Courrier français*, n° 57, 26 février 1829, pp.1-2.
Signed: 'Benjamin Constant'.

D409 'De la liberté de la presse suivant les journaux ministériels', *Le Courrier français*, n° 64, 5 mars 1829, p.1.
('B. Constant' in pen and ink in BN copy).

D410 'A M. le Rédacteur', *Le Courrier français*, n° 71, 12 mars 1829, p.1.
Signed: 'Benjamin Constant'. On the constitutional crisis and party politics.

D411 'De la Séance de ce jour [19 mars 1829]', *Le Courrier français*, n° 79, 20 mars 1829, p.1.
('Benjamin Constant' in pen and ink in BN copy).

D412 'Déclaration de guerre du ministère contre la majorité de la Chambre', *Le Courrier français*, n° 84, 25 mars 1829, pp.1-2.
('Benjamin Constant' in pen and ink in BN copy).

D413 'Des pétitions', *Le Courrier français*, n° 96, 6 avril 1829, p.1.
('Benjamin Constant' in pen and ink in BN copy).

D414 'A M. le Rédacteur', *Le Courrier français*, n° 103, 13 avril 1829, pp.1-2.
Letter, dated 'Paris, 12 avril' and signed 'Benjamin Constant'. On changes in the electoral laws.

D415 'Douleurs de certains journaux à l'occasion de la loi des postes', *Le Courrier français*, n° 105, 15 avril 1829, p.1.
('Benjamin Constant' in pen and ink in BN copy).

D416 'Du déficit sur les produits du trimestre', *Le Courrier français*, n° 112, 22 avril 1829, pp.1-2.
Signed: 'Benjamin Constant'.

D417 'De l'extension de l'amendement de M. Sappey aux pensions au second et au troisième degré', *Le Courrier français*, n° 113, 23 avril 1829, p.1.
('B. Constant' in pen and ink in BN copy).

D418 'A M. le Rédacteur', *Le Courrier français*, n° 117, 27 avril 1829, p.1.
Letter, dated 'Paris 26 avril' and signed 'Benjamin Constant'. On the short-comings of the administration.

D419 'De la terreur qu'inspire aux journaux contre-révolutionnaires la possibilité d'une dissolution de la Chambre', *Le Courrier français*, n° 119, 29 avril 1829, pp.1-2.
('Benjamin Constant' in pen and ink in BN copy).

D420 *Incipit*: 'Les feuilles de la faction continuent leurs clameurs: continuons nos réponses', *Le Courrier français*, n° 121, 1er mai 1829, p.1.
('Benjamin Constant' in pen and ink in BN copy).

D421 *Incipit*: 'La commission du budget a nommé aujourd'hui', *Le Courrier français*, n° 122, 2 mai 1829, p.2.
('Benjamin Constant' in pen and ink in BN copy).

D422 'Coup d'œil sur la position actuelle', *Le Courrier français*, n° 127, 7 mai 1829, pp.1-2.
Signed: 'D.P.' By Constant; see below, D427.

D423 'A M. le Rédacteur', *Le Courrier français*, n° 128, 8 mai 1829, p.1.
Letter, undated, signed 'Benjamin Constant'. On the affaire Leleux and the measures taken by Bourdeau, of the department of Justice.

D424 'A M. le Rédacteur', *Le Courrier français*, n° 129. 9 mai 1829, pp.1-2.
Letter, undated, signed 'Benjamin Constant'. Reply to attacks on liberals by 'counter-revolutionary' newspapers.

D425 'De la responsabilité des ministres relativement aux lois adoptées', *Le Courrier français*, n° 133, 13 mai 1829, p.2.

Signed: 'Benjamin Constant'.

D426   'A M. le Rédacteur', *Le Courrier français*, n° 135, 15 mai 1829, p.1.
Signed: 'Benjamin Constant'. On the responsibility of ministers.

D427   'A M. le Rédacteur', *Le Courrier français*, n° 139, 19 mai 1829, p.1.
Letter, undated, signed 'Benjamin Constant'. Reply to article of 18 May in *Le Courrier français* concerning Constant's article of 7 May in the same newspaper.

D428   *Incipit*: '*Le Messager des Chambres* se plaint', *Le Courrier français*, n° 141, 21 mai 1829, p.1.
('Benjamin Constant' in pen and ink in BN copy). Comparison of the administrations of 1827 and 1829.

D429   *Incipit*: 'Le journal ministériel continue', *Le Courrier français*, n° 143, 23 mai 1829, p.1.
On ministerial corruption. ('B. Constant' in pen and ink in BN copy).

D430   'A M. le Rédacteur', *Le Courrier français*, n° 149, 29 mai 1829, p.1.
Letter, undated, signed 'Benjamin Constant'. On parliamentary procedure regarding the presentation of petitions.

D431   [Two letters by 'le Comte d' ...'], *Le Courrier français*, n° 152, 1er juin 1829, pp.1-2.
('Benj. Constant' in pen and ink in BN copy). Ironic account of the achievements of the administration.

D432   'A M. le Rédacteur', *Le Courrier français*, n° 158, 7 juin 1829, p.1.
Letter, dated 'Paris, 5 mai [*sic*] 1829' and signed 'Benjamin Constant'. On the deletion in published reports of certain passages of speeches on the budget.

D433   'A M. le Rédacteur', *Le Courrier français*, n° 161, 10 juin 1829, p.1.
Letter, undated, signed 'Benjamin Constant'. On censorship of works on religion.

D434   'A M. le Rédacteur', *Le Courrier français*, n° 166, 15 juin 1829, p.1.
Letter, undated, signed 'Benjamin Constant'. On religious liberty.

D435   'Inconvéniens d'une éloquence facile', *Le Courrier français*, n° 169, 18 juin 1829, p.1.
('B. Constant' in pen and ink in BN copy). On the speech of the Minister of the Interior.

D436   'A M. le Rédacteur', *Le Courrier français*, n° 173, 22 juin 1829, p.2.
Letter, undated, signed 'Benjamin Constant'. On censorship of books at Strasbourg.

D437   'Sur la séance de ce jour, [23 juin 1829]', *Le Courrier français*, n° 175, 24 juin 1829, pp.1-2.

('Benjamin C⁰' in pen and ink in BN copy).

D438 'A M. le Rédacteur', *Le Courrier français*, n° 186, 5 juillet 1829, pp.1-2.
Letter, undated, signed 'Benjamin Constant'. On religious freedom.

D439 'Des attaques nouvelles qui se préparent contre le gouvernement repré-sentatif', *Le Courrier français*, n° 187, 6 juillet 1829, pp.1-2.
('B. Constant' in pen and ink in BN copy).

D440 'La Quotidienne grand seigneur', *Le Courrier français*, n° 189, 8 juillet 1829, p.1.
('B. Constant' in pen and ink in BN copy). On Chateaubriand.

D441 'A M. le Rédacteur', *Le Courrier français*, n° 194, 13 juillet 1829, p.1.
Letter, undated, signed 'Benjamin Constant'. France and foreign policy.

D442 'A M. le Rédacteur', *Le Courrier français*, n° 198, 17 juillet 1829, pp.1-2.
Letter, undated, signed 'Benjamin Constant'. On the resignation of d'Argenson and Chauvelin.

D443 *Incipit*: 'Je lis dans la *Gazette de France* ...', *Le Courrier français*, n° 203, 22 juillet 1829, p.2.
Signed: 'Benjamin Constant'. On the same topic as the preceding article.

D444 'A M. le Rédacteur', *Le Courrier français*, n° 208, 27 juillet 1829, pp.1-2.
Letter, undated, signed 'Benjamin Constant'. On the policy of the adminis-tration.

D445 'Des excès dans les luttes politiques', *Le Courrier français*, n° 209, 28 juillet 1829, p.1.
('Benjamin C⁰' in pen and ink in BN copy).

D446 [Au rédacteur], *Le Courrier français*, n° 212, 31 juillet 1829, p.2.
Letter signed 'Benjamin Constant. La Ferté-sous-Jouarre, le 29 juillet 1829'.
On the same topic as the previous article.

D447 'A M. le Rédacteur', *Le Courrier français*, n° 219, 7 août 1829, pp.1-2.
Letter dated 'Lunéville, 2 août 1829' and signed 'Benjamin Constant'. On divisions within the opposition.

D448 'A M. le Rédacteur', *Le Courrier français*, n° 279, 6 octobre 1829, p.3.
Letter, undated, signed 'Un abonné'. ('B. Constant' in pen and ink in BN copy).
On the expulsion of foreigners from France.

D449 'A M. le Rédacteur', *Le Courrier français*, n° 279, 24 octobre 1829, pp.1-2.
Letter, undated, signed 'Benjamin Constant'. Defence of the opposition against the views of the ministry.

D450 'Réflexions sur la tragédie à l'occasion d'une tragédie allemande de M. Robert, intitulée *Du pouvoir des préjugés, premier article*', *Revue de Paris*, VII (octobre 1829), pp.5-21.
Signed: 'Benjamin Constant'.

D451 'Réflexions sur la tragédie ... deuxième et dernier article', *Revue de Paris*, VII (octobre 1829), pp.126-140.
Signed: 'Benjamin Constant'.

D452 'A. M. le Rédacteur', *Le Courrier français*, n° 309, 5 novembre 1829, pp.1-2.
Letter, undated, signed 'Benjamin Constant'. Reply to *Gazette de France* and other newspapers on various issues, including his alleged participation in 18 Fructidor.

D453 'La Quotidienne prêchant pour les jeux', *Le Courrier français*, n° 355, 21 décembre 1829, p.1.
('Benjamin Constant' in pen and ink in BN copy).

D454 'A M. le Rédacteur', *Le Courrier français*, n° 357, 23 décembre 1829, p.1.
Letter, undated, signed 'B. Constant'. On the affaire of *La France méridionale*.

D455 'Quelle conduite doit tenir la Chambre à la prochaine session?', *Le Courrier français*, n°ˢ 360-361, 26-27 décembre 1829, p.1.
Signed: 'Benjamin Constant'.

D456 'Quelle conduite doit tenir la Chambre à la prochaine session?', *Le Courrier français*, n° 363, 29 décembre 1829, pp.1-2.
Signed: 'Benjamin Constant'.

1830

D457 'A M. le Rédacteur', *Le Courrier français*, n° 1, 1ᵉʳ janvier 1830, pp.1-2.
Letter signed 'Benjamin Constant'. On the same topic as the previous article.

D458 'Un dernier mot sur le refus du budget', *Le Courrier français*, n° 5, 5 janvier 1830, pp.1-2.
Signed: 'Benjamin Constant'.

D459 'A M. le Rédacteur', *Le Courrier français*, n° 7, 7 janvier 1830, p.2.
Letter, undated, signed 'Un député signataire d'une association contre le paiement des impôts illégaux'. ('Benjamin Constant' in pen and ink in BN copy).

D460 'Vertige des journaux ministériels', *Le Courrier français*, n° 12, 12 janvier 1830, pp.2-3.
('Benjamin Constant' in pen and ink in BN copy).

D461 'De la prérogative royale', *Le Courrier français*, n° 15, 15 janvier 1830, p.2.
Signed: 'Benjamin Constant'.

D462 'Nouveaux axiomes de politique ministérielle', *Le Courrier français*, n° 16, 16 janvier 1830, p.1.
('Benj. Const.' in pen and ink in BN copy).

D463 *Incipit*: 'En annonçant la correspondance de Garrick', *Le Courrier français*, n° 16, 16 janvier 1830, p.2.
('Benj. Constant' in pen and ink in BN copy). Brief reference to Junius.

D464 'Seconde lettre sur la prérogative royale', *Le Courrier français*, n° 18, 18 janvier 1830, pp.1-2.
Signed: 'Benjamin Constant'.

D465 'De l'art. 14 et de la fausse interprétation qu'on lui a donnée', *Le Courrier français*, n° 21, 21 janvier 1830, pp.1-2.
Signed: 'Benjamin Constant'.

D466 'De la prérogative royale suivant la Charte', *Le Courrier français*, n° 31, 31 janvier 1830, p.2.
Signed: 'Benjamin Constant'.

D467 'Dernière lettre sur la prérogative suivant la Charte et sur l'inviolabilité du serment des rois', *Le Courrier français*, n° 44, 13 février 1830, p.2.
Signed: 'Benjamin Constant'.

D468 'A M. le Rédacteur', *Le Courrier français*, n° 48, 17 février 1830, pp.2-3.
Signed: 'Benjamin Constant'. Defence of opposition députés against charges made by ministerial newspapers.

D469 'A M. le Rédacteur', *Le Courrier français*, n° 52, 21 février 1830, p.2.
Letter, undated, signed 'Benjamin Constant'. On journalism and the freedom of the press.

D470 'Prévisions prouvées par la *Quotidienne*', *Le Courrier français*, n° 55, 22 février 1830, p.2.
('B. Constant' in pen and ink in BN copy).

D471 'Souvenirs historiques à l'occasion de l'ouvrage de M. Bignon. Première lettre', *Revue de Paris*, XI (février 1830), pp.115-125.
Signed: 'Benjamin Constant'. Continued below, items D507-D508.

D472 'Appels à la dictature inspirés par le ministère', *Le Courrier français*, n° 66, 7 mars 1830, p.2.
('B. Constant' in pen and ink in BN copy).

D473 'A M. le Rédacteur', *Le Courrier français*, n° 78, 19 mars 1830, pp.2-3.
Signed: 'Benjamin Constant'. On the political crisis in France.

D474 'A M. le Rédacteur', *Le Courrier français*, n° 81, 22 mars 1830, pp.1-2.
Letter, undated, signed 'Benjamin Constant'. On the same topic as the preceding article.

D475 'A M. le Rédacteur', *Le Courrier français*, n° 82, 23 mars 1830, p.2.
Signed: 'Paris, ce 22 mars 1830. Benjamin Constant'. Reply to *La Quotidienne* concerning allegations that he had not voted for the *Adresse au Roi*.

D476 'Bruits répandus par la faction des absolutistes', *Le Courrier français*, n° 84, 25 mars 1830, pp.1-2.
('Benjamin C^t' in pen and ink in BN copy).

D476a 'Aristophane', *Revue de Paris*, XV, [mars] 1830, pp.239-46. *Signed*: 'Benjamin Constant'.

D477 'Jugement de la *Gazette* sur le jugement prononcé contre elle', *Le Courrier français*, n° 95, 5 avril 1830, pp.1-2.
('B. Constant' in pen and ink in BN copy).

D478 'Nécessité de connaître les députés qui ont voté l'adresse', *Le Courrier français*, n° 101, 11 avril 1830, pp.1-2.
('B. Constant' in pen and ink in BN copy).

D479 'Aptitude des royalistes, suivant la *Quotidienne*', *Le Courrier français*, n° 104, 14 avril 1830, p.2.
('B. Constant' in pen and ink in BN copy).

D480 'Plan du ministère en cas de conservation de la Chambre actuelle', *Le Courrier français*, n° 106, 16 avril 1830, p.2.
('B. Constant' in pen and ink in BN copy).

D481 'Isolement progressif du ministère', *Le Courrier français*, n° 108, 18 avril 1830, p.2.
('Benjamin Constant' [deleted?] in pen and ink in BN copy).

D482 'De la liberté des élections suivant le ministère', *Le Courrier français*, n° 112, 22 avril 1830, p.2. *Signed*: 'Benjamin Constant'.

D483 'Fausse interprétation de l'arrêt de la Chambre des mises en accusation de la Cour royale', *Le Courrier français*, n° 114, 24 avril 1830, p.1.
('B. Constant' in pen and ink in BN copy).

D484 'A M. le Rédacteur', *Le Courrier français*, n° 115, 25 avril 1830, p.2.
Letter, undated, signed 'Benjamin Constant'. On the 'machiavellian' policy of the supporters of the ministry.

D485 'A M. le rédacteur', *Le Courrier français*, n° 121, 1er mai 1830.
Letter, undated, signed 'Benjamin Constant'. On the suspension of the constitution.

D486 'A M. le rédacteur', *Le Courrier français*, n° 127, 7 mai 1830, pp.1-2.
Letter, undated, signed 'Benjamin Constant'. On the same topic as the preceding article.

D487 'De la palinodie de la *Gazette*', *Le Courrier français*, n° 133, 13 mai 1830, pp.1-2.
('B. Constant' in pen and ink in BN copy). On the same topic as the preceding article.

D488 'A M. le Rédacteur', *Le Courrier français*, n° 137, 17 mai 1830, pp.1-2.
Letter, undated, signed 'Benjamin Constant'. On accusations made by the *Gazette de France* against liberals.

D489 'A M. le rédacteur', *Le Courrier français*, n° 149, 29 mai 1830, p.3.
Letter, undated, signed 'Benjamin Constant'. Announces his election for Strasbourg and withdrawal from other candidatures.

D490 'A M. le Rédacteur', *Le Courrier français*, n° 150, 30 mai 1830, p.2.
Letter, dated 'Paris, ce 29 mai 1830' and signed 'Benjamin Constant'. On accusations made by the *Gazette de France* that the liberals are responsible for civil disorder.

D491 'Titres d'un candidat ministériel', *Le Courrier français*, n° 158, 7 juin 1830, p.2.
('B. Constant' in pen and ink in BN copy).

D492 'De la prétendue conspiration d'Orléans', *Le Courrier français*, n° 160, 9 juin 1830, pp.1-2.
('B. Constant' in pen and ink in BN copy).

D493 'Des bulletins ouverts ou fermés suivant la *Gazette de France*', *Le Courrier français*, n° 164, 13 juin 1830, p.1.
('Benjamin C' in pen and ink in BN copy).

D494 'Manœuvres électorales', *Le Courrier français*, n° 167, 16 juin 1830, p.1.
('B. Constant' in pen and ink in BN copy).

D495 'De la circulaire de M. Peyronnet', *Le Courrier français*, n° 169, 18 juin 1830, p.1.
('B. Constant' in pen and ink in BN copy).

D496 *Incipit*: 'La Quotidienne recherche avec curiosité', *Le Courrier français*, n° 170, 19 juin 1830, p.2.

('B. Constant' in pen and ink in BN copy). Short note on article in *La Quotidienne*.

D497   'A M. le rédacteur', *Le Courrier français*, n° 171, 20 juin 1830, pp.3-4.
Letter, undated, signed 'Benjamin Constant'. On the *Nouvelle Revue germanique*.

D498   'Des doctrines opposées du Journal Villèle et du journal Peyronnet, et de l'embarras de ce dernier', *Le Courrier français*, n° 180, 29 juin 1830, pp.2-3.
('B. Constant' in pen and ink in BN copy).

D499   'Encore un mot sur les événemens de Montauban', *Le Courrier français*, n° 186, 5 juillet 1830, pp.1-2.
('B. Constant' in pen and ink in BN copy).

D500   'Nouvelles propositions des journaux ministériels pour le changement de la loi des élections', *Le Courrier français* n°191, 10 juillet 1830, pp.1-2.
('B. Constant' in pen and ink in BN copy).

D501   'De l'intervention populaire', *Le Courrier français*, n° 196, 15 juillet 1830, p.2.
('B. Constant' in pen and ink in BN copy).

D502   'Des procès de tendance redemandés par l'*Universel*', *Le Courrier français*, n° 197, 16 juillet 1830, p.2.
('B.C^t' in pen and ink in BN copy).

D503   'Du silence de l'*Universel*', *Le Courrier français*, n° 199, 18 juillet 1830, p.2.
('B. Constant' in pen and ink in BN copy).

D504   'Nouvelle imposture de l'*Universel*', *Le Courrier français*, n° 201, 20 juillet 1830,
('B. Constant' in pen and ink in BN copy).

D505   *Incipit*: 'Il y a des falsifications', *Le Courrier français*, n° 202, 21 juillet 1830, p.2.
('B. Constant' in pen and ink in BN copy). On *L'Universel*.

D506   'Des causes assignées au résultat des élections', *Le Courrier français*, n° 205, 24 juillet 1830, pp.1-2.
('B. Constant' in pen and ink in BN copy).

D507   'Souvenirs historiques. Deuxième lettre', *Revue de Paris*, XVI (juillet 1830), pp.102-112.
Signed: 'Benjamin Constant'.

D508   'Souvenirs historiques. Troisième lettre', *Revue de Paris*, XVI (juillet 1830), pp.221-233.
Signed: 'Benjamin Constant'.

D509 'A M. le Rédacteur', *Le Courrier français*, n° 219, 7 août 1830, p.4.
Letter signed 'B. Constant'. Concerning subscription of 400 francs by Benjamin and Charlotte de Constant.

D510 'Sur deux arrestations de la *Quotidienne*', *Le Courrier français*, n° 292, 19 octobre 1830, p.1.
('B. Constant' in pen and ink in BN copy).

D511 'Avis à la *Quotidienne* et aux Carlistes', *Le Courrier français*, n° 295, 22 octobre 1830, pp.1-2.
('B. Constant' in pen and ink in BN copy).

D512 'A M. le Rédacteur', *Le Courrier français*, n° 295, 22 octobre 1830.
Letter, undated, signed 'Benjamin-Constant'. On elections in the Var.

D513 'Funerailles de Benjamin Constant', *Le Courrier français*, n° 346, 12 décembre 1830, pp.2-3.
This supernumerary item includes letters from Charlotte de Constant to the President of the Conseil des ministres and Préfet de la Seine.

E Collections and selections

E1 Cours de politique constitutionnelle

1817 Cours de politique constitutionnelle: Prospectus.

Cours de politique constitutionnelle, ou collection complète des ouvrages publiés par M. Benjamin de Constant, sur le gouvernement représentatif et la constitution actuelle de la France. Prospectus. 8° pp.8. Impr. Doublet, [Paris]. Dated at end: 'Paris, ce 9 octobre 1817'.

The Prospectus announces two octavo volumes. 'Le premier volume sera mis en vente à l'ouverture des Chambres. Le second paraîtra à la fin du mois de novembre prochain.' Subscriptions received by Plancher and Delaunay (Paris).

Copy: BN. (C.131).

E1/1 1818 [=1817]   (1) Collection complète des ouvrages publiés sur le gouvernement représentatif et la constitution actuelle de la France, formant une espèce de Cours de politique constitutionnelle; par M. Benjamin de Constant. Premier volume. Première [Seconde] partie. A Paris, chez P. Plancher … 1818. 8° pp.[iv], xxiv, [ii], xii, [13]-250, [ii], 251-478. Impr. Fain, [Paris].

1818   (2) Collection … Deuxième volume. Troisième [Quatrième] partie de l'ouvrage … 1818. 8° pp.[i], 248, [ii], [249]-492. Impr. Poulet, [Paris].

1819   (3) Collection … Troisième volume. Cinquième [Sixième] partie de l'ouvrage. 1819. 8° pp.264, 155, lii. Impr. (part 6) P. Gueffier, [Paris]; (part 7) Mme Jeunehomme-Crémière, [Paris]. Table analytique by Regnault de Warin.

1820   (4) Collection complète des ouvrages publiés sur le gouvernement représentatif et la constitution actuelle, ou Cours de politique constitutionnelle, par M. Benjamin Constant. Quatrième volume. Septième [Huitième] partie. Paris, Béchet aîné … Rouen, Béchet fils … 1820. 8° pp.274, 307. Impr. J.-L. Chanson, [Paris].

Copies: BCU, BL, BN. (C.131a).

Contents of *Cours de politique constitutionnelle*

Vol. I

Avertissement de l'auteur, pp.[iii]-[iv].

Introduction, pp.[i]-xxiv.

[A11] Réflexions sur les constitutions et les garanties, pp.[i]-xii, [13]-170.

[A17] Additions et notes tirées en partie des Principes de politique et autres ouvrages antérieurs. [171]-420.

[A12] De la liberté des brochures, des pamphlets et des journaux, pp.[421]-474.

Table des matières du premier volume, pp.[475]-478.

Vol. II

[A13] Observations sur le discours prononcé par S.E. le Ministre de l'Intérieur, pp.[1]-51.

[A14] De la responsabilité des ministres, pp.[53]-124.

[A19] De la doctrine politique qui peut réunir les partis en France, pp.[125]-158.

[*MF*] Histoire de la Session de la Chambre des Députés, 1816-1817, pp.[159]-392. [Originally published in *MF* in a series of articles from 4 January to 12 April 1817. Here revised].

[A22] Questions sur la législation actuelle de la presse en France, pp.[393]-492.

Vol. III, Cinquième partie de l'ouvrage
[A23] Des élections de 1817, pp.[3]-48.

[A24] Entretien d'un électeur avec lui-même, pp.[49]-62.

[A26] Réponse de Benjamin Constant aux attaques dirigées contre lui durant les élections, pp.[63]-68.

Lettres à M. Odillon-Barrot sur l'affaire de Wilfred Regnault:

[A28] Ière Lettre, pp.[71]-101.

[A29] IIme Lettre, pp.[103]-190. (Including: *Article de la Quotidienne, Encore un mot sur le procès de W. Regnault, Lettre au rédacteur de la Quotidienne, Lettre au Journal du Commerce, Seconde lettre à la Quotidienne, Dernière réponse adressée au Journal du Commerce* and *Article du Moniteur, du 5 avril [1818]*). The second item is reprinted from *La Minerve française*, I, 6, 16-17 March 1818.

[A30] De l'appel en calomnie de M. le Marquis de Blosseville, pp.[191]-200.

[A33] Lettre à M. Odillon-Barrot sur le procès de Lainé, pp.[201]-210.

[*Minerve*] Exposé de la prétendue conspiration de Lyon en 1817, pp.211-235. [originally published in *La Minerve française*, II, 5, (4-5 June 1818), 209-223; II (6), (10-11 June 1818), 265-269].

[A31] Lettres à M. Charles Durand, pp.[237]-264.

Vol. III, Sixième partie de l'ouvrage
[A32] Des élections de 1818, pp.[3]-58.

[A3] Des réactions politiques, pp.[59]-114.

[A8] Essai sur la Contre révolution d'Angleterre en 1660, pp.[115]-156.

Table du troisième volume, pp.[157].

Table analytique, pp.[i]-lii.

Vol. IV, Septième partie
[A36] Eloge de Sir Samuel Romilly, pp.[5]-74.

[A27] Annales de la session de 1817 à 1818, pp.75-231. (Including, pp.196-231, Du discours de M. de Marchangy ... dans la cause de M. Fiévée).

[A37] De la proposition de changer la loi des élections, pp.232-237.

De la liberté des anciens comparée à celle des modernes, pp.238-274.

Vol. IV, Huitième partie
[*Minerve*] Session des Chambres de 1818 à 1819, pp.[5]-222 [Originally published in a series of articles in *La Minerve française* from 15-16 December 1818 to 25-26 March 1819. Here revised].

[A38] Lettre à MM. les habitants de la Sarthe, pp.223-235.

[B14] Opinion sur la nouvelle législation de la presse, prononcée à la Chambre des Députés le 14 avril 1819, pp.236-267.

[A39] Seconde lettre à MM. les habitants du dep^t de la Sarthe, pp.268-286.

Table du quatrième volume, pp.[287].

Table alphabétique et analytique des matières contenues dans le quatrième volume, pp.[289]-307.

Note: The texts printed in the *Collection* have generally been revised. The pre-1814 texts have been abridged.

E1/2 1820-1833   Collection complète des ouvrage publiés sur le gouvernment représentatif et la constitution actuelle, terminée par une table analytique; ou Cours de politique constitutionnelle; par M. Benjamin Constant, député du département de la Sarthe. Seconde édition. Tome premier [second, troisième]. Paris, chez Pierre Plancher ... 1820. [Tome quatrième ... Paris ... Béchet aîné ... 1820 [=1833]].

Vols I-III are a reissue of item E1/1(1-3) with new preliminaries. Imprint, on verso of half-titles, of Mad. Jeunehomme-Crémière, Paris. Vol. IV is a reprint of item E1/1(4), impr. Mme veuve Dubois-Berthault, Meaux. Volume I not located: title page inferred from those of vols II-III.

Copy: BN (vols II-IV). (C.131b).

E1/3 1836   Cours de politique constitutionnelle, par Benjamin Constant. Nouvelle édition, mise en ordre et précédée d'une introduction, par M. J.-P. Pagès (de l'Arriége). Paris: Didier, 1836. 2 vols, pp.[iv], LXIII, 596, + [iv], 705.

A selection and rearrangement of item E1/1.

Copies: BCU, BL, BN, BPU.

E1/4 1837   Cours de politique constitutionnelle ... Troisième édition par J.-P. Pagès (de l'Ariège). Bruxelles: Société belge de librairie, imprimerie, papeterie, etc., Hauman, Cattoir et Comp^{ie}, 1837. pp.[ii], xxvii, 551.

Copies: A, B, BR.

E1/5a 1861   Cours de politique constitutionnelle; ou collection des ouvrages publiés sur le gouvernement représentatif, par Benjamin Constant, avec une introduction et des notes par M. Edouard Laboulaye. Paris: Guillaumin et Cie, 1861. 2 vols, pp.XLIX, VI, 599 + [IV], 573.

Reviews: Sainte-Beuve, *Le Constitutionnel*, 27 janvier 1862; *Nouveaux Lundis*, Paris: Calmann-Lévy, 1863, I, 411-437. L. Wolowski, *Séances et travaux de l'Académie des sciences morales et politiques*, LX (1862), 105-136.

Copies: BL, BN, BPU, VP.

E1/5b 1872   Cours de politique constitutionnelle ... Deuxième édition ... 1872, 2 vols. pp.[iv], LXIV, VI, [7]-563 + [iv], 572.

Contents:
Avertissement de la présente édition, I, I-II
Avertissement de la première édition, I, II-VI
Introduction, I, VII-LXIV
Principes de politique, I, I-IV, 1-165
Réflexions sur les constitutions et les garanties, I, 167-271
Additions et notes, I, 273-381

De la responsabilité des ministres, I, 383-442
De la liberté des brochures, I, 443-475
Observations sur le discours prononcé par S.E. le Ministre de l'Intérieur, I, 477-504
Questions sur la législation actuelle de la presse en France, I, 505-560
Du discours de M. de Marchangy, II, 1-24
Sur le projet de loi relatif à la police de la presse, (Séance du 13 février 1827), II, 25-40
Sur la responsabilité imposée aux imprimeurs (Séance du 10 mars 1827), II, 41-48
Des effets de la terreur, II, 53-69
Des réactions politiques, II, 71-128
De l'esprit de conquête et de l'usurpation, II, 129-282
De la doctrine politique qui peut réunir tous les partis en France, II, 283-308
Des élections prochaines, II, 309-346
Entretien d'un électeur avec lui-même, II, 347-358
Des élections de 1818, II, 359-394
Lettre à Odilon-Barrot sur l'affaire de Wilfrid Régnault, II, 395-421
Appendix (Encore un mot sur le procès de Wilfrid Regnault), II, 423-434
Lettres à M. Charles Durand sur Nîmes en 1815, II, 435-462
Trois lettres à MM. les habitants de la Sarthe, II, 463-491
Des motifs qui ont dicté le nouveau projet de loi sur les élections, II, 493-535
De la liberté des anciens comparée à celle des modernes, II, 537-560
Copies: B, BN, BPU, C.

E1/6 1874 Œuvres politiques de Benjamin Constant avec introduction, notes et index par Charles Louandre. Paris: Charpentier et Cie, 1874. pp.[iv], XXVIII, 432. Bibliography.
A selection and rearrangement of item E1/1.
Review: Barbey d'Aurevilly, *Le Constitutionnel*, 3 février 1875.
Copies: A, B, BL, VP.

Translations

See also items E4/t1-7.

E1/t1 1820 Curso de política constitucional, escrito por Mr Benjamín Constant, traducido por D. Marcial Antonio López. Madrid: Impr. de la Compañía por su regente don Juan José Sigüenza y Vera, 1820. 3 vols.
(Palau y Dulcet; C. Suppl. Add. 4).

E1/t2 1820 Saggio di costituzione. Prima versione italiana corredeta di note relative alla costituzione spagnuola. [Naples: L. Nobile, 1820].
Translation by L.G.C. Issued in parts in *La Biblioteca costituzionale*. (Information based on *National Union Catalog*.)
Copy: MH. (C.131c).

E1/t3 1821 Curso de política constitucional, escrito por Mr Benjamín Constant, traducido libremente al español por D. Marcial Antonio López.

Burdeos: Imprenta de Lawalle jóven y sobrino ... 1821. 12° 3 vols. pp.xxxiv, [35]-395 + 330 + 405.
Copy: BN. (C.131d).

E1/t4 1823   Curso de política constitucional ... segunda edición. Burdeos ... Lawalle jóven ... 1823. 12°. 3 vols. pp.380 + 323 + 389.
Copies: BN, Bx, DLC. (C.131e).

E1/t5 1825   Curso de política constitucional, por M. Benjamín Constant, nuevamente traducido al castellano, por D. J. C. Pages, intérprete real. Paris, en la Librería de Parmantier; Mégico ... Bossange padre, Antoran y comp. 1825. Impr. A. Coniam, [Paris]. 12° 4 vols.
Copies: BN, Bx, NcD, PPL. (C.131f).

E1/t6 1831   O monarchii konstytucyynéy i rękoymiach publicznych, rzecz wyięta z dzieł Benjamina Constant przekładania Wincentego Niemoiowskiego. W Warszawaie, nakładem właścicieli Kuryera Polskiego, druk. A. Gałęzowskiego i spółki, 1831. 8° 2 vols. pp.[viii], 240, + [iv], 322, [12].
Translation of *Reflexions sur les constitutions* from vol. I of *Cours de politique constitutionnelle* (item E1/1(1)).
Copy: Ww. (C.131g).

E1/t7 1837   Over de Goedsdienstige Vrijheid door Benjamin Constant, in leven staatsraad, lid van de kamer der Afgevaardigen van Frankrijk, enz; uit het Fransch. Te Arnhem bij C. A. Thieme, 1837. pp.[ii] II, 30.
Translation of chap. 23 ('De la liberté religieuse') of Pagès's edition edition of the *Cours de politique constitutionnelle*, 1837 (item E1/4).
Copies: A, H.

E1/t8 1849   Corso di politica costituzionale di Beniamino Constant. Tradotto dal francese sulla terza edizione di Brusselles dall'avv. Vincenzo Galeffi, preceduto da una introduzione di J. P. Pagés [sic] (de l'Arriège). Firenze: Enrico Monni, 1849. 2 vols, pp.[iv], 434 + [iv], 487.
(Cordié 176). Cordié also lists an edition, as above, dated 1850 (probably only on the wrappers) and another in which vol. II is dated 1851 on the wrappers (Cordié 176A, 176B).

E1/t9 1850-1851   Corso ... Tomo I, 1850 ... Tomo II, 1851.
Reissue of the preceding item. (Cordié 176C).

E1/t10 1851   Corso ... seconda edizione ... Tomo II ... 1851 ...
(Cordié 176D).

E1/t11 1862   Az alkotmányos politica tana. Irta Constant Benjamin. Fordította Perlaky Sándor. Pest: Nyomatott Trattner-Károlyinál, 1862. (Lauffer V). pp.206.

Copies: Bp, BpFS.

E1/t12 1890   Biblioteca di scienze politiche, scelta collezione delle piú impor-
tanti opere moderne italiane e straniere di scienze politiche diretta da Attilio
Brunialti, vol. V. Torino: Unione Tipografico-Editrice, 1890. pp.CCXXXIX, 1187.
Includes *Della libertà degli antichi paragonata a quella dei moderni*; translation by
[Pietro Fea], pp.454-469. (Cordié 181).

E1/t13 1943   Benjamín Constant. Principios de política; nota preliminar de
Francisco Ayala. [Buenos Aires:] Editorial Americalee, [1943]. (Los Clásicos
políticos, 7). pp.188.
Translation by Antonio Zozaya of extracts from Laboulaye (item E1/5).
Copy: DCL.

E1/t14 1948   Beniamino Constant. Corso di politica costituzionale. Prima
versione italiana di T. Mascitelli. Introd. di J.-P. Pagès. Napoli: Tipogr. di
Porcelli, 1948.

E1/t15 1968   Benjamín Constant. Curso de política constitucional. Madrid:
Taurus, 1968. (Clásicos de la política, 3). pp.317.
Translation by Francisco Luis de Yturbe.
Copy: MBN.

E2 Speeches

1827   Discours de M. Benjamin Constant: Prospectus.
The Prospectus is described as follows in *Bibliographie de la France*, 4 April 1827:
Souscription pour l'impression de deux volumes contenant les *Discours de M.
Benjamin Constant à la Chambre des députés*, avec un portrait de l'auteur et un *fac
simile* de son écriture. (Prospectus.) In-8° d'une demi-feuille. Impr. d'Everat, à
Paris. Les deux volumes coûteront ... 14-0.

1827   A second Prospectus was published by Pinard, and described as follows
in *Bibliographie de la France*, 9 June 1827:
Souscription aux discours de M. Benjamin Constant a la Chambre des députés.
(Prospectus.) Imp. de Pinard, à Paris – A Paris, chez A. Dupont, rue Vivienne,
n. 16; chez Pinard.
La collection formera deux volumes in-8°. Le premier est promis pour le 1er
juillet; le second en octobre. Prix des deux volumes payables à la réception du
premier ... 14-0.
Copy (second prospectus): Florence, Biblioteca Nazionale Centrale (C. Suppl.
Add. 5).

1827   The Prospectus of an earlier projected edition of Constant's Speeches
has been preserved:
Opinions prononcées dans la Chambre des Députés, durant les sessions de 1818,

1819, 1821, par M. Benjamin Constant, député de la Sarthe, auxquelles il a ajouté des éclaircissemens et des notes historiques, 8° pp.2. Impr. Goetschy, [Paris].

This prospectus announced 2 octavo vols each of 400-500 pages; the first to appear in May, the second in June [1822]. Price of each volume 6 fr. Subscriptions payable to M. Coste, rue Saint-Anne, n° 23.

Copy: BN.

E2/1 1827   (1) Discours de M. Benjamin Constant à la Chambre des Députés. Tome premier. Paris. Ambroise Dupont et Compagnie ... J. Pinard, imprimeur et fondeur ... 1827. 8° pp.vi, 580. Avant-propos dated: 'Paris, ce 9 juillet 1827.' Impr. J. Pinard, [Paris].

1828   (2) Discours ... Tome second ... 1828. 8° pp.[v], 644. Impr. J. Pinard, [Paris]. Frontispiece: engraved portrait of B. Constant signed 'Jacques del. Couché fils sculp.'. Folding facsimile page of autograph manuscript of passage from *De l'esprit de conquête* inserted to follow p.[vi].

Copies: BCU, BL, BN. (C.132a).

E2/2(1-2) 1828   Discours ... 1828.

Collation and contents as in E2/1(1-2). Vol. I is a different setting; Vol. II the same setting as E2/1(2). Both volumes are printed on a heavier paper than for E2/1.

Copies: BCU, BL, BN. (C.132b).

Contents of *Discours*

The information given below is reproduced from the tables of contents at the end of each of the two volumes, with dates being added or corrected where necessary. The texts are reprinted from various sources: from the editions listed above in section B, from *Le Moniteur* and from newspapers.

Vol. I:

1. Sur le projet de loi relatif à la répression des délits de la presse (le 14 avril 1819), pp.1-27.
2. Amendement relatif aux brevets des imprimeurs [le 16 avril 1819], pp.28-31.
3. Article additionnel relatif à l'impression des discours des députés dans les journaux (le 21 avril 1819), pp.32-41.
4. Amendement relatif à la diffamation (le 24 avril 1819), pp.41-53.
5. Sur l'admission de la preuve contre les fonctionnaires publics [le 28 avril 1819], pp.53-61.
6. Sur le cautionnement demandé aux journalistes [le 3 mai 1819], pp.61-78.
7. Sur le cautionnement demandé aux journaux de départemens [le 4 mai 1819], pp.78-80.
8. Amendement relatif au moment où les journaux devront être déposés (le 5 mai 1819), pp.81-87.
9. Sur les emprunts de 14 et 24 millions (le 14 mai 1819), pp.88-102.
10. Sur les dépenses appelées accidentelles (le [29] mai 1819), pp.102-109.
11. Sur le traitement des préfets (le 1er juin 1819), pp.109-110.

12. Sur le budget du ministère des finances (le 8 juin 1819), pp.111-136.
13. Sur la loi du 15 mars 1815, relative à l'arriéré de la Légion-d'Honneur (le 18 juin 1819), pp.137-138.
14. Sur la pétition tendant à demander à S.M. le rappel des bannis (le [17 mai] 1819), pp.139-146.
15. Réplique sur la même question, pp.146-151.
16. Sur la pétition des écoles de droit (le 10 juillet 1819), pp.152-156.
17. Sur l'élection de M. Grégoire (le 6 décembre 1819), pp.157-161.
18. Sur la proposition de voter six douzièmes provisoires (le 24 décembre 1819), pp.162-164.
19. Sur les pétitions en faveur de la loi du 5 février 1817, relativement aux élections (le 14 janvier 1820), pp.164-172.
20. Sur une lettre dénonçant les manœuvres pour signer des pétitions (le 15 janvier 1820), pp.172-175.
21. Sur une pétition tendant à prévoir la destitution du roi constitutionnel (le 29 janvier 1820), pp.175-179.
22. Sur la loi relative aux engagistes et aux échangistes (le 9 février 1820), pp.179-182.
23. Sur la rédaction du procès-verbal relativement à une accusation de M. Clausel de Coussergues contre M. Decazes (1er mars 1820), pp.182-185.
24. Sur les mesures à prendre pour constater la fidélité du scrutin (le 6 mars 1820), pp.185-187.
25. Sur la loi d'exception contre la liberté individuelle (le [7] mars 1820), pp.188-205.
26. Sur la même loi d'exception (le 10 mars 1820), pp.206-211.
27. Amendement à la loi d'exception contre la liberté individuelle (le 13 mars 1820), pp.212-223.
28. Sur une proposition relative aux pétitions (le 16 mars 1820), pp.224-228.
29. Sur les améliorations au mode de scrutin (le 20 mars 1820), pp.229-232.
30. Sur la loi d'exception contre la liberté de la presse (le 23 mars 1820), pp.232-248.
31. Amendement tendant à excepter de la censure les ouvrages qui ne paraîtraient qu'une fois par mois (le 27 mars 1820), pp.249-251.
32. Sur un amendement tendant à excepter de la censure le compte rendu des discussions des Chambres (le 28 mars 1820), pp.251-256.
33. Amendement tendant à laisser aux personnes calomniées la faculté de se défendre, malgré la censure (même séance), pp.256-260.
34. Sur un amendement tendant à refuser aux tribunaux le droit d'aggraver les peines pour le simple fait de la publication d'un article rayé par la censure (le 29 mars 1820), pp.261-263.
35. Amendement tendant à libérer de toute poursuite l'auteur d'un article approuvé par la censure (même séance), pp.263-274.
36. Sur un amendement tendant à ne pas conférer la censure à un seul censeur (le 30 mars 1820), pp.274-276.
37. Réponse à M. Blanquart-Bailleul, sur le mode de scrutin et l'appel nominal (le 3 avril 1820), pp.276-280.

38. Sur le projet de loi relatif au règlement des comptes antérieurs à l'exercice 1819 (le 5 avril 1820), pp.280-295.

39. Sur les amendemens proposés à l'article 8 du second projet de loi relatif aux comptes arriérés (le 15 avril 1820), pp.296-305.

40. Sur la pétition de M. Madier-Monjaut, relative au gouvernement occulte et aux assassinats du Midi (le 25 avril 1820), pp.306-309.

41. Sur une pétition accusant M. Decaze de l'assassinat du duc de Berri (le 28 avril 1820), pp.310-318.

42. Discours prononcé à l'occasion de la proposition d'adresse faite à la Chambre des députés par M. Manuel (le 3 mai 1820), pp.318-331.

43. Sur l'usage fait de la censure par le ministère (le 12 mai 1820), pp.332-335.

44. Sur le projet de loi relatif aux élections (le 23 mai 1820), pp.336-365.

45. Réponse à M. de Serre sur le drapeau tricolore, la souveraineté du peuple, les sermens réciproques et M. de La Fayette (le 27 mai 1820), pp.366-372.

46. Sur l'article 1er du projet de loi relatif aux élections (le 3 juin 1820), pp.372-384.

47. Sur les troubles de Paris au mois de juin 1820 (le 5 juin 1820), pp.385-392.

48. Sur les mêmes troubles (le 6 juin 1820), pp.393-395.

49. Sur les troubles de Paris (le 7 juin 1820), pp.396-397.

50. Réponse sur le même sujet [le 10 juin 1820], pp.397-402.

51. Sur la nécessité d'un nouveau code militaire (le 21 juin 1820), pp.403-406.

52. Sur la spécialité (le 30 juin 1820), pp.407-409.

53. Sur les six douzièmes provisoires (le 8 janvier 1821), pp.410-416.

54. Développement d'une proposition sur la clôture (le 2[7] janvier 1821), pp.416-424.

55. Sur la cocarde tricolore (le 7 février 1821), pp.425-429.

56. Sur l'amendement, proposé par M. Bertin-Devaux, au projet de loi relatif au remboursement du premier cinquième des reconnaissances de liquidation (le 19 février 1821), pp.429-444.

57. Sur l'interdiction de la parole, par suite du rappel à l'ordre et à la question (le 6 avril 1821), pp.445-466.

58. Sur le même objet (le 14 avril 1821), pp.466-480.

59. Sur les mesures tendant à faire renchérir les grains (le 28 avril 1821), pp.481-484.

60. Sur un article additionnel à la loi sur le prix des grains (le 30 avril 1821), pp.485-490.

61. Sur un amendement au projet de loi relatif aux grains (le 4 mai 1821), pp.490-493.

62. Contre le projet de loi tendant à changer l'article 351 du code pénal, concernant les décisions du jury (le 7 mai 1821), pp.493-502.

63. Sur le projet de loi relatif aux pensions ecclésiastiques et aux sièges épiscopaux (le [14] mai 1821), pp.502-522.

64. Sur une pétition relative à l'influence du clergé catholique sur l'éducation des protestans (le 19 mai 1821), pp.522-523.

65. Sur les attaques dirigées contre les donataires français (le 28 mai 1821), pp.523-526.

66. Sur le même sujet (le 29 mai 1821), pp.526-527.

67. Sur un discours de M. de La Fayette (le 4 juin 1821), pp.528-530.
68. Sur les frais de justice (le 7 juin 1821), pp.530-537.
69. Sur le code militaire (le 23 juin 1821), pp.537-548.
70. Opinion relative à la traite des noirs (le 27 juin 1821), pp.548-560.
71. Sur la censure des journaux (le 7 juillet 1821), pp.560-570.
72. Sur le même sujet (le 9 juillet 1821), pp.571-574.
73. Sur l'amendement de M. Darrieux, tendant à proportionner le cens électoral aux dégrèvemens [le 19 juillet 1821], pp.575-576.

Vol. II:
1. Sur une pétition tendant à soustraire au jury les causes de la presse (11 janvier 1822), pp.1-5.
2. Sur la fixation du jour pour la discussion du projet de loi sur la presse (14 janvier 1822), pp.6-8.
3. Sur l'article 1er du projet de loi sur la presse (25 janvier 1822), pp.9-13.
4. Sur un amendement à ce projet de loi (même séance), pp.13-16.
5. Sur les procès relatifs aux troubles du mois de juin 1820 (29 janvier 1822), pp.17-20.
6. Sur l'article 6 du projet de loi sur la presse (même séance), pp.20-24.
7. A l'appui d'un amendement à l'article 7 de la loi sur la presse (30 janvier 1822), pp.24-29.
8. Sur l'article 9 de la loi sur la presse (31 janvier 1822), pp.29-40.
9. Sur la censure proposée contre les journaux en cas de récidive (1er février 1822), pp.41-43.
10. Sur la question de savoir si les écrivains accusés par la Chambre auraient des défenseurs (2 février 1822), pp.43-47.
11. Sur le refus de la preuve testimoniale contre les fonctionnaires, dans le projet de loi sur la presse (6 février 1822), pp.47-55.
12. Sur le même objet (9 février 1822), pp.56-72.
13. A l'appui d'un amendement à l'article 3 du projet sur les journaux (14 février 1822), pp.73-84.
14. A l'appui d'un amendement tendant à obliger les ministres à rendre compte aux Chambres de leurs motifs pour le rétablissement de la censure (16 février 1822), pp.84-95.
15. Pour la réduction des frais de justice criminelle (2 mars 1822), pp.96-101.
16. Sur la pétition de M. Sauquaire-Souligné (11 mars 1822), pp.101-107.
17. Opinion sur la loi des comptes (13 mars 1822), pp.108-130.
18. En réponse à une accusation de M. Dudon (même séance), pp.130-131.
19. Sur les frais de tenue des collèges électoraux (27 mars 1822), pp.131-137.
20. Contre la traite des noirs ([3] avril 1822), pp.137-144.
21. Proposition pour accélérer le rapport des pétitions (12 juillet 1822), pp.145-152.
22. Sur les fraudes pratiquées dans les élections [le 20 juillet 1822], pp.152-155.
23. Sur le budget du ministère de la justice (22 juillet 1822), pp.155-163.
24. Sur le cordon sanitaire et les préparatifs de la guerre d'Espagne (25 juillet 1822), pp.164-169.
25. Sur les fonds de la police secrète (27 juillet 1822), pp.169-178.

26. Sur la traite des noirs (31 juillet 1822), pp.179-181.
27. Sur le budget de la Chambre des pairs et le réquisitoire de M. Mangin dans le procès de Berton (1ᵉʳ août 1822), pp.182-187.
28. Sur le retard des rapports de pétitions (3 août 1822), pp.188-190.
29. Sur la proposition de réduire les salaires et traitemens des fonctionnaires publics ([6] août 1822), pp.190-196.
30. Contre la taxe des journaux (7 août 1822), pp.197-202.
31. Sur l'éligibilité des descendans de religionnaires fugitifs (27 mars 1824), pp.203-215.
32. Sur la même question (22 mai 1824), pp.216-243.
33. Sur la septennalité (8 juin 1824), pp.243-273.
34. Sur le budget (8 juillet 1824), pp.274-289.
35. Sur les déportés de la Martinique ([17] juillet 1824), pp.289-300.
36. Sur la pétition des déportés de la Martinique (8 janvier 1825), pp.301-305.
37. Sur une pétition relative à la loi d'indemnité (26 janvier 1825), pp.305-309.
38. Sur la loi d'indemnité pour les émigrés (23 février 1825), pp.309-330.
39. Sur la proposition de réduire les droits d'enregistrement en faveur des émigrés qui rachèteraient leurs biens (15 mars 1825), pp.331-336.
40. Sur l'application des achats de la Caisse d'amortissement exclusivement au 3 pour 100 (24 mars 1825), pp.336-346.
41. Sur le projet relatif au sacrilège (14 avril 1825), pp.347-365.
42. Sur le projet de loi portant réglement des crédits et des dépenses de l'exercice 1823 (28 avril 1825), pp.366-382.
43. Sur le procès du *Journal du Commerce* ([21] février 1826), pp.383-387.
44. Sur le droit réclamé par les ministres de céder des portions du territoire français (20 mars 1826), pp.387-400.
45. Sur les frais de la guerre d'Espagne ([20] avril 1826), pp.400-407.
46. Sur les dépenses de la guerre d'Espagne (24 avril 1826), pp.408-425.
47. Sur la même question (27 avril 1826), pp.426-432.
48. Sur une pétition des écoles, relativement au droit d'aînesse (29 avril 1826), pp.433-438.
49. Contre le projet de loi sur les substitutions (9 mai 1826), pp.438-462.
50. Sur le budget de 1827 (17 mai 1826), pp.462-474.
51. Sur l'amovibilité des conseillers d'Etat (23 mai 1826), pp.475-480.
52. Sur la proposition de M. de Noailles en faveur des Grecs ([24] mai 1826), pp.480-483.
53. Sur le rétablissement de la censure (29 mai 1826), pp.483-489.
54. Sur l'administration des colonies et les déportés de la Martinique ([6] juin 1826), pp.490-498.
55. Sur la loterie (9 juin 1826), pp.499-501.
56. En réponse à M. de la Boëssière sur une pétition contraire à la liberté de la presse (10 juin 1826), pp.501-509.
57. Discours sur l'adresse ([28 décembre] 1826), pp.510-518.
58. Sur la loi des postes (1ᵉʳ février 1827), pp.519-530.
59. Sur les calculs de M. de Villèle relativement aux journaux ([3] février 1827), pp.531-537.

60. Sur le projet de loi relatif à la police de la presse (13 février 1827), pp.538-557.
61. Sur la responsabilité imposée aux imprimeurs (10 mars 1827), pp.558-566.
62. De l'assimilation des écrivains avec les hommes condamnés pour crime à des peines infamantes (12 mars 1827), pp.566-569.
63. Sur le projet de loi relatif à la traite des noirs (13 mars 1827), pp.569-573.
64. Sur la proposition de M. de la Boëssière (15 mars 1827), pp.574-582.
65. Sur les outrages faits au cercueil de M. le duc de Liancourt (2 avril 1827), pp.583-586.
66. Développement d'un article additionnel tendant à investir la commission des droits de la Chambre du droit de lui déférer les ministres qui l'outrageraient (23 avril 1827), pp.587-603.
67. Sur le budget ([8] mai 1827), pp.604-624.
68. Sur le budget de l'instruction publique ([18] mai 1827), pp.624-634.
69. Sur le prochain rétablissement de la censure (29 mai 1827), pp.634-640.

E2/3 1832   Choix de rapports, opinions et discours prononcés à la Chambre des Députés, par MM. Benjamin Constant, Foy, Manuel, Casimir Perrier, Girardin, Camille Jordan, Lafayette, Dupont (de l'Eure), Pasquier, De la Bourdonnaye, de Serre, Lainé, de Villèle, etc., etc. Paris: chez les principaux libraires, 1832. 8° pp.10, 746. On p.[2] imprint of Ad. Morssard, [Paris]; on p.746 imprint of Cosson, [Paris].

Reissue of: Choix de rapports, opinions et discours prononcés à la Tribune nationale; recueillis dans un ordre historique, et imprimés après des pièces originales ... Session de 1819. Paris: Alex Eymery ... 1820. 8° pp.10, 746.

Copy: H. (C.136a).

Other selections: Adolphe et choix de discours, Paris: Guillequin [1907], item A18/30; Adolphe et choix de discours, Londres: Dent: Paris: Mignot, [1912], item A18/33. See also Laboulaye (items E1/5a-b) and works listed in section E4.

Translation

See also item E4/t1(1).

E2/t1 1828   Reden und Meinungen der Deputirten des Niederrheinischen Departements. Session vom Jahr 1828. Aus dem Französischen übersetzt von Ehrenfried Stöber. Strassburg. Gedruckt und zu finden bei G. L. Schuler, kleine Gewerbslaube. 8° pp.[iv], 196.

Includes the following speeches by Constant (normally with caption title):

Sitzung vom 5ten April 1828. Rede des Herrn Benjamin Constant, Deputirten des Niederrheins, pp.5-11.
Sitzung vom 21ten April 1828. Worte des Herrn Benjamin Constant, über eine Bittschrift des Herrn Sarat, Herrn von Villele betreffend, pp.13-14.
Sitzung vom 26ten April. Rede des Herrn Benjamin Constant, zu Gunsten einer Bittschrift der Mulatten Bissette und Fabian, pp.15-27.
Sitzung vom 28ten April. Nach Ablesung Protokolls über die letztere Sitzung,

begehrt Herr Benjamin Constant das Wort um einer Berichtigung willen, p.28.

Sitzung vom 2ten Mai 1828. Vorschlag eines Zusatz-Artikels zum neuen Gesetze über die Wahllisten, von Herrn Benjamin Constant, pp.29-30.

Sitzung vom 3ten Mai 1828. Worte des Herrn Benjamin Constant über eine Bittschrift die Septennalität betreffend, pp.31-32.

Sitzung vom 6ten Mai 1828. Worte des Herrn Benjamin Constant, wegen einem Zusatz-Artikel des Herrn von Formond, den Gesetz-Entwurf über die Wahllisten betreffend, pp.33-36.

Sitzung vom 7ten Mai 1828. Rede des Herrn Benjamin Constant über eine von ihm vorgeschlagene Reglementar-Verfügung die saumseligen Deputirten betreffend, pp.37-44.

Sitzung vom 12ten Mai 1828. Berathschlagung über das Gesetz wegen den Wahllisten, p.45.

Worte des Herrn Benjamin Constant, über diesen Zusatz-Artikel, p.45.

Sitzung vom 14ten Mai 1828. Rede des Herrn Benjamin Constant über das von den Ministern vorgeschlagene Anleihen von 80 Millionen, pp.46-56.

Sitzung vom 17ten Mai 1828. [Desselben Worte wegen einer Bittschrift der Einwohner von Sessenheim], pp.57-58.

[Sitzung vom 17ten Mai 1828. Desselben Worte wegen einer Bittschrift des Advocaten Grand], pp.58-60.

Sitzung vom 24ten Mai 1828. [Desselben Worte über eine Bittschrift wegen den Pensionen für die Wittwen aller Mitglieder der königlichen Universität], pp.61-63.

Sitzung vom 30ten Mai 1828. Berathung über das Pressgesetz, pp.69-88.

Sitzung vom 31ten Mai 1828. [Desselben Worte über eine Bittschrift des Advocaten Marchand], pp.89-90.

Sitzung vom 2ten Juni 1828. [Desselben Rede wegen einer Persönlichkeit gegen den Minister des Innern], pp.91-99.

Sitzung vom 4ten Juni 1828. Berathung über das Press-Gesetz, pp.100-103.

Sitzung vom 11ten Juni 1828. Berathung über das Press-Gesetz, pp.103-104.

Sitzung vom 12ten Juni 1828. Berathung über das Press-Gesetz, pp.104-109.

Sitzung vom 13ten Juni 1828. Fortsetzung der Berathung über das Press-Gesetz, pp.109-111.

Sitzung vom 30ten Juni 1828. Berathung über das Budget die Ausgaben betreffend, pp.112-131.

Sitzung vom 12ten Juli 1828. Berathung die Bittschriften über die Nationalgarden betreffend. Worte des Herrn Benjamin Constant, pp.157-158.

Sitzung vom 15ten Juli. Fortsetzung der Berathung über das Budget, pp.159-162.

Sitzung vom 19ten Juli 1828. Fortsetzung der Verhandlung über das Budget, pp.163-166.

Sitzung vom 25ten Juli 1828. Fortsetzung der Berathung über das Budget. (Finanz-Ministerium). Rede des Herrn Benjamin Constant, pp.167-184.

Imprint of G. L. Schuler, Strassburg, at foot of pp.11, 28, 36, 44, 60, 88, 99, 111, 131, 166, 184. This would seem to indicate that speeches (or groups of speeches) were issued separately before being issued as a volume. Two of the copies located (see below) are simply parts containing one speech.

Copies: Sor (HJm 346(10) 8°: incomplete, contains *Vorwort* and speech of 5 April only), St (M 7137; M 117782; D 121447: three copies, of which only the first is complete). (C.133a).

E3 Mélanges de littérature et de politique

E3/1 1829   Mélanges de littérature et de politique, par M. Benjamin-Constant. Paris, Pichon et Didier … 1829. 8° pp.xiv, [ii], 483. Impr. Huzard-Courcier, [Paris].

Copies: BCU, BL, BN. (C.134a).

Contents of *Mélanges de littérature et de politique*

I. Aperçus sur la marche et les révolutions de la philosophie à Rome, pp.1-27. [Published in *La Minerve française*, I(13), 29 April-1 May 1818, 602-611; II(2), 14-15 May 1818, 71-77. Here revised.]

II. De la puissance de l'Angleterre durant la guerre, et de sa détresse à la paix, jusqu'en 1818, pp.28-45. [Published in *La Minerve française*, II(1), 6-7 May 1818, 42-50. Here revised and with addition of P.S.]

III. Du Parlement anglais sous Cromwell, et du Tribunat, dans la constitution de l'an VIII, jusqu'à son épuration, pp.46-54.

IV. Lettre sur Julie, pp.55-74.

V. Fragmens sur la France, du 14 juillet 1789 au 31 mars 1814, pp.75-92.

VI. Du développement progressif des idées religieuses, pp.93-127. [From *Religion*, item A62/1.]

VII. De M. Dunoyer, et de quelques-uns de ses ouvrages, pp.128-162. [Published in the *Revue encyclopédique*, XXIX (1826), 416-435.]

VIII. De madame de Staël et de ses ouvrages, pp.163-210. [Published in part in *Le Publiciste*, 12, 14, 16 May 1807; *MF*, 19 July 1817, 136-137; *MF*, 26 July 1817, 175-180; *La Minerve française*, II(3), 25-26 May 1818, 105-110; II(7) 16-17 June 1818, 316-325; II(13), 28-29 July 1818, 601-610.]

IX. De Godwin, et de son ouvrage sur la justice politique, pp.211-224. [*MF*, 27 April 1817, 161-173. Here revised and with two additional final paragraphs.]

X. De la Littérature dans ses rapports avec la liberté, pp.225-239. [*MF*, 13 September 1817, 485-495. Here revised and with Latin quotations.]

XI. De la juridiction du gouvernement sur l'éducation, pp.240-254. [*MF*, 11 October 1817, 53-63. Here revised.]

XII. De la guerre de trente ans, de la tragédie de Wallstein, par Schiller, et du théâtre allemand, pp.255-321. [Published as preface to *Wallstein*, item A9/1, ('Quelques réflexions sur la tragédie de Wallstein et sur le théâtre allemand'). Here revised and with addition of 'Notes sur la guerre de trente ans'.]

XIII. De M. Fox et de M. Pitt, pp.322-331. [*La Minerve française*, VII(1), 6-7 August 1819, 6-13. Here abridged.]

XIV. De la révolution d'Angleterre, de 1640 à 1688, pp.332-342.

XV. De l'effet du régime qu'on a nommé *révolutionnaire*, relativement au salut et à la liberté de la France, pp.343-353. [*Des effets de la terreur*, item A4/1. Here abridged and with P.S.]

XVI. Des causes humaines qui ont concouru à l'établissement du christianisme, pp.354-386. [Adapted from *Christianisme*, item A59.]

XVII. De la perfectibilité de l'espèce humaine, pp.387-415.

XVIII. De la division des propriétés foncières, pp.416-428. [*La Minerve française*, VI(9), 3-5 July 1819, 409-415. Here revised and enlarged.]

XIX. Des erreurs que l'histoire favorise sur les gouvernemens absolus et les gouvernemens populaires, pp.429-436.

XX. Pensées détachées, pp.437-472. [*MF*, 24 May 1817, 346-352; 14 June 1817, 509-523; *MF*, 28 June 1817, 584-591. Here revised and, in the case of the last *pensée*, enlarged.]

E3/2 1829   Mélanges de littérature et de politique, par M. Benjamin-Constant. Tome premier [second]. Bruxelles, Imprimerie romantique ... Londres, même maison, 1829. 18°, 2 vols. pp.[iii], VII, 205 + [iii], 211.

Copy: OT. (C.134b).

E3/3 1830   Mélanges de littérature et de politique, par Benjamin-Constant. Tome premier [second]. Louvain, chez F. Michel ... 1830. 8° 2 vols. pp.x, 165 + [iii], 163.

Copies: AR, BR, H, L, T. (C.134c).

E3/4 1838   Mélanges de littérature et de politique, par Benjamin-Constant. Bruxelles: Société belge de librairie, etc., Hauman et Compagnie, 1838. pp.[iv], VI, 402.

Copies: A, BCU, BR, OT.

E3/5 1840   Mélanges de littérature et de politique, par M. Benjamin-Constant. Bruxelles: Imprimerie-librairie romantique; Londres: même maison, 1840. 18° 2 vols. pp.[iv], VII, 205 + [iv], 211.

Copy: BCU.

E3/6 1928   Benjamin Constant. Réflexions sur le théâtre allemand. Bearb. von W. Waterstradt. [Nebst] Wörterb. Braunschweig: G. Westermann, [1928]. (Westermann-Texte. Franzos. Reihe, 54). pp.47; 19.

(*Gesamtverzeichnis des deutschsprachigen Schrifttums (GV) 1911-1915*, Munich: Verlag Dokumentation, 1976.)

E3/7 1967   Benjamin Constant. De la perfectibilité de l'espèce humaine. Lausanne: Editions l'Age d'Homme, 1967. (La Merveilleuse Collection, dirigée par Jacques Chessex et Vladimir Dimitrijevic, 6). pp.130.

1217 numbered copies printed.

Includes selection from *Mélanges*: *Préface*, pp.35-39; *De la perfectibilité de l'espèce humaine*, pp.41-65; *De M. Dunoyer et de quelques-uns de ses ouvrages*, pp.66-95; *Pensées détachées*, pp.96-126. Introduction and notes par Pierre Deguise.

Other editions: Pléiade 1957, 1964, 1979: extracts (E4/5), Gauchet 1980: extracts (E4/11).

Translations

E3/t1 1838   Philosophical Miscellanies translated from the French of Cousin, Jouffroy, and B. Constant. With introductory and critical notices. By George Ripley. Boston: Hilliard, Gray, and Company, 1838. 2 vols (Specimens of foreign standard literature, I-II).

In II, 292-376: translation of extracts from *Mélanges*. Introductory notice: pp.249-291.

Copies: BL, DLC.

E3/t2 1976   Benjamín Constant. Reflexiones sobre el teatro alemán. Buenos Aires: Hachette, 1976. (Las ideas y las formas). pp.88.

E4 Other collections and selections

E4/1 1829   Œuvres diverses sur la politique constitutionnelle, par Benjamin Constant. A Paris, chez J. P. Aillaud, 1829. 8° 2 vols.

Contents: (vol. I): *Lettres sur les Cent Jours*; (vol. II): *Eloge de Sir S. Romilly, Des Motifs qui ont dicté le nouveau projet de loi sur les élections, Des Élections de 1818, Annales de la Session de 1817 à 1818 – 5ᵉ livraison du tome 1ᵉʳ*.

Copies: MU, NSchU. (C.135a).

E4/2 [1892]   Benjamin Constant. Les Cent jours. La souveraineté du peuple. Edité par Henri Gautier. Paris: Henri Gautier, [1892]. (Nouvelle bibliothèque populaire, 363). pp.[37]-72. (Also paginated 1-36).

Contents:

'Benjamin Constant', by Charles Simond, p.1

'La souveraineté du peuple', pp.2-12

'Madame Récamier, Première année de mariage', pp.13-14

'Madame Récamier, Madame de Staël', pp.14-17

Eleven letters from Constant to Mᵐᵉ de Nassau (1808), pp.18-36

Copy: B.

E4/3 1944   Cordié, Carlo. Gli scritti politici giovanili di Benjamin Constant (1796-97). (Introduzione, bibliografia e testi). Como: Carlo Marzorati, [1944]. (Testimonia: Raccolta di testi e documenti per l'Insegnamento Superiore). pp.LXXV, 241. Bibliography [reprinted and revised in item E4/4].

Contents:

Introduzione, pp.IV-XXX.

Nota bibliografica, pp.XXXI-LXXV.

De la force du gouvernement actuel de la France et de la nécessité de s'y rallier, pp.3-91.

Des réactions politiques ... Des effets de la terreur, pp.93-211.

Discours prononcé au cercle constitutionnel pour la plantation de l'arbre de la liberté le 30 fructidor an 5, pp.213-233.

Indici, 235-241.

E4/4 1946   Benjamin Constant a cura di Carlo Cordié. Con 33 tavole fuori testo. Milano: Ulrico Hoepli, 1946. (I Propilei. Guide storico-letterarie a autori, scuole, movimenti culturali, 1). pp.VII, 449. Frontispiece (portrait), illus., facsimiles.

Selection from full range of Constant's writings. Important bibliographies.

Reviews: F. Flora, *Corriere d'informazione*, 29 marzo 1946, p.1. F. Neri, *L'Opinione*, (Torino), 15 marzo 1946, 'Tutto Constant'.

E4/5 1957   Benjamin Constant. Œuvres. Texte présenté et annoté par Alfred Roulin [et Charles Roth]. Paris: Gallimard, 1957. (Bibliothèque de la Pléiade, 123). pp.1681. Bibliography.

Contents:
Préface, pp.7-11
Chronologie de la vie de Benjamin Constant, pp.13-24
Bibliographie, pp.25-34
Adolphe, pp.37-117
Le Cahier rouge, pp.119-167
Cécile, pp.169-219
Journaux intimes, pp.221-823
Fragments du carnet disparu, pp.825-830
Mélanges de littérature et de politique [selection], pp.833-931:
Preface, pp.835-838
I. *Lettre sur Julie*, pp.839-850
II. *Fragments sur la France, du 14 juillet 1789 au 31 mars 1814*, pp.850-859
III. *De Mme de Staël et de ses ouvrages*, pp.859-886
IV. *De la littérature dans ses rapports avec la liberté*, pp.886-894
V. *De la guerre de Trente Ans. De la tragédie de Wallstein, par Schiller, et du théâtre allemand*, pp.894-919; *Notes sur la guerre de Trente Ans*, pp.919-931
Réflexions sur la tragédie, pp.933-962
Fragments des mémoires de Madame Récamier, pp.963-982
De l'esprit de conquête et de l'usurpation, pp.983-1096
Principes de politique, pp.1097-1249
De la liberté des brochures, pp.1251-1277
Observations sur le discours prononcé par S.E. le Ministre de l'Intérieur en faveur du projet de loi sur la liberté de la presse, pp.1279-1305
Discours à la Chambre des députés, pp.1307-1393:
Speech of 7 March 1820 ('Sur la loi d'exception contre la liberté individuelle'), pp.1309-1321
Speech of 27 June 1821 ('Opinion relative à la traite des noirs'), pp.1321-1329
Speech of 7 July 1821 ('Sur la censure des journaux'), pp.1329-1336
Speech of 5 [=3] April 1822 ('Contre la traite des noirs'), pp.1337-1341
Speech of 27 March 1824 ('Sur l'éligibilité des descendants de religionnaires fugitifs'), pp.1342-1350
Speech of 22 May 1824 ('Sur la même question'), pp.1350-1368
Speech of 23 March 1820 ('Sur la loi d'exception contre la liberté de la presse'), pp.1369-1380
Speech of 13 February 1827 ('Sur le projet de loi relatif à la police de la presse'), pp.1380-1393

De la Religion, [Liv. I, chaps 1-2], pp.1397-1429
Notices et Notes, pp.1431-1648
Index, pp.1649-1669
Table des matières, pp.1671-1681

Review: P. Serini, 'Constant nella Pléiade', *Il Mondo*, IX (16 luglio 1957), p.8.

Reprinted: 1964, 1979. pp.1657. Contents identical to 1957 edition, but with slightly different arrangement. Bibliography at end of volume.

1964   See also item E4/5 (reprint of Œuvres ... Paris: Bibliothèque de la Pléiade, 1957).

E4/6 1964   Ecrits et discours politiques par Benjamin Constant. Présentation, notes et commentaires par O. Pozzo di Borgo. [Paris]: Jean-Jacques Pauvert, 1964. 2 vols, pp.XXXII, 244 + 251. Portraits, facsimiles. Bibliography.

Contents: Eight chapters in which text and comment are interspersed. The following texts are included:
Des réactions politiques, I, 21-91
Des effets de la terreur, I, 93-112
Discours prononcé au Cercle constitutionnel pour la plantation de l'arbre de la liberté, le 30 fructidor an 5, I, 115-128
Speech of 15 nivôse an VIII [5 January 1800] ('Sur le projet concernant la formation de la loi'), I, 139-153
Speech of 5 pluviôse an IX [25 January 1801] ('Sur le projet de loi concernant l'établissement de tribunaux criminels spéciaux'), I, 156-189
De l'esprit de conquête [chap. 8], *De l'usurpation* [chap. 11], I, 206-212
De la doctrine politique qui peut réunir les partis en France, II, 32-56
Speech of 17 July 1824 ('Sur les déportés de la Martinique'), II, 65-74
Speech of 14 April 1825 ('Sur le projet de loi relatif au sacrilège'), II, 80-95
Speech of 23 February 1825 ('Sur la loi d'indemnité pour les émigrés'), II, 97-116
Speech of 6 April 1829 ('Sur le projet de loi relatif à l'organisation départementale'), II, 125-144
Speech of 15 March 1830 ('Sur le projet d'adresse au Roi'), II, 151-154
Speech of 19 November 1830 ('Sur le projet de résolution relatif à l'affaire de M. de Lameth'), II, 161-169

Reviews: Jean Guéhenno, *Le Figaro*, 7 octobre 1964, 'La liberté endormie'. David Thomson, *FS*, XIX (1965), 299-300. Patrice Thompson, *RSH*, 1965, 129-145. *TLS*, 6 May 1965, p.354, 'Arbiter Constant'. Samuel S. de Sacy, *QL*, n° 12 (15-30 septembre 1966), 14-15, 'Un citoyen contre les pouvoirs'. Paul Delbouille, *RLV*, XXXII (1966), 424-430. H. Perrochon, *Culture française*, XIII (1966), 19-20. René Le Grand Roy, *CBC*, sér. I, n° 4 (1967), 164-165. Pierre Deguise, *RR*, LVIII (1967), 200-203.

E4/7 1965   Benjamin Constant. Choix de textes politiques. Présentation et notes par Olivier Pozzo di Borgo. [Paris]: Jean-Jacques Pauvert, 1965. (Libertés, Collection dirigée par Jean-François Revel, 32). pp.220. Bibliography.
Contents:

Speech of 5 January 1800 [extract], pp.25-28
Speech of 25 January 1801 [extract], pp.29-41
De l'esprit de conquête et de l'usurpation [extracts], pp.48-52, 53-57
Mémoire apologétique [extracts], pp.70-73
Entretien d'un électeur avec lui-même, pp.78-91
De la liberté des anciens comparée à celle des modernes [extract], pp.92-105
Speech of 14 April 1825 ('Sur la loi relative au sacrilège'), pp.113-132
Speech of 23 February 1825 ('Sur la loi d'indemnité pour les émigrés'), pp.135-156
Speech of 30 May 1828 ('Sur la loi concernant la presse périodique'), pp.164-184
Reviews: René Le Grand Roy, *CBC*, sér. I, n° 4 (1967), 165-166. Max Milner, *IL*, XIX (1967), 122.

E4/8 1972   Benjamin Constant. Recueil d'articles. *Le Mercure, La Minerve et La Renommée*. Introduction, notes et commentaires par Ephraïm Harpaz. Genève: Droz, 1972. 2 vols. (Travaux d'histoire éthico-politique, 22). pp.xix, 1566.
Reviews: A. Delorme, *Revue de synthèse*, XCIV (1973), 398-400. P. Guiral, *Revue historique*, CCL (1973), 546-547. Carlo Pellegrini, *RLMC*, XXVI (1973), 141-156. R. Pouillart, *Les Lettres romanes*, XXVII (1973), 91-92. M. Salamin, *Revue suisse d'histoire*, XXIII (1973), 191-194. Kurt Kloocke, *RF*, LXXXV (1973), 598-601. Jean-René Derré, *SF*, XVII (1973), 369-370. Pierre Deguise, *FR*, XLVII (1973-1974), 197-199. Norman King, *FS*, XXVIII (1974), 83-85. Patrice Thompson, *RHLF*, LXXIV (1974), 512-514.

E4/9 1978   Benjamin Constant. Recueil d'articles, 1795-1817. Introduction, notes et commentaires par Ephraïm Harpaz. Genève: Droz, 1978. (Travaux d'histoire éthico-politique, 32). pp.276.
Review: Kurt Kloocke, *ZFSL*, XC (1980), 80-84.

1979   See also item E4/5 (reprint of Œuvres, Paris: Bibliothèque de la Pléiade, 1957).

E4/10 1979   Benjamin Constant. L'affaire Regnault. Textes présentés et commentés par René Bourgeois. Publications de l'Université des langues et lettres de Grenoble, 1979. pp.161. Facsimiles, illus.
Contents:
Lettre à Odilon Barrot (facsimile reprint), pp.19-68
Deuxième lettre à Odilon Barrot, pp.69-128
De l'appel en calomnie, pp.129-140
Extrait de *La Minerve française*, mars 1818, 261-273, pp.141-152 (*Encore un mot sur le procès de Wilfred Regnault*)
Extraits des *Mémoires posthumes* d'Odilon Barrot, pp.155-159

E4/11 1980   Benjamin Constant. De la liberté chez les modernes. Ecrits politiques. Textes choisis, présentés et annotés par Marcel Gauchet. Paris: Le Livre de poche, 1980. (Le Livre de poche 8346, Collection Pluriel, dirigée par Georges Liébert). pp.703.

Contents:
Préface, pp.11-91
Avertissement, pp.93-103
De l'esprit de conquête et de l'usurpation, pp.107-261
Principes de politique, pp.263-427
Annexes aux Principes de politique, pp.429-490
De la liberté des anciens, pp.491-515
Mélanges de littérature et de politique [selected articles], pp.517-612
Notes, pp.613-703

Reviews: François Furet, *Le Nouvel Observateur*, 16-22 août 1980. ('Constant l'insaisissable'). Jean-Marie Gobert, *L'Express*, 13 septembre 1980. ('Benjamin Constant: la lucidité libérale').

E4/12 1981   Benjamin Constant. Recueil d'articles, 1820-1824. Introduction, notes et commentaires par Ephraïm Harpaz. Genève: Droz, 1981. (Travaux d'histoire éthico-politique, 35). pp.362.

Reviews: M.A. Wégimont, *Nineteenth-century French studies*, X (1982), 361-362. Kurt Kloocke, *ZFSL*, XCIII (1983), 106-111.

Translations

See also items A10/t6, A17/t3 and A17/t4.

E4/t1 1834-1835   Benjamin Constant. Sämmtliche politischen Werke, übersetzt und mit Anmerkungen begleitet von F. J. Buß. Freiburg: Wagner, 1834-1835. Vols I & IV.

Only two volumes published: I. B. Constant: Reden in der Kammer der Deputirten; IV. B. Constant: Vollständige Sammlung der über die repräsentative Regierungsform und die gegenwärtige Constitution Frankreichs herausgegebenen Werke, bildend eine Art Lehrgang der constitutionellen Politik.
Copy: Graz. (Fromm 5696).

E4/t2 1883   Benžamen Konstan. Načela politike i O ministarskoj odgovornosti. Beograd, 1883. pp.x, 243.

Published by Royal Serbian State Press. Translation by Dj. S. Simić of *Principes de politique* and *De la responsabilité des ministres*.
Copy: DCL.

E4/t3 1934   Constant, Benjamin. Scritti politici, a cura di Salvatore Valitutti. Bologna: Cappelli, 1934. (Istituto Nazionale Fascista: Classici del pensiero politico).

Announced, but apparently never published.

E4/t4 1946   Benjamin Constant. Über die Freiheit. [Eingeleitet und übertragen von Walther Lüthi]. Klosterberg, Basel: Verlag Benno Schwabe & Co, [1946]. (Sammlung Klosterberg, schweizerische Reihe, herausgegeben von Walter Muschg). pp.[iv], 139. Frontispiece (portrait).

Extracts from *Cours de politique constitutionnelle* and *Mélanges*.

Copies: B, T. (Fromm 5705).

E4/t5 1954   Beniamino Constant. Discorso sulla libertà degli antichi paragonata a quella dei moderni. Studio introduttivo, traduzione e note di Lucia Nutrimento. Treviso: Canova, [1954]. (Testi filosofici ad uso delle scuole). pp.133. Bibliography.

Includes *Discorso*, pp.45-83, and selections from other political writings of Constant.

Copy: BPU. (Cordié 220).

E4/t6 1962   Antologia degli scritti politici di Benjamin Constant, a cura di Antonio Zanfarino. Estratta da: Discorso sulla libertà degli antichi paragonata a quella dei moderni – Principi di Politica – Riflessioni sulle costituzioni e le garanzie – Le reazioni politiche – Lo spirito di conquista e d'usurpazione – Miscellanea di politica e letteratura – Sulle religione – Commento all'opera del Filangieri – Discorsi alla Camera dei deputati. Traduzione di Giannina Zanfarino-Bonacci. [Bologna]: Il Mulino, [1962]. (Classici della democrazia moderna, a cura di Vittorio Caprariis, 10). pp.208. Bibliography.

Includes *La libertà degli antichi paragonata a quella dei moderni*, pp.36-58 and extracts from *Mélanges*, political and religious writings.

Copy: BCU. (Cordié 228).

E4/t7 1970-1972   Benjamin Constant. Werke in vier Bänden. Herausgegeben von Axel Blaeschke und Lothar Gall. Deutsch von Eva Rechel-Mertens. Berlin: Propyläen Verlag, 1970-1972. 4 vols.

Bd. I-II: Autobiographische und kritische Schriften. Ausgewählt, eingeleitet und kommentiert von Axel Blaeschke, 1970. pp.483 + 561.

Bd. III-IV: Politische Schriften. Ausgewählt, eingeleitet, ergänzend übertragen und kommentiert von Lothar Gall, 1972. pp.460 + 529.

Contents Bd. I:
Einführung, pp.9-61
Adolphe, pp.63-187
Cécile, pp.189-267
Das rote Heft, pp.269-341
Schillers Trauerspiel "Wallenstein" und das deutsche Theater, pp.343-380
Gedanken über die Tragödie, pp.381-426
Anmerkungen, pp.427-483

Bd. II:
Tagebuch I, Amélie und Germaine (6. Januar bis 10. April 1803), pp.11-60
Tagebuch II, 22. Januar 1804 bis 7. Mai 1805 (Auswahl), pp.61-248
Tagebuch III 22. Januar 1804 bis 27. Dezember 1807 (Auswahl), pp.249-331
Tagebuch IV 15. Mai bis 26. September 1816 (Auswahl), pp.333-432
Anmerkungen, pp.433-561

Bd. III:

Einführung, pp.9-32

Über die Stärke der gegenwärtigen Regierung Frankreichs und die Notwendigkeit, sich ihr anzuschliessen, pp.33-117

Über politische Reaktion, pp.119-202

Über die Auswirkungen der Schreckensherrschaft, pp.203-229

Vom Geist der Eroberung und der Usurpation in ihrem Verhältnis zur europäischen Zivilisation, pp.231-406

Anmerkungen, pp.407-460

Bd. IV:

Grundprinzipien der Politik, die auf alle repräsentativen Regierungssysteme und inbesondere auf die gegenwärtige Verfassung Frankreichs angewandt werden können, pp.9-244

Über die Freiheit der Broschüren, Flugschriften und Zeitungen, betrachtet unter dem Gesichtspunkt des Interesses der Regierung, pp.245-286

Betrachtungen über die Rede Seiner Exzellenz des Ministers des Innern zugunsten des Gesetzentwurfs über die Pressefreiheit, pp.287-325

Über die politische Doktrin, die alle Parteien Frankreichs einigen kann, pp.325-362

Über die Freiheit der Alten in Vergleich zu der her Heutigen pp.363-396

Über die Perfektibilität des Menschengeschlechts, pp.397-422

Anmerkungen, pp.423-478

Personenregister, pp.479-529

F Correspondence

I Collections

F1 1864   Colet, Louise. Lettres de Benjamin Constant à Mme Récamier avec introduction et épilogue par Mme Louise Colet. Paris: E. Dentu, 1864. pp.XLVII, 216.

Seventy-five letters to Juliette Récamier (including three in the introduction); letter to Béranger, 'ce 29 janvier 1829' (p.VII), letter to Claude Hochet, Hardenberg, ce 11 octobre 1811 (pp.IX-XI), and letter to Germaine de Staël, Paris, 6 septembre 1810 (pp.XXXIII-XXXVI). See items F116 (Béranger), F4 and F16 (Récamier) and F11 (Hochet).

F2a 1879   Isler, M. Briefe von Benj. Constant – Görres – Goethe – Jac. Grimm – Guizot – F. H. Jacobi – Jean Paul – Klopstock – Schelling – Mad. de Staël – J. H. Voss und vielen Anderen. Auswahl aus dem handschriftlichen Nachlasse des Ch. de Villers herausgegeben von M. Isler. Hamburg: Otto Meissner, 1879. pp.XX, 320.

Thirty-one letters (1804-1814) to Charles de Villers from manuscripts in Stadts- und Universitätsbibliothek, Hamburg. See also Rudler, *Bibliographie* (item F164).

Review: A. Chuquet, *Revue critique d'histoire et de littérature*, X (1880), 186-189.

F2b 1883   Isler, M. Briefe an Ch. de Villers von Benj. Constant ... Zweite vermehrte Ausgabe ... 1883. pp.XX, 376.

Includes reprint of the letters to Villers referred to in the preceding item.

F3 1879   Strodtmann, Adolf. Dichterprofile, Literaturbilder aus dem neunzehnten Jahrhundert. Stuttgart: Abendheim'sche Verlagsbuchhandlung, 1879. 2 vols.

In vol. II, 1-42: 'Frau von Staël und Benjamin Constant, nach bisher ungedruckten Briefen derselben geschildert': forty-two letters or documents (in German translation) from Germaine and Albertine de Staël to Constant (1813-1816) from the Mahrenholz archives, Groß-Schwülper, Hanover. See item F8.

F4a 1882 [=1881]   [Lenormant, Amélie]. Lettres de Benjamin Constant à Madame Récamier, 1807-1830, publiées par l'auteur des Souvenirs de Mme Récamier. Paris: Calmann Lévy, 1882 [=1881]. pp.[iv], XL, 365.

Includes letter, Paris, 28 mai 1815, from Constant to Napoleon, pp.181-183. (Manuscripts now in BN, N.a.fr. 13265).

This edition was in fact published in 1881, as can be seen from the date of the reviews: A. de Pontmartin, *GF*, 6 novembre 1881. A. Laugel, *The Nation* (New York), XXXIII (17 novembre 1881), 391-392. J.-A. Barbey d'Aurevilly, *Le Constitutionnel*, 19 décembre 1881. A. Mézières, *Le Temps*, 1er janvier 1882. Arvède Barine, *Bibliothèque universelle et revue suisse*, XIII (1882), 108-130. Anon., *American*

(Philadelphia), III (1882), 394-395. Anon., *Temple Bar* (London), LXIV (1882), 510-519; also in *The Eclectic Magazine*, XCVIII (1882), 811-817. Gaston Boissier, *RDM*, 15 janvier 1882, 461-466.

F4b 1882 [Lenormant, Amélie]. Lettres ... deuxième édition ... 1882.

1882 See item F4b (Lenormant, Lettres ... deuxième édition ... 1882).

1883 See item F2b (Isler, Briefe ... Zweite vermehrte Ausgabe, 1883).

F5 1888 Menos, Jean-H. Lettres de Benjamin Constant à sa famille, 1775-1830, précédées d'une introduction, d'après des lettres et des documents inédits, par Jean-H. Menos. Paris: Albert Savine, 1888. pp.[iv], 598.

Includes letters to Rose-Susanne, Louis-Arnold-Juste, Rosalie, Lisette, Charles, and Juste de Constant and to Mme de Nassau, from manuscripts in BPU.

Reviews: [A. Laugel?], *The Nation* (New York), XLVII (1888), 168-169. A. de Pontmartin, *GF*, 28 octobre 1888.

Reprint: Paris: Stock, Delamain et Boutelleau, 1931.

F6 1895 Melegari, Dora. Journal intime de Benjamin Constant et lettres à sa famille et à ses amis, précédés d'une introduction par D. Melegari. Paris: Paul Ollendorff, 1895. pp.LXXI, 447. Portraits, facsimile. Bibliography.

Includes letters to Mme de Nassau, Isabelle de Charrière and others. Published from manuscripts now in BN and BCU (apart from letters from Isabelle de Charrière, for which the originals have not been found). Also includes letter from François de Neufchâteau, [14 April 1789]; see item A66/1.

Reprints: Paris: Albin Michel, [1928]; Paris: Stock, 1931.

Reviews and notices: see above, item A66/2.

F7 1906 Glachant, Victor. Benjamin Constant sous l'œil du guet. Paris: Plon-Nourrit et Cie, 1906. pp.[vii], xxxix, 600. Frontispiece (portrait), facsimiles. Bibliography.

Includes thirty-six letters from Constant to Claude Fauriel and a letter from Constant to Sophie de Condorcet. (Manuscripts in Bibliothèque de l'Institut, Paris). Also includes survey of letters listed in sale catalogues and prints texts of the following: from Constant to Charles Coquerel, Ce 18 may 1823 (p.152); to Juliette Récamier, Paris, le 1er mars 1823 (p.203; see items F4 and F16); to Bernard van Praet, Paris, ce 10 octobre 1825 (p.204, note 2); to François Raynouard, Paris, ce 5 février 1829 (pp.257-258; BCU, Co 3234); to Maréchal Gérard, Paris, 3 octobre (p.285); to Sieyès, Ce 24 brumaire an VIII, 15 novembre 1799 (pp.310-311; see items F182, F249, F251 and F307); to Juliette Récamier, 17 août 1816 (pp.314-315; see items F4 and F16); to the commissaire de police at Calais, Spa, ce 16 Aoust 1816 (pp.315-316; AN, F^7 6719/8371); to Jean-Jacques Coulmann, Münster, ce 22 octobre 1827 (pp.429-431; see item F122); to Martignac, Paris, ce 23 janvier 1829 (facsimile following p.456); to Ravez, 16 avril 1824; (pp.518-519); to d'Osmond, [Londres], Ce 21 juillet 1816 (pp.520-521); to P.-F. Tissot, [1822] (p.550).

Reviews: Maurice Dumoulin, *Petit Temps*, 22 février, 1906. J. Ernest-Charles, *Revue politique et littéraire (Revue bleue)*, 10 mars 1906, pp.312-313. Michel Salomon, *JD*, 24 mars 1906. G. Weill, *Revue de synthèse historique*, XII (1906), 117. Fernand Baldensperger, *Revue critique d'histoire et de littérature*, LXI (1906), 340-341. Gustave Lanson, *Revue universitaire*, juin 1906. Emile Faguet, *Revue latine*, VII (25 juillet 1906), 408-410. J. Ladreit de Lacharrière, *Revue des études historiques*, LXXII (1906), 523-525. Emile Couvreu, *Gazette de Lausanne*, 27 octobre 1906, p.1. A. d'Ochsenfeld, *Revue d'Alsace*, LXXVII (1906), 281-295. L. Rocheblave, *Revue internationale de l'enseignement*, LII (1906), 546-547. Anon., *Les Annales romantiques*, III (1906), 71-72. Anon., *Bibliothèque universelle et revue suisse*, XLII (1906), 196-197. Ch.-M. Des Granges, *Bulletin critique*, XII (1906), 334-337; *La Quinzaine*, LXXIV (1907), 557-565. Edmond Biré, *Ecrivains et soldats*, Paris: M. Falque, 1907, pp.49-67. J.L., *Revue des questions historiques*, XXXVII (1907), 343-344.

Reprint: 1931.

F8a 1907   Nolde, Elisabeth de. Madame de Staël and Benjamin Constant. Unpublished Letters together with other Mementos from the Papers left by Mme. Charlotte de Constant. Edited by Mme. de Constant's Great-Granddaughter Baroness Elisabeth de Nolde. Translated from the French by Charlotte Harwood. New York and London: G. P. Putnam's Sons, 1907. pp.vii, 298. Frontispiece (portrait), facsimile, illus.

See the following item.

F8b 1928   Nolde, Elisabeth de, & Léon, Paul L. Lettres de Madame de Staël à Benjamin Constant publiées pour la première fois en original par Madame la Baronne de Nolde avec une Introduction et des Notes par Paul L. Léon. Avant-propos de Gustave Rudler. Paris: Kra, 1928. pp.165. Illus., facsimile.

Letters published from the Mahrenholz archives, including a number of items retranslated from Strodtmann, item F3. Includes facsimile of letter from Germaine de Staël (dimanche soir 7 août [1796]) to Pictet-Diodati, with postscript by Constant. See items F194 and F284a.

Reviews: Daniel Mornet, *RHLF*, XXXVII (1930), 460. J. Prévost, *NRF*, 1er mars 1930, 420-422.

1928   See also item F6 (reprint of Melegari, Journal intime ... 1895).

1931   See items F5 (reprint of Menos, Lettres ... 1888), F6 (reprint of Melegari, Journal intime ... 1895) and F7 (reprint of Glachant ... 1906).

F9 1933   Constant de Rebecque, Baronne [L.]. L'Inconnue d'Adolphe. Correspondance de Benjamin Constant et d'Anna Lindsay, publiée par la baronne Constant de Rebecque. Préface de Fernand Baldensperger. Paris: Plon, [1933]. (La Palatine). pp.[iv], XXIX, 240. Frontispiece (portrait), illus. Bibliography.

Published from manuscripts now in BCU, Fonds Constant II.

Reviews: C.P., *JG*, 30 janvier 1933, p.1. Jeanne Cappe, *La Nation belge*, 12 février 1933. H. Colleye, *L'Essor colonial et maritime* (Bruxelles), 12 février 1933, p.2.

George Bergner, *L'Alsace française*, 19 février 1933, pp.149-150. Emile Henriot, *NL*, 15 juillet 1933, pp.1-2. Emile Magne, *MF*, 15 novembre 1933, pp.144-146. Benjamin Jarnes, *Revista de Occidente*, XLI (1933-1934), 362-368. Pierre Kohler, *RHLF*, XLI (1934), 605-606. Pierre Kohler, *GL*, 2 avril 1933, p.1. Gabriel Marcel, *L'Europe nouvelle*, 30 septembre 1933, pp.935-936.

F10 1933 Constant de Rebecque, Baronne [L.]. Lettres de Julie Talma à Benjamin Constant, publiées avec une introduction biographique et des notes par la baronne Constant de Rebecque. Paris: Plon, 1933. (La Palatine). pp.[vi], LXVIII, 254. Frontispiece (portrait), facsimiles, illus. Bibliography.

Published from manuscripts now in BCU, Fonds Constant II. Includes the *Lettre sur Julie* and letter to Napoleon Bonaparte, 15 April 1803, pp.155-157.

Reviews: Emile Henriot, *NL*, 15 juillet 1933, pp.1-2. G. Molteni, *Rivista di letture*, 15 marzo 1934, pp.69-71. Gabriel Marcel, *L'Europe nouvelle*, 30 septembre 1933, pp.935-936. Emile Magne, *MF*, 15 novembre 1933, pp.144-146.

F11 1949 Mistler, Jean. Benjamin Constant et Madame de Staël. Lettres à un ami. Cent onze lettres inédites à Claude Hochet, publiées avec une introduction et des notes par Jean Mistler. Neuchâtel: à la Baconnière, [1949]. pp.253. Portrait.

Published from manuscripts now in BN, N.a.fr. 11909.

Review: Robert Kemp, *NL*, 15 septembre 1949, p.3.

F12 1952 Hasselrot, Bengt. Benjamin Constant. Lettres à Bernadotte. Sources et origine de l'Esprit de conquête et de l'usurpation, publiées par Bengt Hasselrot. Genève: Droz; Lille: Giard, 1952. (Textes littéraires français). pp.LXIV, 46. Facsimiles.

Published from Swedish sources.

Reviews: J. Dechamps, *FS*, VI (1952), 371-373. Pierre Reboul, *AUS*, philosophie-lettres, II (1953), 138-142. Antoine Adam, *RSH*, LXVI (1952), 173-174. J.M.T., *EHR*, LXVII (1952), 615. A. Götze, *Archiv für das Studium der neueren Sprachen*, CXC (1953-1954), 165. I.W. Alexander, *MLR*, XLVIII (1953), 473-474.

F13 1955 Roulin, Alfred & Suzanne. Benjamin et Rosalie de Constant. Correspondance, 1786-1830, publiée avec une introduction et des notes par Alfred et Suzanne Roulin. Paris: Gallimard, 1955. pp.XXIII, 369.

Published from manuscripts in BCU and BPU.

Reviews: Guido Saba, *Nuova Antologia*, CDLXV (1955), 265-270. Carlo Pellegrini, *L'Italia che scrive*, XXXVIII (1955), 201.

F14 1973 Harpaz, Ephraïm. Benjamin Constant et Goyet de la Sarthe. Correspondance, 1818-1822, publiée avec une introduction, des notes et un index par Ephraïm Harpaz. Genève: Droz, 1973. (Travaux d'histoire éthico-politique, 26). pp.758.

Published from manuscripts in BN and BCU.

Reviews: S. Dontenwill, *Cahiers d'histoire*, XIX (1974), 201-203. B. Sachter, *Annales de Bretagne*, LXXXI (1974), 771-775. J.-R. Derré, *SF*, XVIII (1974), 359-360. Anon., *Cahiers staëliens*, XVIII (1974), 48. Kurt Kloocke, *ZFSL*, LXXXV (1975), 378-380. J. Waquet, *Bibliothèque de l'Ecole des Chartes*, CXXXIII (1975), 366-374. Max Milner, *IL*, 28ᵉ année, janvier-février 1976, 30-31. Norman King, *MLR*, LXXI (1976), 419-420.

F15 1974   Cordey, Pierre. Benjamin Constant. Cent lettres choisies et présentées par Pierre Cordey. Lausanne: Bibliothèque romande, 1974. pp.254.

Includes two previously unpublished letters from private collections: Constant to the Rédacteur du *Moniteur*, Paris, ce 16 septembre 1817; to Isabelle Morel (née de Gélieu), ce 22 juillet 1818.

F16 1977   Harpaz, Ephraïm. Benjamin Constant. Lettres à Madame Récamier (1807-1830). Edition critique, avec introduction et commentaires par Ephraïm Harpaz. Paris: Klincksieck, 1977. (Bibliothèque du XIXᵉ siècle, 6). pp.309. Portrait.

Published from manuscripts in BN. Includes *Idées sur la conservation du royaume de Naples* (item A74/2) and three letters from Constant to Mme Degérando (item F173).

Reviews: Anita Brookner, *TLS*, 6 May 1977, p.552, 'The romantic lover's handbook'. Alison Fairlie, *FS*, XXXII (1978), 84-86. K. Kloocke, *ZFLS*, LXXXVIII (1978), 84-87. G. Mercken-Spaas, *Nineteenth-century French studies*, VII (1979), 272-273. Paul Delbouille, *RHLF*, LXXX (1980), 303-305.

Translations

See items A66/t1 and A66/t3. See also items F3 and F8a.

F/t1 1954   Betocchi, Carlo. Festa d'amore. Le piú belle lettere d'amore di tutti i tempi e di tutti i paesi, a cura di Carlo Betocchi. [Firenze]: Vallecchi, [1954]. pp.xxviii, 713. Illus.

Includes, pp.429-433, translation of six letters from Constant to Mme Récamier, 1814-1815. (Cordié 221).

F/t2 1962   Talma, Julie. Erotisch schimmenspel. Brieven aan Benjamin Constant. Amsterdam: G. A. van Oorschot, 1962. (Stoa-reeks). pp.237.

Translation, introduction and notes by H. L. Mulder.

F/t3 1971   Dubois, Simone. Rebels en Beminnelijk. Brieven van Belle van Zuylen-Madame de Charrière aan Constant d'Hermenches, James Boswell, Benjamin Constant en anderen, 1760-1805. Amsterdam: De Arbeiderspers, 1971. (Privé-Domein, 18). pp.179.

Translations and introductions by Simone Dubois. Reprinted: 1971, 1972, 1978, 1979.

F/t4 1982   Benjamin Constant. La porta chiusa. Lettere a Juliette Récamier (1814-1816). Postfazione e apparati critici di Lucia Omacini. Milano: Serra e

Riva, 1982. (Biblioteca del Minotauro, 32). pp.267.

Translation by Laura Este Bellini.

II Separate letters

See also items A18/44 (Adolphe ... Lausanne: Spes, 1921), A18/54 (Adolphe ... Paris: Payot, 1929); A18/101 (Adolphe ... Paris: Garnier, 1955); A66/1 (Le Journal intime ... 1887); A68/2 (Le Cahier rouge, Paris: Calmann-Lévy, [1907]); A74/9a ('B. Constant prophète' ... 1968); E4-2 (Les Cent Jours ... Paris: H. Gautier, 1892); A66/t1 (Reise durch die deutsche Kultur ... Potsdam: Kiepenheuer, 1919); A68/t1 (Czerwony Kajet, Warszawa: Bibl. Boya, 1932).

F101 1831 Constant, Charles de. [Letter of 2 June 1831 to the Editors], *JG*, n° 24, sixième année, 16 juin 1831, p.103.

Letter from Benjamin Constant to Rose-Susanne de Constant, Brusselles, le 19 novembre 1779, reprinted in Menos, item F5.

F102 1831 Constant, Charles de. [Letter of 2 June 1831 from Charles de Constant to the Editors], *Le National*, n° 173, 22 juin 1831, p.[4].

Letter from Benjamin Constant to Rose-Susanne de Constant, Brusselles, le 19 novembre 1779, as in preceding item.

F103 1835 Mackintosh, Sir James. Memoirs of the Life of the Right Honourable Sir James Mackintosh, edited by his son, Robert James Mackintosh: London: Edward Moxon, 1835. 2 vols.

Letter from Constant to Mackintosh, Liège, March 27th, 1814, II, 270-272. Also in second edition, London: Moxon, 1836, II, 275-277. Reprinted in Nicolson, item F223.

F104 1835 Pagès, Jean-Piere. Dictionnaire de la conversation et de la lecture. Paris: Belin Mandar, 1835, XVI, 332-337; second edition, 1860, VI, 349.

Includes extract from a letter from Constant, 1er avril 1815, to an unnamed correspondent.

F105 1838 Chateaubriand, François-René de. Congrès de Vérone. Guerre d'Espagne. Négociations: colonies espagnoles. Paris: Delloye; Leipzig: Brockhaus et Avenarius, 1838. 2 vols.

Includes letter from Constant to Chateaubriand, Paris, ce 31 mai 1824, II, 454-455. Reprinted in items F201, F189a and F285.

F105a 1838 Lafayette, Marie-Joseph Du Motier, marquis de. Mémoires, correspondance et manuscrits du général Lafayette, publiés par sa famille. Paris: H. Fournier aîné; Leipzig: Brockhaus & Avenarius, 1837-1838. 6 vols.

In vol. V (1838), pp.406-412, letter from Lafayette to Constant, Lagrange, le 9 avril 1815.

F106 1842 Dorow, Wilhelm. Reminiszenzen Goethe's Mutter, nebst Briefen und Aufzeichnungen zur Charakteristik anderer merkwürdiger Männer und Frauen. Leipzig: Hinrich, 1842.

Letter from Constant to Ludwig Robert, Paris, 18 juin 1826, pp.92-93. See item F300.

F107 1844   Gaullieur, Eusèbe H. [Correspondance of Benjamin Constant and Isabelle de Charrière], *Revue suisse*, VII (1844), 181-187; 245-251.

Letters and extracts, 1787-1794. See item F292.

F108 1844   Sainte-Beuve, C.-A. 'Benjamin Constant et Mme de Charrière, lettres inédites', *RDM*, 15 avril 1844, 193-264.

Reprinted, with some revisions, in *Caliste ou Lettres écrites de Lausanne*, roman par Mme de Charrière, Paris: Jules Labitte, 1845, pp.217-315. Also in Sainte-Beuve, *Derniers portraits littéraires*, Paris: Didier, 1852, pp.180-276; *Portraits littéraires*, nouvelle édition, Paris: Garnier frères, 1864, III, 185-283; Sainte-Beuve, *Œuvres*, texte présenté et annoté par Maxime Leroy, Paris: Gallimard, 1960 (Bibliothèque de la Pléiade), II, 677-763. See item F292.

F109 1845   Gaullieur, Eusèbe-H. 'Fragment d'une course en Angleterre; Extrait des Mémoires inédits de Benjamin Constant. – 1787', *Album de la Suisse romane*, 1845, III, 49-52.

Letter to Isabelle de Charrière, 6-7 septembre 1787. See item F292.

F110 1847   Gaullieur, Eusèbe-H. 'La jeunesse de Benjamin Constant (d'après de nouvelles lettres inédites)', *Bibliothèque universelle et Revue suisse*, 4e série, VI (1847), 236-267; 344-375.

Letters and extracts of letters to Isabelle de Charrière, 1789-1790. First part reprinted, with some cuts, in Gaullieur, E.-H., *Etrennes nationales*, Genève: Gruaz, 1854, II, 95-138; both parts reprinted in Gaullieur, E.-H., *Mémoires historiques et littéraires sur la Suisse française*, Paris-Genève: J. Cherbuliez, 1855. See item F292.

F111 1848   Gaullieur, Eusèbe-H. 'Benjamin Constant pendant la Révolution (d'après de nouvelles lettres inédites), 1791-1796', *Bibliothèque universelle et Revue suisse*, 4e série, VIII (1848), 50-84; 271-293.

Letters and extracts of letters to Isabelle de Charrière, 1791-1796. See item F292.

F112 1849   Colet, Louise. 'Lettres intimes de Benjamin Constant à Madame Récamier, avec une introduction et une conclusion, par Mme Louise Colet, *La Presse*, 3-5 juillet 1849.

Includes selection of letters reprinted in item F1 and letter from Constant to Claude Hochet, Hardenberg, ce 11 octobre 1811.

F113 1849   Chateaubriand, François-René de. Mémoires d'Outre-Tombe. Paris: E. et V. Penaud frères, 1849-1851. 12 vols.

Includes letter from Constant to Chateaubriand, Paris, ce 21 mai 1827 and a number of letters from Constant to Juliette Récamier. See *Mémoires d'Outre-Tombe*, édition du Centenaire, établie par Maurice Levaillant, Paris: Flammarion, 1949, III, 286-288, 379-383, 394-395. See also items F1, F4 and F16.

F114 1853 Grille, François-Joseph. Le Bric-à-brac, avec son catalogue raisonné. Paris: Ledoyen, 1853. 2 vols.

Four letters from Constant: to Mme Paschoud, Paris, 21 janvier [1809], II, 28-29; to J.-J. Paschoud, Dôle, ce 16 décembre 1808, II, 30-32; to the same, Coppet, 15 novembre 1808, II, 32-34; to the same, Coppet, le 19 novembre 1808, II, 34-36.

F115 1855 Gaullieur, Eusèbe-H. Etudes sur l'histoire littéraire de la Suisse française, particulièrement pendant la seconde moitié du XVIIIe siècle, *Bulletin de l'Institut national genevois*, III (1855). pp.318.

Includes extracts from letters to Isabelle de Charrière. Also published separately as: Gaullieur, E.-H., *Etudes sur l'histoire littéraire de la Suisse française, particulièrement dans la seconde moitié du XVIIIe siècle*, Genève: Gruaz, Cherbuliez; Paris: Cherbuliez, 1856. pp.318. See item F292.

F116 1857 Béranger, P.-J. de. Ma Biographie. Paris: Perrotin, 1857. pp.332.

Letter from Constant to Béranger, 29 janvier 1829, pp.157-161. Also in second edition (1858), third edition (1859) and in *Correspondance de Béranger*, recueillie par Paul Boiteau, Paris: Perrotin, 1860, I, 354-356. See item F1.

F117 1857 Castille, Hippolyte. Benjamin Constant. Paris: Ferdinand Sartorius, 1857. (Portraits historiques au dix-neuvième siècle, 26). pp.63.

Includes facsimile of letter, Paris ce 30 Juillet 1828, from Constant to an unidentified correspondent.

F118 1859 Guizot, François. Mémoires pour servir à l'histoire de mon temps. Paris: Michel Lévy frères, 1858-1867. 8 vols.

Includes letter from Constant to Guizot, 24 octobre 1830, II (1859), 145. Reprinted in item F204.

F118a 1863 Hugo, Victor. Victor Hugo raconté par un témoin de sa vie. Bruxelles et Leipzig: A. Lacroix, Verboeckhoven, 1863. 2 vols.

Vol. II includes letter from Constant to Hugo, ce 12 janvier 1830.

F119 1863-1864 'Charles Nodier à Benjamin Constant', *Revue littéraire de la Franche-Comté*, I (1863-1864), 309-311.

Letter, Paris, le 5 janvier 1830, from Ms 272 in Bibliothèque municipale, Dôle.

F120 1867 Crépet, Eugène. 'Benjamin Constant, d'après une correspondance de famille complètement inédite', *Revue nationale et étrangère*, XXVII (1867), 161-188; 415-459.

Letters later published in Menos, item F5.

F121 1868 Crépet, Eugène. 'Une correspondance inédite de Benjamin

Constant', *Revue moderne*, XLV (1868), 531-552; XLVI (1868), 241-259.

Letters to Fauriel, later published in Glachant, item F7.

F122 1869   Coulmann, Jean-Jacques. Réminiscences. Paris: Michel Lévy frères, 1862-1869, 3 vols.

Fifty-five letters from Constant to Coulmann (1823-1830), III, 90-124 (BN, N.a.fr. 24914); letter from Constant to Goethe (Baden, 14 septembre 1827), III, 174.

F123 1875   Bouniol, Batild. 'La vérité sur Benjamin Constant', *Revue du monde catholique*, XLIV (1875), 188-192.

Letter from Constant to Claude Hochet, ce 11 octobre 1811. See items F1 and F11.

F124 1876   'En temps d'élections. Lettre inédite de Benjamin Constant', *ICC*, IX, n° 186, 10 février 1876, cols. 94-95.

Letter to Pictet-Diodati, 27 vendémiaire an VII, (18 octobre 1798). Copies, with variants, in BPU, Ms 2256, ff.38-40 and Ms 2265, ff.11-14.

F125 1877   Adolphe, par Benjamin Constant. Préface de A. J. Pons. Paris: Jules Claye, A. Quantin, 1877. pp.228. (Items A18/16-17).

Includes facsimile of letter of 'ce 22 May' from Constant to an unidentified correspondent and selection of letters from Constant to Isabelle de Charrière and others.

F126 1879   E.D. 'La correspondance amoureuse de Madame de Staël avec Benjamin Constant', *ICC*, XII, n° 271, 25 août 1879, col. 485.

Constant sold his letters to Mme de Staël to the duchesse de Broglie for 100.000 francs: A. J. Pons, *Sainte-Beuve et ses inconnues*, Paris: Ollendorff, 1879, p.137. See also Ellick, 'Lettres d'amour à Benjamin Constant', *ICC*, XXIV, n° 556, 10 juillet 1891, col. 495.

F126a 1879   Pictet de Sergy, J. Notice biographique sur feu Marc Pictet de Sergy (Monsieur Pictet-Diodati). Genève, 1879.

Includes letter from Constant to Pictet-Diodati, [1799], p.14. Quoted by Jasinski, item F305.

F127 1880   'Quelques lettres de Benjamin Constant et de Mme de Staël sur l'Allemagne (1802-1814)', *Revue politique et littéraire, Revue des cours littéraires*, 2e série, 9e année (27 mars 1880), 909-914.

Extracts from Isler, item F2.

F128 1880   [Letter to M. Johanys, 16 juillet 1829]. *Revue des documents historiques, suite de pièces curieuses et inédites avec des notes et des commentaires* par Etienne Charavay, VII (1880), 150-151.

F129 1881   Rousset, A. La Société en robe de Chambre, 1881. Facsimiles.

Cahier 1, n° 1: facsimile of letter from B. Constant to Rillet & Ce, Neufchatel ce 4 Septembre 1793.

F130 1884 Frossard, Frédéric. 'Mme de Krüdener d'après des documents inédits', *Bibliothèque universelle et Revue suisse*, XXIV (1884), 302-321, 503-532.

On pp.519-532: quotations from letters later published in *JG*, 1908, item F159.

F131 1886 Ego E.-G. 'Benjamin Constant et Mme Récamier', *ICC*, XIX, n° 431, 25 avril 1886, col. 229.

Comments on Louise Colet's edition, item F1. See also O'Realy, 'Benj. Constant et Madame Récamier', *ICC*, XIX n° 432, 10 mai 1886, col. 283.

F132 1887 [Melegari, Dora]. 'Lettres de Benjamin Constant à sa famille', *Revue internationale*, XIV (1887), 24-53; 200-232; 355-379; 584-605.

Reprinted in Melegari, item F6.

F133 1887 'Lettres inédites de Benjamin Constant', *La Nouvelle Revue*, XLVIII (1887), 446-470; 712-737.

Letters from Constant to the comtesse de Nassau published in Menos, item F5.

F134 1887 Charavay, Etienne. Lettres autographes composant la collection de M. Alfred Bovet, Paris: Charavay frères, 1887. 2 vols.

Letter from Constant to Casimir Périer, ce samedi [27 mars 1824], I, 72, n° 188.

F135 1888 Ernouf, baron. 'Une lettre inédite de Benjamin Constant', *BB*, 1888, 530-533.

Letter, Paris, 6 août 1819, to Bignon.

F136 1889 [Melegari, Dora]. 'Benjamin Constant: Lettres à sa tante, la comtesse de Nassau', *Revue internationale*, XXI (1889), 5-32; 149-177; 302-324.

Reprinted in Melegari, item F6.

F137 1889 Asse, Eugène. 'Benjamin Constant et le Directoire', *Revue de la Révolution*, XV (1889), 337-356; 433-453, XVI (1889), 5-26, 105-125.

Includes, XVI, 107-108, letter from Constant 'au citoyen G', Hérivaux, 15 germinal an VI (4 April 1798), reprinted from *Le Républicain*, n° 2, 2 floréal an VI (21 April 1798). See item D21.

F138 1890 'Deux lettres de Benjamin Constant', *Revue rétrospective*, Nouvelle série, XII (janvier-juillet 1890), 138-141.

Letter to Fauriel, Leipsic, 9 mars 1804; to Kératry, ce 12 may 1827, from Bibliothèque de la ville d'Avignon, collection Requien.

F138a 1891 Talleyrand. Mémoires du Prince de Talleyrand, publiés avec une préface et des notes par le duc de Broglie. Paris: Calmann Lévy, 1891-1892. 5 vols.

Includes, vol. II (1891), p.261, letter from Constant to Talleyrand, [8 April 1814].

F138b 1891   Smiles, Samuel. A Publisher and his friends. Memoir and Correspondence of the late John Murray. London: John Murray, 1891. 2 vols.

Includes extract of letter from Constant to Murray. Brussels [4 November 1815], vol. I, p.281.

F139 1892-1893   Barante, Amable-Guillaume-Prosper Brugière de. Souvenirs du baron de Barante, publiés par son petit-fils Claude de Barante. Paris: Calmann-Lévy, 1890-1901. 8 vols.

Letters from Constant to Barante: Paris, 27 janvier 1820, II (1892), 395-397; Paris, juin 1820, II, 440; Paris , 4 décembre 1821, II, 542-543; Paris, novembre 1822, III (1893), 59-61; Paris, 18 mars 1823, III, 173-174.

F140 1894   Melegari, Dora. 'Lettres à Madame de Charrière, 1792-1795', *RP*, 15 octobre 1894, pp.673-718.

Reprinted in Melegari, item F6. See item F292.

F141 1895   Barthélemy-Saint-Hilaire, Jules. M. Victor Cousin, sa vie et sa correspondance. Paris: Hachette, Alcan, 1895. 3 vols.

Letters from Constant to Cousin: Paris, le 10 juin 1823, II, 268-269; le 11 juillet [1824], II, 270; le 30 juillet 1824, II, 270-271; Cousin to Constant: Orbec, le 4 novembre 1825, II, 272-274; Constant to Cousin: Paris, le 10 septembre 1830, II, 278-279. (Manuscripts in Bibliothèque de la Sorbonne, Cousin 223).

F142 1895-1896   Barras, Paul, vicomte de. Mémoires de Barras, publiés avec une introduction générale, des préfaces et des appendices, par Georges Duruy. Paris: Hachette, 1895-1896. 4 vols.

Letter from Constant to Citoyens Directeurs, Paris, ce 30 frimaire an VI, 20 December 1797, III, 128-131, (BCU, IS 4219/2) and from Constant to Barras, Hérivaux, le 7 germinal an VI (27 March 1798), III, 200.

F143 1897   Geiger, Ludwig. Aus Alt-Weimar: Mittheilungen von Zeitgenossen nebst Skizzen und Ausführungen. Berlin: Paetel, 1897. pp.xvi, 369.

Extract of a letter from Constant to Karl August Böttiger, 15 août, 1804, p.53. See item F157.

F144 1901   Leroux-Cesbron, E. 'Benjamin Constant à Saumur (1820)', *Nouvelle Revue rétrospective*, 2ᵉ série, XVIIᵉ année, n° 79, 10 janvier 1901, pp.1-36.

Includes letters from Constant to Gentil de Saint-Alphonse, Jacques Lofficial and editor of *Le Courrier français*, 1820-1830. Extracts from texts reprinted in full in Harpaz, item F14.

F145 1902   Glachant, Paul et Victor. 'Benjamin Constant, Cabanis, Manzoni, etc., etc., Lettres à Fauriel', *La Nouvelle Revue*, XIV (1902), 63-78.

Reprinted in Glachant, item F7.

F146 1903   'Lettres à Rosalie', *La Nouvelle Revue*, Nouvelle série, Tome XXIV, 25ᵉ année, 1ᵉʳ octobre 1903, 289-295.

Seven letters to Rosalie de Constant, 1809-1810. Reprinted in Roulin, item F13.

F147 1904 Herriot, Edouard. *Madame Récamier et ses amis*. Paris: Plon-Nourrit, 1904. 2 vols. pp.LXXIX, 363 + IV, 424.

Includes letters and extracts of letters from Constant to Juliette Récamier, I, 115, 333. See items F1, F4 and F16.

F148 1904 Lauris, Georges de. 'Benjamin Constant: Lettres inédites', *La Revue*, 1er mai 1904, pp.1-18; 15 mai 1904, pp.151-159.

Extracts of thirty-two letters from Constant to Claude Hochet, 1800-1830. Published in full in Mistler, item F11.

F149 1904 Melegari, Dora. 'Lettres inédites de Mme de Staël', *JG*, 21 novembre 1904, p.1; 5 décembre 1904, p.1; 12 décembre 1904, p.1.

Letter from Germaine de Staël to Constant, 17 fév. [1813], Stoc[kholm], and three undated letters to Constant from an unidentified female correspondent.

F150 1905 Rudler, Gustave. 'Un "portrait littéraire" de Sainte-Beuve. Notes historiques et critiques', *RHLF*, XII (1905), 177-202.

Includes corrections to letters published by Sainte-Beuve, item F108.

F151 1906 [Glachant, Victor]. 'Lettres de Benjamin Constant à Fauriel (1802-1823)', *Revue politique et littéraire (Revue bleue)*, 13 janvier 1906, pp.36-41; 20 janvier 1906, pp.65-70.

Reprinted in Glachant, item F7.

F152 1906 Dierolf, Georges. 'Lettres inédites de Benjamin Constant', *Le Gaulois du dimanche*, 27-28 janvier 1906, pp.1-2.

Five letters from Constant: to Reinhard, Göttingue, ce 10 avril 1813 (BN, N.a.fr. 13627, ff.9-10); Göttingue, ce [15] septembre 1813; (*ibid*, ff.13-14), Paris, ce 12 octobre 1819; to [Dommequère], Bade, ce 21 novembre 1829 (*ibid*, ff.131-132; to an unidentified correspondent, ce 13 juillet [s.a].

F153 1906 Barante, Baron de. 'Lettres de Benjamin Constant à Prosper de Barante', *RDM*, 15 juillet 1906, pp.241-272; 1er août 1906, pp.528-567.

Thirty-six letters to Barante, [1805]-1830.

F154 1906 Nolde, Baroness de. 'Love letters of Mme de Staël to Benjamin Constant', translated by Charlotte Harwood, *The Critic and the literary world*, (New York), XLVIII (March-May 1906), pp.273-280; 357-364; 444-450.

Reprinted in Nolde, item F8a.

F155 1906 Godet, Philippe. *Madame de Charrière et ses amis, d'après de nombreux documents inédits (1740-1805)*. Genève: A. Jullien, 1906. 2 vols.

Includes extracts from correspondence between Isabelle de Charrière and Constant. See item F292. Reprinted (and abridged): Edition abrégée établie par Gabrielle Godet, Lausanne: Spes, 1927.

F156 1906   Pélissier, L.-G. 'Lettres de divers écrivains français: Lettres de Benjamin Constant', *BB*, 1906, pp.357-359.

Three letters from Biblioteca Civica, Turin: Constant to Fontanes, 28 mai 1795; to Fanny Randall, n.d.; to Laguionie, [12 May 1824: see item F298].

F157 1908   Baldensperger, Fernand. 'Lettres à Böttiger (1804-1814)', *Revue politique et littéraire (Revue bleue)*, 5e série, IX (18 avril 1908), pp.481-486.

Ten letters from Constant to Böttiger, 1804-1814, from manuscripts in Sächsische Landesbibliothek, Dresden.

F158 1908   Gautier, Paul. Mathieu de Montmorency et Madame de Staël, d'après des lettres inédites de M. de Montmorency à Mme Necker de Saussure. Paris: Plon-Nourrit, 1908. pp.VII, 311.

Letter from Constant to Mme Necker de Saussure, Paris, 19 pluviôse (8 février 1805), pp.210-216; letter from Germaine de Staël to Mme Necker de Saussure, Weimar, le 23 avril [1804], with postscript by Constant, p.193.

F159 1908   [Privat, Raoul]. 'Trois lettres inédites de Benjamin Constant [à Mme de Krüdener]', *JG*, 9 mars 1908.

Included in collection published by Ley, 1967, item F270.

F160 1908   Souriau, Maurice. Népomucène Lemercier et ses correspondants. Paris: Vuibert et Nony, 1908. pp.XII, 308.

Letters from Constant: Paris, ce 9 septembre 1830, pp.261-262; 20 novembre 1830, p.264.

F161 1909   Ettlinger, Josef. Benjamin Constant: der Roman eines Lebens. Berlin: E. Fleischel, 1909. pp.xvi, 324.

Facsimile of letter from Constant to Goethe, [Weimar, 1804], following p.136, from Goethe-Schiller Archiv, Weimar. See items F194, F219 and F300.

F162 1909   Galley, Jean-Baptiste. Claude Fauriel, membre de l'Institut, 1772-1843. Sainte-Etienne: Impr. de la 'Loire républicaine', 1909. pp.xxiv, 512.

Includes extracts from letters from Constant to Fauriel, 1802-1809. See item F7.

F163 1909   Rudler, Gustave. La jeunesse de Benjamin Constant, 1767-1794. Paris: Armand Colin, 1909. pp.xi, 542.

Includes letters to members of the Constant family and to Isabelle de Charrière.

F164 1909   Rudler, Gustave. Bibliographie critique des œuvres de Benjamin Constant. Paris: Armand Colin, 1909. pp.108.

Includes survey of Constant's manuscripts (including letters to Huber and Villers) and prints texts of several letters of the period 1774-1794.

F165 1909   Godet, Philippe. 'La jeunesse de Benjamin Constant', *Bibliothèque universelle et Revue suisse*, LIV (1909), 449-470.

Includes, pp.469-470, letter from Constant to Isabelle de Charrière, Lausanne, ce 7 octobre 94. See item F292.

F166 1910   B[onnefon], Paul. 'A travers les autographes. Un billet inédit de Benjamin Constant'. *RHLF*, XVII (1910), 398.

Letter, ce 16 juillet 1827, to Ambroise Dupont.

F167 1910   Chapuisat, Edouard. La municipalité de Genève pendant la domination française. Extraits de ses registres et de sa correspondance (1798-1814). Genève: Kündig; Paris: Champion, 1910. 2 vols.

Includes letter to the Ministre de l'Intérieur, 17 mai 1799 (AN, F^{IC} III, Léman 2), I, 238-243; letter to the Administration municipale de Genève, 3 janvier 1800 (Arch. munic. XV A'22), II, 11; further letter of 31 janvier 1800 (II, 18-19) and reply from the Administration municipale, 29 août 1800 (II, 80-82).

F168 1910   Rudler, Gustave. 'Robespierre et les Jacobins dans la correspondance de Benjamin Constant (1793-1794)', *Annales révolutionnaires*, III (1910), 92-103.

Extracts of letters from Constant to Isabelle de Charrière and Mme de Nassau, 1793-1794.

F169 1911   Rudler, Gustave. 'Deux lettres d'Edgar Quinet à B. Constant et une lettre sur Benjamin Constant', *RHLF*, XVIII (1911), 941-943.

Letters from Quinet to Constant: Heidelberg, le 11 mars 1827; Paris, 12 7bre 1830 (BCU, Co 982-983); letter from Rivier to Juste de Constant, Londres, le 20 juillet 1787; and receipt signed by B. Constant, Londres, ce 20 juillet 1787.

F170 1911-1912   Charrière de Sévery, [William & Clara de]. La vie de société dans le Pays de Vaud à la fin du dix-huitième siècle. Lausanne: Georges Bridel; Paris: Fischbacher, 1911-1912. 2 vols.

Includes letters from Constant to members of the Charrière de Sévery family and to the comtesse de Nassau.

F171 1912   Daudet, Ernest. La police politique: chronique des temps de la Restauration, d'après les rapports des agents secrets et les papiers du cabinet noir, 1815-1820. Paris: Plon-Nourrit, 1912. pp.XXVII, 392.

Letter from Constant to Alexander von Humboldt, [1817], pp.309-310.

F172 1912   Rudler, Gustave. 'Une correspondance inédite: Benjamin Constant et Louvet', *Bibliothèque universelle et Revue suisse*, LXVII (1912), 225-247.

Text of letters, 1795-1796, from manuscripts now in BCU, Ms 274.

F173 1913   Rudler, Gustave. 'Lettres de B. Constant à M. et Mme Degérando', *Bibliothèque universelle et Revue suisse*, LXIX (1913), 449-485.

Text of letters, 1814-1825, now in BCU, Ms 282-283. See item F16.

F174 1913   Rudler, Gustave. Benjamin Constant, député de la Sarthe (1819-

1822). Le Mans: Association ouvrière de l'imprimerie Drouin, 1913. pp.[vi], 64. (Extrait de *La Révolution dans la Sarthe et les départements voisins*, VIII (1913), 64-125).

Includes letter from Chateaubriand to Constant, Paris, le 27 mai 1827, (BCU, Co 1055) and extracts from letters to Constant from Goyet, Thoré and others, later published by Harpaz, item F14. See item F225.

F175 1913　Thomas, Louis. 'Un projet de mariage de Benjamin Constant', *La Semaine littéraire*, 8 novembre 1913, pp.536-537.

Two letters from Constant to Rosalie de Constant, 1802-1803, reprinted in Roulin, item F13.

F175a 1913　Chateaubriand, François-René de. Correspondance générale, publiée avec introduction, indication des sources, notes et tables doubles, par Louis Thomas. Tome IV. Paris: Honoré et Edouard Champion, 1913.

Includes, pp.364-365, letter from Chateaubriand to Constant, Paris le 13 août 1823. See item F225.

F175b 1914　Chapuisat, Edouard. 'De Genève française à Genève suisse', *MF*, CIX (1914), 484-498.

Includes letter from Constant to H.-A. Gosse, Paris, ce 25 frimaire an IX (16 December 1800), p.491 (BPU, Ms 2628).

F176 1914　Thomas, Louis. 'Lettres inédites de Benjamin Constant', *Revue politique et littéraire (Revue bleue)*, 52ᵉ année, n° 16, 18 avril 1914, pp.481-486; 25 avril 1914, 519-524.

Twenty-two letters (1799-1809) from manuscripts in BPU omitted by Menos, item F5.

F177 1915　Rudler, Gustave. 'Une créance de Talleyrand', *Revue des études napoléoniennes*, VII (1915), 425-431.

Includes letter from Constant to Archambaud-Joseph de Talleyrand, ce 21 novembre 1818 (BCU, Co 166); to Talleyrand, Paris, ce 4 février 1821; from Rihouet, Paris, 23 avril 1829 (BCU, Co, 194).

F178 1916　Kohler, Pierre. Madame de Staël et la Suisse. Lausanne-Paris: Payot, 1916, pp.x, 720.

Includes extract from letter of 19 mars 1797 from Constant to Pictet-Diodati, p.230, and extracts of letters from Constant to the same, 26 juin 1801, pp.404-405; 28 octobre 1801, p.405.

F179 1919　Rudler, Gustave. Benjamin Constant. Adolphe. Edition historique et critique. Manchester: Imprimerie de l'Université, 1919. (Modern Language Texts. French series: modern section). pp.lxxxvi, xxi, 168. (Item A18/42).

Includes, in Introduction, contract with Brissot-Thivars, Paris, 8 mars 1824; letters from Mme Brissot-Thivars to Constant, 2 juin 1824; Paris, 7 juin 1824; Paris, le 14 Xʳᵉ 1827; Paris, le 2 avril 1828. Includes in Appendix A,

'Correspondance relative à *Adolphe*': letter from Constant to the Editor of the *Morning Chronicle*, June 23, 1816; letter from Constant to Alexander Walker, Spa, 10 September 1816; letter from Frédérique to Constant, Londres, ce 19ᵉ juin 1816; from Walker, July 1816.

F180 1920   Rudler, Gustave. 'Un chapitre de la tragédie-comédie académique: les candidatures de Benjamin Constant', *Bibliothèque universelle et Revue suisse*, XCVIII (1920), 29-38, 189-202.

Includes the following letters: Regnaut de Saint-Jean d'Angély to Constant, n.d.; J.-B. Suard to Constant, 7 juillet [1817] (BCU, Co 1113); Constant to Raynouard, Paris, 18 août 1817; Paris, 27 août 1817; Béranger to Constant, 22 mai 1830 (BCU, 1042); Jouy to Constant, [1ᵉʳ ou 8 septembre 1830] (BCU, Co 1029); Constant to Lemercier, 9 septembre 1830] (Bayeux, Bibl, mun.); Lemercier to Constant, 11 septembre 1830; Constant to Raynouard, 11 novembre 1830 (BCU, Ms 317); La Berge to Constant, 20 novembre 1830 (BCU, Co 1229).

F181 1920   Nescio. 'La correspondance de Benjamin Constant', *ICC*, LXXII, nᵒ 1530, 20-30 décembre 1920, cols 402-403.

Request for information about whether Nolde (item F8a) has been published in French. A similar request by the same author was published in *ICC*, LVIII, nᵒ 1200, 30 octobre 1908, cols 612-613.

F182 1920   Vauthier, Gabriel. 'Une lettre inédite de Benjamin Constant', *Annales révolutionnaires*, XIII (1921), 413-418.

Letter of 24 brumaire an 8 (15 November 1799) to [Sieyès]. Also published in Glachant (item F7) and Guillemin (items F249, F251 and F307).

F183 1924   Bergner, Georges. 'Benjamin Constant député de Strasbourg', *L'Alsace française*, 4ᵉ année, nᵒ 15 (12 avril 1924), 353-356; nᵒ 16, (19 avril 1924), 376-380.

Letter from Constant to Véron, 1ᵉʳ juin 1830, p.380.

F184 1924   Lods, Armand. 'Benjamin Constant. En Alsace. Sa correspondance', *ICC*, LXXXVII, nᵒ 1606, 10-30 août 1924, cols 626-627.

Includes letter from Constant to 'un ami', 31 octobre 1827.

F185 1924   Rudler, Gustave. 'Quelques lettres écrites d'Angleterre à Benjamin Constant', *FQ*, VI (1924), 101-114.

Letters to Constant, [1816]-1830 from Mrs Cullum, Thomas John Hussey, Thomas W. Stonow, Sir James Mackintosh, R. W. Norton, Sismondi, John Cam Hobhouse, W. E. Frye, Alphonse Varnier, George Morton and an anonymous Englishman. Also includes a letter from Constant to Charles de Rebecque (Paris, ce 14 mars 1830).

F186 1925   Rudler, Gustave. 'Pour mon édition d'*Adolphe*', *FQ*, VII (1925), 65-68.

Includes letter from Charles Dumont to Constant, Paris, ce 27 7bre 1827 (BCU, Fonds Constant I, Co 3401).

F187 1926   Mistler, Jean. *Madame de Staël et Maurice O'Donnell, 1805-1817, d'après des lettres inédites.* Paris: Calmann-Lévy, [1926]. pp.ii, 332.

Includes, pp.99-109, two letters from Constant to Germaine de Staël, from Archives de la police (Vienna): Des Herbages, ce 25 avril [1808]; ce 27 avril [1808]; and letter, Vienne, le 15 mai 1808, from [Germaine de Staël] to Constant.

F188 1926   Vandérem, F. 'La première préface d'*Adolphe*. Une lettre inédite de Benjamin Constant', *BB*, nouvelle série, V (1926), 501-502.

Letter from Constant to Würtz, 'ce mardi' [July 1816].

F189 1926   [Facsimile of letter, ce 18 Aoust, from Constant to Lacretelle]. *Le Manuscrit autographe*, mai-juin 1926.

F189a 1926   'Trois billets de Chateaubriand', *Le Figaro*, 17 août 1926, p.4.

Letter from [Constant], 31 mai 182[4]. See items F105, F201 and F285.

F190 1928   Léon, Paul-Léopold. 'Lettres de Madame de Staël à Benjamin Constant', *RP*, 1er mars 1928, pp.5-26; 15 mars 1928, pp.303-340.

Reprinted in Léon, item F8b.

F191 1928   Lods, Armand. 'Benjamin Constant, député de Strasbourg', *ICC*, XCI, n° 1691, 10-30 septembre 1928, col. 667.

Letter from Constant to a friend, Paris, 18 janvier 1828 (Neuchâtel, Collection Th. Bringolf).

F191a 1929   Thomas, Louis. 'Une propriété de Benjamin Constant', *MF*, CCX (1929), 726-729.

Includes letter from Constant to an unidentified correpondent. Paris ce 21 Prairial an 7 (9 June 1799).

F192 1930   Constant de Rebecque, Baronne [L.]. 'Benjamin Constant: Lettres à Anna Lindsay', *RDM*, 15 décembre 1930, pp.781-818; 1er janvier 1931, pp.62-97; 15 janvier 1931, pp.373-404.

Reprinted in item F9.

F192a 1930   Centenaire de Benjamin Constant, 1767-1830. Discours prononcés à la séance commémorative du 14 juin 1930 à l'Aula de l'Université de Lausanne. Lausanne: Editions de la Gazette de Lausanne, 1930. pp.71.

Includes facsimiles of letters from Constant: to Isabelle de Charrière, ce 13e Juin [1797]; to Verly, à Strasbourg, Paris ce 15 Mars 1830.

F193 1930   Hawkins, Richmond Laurin. 'Unpublished letters written in English by Brillat-Savarin and Benjamin Constant', *Modern language notes*, XLV (1930), 1-7.

Letter to W. C. Somerville, reprinted in item F207.

F194 1930 Léon, Paul L. Benjamin Constant. Paris: Rieder, 1930. (Maîtres des littératures, 6). pp.100.

Includes facsimiles of letters from Constant: to Rose-Susanne de Constant, 19 novembre 1779 (see item F5); to Isabelle de Charrière, 26 mars 1796 (see item F292); to Goethe, [1804] (see items F161, F219 and F300); also includes letter from Germaine de Staël with a postcript by Constant, dimanche soir 7 aoust (see items F8a and F284a).

F195 1930 Leuilliot, Paul, 'Benjamin Constant et l'Alsace', *La Vie en Alsace*, Strasbourg, 1930, pp.283-285.

Includes facsimile of letter from Constant to Louis Schertz, Paris, ce 23 novembre 1827 (Strasbourg, Bibliothèque nationale et universitaire, Ms 1534).

F196 1930 Lods, Armand. 'Les derniers jours de Benjamin Constant, d'après des documents inédits', *Le Figaro*, 6 décembre 1930, p.6.

Letter from Constant to Scipion Mourgue, 1er septembre 1830.

F197 1930 'Un Publiciste'. 'Une lettre inédite de Benjamin Constant à Talleyrand', *ICC*, XCIII, n° 1720, 20-30 janvier 1930, col. 44.

Letter of 13 juin 1827 (BCU, Co 1).

F198 1930 Lods, Armand. 'Une lettre inédite de Benjamin Constant à Talleyrand', *ICC*, XCIII, n° 1723, 10 mars 1930, cols. 208-209.

Comments on the preceding item.

F199 1931 Levaillant, Maurice. 'La confidente d'*Adolphe*, ou Julie Talma et Benjamin Constant', *Le Figaro*, 31 juillet 1931, p.5.

Extracts of letters published in item F200.

F200 1931 Constant de Rebecque, [Baronne] L. 'Julie Talma: Lettres à Benjamin Constant (1798-1808)', *RDM* 1er août 1931, pp.541-574; 15 août 1931, pp.807-833; 1er septembre 1931, pp.97-127.

Reprinted in item F10.

F201 1931 Lods, Armand. 'Une lettre de Benjamin Constant à Chateaubriand', *ICC*, XCIV, n° 1748, 15 mai, n° 1751, 30 juin 1931, cols. 423-424, 556-557.

Letter dated Paris, ce 31 mai 1824. See items F105, F189a and F285.

F202 1931 Paquot, Marcel. 'Benjamin Constant et la peine de mort aux Pays-Bas', *Le Flambeau, revue belge des questions politiques et littéraires*, 14e année, n° 8, août 1931, pp.89-99.

Letter from Constant to C. de Brouckere, Paris ce 28 avril 1828 (BR, Stassart MSS).

F203 1932 Lods, Armand. 'La correspondance de Benjamin Constant', *ICC*, XCV, n° 1767, 15 avril 1932, cols. 315-316.

Refers to letters published by Grille, item F114.

F204 1932   Lods, Armand. 'Benjamin Constant, candidat à l'Académie Française', *ICC*, XCV, n° 1770, 30 mai 1932, cols. 443-444.
Letter from Constant to Guizot, Paris, 24 octobre 1830. See item F118.

F205 1932   Pellegrini, Carlo. 'Lettere inedite di Benjamin Constant al Sismondi', *Pègaso*, IV (1932), 641-660.
Sixteen letters from Constant to Sismondi, 1801-1827, from Sismondi manuscripts, Biblioteca di Pescia. Reprinted 1938 (item F214). See item F296.

F206 1933   Duchon, Paul. 'Parmi les papiers de Laffitte: souvenirs sur Louis-Philippe et Benjamin Constant', *RP*, 15 juillet 1933, pp.266-293.
Three letters from Constant to Laffitte: ce 27 octobre 1830; Bains de Tivoli, 17 november 1830; ce 25 novembre 1830.

F207 1933   Hawkins, Richmond Laurin. *Newly discovered French Letters of the seventeenth, eighteenth and nineteenth centuries*. Cambridge, Massachusetts: Harvard University Press, 1933. (Harvard Studies in Romance Languages, vol. IX).
N° 55 (pp.127-130): Benjamin Constant to William Clarke Somerville, Baltimore, United States, Paris, February 1825. In English. From Historical Society of Pennsylvania, Dreer Collection. First published in *MLN*, XLV (1930): see above, item F193.

F208 1934   Constant de Rebecque, [Baronne] L. 'Lettres [de Charlotte de Hardenberg] à Benjamin Constant', *RDM*, 1er mai 1934, pp.50-79: 15 mai 1934, pp.336-369; 1er juin 1934, pp.605-635.
Ninety-six letters of the period 1793-1810. Manuscripts in BCU, Fonds Constant II. *Review*: Emile Henriot, *Le Temps*, 15 mai 1934.

F209 1934   Rudler, Gustave. 'Benjamin Constant et Philippe-Albert Stapfer', *Mélanges de philologie, d'histoire et de littérature offerts à Joseph Vianey*. Paris: Les Presses françaises, 1934, pp.321-331.
Four letters from Constant to Stapfer, 1821-1822 (BN, N.a.fr. 23640), and four from Stapfer to Constant, 1824-1826.

F210 1935   Lassaigne, Jacques. 'Lettres inédites de Benjamin Constant', *La Revue mondiale*, XLVI, n° 9, 1er mai 1935, pp.5-9.
Ten letters, 1823-1830, from Constant to J.-P. Pagès.

F211 1935   Lods, Armand. 'Une lettre inédite de Benjamin Constant relative à ses cours à l'Athénée', *ICC*, XCVIII, n° 1837, 15-30 août, 1935, cols. 624-625.
Letter [1818 or 1819] to 'mon cher Victor' and fragment of letter of 25 janvier [1819].

F212 1935   Rudler, Gustave. 'Comment un règne se prépare: Benjamin

Constant et le Palais-Royal', *Mélanges de littérature, d'histoire et de philologie offerts à Paul Laumonier*, Paris: Droz, 1935, 507-514.

Includes letters from Constant to Chevalier de Broval: Paris, ce 22 août 1830; Paris, ce 20 février 1827; and letter from Broval to Constant, 14 janvier 1825. Manuscripts in BCU, Fonds Constant I.

F213 1936   Sismondi, G.C.L. Epistolario, raccolto, con introduzione e note, a cura di Carlo Pellegrini. Firenze: La Nuova Italia, vol. III, 1936.

Includes, p.47, letter from Sismondi to Constant, Chêne, 15 juillet 1827. See item F296.

F213a 1937   Samie, Mme Paul de. 'Chateaubriand et la marquise de Custine', *RHLF*, XLIV (1937), 208-228.

Includes, p.225, letter from Constant to Chênedollé, Gottingen, 10 juillet 1813, from archives d'Annoville.

F214 1938   Pellegrini, Carlo. Madame de Staël. Il gruppo cosmopolita di Coppet. L'influenza delle sue idee critiche. Con appendice di documenti. Firenze: Le Monnier, 1938. (Pubblicazioni della R. Università degli studi di Firenze, Facoltà di Magistero, I). pp.[iv], 221.

Reprinted from item F205, with addition of letters from Constant to Sismondi and Fanny Randall, May 1814.

Second edition: *Madame de Staël e il Gruppo di Coppet*, Bologna: Pàtron, 1974. (Testi e saggi di letterature moderne: saggi, 18).

F215 1938   Sloog, Maurice. 'L'édition originale d'*Adolphe*', *BB*, nouvelle série, XVII (1938), 481-483.

Letter from Constant to Henry Colburn, 27 May [1816]. See item F231.

F216 1939   Efros, Abraham. 'Yuliya Kryudener: frantsuzkie pisateli', *Literaturnoe nasledstvo*, XXXIII-XXXIV (1939), 142-181, 191-194.

Seventeen letters from Constant to Mme de Krüdener; French text published by Ley, item F270.

F216a 1939   Kientz, Louis. J. H. Campe et la Révolution française, avec des lettres et des documents inédits. Paris: Didier, 1939. pp.147.

Includes two letters from Constant to J. H. Campe: B[raunschweig], d. 6ten May 1794 and Braunschweig, den 6. May 1794, from Wolfenbüttel, Herzog August Bibliothek (p.123), See item F310.

F217 1943   Berthoud, Dorette. La seconde Madame Benjamin Constant d'après ses lettres. Lausanne: Payot, 1943. pp.256.

Includes text of letters from Charlotte de Constant, née Hardenberg, to Constant and letter from Germaine de Staël to Constant, Lyon, 15 juin 1809, pp.193-194. Manuscripts in BCU, Fonds Constant II.

F218 1945   Levaillant, Maurice. 'Benjamin Constant et Madame Récamier', *RP*, juillet 1945, pp.15-32.

Includes letter from Constant to Mme de Catellan. Reprinted in Levaillant, *Les amours de Benjamin Constant*, pp.238-239, item F252.

F219 1946   Cordié, Carlo. Benjamin Constant a cura di Carlo Cordié. Milano: Ulrico Hoepli, 1946. (I Propilei, 1).

Includes, p.98, letter from Constant, Genève, le 6 février 1813, to the Editors of the *Bibliothèque britannique* (see item D41). Also, facsimiles of letters published by Léon, item F194.

F220 1947   Bressler, Henri. 'Lettres inédites de Benjamin Constant'. *JG*, 19-20 avril 1947, pp.3-4; 26-27 avril 1947, p.3; 3-4 mai 1947, pp.3-4.

Undated letter from Constant to Sieyès [13 décembre 1799: see items F249, F251 and F307]; extracts from 18 letters to Rousselin de Saint-Albin, 1802-1810 (BN, N.a.fr. 13123).

F221 1947   Pelet, P.-L. 'Le premier duel de Benjamin Constant', *Etudes de lettres*, Lausanne, XXI (1947), 25-36.

Also published, with illustrations, by F. Rouge & Cie, Lausanne, [1947], pp.12. Includes letter from Constant, Colombier, 10 janvier 178[8], to François Du Plessis-Gouret, from Archives Du Plessis, Archives cantonales vaudoises, Lausanne. Reprinted in item E4/5, pp.1467-1468,

F222 1948   Mistler, Jean. 'Lettres de Benjamin Constant à Claude Hochet', *RDM*, 15 mai 1948, pp.193-200; 1er juin 1948, pp.400-422; 15 juillet 1948, 217-233; 1er septembre 1948, pp.124-142.

Reprinted in item F11.

F223 1949   Nicolson, Harold. Benjamin Constant. London: Constable, 1949. pp.x, 290.

Includes letter from Constant to Sir James Mackintosh, Liège, March 27, 1814, pp.213-214. See item F103.

F224 1950   Hasselrot, Bengt. Benjamin Constant og Bernadotte: 'De l'Esprit de conquête et de l'usurpation' og dens tilblivelse. København: Bianco Lunos Bogtrykkeri, 1950. pp.95. (Festskrift udgivet af Københavns Universitet, Marts 1950).

French texts reprinted in item F12.

F225 1950   Letessier, Fernand. 'Quelques faits manceaux dans la vie et l'œuvre de Chateaubriand', *Bulletin de l'Association Guillaume Budé*, n.s. n° 11 (octobre 1950), 40-80.

Two letters from Chateaubriand to Constant: Paris, le 13 août 1823, Paris, le 27 mai 1827, pp.52-53 (BCU, Co 1054-1055). See items F174 and F175a.

F226 1950   Mistler, Jean. 'Benjamin Constant et Mme Récamier', *RDM*, 1er septembre 1950, pp.81-96.

Fourteen letters omitted by Lenormant, item F4.

F227 1950-1951   Leuilliot, Paul. 'Benjamin Constant en Alsace: politique et finances, avec des lettres inédites', *Revue d'Alsace*, XC (1950-1951), 111-130.

Fourteen letters and extracts of letters from Constant to Frédéric Hartmann, 1827-1830.

F228 1951   Cordié, Carlo. 'Spigolature intorno al gruppo di Coppet', *Convivium*, 1951, n° 4 (luglio-agosto), 506-516.

Includes, pp.506-509, 'Due lettere poco note di Benjamin Constant': to the *Bibliothèque britannique*: Genève, le 6 février 1813 [see above, item F219]; to Béchet, Ce 13 9bre 1821, from BN (Rés. 8° Lb^{46} 38B). Reprinted in item F235.

F229 1952   Hasselrot, Bengt. 'Benjamin Constant et ses amitiés scandinaves', *Mélanges de philologie romane offerts à M. Karl Michaëlsson par ses amis et ses élèves*. Göteborg: Bergendahl, 1952, pp.240-249.

Reprinted in the following item.

F230 1952   Hasselrot, Bengt. Nouveaux documents sur Benjamin Constant et Mme de Staël. Copenhague: Ejnar Munksgaard, 1952. pp.83.

Includes 'Benjamin Constant et ses amitiés scandinaves', pp.67-82. Three letters from Constant to Carl Gustav von Brinkman: ce 17 Messidor an 7 (5 July 1799); ce 20 Messidor (8 July [1799]); Genève, ce 1er Juin 1804. Published from archives of Count Carl-Axel Trolle-Wachtmeister, Trolle-Ljungby.

F231 1952   Seznec, Jean. 'Deux lettres de Benjamin Constant sur *Adolphe* et *Les Cent Jours*'. In: *The French Mind: Studies in honour of Gustave Rudler*, edited by Will Moore, Rhoda Sutherland, Enid Starkie, Oxford: Clarendon Press, 1952, pp.208-219.

Includes letter from Constant to John Cam Hobhouse, May 17 1816 from the Curzon Collection, Bodleian Library, Oxford and letter to Henry Colburn, 27 May [1816], from Harvard University.

F232 1953   Cordié, Carlo. 'Alcune lettere inedite o poco note di Benjamin Constant', *Paideia*, VIII (1953), 261-268.

Letters from Constant: to L. F. Huber, 1799 (BN, Rés p.Y^2 2037); to Victor de Bonstetten, 19 juin 1821 (*ibid*); to Sainte-Aulaire, 1825 (private collection: C. Cordié); to Casimir Périer, 1825 (*ibid*); to Président de la Chambre [Ravez], 29 décembre 1824 (*Le Moniteur*, 1er janvier 1825). Reprinted in Cordié *Ideali e figure d'Europa*, pp.249-265, item F235.

F233 1954   Fourcassié, Jean. Villèle. Paris: Arthème Fayard, 1954. pp.486.

Includes letter from Constant to Villèle: Paris, 5 octobre 1822, pp.220-223; and letter to Richemont: ce 14 may [1824], pp.273-274. See items F236 and F279.

F234 1954   Roulin, Alfred. 'Lettres inédites de Benjamin Constant à sa cousine Rosalie', *Nouvelle NRF*, n° 14 (février 1954), pp.370-384.

Seven letters reprinted in item F13.

F235 1954   Cordié, Carlo. Ideali e figure d'Europa. Pisa: Nistri-Lischi, 1954. (Saggi di varia umanità. Collana diretta da Francesco Flora, 7).

On pp.249-265, reprint of letters in item F232, with addition of two letters published in *Convivium*, 1951, item F228.

F236 1955   Guillemin, Henri. 'Cet étrange Benjamin Constant', *JG*, 16-17 avril 1955, p.4.

Letter, 5 octobre 1822, to Villèle. Reprinted in Guillemin, *Pas à pas*, pp.54-56, item F279. See also item F233.

F237 1955   Guillemin, Henri. 'Benjamin Constant et son biographe', *Tribune de Lausanne*, 6 novembre 1955, p.15.

Includes letter from Constant to Alphonse Rabbe, Paris, 23 avril 1827. See item F253.

F238 1956   Guillemin, Henri. 'Un écrivain en quête d'une position politique. Les pénibles aventures de Benjamin Constant dans le Paris du Directoire', *FL*, 15 septembre 1956, pp.1, 5-6.

Letter from Constant of 'ce 28' [14 September 1797] to Sottin, ministre de la police, from AN, F^7 7234A d^r 6530. Reprinted in Guillemin, *Benjamin Constant muscadin*, item F251, pp.175-176.

F239 1956   Levaillant, Maurice. Une amitié amoureuse: Madame de Staël et Madame Récamier. Lettres et documents inédits. Paris: Hachette, 1956. pp.383.

Includes letter from Constant to Germaine de Staël, Paris, 6 septembre 1810 (Archives Lenormant), pp.241-243; will by Constant dated Genève, ce 19 avril 1811, pp.283-285; and letter from Germaine de Staël, [1809], p.191.

F240 1957   Bressler, Henri. 'Une lettre peu véridique sur un épisode du "Cahier Rouge"', *CBC* série I, n° 2, (1957), 43-47.

Letter from Louis-Arnold-Juste de Constant to Grand, Bois le Duc, le 27 7bre 1787.

F241 1957   Constant, Adolphe. Paris: Lucien Mazenod, [1957]. (Item A18/103).

Facsimile of letter of 31 August 1830, Bains de Tivoli, to Jouy (Arsenal, autogr. P. Lacroix).

F242 1957   Guillemin, Henri. 'Benjamin Constant muscadin', *Les Lettres nouvelles*, n° 49 (mai 1957), 678-690; n° 50 (juin 1957), 862-877; n° 51 (juillet-août 1957), 64-80; n° 52 (septembre 1957), 249-258.

Reprinted in Guillemin, *Benjamin Constant muscadin*, item F251.

F243 1957   Guillemin, Henri. 'Douze lettres autographes de Benjamin Constant', *TR*, n° 115-116 (juillet-août 1957), 7-28.

Twelve letters to Mme de Nassau, 1796-1803. Manuscripts in BCU.

F244 1957   Guillemin, Henri. 'Quand Benjamin Constant voulait être "commissaire" à Genève', *JG*, 31 août-1ᵉʳ septembre 1957, p.3.

Lettre from Constant to François de Neufchâteau, 17 mai 1799 from AN, FᴵC III, Léman 2: also in Guillemin, *Benjamin Constant muscadin*, item F251, p.250.

F245 1957   Le Grand Roy, René. 'La querelle du printemps 1811 entre Benjamin Constant et son père', *CBC*, série I, n° 2 (1957), 48-53; série I, n° 3 (1961), 69-82.

Letters from Louis-Arnold-Juste de Constant to Benjamin Constant from Archives Payot-Rilliet, Geneva.

F246 1957   Mistler, Jean. 'Deux inédits de Constant', *L'Aurore*, 18 juin 1957, p.11.

Letter from Constant to Emilie de Rebecque, 24 mars 1830. Reprinted in Levaillant, *Les Amours de Benjamin Constant* (item F252), p.246.

F247 1957   Monglond, André. La France révolutionnaire et impériale. Tome VIII. Années 1809-1810. Paris: Imprimerie nationale, 1957.

Letter from Constant to Prosper de Barante, Paris, ce 22 janvier [1809], pp.406-408.

F248 1957   Pange, comtesse Jean de. 'La "Notice" de Mᵐᵉ Necker de Saussure et Benjamin Constant', *CBC*, série I, n° 2 (1957), 39-42.

Includes letter from Constant, ce 25 9bre 1818 [=1819], to Auguste de Staël from Archives de Broglie. See item F275.

F249 1958   Guillemin, Henri. 'Benjamin Constant et le 18 Brumaire', *La Nef*, n° 18, juin 1958, 45-50.

Includes two letters from Constant to Sieyès, 24 brumaire an VIII (15 November 1799) and 22 [frimaire an VIII] (13 December 1799), from AN, AA 63 220 and BN, N.a.fr. 13123. Reprinted in Guillemin, *Benjamin Constant muscadin*, item F251, pp.276-279. See items F7, F182, F220 and F307.

F250 1958   Guillemin, Henri. 'Trois lettres autographes de Benjamin Constant', *JG*, 1ᵉʳ-2 novembre 1958.

Letters to Réal, 17 nivôse (7 janvier [1800]); Rousselin de Saint-Albin, ce 28 floréal an 10 (18 mai 1802); to the same, ce 13 [1802]. The first letter is reprinted in Guillemin, *Madame de Staël*, item F255, p.12, and in Hofmann, item F295, p.209.

F251 1958   Guillemin, Henri. Benjamin Constant muscadin, 1795-1799. Paris: Gallimard, 1958. pp.299.

Includes numerous letters of the period 1795-1799. See above, items F238, F242, F244, F249.

F252 1958   Levaillant, Maurice. Les Amours de Benjamin Constant. Lettres et documents, avec un opuscule inédit. Paris: Hachette, 1958. pp.279.

Includes letter to Emilie de Rebecque published in item F246, p.246 and fragment of a letter to Mme de Catellan, [1819], pp.238-239. See item F218.

F253 1959   Durry, Marie-Jeanne. Autographes de Mariemont, deuxième partie, tome II: De Marchangy à Victor Hugo. Paris: Nizet, 1959.

Includes, pp.433-444, three letters from Constant: to C. Marchand, Ce 30 janvier [1819]; to C[harles] Coquerel, Ce 13 8bre 1825; to [Alphonse Rabbe], Paris ce 23 avril 1827 (see item F237).

F254 1959   Guillemin, Henri. 'Une correspondance inédite de Benjamin Constant', *TR*, n° 135 (mars 1959), 57-95.

Twenty-three letters to Mme de Nassau from manuscripts in BPU. Reprinted in Guillemin, *Eclaircissements*, 1961, pp.119-160, item F257.

F255 1959   Guillemin, Henri. Madame de Staël, Benjamin Constant et Napoléon. Paris: Plon, 1959. pp.III, 210.

Includes letters of the period 1800-1815. See above, item F250.

F256 1960   Aleekseev, M. P. Neizdannye pis'ma inostrannykh pisateley XVIII-XIX vekov iz leningradskikh rukopisnykh sobraniy. Pod redaktsiey akademika M. P. Alekseeva. Moskva-Leningrad. Isdatel'stvo Akademii Nauk SSSR, 1960. pp.380.

Includes, pp.248-249, letter, Paris, ce 9 9bre 1826, from Constant to Joseph-Basile-Bernard van Praet.

F257 1961   Guillemin, Henri. Eclaircissements. Paris: Gallimard, 1961. pp.290.

Includes, pp.119-160, 'Benjamin et sa "bonne tante"'. Reprint of item F254.

F258 1962   Guillemin, Henri. 'Documents inédits: trois lettres "politiques" de Benjamin Constant', *JG*, 19-20 mai 1962.

Letters to the comtesse de Nassau: [early summer 1802]; Genève, 11 février 1803; Herbages, 22 Messidor an 11 (11 July 1803). Reprinted in Guillemin, *Pas à pas*, pp.49-53, item F279.

F259 1963   Luppé, Albert de. 'Constant juge *Adolphe*'. Inédits présentés par Albert de Luppé, *NL*, 6 juin 1963, p.7.

Letter from Constant to Sophie Gay, Paris, ce 26 février 1807.

F260 1964   Berthoud, Dorette. 'Belle et Benjamin: Lettres inédites de Benjamin Constant', *RP*, octobre 1964, pp.65-75.

Letters to Isabelle de Charrière, 1793-1794, from manuscripts in Bibliothèque publique de la Ville, Neuchâtel. See item F292.

F261 1965   Baelen, Jean. Benjamin Constant et Napoléon. Paris: J. Peyronnet, 1965. pp.248.

Letter from Constant to Masclet, Paris, ce [5] May 1830, p.243, and facsimile between pp.196 and 197.

F262 1965 Guillemin, Henri. 'Dossiers secrets: Compléments pour Benjamin', *JG*, 13-14 février 1965.

Letters from Constant: to Laporte 8 germinal an 6 (28 mars 1798); to Jouy, 15 novembre 1830; and letter to Constant from Jouy, [*post* 15 November 1830]. Published from the collection of M. Th. Bringolf, Neuchâtel. Reprinted in item F279.

F263 1966 Letessier, Fernand. 'Trois notes historiques et littéraires. I. A propos de Benjamin Constant député de la Sarthe', *Revue historique et archéologique du Maine*, XLVI (1966), 84-90.

Includes letter from Pierre Thoré to Constant, Le Mans 10 juin 1822, and four letters from Constant to Thoré: Paris, ce 2 Novembre 1820; ce 12 août [1821]; Ce 15 8bre 1822; Paris, ce 15 Juin 1827.

F264 1966 Courtney, C. P. 'Benjamin Constant et Nathaniel May: documents inédits', *RHLF*, LXVI (1966), 162-178.

Seven letters from Constant to May, 1816-1823 from manuscripts now in BCU.

F265 1966 Deguise, Pierre. Benjamin Constant méconnu: le livre 'De la religion'. Genève: Droz, 1966. pp.x, 308.

Includes letter from Barante to Constant, [août 1813], pp.271-272; letter from P.-A. Stapfer to Constant, 1er mai [1823 or 1825], pp.286-287; letter from Eckstein to Constant, [octobre, 1827], p.288; and letter from Guigniaut to Constant, 12 août [1826], pp.288-289. Manuscripts in BCU.

F266 1966 Mistler, Jean. 'Le salon de l'Europe: Madame de Staël à Coppet'. *Historia*, n° 233, avril 1966, pp.109-115.

Letter from Benjamin to Louis-Arnold-Juste de Constant [11 décembre 1807].

F267 1967 Cordey, Pierre. 'Deux billets inédits de Benjamin Constant', *RHV*, LXXV (1967), 174-176.

Letters of 12 and 30 June 1830 to Paul-François Dubois, Directeur of *Le Globe*. *Review*: P. Ciureanu, *SF*, XII (1968), 372.

F268 1967 Courtney, C. P. 'Autour de Benjamin Constant: lettres inédites de Juste de Constant à Sir Robert Murray Keith', *RHLF*, LXVII (1967), 97-100.

Three letters (18 avril 1783; 2 juin 1783; 29 juin 1784) from BL, Add. MSS. 35528, 35529, 35532.

F269 1967 Courtney, C. P. 'New light on Benjamin Constant: three unpublished letters from Juste de Constant to J.-B. Suard', *Neophilologus*, LI (1967), 10-14.

Three letters: (16 juin 1784; 12 juillet 1787; 13 août 1787) from Suard manuscripts, AN, AB XIX 3066.

F270 1967   Ley, Francis. Bernardin de Saint-Pierre, Madame de Staël, Chateaubriand, Benjamin Constant et Madame de Krüdener (d'après des documents inédits). Préface de Jean Fabre. Paris: Aubier, Editions Montaigne, 1967. pp.270.

Chapitre 4: 'Benjamin Constant et Julie de Krüdener ou l'amour profane et l'amour divin', pp.205-257. Includes 21 letters from Constant to Mme de Krüdener (1815) and a letter from Julie de Krüdener to Constant, from Saltykov-Shchedrin Public Library, Central State Archives, Moscow, Kiev State Museum, and Collection F. Ley.

Review: Béatrice Didier, *RHLF*, LXXII (1972), 319.

F271 1967   Roulin, Alfred. 'Lettres de Benjamin Constant à Jean-Samuel de Loys, 1811-1816', *RHV*, LXXV (1967), 159-173.

Ten letters (1811-1816) from Fonds Loys, Archives cantonales vaudoises, Lausanne.

Review: P. Ciureanu, *SF*, XII (1968), 371-372.

F272 1968   Benjamin Constant. Actes du Congrès Benjamin Constant (Lausanne, octobre 1967), édités par Pierre Cordey et Jean-Luc Seylaz. Genève: Droz, 1968. (Histoire des idées et critique littéraire, 91). pp.225.

See below items F273-F275.

F273 1968   Berthoud, Dorette. 'Lettres de Charlotte de Hardenberg', *Actes du Congrès de Lausanne*, (item F272) pp.137-143.

Extracts of letters, 1806-1808; manuscripts in BCU, Fonds Constant II.

F274 1968   Ley, Francis. 'Présentation des lettres inédites de Benjamin Constant à Mme de Krüdener', *Actes du Congrès de Lausanne*, (item F272) pp.129-135.

Discussion of the letters published in item F270.

F275 1968   Pange, comtesse Jean de. 'Quelques lettres inédites de Benjamin Constant à Auguste et Albertine de Staël entre 1815 et 1830', *Actes du Congrès de Lausanne*, (item F272) pp.119-127.

Thirteen letters from Constant to Auguste de Staël and one from Constant to Albertine de Broglie, from Archives de Broglie.

F276 1968   Balayé, Simone. 'La nationalité de Madame de Staël. Textes inédits de Mme de Staël et de Benjamin Constant', *Humanisme actif; Mélanges d'art et de littérature offerts à Julien Cain*. Paris: Hermann, 1968, I, 73-85.

Letter from Constant to Minister of Justice, Paris, le 15 nivôse an 5 (4 January 1797); letter to Barras, same date. Published from Archives nationales, BB[16] 709.

F277 1969   Anthologie de la correspondance française, établie, préfacée et annotée par André Maison, vol. V: 1766-1803, De Madame de Staël à Edgar Quinet. [Lausanne]: Rencontre, 1969. pp.511.

Reprints ten letters from Constant, pp.31-54.

F278 1969 Balayé, Simone. 'Benjamin Constant et la mort de Madame de Staël', *Cahiers staëliens*, n° 9, décembre 1969, pp.17-38.

Includes letter from Constant to the *Journal général*, Paris, 25 juillet 1817. See items D100 and D102.

F279 1969 Guillemin, Henri. Pas à pas. Paris: Gallimard, 1969. pp.464.

Includes 'Benjamin Constant: documents', pp.41-58: letters from Constant: to Villèle, 5 octobre 1822; to Laporte, 8 germinal an VI (28 March 1798); to Rousselin de Saint-Albin, Genève, ce 28 floréal an 10 (18 May 1802); to Mme de Nassau, [1802], 11 février 1803; 22 Messidor an 11 (11 July 1803); to Jouy, 15 novembre 1830, and reply from Jouy. See above, items F233, F236, F258 and F262.

F280 1969 Senelier, Jean. 'Benjamin Constant et Eusèbe de Salverte (deux lettres inédites)', *SF*, XIII (1969), 267-270.

Letter from Salverte to Constant, [12 mars 1829]; from Constant to Salverte, Paris, le 25 mars 1829; and from Constant to Cauchois-Lemaire, ce 20 8ᵇʳᵉ 1825, from manuscripts in Bibliothèque de la ville de Senlis.

F281 1970 King, Norman. '"The airy form of things forgotten": Madame de Staël, l'utilitarisme et l'impulsion libérale', *Cahiers staëliens*, n° 11 (1970), 5-26.

Two letters from Constant to Jeremy Bentham: Paris, 27th July 1821; Paris, 29 7ᵇʳᵉ [18]24, from Bentham manuscripts in University College, London.

F281a 1970 Solovieff, Georges. Madame de Staël, ses amis, ses correspon-dants: choix de lettres (1778-1817) présenté et commenté par Georges Solovieff. Préface de la comtesse Jean de Pange. Paris: Klincksieck, 1970. pp.XII, 566.

Includes selection of letters published by Léon (item F8b) and Berthoud (item F217). Preface includes letter from Constant to Victor de Broglie, Ce 6 août, and to Charlotte de Constant, Paris ce 9 may, along with a document relating to the destruction by Albertine de Broglie of Germaine de Staël's letters to Constant.

F282 1970 Staël, Anne-Louise-Germaine de. Lettres à Louis de Narbonne, Adolphe de Ribbing et Benjamin Constant. Choix de Jean-Luc Benoziglio. Paris: Tchou, 1970. (Le Livre de chevet). pp.188.

Reprints thirteen letters to Constant, 1813-1815, pp.139-188.

F283 1971 Delbouille, Paul. Genèse, structure et destin d'*Adolphe*. Paris: Les Belles Lettres, 1971. (Bibliothèque de la Faculté de Philosophie et Lettres de l'Université de Liège, 195). pp.643.

Includes correspondence relating to the composition, publication and reception of *Adolphe*.

F284 1971 Jasinski, Béatrice W. L'Engagement de Benjamin Constant.

Amour et politique (1794-1796). Paris: Minard, 1971. pp.292.

Includes the following letters from Constant: to Citoyen Président [La Révellière Lépeaux], Paris, 24 floréal l'an 4ᵉ (13 May 1796), (AN, AF III 370, dr 1812, fᵒ 114), p.207; to the same, 27 floréal quatrième année (16 May 1796), (AN, AF III 370, dr 1812, fᵒ 115), pp.208-209; to Citoyens Directeurs, Paris, 30 prairial l'an 4ᵉ de la République française (18 June 1796), (AN, BB¹⁶ 708 dr B4931), pp.235-243; to Commecy, 6 thermidor an VII (24 July 1799), (BCU, Co 2060), pp.273-274; to the same, Paris, ce 25 nivôse an 8 (15 January 1800), (BCU, Co 2058), p.274; to Fontanes, 25 floréal l'an III (14 May 1795), p.93 (BCU, Co 2057).

F284a 1974   Madame de Staël. Correspondance générale, tome III, deuxième partie, texte établie et présenté par B. W. Jasinski. Paris: Jean-Jacques Pauvert, 1974.

Includes, p.227, letter from Germaine de Staël to Pictet-Diodati, dimanche soir 7 aoust [1796] with postscript by B. Constant. See items F8b and F194.

F285 1974   Riberette, Pierre. 'Une lettre inédite de Chateaubriand à Benjamin Constant', *Société Chateaubriand, Bulletin*, nouvelle série, nᵒ 17, 1974, 36-39.

Letter, Paris, 1ᵉʳ février 1809; and letter from Constant, Paris, 31 mai 1823 [=1824], from BCU, Fonds Constant II. See items F20, F105, F189a and F287a.

F286 1975   Courtney, C. P. 'Alexander Walker and Benjamin Constant: a note on the English translator of *Adolphe*', *FS*, XXIX (1975), 137-150.

Includes letter from Constant to the editor of the *Revue européenne*, août 1824 (item D368) and two letters to Constant from Walker, 3 September 1824 and 19 October 1824, from BCU, Fonds Constant I.

F287 1976   Kloocke, Kurt. 'Un billet de Madame de Staël à Benjamin Constant et trois lettres de Benjamin Constant; documents inédits', *RF*, LXXX-VIII (1976), 412-416.

Letters published from manuscripts in Bibliothèque municipale de Laon: Germaine de Staël to Constant [June 1795?]; two letters from Constant to Méchin (ce 5 juillet 1825; ce 9 Aout 1828); letter from Constant to Visme (ce 2 juillet 1825).

F287a 1977   Chateaubriand, François-René. Correspondance générale. Paris: Gallimard, 1977-[in progress].

Vol.II, 1808-1814, textes établis et annotés par Pierre Riberette (1979), includes letter to Constant, Paris, ce 1ᵉʳ février 1809, pp.38-39. See above, item F285.

F288 1978   Jequier, Marie-Claude. 'Frédéric-César Laharpe, Benjamin Constant et Mᵐᵉ de Staël face à la Suisse (1797-1814)', *RHV*, LXXXVI (1978), 39-56.

Includes two letters from Constant to Laharpe from BCU, Fonds Laharpe: le 21 avril 1814 and Paris, le 26 mai 1814.

F289 1978 King, Norman. 'Coppet en 1809-1810', *Cahiers staëliens*, n° 24, 1er semestre 1978, 37-62.

Three letters from Constant to Louis-Arnold-Juste de Constant: Coppet, ce 16 may 1809; ce 4 août [1809]; [January 1810]; Constant to Mme de Nassau, [Coppet, 16 mai 1809], from Fonds Monamy-Valin (copies in Rudler papers).

F290 1978 King, Norman. 'Après les Cent-Jours: trois lettres de Benjamin Constant écrites en 1815', *Cahiers staëliens*, n° 25, 2ème semestre 1978, 25-44.

Letters to Sir James Mackintosh from BL, Add. MS 52452: Paris, ce 4 Aoust 1815; Brussels, Nov[em]ber 4th 1815; Brussels, December 17th 1815.

F291 1978 Schnetzler, Barbara. 'Kreuzpunkt Weimar 1804 – Benjamin Constant an Johannes von Müller', *Schaffhauser Beiträge zur Geschichte*, LV (1978), 34-43.

Letter from Constant to Jean de Muller, Leipsick, ce 5 mars 1804, from manuscript in Stadtbibliothek, Schaffhausen.

F292 1979 Charrière, Isabelle de/Belle de Zuylen. *Œuvres complètes*, édition critique publiée par Jean-Daniel Candaux, C. P. Courtney, Pierre H. Dubois, Simone Dubois-De Bruyn, Patrice Thompson, Jeroom Vercruysse et Dennis M. Wood. Amsterdam: G. A. van Oorschot; Genève: Editions Slatkine, 1979-1984. 10 vols.

Vols. III-VI include Constant's correspondence with Isabelle de Charrière.

F293 1979 Kloocke, Kurt. [Review of *Adolphe*, éd. Delbouille, Paris, 1977], *ZFSL*, LXXXIX (1979), 88-92.

Includes letter from Constant to Henry Colburn, [12 May 1816], from manuscript in Bibliothèque de Nantes.

F294 1980 Delbouille, Paul. 'Lettres inédites de Benjamin Constant à ses grands-tantes Villars et Chandieu et à sa tante Nassau', *Etudes de philologie romane et d'histoire littéraire offertes à Jules Horrent*, éditées par Jean Marie d'Heur et Nicoletta Cherubini, Liège: Gédet, 1980, pp.623-633.

Includes letter from Constant to Angletine-Charlotte and Antoinette-Madeleine de Chandieu, Bruxelles, le 2 novembre 1779 and seven letters, [1788]-1808 to the comtesse de Nassau, from BCU, Fonds Constant I.

F295 1980 Hofmann, Etienne. Les 'Principes de politique' de Benjamin Constant: la genèse d'une œuvre et l'évolution de la pensée de leur auteur (1789-1806). Genève: Droz, 1980. pp.419.

Includes letter from Constant to Sieyès [10 novembre 1799], from AN, 284 AP 16/3 (p.189); and letter from Réal to Constant, ce 23 nivôse an 8 (13 janvier 1800) from BCU, Fonds Constant II 34/4 (pp.209-210). See items F250 and F255.

F296 1980 King, Norman, & Candaux, J.-D. 'La correspondance de Benjamin Constant et de Sismondi (1801-1830)', *ABC*, n° 1 (1980), 81-172.

Includes thirty-five letters from Constant to Sismondi, 1801-1827 and four letters from Sismondi to Constant, mainly from manuscripts in Biblioteca comunale, Pescia, BCU and Wedgwood archives, University of Keele.

Review: Carlo Cordié, *SF*, XXV (1981), 369-370.

F296a 1980   Kloocke, Kurt. [Review of Harpaz, *Recueil d'articles, 1795-1817*, 1978, item E4/9], *ZFSL*, XC (1980), 80-84.

Includes two letters from Constant: to M.-C.-J. Pougens, Paris ce 30 juillet 1819, from manuscript in Bibl. municipale, Lille; to A. Eymery, [1829], from manuscript in Bibl. municipale, Nantes.

F297 1980   Zabarov, P. R. Neskol'ko pisem frantsuzskikh pisatelei iz kollektsii G. V. Orlova. Russkie istochniki dlya istorii zarubezhnykh literatur: sbornik issledoraniy i materialov. Leningrad: Nauka, 1980.

Includes letter from Constant to comte G. Orloff, ce 8 juillet [s.a.], pp.112-113.

F298 1981   Courtney, C. P. A Bibliography of Editions of the Writings of Benjamin Constant to 1833. London: Modern Humanities Research Association, 1981. pp.xxxiv, 267.

Includes the following letters from Constant: to the Director of the *Journal de la librairie*, Paris ce 13 Juillet 1817, p.72 (VP, CP 6345); to Lady Morgan (extract), 2 November 1818, p.100 (Yale University Library); to the marquis de Vaulchier, Directeur général des douanes (extract), 14 octobre 1824, pp.134-135 (BN, N.a.fr. 13627); to Tarlier (extract), 31 juillet 1824, p.138 (BCU, Co 2826); to the same, 20 août 1824 (extract from Catalogue Blancheteau n° 25); to a printer [Laguionie] (extract), [May 1824], p.166 (Rudler papers); to Laguionie, ce mercredi [12 May 1824] (extract), p.166 (Bibl. Civiche, Turin, Coll. Cossilla); to Michaud, 26 mars 1810, pp.209-210 (BCU, Ms 280/1); to the same, Paris ce 19 avril 1810, pp.210-211 (VP, CP 6345); to Antoine Roux de Laborie, [1814?], p.211 (BCU, Ms 278/2); to Louise d'Estournelles (extracts), [5 December 1819], 17 avril [1821], 11 juin 1821, 23 juillet 1821, pp.215-216. (BCU, Co 279, 298, 300).

F299 1981   Hofmann, Etienne. 'Lettres [de Benjamin Constant] à Louis-Ferdinand Huber et à Therese Huber (1798-1806)', *Cahiers staëliens*, n°s 29-30, 1981, pp.77-122.

Fifteen letters (1798-1806) from various sources, including manuscripts formerly in the Preussische Staatsbibliothek, Berlin. Also includes letter, Paris ce 8 nivôse an 6 (28 December 1797) from Constant to Rewbell, pp.89-90, note (BCU, Co 2).

F300 1981   Kloocke, Kurt. 'Documents inédits ou peu connus de et sur Benjamin Constant', *SF*, n° 75, 1981, 459-472.

Includes three letters from Ludwig Robert to Constant: Paris, den 12 Mai 1826 (BCU, Co 3686), Paris, ce 30 juin 1826 (Co 1141) and Berlin, ce 26 févr. 1830 (Co 3687); letter from Constant to Robert, Paris, le 18 juin 1826 (Dorow, item F106); letter from Constant to J. G. Cotta, Bade, ce 20 Aoust 1829 (Marbach,

Schiller-Nationalmuseum); letter from J. C. Leist to Constant, Cassel, le 14 décembre 1812 (BN, Fonds Monamy); letter from J. F. Blumenbach to Constant, den 18ᵗᵉⁿ Dec. 1812 (*ibid.*); letter from Constant to Blumenbach, Cassel, ce 23 décembre 1812 (Göttingen, Staats- und Universitätsbibliothek); five letters from Constant to K. A. Böttiger [1804] (Nürnberg, Germanisches National Museum; Weimar, Goethe-Schiller Archiv; Marbach, Schiller-Nationalmuseum); letter to Goethe [17 March 1804] (Weimar, Goethe-Schiller Archiv: see items F161, F194 and F219) letters from Constant to Sophie von Schardt, [15 March 1804] and Charlotte von Schiller, [23-30 April 1804] (*ibid.*).

F301 1982 Balayé, Simone. 'Une lettre inédite de Benjamin Constant à Madame Talma', *ABC*, n° 2 (1982), pp.111-112.

Letter of 25 germinal (15 April [1804]) from manuscript in BPU, Dossiers ouverts.

F302 1982 Courtney, C. P. 'Isabelle de Charrière and the "Character of H. B. Constant": a false attribution', *French Studies*, XXXVI (1982) pp.282-289.

Includes three letters to Constant from Marie-Charlotte Johannot [1785] from manuscripts in BCU.

F303 1982 Kloocke, Kurt. 'Benjamin Constant et Mina von Cramm: documents inédits', *ABC* n° 2, (1982), pp.81-109.

Letters from Constant to K. J. von Preen: Bronsvic, ce 24 mars 1793, Bronsvic, ce 26 mars 1793, Bronsvic, ce 27 mars 1793, Bronsvic, ce 27 mars 1793, Bronsvic, ce 28 mars 1793; letters from von Preen to Constant: Bronsvic, ce 25 mars 1793, Bronsvic, ce 26 mars 1793, Bronsvic, ce 27 mars 1793; letter from Constant to his wife, Minna, 10 avril [1793] and reply; letter from Constant to J.-B. Féronce von Rosencreutz, Brunsvic, ce 10 avril 1793; letters from Constant to the Duke and Duchess of Brunswick, Bronsvic, ce 13 avril, [*c.* 20 April 1793]; letter from Constant to E. G. von Münchhausen, Bronsvic, ce 15 avril 1793 and reply, 16 avril 1793. These, and other documents, published from manuscripts in BCU, Fonds Constant II, 34.

F304 1982 Harpaz, Ephraïm. 'Lettres du docteur Véron à Benjamin Constant', *SF*, n° 77 (1982), 257-264.

Nine letters (1829-1830), from BN, Fonds Monamy.

F305 1982 Jasinski, Béatrice W. 'Benjamin Constant tribun', *Benjamin Constant, Madame de Staël et le groupe de Coppet: Actes du deuxième congrès de Lausanne à l'occasion du 150ᵉ anniversaire de la mort de Benjamin Constant et du troisième colloque de Coppet, 15-19 juillet 1980*, publiés sous la direction d'Etienne Hofmann. Oxford, The Voltaire Foundation; Lausanne: Institut Benjamin Constant, 1982, pp.63-88.

Includes letter from Constant to Sieyès, [10 novembre 1799] (AN, 284 AP 16, dossier 3); to Pictet-Diodati, (24 novembre 1799: see items F126a and F307).

F306 1983 Deguise, Pierre. 'Lettres de Prosper de Barante à Benjamin

Constant suivies d'additions inédites aux lettres de Constant à Barante, *ABC*, n° 3 (1983), pp.33-88.

Includes 24 letters from Barante to Constant, from BCU, Fonds Constant II and additions to letters from Constant to Barante published in items F139, F153 and F247.

F307 1983   King, Norman & Hofmann, Etienne. 'Les lettres de Benjamin Constant à Sieyès avec une lettre de Constant à Pictet-Diodati', *ABC*, n° 3 (1983), pp.89-110.

Eight letters to Sieyès, including those published in items F7, F182, F220, F249, F251, F295 and F305. Letter to Pictet-Diodati, [25 December 1799] from Archives Edmond Pictet (facsimile in J.-D. Candaux, *Histoire de la famille Pictet, 1474-1974*, Genève: Braillard, 1974, II, following p.316).

F308 1983   Olzien, Otto. 'Benjamin Constant, Göttingen et la Bibliothèque universitaire', *ABC*, n° 3 (1983), pp.123-139.

Includes letter from Constant to Blumenbach, Cassel, ce 23 Décembre 1812. See item F300.

F309 1983   Kloocke, Kurt. [Review of Courtney, *Bibliography of editions*, 1981]. *ZFSL*, XCIII (1983), 317-322.

Includes five letters from Constant to Erasme Kleffer (1821) and one to the same (1829), from manuscripts in Bibliothèque municipale de Versailles.

F310 1984   Kloocke, Kurt. Benjamin Constant. Une biographie intellectuelle. Genève: Droz, 1984. pp.[x], 374.

Includes letters from Constant: to M. and Mme de Prony, ce 8 avril [1829], BN, N.a.fr. 15778, f. 95 (p.17, note 11); to Ernest Theodor Langer, Brunsvic ce 26 avril 1794, Wolfenbüttel, Herzog August Bibliothek (p.47, note 116); to the same, Brunsvic ce 2 Aout 1794, *ibid.* (pp.47-48, note 116); to Friedrich Schlichtegroll, Gotha, [13 or 14 December 1803], Wolfenbüttel, Staatsarchiv 298 N 628 (p.54, note 137); to J.H. Campe, B[raunschweig] d. 6ten May 1794 and Braunschweig, den 6. May 1794, Wolfenbüttel, Herzog August Bibliothek (p.55, note 139); to Petit-Radel, Paris, 13 mai 1824, Versailles, Bibliothèque municipale (p.274, note 179); to Richmont, Ce 14 may 1824, Jean Fourcassié, *Villèle*, item F233 (pp.274-275, note 179); to Chateaubriand, Paris ce 1er février 1809, items F285 and F287a (p.337, note 174).

G The *Acte additionnel aux constitutions de l'Empire* 1815

The *Acte additionnel* of 22 April 1815, which was composed at least in part by Constant, was published on 23 April 1815 in the *Moniteur* and *Bulletin des lois*. Separate editions of the *Acte additionnel* include the following:

G1/1 1815 Acte additionnel aux Constitutions de l'Empire. 8° pp.27. Paris, Imprimerie impériale. Avril 1815.

Copy: AN (AF IV 859¹², plaq. 6989 p.17: proof copy with corrections possibly in Constant's hand). (C. Appendix A1a).

G1/2 1815 Acte additionnel aux constitutions de l'Empire. Paris, le 22 avril 1815. Extrait du *Moniteur*. 8° pp.16. 1815.

Copy: BL. (C. Appendix A1b).

G1/3 1815 Acte additionnel aux constitutions de l'Empire. A Brest, de l'imprimerie de Michel. Avril 1815. 8° pp.[ii], 14.

Copy: BN. (C. Appendix A1c).

Chronology of the works of Benjamin Constant

[1774-1775]

[1774-1775]   *Prière au créateur du monde à celui que nous devons adorer et aimer comme notre père,* [*ca.*1774-1775]. Rudler, *Bibliographie* 2. Published in Rudler, *Jeunesse* (1909), p.88, from BPU, Ms Constant 35. *Checklist* A74/4.

[1774-1775]   *Sur l'homme juste,* [*ca.*1774-1775]. Rudler, *Bibliographie* 3. Published in Rudler, *Jeunesse* (1909), p.88, from BPU, Ms Constant 35. *Checklist* A74/4.

[1775-1776]

[1775-1776]   *Dialogue. Frugalité et Bombance,* [*ca.*1775-1776]. Rudler, *Bibliographie* 11. Published in Rudler, *Jeunesse* (1909), p.89, from BPU, Ms Constant 35. *Checklist* A74/4.

[1777]

[1777]   Novel, [*ca.*1777]. Not extant. Rudler, *Bibliographie* 7. The 'roman' is mentioned by Constant in a letter of 24 December 1777 to Rose-Susanne de Constant.

[1777]   *Didon, fragment de tragédie,* [*ca.*1777]. Rudler, *Bibliographie* 12. Published in Rudler, *Jeunesse* (1909), pp.90-91, from BPU, Ms Constant 35. *Checklist* A74/4.

1779

[1779]/[03-04]/-   *Pastorale,* [*ca.* spring 1779]. Rudler, *Bibliographie* 13. Published in Rudler, *Jeunesse* (1909), pp.94-95, from BPU, Ms Constant 35. *Checklist* A74/4.

[1779]/[03-04]/-   *Bouts rimés,* [*ca.* spring 1779]. Rudler, *Bibliographie* 14. By Benjamin Constant, Rosalie de Constant and Mlle Gallatin. Published in Rudler, *Jeunesse* (1909), p.96, from BPU, Ms Constant 35. *Checklist* A74/4.

[1779]/[03-04]/-   *Bouts rimés,* [*ca.* spring 1779]. Rudler, *Bibliographie* 15. Extract published in Lucie Achard, *Rosalie de Constant, sa famille et ses amis,* Genève: Eggiman; Paris: Fischbacher, 1901-1902, I, 122; full text in Rudler, *Jeunesse* (1909), p.96, from BPU, Ms Constant 35. 'Benjamin a au moins pu collaborer à ces vers, qui se trouvent au verso d'une lettre de Rosalie à son père' (Rudler, *Bibliographie* 15). *Checklist* A74/4.

[1779]   *Des mortels voïez la chimère,* [*ca.*1779]. Rudler, *Bibliographie* 16. Published in Rudler, *Jeunesse* (1909), pp.91-92, from BPU, Ms Constant 35. *Checklist* A74/4.

[1779]   *Le dévouement de Décius,* [*ca.*1779]. Rudler, *Bibliographie* 17. Published in Rudler, *Jeunesse* (1909), pp.92-94, from BPU, Ms Constant 35. *Checklist* A74/4.

1779   *Les Chevaliers. Roman héroïque par H .... B ... . C ... . de R ... . ingenium – misera fortunatus arté à Brusselles 1779.* Rudler, *Bibliographie* 18. Edition: *Les Chevaliers;* avant-propos de G. Rudler, Paris: Kra, 1927. Manuscript in BCU (Co 3274). *Checklist* A69/1.

1785

1785/[08-11]/-   *Histoire du polythéisme,* [*ca.* August-November 1785]. Not extant. Rudler, *Bibliographie* 22bis. Nothing has survived of the first draft of the work which was to become *De la religion* (1824-1831). See *Le Cahier rouge,* Pléiade, p.129.

[1786]

[1786]/[04-05]/-   *De la discipline militaire des Romains,* [*ca.* April-May 1786]. Not extant. Rudler, *Bibliographie* 26. Referred to in a letter of 2 May 1786 from Benjamin to Samuel de Constant. A later (revised) copy has been preserved in the *Œuvres manuscrites* of 1810 (BN, N.a.fr. 14362).

1787

1787/04/[ca.24]   *Essai sur les mœurs des tems héroïques de la Grèce, tiré de l'Histoire grecque de M. Gillies*, Londres; Paris: Lejay, 1787. Announced in *Gazette de France*, 24 Avril 1787. Rudler, *Bibliographie* 28. C.1a. *Checklist* A1/1.

[1787]/[07-09]/-   *Lettres écrites de Patterdale à Paris, dans l'été de 1787, adressées à Mme de C[harrière] de Z[uylen]*, [ca. July-September 1787]. Not extant. Rudler, *Bibliographie* 37. For references to this work (originally conceived as a novel, but to be recast with the title as above), see Constant's letters to Isabelle de Charrière of the period July-September 1787.

[1787]/[12]/-   *Poème épique sur les Duplessis*. [ca. December 1787]. Not extant. Rudler, *Bibliographie* 41. For references to this work see Constant's letters of this date to Isabelle de Charrière.

[1787]/[12]/-   *Feuilles*, [ca. end of December 1787]. Not extant. Rudler, *Bibliographie* 44. Rudler suggests that the 'feuilles' may be identical to the *Lettres sur l'histoire* of 1788 (see below under 1788).

[1787-1788]   *Lettres de d'Arsillé fils, de Sophie Durfé et autres*, [ca. end of 1787 and early 1788]. Isabelle de Charrière/Belle de Zuylen, *Romans, contes et nouvelles, II, 1798-1806*, Amsterdam: Van Oorschot, 1981, pp.651-678; published from manuscript in Bibliothèque publique de la Ville, Neuchâtel. Attributed to Isabelle de Charrière and Benjamin Constant: see introduction by Dennis M. Wood. *Checklist* A74/11.

[1788]

[1788]/[03]/-   *Réfutation de l'Importance des Opinions religieuses de Necker*, [ca. March 1788]. Not extant. Rudler, *Bibliographie* 61bis. The work, referred to in letters of March 1788 to Isabelle de Charrière, may never have been written.

[1788]/[03-04]/-   *Petits Grecs* (Projet d'une histoire de la civilisation graduelle des Grecs par les colonies égyptiennes, etc.), [ca. March-April 1788]. Not extant. Rudler, *Bibliographie* 61ter. In letters of March 1788 to Isabelle de Charrière, Constant refers to this work, which he distinguishes from the translation of Gillies published in the previous year.

[1788]/[04]/-   *Lettres sur l'histoire*, [ca. April 1788]. Rudler, *Bibliographie* 63. Only a fragment of the preface is extant; cited by Constant in a letter of 4-5 April 1788 to Isabelle de Charrière.

[1788]/-/-   *Monument de la Sagesse des Tribunaux Suisses. Première partie. Observations et examen historique d'un procès jugé par un Conseil de Guerre National Suisse au mois d'août 1788, à Amsterdam*, [1788]. Rudler, *Bibliographie* 87. Date and authorship uncertain; see Rudler, who refers to the manuscript (BCU, Fonds Constant I).

1789

1789/10/19   *A Leurs Nobles Puissances les Seigneurs du Conseil d'Etat des Pays-Bas-Unis*. 4° pp.4. Dated 'La Haye ce 19 Octobre 1789' and signed 'H.B. de Constant, Gentilhomme de S.A. le Duc de Bronsvic'. Rudler, *Bibliographie* 107. Autograph manuscript in BCU, Fonds Constant I; printed text in BPU. Analysed by Rudler, *Jeunesse* (1909), p.366.

[1789]/[11-12]/-   *Dialogue humoristique* [ca. November-December 1789]. Rudler, *Bibliographie* 113. Unpublished (manuscript in BCU, Fonds Constant I); analysed by Rudler, *Jeunesse* (1909), p.366 note 2.

1790

1790/05/05   *Pièces détachées concernant les procédures, entamées contre J. Constant de Rebecque, collonel-commandant du régiment suisse de Mr. le général-major May, depuis le 2 Juin 1788.* 4° pp.[i], VI, 24. Contents: *Réflexions sur une procédure* (pp.I-IV), *Pièces relatives aux Réflexions précédentes* (pp.V-VI) and *Pièces justificatives* (pp.1-24). The first part includes (p.VI) letter from Benjamin Constant to General-Major May dated 'La Haye ce 5 May 1790' and signed 'De Constant, Gentilh. de S.A.S. le Duc de Brunswick'. Copies in BCU and BPU.

[1790]/[09]/-   *De la Révolution du Brabant en 1790,* [*ca.* September 1790]. Rudler, *Bibliographie* 117bis. Referred to in a letter of 17 September 1790 to Isabelle de Charrière. On 10 December 1790 Constant wrote to her, 'Mes Brabançons se sont en allés en fumée'. However a copy has survived in the *Œuvres manuscrites* of 1810 (BN, N.a.fr. 14362).

[1790]/[12]/-   *Réfutation des Réflexions sur la Révolution française de Burke,* [*ca.* December 1790]. Not extant. Mentioned by Rudler, *Bibliographie* 118, with reference to a letter of 10 December 1790 from Constant to Isabelle de Charrière.

1792

[1792]/[08-09]/-   *Mémoire pour Juste Constant de Rebecque,* [*ca.* August-September 1792]. Rudler, *Bibliographie* 128. Unpublished (manuscripts in BN, Fonds Monamy and in BCU, Fonds Constant I); analysed by Rudler, *Jeunesse* (1909), p.381.

1793

[1793]/[01-03]/-   *Commencement de l'histoire de ma vie,* [*ca.* January-March 1793]. Not extant. Rudler, *Bibliographie* 133. Rudler (*Jeunesse,* p.404) suggests that the work was written at Brunswick between 11 January and 25 March 1793 for Charlotte de Marenholz.

[1793]/[11]/-   *Dialogue entre Louis XVI, Brissot et Marat,* [*ca.* November 1793]. Not extant. Rudler, *Bibliographie* 170bis. Referred to in a letter of 9 November 1793 to Isabelle de Charrière. On 19 November 1793 Constant wrote to her, 'Mon dialogue est au diable'; the project may never have been executed. See Rudler, *Jeunesse* (1909), pp.423, 484.

1794

1794/[03]/[ante 08]   *Pièces relatives à mes différends avec Madame de Constant née de Cramm.* Kurt Kloocke, 'Benjamin Constant et Minna von Cramm: documents inédits', *Annales Benjamin Constant,* n° 2 (1982), pp.81-109 (from manuscript copy in Constant's hand in BCU, Fonds Constant II). For date (*ante* 8 March 1794), see Kloocke, p.82. *Checklist* A74/13.

[1794]/[01-06]/-   *Vie de Mauvillon,* [*ca.* January-June 1794]. Not extant. Rudler, *Bibliographie* 241. Work on this biography is frequently referred to in Constant's letters to Isabelle de Charrière of January-June 1794.

[1794]/[05-07]/-   *Dissertation sur le décret religieux du Roi de Prusse,* [*ca.* May-July 1794]. Not extant. Rudler, *Bibliographie* 263. It is not clear whether this work was actually written; for discussion see Rudler.

1795

1795/06/24   'Lettre à un Député à la Convention', *Nouvelles politiques nationales et étrangères,* n° 276, 6 messidor an III, 24 juin 1795, pp.1101-1102. *Checklist* D1.

1795/06/25   'Seconde lettre à un député', *Nouvelles politiques nationales et étrangères,* n° 277,

7 messidor an III, 25 juin 1795, pp.1106-1107. *Checklist* D2.

1795/06/26   'Troisième lettre à un député', *Nouvelles politiques nationales et étrangères*, n°
278, 8 messidor an III, 26 juin 1795, pp.1110-1112. *Checklist* D3.

1795/07/24   'A Charles His, rédacteur du Républicain français', *Le Républicain français*,
6 thermidor an III, 24 juillet 1795. *Checklist* D4.

1795/08/20-21   Discours de Jean-Baptiste Louvet à la Convention, 3-4 fructidor an III,
20 août 1795, *Le Moniteur universel*, 9 fructidor an III, 26 août 1795. *Checklist* D5.

1796

1796/02/18   *Rapport du Comité de l'Union, fait le 18 février 1796 et Résolution de Leurs Hautes
Puissances les Etats Généraux des Provinces unies des Pays bas, du 19 février 1796 sur l'affaire du
Colonel Juste Constant de Rebecque.* Autograph manuscript in BCU, Fonds Constant I; copy
with corrections in the hand of Juste de Constant in BPU.

1796/04/[ca.15]   *De la force du gouvernement actuel de la France et de la nécessité de s'y rallier*,
[Lausanne: Mourer], 1796. Published *ca.*15 April 1796. C.2a. *Checklist* A2/1.

1796/04/30-1796/05/04   'De la force du gouvernement actuel de la France', *La Sentinelle*,
11-15 floréal an IV, 30 avril-4 mai 1796. *Checklist* D6.

1796/05/01-09   'De la force du gouvernement actuel de la France', *Le Moniteur universel*,
12-20 floréal an IV, 1-9 mai 1796. *Checklist* D7.

1796/07/27   *Aux Citoyens représentans du peuple composant le Conseil des Cinq-Cents. Séance du
9 thermidor an IV, [27 juillet 1796]*, [Paris]: Imprimerie nationale. C.64a. *Checklist* B1/1.

1796/07/29   'Aux citoyens représentans du peuple composant le Conseil des Cinq-
Cents', *Le Républicain français*, 11 thermidor an IV, 29 juillet 1796. *Checklist* D8.

1796/08/01   'Aux Citoyens représentans du peuple composant le Conseil des Cinq-
Cents', *Le Moniteur universel*, 14 thermidor an IV, 1er août 1796. *Checklist* D9.

1796/08/26   'De la restitution des droits politiques aux descendans des religionnaires
fugitifs', *Le Moniteur universel*, 9 fructidor an IV, 26 août 1796. *Checklist* D10.

1796/[04-09]/-   De la force du gouvernememt [*sic*] actuel de la France et de la nécessité
de s'y rallier, Besançon: Couche, an IV. Reprint, presumably published before the end
of an IV (21 September 1796). C.2c. *Checklist* A2/3.

1796/[04-10]/-   'Ueber die Kraft der gegenwärtigen Regierung Frankreichs und über
die Nothwendigkeit, sich an sie anzuschließen', *Klio. Eine Monatschrift für die französische
Zeitgeschichte*, 1796, Bd. II, 5. Heft, 106-134; 6. Heft, 137-204. C.2e. *Checklist* A2/t1, D11.

1796/10/26   *'De l'influence des passions sur le bonheur des individus et des nations*, par Madame
de Staël', *Le Moniteur universel*, 5 brumaire an V, 26 octobre 1796. *Checklist* D12.

1796/[04-12]/-   *De la force du gouvernement actuel de la France et de la nécessité de s'y rallier*,
[Lausanne: Mourer], 1796. Reissue (and in part a reprint). C.2b. *Checklist* A2/2.

1796/[04-12]/-   'Von der Stärke der gegenwärtigen Regierung Frankreichs und von der
Nothwendigkeit sich derselben anzuschliessen', *Frankreich im Jahr 1796*, 1796, Bd. II, 7.
St., 211-244; 8. St., 291-324. C.2f. *Checklist* A2/t2, D13.

1796/[07-12]/-   'Bittschrift von Benjamin Constant Rebecque an den Rath der Fünfhundert', *Frankreich im Jahr 1796*, 1796 Bd. II, 8. St., 363-367. C.64b. *Checklist* B1/t1, D14.

1797

1797/[01-02]/- *Observations on the strength of the present government of France, and upon the necessity of rallying round it*, translated by James Losh, London: Robinson, 1797. Translator's preface dated 26 January 1797. C.2g. *Checklist* A2/t3.

1797/04/[ca.05] *Des réactions politiques*, [Paris: Mourer et Pinparé], an V. Preface dated 10 germinal an V [30 March 1797]. Announced in *La Sentinelle*, 5 April 1797. C.3a. *Checklist* A3/1.

1797/04/05-11 'Des réactions politiques', *La Sentinelle*, 16-22 germinal an V, 5-11 avril 1797. *Checklist* D15.

1797/06/[ante 08] *Des réactions politiques, seconde édition, augmentée de l'examen des effets de la terreur*, [Paris: Mourer et Pinparé], an V. Addition dated 10 prairial an 5 [29 May 1797]. Reviewed in *La Décade*, 8 June 1797. C.3b. *Checklist* A3/2.

1797/07/[ante 08] *Des effets de la terreur*, [Paris: Mourer et Pinparé], an V. Reviewed in *La Décade*, 20 messidor an V, 8 juillet 1797. C.4a. *Checklist* A4/1.

1797/08/28 [Obituary notice on J.-B. Louvet], *La Sentinelle*, 11 fructidor an V, 28 août 1797. *Checklist* D15a.

1797/09/16 *Discours prononcé au Cercle constitutionnel, pour la plantation de l'arbre de la liberté, le 30 fructidor an 5* [16 septembre 1797], [Paris]: impr. Lemaire, [1797]. Presumably published shortly after 16 September 1797. C.5a. *Checklist* A5/1.

1797/09/16 *Extrait du discours de Benjamin Constant, prononcé le 30 fructidor, au Cercle constitutionnel*, [Paris]: impr. Lemaire, [1797]. Presumably published at the same time as the preceding item. C.5b. *Checklist* A5/2.

1797/09/21 'Discours prononcé au Cercle constitutionnel … le 30 fructidor', *Echo des cercles patriotiques*, n° 14 [21 septembre 1797]. *Checklist* D16.

1797/10/03 'Discours prononcé au Cercle constitutionnel … le 30 fructidor', *La Sentinelle*, 3 octobre 1797. *Checklist* D16a.

1797/10/16 'Discours prononcé au Cercle constitutionnel … le 30 fructidor', *Echo des cercles patriotiques*, n° 15 [16 octobre 1797]. *Checklist* D17.

1797/[04-12]/- 'Von den politischen Gegenwirkungen', *Frankreich im Jahr 1797*, 1797, Bd. II, 5. St., 3-27; 6. St., 99-127; 7. St., 200-213; 8. St., 291-298. C.3c. *Checklist* A3/t1, D18.

1797/[07-12]/- 'Ueber die Wirkungen des Schreckens', *Frankreich im Jahr 1797*, 1797, Bd. III, 9. St., 3-24. C.4b. *Checklist* A4/t1, D19.

1797/11/13 Discours de Benjamin Constant, président de l'administration municipale de Luzarches, 13 novembre 1797. Published from Archives départementales de Seine-et-Oise by Ernest Tambour, 'Benjamin Constant à Luzarches', *Revue de l'histoire de Versailles et de Seine-et-Oise*, 1906, pp.169-172. *Checklist* A74/3.

1797/-/- *De la force du gouvernement actuel de la France et de la nécessité de s'y rallier*, Strasbourg: Levrault, 1797. C.2d. *Checklist* A2/4.

1798

1798/02/27 *Discours prononcé au Cercle constitutionnel, le 9 ventôse an VI* [27 février 1798], [Paris]: impr. veuve Galletti, [1798]. Presumably published almost immediately after 27 February 1798. C.6a. *Checklist* A6/1.

1798/03/11-12 'Discours prononcé au Cercle constitutionnel, le 9 ventôse an VI', *Le Moniteur universel*, 21-22 ventôse an VI, 11-12 mars 1798. *Checklist* D20.

1798/03/- *Discours prononcé au Cercle constitutionnel le 9 ventôse an VI*, Marseille: impr. Bertrand. Reprint, presumably published shortly after the original edition. C. Suppl. Add. 1. *Checklist* A6/2.

1798/04/10 *Benjamin Constant à ses collègues de l'assemblée électorale du département de Seine et Oise*, [1798]. Text signed: 'Versailles, le 21 germinal, an 6 de la république [10 April 1798]. Benjamin Constant.' C.7a. *Checklist* A7/1.

1798/04/21 'Au citoyen G ...', *Le Républicain*, n° 2, 2 floréal an VI, [21 avril 1798]. *Checklist* D21.

1799

1799/07/[*ante* 12] *Des suites de la contre-révolution de 1660 en Angleterre*, Paris: Buisson, an VII. Announced in *Journal typographique et bibliographique*, 20 messidor an VII, 8 juillet 1799. Reviewed in *Journal de Paris*, 24, 27 messidor an VII, 12, 15 juillet 1799. C.8a. *Checklist* A8/1.

1799/[07-09]/- *Des suites de la contre-révolution de 1660 en Angleterre, seconde édition*, Paris: Buisson, an VII. Published before the end of an VII (22 September 1799). C.8b. *Checklist* A8/2.

1799/10/17 [Obituary notice on Baudin], *Journal de Paris*, 25 vendémiaire an VIII, 17 octobre 1799. *Checklist* D21a.

1799/10/18 [Obituary notice on Baudin], *Le Rédacteur*, 26 vendémiaire an VIII, 18 octobre 1799. *Checklist* D21b.

1799/[10]/- 'Ueber den jungverstorbenen Rapräsentanten Baudin. Von Benjamin Constant', *Frankreich im Jahr 1799*, 1799, Bd. III, 11. St., 195-197. *Checklist* D22.

1799/-/- 'Weder die Folgen der Gegenrevolution 1660 in England. Von Benjamin Constant. (In Auszuge)', *Frankreich im Jahr 1799*, 1799, Bd. II, 8. St., 291-297. *Checklist* D23.

1799/-/- *Van Wederwerkingen in den Staat. (Politieke Réactien.)* Naar het Fransch door J. G. H. Hahn, In de Haag: van Cleff, 1799. C.3d. *Checklist* A3/t2.

1799/-/- *De la justice politique.* [1799] Translation of William Godwin's *Political Justice* (1793). Announced by Constant as forthcoming in *Des suites de la contre-révolution de 1660 en Angleterre*. Published from *Œuvres manuscrites* of 1810 (BN, N.a.fr. 14360-14362): *De la justice politique. Traduction inédite de l'ouvrage de William Godwin, 'Enquiry concerning Political Justice and its Influence on General Virtue and Happiness'*, éditée by Burton R. Pollin, Québec: Presses de l'Université Laval, 1972. C. Appendix D1. *Checklist* A72/1.

[1799-1810] *De Godwin, de ses principes, et de son ouvrage sur la justice politique.* [1799-1810]. Published from Constant's *Œuvres manuscrites* of 1810, BN, N.a.fr. 14362, by Pollin (1972), pp.357-362. *Checklist* A72/1.

[1799-1810] *Fragmens d'un essai sur la perfectibilité de l'espèce humaine.* [1799-1810]. Published from Constant's *Œuvres manuscrites* of 1810, BN, N.a.fr. 14362, by Pollin (1972), pp.363-373. Some of the material was used by Constant in the 'Pensées détachées' of *Mélanges* (1829). *Checklist* A72/1.

1800

1800/01/05 Tribunat. Sur le projet de loi relatif aux opérations et communications respectives des autorités chargées de faire la loi. Séance du 15 nivôse an 8 [5 janvier

1800]. *Archives parlementaires*, I, 30-44. Editions: *Discours sur le projet concernant la formation de la loi*, [Paris]: Imprimerie nationale, nivôse an 8; Pozzo di Borgo (1964), I, 139-153. C.65a. *Checklist* B2.

1800/02/01 Tribunat. Sur le mode de rendre compte des pétitions. Séance du 12 pluviôse an 8 [1er février 1800]. *Archives parlementaires*, I, 132-136. Edition: *Opinion sur le mode à adopter pour prendre en considération les pétitions adressées au Tribunat*, [Paris]: Imprimerie nationale, pluviôse an 8. C.66a. *Checklist* B3.

1800/02/23 Tribunat. Sur une pétition de citoyens détenus à Perpignan. Séance du 4 ventôse an 8 [23 février 1800]. *Archives parlementaires*, I, 244.

1800/03/06 Tribunat. Sur le projet de loi relatif à la levée de la première classe de la conscription militaire. Séance du 15 ventôse an 8. [6 mars 1800]. *Archives parlementaires*, I, 310-314. Edition: *Opinion sur le projet de loi* ... [Paris]: Imprimerie nationale, ventôse an 8. C.67a. *Checklist* B4.

1800/03/08 Tribunat. Sur le projet de loi relatif à la levée de la première classe de la conscription militaire. Séance du 17 ventôse an 8 [8 mars 1800]. *Archives parlementaires*, I, 321-322. Edition: *Discours sur le projet de loi tendant à mettre à la disposition du gouvernement les citoyens qui ont atteint l'âge de 20 ans*, [Paris]: Baudouin, [1800]. C.68a. *Checklist* B5.

1800/03/18 Tribunat. Sur le projet de loi relatif aux rentes foncières. Séance du 27 ventôse an 8 [18 mars 1800]. *Archives parlementaires*, I, 460-462. Edition: *Opinion sur le projet de loi* ... [Paris]: Imprimerie nationale, ventôse an 8. C.69a. *Checklist* B6.

1800/03/20 Tribunat. Sur le projet de loi relatif à la faculté de disposer. Séance du 29 ventôse an 8 [20 mars 1800]. *Archives parlementaires*, I, 486-88. Edition: *Opinion sur le projet de loi* ... [Paris]: Imprimerie nationale, germinal an 8. C.70a. *Checklist* B7.

1800/03/28 Tribunat. Sur la proposition de procéder à un scrutin d'instruction pour l'élection d'un candidat à présenter au Sénat conservateur. Séance du 7 germinal an 8 [28 mars 1800]. *Archives parlementaires*, I, 553.

1800/05/22 Tribunat. Sur la motion d'ordre de Ganilh, sur la publicité des jugements de cassation et leur distribution aux diverses branches du pouvoir législatif. Séance du 2 prairial an 8 [22 mai 1800]. *Archives parlementaires*, I, 579.

1800/05/26 '*De la littérature considérée dans ses rapports avec les institutions sociales*: par madame de Staël de Holstein', *Le Publiciste*, 6 prairial an VIII, 26 mai 1800. *Checklist* D24.

1800/05/31 '*De la littérature* ... par madame de Staël de Holstein, Second extrait', *Le Publiciste*, 11 prairial an VIII, 31 mai 1800. *Checklist* D25.

1800/06/22 Tribunat. Sur les événements qui ont précédé et suivi la victoire de Marengo. Séance du 3 messidor an 8, [22 juin 1800]. *Archives parlementaires*, I, 596-597. Edition: *Discours sur les victoires* ... [Paris]: Imprimerie nationale, messidor an 8. C.71a. *Checklist* B8.

1800/[06]/- 'Sitzung des Tribunats vom 3ten Messidor', *Frankreich im Jahr 1800*, 1800, Bd. II, 7. St., 195-213. *Checklist* B8/t1, D26.

1800/10/22 'Extrait d'une lettre de Genève', *Le Citoyen français*, 30 vendémiaire an IX, 22 octobre 1800. *Checklist* D27.

1800/10/23 [Samuel de Constant], *Le Journal de Paris*, 1er brumaire an IX, 23 octobre 1800. *Checklist* D28.

1800/10/24   [Samuel de Constant], *Le Publiciste*, 2 brumaire an IX, 24 octobre 1800. *Checklist* D29.

1800/11/07   Tribunat. Sur la modification de l'article 43 du règlement. Séance du 16 brumaire an 9 [7 novembre 1800]. *Archives parlementaires*, I, 661.

1801

1801/01/21   Tribunat. Sur le projet de loi portant réduction des justices de paix. Séance du 1er pluviôse an 9 [21 janvier 1801]. *Archives parlementaires*, II, 129-132. Edition: *Opinion sur le projet de loi* ... [Paris]: Imprimerie nationale, pluviôse an 9. C.72a. *Checklist* B9.

1801/01/24   Tribunat. Sur le projet de loi relatif à la réduction des justices de paix. (Opposition à l'impression du discours de Girardin). Séance du 4 pluviôse an 9 [24 janvier 1801]. *Archives parlementaires*, II, 162.

1801/01/25   Tribunat. Sur le projet de loi concernant l'établissement d'un tribunal criminel spécial. Séance du 5 pluviôse an 9 [25 janvier 1801]. *Archives parlementaires*, II, 179-188. Editions: *Opinion sur le projet de loi* ... [Paris]: Imprimerie nationale, pluviôse an 9; Pozzo di Borgo (1964), I, 156-189. C.73a. *Checklist* B10.

1801/02/03   Tribunat. Sur le projet de loi concernant l'établissement d'un tribunal criminel spécial. (Contre la clôture de la discussion). Séance du 14 pluviôse an 9 [3 février 1801]. *Archives parlementaires*, II, 302.

1801/03/14   Tribunat. Sur un incident relatif à la dette publique. Séance du 23 ventôse an 9 [14 mars 1801]. *Archives parlementaires*, II, 574.

1801/03/19   Tribunat. Sur le projet de loi relatif à la dette publique et aux domaines nationaux. Séance du 28 ventôse an 9 [19 mars 1801]. *Archives parlementaires*, II, 652-660. Edition: *Opinion sur le projet de loi* ... [Paris]: Imprimerie nationale, germinal an 9. C.74a. *Checklist* B11.

1801/03/21   Tribunat. Sur le projet de loi relatif à la dette publique et aux domaines nationaux. Séance du 30 ventôse an 9 [21 mars 1801]. *Archives parlementaires*, II, 680-81.

1801/12/25   Tribunat. Sur la pétition du citoyen Rouppe, maire de Bruxelles, contre un ordre du ministre de la Police générale. Séance du 4 nivôse an 10 [25 décembre 1801]. *Archives parlementaires*, III, 255.

1801/12/25   Tribunat. Sur le projet de loi relatif aux actes de l'état civil. Séance du 4 nivôse an 10 [25 décembre 1801]. *Archives parlementaires*, III, 259-265. Edition: *Opinion sur le projet de loi* ... [Paris]: Imprimerie nationale, frimaire an 10. C.75a. *Checklist* B12.

1801/12/28   Tribunat. Sur le projet de loi relatif aux actes de l'état civil. Séance du 7 nivôse an 10 [28 décembre 1801]. *Archives parlementaires*, III, 305-309. Edition: *Seconde opinion* ... [Paris]: Imprimerie nationale, nivôse an 10. C.76a. *Checklist* B13.

1803

1803/01/06-1803/04/10   *Amélie et Germaine*, 6 janvier-10 avril 1803. Alfred Roulin, *Les Cahiers de la Pléiade* (1951-1952); Pléiade (1957), pp.225-255. Date of composition uncertain.

1803/01/16   Review of *Delphine* by Germaine de Staël, *Le Citoyen français*, 16 janvier 1803. *Checklist* D29a.

1803-1804

[1803-1804]   *Des rapports de la morale avec les croyances religieuses. De l'intervention de l'autorité dans ce qui a rapport à la religion*, [1803-1804]. *Deux chapitres inédits de l'Esprit des religions*

(1803-1804) ... publiés avec une introduction et des notes par Patrice Thompson, Neuchâtel: Faculté des Lettres; Genève: Droz 1970. (Université de Neuchâtel, Recueil de travaux publiés par la Faculté des Lettres, 33). *Checklist* A71/1.

1804

1804/01/22-1804/12/31   *Journal*, 22 janvier-31 décembre 1804. Roulin & Roth (1952); Pléiade (1957).

1804/01/22-1804/12/31   *Journal abrégé*, 22 janvier-31 décembre 1804. Roulin & Roth (1952); Pléiade (1957).

1805

1805/01/01-1805/05/08   *Journal*, 1er janvier-8 mai 1805. Roulin & Roth (1952); Pléiade (1957).

1805/01/01-1805/12/31   *Journal abrégé*, 1er janvier-31 décembre 1805. Roulin & Roth (1952); Pléiade (1957).

1805/02/25   [Article for a newspaper, *ca.* 25 February 1805]. Not identified. *Checklist* D29.

1805/03/02   [Article for *Le Publiciste*, *ca.* 2 March 1805]. Not identified. *Checklist* D29a.

1805/04/16   'Dialogue entre deux hommes d'autrefois sur des hommes d'aujourd'hui', *Le Publiciste*, 16 avril 1805. *Checklist* D30.

1805/05/26   'Aux auteurs du Publiciste', *Le Publiciste*, 26 mai 1805. *Checklist* D31.

1805/06/17   '*Essai sur les causes de la supériorité des Grecs dans les arts d'imagination*; par M. Leulliette', *Le Publiciste*, 17 juin 1805, pp.3-4. *Checklist* D32.

1805/07/03   '*Essai sur les causes de la supériorité des Grecs dans les arts d'imagination*. Deuxième et dernier extrait', *Le Publiciste*, 3 juillet 1805, pp.3-4. *Checklist* D33.

1805-1807

[1805-1807]   *Lettre sur Julie*. [*ca.* 1805-1807]. Written after the death of Julie Talma (5 May 1805). *Mélanges* (1829); Pléiade (1957).

[1805-1807]   *Fragmens d'un essai sur la littérature dans ses rapports avec la liberté*. Kurt Kloocke, 'Une étude littéraire inachevée de Benjamin Constant', *Annales Benjamin Constant*, n° 1 (1980), pp.173-200. For date [1805-1807?] see Kloocke, p.176. (Published from *Œuvres manuscrites* of 1810: BN, N.a.fr. 14362.) *Checklist* A74/10.

1806/01/01-1806/12/31   *Journal abrégé*, 1er janvier-31 décembre 1806. Roulin & Roth (1952); Pléiade (1957).

[1806]/-/-   *Principes de politique applicables à tous les gouvernements*. Benjamin Constant, *Principes de politique applicables à tous les gouvernements*, texte établi d'après les manuscrits de Lausanne et de Paris avec une introduction et des notes, par Etienne Hofmann, Genève: Droz, 1980. *Checklist* A73/1.

1807

1807/01/01-1807/12/27   *Journal abrégé*, 1er janvier-27 décembre 1807. Roulin & Roth (1952); Pléiade (957).

1807/02/*ca.*16   [Article for a newspaper, *ca.* 16 February 1807]. Not identified. *Checklist* D34.

1807/02/21   'Observations sur un article du *Journal de l'Empire* du 21 février 1807'. *Checklist* D35.

1807/05/12   '*Corinne ou l'Italie*, par Mme de Staël Holstein. Premier extrait', *Le Publiciste*, 12 mai 1807. *Checklist* D36.

1807/05/14   '*Corinne ou l'Italie*. Second extrait', *Le Publiciste*, 14 mai 1807. *Checklist* D37.

1807/05/16   '*Corinne ou l'Italie*. Troisième et dernier extrait', *Le Publiciste*, 16 mai 1807. *Checklist* D38.

[1807]/[07]/[24]   *Esquisse d'un essai sur la littérature du 18e siècle*, [24 juillet 1807]. S. Balayé *Europe*, n° 467 (mars 1968) pp.18-21. (Published from *Œuvres manuscrites* of 1810 (BN, N.a.fr. 14362). For date see Balayé, who quotes from Constant's *Journal* of 24 July 1807: 'Commencé un tableau littéraire du XVIIIe siècle pour concourir à l'Institut'.) *Checklist* A74/8.

1809

1809/01/26   *Wallstein, tragédie en cinq actes et en vers*, Paris-Genève: Paschoud, 1809. Published 26 January 1809. C.9a. *Checklist* A9/1.

1809/02/25   '*Lettres & Pensées du maréchal Prince de Ligne*', publiées par Mme la baronne de Staël-Holstein', *Le Publiciste*, 25 février 1809, pp.3-4. *Checklist* D39.

1809/03/02   '*Lettres & Pensées du maréchal Prince de Ligne*. Deuxième et dernier extrait', *Le Publiciste*, 2 mars 1809, pp.3-4. *Checklist* D40.

1810

1810/-/-   *Œuvres manuscrites, 1810*. BN, N.a.fr. 14358-14364. Copy (with autograph additions and corrections) of works written *ca.* 1786-1810. Vol. I (N.a.fr. 14358) Articles for the *Biographie universelle*, ff.2-30. (C.B1. *Checklist* C1/1). *Adolphe*, ff.32-83. This is an earlier state than the version published in 1816. (C.18a. *Checklist* A18/1). *Principes de politique*, I-VII, ff.86-182. Continued below. Vol. II (N.a.fr. 14359) *Principes de politique*, VIII-XV, ff.2-179. Continued below. Vol. III (N.a.fr. 14360) *Principes de politique*, XVI-XVIII, ff.2-66. (*Checklist* A73/1). *De la justice politique* (Godwin), I-III, ff.67-145. Continued below. Vol. IV (N.a.fr. 14361) *De la justice politique*, IV-VI, ff.2-188. Continued below. Vol. V (N.a.fr. 14362) *De la justice politique*, VII-VIII, ff.2-23. (*Checklist* A72/1). *De Godwin, de ses principes ...* ff.24-30. (*Checklist* A72/1). *Fragmens d'un essai sur la littérature*, ff.31-51. (*Checklist* A74/10). *Corinne ou l'Italie*, ff.53-64. (*Checklist* D36-D38). *De la perfectibilité de l'espèce humaine*, ff.66-83. (C.134a. *Checklist* E3/1). *Fragmens d'un essai sur la perfectibilité*, ff.83-94. (*Checklist* A72/1). *Lettre sur Julie*, ff.96-107. (C.134a. *Checklist* E3/1). *Esquisse d'un essai sur la littérature du 18e siècle*, ff.109-112. (*Checklist* A74/8). *Apologie du parlement anglais*, ff.113-117. *Ferdinand de Brunswick*, ff.119-122. (C.B1a. *Checklist* C1/1). *Observations sur un article du Journal de l'Empire*, ff.124-127. (*Checklist* D35). *De la révolution du Brabant en 1790*, ff.128-139. (See above under 1790). *De la discipline militaire des Romains*, ff.140-148. (See above under 1786). *Histoire de Frédéric le Grand*, ff.149-172. *Morceau de Filangieri sur la religion*, ff.172-182. Vol. VI (N.a.fr. 14363) *Fragmens d'un ouvrage abandonné sur la possibilité d'une constitution républicaine dans un grand pays*, I-VIII, ff.3-205. Continued below. Vol. VII (N.a.fr. 14364) *Fragmens d'un ouvrage abandonné ...* VIII, ff.2-26. *Additions à l'ouvrage intitulé Principes de politique*, ff.28-92. (*Checklist* A73/1). *Additions à l'ouvrage intitulé Des moyens de constituer une république dans un grand pays*, ff.93-104. *Table des matières des sept premiers volumes*, ff.162-174.

1811

1811/04/11-12 *Biographie universelle*, tome I, Paris: Michaud, 1811. Includes seven articles signed 'B. C-t': 'Adolphe de Nassau', 'Agnès d'Autriche', 'Albert Ier', 'Albert II', 'Albert III', 'Albert IV' and 'Albert V'. Dépôt légal: 11-12 April 1811. Harpaz (1978), pp.101-121. C.B1a. *Checklist* C1/1.

1811/04/11-12 *Biographie universelle*, tome II, Paris: Michaud, 1811. Includes one article by Constant: 'Arnoul'. Dépôt legal: 11-12 April 1811. Harpaz (1978), p.122. C.B1. *Checklist* C1/1.

1811/05/15-1811/12/31 *Journal*, 15 mai-31 décembre 1811. Roulin & Roth (1952); Pléiade (1957).

[1811]/[08-10]/- *Ma vie (1767-1787)*, [August-October 1811]. Published as *Le Cahier rouge* by Adrien de Constant, *Revue des deux mondes*, 1er-15 janvier 1907. Pléiade (1957). For date of composition [August-October 1811?], see Roulin, Pléiade (1957), p.1454. *Checklist* A68/1.

[1811]/[11-12]/- *Cécile*, [November-December 1811]. *Cécile*, présenté et annoté par Alfred Roulin, Paris: Gallimard, 1951; Pléiade (1957). For date of composition [November-December 1811?], see Roulin, Pléiade (1957), p.1470. *Checklist* A70.

1812

1812/01/01-1812/12/31 *Journal*, 1er janvier-31 décembre 1812. Roulin & Roth (1952); Pléiade (1957).

1812/09/26-28 *Biographie universelle*, tome VI, Paris: Michaud, 1812. Includes one article by Constant: 'Ferdinand, duc de Brunswick'. Dépôt légal: 26-28 September 1812. Harpaz (1978), pp.123-124. C.B1a. *Checklist* C1/1.

1813

1813/01/01-1813/12/31 *Journal*, 1er janvier-31 décembre 1813. Roulin & Roth (1952); Pléiade (1957).

1813/02/06 'Lettre de Mr. Constant aux Rédacteurs', *Bibliothèque britannique*, LII (1813), 266-267. Letter dated 'Genève, le 6 février 1813' and signed 'Constant'. *Checklist* D41.

[1813]/[03]/[15]-[1815]/-/- *Florestan ou le Siège de Soissons*, [15 March 1813-1815]. V. Waille, *Le Siège de Soissons*, *Bulletin de la société d'agriculture, sciences et arts de Poligny*, 1890-1892; and edition, Poligny: impr. Cottez, 1892. For date of composition see *Journal* from 15 March 1813 to 1815. *Checklist* A67.

1813/04/27-28 *Biographie universelle*, tome VIII, Paris: Michaud, 1813. Includes two articles by Constant: 'Charles III, dit le Gros' and 'Charles IV'. Dépôt légal: 27-28 April 1813. Harpaz (1978), pp.125-132. C.B1a. *Checklist* C1/1.

1813/11/[14] *Commentaire sur la réponse faite par Buonaparté*, [14] novembre 1813. Hasselrot (1952), pp.7-14. Published in *L'Ambigu*, 20 February 1814 (see below). *Checklist* A74/6, D42.

[1813]/[12]/13 *Mémoire sur les communications à établir avec l'intérieur de la France*, [novembre 1813]. Hasselrot (1952), pp.3-6. *Checklist* A74/6.

1813/12/08-09 *Biographie universelle*, tome IX, Paris: Michaud, 1813. Includes three articles by Constant: 'Conrad Ier', 'Constant de Rebecque (David)-Constant de Rebecque (Samuel)'. Dépôt légal: 8-9 December 1813. Harpaz (1978), pp.133-136. C.B1a. *Checklist* C1/1.

1814

1814/01/01-1814/12/31   *Journal*, 1er janvier-31 décembre 1814. Roulin & Roth (1952); Pléiade (1957).

1814/01/30   *De l'esprit de conquête et de l'usurpation*, [Hanover: Hahn], 1814. Published on 30 January 1814. C.10a. *Checklist* A10/1.

[1814]/[02]/[04-05]   *Projet corrigé*, [4-5 February 1814]. Franklin D. Scott, 'Benjamin Constant's 'Projet' for France in 1814', *Journal of British History*, VII (1935), 41-48; Hasselrot (1952), pp.14-21. *Checklist* A74/6.

1814/02/20   'Sur la réponse faite par Buonaparté à la députation du Sénat, le [14] novembre 1813', *L'Ambigu*, 20 février 1814. Hasselrot (1952); Harpaz (1978), pp.137-140. *Checklist* A74/6b, D42.

1814/03/[ca.15]   *De l'esprit de conquête et de l'usurpation*, Londres: Murray, 1814. Published *ca.* 15 March 1814. C.10b. *Checklist* A10/2.

1814/03/22   *Notes instructives*, 22 mars 1814. Hasselrot (1952), pp.21-24. *Checklist* A74/6.

[1814]/[ca.04]/-   *Ueber den Eroberungsgeist und die Usurpation*, aus dem Französischen übersetzt von J.J. Stolz, Hanover: Hahn, 1814. Translator's introduction signed: 'Bremen am Ende des März 1814. Stolz.' C.10e. *Checklist* A10/t1.

1814/04/18   'Au Rédacteur', *Journal des débats*, 18 avril 1814. *Checklist* D43.

1814/04/19   Pamphlet sur le Sénat, [April 1814]. Not extant. 'Fait énormément de petites choses. Pamphlet sur le Sénat' (*Journal*, 19 April 1814).

1814/04/21   'Des révolutions de 1660 et de 1688 en Angleterre, et de celle de 1814 en France', *Journal des débats*, 21 avril 1814. *Checklist* D44.

1814/05/11-12   *De l'esprit de conquête et de l'usurpation, troisième édition*, Paris: Lenormant, Nicolle, 1814. Dépôt légal: 11-12 May 1814. C.10c. *Checklist* A10/3.

1814/05/25-26   *Réflexions sur les constitutions, la distribution des pouvoirs, et les garanties, dans une monarchie constitutionnelle*, Paris: Nicolle, Gide, 1814. Dépôt légal: 25-26 May 1814. C.11a. *Checklist* A11/1.

1814/06/27-30   Discours de Durbach sur la liberté de la presse, 27-30 juin 1814. On 26 June 1814 Constant wrote in his *Journal*, 'Fini le discours de D.' and on 30 June, 'Corps législatif. Mauvais succès de D. Je ne fais plus de discours pour d'autres'. Constant is referring probably to the speeches made by Durbach in the Chambre des députés on 27 and 30 June 1814. *Archives parlementaires*, XII, 64-65, 87-88. See also below under 6 August 1814.

1814/07/09-10   *De la liberté des brochures, des pamphlets et des journaux*, Paris: Nicolle, 1814. Dépôt légal: 9-10 July 1814. C.12a. *Checklist* A12/1.

1814/[07]/-   *De l'esprit de conquête et de l'usurpation, quatrième édition*, Paris: Nicolle, Lenormant, 1814. Published before August 1814. C.10d. *Checklist* A10/4.

1814/08/03-04   *De la liberté des brochures, des pamphlets et des journaux, seconde édition*, Paris: Nicolle, 1814. Dépôt légal: 3-4 August 1814. C.12b. *Checklist* A12/2.

1814/08/04   'Au Rédacteur', *Journal des débats*, 4 août 1814. *Checklist* D45.

1814/08/06   Discours de Durbach sur la liberté de la presse, 6 août 1814. On 4 August 1814 Constant wrote in his *Journal*, 'Fait un discours excellent, je crois, pour Durbach'. Durbach's speech was made in the Chambre des députés on 6 August (*Archives parlementai-*

res, XII, 250-253) and was printed by order of the Chambre: *Opinion de M. Durbach sur la liberté de la presse. Séance du 6 août 1814*, [Paris]: impr. Hacquart, [1814], 8° pp.15. (Impressions ordonnées. Session de 1814, I, n° 32).

1814/08/10   [Article for a newspaper, *ca.* 10 August 1814]. Not identified. *Checklist* D45a.

1814/08/24-26   *Observations sur le discours prononcé par S.E. le Ministre de l'Intérieur en faveur du projet de loi sur la liberté de la presse*, Paris: Nicolle, 1814. Dépôt légal: 24-26 August 1814. C.13a. *Checklist* A13/1.

1814/08/[*ante* 27]   *Observations sur le discours prononcé par S.E. le Ministre de l'Intérieur en faveur du projet de loi sur la liberté de la presse, seconde édition*, Paris: Nicolle, 1814. *Bibliographie de la France*, 27 August 1814. C.13b. *Checklist* A13/2.

1814/09/13-14   *Idées sur la conservation du royaume de Naples au roi Joachim Ier*. Written 13-14 September 1814 (see *Journal*). *Checklist* A74/2.

1814/09/27   [Article for a newspaper, *ca.* 27 September 1814]. Not identified. *Checklist* D45b.

1814/10/-   *Betrachtungen über Constitutionen, über die Vertheilung der Gewalten, und die Bürgschaften in einer constitutionellen Monarchie, aus dem Französischen übersetzt* von J.J. Stolz, Bremen: Heyse, 1814. Published by October 1814. C.11b. *Checklist* A11/t1.

1814/12/[29]   [Reply to the *Journal des débats*, 29 December 1814]. Not identified. *Checklist* D46.

1815

1815/01/01-1815/12/31   *Journal*, 1er janvier-31 décembre 1815. Roulin & Roth (1952); Pléiade (1957).

1815/02/09-10   *De la responsabilité des ministres*, Paris: Nicolle, 1815. Dépôt légal: 9-10 February 1815. C.14a. *Checklist* A14/1.

[1815]/[01-02]/-   *Mémoires de Madame Récamier*, [January-February 1815]. For date of composition see *Journal*, 27 January-25 February 1815. 'Portraits et souvenirs contemporains', *Paris, ou le livre des Cent-et-un*, VII, Paris: Ladvocat, 1832; Pléiade (1957), pp.965-982. C.B5a. *Checklist* C8/1.

1815/02/28   'Travaillé à l'extrait de Ballanche', *Journal*, 28 February 1815. Not extant.

1815/03/11   *Incipit*: 'Nous avons été opprimés pendant douze années par un seul homme', *Journal de Paris*, 11 mars 1815. *Checklist* D47.

1815/03/19   *Incipit*: 'Les représentans de la nation ont porté au pied du trône l'expression de leur dévouement', *Journal des débats*, 19 mars 1815. *Checklist* D48.

1815/04/04   'Observations sur une déclaration du Congrès de Vienne', *Journal de Paris*, 4 avril 1815. *Checklist* D49.

1815/04/22   *Acte additionnel aux constitutions de l'Empire*, (22 avril 1815). Composed in part by Constant. Published in *Le Moniteur universel* and *Bulletin des lois*, 23 avril 1815. C.A1. *Checklist* G1.

1815/[04]/[30]   *A Sa Majesté l'Empereur Napoléon*, [30 April 1815]. Printed *ca.*30 April 1815, but apparently not published. C. Suppl. Add. 2. *Checklist* A74/12.

1815/04/30   *Le Transfuge Benjamin de Constant, au peuple français. Extrait du Journal des débats du 19 mars 1815*, [Paris, 1815]. Unauthorized reprint of Constant's article of 19 March

1815. For date of publication see *Journal*, 29-30 April 1815. C.15a. *Checklist* A15/1.

1815/05/01   'Comparaison de l'ordonnance de réformation de Louis XVIII avec la constitution proposée à la France le 22 avril 1815', *Journal des débats*, 1ᵉʳ mai 1815. *Checklist* D50.

[1815]/[05]/-   *Note sur les droits de Cité appartenant à la famille Constant de Rebecque*, [Paris, 1815]. For date [May 1815] see C.16a, note. Reprinted possibly in the same year. C.16a-b. *Checklist* A16/1-2.

1815/05/-   'On the Responsibility of Ministers', *The Pamphleteer*, V, n° 10 (May 1815), 299-330, 315*-329*. C.14b. *Checklist* A14/t1, D51.

1815/06/02-03   *Principes de politique, applicables à tous les gouvernemens représentatifs et particulièrement à la constitution actuelle de la France*, Paris: Eymery, mai 1815. Dépôt légal: 2-3 June 1815. C.17a. *Checklist* A17/1.

1815/06/9-12   Manifesto for Napoleon. Not extant. Referred to in *Journal*, 9-12 June 1815.

1815/06/14   'Sur les discours écrits', [June 1815]. Not extant. *Checklist* D52.

1815/07/21   *Mémoire de M. Benjamin de Constant*, 21 juillet 1815. P.F. Réal, *Indiscrétions 1780-1830*, Paris: Dufey, 1835, II, 152-172. *Checklist* A74/1.

1815/07/28   [Article for *L'Indépendant*, July 1815]. Not identified. *Checklist* D53.

1815/08/01   [Article for *L'Indépendant*, August 1815]. Not identified. *Checklist* D54.

1815/08/04   'Au Rédacteur'. *Incipit*: 'Je réfléchissais hier aux circonstances dans lesquelles se trouvent la France et l'Europe', *L'Indépendant*, 4 août 1815. *Checklist* D55.

1815/08/06   'Au Rédacteur'. *Incipit*: 'Puisque vous avez jugé ma lettre d'avant-hier digne d'être insérée', *L'Indépendant*, 6 août 1815. *Checklist* D56.

1815/08/13   'Petit morceau pour L[a] B[édoyère]', *Journal*, 13 August 1815. Not extant.

1815/08/17   *Comparaison du jacobisme ancien et moderne*, [August 1815]. Not extant. 'Travaillé à une comparaison assez piquante du jacobisme ancien et moderne. Je la publierai sans me nommer' (*Journal*, 17 August 1815).

1815/09/08   [Article for the *Journal des arts*, September 1815]. Not identified. *Checklist* D57.

1815/09/09   [Article for *Le Courrier*, September 1815]. Not identified. *Checklist* D58.

1815/09/12   [Articles for the *Journal [des arts]*, September 1815]. Not identified. *Checklist* D59.

1815/09/15   'Sur les assemblées électorales, et les discours de leurs présidens', *Journal des arts*, 15 septembre 1815. *Checklist* D60.

1815/09/18   'Sur les assemblées électorales et sur les discours de leurs présidens. (Second article)', *Journal des arts*, 18 septembre 1815. *Checklist* D61.

1815/09/21   'Sur les assemblées électorales et sur les discours de leurs présidens. (Troisième et dernier article)', *Journal des arts*, 21 septembre 1815. *Checklist* D62.

[1815]/[09-10]/-   *Prière*, [September-October 1815]. Henri Lavedan, *Avant l'oubli*, Paris: Plon, 1933, I, 46-51. *Checklist* A74/5.

1815/10/01   '*Des désordres actuels de la France et des moyens d'y remédier*, par M. le comte de

Montlosier. (Premier article)', *Le Courrier*, 1ᵉʳ octobre 1815. *Checklist* D63.

1815/10/01   [Article for the *Journal des arts*, October 1815]. Not identified. *Checklist* D64.

1815/10/02   [Article for the *Journal des arts*, October 1815]. Not identified. *Checklist* D65.

1815/10/03   *Incipit*: 'Le Journal Général nous attaque aujourd'hui', *Journal des arts*, 3 octobre 1815. *Checklist* D66.

1815/10/18   '*Des désordres actuels de la France et des moyens d'y remédier*. (Second article)', *Le Courrier*, 18 octobre 1815. *Checklist* D67.

1815/10/[19]   'La liberté politique, essentielle à la liberté civile. De la liberté en général', *Mercure de France*, n° 3, [19] octobre 1815. *Checklist* D68.

1815/-/-   *Om Eröfrings-Systemet och om Usurpationen uti deras samband med odlingen i Europa*, Stockholm: Gadelius, 1815. C.10f. *Checklist* A10/t2.

1815/-/-   'On the Liberty of the Press', *The Pamphleteer*, VI (1815), 205-238. C.12c. *Checklist* A12/t1, D69.

1816

1816/01/01-1816/09/26   *Journal*, 1ᵉʳ janvier-26 septembre 1816. Roulin & Roth (1952); Pléiade (1957).

1816/06/07   *Adolphe; anecdote trouvée dans les papiers d'un inconnu*, Londres: Colburn; Paris: Tröttel et Wurtz, 1816. Entered at Stationers' Hall: 7 June 1816. C.18a. *Checklist* A18/1.

1816/06/[ca.15]   *Adolphe, anecdote trouvée dans les papiers d'un inconnu*, Paris: Treuttel et Würtz; Londres: Colburn, 1816. Published *ca*.15 June 1816. C.18b. *Checklist* A18/2.

1816/06/24   'To the Editor', 23 June 1816, *Morning Chronicle*, 24 June 1816. *Checklist* D70.

1816/06/25   [Summary of preceding item]. *Courrier de Londres*, 25 juin 1816. *Checklist* D71.

1816/06/30   [Summary of same item]. *Journal des débats*, 30 juin 1816. *Checklist* D72.

1816/07/[ante 22]   *Adolphe; anecdote trouvée dans les papiers d'un inconnu*, seconde édition, Londres: Colburn; Paris: Treuttel et Würtz, 1816. Published before 22 July 1816. C.18c. *Checklist* A18/3.

1816/07-08/-   'Adolphe, Anecdote trouvée dans les papiers d'un inconnu', *Le Nouvelliste français*, Pesth: Hartleben, tome X, livr. 14 (31 juillet 1816); livr. 15 (15 août 1816); livr. 16 (31 août 1816). C.18d. *Checklist* A18/4, D73.

1816/08-09/-   *Adolphe*, *Morgenblatt*, 1816, nᵒˢ 199-217 (19 August-9 September). C. Suppl. Add. 3. *Checklist* A18/t1a, D74.

1816/09/03   *Adolphe: an anecdote found among the papers of an unknown person*, London: Colburn, 1816. Entered at Stationers' Hall: 3 September 1816. C.18i. *Checklist* A18/t1.

1816/12/31-1817/01/02   *De la doctrine politique, qui peut réunir les partis en France*, Paris: Delaunay, décembre 1816. Dépôt légal: 31 December 1816-2 January 1817. C.19a. *Checklist* A19/1.

1817

1817/01/04   'Des Chambres, depuis leur convocation jusqu'au 31 décembre 1816', *Mercure de France*, I, 4 janvier 1817, pp.28-32. *Checklist* D75.

1817/01/11   'Des Chambres, depuis leur convocation jusqu'au 31 décembre 1816. (IIe article)', *Mercure de France*, I, 11 janvier 1817, pp.69-77. *Checklist* D76.

1817/01/15-16   *De la doctrine politique, qui peut réunir les partis en France, seconde édition*, Paris: Delaunay, janvier 1817. Dépôt légal: 15-16 January 1817. C.19b. *Checklist* A19/2.

1817/01/18   'Tableau politique de l'Europe', *Mercure de France*, I, 18 janvier 1817, pp.104-113. *Checklist* D77.

1817/01/18   'Des Chambres. (IIIe article). Loi sur les élections', *Mercure de France*, I, 18 janvier 1817, pp.113-127. *Checklist* D78.

1817/01/22-23   *Considérations sur le projet de loi relatif aux élections, (Extrait du Mercure de France du 18 janvier)*, Paris: Delaunay, 1817. Dépôt légal: 22-23 January 1817. C.20a. *Checklist* A20/1.

1817/01/25   'Des Chambres. (IVe article). Projet de loi relatif à la liberté individuelle', *Mercure de France*, I, 25 janvier 1817, pp.155-171. *Checklist* D79.

1817/02/01   'Des Chambres. (V^e article). Projet de loi sur la liberté de la Presse', *Mercure de France*, I, 1er février 1817, pp.203-215. *Checklist* D80.

1817/02/01   'Réponse à la lettre de M***, à M. B. de Constant, insérée dans le dernier numéro', *Mercure de France*, I, 1er février 1817, pp.215-221. *Checklist* D81.

1817/[01-02]/-   *On the political doctrine calculated to unite parties in France*, translated by Thomas Elde Darby, London: Ridgways, 1817. Cited by *Bibliographie de la France*, 8 February 1817. C.19c. *Checklist* A19/t1.

1817/02/08   'Des Chambres. (VIe article). Projet de loi sur les Journaux', *Mercure de France*, I, 8 février 1817, pp.262-272. *Checklist* D82.

1817/02/15   'Des Chambres. (VIIe article). Projet de loi sur les Journaux', *Mercure de France*, I, 15 février 1817, pp.301-319. *Checklist* D83.

1817/02/22   'Tableau politique de l'Europe. (Deuxième article)', *Mercure de France*, I, 22 février 1817, pp.354-365. *Checklist* D84.

1817/03/01   'Des Chambres. Discussion sur le Budget', *Mercure de France*, I, 1er mars 1817, pp.401-415. *Checklist* D85.

1817/03/08   'Des Chambres. (Art. IX). Projet de loi sur le Budget, (Continuation)', *Mercure de France*, I, 8 mars 1817, pp.450-462. *Checklist* D86.

1817/03/15   'Des Chambres. (article X). Projet de loi sur le Budget. (Continuation)', *Mercure de France*, I, 15 mars 1817, pp.497-509. *Checklist* D87.

1817/03/22   'Des Chambres. (article XI). Continuation du budget', *Mercure de France*, I, 22 mars 1817, pp.547-555. *Checklist* D88.

1817/03/29   'Des Chambres. (XIIe article). Projet de loi sur le Budget. (Continuation)', *Mercure de France*, I, 29 mars 1817, pp.599-603. *Checklist* D89.

1817/04/05   'Lettre de M. Saint-Aubin, relativement à la dette publique de l'Angleterre', *Mercure de France*, II, 5 avril 1817, pp.33-44. *Checklist* D90.

1817/04/12   'Des Chambres. (Article XIIIe). Continuation et fin du budget', *Mercure de France*, II, 12 avril 1817, pp.76-85. *Checklist* D91.

1817/04/19   'Tableau politique de l'Europe. (Article III)', *Mercure de France*, II, 19 avril 1817, pp.131-139. *Checklist* D92.

1817/04/26 'De Godwin et de son ouvrage sur la justice politique', *Mercure de France*, II, 26 avril 1817, pp.161-173. *Checklist* D93.

1817/05/10 'Tableau politique de l'Europe. (Art. IV^c)', *Mercure de France*, II, 10 mai 1817, pp.278-285. *Checklist* D94.

1817/05/24 'Pensées détachées', *Mercure de France*, II, 24 mai 1817, pp.346-352. *Checklist* D95.

1817/05/30 'De Madame de Krudener', *Journal de Paris*, 30 mai 1817. *Checklist* D96.

1817/05/31 '*Eloge de Saint-Jérôme*', *Mercure de France*, II, 31 mai 1817, pp.401-413. *Checklist* D97.

1817/[05-06]/- *Tableau politique du royaume des Pays-Bas*, Paris [= Bruxelles], 1817. Reprinted from *Mercure de France*, 19 avril, 10 mai 1817. Cited in *Bibliographie de la France*, 7 June 1817. C.21a. *Checklist* A21/1.

1817/06/14 'Pensées détachées', *Mercure de France*, II, 14 juin 1817, pp.509-523. *Checklist* D98.

1817/06/28 '*Théorie des Révolutions* ... [par Antoine-François-Claude Ferrand], (1er Article)', *Mercure de France*, II, 28 juin 1817, pp.581-591. *Checklist* D99.

1817/07/12-14 *Questions sur la législation actuelle de la presse en France*, Paris: impr. Renaudière, 1817. Dépôt légal: 12-14 July 1817. C.22a. *Checklist* A22/1.

1817/07/18 'Sur Madame de Staël', *Journal général de France*, 18 juillet 1817. *Checklist* D100.

1817/07/18-19 *Questions sur la législation actuelle de la presse en France, seconde édition*. Paris: Delaunay 1817. Dépôt légal: 18-19 July 1817. C.22b. *Checklist* A22/2.

1817/07/19 [Nécrologie: Germaine de Staël-Holstein], *Mercure de France*, III, 19 juillet 1817, pp.136-137. *Checklist* D101.

1817/07/26 [Nécrologie: Germaine de Staël-Holstein], *Mercure de France*, III, 26 juillet 1817, pp.175-180. *Checklist* D101a.

1817/07/26 *Incipit*: 'J'ai lu hier, Monsieur, avec un sentiment très pénible, un article du journal relatif à madame de Staël', *Journal général de France*, 26 juillet 1817. *Checklist* D102.

1817/08/16 '*Théorie des Révolutions*, (Deuxième Article)', *Mercure de France*, III, 16 août 1817, pp.307-313. *Checklist* D103.

1817/09/[*ante* 13] *Des élections prochaines*, Paris: Plancher, Delaunay, Hubert, 1817. Printer's declaration: 29 août 1817; *Bibliographie de la France*, 13 septembre 1817. C.23a. *Checklist* A23/1.

1817/09/13 'De la Littérature dans ses rapports avec la Liberté', *Mercure de France*, III, 13 septembre 1817, pp.485-495. *Checklist* D104.

1817/09/17-18 *Entretien d'un électeur avec lui-même*, Paris: Plancher, Delaunay, 1817. Dépôt légal: 17-18 September 1817. C.24a. *Checklist* A24/1.

1817/09/18 'Au Rédacteur', *Le Moniteur universel*, 18 septembre 1817, p.1030. *Checklist* D104a.

1817/09/[*post* 16] *Notes sur quelques articles de journaux*, Paris: Plancher, Delaunay, 1817. Printer's declaration: 16 September 1817. C.25a. *Checklist* A25/1.

1817/09/22   Summary of letter of 21 September 1817 from Constant, *Le Moniteur universel*, 22 septembre 1817. *Checklist* D104b.

[1817]/[09]/[*post* 26]   *Seconde réponse de Benjamin Constant*, [Paris]: Porthmann, [1817]. Published probably at the end of September 1817. C.26a. *Checklist* A26/1.

[1817]/[09]/-   *Note sur les droits de Cité appartenant à la famille de Constant-Rebecque*, [Paris, 1817]. Published probably in September 1817. C.16c. *Checklist* A16/3.

1817/[09]/-   *Des élections prochaines, édition entièrement conforme à celle de Paris*, Bruxelles: impr. Maubach, 1817. Presumably an unauthorized reprint published shortly after the Paris edition. C.23b. *Checklist* A23/2.

1817/10/11   'De la Juridiction du gouvernement sur l'Education', *Mercure de France*, IV, 11 octobre 1817, pp.53-63. *Checklist* D105.

1817/10/11-13   *Cours de politique constitutionnel; Prospectus*, Paris: impr. Doublet, 1817. Text dated: 'ce 9 octobre 1817'. Dépôt légal: 11-13 October 1817. C.131. *Checklist* E1.

1817/10/[*ante* 18]   *Constitutions des différens peuples, ou Textes de tous les actes constitutionnels en vigueur; avec des discours historiques et politiques sur les principes qui en font la base*. Par MM. Benjamin de Constant, Esménard, Jay, le comte Lanjuinais, pair de France, Letellier, Grégoire, ancien évêque de Blois, Theremin, ancien consul à Leipsick, etc., etc. (Prospectus des), Paris: impr. Fain, 1817. *Bibliographie de la France*, 18 October 1817. Constant's projected contribution is not extant. See C.D2.

1817/11/08   'De l'obéissance à la loi. Fragmens d'un chapitre extrait des additions inédites à la collection des ouvrages politiques de M. B. de Constant', *Mercure de France*, IV, 8 novembre 1817, pp.244-255. *Checklist* D106.

1817/12/01-02   *Annales de la session de 1817 à 1818*, 1ère livraison, Paris: Béchet, 1817. Dépôt légal: 1-2 December 1817. C.27a(1). *Checklist* A27/1.

1817/12/05-06   *Collection complète des ouvrages publiés sur le gouvernement représentatif et la Constitution actuelle de la France, formant une espèce de Cours de politique constitutionnelle*, vol. I, première partie, Paris: Plancher, 1818[=1817]. Dépôt légal: 5-6 December 1817. C.131a(1). *Checklist* E1/1(1).

1817/12/13   'Du Théâtre français et du Théâtre étranger', *Mercure de France*, IV, 13 décembre 1817, pp.484-490. *Checklist* D107.

1817/12/23   *Mémoires sur la vie privée de mon père*, par Mme la baronne de Staël-Holstein ... Paris-Londres: Colburn 1818[=1817]. Includes 'Notice sur Mme de Staël Holstein' by Benjamin Constant, reprinted from *Mercure de France*, 26 July 1817. Entered at Stationers' Hall: 23 December 1817. C. Suppl. Add. 6. *Checklist* C2/1.

1817/12/23   *Memoirs of the private life of my father*, by the Baroness de Staël-Holstein ... London: Colburn 1818[=1817]. Translation of the preceding item. Entered at Stationers' Hall: 23 December 1817. C. Suppl. Add. 7. *Checklist* C2/t1.

1817/[06-12]/-   *Adolphe, histoire trouvée dans les papiers d'un inconnu*, Vienne: Schrämbl, 1817. C.18e. *Checklist* A18/5.

1817/[06-12]/-   *Adolf, eine Erzählung, aus den gefundenen Papieren eines Unbekannten*, Pesth: Hartleben, 1817. C.18k. *Checklist* A18/t3.

1817/[09-12]/-   *Adolphe: an anecdote found among the papers of an unknown person*, Philadelphia: Carey and Son, 1817. Reprint. C.18j. *Checklist* A18/t2.

1818

1818/01/22-23 *Lettre à M. Odillon-Barrot, avocat en la cour de cassation, sur l'affaire de Wilfrid Regnault, condamné à mort*, Paris: Plancher, Delaunay, 1818. Dépôt légal: 22-23 January 1818. C.28a. *Checklist* A28/1.

1818/02/06-07 *Collection complète des ouvrages publiés sur le gouvernement représentatif et la constitution actuelle de la France, formant une espèce de Cours de politique constitutionnelle*, vol. I, seconde partie, Paris: Plancher, 1818. Dépôt légal: 6-7 February 1818. C.131a(1). *Checklist* E1/1(1).

1818/02/23-24 'Sur les provocations au crime pour le dénoncer', *La Minerve française*, I, cahier 2 [23-24 février 1818], pp.70-72. *Checklist* D108.

1818/02/24-26 *2ᵐᵉ lettre à M. Odillon-Barrot, avocat en la cour de cassation, sur le procès de Wilfrid Regnault, condamné à mort*, Paris: Béchet, Plancher, Delaunay, 1818. Dépôt légal: 24-26 February 1818. C.29a. *Checklist* A29/1.

1818/03/02-03 'D'une assertion de M. Bailleul dans sa brochure contre M. de Chateaubriand', *La Minerve française*, I, cahier 4 [2-3 mars 1818], pp.165-169. *Checklist* D109.

1818/03/16-17 'Encore un mot sur le procès de Wilfrid Regnault, ou Réflexions sur cette question: L'examen public des actes de l'autorité judiciaire est-il contraire à l'esprit de la charte, et blesse-t-il le respect dû aux tribunaux et à leurs sentences?', *La Minerve française*, I, cahier 6 [16-17 mars 1818], pp.261-273. *Checklist* D110.

1818/03/28-30 *Collection complète des ouvrages publiés sur le gouvernement représentatif et la constitution actuelle de la France, formant une espèce de Cours de politique constitutionnelle*, vol. II, 3ᵉ partie, Paris: Plancher, 1818. Dépôt légal: 28-30 March 1818. C.131a(2). *Checklist* E1/1(2).

1818/04/03-04 'Des égards que, dans les circonstances présentes, les écrivains se doivent les uns aux autres', *La Minerve française*, I, cahier 9 [3-4 avril 1818], pp.413-420. *Checklist* D111.

1818/04/17-20 'Introduction à l'*Histoire des Républiques italiennes*, par M. de Sismondi', *La Minerve française*, I, cahier 11 [17-20 avril 1818], pp.508-517. *Checklist* D112.

1818/04/25-27 *Annales de la session de 1817 à 1818, 5ᵉ livraison du tome Iᵉʳ; partie politique*, Paris: Béchet, 1818. Includes Constant's *Du Discours de M. de Marchangy, avocat du Roi, devant le tribunal de police correctionnelle, dans la cause de M. Fiévée*. Dépôt légal: 25-27 April 1818. C.27a(5). *Checklist* A27/1.

1818/04/25-27 *Du Discours de M. de Marchangy, avocat du Roi, devant le tribunal de police correctionnelle, dans la cause de M. Fiévée*. See the preceding item.

1818/04/29-1818/05/01 'Aperçus sur la marche et les révolutions de la philosophie à Rome. (Extrait d'un ouvrage inédit)', *La Minerve française*, I, cahier 13 [29 avril-1ᵉʳ mai 1818], pp.602-611. *Checklist* D113.

1818/05/06-07 'De l'Angleterre', *La Minerve française*, II, cahier 1 [6-7 mai 1818], pp.42-50. *Checklist* D114.

1818/05/14-15 'Aperçus sur la marche et les révolutions de la philosophie à Rome. (Extrait d'un ouvrage inédit). – Deuxième et dernier article', *La Minerve française*, II, cahier 2 [14-15 mai 1818], pp.71-77. *Checklist* D115.

1818/05/16-22 *Collection complète des ouvrages publiés sur le gouvernement représentatif et la constitution actuelle de la France, formant une espèce de Cours de politique constitutionnelle*, vol. II,

4ᵉ partie, Paris: Plancher, 1818. Dépôt légal: 16-22 May 1818. C.131a(2). *Checklist* E1/1(2).

1818/05/17 'Au Rédacteur', *Le Moniteur universel*, 17 mai 1818, p.610. *Checklist*, D115a

1818/05/25-26 '*Considérations sur les principaux événemens de la Révolution française*, ouvrage posthume de madame la baronne de Staël, publié par M. le duc de Broglie et M. le baron de Staël', *La Minerve française*, II, cahier 3 [25-26 mai 1818], pp.105-110. *Checklist* D116.

1818/05/25-26 'Quelques réflexions sur la brochure de M. Aignan, *de l'Etat des Protestans en France*, et sur des critiques dirigées contre cette brochure', *La Minerve française* II, cahier 3 [25-26 mai 1818], pp.119-123. *Checklist* D117.

1818/05/25-26 '*Antiquités romaines, ou Tableau des mœurs, usages et institutions des Romains*, etc., traduites de l'anglais par Alexandre Adam, recteur de la grande école d'Edimbourg', *La Minerve française*, II, cahier 3 [25-26 mai 1818], pp.159-160. *Checklist* D118.

1818/06/04-05 '*Compte rendu des événemens qui se sont passés à Lyon*, par M. Charrier Sainneville, ancien lieutenant de police à Lyon', *La Minerve française*, II, cahier 5 [4-5 juin 1818], pp.209-223. *Checklist* D119.

1818/06/10-11 '*Compte rendu des événemens qui se sont passés à Lyon*, par M. Charrier-Sainneville, ancien lieutenant de police à Lyon, (Second article)', *La Minerve française*, II, cahier 6 [10-11 juin 1818], pp.265-279. *Checklist* D120.

1818/06/16-17 '*Considérations sur les principaux événemens de la Révolution française*, ouvrage posthume de madame la baronne de Staël, (Second article)', *La Minerve française*, II, cahier 7 [16-17 juin 1818], pp.316-325. *Checklist* D121.

1818/06/16-17 '*Le dernier cri d'un dépositaire de la charte, ou coup d'œil rapide sur l'état actuel des libertés nationales*; par J.-B. Mailhos, avocat à la cour royale de Paris', *La Minerve française*, II, cahier 7 [16-17 juin 1818], pp.325-326. *Checklist* D122.

1818/07/11-13 'De la nécessité et des moyens de nous faire une juste idée des doctrines du ministère public, dans les causes relatives aux délits de la presse', *La Minerve française*, II, cahier 10 [11-13 juillet 1818], pp.474-480. *Checklist* D123.

1818/07/18-20 *De l'appel en calomnie de M. le Marquis de Blosseville, contre Wilfrid-Regnault*, Paris: Béchet, juillet 1818. Dépôt légal: 18-20 July 1818. C.30a. *Checklist* A30/1.

1818/07/28-29 '*Considérations sur les principaux événemens de la Révolution française*, ouvrage posthume de madame la baronne de Staël, (Troisième article)', *La Minerve française*, II, cahier 13 [28-29 juillet 1818], pp.601-610. *Checklist* D124.

1818/08/14-17 'Première lettre de M. Benjamin Constant à M. Charles Durand, avocat, en réponse aux questions contenues dans la troisième partie de son ouvrage, intitulé: *Marseille, Nîmes et ses environs, en 1815*', *La Minerve française*, III, cahier 2 [14-17 août 1818], pp.49-63. *Checklist* D125.

1818/08/21-22 '*Précis historique, militaire et critique des batailles de Fleurus et de Waterloo* ..., par le maréchal-de-camp Berton', *La Minerve française*, III, cahier 3 [21-22 août 1818], pp.107-112. *Checklist* D126.

1818/08/21-22 '*Question judiciaire*', *La Minerve française*, III, cahier 3 [21-22 août 1818], pp.118-121. *Checklist* D127.

1818/08/29-31 'Seconde lettre de M. Benjamin Constant à M. Charles Durand, avocat, en réponse aux questions contenues dans la troisième partie de l'ouvrage intitulé:

Marseille, Nîmes et ses environs en 1815', *La Minerve française*, III, cahier 4 [29-31 août 1818], pp.145-157. *Checklist* D128.

1818/09/08-09 'Réflexions sur les pièces ci-dessus' [documents sur Charles Lainé: *Tribunaux: Département du Pas-de-Calais*], *La Minerve française*, III, cahier 5 [8-9 septembre 1818], pp.219-221. *Checklist* D129.

1818/09/11-12 *Lettres à M. Charles Durand, avocat, en réponse aux questions contenues dans la troisième partie de son ouvrage, intitulé: Marseille, Nîmes et ses environs, en 1815*, Paris: Béchet, 1818. Originally published in *La Minerve française*, 14-17, 29-31 août 1818. Dépôt légal: 11-12 September 1818. C.31a. *Checklist* A31/1.

1818/09/21-22 '*Revue de la session de 1817*; par le vicomte de Saint-Chamans', *La Minerve française*, III, cahier 7 [21-22 septembre 1818], pp.302-313. *Checklist* D130.

1818/09/21-22 '*Eclaircissemens historiques en réponse aux calomnies dont les protestans du Gard sont l'objet, et Précis des agitations et des troubles de ce département, depuis 1790 jusqu'à nos jours*; par P.-J. Lauze de Perret, avocat à la cour royale de Nîmes', *La Minerve française*, III, cahier 7 [21-22 septembre 1818], p.314. *Checklist* D131.

1818/10/02-03 '*Coup d'œil sur les démêlés des cours de Bavière et de Bade ...*, par M. Bignon', *La Minerve française*, III, cahier 9 [2-3 octobre 1818], pp.385-391. *Checklist* D132.

1818/10/02-03 [Letter from Gamot to the editors], *La Minerve française*, III, cahier 9 [2-3 octobre 1818], p.425. *Checklist* D133.

1818/10/05-06 *Des élections de 1818*, Paris: Béchet, 1818. Dépôt légal: 5-6 October 1818. C.32a. *Checklist* A32/1.

1818/10/08-09 *Lettre de M. Benjamin Constant, à M. Odillon Barrot, sur le procès de Lainé, serrurier, entraîné au crime de fausse monnaie, par un agent de la gendarmerie, et condamné à mort*, Paris: Béchet, 1818. Dépôt légal: 8-9 October 1818. C.33a. *Checklist* A33/1.

1818/10/14-15 *Entretien d'un électeur avec lui-même, recueilli et publié par M. Benjamin-Constant, éligible, [seconde édition]*, Paris: Plancher, 1818. Dépôt légal: 14-15 October 1818. C.24b-c. *Checklist* A24/2-3.

1818/10/15-16 '*Réponse à M. Benjamin Constant*, par M. Duvergier de Hauranne, député de la Seine-Inférieure', *La Minerve française*, III, cahier 11 [15-16 octobre 1818], pp.493-497. *Checklist* D134.

1818/10/15-16 '*Lettre à M. Benjamin Constant sur l'ordonnance du 20 mai*, par M. Delapoterie, officier en non-activité, chevalier de la Légion d'Honneur', *La Minerve française*, III, cahier 11 [15-16 octobre 1818], pp.497-502. *Checklist* D135.

1818/10/15-16 '*Rosaure, ou l'Arrêt du Destin*, traduit de l'allemand, d'Auguste Lafontaine; par madame la comtesse de M ....', *La Minerve française*, III, cahier 11 [15-16 octobre 1818], pp.503-504. *Checklist* D136.

1818/10/21-22 [Les protestants de Vaucluse, de la Drôme et de la Lozère], *La Minerve française*, III, cahier 12 [21-22 octobre 1818], pp.542-544. *Checklist* D137.

1818/10/21-22 'Pensées diverses sur les élections', *La Minerve française*, III, cahier 12 [21-22 octobre 1818], pp.544-552. *Checklist* D138.

1818/10/24-26 *A Messieurs les électeurs de Paris*, [Paris: Renaudière], 1818. *Signed*: 'Benjamin Constant. Paris, le 23 octobre 1818'. Dépôt légal: 24-26 October 1818. C.34a. *Checklist* A34/1.

1818/10/26-27 'Sur les élections', *La Minerve française*, III, cahier 13 [26-27 octobre 1818], pp.610-615. *Checklist* D139.

1818/10/29   Benjamin Constant. *A Messieurs les électeurs de Paris*, [Paris], 1818. *Signed*: 'Benjamin Constant. Paris, le 29 octobre 1818'. C.35a-b; *Checklist* A35/1-2.

1818/11/04-05   'Des élections, du ministère, de l'esprit public et du parti libéral en France', *La Minerve française*, IV, cahier 1 [4-5 novembre 1818], pp.14-22. *Checklist* D140.

1818/11/12-13   [Sur la circulaire du Préfet de la Seine aux maires des communes rurales], *La Minerve française*, IV, cahier 2 [12-13 novembre 1818], pp.91-92. *Checklist* D141.

1818/11/19-20   '*A M. le vicomte de Châteaubriant, pair de France, sur ses projets politiques et sur la situation actuelle des choses et des esprits*; par M. Azaïs', *La Minerve française*, IV, cahier 3 [19-20 novembre 1818], pp.97-104. *Checklist* D142.

1818/12/02-03   'Affaire du sieur Raman [Roman de Lourmarin], condamné par le tribunal de police correctionnelle de Gap, pour avoir résisté à l'ordre de tapisser sa maison pendant la procession de la Fête-Dieu', *La Minerve française*, IV, cahier 4 [2-3 décembre 1818], pp.161-162. *Checklist* D143.

1818/12/11-12   'D'un article de M. de Bonald contre M. Camille Jordan', *La Minerve française*, IV, cahier 5 [11-12 décembre 1818], pp.193-202. *Checklist* D144.

1818/12/11-12   [Note sur l'affaire Lainé], *La Minerve française*, IV, cahier 5 [11-12 décembre 1818], pp.226-227. *Checklist* D145.

1818/12/11-12   '*Petit cours de jurisprudence littéraire, ou Répertoire de police correctionnelle, à l'usage des gens de lettres*; par M. Jouslin de La Salle. Tome premier, première et deuxième partie', *La Minerve française*, IV, cahier 5 [11-12 décembre 1818], p.228. *Checklist* D146.

1818/12/15-16   'Session des Chambres', *La Minerve française*, IV, cahier 6 [15-16 décembre 1818], pp.289-296. *Checklist* D147.

1818/12/19-21   *Incipit*: 'Le *Journal du commerce* a parlé déjà du dîner patriotique', *La Minerve française*, IV, cahier 7 [19-21 décembre 1818], pp.326-327. *Checklist* D148.

1818/12/19-21   'Session des Chambres', *La Minerve française*, IV, cahier 7 [19-21 décembre 1818], pp.327-330. *Checklist* D149.

1818/12/26   *Eloge de Sir Samuel Romilly, prononcé à l'Athénée royal de Paris, le 26 décembre 1818*. See below under 19-20 January 1819.

1818/12/28-29   '*Charlemagne ou la Caroléide*; par M. Victor d'Arlincourt', *La Minerve française*, IV, cahier 8 [28-29 décembre 1818], pp.349-356. *Checklist* D150.

1818/12/28-29   'Session des Chambres', *La Minerve française*, IV, cahier 8 [28-29 décembre 1818], pp.379-384. *Checklist* D151.

1818/-/-   *Adolphe*. [Russian translation], Orel: Provincial Press, 1818. C.18l. *Checklist* A18/t4.

1819

1819/01/04-05   'Session des Chambres', *La Minerve française*, IV, cahier 9 [4-5 janvier 1819], pp.430-436. *Checklist* D152.

1819/01/08-09   'Session des Chambres', *La Minerve française*, IV, cahier 10 [8-9 janvier 1819], pp.477-486. *Checklist* D153.

1819/01/14-15   'Session des Chambres', *La Minerve française*, IV, cahier 11 [14-15 janvier 1819], pp.541-545. *Checklist* D154.

1819/01/19-20   *Eloge de Sir Samuel Romilly, prononcé à l'Athénée royal de Paris, le 26 décembre 1818*, Paris: Béchet aîné; Bruxelles: Lecharlier, Demat, 1819. Dépôt légal: 19-20 January 1819. C.36a. *Checklist* A36/1.

1819/01/[*post* 20]   *An Eulogium on Sir Samuel Romilly* ... edited by Sir T.C. Morgan, London: Colburn, [1819]. Translator's preface dated 20 January 1819. C.36b. *Checklist* A36/t1.

1819/01/23-25   'Session des Chambres', *La Minerve française*, IV, cahier 12 [23-25 janvier 1819], pp.581-585. *Checklist* D155.

1819/01/28-29   'Session des Chambres', *La Minerve française*, IV, cahier 13 [28-29 janvier 1819], pp.631-637. *Checklist* D156.

1819/02/05-06   '*Lettre au général Gourgaud, sur la relation de la campagne de 1815, écrite à Sainte-Hélène*; par M. Marchand, ex-adjoint aux commissaires des guerres', *La Minerve française*, V, cahier 1 [5-6 février 1819], pp.12-13. *Checklist* D157.

1819/02/05-06   'Session des Chambres', *La Minerve française*, V, cahier 1 [5-6 février 1819], pp.31-44. *Checklist* D158.

1819/02/15-16   'Session des Chambres', *La Minerve française*, V, cahier 2 [15-16 février 1819], pp.76-91. *Checklist* D159.

1819/02/19-20   'Session des Chambres', *La Minerve française*, V, cahier 3 [19-20 février 1819], pp.141-150. *Checklist* D160.

1819/02/22-23   *De la proposition de changer la loi des élections*, Paris: Poulet, 1819. Dépôt légal: 22-23 February 1819. C.37a-b. *Checklist* A37/1-2.

1819/02/24-25   'Session des Chambres', *La Minerve française*, V, cahier 4 [24-25 février 1819], pp.181-186. *Checklist* D161.

1819/03/[03-04]   'Session des Chambres', *La Minerve française*, V, cahier 5 [3-4 mars 1819], pp.242-257. *Checklist* D162.

1819/03/09-10   'Session des Chambres', *La Minerve française*, V, cahier 6 [9-10 mars 1819], pp.289-310. *Checklist* D163.

1819/03/09-11   *Collection complète des ouvrages publiés sur le gouvernement représentatif et la constitution actuelle de la France, formant une espèce de Cours de politique constitutionnelle*, vol. III (5-6), Paris: Plancher, 1819. Dépôt légal: 9-10 March 1819 (5ᵉ partie); 10-11 March 1819 (6ᵉ partie). C.131a(3). *Checklist* E1/1(3).

1819/03/17-18   'Session des Chambres', *La Minerve française*, V, cahier 7 [17-18 mars 1819], pp.337-347. *Checklist* D164.

1819/03/25-26   'Session des Chambres', *La Minerve française*, V, cahier 8 [25-26 mars 1819], pp.382-405. *Checklist* D165.

1819/04/01-02   'Lettre à MM. les habitans du département de la Sarthe', *La Minerve française*, V, cahier 9 [1-2 avril 1819], pp.447-455. *Checklist* D166.

1819/04/04-05   *Lettre à Messieurs les habitans du département de la Sarthe*, [Paris]: impr. Fain, 1819. Dépôt légal: 4-5 April 1819. Reprinted from *La Minerve française*, V, cahier 9 [1-2 avril 1819], pp.447-455. C.38a. *Checklist* A38/1.

1819/04/09-10   [Pétition du commerce de Bordeaux en faveur de la loi des élections], *La Minerve française*, V, cahier 10 [9-10 avril 1819], pp.493-497. *Checklist* D167.

1819/04/14   Chambre des Députés. Sur le projet de loi relatif aux crimes et délits de la presse. Séance du 14 avril 1819. *Archives parlementaires*, XXIII, 622-29. Editions: *Opinion* ... [Paris]: impr. Hacquart, 1819 (C.77a. *Checklist* B14); *Amendemens* ... [Paris]: impr. Hacquart, 1819 (C.78a. *Checklist* B15); *Cours de politique*, IV (1820), 236-267; *Discours* (1827-1828), I, 1-31.

1819/04/15   Chambre des Députés. Sur le projet de loi relatif aux crimes et délits de la presse. Séance du 15 avril 1819. *Archives parlementaires*, XXIII, 645.

1819/04/16   Chambre des Députés. Sur le projet de loi relatif aux crimes et délits de la presse. Séance du 16 avril 1819. *Archives parlementaires*, XXIII, 651-652. *Discours* (1827-1828), I, 28-31. Editions: see above under 14 April 1819.

1819/04/16-17   'D'un amendement proposé à la loi sur la liberté de la presse', *La Minerve française*, V, cahier 11 [16-17 avril 1819], pp.538-541. *Checklist* D168.

1819/04/17   Chambre des Députés. Sur le projet de loi relatif aux crimes et délits de la presse. Séance du 17 avril 1819. *Archives parlementaires*, XXIII, 680.

1819/04/19   Chambre des Députés. Sur le projet de loi relatif aux crimes et délits de la presse. Séance du 19 avril 1819. *Archives parlementaires*, XXIII, 692, 702.

1819/04/21   Chambre des Députés. Sur le projet de loi relatif aux crimes et délits de la presse. Séance du 21 avril 1819. *Archives parlementaires*, XXIII, 718-720, 724, 725, 730. *Discours* (1827-1828), I, 32-41.

1819/04/21-22   'De la religion et de la morale religieuse', *La Minerve française*, V, cahier 12 [21-22 avril 1819], pp.583-590. *Checklist* D169.

1819/04/22   Chambre des Députés. Sur le projet de loi relatif aux crimes et délits de la presse. Séance du 22 avril 1819. *Archives parlementaires*, XXIII, 768.

1819/04/23   Chambre des Députés. Sur le projet de loi relatif aux crimes et délits de la presse. Séance du 23 avril 1819. *Archives parlementaires*, XXIII, 780.

1819/04/24   Chambre des Députés. Sur le projet de loi relatif à la répression des délits de la presse. Séance du 24 avril 1819. *Archives parlementaires*, XXIV, 30-33. *Discours* (1827-1828), I, 41-53.

1819/04/28   Chambre des Députés. Sur le projet de loi relatif à la répression des délits de la presse. Séance du 28 avril 1819. *Archives parlementaires*, XXIV, 86-87. *Discours*, (1827-1828), I, 53-61.

1819/05/03   Chambre des Députés. Sur le projet de loi relatif aux journaux et écrits périodiques. Séance du 3 mai 1819. *Archives parlementaires*, XXIV, 167-171. *Discours*, (1827-1828), I, 61-78.

1819/05/04   Chambre des Députés. Sur le projet de loi relatif aux journaux et écrits périodiques. [Lecture de l'amendement de M. Benjamin Constant]. Séance du 4 mai 1819. *Archives parlementaires*, XXIV, 197, 203. *Discours* (1827-1828), I, 78-80.

1819/05/05   Chambre des Députés. Sur le projet de loi relatif aux journaux et écrits périodiques. Séance du 5 mai 1819. *Archives parlementaires*, XXIV, 207-208, 213. *Discours* (1827-1828), I, 81-87.

1819/05/07-08   '*Constitutions de la nation française*; par M. le comte Lanjuinais. (Premier article.)', *La Minerve française*, VI, cahier 1 [7-8 mai 1819], pp.5-12. *Checklist* D170.

1819/05/14   Chambre des Députés. Sur le projet de loi relatif à la fixation des comptes des années 1815, 1816, 1817 et 1818. Séance du 14 mai 1819. *Archives parlementaires*, XXIV, 409-412. Edition: *Opinion sur le projet de loi relatif à la fixation des budgets* ... [Paris]:

impr. Hacquart, 1819 (C.79a. *Checklist* B16). *Discours* (1827-1828), I, 88-102.

1819/05/17 Chambre des Députés. Sur les pétitions demandant le rappel des bannis. Séance du 17 mai 1819. [Opinion non prononcée]. *Archives parlementaires*, XXIV, 449-551. Edition: *Opinion sur la pétition tendant à demander le rappel des bannis*, Paris: Brissot-Thivars, 1819; dépôt légal: 26-27 May 1819 (C.80a. *Checklist* B17). *Discours* (1827-1828), I, 139-151.

1819/05/21 Chambre des Députés. Sur le projet de loi relatif à la fixation des comptes des années 1815, 1816, 1817 et 1818. Séance du 21 mai 1819. *Archives parlementaires*, XXIV, 497.

1819/05/22 Chambre des Députés. Sur des pétitions. Séance du 22 mai 1819. *Archives parlementaires*, XXIV, 515.

1819/05/22-24 '*Constitution de la nation française*, par M. le comte Lanjuinais. (Second article.)', *La Minerve française*, VI, cahier 3 [22-24 mai 1819], pp.110-119. *Checklist* D171.

1819/05/24 Chambre des Députés. Sur le projet de loi relatif à la fixation des comptes des années 1815, 1816, 1817 et 1818. Séance du 24 mai 1819. *Archives parlementaires*, XXIV, 548.

1819/05/27 Chambre des Députés. Sur le projet de loi relatif aux dépenses de l'exercice 1819. Séance du 27 mai 1819. *Archives parlementaires*, XXIV, 614, 620.

1819/05/28 Chambre des Députés. Sur le projet de loi relatif aux dépenses de l'exercice 1819. Séance du 28 mai 1819. *Archives parlementaires*, XXIV, 634, 637, 642.

1819/05/28-29 'De l'examen des emprunts de 16 et de 24 millions dans le budget de 1819, avec quelques observations sur l'ancien et le nouveau ministère', *La Minerve française*, VI, cahier 4 [28-29 mai 1819], pp.149-155. *Checklist* D172.

1819/05/29 Chambre des Députés. Sur le projet de loi relatif aux dépenses de l'exercice 1819. Séance du 29 mai 1819. *Archives parlementaires*, XXIV, 648, 650, 654. *Discours* (1827-1828), I, 102-109.

1819/05/31 Chambre des Députés. Sur deux rapports de la commission du budget des dépenses à laquelle diverses pétitions avaient été successivement renvoyées. Séance du 31 mai 1819. *Archives parlementaires*, XXIV, 667.

1819/06/01 Chambre des Députés. Sur le budget des dépenses de 1819. Séance du 1er juin 1819. *Archives parlementaires*, XXIV, 686, 690. *Discours* (1827-1828), I, 109-110.

1819/06/02 Chambre des Députés. Sur le budget des dépenses de 1819. Séance du 2 juin 1819. *Archives parlementaires*, XXIV, 703.

1819/06/08 Chambre des Députés. Sur le budget des dépenses de 1819. Séance du 8 juin 1819. *Archives parlementaires*, XXV, 34-40. Edition: *Opinion sur le budget des dépenses à ordonnancer par le Ministre des Finances pour l'exercice 1819*, [Paris]: impr. Hacquart, 1818 (C.81a. *Checklist* B18). *Discours* (1827-1828), I, 111-136.

1819/06/10 Chambre des Députés. Sur le budget des dépenses de 1819. Séance du 10 juin 1819. *Archives parlementaires*, XXV, 82.

1819/06/10-11 'De la formation d'un nouveau ministère', *La Minerve française*, VI, cahier 6 [10-11 juin 1819], pp.245-251. *Checklist* D173.

1819/06/12 Chambre des Députés. Sur le budget des dépenses de 1819. Séance du 12 juin 1819. *Archives parlementaires*, XXV, 112-113.

1819/06/15   Chambre des Députés. Sur le budget des dépenses de 1819. Séance du 15 juin 1819. *Archives parlementaires*, XXV, 147.

1819/06/15   'De l'état constitutionnel de la France', *La Renommée*, n° 1, 15 juin 1819. *Checklist* D174.

1819/06/16   Chambre des Députés. Sur le budget des dépenses de 1819. Séance du 16 juin 1819. *Archives parlementaires*, XXV, 156-58. Edition: *Opinion ... sur les douanes. Séance du 15 [sic] juin 1819*, [Paris]: impr. Hacquart, 1819, C.82a. *Checklist* B19.

1819/06/17   Chambre des Députés. Sur le budget des dépenses de 1819. Séance du 17 juin 1819. *Archives parlementaires*, XXV, 185-89, 191, 193, 195. Edition: *Opinion ... sur l'administration des contributions indirectes. Séance du 16 [sic] juin 1819*, [Paris]: impr. Hacquart, 1819. C.83a; *Checklist* B20.

1819/06/18   Chambre des Députés. sur le budget des dépenses de 1819. Séance du 18 juin 1819. *Archives parlementaires*, XXV, 218. *Discours* (1827-1828), I, 137-138.

1819/06/18-19   '*Constitution de la nation française*, par M. le comte Lanjuinais. (Troisième et dernier article.)', *La Minerve française*, VI, cahier 7 [18-19 juin 1819], pp.312-317. *Checklist* D175.

1819/06/19   Chambre des Députés. sur le budget des dépenses de 1819. Séance du 19 juin 1819. *Archives parlementaires*, XXV, 229, 230, 231-232.

1819/06/21   Chambre des Députés. Sur le budget des dépenses de 1819. Séance du 21 juin 1819. *Archives parlementaires*, XXV, 242-245. Edition: *Opinion ... sur les pensions*, [Paris]: impr. Hacquart, 1819. C.84a. *Checklist* B21.

1819/06/25   *Incipit*: 'Un des symptômes les plus satisfaisans qu'on puisse remarquer dans notre situation politique', *La Renommée*, n° 11, 25 juin 1819. *Checklist* D176.

1819/06/26   Chambre des Députés. Sur le budget des recettes de l'exercice 1819. Séance du 26 juin 1819. *Archives parlementaires*, XXV, 390.

1819/06/27   'Aux rédacteurs de la Renommée', *La Renommée*, n° 13, 27 juin 1819. *Checklist* D177.

1819/06/30   Chambre des Députés. Sur le budget des recettes de l'exercice 1819. Séance du 30 juin 1819. *Archives parlementaires*, XXV, 445-49. Edition: *Opinion ... sur le titre IV du projet de loi des voies et moyens de 1819. Séance du 28 [sic] juin 1819*, [Paris]: impr. Hacquart, 1819. C.85a. *Checklist* B22.

1819/07/01   'Aux rédacteurs de la Renommée', *La Renommée*, n° 17, 1er juillet 1819. *Checklist* D178.

1819/07/03-05   'Des rapports de la grande propriété avec nos institutions', *La Minerve française*, VI, cahier 9 [3-5 juillet 1819], pp.409-415. *Checklist* D179.

1819/07/05   'Aux rédacteurs de la Renommée', *La Renommée*, n° 21, 5 juillet 1819. *Checklist* D180.

1819/07/07   Chambre des Députés. Sur la pétition du sieur Rauthal, détenu à Pierre-Châtel. Séance du 7 juillet 1819. *Archives parlementaires*, XXV, 593.

1819/07/10   Chambre des Députés. Sur la pétition des étudiants en droit relative au professeur Bavoux. Séance du 10 juillet 1819. *Archives parlementaires*, XXV, 652-653. *Discours* (1827-1828), I, 152-156.

1819/07/16-17   'Du ministère pendant la session qui vient de finir', *La Minerve française*,

VI, cahier 11 [16-17 juillet 1819], pp.497-507. *Checklist* D181.

1819/07/18   'Aux Auteurs de la Renommée', *La Renommée*, n° 32, 18 juillet 1819. *Checklist* D182.

1819/07/22   'Aux Auteurs de la Renommée', *La Renommée*, n° 38, 22 juillet 1819. *Checklist* D183.

1819/07/23-24   '*Trois règnes de l'Histoire d'Angleterre*; par M. Sauquaire-Souligné', *La Minerve française*, VI, cahier 12 [23-24 juillet 1819], pp.568-576. *Checklist* D184.

1819/07/25   'Aux Auteurs de la Renommée', *La Renommée*, n° 41, 25 juillet 1819. *Checklist* D185.

1819/07/31-1819/08/02   'De l'état de l'Europe sous le point de vue constitutionnel', *La Minerve française*, VI, cahier 13 [31 juillet-2 août 1819], pp.593-605. *Checklist* D186.

1819/08/01   'Aux Auteurs de la Renommée', *La Renommée*, n° 48, 1er août 1819. *Checklist* D187.

1819/08/02   'Aux Auteurs de la Renommée', *La Renommée*, n° 49, 2 août 1819. *Checklist* D188.

1819/08/06-07   '*Recueil de discours prononcés au parlement d'Angleterre par J.-C. Fox et W. Pitt*, par MM. H …, de J[anvry] et de Jussieu', *La Minerve française*, VII, cahier 1 [6-7 août 1819], pp.6-13. *Checklist* D189.

1819/08/09   'Aux Auteurs de la Renommée', *La Renommée*, n° 56, 9 août 1819. *Checklist* D190.

1819/08/10   'Aux Auteurs de la Renommée', *La Renommée*, n° 57, 10 août 1819. *Checklist* D191.

1819/08/14-16   'De l'état de l'Europe sous le point de vue constitutionnel', *La Minerve française*, VII, cahier 2 [14-16 août 1819], pp.49-58. *Checklist* D192.

1819/08/18-23   'De la traite des nègres au Sénégal', *La Minerve française*, VII, cahier 3 [18-23 août 1819], pp.113-124. *Checklist* D193.

1819/08/27   'Aux Auteurs de la Renommée', *La Renommée*, n° 73, 27 août 1819. *Checklist* D194.

1819/08/28-30   'Des accusateurs de la France', *La Minerve française*, VII, cahier 4 [28-30 août 1819], pp.154-160. *Checklist* D195.

1819/09/04-06   'Lettres sur les Cent Jours. (Première lettre.)', *La Minerve française*, VII, cahier 5 [4-6 septembre 1819], pp.193-199. *Checklist* D196.

1819/09/05   'Aux Auteurs de la Renommée', *La Renommée*, n° 82, 5 septembre 1819. *Checklist* D197.

1819/09/11-13   'Lettres sur les Cent Jours. (Seconde lettre.)', *La Minerve française*, VII, cahier 6 [11-13 septembre 1819], pp.241-249. *Checklist* D198.

1819/09/18-20   'Lettres sur les Cent Jours. (Troisième lettre.)', *La Minerve française*, VII, cahier 7 [18-20 septembre 1819], pp.292-303. *Checklist* D199.

1819/09/19   'Aux Auteurs de la Renommée', *La Renommée*, n° 96, 19 septembre 1819. *Checklist* D200.

1819/09/24   'Aux Auteurs de la Renommée', *La Renommée*, n° 101, 24 septembre 1819. *Checklist* D201.

1819/09/25-27 'Lettres sur les Cent Jours. (Quatrième lettre.)', *La Minerve française*, VII, cahier 8 [25-27 septembre 1819], pp.337-347. *Checklist* D202.

1819/10/02-04 'Lettres sur les Cent Jours. (Cinquième lettre.)', *La Minerve française*, VII, cahier 9 [2-4 octobre 1819], pp.385-394. *Checklist* D203.

1819/10/10 'Aux Auteurs de la Renommée', *La Renommée*, n° 117, 10 octobre 1819. *Checklist* D204.

1819/10/09-11 'Lettres sur les Cent Jours. (Sixième lettre.)', *La Minerve française*, VII, cahier 10 [9-11 octobre 1819], pp.433-443. *Checklist* D205.

1819/10/14 'Aux Auteurs de la Renommée', *La Renommée*, n° 121, 14 octobre 1819. *Checklist* D206.

1819/10/16-18 'Lettres sur les Cent Jours. (Septième lettre.)', *La Minerve française*, VII, cahier 11 [16-18 octobre 1819], pp.481-491. *Checklist* D207.

1819/10/22 'Aux Auteurs de la Renommée', *La Renommée*, n° 129, 22 octobre 1819. *Checklist* D208.

1819/10/23-25 'Lettres sur les Cent Jours. (Huitième lettre.)', *La Minerve française*, VII, cahier 12 [23-25 octobre 1819], pp.531-540. *Checklist* D209.

1819/10/28 'Aux Auteurs de la Renommée', *La Renommée*, n° 135, 28 octobre 1819. *Checklist* D210.

1819/10/30 'Aux Auteurs de la Renommée', *La Renommée*, n° 137, 30 octobre 1819. *Checklist* D211.

1819/10/30-1819/11/02 'Lettre à MM. les habitans de la Sarthe', *La Minerve française*, VII, cahier 13 [30 octobre-2 novembre 1819], pp.577-590. *Checklist* D212.

1819/10/31 *Incipit*: 'La *Minerve* qui doit paraître demain contient une lettre de M. Benjamin Constant aux habitans de la Sarthe', *La Renommée*, n° 138, 31 octobre 1819. *Checklist* D213.

1819/11/02-03 *[Seconde] Lettre à Messieurs les habitans de la Sarthe*, [Paris]: impr. Fain, [1819]. Dépôt légal: 2-3 November 1819. Reprinted from *La Minerve française*, VII, cahier 13 [30 octobre-2 novembre 1819], pp.577-590. C.39a. *Checklist* A39/1.

1819/11/05 'Aux Auteurs de la Renommée', *La Renommée*, n° 143, 5 novembre 1819. *Checklist* D214.

1819/11/08-09 'Lettres sur les Cent Jours. (Neuvième lettre.)', *La Minerve française*, VIII, cahier 1 [8-9 novembre 1819], pp.3-11. *Checklist* D215.

1819/11/10 'Aux Auteurs de la Renommée', *La Renommée*, n° 148, 10 novembre 1819. *Checklist* D216.

1819/11/11 'De l'état de la France et des rumeurs qui circulent', *La Renommée*, n° 149, 11 novembre 1819. *Checklist* D217.

1819/11/12-13 *De l'état de la France et des bruits qui circulent*, Paris: Brissot-Thivars, Béchet aîné, 1819. Dépôt légal: 12-13 November 1819. C.40a. *Checklist* A40/1.

1819/11/14-15 'Lettres sur les Cent Jours. (Dixième lettre.)', *La Minerve française*, VIII, cahier 2 [14-15 novembre 1819], pp.49-59. *Checklist* D218.

1819/11/19 *Incipit*: 'Le *Courrier* d'hier reproche à la brochure de M. B. Constant de contenir des idées à la portée de tout le monde', *La Renommée*, n° 157, 19 novembre 1819. *Checklist* D219.

1819/11/20   'Napoléon et les 100 jours', *La Renommée*, n° 158, 20 novembre 1819. ['Le fragment fait partie de la 94ᵉ livraison de la *Minerve*, qui doit paraître demain, 20 novembre']. *Checklist* D220.

1819/11/20-22   'Lettres sur les Cent Jours. (Onzième lettre.)', *La Minerve française*, VIII, cahier 3 [20-22 novembre 1819], pp.97-105. *Checklist* D221.

1819/11/22   'Aux Auteurs de la Renommée', *La Renommée*, n° 160, 22 novembre 1819. *Checklist* D222.

1819/11/25   'Aux Auteurs de la Renommée', *La Renommée*, n° 163, 25 novembre 1819. *Checklist* D223.

1819/11/26-27   'De l'inviolabilité de la Charte', *La Minerve française*, VIII, cahier 4 [26-27 novembre 1819], pp.145-153. *Checklist* D224.

1819/11/29   'Aux Auteurs de la Renommée', *La Renommée*, n°167, 29 novembre 1819. *Checklist* D225.

1819/[11]/-   *Alphonse et Mathilde*, par Madame L. D'E****, Paris: Brissot-Thivars, 1819. 2 vols. By Louise d'Estournelles, with corrections by Constant. *Bibliographie de la France*, 4 December 1819. C.C1. *Checklist* C3/1.

1819/12/02-03   'Du projet de conférer aux Chambres le droit de s'épurer, et de quelques autres projets de même nature', *La Minerve française*, VIII, cahier 5 [2-3 décembre 1819], pp.193-202. *Checklist* D226.

1819/12/03   'Aux Auteurs de la Renommée', *La Renommée*, n° 171, 3 décembre 1819. *Checklist* D227.

1819/12/04   'Aux Auteurs de la Renommée', *La Renommée*, n° 172, 4 décembre 1819. *Checklist* D228.

1819/12/06   Chambre des Députés. Sur les dernières opérations du collège électoral de l'Isère. (Sur l'élection de Grégoire). Séance du 6 décembre 1819. *Archives parlementaires*, XXV, 728-729. *Discours* (1827-1828), I, 157-161.

1819/12/11   'Aux Auteurs de la Renommée', *La Renommée*, n° 179, 11 décembre 1819. *Checklist* D229.

1819/12/11-13   'De la responsabilité des ministres dans la proposition des lois', *La Minerve française*, VIII, cahier 6 [11-13 décembre 1819], pp.241-251. *Checklist* D230.

1819/12/22   'Aux Auteurs de la Renommée', *La Renommée*, n° 190, 22 décembre 1819. *Checklist* D231.

1819/12/22-23   'De l'adresse au Roi', *La Minerve française*, VII, cahier 7 [22-23 décembre 1819], pp.289-295. *Checklist* D232.

1819/12/24   Chambre des Députés. Sur le projet de loi tendant à autoriser le recouvrement des six premiers douzièmes des contributions de 1820 sur les rôles de 1819. Séance du 24 décembre 1819. *Archives parlementaires*, XXV, 770. *Discours* (1827-1828), I, 162-164.

1819/12/26   'Aux Auteurs de la Renommée', *La Renommée*, n° 194, 26 décembre 1819. *Checklist* D233.

1819/12/27-28   'Lettres sur les Cent Jours. (Douzième lettre.)', *La Minerve française*, VIII, cahier 8 [27-28 décembre 1819], pp.337-343. *Checklist* D234.

1819/12/30   Chambre des Députés. Sur la rédaction du procès-verbal de la séance du 24 décembre 1819. Séance du 30 décembre 1819. *Archives parlementaires*, XXVI, 10-11.

1819/12/31-1820/01/03   'Lettres sur les Cent Jours. (Treizième lettre.)', *La Minerve française*, VIII, cahier 9 [31 décembre 1819-3 janvier 1820], pp.385-396. *Checklist* D235.

1820

1820/01/02   'Aux Auteurs de la Renommée', *La Renommée*, n° 201, 2 janvier 1820. *Checklist* D236.

1820/01/08-10   'Lettres sur les Cent Jours. (Quatorzième lettre.)', *La Minerve française*, VIII, cahier 10 [8-10 janvier 1820], pp.433-438. *Checklist* D237.

1820/01/11   'Aux Auteurs de la Renommée', *La Renommée*, n° 210, 11 janvier 1820. *Checklist* D238.

1820/01/12   'Aux Auteurs de la Renommée', *La Renommée*, n° 211, 12 janvier 1820. *Checklist* D239.

1820/01/13-14   *Collection complète des ouvrages publiés sur le gouvernement représentatif et la constitution actuelle, ou Cours de politique constitutionnelle*, vol. IV (7-8), Paris: Béchet aîné; Rouen: Béchet fils, 1820. Dépôt légal: 13-14 January 1820. C.131a(4). *Checklist* E1/1(4).

1820/01/14   Chambre des Députés. Sur les pétitions relatives à la Charte et aux élections. Séance du 14 janvier 1820. *Archives parlementaires*, XXVI, 49-51. Edition: *Développemens de la proposition de M. Benjamin-Constant … tendant à améliorer le mode de scrutin*, [Paris]: impr. Hacquart, 1820. C.86a. *Checklist* B23. *Discours*, (1827-1828), I, 164-172.

1820/01/15   Chambre des Députés. Sur les pétitions relatives à la Charte et aux élections. Séance du 15 janvier 1820. *Archives parlementaires*, XXVI, 73-74. *Discours* (1827-1828), I, 172-175.

1820/01/15-17   'Lettres sur les Cent Jours. (Quinzième lettre.)', *La Minerve française*, VIII, cahier 11 [15-17 janvier 1820], pp.481-488. *Checklist* D240.

1820/01/19   Chambre des Députés. Sur le droit de pétition. Séance du 19 janvier 1820. *Archives parlementaires*, XXVI, 108.

1820/01/21   'Aux Auteurs de la Renommée', *La Renommée*, n° 220, 21 janvier 1820. *Checklist* D241.

1820/01/22-24   'Des aveux échappés aux ennemis de la loi des élections', *La Minerve française*, VIII, cahier 12 [22-24 janvier 1820], pp.529-543. *Checklist* D242.

1820/01/24-25   *Aux auteurs de La Renommée*, [Paris]: impr. Plassan, [1820]. Text signed: 'Benjamin Constant. (Extrait de la *Renommée* du 20 [=21] janvier)'. Dépôt légal: 24-25 January 1820. C.41a. *Checklist* A41/1.

1820/01/26   'Aux Auteurs de la Renommée', *La Renommée*, n° 225, 26 janvier 1820. *Checklist* D243.

1820/01/28   'Aux Auteurs de la Renommée', *La Renommée*, n° 227, 28 janvier 1820. *Checklist* D244.

1820/01/29   Chambre des Députés. Sur la pétition de J.-P. Arbaud, ancien juge au tribunal du Var, sollicitant une loi portant qu'en cas de mort, de démission ou destitution d'un roi de France, toutes les fonctions publiques soient suspendues jusqu'à ce qu'il soit autrement ordonné par la Chambre des Députés. Séance du 29 janvier 1820. *Archives parlementaires*, XXVI, 126-127. *Discours* (1827-1828), I, 175-179.

1820/01/29   Chambre des Députés. Sur la proposition du général Demarçay, relative à la convocation des collèges électoraux. Séance du 29 janvier 1820. *Archives parlementaires*, XXVI, 130.

1820/01/29-31   'Lettres sur les Cent Jours (Seizième lettre.)', *La Minerve française*, VIII, cahier 13 [29-31 janvier 1820], pp.593-601. *Checklist* D245.

1820/02/05-07   'Du plan de la faction contre-révolutionnaire', *La Minerve française*, IX, cahier 1 [5-7 février 1820], pp.3-11. *Checklist* D246.

1820/02/07   Chambre des Députés. Proposition de M. B. Constant tendant à modifier l'art. 151 de la loi des finances du 25 mars 1817. Séance du 7 février 1820. *Archives parlementaires*, XXVI, 157.

1820/02/08   Chambre des Députés. Sur le projet de loi concernant les acquéreurs de domaines nationaux. Séance du 8 février 1820. *Archives parlementaires*, XXVI, 163.

1820/02/09   Chambre des Députés. Sur le projet de loi concernant les acquéreurs de domaines nationaux. Séance du 9 février 1820. *Archives parlementaires*, XXVI, 179-180, 184. *Discours* (1827-1828), I, 179-182.

1820/02/14   'Aux Auteurs de la Renommée', *La Renommée*, n° 214, 14 février 1820. *Checklist* D247.

1820/02/14-15   'De l'influence de la faction contre-révolutionnaire sur les projets de loi des ministres', *La Minerve française*, IX, cahier 2 [14-15 février 1820], pp.49-56. *Checklist* D248.

1820/02/19-21   'Reflexions sur le moment présent', *La Minerve française*, IX, cahier 3 [19-21 février 1820], pp.97-103. *Checklist* D249.

1820/02/24   'Aux Auteurs de la Renommée', *La Renommée*, n° 224, 24 février 1820. *Checklist* D250.

1820/02/27-28   'Du rétablissement de la censure des journaux', *La Minerve française*, IX, cahier 4 [27-28 février 1820], pp.133-143. *Checklist* D251.

1820/03/01   Chambre des Députés. Incident sur le procès-verbal au sujet d'une expression adressée à M. Clausel de Coussergues. Séance du 1er mars 1820. *Archives parlementaires*, XXVI, 294. *Discours* (1827-1828), I, 182-185.

1820/03/03   Chambre des Députés. Sur la pétition du sieur Hottin, ancien notaire à Anizy-le-Château (Aisne), relative à l'article additionnel de la loi des décomptes. Séance du 3 mars 1820. *Archives parlementaires*, XXVI, 322.

1820/03/03   Chambre des Députés. Sur le projet de loi relatif à la liberté individuelle. Séance du 3 mars 1820. *Archives parlementaires*, XXVI, 326, 329.

1820/03/03   Chambre des Députés. Sur la proposition de Manuel relative au jury. Séance du 3 mars 1820. *Archives parlementaires*, XXVI, 335.

1820/03/[03-04]   'Lettres sur les Cent Jours. Dix-septième lettre', *La Minerve française*, IX, cahier 5 [3-4 mars 1820], pp.197-207. *Checklist* D252.

1820/03/04   'Aux Auteurs de la Renommée', *La Renommée*, n° 233, 4 mars 1820. *Checklist* D253.

1820/03/06   Chambre des Députés. Proposition de B. Constant concernant le règlement. Séance du 6 mars 1820. *Archives parlementaires*, XXVI, 345, 346. *Discours* (1827-1828), I, 185-187.

1820/03/07   Chambre des Députés. Sur le projet de loi relatif à la liberté individuelle. Séance du 7 mars 1820. *Archives parlementaires*, XXVI, 374-378. Edition: *Opinion ... sur le projet de loi relatif à la suspension de la liberté individuelle*, [Paris]: impr. Plassan, 1820; dépôt légal: 8-9 March 1820. C.87a. *Checklist* B24. *Discours* (1827-1828), I, 188-205; Pléiade (1957), pp.1309-1321.

1820/03/10   Chambre des Députés. Sur le projet de loi relatif à la liberté individuelle. Séance du 10 mars 1820. *Archives parlementaires*, XXVI, 433-35. *Discours* (1827-1828), I, 206-211.

1820/03/13   Chambre des Députés. Sur le projet de loi relatif à la liberté individuelle. (Sur la demande de rappel à l'ordre formulée par Castelbajac contre Manuel). Séance du 13 mars 1820. *Archives parlementaires*, XXVI, 472. Edition: *Opinion ... sur le projet de loi relatif à la suspension de la liberté individuelle*. [Paris]: Plassan, 1820; dépôt légal: 14-16 March 1820. C.88a. *Checklist* B25. *Discours* (1827-1828), I, 212-223.

1820/03/14   'De la contre-révolution et du ministère', *La Minerve française*, IX, cahier 6 [14 mars 1820], pp.229-237. *Checklist* D254.

1820/03/15   Chambre des Députés. Sur le projet de loi relatif à la liberté individuelle. (Incident sur le point de savoir si un ministre peut parler entre deux épreuves). Séance du 15 mars 1820. *Archives parlementaires*, XXVI, 483.

1820/03/15   Chambre des Députés. Sur le projet de loi relatif à la liberté individuelle. Séance du 15 mars 1820. *Archives parlementaires*, XXVI, 493.

1820/03/16   Chambre des Députés. Sur la proposition de Maine de Biran, relative au droit de pétition. Séance du 16 mars 1820. *Archives parlementaires*, XXVI, 522-23. *Discours* (1827-1828), I, 224-228.

1820/03/16-17   'Symptômes du moment', *La Minerve française*, IX, cahier 7 [16-17 mars 1820], pp.285-291. *Checklist* D255.

1820/03/17   Chambre des Députés. Sur la pétition du sieur Tholard, propriétaire à La Chapelle (près Paris), réclamant contre un arrêté du préfet de la Seine qui lui ordonne de démolir un hangar sous lequel il tient un jeu de Siam. Séance du 17 mars 1820. *Archives parlementaires*, XXVI, 526.

1820/03/18-20   *Mémoires sur les Cent Jours, en forme de lettres*, Paris: Béchet aîné; Rouen: Béchet fils, 1820. Dépôt légal: 18-20 March 1820. Originally published in *La Minerve française*; see above. C.42a(1). *Checklist* A42/1.

1820/03/20   Chambre des Députés. Rapport, par M. Benjamin Constant, sur sa proposition relative au règlement. Séance du 20 mars 1820. *Archives parlementaires*, XXVI, 564-565. Edition: *Rapport fait au nom de la commission centrale ... sur la proposition tendant à améliorer les articles 15, 22 et 33 du règlement*, [Paris]: impr. Hacquart, 1820. C.89a; *Checklist* B26. *Discours* (1827-1828), I, 229-232.

1820/03/23   Chambre des Députés. Sur le projet de loi relatif aux journaux. Séance du 23 mars 1820. *Archives parlementaires*, XXVI, 644-648. Edition: *Opinion ... sur le projet de loi relatif à la censure des journaux*, [Paris]: impr. Plassan, 1820; dépôt légal: 25 March 1820. C.90a. *Checklist* B27. *Discours* (1827-1828), I, 232-248; Pléiade (1957), pp.1369-1380.

1820/03/22-24   'Troisième lettre à Messieurs les habitans du département de la Sarthe', *La Minerve française*, IX, cahier 8 [22-24 mars 1820], pp.333-339. *Checklist* D256.

1820/03/25   *Troisième lettre à MM. les habitans du département de la Sarthe. (Extrait de la 112ᵉ livraison de La Minerve française. Signed:* 'Benjamin Constant. Paris, le 21 mars 1820'. Dépôt légal: 25 March 1820. C.43a. *Checklist* A43/1.

1820/03/27   Chambre des Députés. Sur le projet de loi relatif aux journaux. Séance du 27 mars 1820. *Archives parlementaires*, XXVI, 729-730. *Discours* (1827-1828). I, 249-251.

1820/03/28 Chambre des Députés. Sur le projet de loi relatif aux journaux. Séance du 28 mars 1820. *Archives parlementaires*, XXVI, 752, 756-757, 763. *Discours* (1827-1828), I, 251-260.

1820/03/29 'Conspiration des contre-révolutionnaires contre le trône et la vie du Roi d'Espagne', *La Minerve française*, IX, cahier 9 [29 mars 1820], pp.381-386. *Checklist* D257.

1820/03/29 Chambre des Députés. Sur le projet de loi relatif aux journaux. Séance du 29 mars 1820. *Archives parlementaires*, XXVI, 773-777. *Discours* (1827-1828), I, 261-274.

1820/03/30 Chambre des Députés. Sur la pétition du sieur Paul Lehr, manufacturier et adjoint au maire de Saint-Dié (Vosges), sur les demandes faites par le sous-préfet pour le porter à donner sa démission. Séance du 30 mars 1820. *Archives parlementaires*, XXVII, 2.

1820/03/30 Chambre des Députés. Sur le projet de loi relatif aux journaux. Séance du 30 mars 1820. *Archives parlementaires*, XXVII, 8-10, 12. *Discours* (1827-1828), I, 274-276.

1820/03/31 'Aux Auteurs de la Renommée', *La Renommée*, n° 259, 31 mars 1820. *Checklist* D258.

1820/03-05/- *De la Charte constitutionnelle telle que le ministère de 1820 l'a faite*, [March-May 1820]. Not extant. See the preceding item and also under 8 May 1820. The printer's declaration (by Plassan, 5 May 1820) gives the title recorded above. C.D3.

1820/04/03 Chambre des Députés. Proposition de M. Benjamin Constant relative au règlement. Séance du 3 avril 1820. *Archives parlementaires*, XXVII, 20-21, 22. *Discours* (1827-1828), I, 276-280.

1820/04/05 Chambre des Députés. Sur le projet de loi relatif aux comptes arriérés des exercices antérieurs à 1819. Séance du 5 avril 1820. *Archives parlementaires*, XXVII, 51-54. Edition: *Opinion ... sur le projet de loi relatif au règlement définitif des comptes antérieurs à l'exercice, 1819*, [Paris]: impr. Hacquart, 1820. C.91a. *Checklist* B28. *Discours* (1827-1828), I, 280-295.

1820/04/06 Chambre des Députés. Sur le projet de loi relatif aux comptes arriérés des exercices antérieurs à 1819. Séance du 6 avril 1820. *Archives parlementaires*, XXVII, 77-78.

1820/04/08 Chambre des Députés. Sur le projet de loi relatif aux comptes arriérés des exercices antérieurs à 1819. Séance du 8 avril 1820. *Archives parlementaires*, XXVII, 132-133, 136, 137.

1820/04/09 'Aux Auteurs de la Renommée', *La Renommée*, n° 269, 9 avril 1820. *Checklist* D259.

1820/04/10 *Lettres sur la situation de la France*, Paris: impr. Plassan, avril 1820. Includes: 'Lettre à M. Lacretelle aîné, sur les attaques autorisées par les ministres, dans les journaux censurés, contre les individus et les grands corps de l'état', dated '5 avril 1820' and signed 'Benjamin Constant'. Dépôt légal: 10 avril 1820. C.B2. *Checklist* C4/1.

1820/04/14 Chambre des Députés. Sur la pétition du sieur de Voisins, propriétaire à Damiatte (Tarn), relative aux élections. Séance du 14 avril 1820. *Archives parlementaires*, XXVII, 207.

1820/04/15 Chambre des Députés. Sur diverses pétitions. Séance du 15 avril 1820. *Archives parlementaires*, XXVII, 228, 229.

1820/04/15 Chambre des Députés. Sur le projet de loi relatif au règlement des comptes de 1818. Séance du 15 avril 1820. *Archives parlementaires*, XXVII, 236-38; Edition:

Opinion ... sur les amendemens proposés à l'art. 8 du second projet de loi relatif aux comptes arriérés, [Paris]: impr. Hacquart, 1820. C.92a. *Checklist* B29. *Discours*, (1827-1828), I, 296-305.

1820/04/17   Chambre des Députés. Présentation par M. le comte Siméon, ministre de l'intérieur, d'un nouveau projet de loi sur les collèges électoraux. (Incident au sujet de la présentation de ce projet de loi). Séance du 17 avril 1820. *Archives parlementaires*, XXVII, 251, 252, 254, 256.

1820/04/17   Chambre des Députés. Sur le nouveau projet de loi sur les collèges électoraux. Séance du 17 avril 1820. *Archives parlementaires*, XXVII, 260, 261.

1820/04/18   Chambre des Députés. Sur le projet de loi relatif au règlement des comptes de 1818. Séance du 18 avril 1820. *Archives parlementaires*, XXVII, 272, 278-279, 281. Edition: *Opinion ... sur le deuxième projet de loi relatif aux comptes arriérés*, [Paris]: impr. Hacquart, 1820. C.93a. *Checklist* B30.

1820/04/19   Chambre des Députés. Sur la pétition des habitants du canton de Pontrieux (Côtes-du-Nord), relative aux lois d'exception. Séance du 19 avril 1820. *Archives parlementaires*, XXVII, 282.

1820/04/25   Chambre des Députés. Rapport, par M. Saulnier, sur une pétition de M. Madier de Montjau, relative à l'état de la ville de Nîmes et du département du Gard. Séance du 25 avril 1820. *Archives parlementaires*, XXVII, 368. *Discours* (1827-1828), I, 306-309.

1820/04/28   Chambre des Députés. Sur les pétitions des sieurs Pinet, Gallay et Le Joyant, relative au renvoi de M. Decazes. Séance du 28 avril 1820. *Archives parlementaires*, XXVII, 398-400, 406. Edition: *Opinion ... sur trois pétitions relatives au renvoi de M. Decazes*, [Paris]: impr. Plassan, 1820; dépôt légal: 4 May 1820. C.94a. *Checklist* B31. *Discours* (1827-1828), I, 310-318.

1820/05/03   Chambre des Députés. Sur la proposition de M. Manuel, d'un projet d'adresse au Roi. Séance du 3 mai 1820. *Archives parlementaires*, XXVII, 472-75. Edition: *Discours prononcé ... dans le comité secret du 3 mai, à l'occasion de la proposition d'adresse, faite à la Chambre des Députés par M. Manuel*, [Paris]: impr. Plassan, 1820; dépôt légal: 6 May 1820. C.95a. *Checklist* B32. *Discours* (1827-1828), I, 318-331.

1820/05/05   Chambre des Députés. Incident sur la fixation de l'ordre du jour. Séance du 5 mai 1820. *Archives parlementaires*, XXVII, 503.

1820/05/06   Chambre des Députés. Discussion pour fixer l'ouverture de la discussion. Séance du 6 mai 1820. *Archives parlementaires*, XXVII, 528.

1820/05/08   'Aux Auteurs de la Renommée', *La Renommée*, n° 298, 8 mai 1820. *Checklist* D260.

1820/05/12   Chambre des Députés. Sur diverses pétitions. Séance du 12 mai 1820. *Archives parlementaires*, XXVII, 549-550, 551-552. *Discours* (1827-1828), I, 332-335.

1820/05/15   Chambre des Députés. Incident sur le procès-verbal au sujet de la censure. Séance du 15 mai 1820. *Archives parlementaires*, XXVII, 593.

1820/05/17   *Des motifs qui ont dicté le nouveau projet de loi sur les élections*, Paris: Béchet aîné, mai 1820. Dépôt légal: 17 May 1820. C.44a. *Checklist* A44/1.

1820/05/20   Chambre des Députés. Sur le projet de loi relatif aux élections. Séance du 20 mai 1820. *Archives parlementaires*, XXVII, 717.

1820/05/22-23   'Au Rédacteur', *Le Courrier français*, n°s 337-338, 22-23 mai 1820, p.4. *Checklist* D261.

1820/05/23 Chambre des Députés. Sur le projet de loi relatif aux élections. Séance du 23 mai 1820. *Archives parlementaires*, XXVIII, 54-61. Editions: *Opinion sur le projet de loi …* [Paris]: impr. Agasse, 1820; *Discours …* Grenoble: impr. Barnel, [1820]. C.96a-b. *Checklist* B33/1-2. *Discours* (1827-1828), I, 336-365.

1820/05/27 Chambre des Députés. Sur le projet de loi relatif aux élections. Séance du 27 mai 1820. *Archives parlementaires*, XXVIII, 155-57. *Discours* (1827-1828), I, 366-372.

1820/05/29 Chambre des Députés. Sur le projet de loi relatif aux élections. Séance du 29 mai 1820. *Archives parlementaires*, XXVIII, 189-190.

1820/05/31 Chambre des Députés. Sur le projet de loi relatif aux élections. Séance du 31 mai 1820. *Archives parlementaires*, XXVIII, 232.

1820/06/01 Chambre des Députés. Sur le projet de loi relatif aux élections. (Sur le rappel à l'ordre du général Foy). Séance du 1er juin 1820. *Archives parlementaires*, XXVIII, 240-241.

1820/06/02 Chambre des Députés. Sur la pétition du sieur Paul Bertaux (Paris), relative au titre de pair. Séance du 2 juin 1820. *Archives parlementaires*, XXVIII, 247.

1820/06/02 Chambre des Députés. Sur le projet de loi relatif aux élections. Séance du 2 juin 1820. *Archives parlementaires*, XXVIII, 256.

1820/06/02 Chambre des Députés. Incident sur l'ordre de la discussion et la priorité à donner aux diverses propositions. Séance du 2 juin 1820. *Archives parlementaires*, XXVIII, 260.

1820/06/03 Chambre des Députés. Sur le projet de loi relatif aux élections. Séance du 3 juin 1820. *Archives parlementaires*, XXVIII, 266-269. Editions: *Opinion … sur l'article premier du projet de loi relatif aux élections; prononcé dans la séance du 3 juin 1820*, [Paris]: impr. Agasse, 1820; *Second discours …* Grenoble: impr. Barnel, 1820. C.97a-b. *Checklist* B34/1-2. *Discours* (1827-1828), I, 372-384.

1820/06/05 Chambre des Députés. Sur les troubles survenus autour du palais de la Chambre. Séance du 5 juin 1820. *Archives parlementaires*, XXVIII, 277, 287-289, 290, 292. *Discours* (1827-1828), I, 385-392.

1820/06/06 Chambre des Députés. Incident au sujet du procès-verbal. Séance du 6 juin 1820. *Archives parlementaires*, XXVIII, 293. *Discours* (1827-1828), I, 393-395.

1820/06/06 Chambre des Députés. Sur le projet de loi relatif aux élections. Séance du 6 juin 1820. *Archives parlementaires*, XXVIII, 303-304.

1820/06/07 Chambre des Députés. Sur les troubles survenus autour du palais de la Chambre. Séance du 7 juin 1820. *Archives parlementaires*, XXVIII, 308, 314. *Discours* (1827-1828), I, 396-397.

1820/06/10 Chambre des Députés. Incident sur les troubles de Paris. Séance du 10 juin 1820. *Archives parlementaires*, XXVIII, 358, 359-62. *Discours*, (1827-1828), I, 397-402.

1820/06/12 Chambre des Députés. Sur le projet de loi relatif aux élections. Séance du 12 juin 1820. *Archives parlementaires*, XXVIII, 380, 386.

1820/06/15 Chambre des Députés. Sur le budget des dépenses de 1820. Séance du 15 juin 1820. *Archives parlementaires*, XXVIII, 543.

1820/06/16 Chambre des Députés. Sur le budget des dépenses de 1820. Séance du 16 juin 1820. *Archives parlementaires*, XXVIII, 557, 558-559, 560, 562.

1820/06/17   Chambre des Députés. Sur le budget des dépenses de 1820. Séance du 17 juin 1820. *Archives parlementaires*, XXVIII, 577.

1820/06/19   Chambre des Députés. Sur le budget des dépenses de 1820. Séance du 19 juin 1820. *Archives parlementaires*, XXVIII, 606.

1820/06/19   'A M. Kératry, membre de la Chambre des Députés et homme de lettres', *Le Courrier français*, n° 365, 19 juin 1820, p.3. *Checklist* D262.

1820/06/21   Chambre des Députés. Sur le budget des dépenses de 1820. Séance du 21 juin 1820. *Archives parlementaires*, XXVIII, 638. *Discours* (1827-1828), I, 403-406.

1820/06/26   Chambre des Députés. Sur le budget des dépenses de 1820. Séance du 26 juin 1820. *Archives parlementaires*, XXVIII, 777, 780.

1820/06/27   Chambre des Députés. Sur le budget des dépenses de 1820. Séance du 27 juin 1820. *Archives parlementaires*, XXIX, 50-52, 53-54.

1820/06/30   'Au rédacteur', *Le Moniteur universel*, 30 juin 1820. *Checklist* D263.

1820/06/30   Chambre des Députés. Sur la pétition du chevalier Bacheville (Paris) concernant l'affaire des frères Bacheville. Séance du 30 juin 1820. *Archives parlementaires*, XXIX, 118, 119, 120.

1820/06/30   Chambre des Députés. Sur le budget des dépenses de 1820. Séance du 30 juin 1820. *Archives parlementaires*, XXIX, 125-26. *Discours* (1827-1828), I, 407-409.

1820/07/01   Chambre des Députés. Proposition de M. Benjamin Constant relative aux contreseing des actes de la direction générale de la police. Comité secret du 1er juillet 1820. *Archives parlementaires*, XXIX, 157.

1820/07/02   'A M. Kératry, député du Finistère', *Le Courrier français*, n° 378, 2 juillet 1820, p.2. *Checklist* D264.

1820/07/02   'Au Rédacteur', *Le Courrier français*, n° 378, 2 juillet 1820, pp.2-3. *Checklist* D265.

1820/07/04   'Au Rédacteur', *Le Courrier français*, n° 380, 4 juillet 1820, p.3. *Checklist* D266.

1820/07/04   Chambre des Députés. Sur le budget des recettes de 1820. Séance du 4 juillet 1820. *Archives parlementaires*, XXIX, 201.

1820/07/05   Chambre des Députés. Sur le budget des recettes de 1820. Séance du 5 juillet 1820. *Archives parlementaires*, XXIX, 221-222.

1820/07/06   'Au Rédacteur', *Le Courrier français*, n° 382, 6 juillet 1820, pp.3-4. *Checklist* D267.

1820/07/06   Chambre des Députés. Sur le budget des recettes de 1820. Séance du 6 juillet 1820. *Archives parlementaires*, XXIX, 241.

1820/07/08   Chambre des Députés. Sur la discussion du budget des recettes de 1820. Séance du 8 juillet 1820. *Archives parlementaires*, XXIX, 267, 275, 276.

1820/07/10   Chambre des Députés. Sur le budget des recettes de 1820. Séance du 10 juillet 1820. *Archives parlementaires*, XXIX, 323.

1820/07/11   'Au Rédacteur', *Le Courrier français*, n° 387, 11 juillet 1820, p.4. *Checklist* D268.

1820/07/11   *Pièces relatives à la saisie de lettres et de papiers dans le domicile de MM. Goyet et*

Pasquier, *l'un juge et l'autre agréé au tribunal de commerce du Mans, avec quelques réflexions sur la direction de la police générale*, Paris: impr. Plassan, 1820. Dépôt légal: 11 July 1820. C.45a. *Checklist* A45/1.

1820/07/11   Chambre des Députés. Sur la pétition des habitants de Gogolin (Var). Séance du 11 juillet 1820. *Archives parlementaires*, XXIX, 340-341.

1820/07/11   Chambre des Députés. Incident au sujet de l'accusation portée par M. Clausel de Coussergues contre M. le comte Decazes. Séance du 11 juillet 1820. *Archives parlementaires*, XXIX, 343.

1820/07/11   Chambre des Députés. Sur le projet de loi relatif au traité conclu avec le dey d'Alger. Séance du 11 juillet 1820. *Archives parlementaires*, XXIX, 351-352.

1820/07/12   Chambre des Députés. Sur le projet de loi concernant la ville du Mans, relative au rapport de M. Picot-Desormaux. Séance du 12 juillet 1820. *Archives parlementaires*, XXIX, 353.

1820/07/13   Chambre des Députés. Sur le rapport de M. Picot-Desormaux concernant Le Mans. Séance du 13 juillet 1820. *Archives parlementaires*, XXIX, 392.

1820/07/15   *Pensieri sugli ultimi avvenimenti, seguiti dal Ragionamento di un elettore con se stesso*, pubblicati da V. Balsamo, Lecce il 15 luglio 1820. C.24d. *Checklist* A24/t1.

1820/07/18   *Collection complète des ouvrages publiés sur le gouvernement représentatif et la constitution actuelle, terminée par une table analytique; ou Cours de politique constitutionnelle*, vols. I-III, Paris: Plancher, 1820. Reissue. Dépôt légal: 18 July 1820. C.131b(1-3). *Checklist* E1/2(1-3).

1820/07/19   'Au Rédacteur', *Le Courrier français*, n° 395, 19 juillet 1820, pp.2-3. *Checklist* D269.

1820/07/20   'Au Rédacteur', *Le Courrier français*, n° 396, 20 juillet 1820, p.2. *Checklist* D270.

1820/08/29   'Au Rédacteur' *Le Courrier français*, n° 436, 29 août 1820, p.2. *Checklist* D271.

1820/09/01   'Au Rédacteur', *Le Courrier français*, n° 439, 1ᵉʳ septembre 1820, p.3. *Checklist* D272.

1820/09/[*ante* 16]   *Commentaire sur l'ouvrage de Filangieri*. Prospectus. Printer's declaration: 5 September 1820; *Bibliographie de la France*, 16 September 1820. C.50. *Checklist* A50.

1820/09/20   *De la dissolution de la Chambre des Députés, et des résultats que cette dissolution peut avoir pour la nation, le gouvernement et le ministère*, Paris: Béchet aîné; Rouen: Béchet fils, 1820. Dépôt légal: 20 September 1820. C.46a. *Checklist* A46/1.

1820/10/02   *De la dissolution de la Chambre des Députés, et des résultats que cette dissolution peut avoir pour la nation, le gouvernement et le ministère, deuxième édition, revue et corrigée*, Paris: Béchet aîné; Rouen: Béchet fils, 1820. Dépôt légal: 2 October 1820. C.46b. *Checklist* 46/2.

1820/10/18   'A M. le Rédacteur', *Le Courrier français*, n° 486, 18 octobre 1820, p.2. *Checklist* D273.

1820/10/19   *Lettre à M. le marquis de Latour-Maubourg, ministre de la guerre, sur ce qui s'est passé à Saumur les 7 et 8 octobre 1820*, Paris: Béchet aîné; Rouen: Béchet fils, 1820. Dépôt légal: 19 October 1820. C.47a. *Checklist* A47/1.

1820/10/26   *Lettre à M. le marquis de Latour-Maubourg, ministre de la guerre, sur ce qui s'est passé à Saumur les 7 et 8 octobre 1820, seconde édition*, Paris: Béchet aîné; Rouen: Béchet fils,

1820. Dépôt légal: 26 October 1820. C.47b. *Checklist* A47/2.

1820/11/04   'Au Rédacteur', *Le Courrier français*, n° 503, 4 novembre 1820, p.2. *Checklist* D274.

1820/11/04   *Lettre à M. le marquis de Latour-Maubourg, ministre de la guerre, sur ce qui s'est passé à Saumur les 7 et 8 octobre 1820, troisième édition*, Paris: Béchet aîné; Rouen: Béchet fils, 1820. Dépôt légal: 4 November 1820. C.47c. *Checklist* A47/3.

1820/11/07   'Au Rédacteur', *Le Courrier français*, n° 506, 7 novembre 1820, p.2. *Checklist* D275.

1820/11/09   *Réponses aux articles du Moniteur et à un pamphlet du 2ᵉ adjoint au maire de Saumur, sur ce qui s'est passé dans cette ville les 7 et 8 octobre 1820*, Paris: Béchet aîné; Rouen: Béchet fils, 1820. Dépôt légal: 9 November 1820. C.47d. *Checklist* A47/4.

1820/11/13-16   *Lettre à Monsieur Goyet électeur de la Sarthe*, Le Mans: impr. Renaudin. *Signed*: 'Benjamin Constant. Paris, ce 6 novembre 1820'. Dépôt légal: 13-16 November 1820. C.48a. *Checklist* A48/1.

1820/12/21   Chambre des Députés. Sur la vérification des pouvoirs (élection de MM. Dussumier-Fonbrune et Pilastre). Séance du 21 décembre 1820. *Archives parlementaires*, XXIX, 469-470; 471.

1820/12/23   Chambre des Députés. Sur la vérification des pouvoirs. (Sur les élections de la Sarthe). Séance du 23 décembre 1820. *Archives parlementaires*, XXIX, 488, 489, 490.

1820/12/25   *Eclaircissemens sur quelques faits, adressés à MM. les membres de la Chambre des Députés*, [Paris]: impr. Moreau. *Signed*: 'Benjamin Constant. Paris, ce 25 Décembre 1820'. C.98a. *Checklist* B35.

1820/12/30   Chambre des Députés. Sur le projet d'une adresse au Roi. Comité secret du 30 décembre 1820. *Archives parlementaires*, XXIX, 513-514.

1820/-/-   *Curso de política constitucional*, traducido per D. Marcial Antonio López, Madrid: Impr. de la Compañía por su regente don Juan José Sigüenza y Vera, 1820. 3 vols. C. Suppl. Add. 4. *Checklist* E1/t1.

1820/-/-   *Saggio di costituzione. Prima versione italiana corredata di note relative alla costituzione spagnuola*, [Naples: L. Nobile, 1820]. Issued in parts in *La Biblioteca costituzionale*. C.131c. *Checklist* E1/t2, D276.

1821

1821/01/02   '*Notice sur M. Necker*, par A. de Staël, son petit-fils. A Paris, chez Treuttel et Wurtz ...', *Le Courrier français*, n° 2, 2 janvier 1821, pp.3-4. *Checklist* D277.

1821/01/05   '*Sur la vie de Jacques II, roi d'Angleterre, écrite de sa propre main*', *Le Courrier français*, n° 5, 5 janvier 1821, pp.3-4. *Checklist* D278.

1821/01/05   Chambre des Députés. Incident relatif à la proposition de M. Maine de Biran concernant le règlement. Séance du 5 janvier 1821. *Archives parlementaires*, XXIX, 543, 544, 546-547.

1821/01/08   Chambre des Députés. Sur le projet de loi relatif aux douzièmes provisoires. Séance du 8 janvier 1821. *Archives parlementaires*, XXIX, 557-558. *Discours* (1827-1828), I, 410-416.

1821/01/09   Chambre des Députés. Sur le projet de loi relatif aux douzièmes provisoires. Séance du 9 janvier 1821. *Archives parlementaires*, XXIX, 581.

1821/01/16   Chambre des Députés. Incident au sujet de l'impression des motifs du projet de budget de 1821. Séance du 16 janvier 1821. *Archives parlementaires*, XXIX, 627-628.

1821/01/19   'Au Rédacteur', *Le Constitutionnel*, 19 janvier 1821. *Checklist* D279.

1821/01/22   Chambre des Députés. Sur un projet de loi relatif à la halle de la ville du Mans. Séance du 22 janvier 1821. *Archives parlementaires*, XXIX, 642-643.

1821/01/27   Chambre des Députés. Développements d'une proposition relative au règlement. Séance du 27 janvier 1821. *Archives parlementaires*, XXIX, 665-666. *Discours* (1827-1828), I, 416-424.

1821/01/31   Chambre des Députés. Sur l'adresse au Roi, au sujet de l'événement du 27 janvier. Comité secret du 31 janvier 1821. Edition: *Discours prononcés dans le Comité secret du 31 janvier 1821* ... Paris: Brissot-Thivars, 1821; dépôt légal: 26 February 1821. C.99a. *Checklist* B36.

1821/02/02   Chambre des Députés. Incident à propos de l'ordre du jour. Séance du 2 février 1821. *Archives parlementaires*, XXIX, 700.

1821/02/05   Chambre des Députés. Incident à propos d'un écrit de M. Prosper Ribard. Séance du 5 février 1821. *Archives parlementaires*, XXIX, 723-724, 730.

1821/02/07   Chambre des Députés. Discusssion à propos de la cocarde tricolore. Séance du 7 février 1821. *Archives parlementaires*, XXIX, 736-737. *Discours* (1827-1828), I, 425-429.

1821/02/12   Chambre des Députés. Incident à l'occasion de la lecture du procès-verbal. Séance du 12 février 1821. *Archives parlementaires*, XXX, 1-2, 4-5.

1821/02/16   Chambre des Députés. Sur le projet de loi relatif aux reconnaissances de liquidation. (Sur l'impression du discours de M. Pardessus). Séance du 16 février 1821. *Archives parlementaires*, XXX, 43.

1821/02/19   Chambre des Députés. Sur le projet de loi relatif aux reconnaissances de liquidation; amendement de M. Bertin de Vaux. Séance du 19 février 1821. *Archives parlementaires*, XXX, 88-91. Edition: *Opinion ... sur l'amendement proposé par M. Bertin de Vaux au projet de loi relatif au remboursement du premier cinquième des reconnaissances de liquidation*, [Paris]: impr. Hacquart, 1821. C.100a. *Checklist* B37. *Discours* (1827-1828), I, 429-444.

1821/02/21   Chambre des Députés. Incident à propos de la discussion de diverses pétitions. (Sur le rappel à l'ordre du général Maynaud de Lavaux; sur la suppression des discussions). Séance du 21 février 1821. *Archives parlementaires*, XXX, 113, 118, 119, 120.

1821/02/22   'A M. le rédacteur', *Le Courrier français*, n° 52, 22 février 1821, p.4. *Checklist* D280.

1821/02/23   Chambre des Députés. Sur le projet de loi relatif à la circonscription des arrondissements électoraux. (Incident au sujet du discours de M. Bignon). Séance du 23 février 1821. *Archives parlementaires*, XXX, 145-148

1821/02/28   Chambre des Députés. Sur le projet de loi relatif à la circonscription des arrondissements. Article 44 (Maine-et-Loire). Séance du 28 février 1821. *Archives parlementaires*, XXX, 215-216, 222.

1821/03/01   Chambre des Députés. Sur le projet de loi relatif à la circonscription des arrondissements électoraux. Article 65 (Sarthe). Séance du 1er mars 1821. *Archives parlementaires*, XXX, 228-231.

1821/03/27   'Etat actuel de la Corse, caractère et mœurs de ses habitans, par P. P. Pompei', *Le Courrier français*, n° 85, 27 mars 1821, p.4. *Checklist* D281.

[1821]/[03]/-   *Carnet*, [3 March 1821?]. Sainte-Beuve (1852, 1881); Pierre Deguise (1963). *Checklist* A64.

1821/04/02-03   *Du triomphe inévitable et prochain des principes constitutionnels en Prusse, d'après un ouvrage imprimé, traduit de l'allemand de M. Koreff, conseiller intime de Régence, par M.****; avec un avant-propos et des notes de M. Benjamin-Constant*, Paris: impr. P. Didot l'aîné, mars 1821. Dépôt légal: 2-3 April 1821. C.49a. *Checklist* A49/1.

1821/04/06   Chambre des Députés. Sur la proposition de M. Sirieys de Mayrinhac, relative au règlement. Séance du 6 avril 1821. *Archives parlementaires*, XXX, 607-612. Edition: see below under 14 April 1821.

1821/04/06   'Au Rédacteur', *Le Courrier français*, n° 95, 6 avril 1821, p.3. *Checklist* D282.

1821/04/12   'Au Rédacteur', *Le Courrier français*, n° 101, 12 avril 1821, p.4. *Checklist* D283.

1821/04/14   Chambre des Députés. Sur la proposition de M. Sirieys de Mayrinhac, relative au règlement, art. 2. Séance du 14 avril 1821. *Archives parlementaires*, XXXI, 6-9. 17. Edition: *Opinion ... sur l'interdiction de la parole, par suite du rappel à l'ordre et à la question, ... avec un avertissement et des notes de l'auteur*, Paris: Kleffer, Moreau, Mongie, Béchet aîné, Delaunai, Pélicier et Ponthieu, mai 1822. Dépôt légal: 10 May 1821. C.101a. *Checklist* B38. *Discours* (1827-1828), I, 445-480.

1821/04/16   Chambre des Députés. Sur la proposition de M. Sirieys de Mayrinhac relative au règlement, art. 3. Séance du 16 avril 1821. *Archives parlementaires*, XXXI, 30-31.

1821/04/26   'Au Rédacteur', *Le Courrier français*, n° 114, 26 avril 1821, p.4. *Checklist* D284.

1821/04/28   'Précis historique des principaux événemens politiques et militaires qui ont amené la Révolution d'Espagne, par M. Louis Jullian', *Le Courrier français*, n° 116, 28 avril 1821, p.4. *Checklist* D285.

1821/04/28   Chambre des Députés. Sur le projet de loi relatif aux grains, art. 8. Séance du 28 avril 1821. *Archives parlementaires*, XXXI, 222-223. *Discours* (1827-1828), I, 481-484.

1821/04/30   'Au Rédacteur', *Le Courrier français*, n° 118, 30 avril 1821, p.3. *Checklist* D286.

1821/04/30   Chambre des Députés. Sur des pétitions. Séance du 30 avril 1821. *Archives parlementaires*, XXXI, 231, 232.

1821/04/30   Chambre des Députés. Sur le projet de loi relatif aux grains. Articles additionnels. Séance du 30 avril 1821. *Archives parlementaires*, XXXI, 239-240. *Discours* (1827-1828), I, 485-493.

1821/05/01   'Au Rédacteur', *Le Courrier français*, n° 119, 1er mai 1821, p.3. *Checklist* D287.

1821/05/04   Chambre des Députés. Sur le projet de loi relatif aux grains. Amendement de M. Basterrèche. Séance du 4 mai 1821. *Archives parlementaires*, XXXI, 252. *Discours* (1827-1828), I, 490-493.

1821/05/05   Chambre des Députés. Sur l'article 44 du projet de loi concernant les circonstances électorales. Séance du 5 mai 1821. *Archives parlementaires*, XXXI, 273-274.

1821/05/07   Chambre des Députés. Sur le projet relatif à l'article 351 du Code d'instruction criminelle. Séance du 7 mai 1821. *Archives parlementaires*, XXXI, 296-298. *Discours* (1827-1828), I, 493-502.

1821/05/08   Chambre des Députés. Sur la pétition du sieur Arnoux, ancien capitaine à Saint-Paul (Var). Séance du 8 mai 1821. *Archives parlementaires*, XXXI, 300, 302.

1821/05/14   Chambre des Députés. Sur le projet de loi relatif aux pensions ecclésiastiques. Séance du 14 mai 1821. *Archives parlementaires*, XXXI, 414-418. *Discours* (1827-1828), I, 502-522.

1821/05/16   'Au Rédacteur', *Le Courrier français*, n° 133, 16 mai 1821, p.4. *Checklist* D288.

1821/05/19   Chambre des Députés. Sur la pétition des sieurs Haker (Strasbourg) et Germain (professeur à Paris), relative à l'ordonnance royale qui met toutes les écoles sous la surveillance des évêques. Séance du 19 mai 1821. *Archives parlementaires*, XXXI, 504, 506. *Discours* (1827-1828), I, 522-523.

1821/05/19   Chambre des Députés. Sur le projet de loi relatif aux pensions ecclésiastiques, art. 2. Séance du 19 mai 1821. *Archives parlementaires*, XXXI, 508.

1821/05/21   Chambre des Députés. Sur le projet de loi relatif aux pensions ecclésiastiques, art. 2. Séance du 21 mai 1821. *Archives parlementaires*, XXXI, 530.

1821/05/22   'Au Rédacteur', *Le Courrier français*, n° 139, 22 mai 1821, p.4. *Checklist* D289.

1821/05/22   Chambre des Députés. Sur le procès-verbal. Séance du 22 mai 1821. *Archives parlementaires*, XXXI, 550-551.

1821/05/24   'Au Rédacteur', *Le Courrier français*, n° 141, 24 mai 1821, p.4. *Checklist* D290.

1821/05/25   Chambre des Députés. Sur le projet de loi relatif au domaine extraordinaire. Séance du 25 mai 1821. *Archives parlementaires*, XXXI, 608.

1821/05/28   Chambre des Députés. Sur le projet de loi relatif au domaine extraordinaire. Séance du 28 mai 1821. *Archives parlementaires*, XXXI, 661, 667. *Discours* (1827-1828), I, 523-526.

1821/05/29   Chambre des Députés. Sur le projet de loi relatif au domaine extraordinaire. Séance du 29 mai 1821. *Archives parlementaires*, XXXI, 672-673, 683-684. *Discours* (1827-1828), I, 526-527.

1821/06/04   Chambre des Députés. Sur la discussion du budget des dépenses de 1821. Séance du 4 juin 1821. *Archives parlementaires*, XXXI, 758-759. *Discours* (1827-1828), I, 528-530.

1821/06/06   Chambre des Députés. Sur le budget des dépenses de 1821. Article additionel à l'article 2 proposé par M. Delessert. Séance du 6 juin 1821. *Archives parlementaires*, XXXII, 23, 32-33.

1821/06/07   Chambre des Députés. Sur le budget des dépenses de 1821. Amendement de M. Labbey de Pompières au paragraphe concernant le conseil du Roi. Séance du 7 juin 1821. *Archives parlementaires*, XXXII, 48-50. *Discours* (1827-1828), I, 530-537.

1821/06/08   Chambre des Députés. Sur le budget des dépenses de 1821. Séance du 8 juin 1821. *Archives parlementaires*, XXXII, 67.

1821/06/09   Chambre des Députés. Sur le budget des dépenses de 1821. Séance du 9 juin 1821. *Archives parlementaires*, XXXII, 85-86.

1821/06/13   Chambre des Députés. Sur le budget des dépenses de 1821. Séance du 13 juin 1821. *Archives parlementaires*, XXXII, 144-145.

1821/06/15   Chambre des Députés. Sur le budget des dépenses de 1821. Séance du 15 juin 1821. *Archives parlementaires*, XXXII, 189-190.

1821/06/16   Chambre des Députés. Sur le budget des dépenses de 1821; chapitre XV: secours aux colons et autres réfugiés, théâtres, etc. Séance du 16 juin 1821. *Archives parlementaires*, XXXII, 206.

1821/06/18   Chambre des Députés. Sur le budget des dépenses de 1821; dépenses de l'instruction publique. Séance du 18 juin 1821. *Archives parlementaires*, XXXII, 225, 231-232.

1821/06/19   *Curso de política constitucional, escrito por Mr Benjamín Constant, traducido libremente al español par D. Marcial Antonio López*, Burdeos: impr. Lawalle jóven y sobrino, 1821. Dépôt légal: 19 June 1821. C.131d. *Checklist* E1/t3.

1821/06/23   Chambre des Députés. Sur le budget des dépenses de 1821. Séance du 23 juin 1821. *Archives parlementaires*, XXXII, 315-318. *Discours* (1827-1828), I, 537-548.

1821/06/26   'Au Rédacteur', *Le Courrier français*, n° 173, 26 juin 1821, p.4. *Checklist* D291.

1821/06/27   Chambre des Députés. Sur le budget des dépenses de 1821. Ministère de la marine. Chapitre XI. Séance du 27 juin 1821. *Archives parlementaires*, XXXII, 414-416. Edition: *Opinion* ... Paris: impr. Constant-Chantpie, 1821; dépôt légal: 29 June 1821. C.102a. *Checklist* B39. *Discours* (1827-1828), I, 548-560; Pléiade (1957), pp.1321-1329.

1821/07/02   Chambre des Députés. Sur le projet de loi relatif à l'achèvement de divers canaux. Séance du 2 juillet 1821. *Archives parlementaires*, XXXII, 518-519.

1821/07/03   'Au Rédacteur', *Le Courrier français*, n° 180, 3 juillet 1821, p.2. *Checklist* D292.

1821/07/07   Chambre des Députés. Sur le projet de loi relatif à la censure des journaux. Séance du 7 juillet 1821. *Archives parlementaires*, XXXII, 613-615. *Discours* (1827-1828), I, 560-570; Pléiade (1957), pp.1329-1336.

1821/07/09   Chambre des Députés. Sur le projet de loi relatif à la censure des journaux. Amendement de M. Benjamin Constant. Séance du 9 juillet 1821. *Archives parlementaires*, XXXII, 648-650. *Discours* (1827-1828), I, 571-574.

1821/07/11   Chambre des Députés. Sur le budget des recettes de l'exercice 1821. Séance du 11 juillet 1821. *Archives parlementaires*, XXXII, 748.

1821/07/12   Chambre des Députés. Sur le budget des recettes de 1821. Amendement de M. Humbert de Sesmaisons. Séance du 12 juillet 1821. *Archives parlementaires*, XXXII, 762-763.

1821/07/16   Chambre des Députés. Sur le budget des recettes de 1821. Séance du 16 juillet 1821. *Archives parlementaires*, XXXIII, 38-40.

1821/07/19   Chambre des Députés. Sur le budget des recettes de 1821. Amendements relatifs au dégrèvement par rapport au cens électoral. Séance du 19 juillet 1821. *Archives parlementaires*, XXXIII, 135. *Discours* (1827-1828), I, 575-576.

1821/07/21   Chambre des Députés. Sur le budget des recettes de 1821. Séance du 21 juillet 1821. *Archives parlementaires*, XXXIII, 170.

1821/07/21   Chambre des Députés. Sur le projet de loi tendant à augmenter le nombre de juges du tribunal de première instance de la Seine. Séance du 21 juillet 1821. *Archives parlementaires*, XXXIII, 176, 177.

1821/[07]/[ante 30]   *Pascaline, par Mme L. D'E**, auteur d'Alphonse et Mathilde*, Paris: Ch.

Villet, 1821. 2 vols. By Louise d'Estournelles, with corrections by Constant. *Bibliographie de la France*, 12 January 1822. See the following item. C.C2. *Checklist* C5/1.

1821/07/30 '*Pascaline*, par Madame L. d'E** auteur d'*Alphonse et Mathilde*', *Le Courrier français*, n° 208, 30 juillet 1821, p.4. *Checklist* D293.

1821/08/09 'Au Rédacteur', *Le Courrier français*, n° 218, 9 août 1821, p.3. *Checklist* D294.

1821/08/12 *Incipit*: 'La cour d'assises de Paris', *Le Courrier français*, n° 221, 12 août 1821, pp.2-3. *Checklist* D295.

1821/08/22 '*Histoire de l'Assemblée constituante*; par M. Ch. Lacretelle', *Le Courrier français*, n° 230, 22 août 1821, pp.3-4. *Checklist* D296.

1821/08/30 '*Histoire de l'Assemblée constituante*, par M. Ch. Lacretelle', *Le Courrier français*, n° 238, 30 août 1821, pp.3-4. *Checklist* D297.

1821/09/21 '*Voyage aux Alpes et en Italie*, par M. Albert Montémont', *Le Courrier français*, n° 258, 21 septembre 1821, p.4. *Checklist* D298.

1821/09/29 '*Histoire de la session de 1820*, par J. Fiévée', *Le Courrier français*, n° 266, 29 septembre 1821, pp.2-3. *Checklist* D299.

1821/09/29 *Incipit*: '*Le Drapeau blanc* prend occasion d'une brochure', *Le Courrier français*, n° 226, 29 septembre 1821, p.3. *Checklist* D300.

1821/10/02 *Incipit*: 'Nous avons sous les yeux le journal du fameux Cobbet', *Le Courrier français*, n° 269, 2 octobre 1821, p.4. *Checklist* D301.

1821/10/07 *Incipit*: 'Au moment où nous prenions la plume', *Le Courrier français*, n° 274, 7 octobre 1821, p.2. *Checklist* D302.

1821/10/22 'A Monsieur le rédacteur', *Le Courrier français*, n° 288, 22 octobre 1821, pp.3-4. *Checklist* D303.

1821/11/24 *Incipit*: '*Le Journal des Débats*, en rapportant le jugement', *Le Courrier français*, n° 320, 24 novembre 1821, pp.2-3. *Checklist* D304.

1821/12/08 Chambre des Députés. Sur la nomination de deux commissions pour l'examen des deux projets de loi sur les délits de la presse et la censure des journaux. Séance du 8 juillet 1821. *Archives parlementaires*, XXXIII, 679.

1821/12/20 Chambre des Députés. Sur la pétition du sieur Touquet, éditeur, relative à la censure. Séance du 20 décembre 1821. *Archives parlementaires*, XXXIII, 738.

1821/12/22 Chambre des Députés. Proposition de M. Benjamin Constant relative au règlement. Séance du 22 décembre 1821. *Archives parlementaires*, XXXIII, 752-53. Edition: *Opinion* ... [Paris]: impr. Constant-Chantpie, 1821; dépôt légal: 26 December 1821. C.103a. *Checklist* B40.

1821/-/- 'On the Dissolution of the Chamber of Deputies, and on the possible consequence of this dissolution to the nation, the gouvernement, and the ministry', *The Pamphleteer*, XVIII (1821), 97-128. C.46c. *Checklist* A46/t1, D305.

1822

1822/01/09 *Commentaire sur l'ouvrage de Filangieri*, Paris: Dufart, 1822. Dépôt légal: 9 January 1822. C.50a(1). *Checklist* A50/1.

1822/01/11 Chambre des Députés. Sur la pétition du sieur Spy (Châlons-sur-Marne), demandant que les délits de la presse soient portés devant les juges et non devant les jurys. Séance du 11 janvier 1822. *Archives parlementaires*, XXXIV, 25-26. Edition: *Opinion ...* [Paris]: impr. Constant-Chantpie, 1822; dépôt légal: 14 January 1822. C.104a. *Checklist* B41. *Discours* (1827-1828), II, 1-5.

1822/01/11   Chambre des Députés. Sur le projet de loi portant modification du budget de 1822. (Demande de M. Benjamin Constant de la nomination d'une commission spéciale pour l'examen du projet de loi). Séance du 11 janvier 1822. *Archives parlementaires*, XXXIV, 43-44.

1822/01/13   'Œuvres de Filangieri, traduites de l'italien, nouvelle édition, accompagnée d'un commentaire, par M. Benjamin Constant ...', *Le Courrier français*, n° 13, 13 janvier 1822, p.4. *Checklist* D306.

1822/01/14   Chambre des Députés. Sur le projet de loi relatif à la répression des délits de la presse. (Sur la fixation du jour pour la discussion du projet de loi). Séance du 14 janvier 1822. *Archives parlementaires*, XXXIV, 68. *Discours* (1827-1828), II, 6-8.

1822/01/19   Chambre des Députés. Sur le projet de loi relatif à la répression des délits de la presse. (Contre l'impression du rapport de Martignac). Séance du 19 janvier 1822. *Archives parlementaires*, XXXIV, 103.

1822/01/25   Chambre des Députés. Sur le projet de loi relatif à la repression des délits de la presse. Séance du 25 janvier 1822. *Archives parlementaires*, XXXIV, 179, 194-195. *Discours* (1827-1828), II, 9-16.

1822/01/28   *A Messieurs les électeurs du premier arrondissement du département de la Seine*, [Paris, 1822]. *Signed*: 'Benjamin Constant ... ce 28 janvier 1822'. C.51a. *Checklist* A51/1.

1822/01/28   Chambre des Députés. Sur le projet de loi relatif à la répression des délits de la presse. Article 4. Amendement de M. Darrieux. Séance du 28 janvier 1822. *Archives parlementaires*, XXXIV, 258.

1822/01/29   Chambre des Députés. Sur le projet de loi relatif à la répression des délits de la presse. Article 5. Séance du 29 janvier 1822. *Archives parlementaires*, XXXIV, 277. *Discours* (1827-1828), II, 17-24.

1822/01/30   Chambre des Députés. Sur le projet de loi relatif à la répression des délits de la presse. Articles 7 et 8. Séance du 30 janvier 1822. *Archives parlementaires*, XXXIV, 288, 291-292. *Discours* (1827-1828),II, 24-29.

1822/01/31   Chambre des Députés. Sur le projet de loi relatif à la répression des délits de la presse. Article 9. Séance du 31 janvier 1822. *Archives parlementaires*, XXXIV, 308-10. Edition: *Opinion ... dans la discussion sur le projet de loi relatif à la presse*, [Paris]: impr. Constant-Chantpie, 1822; dépôt légal: 2 February 1822. C.105a. *Checklist* B42. *Discours* (1827-1828), II, 29-40.

1822/02/01   Chambre des Députés. Sur le projet de loi relatif à la répression des délits de la presse. Article 11. Séance du 1er février 1822. *Archives parlementaires*, XXXIV, 337-338. *Discours* (1827-1828), II, 41-43.

1822/02/02   Chambre des Députés. Sur le projet de loi relatif à la répression des délits de la presse. Article 13. Séance du 2 février 1822. *Archives parlementaires*, XXXIV, 356-357. *Discours* (1827-1828), II, 43-47.

1822/02/03   'A M. le Rédacteur', *Le Courrier français*, n° 34, 3 février 1822, p.4. *Checklist* D307.

1822/02/04   Chambre des Députés. Sur le projet de loi relatif à la répression des délits de la presse. Article 14. Séance du 4 février 1822. *Archives parlementaires*, XXXIV, 372.

Edition: *Opinion ... dans la discussion sur le projet de loi relatif au jury*, [Paris]: impr. Constant-Chantpie, 1822; dépôt légal: 11 February 1822. C.106a. *Checklist* B43.

1822/02/06   Chambre des Députés. Sur le projet de loi relatif à la répression des délits de la presse. Séance du 6 février 1822. *Archives parlementaires*, XXXIV, 404-406. *Discours* (1827-1828), II, 47-55.

1822/02/07   'Au Rédacteur', *Le Courrier français*, n° 38, 7 février 1822, pp.3-4. *Checklist* D308.

1822/02/09   Chambre des Députés. Sur le projet de loi relatif à la presse périodique. Séance du 9 février 1822. *Archives parlementaires*, XXXIV, 501-502. Edition: *Opinion ... sur le projet de loi relatif à la police des journaux*, [Paris]: Constant-Chantpie, 1822; dépôt légal: 15 February 1822. C.107a. *Checklist* B44. *Discours* (1827-1828), II, 56-72.

1822/02/09   Chambre des Députés. Sur le projet de loi relatif à la presse périodique: amendements. Séance du 9 février 1822. *Archives parlementaires*, XXXIV, 509.

1822/02/11   Chambre des Députés. Sur la pétition des habitants de Magny-le-Freulle (Calvados). Séance du 11 février 1822. *Archives parlementaires*, XXXIV, 511.

1822/02/13   Chambre des Députés. Sur le projet de loi relatif à la presse périodique. Séance du 13 février 1822. *Archives parlementaires*, XXXIV, 552-553.

1822/02/14   Chambre des Députés. Sur le projet de loi relatif à la presse périodique. Article 3. Amendement de M. Benjamin Constant. Séance du 14 février 1822. *Archives parlementaires*, XXXIV, 567-570, 579. *Discours* (1827-1828), II, 73-84.

1822/02/16   Chambre des Députés. Sur le projet de loi relatif à la presse périodique. Article 4. Amendement de M. Benjamin Constant. Séance du 16 février 1822. *Archives parlementaires*, XXXIV, 614-616. *Discours* (1827-1828), II, 84-95.

1822/02/22   Chambre des Députés. Sur la pétition du sieur Clausel, prêtre, propriétaire à Nogent-le-Roi. Séance du 22 février 1822. *Archives parlementaires*, XXXIV, 699.

1822/02/23   'A M. le Rédacteur', *Le Courrier français*, n° 54, 23 février 1822, pp.1-2. *Checklist* D309.

1822/02/23   Chambre des Députés. Sur le projet de loi portant règlement définitif du budget de 1820. (Sur l'impression du discours de Caumartin). Séance du 23 février 1822. *Archives parlementaires*, XXXIV, 727.

1822/03/01   Chambre des Députés. Sur le projet de loi relatif au règlement définitif du budget de 1820. 2ᵉ projet de loi. (Sur l'impression d'un discours du chevalier de Berbis). Séance du 1ᵉʳ mars 1822. *Archives parlementaires*, XXXV, 158-159.

1822/03/02   Chambre des Députés. Sur le projet de loi relatif au règlement définitif du budget de 1820. 4ᵉ projet de loi. Séance du 2 mars 1822. *Archives parlementaires*, XXXV, 186-188. *Discours* (1827-1828), II, 96-101.

1822/03/06   'Au rédacteur', *Le Courrier français*, n° 65, 6 mars 1822, pp.1-2. *Checklist* D310.

1822/03/08   Chambre des Députés. Sur le projet de loi portant règlement définitif du budget de 1820. Séance du 8 mars 1822. *Archives parlementaires*, XXXV, 327, 328.

1822/03/11   Chambre des Députés. Sur la pétition du sieur Sauquaire-Souligné. Séance du 11 mars 1822. *Archives parlementaires*, XXXV, 367-68. *Discours* (1827-1828), II, 101-107.

1822/03/13   Chambre des Députés. Sur le budget des dépenses de l'exercice 1822.

Séance du 13 mars 1822. *Archives parlementaires*, XXXV, 443-48. Editions: *Discours ...sur la loi relative aux finances*, Paris: Plancher 1822; dépôt légal: 16 March 1822; *Discours ...* [Paris]: impr. Constant-Chantpie, 1822; dépôt légal: 21 March 1822. C.108a-b. *Checklist* B45/1-2. *Discours* (1827-1828), II, 108-130, 131.

1822/03/18   'Au rédacteur', *Le Courrier français*, n° 77, 18 mars 1822, p.3. *Checklist* D311.

1822/03/20   Chambre des Députés. Sur le projet de loi relatif à la répression des délits de la presse. Incident sur la communication de ce projet de loi, amendé par la Chambre des Pairs. Séance du 20 mars 1822. *Archives parlementaires*, XXXV, 553, 554-555.

1822/03/22   Chambre des Députés. Sur le budget des dépenses de l'exercice 1822. Séance du 22 mars 1822. *Archives parlementaires*, XXXV, 582, 583.

1822/03/24   *Incipit*: 'Le roi d'Espagne, à peine arrivé à Aranjuez', *Le Courrier français*, n° 83, 24 mars 1822, p.3. *Checklist* D312.

1822/03/25   *Incipit*: '*L'Etoile* réfute l'assertion d'un député', *Le Courrier français*, n° 84, 25 mars 1822, p.2. *Checklist* D313.

1822/03/27   Chambre des Députés. Sur le budget des dépenses de de l'exercice 1822. Ministère de l'intérieur. Chapitre XIII. Dépenses variables des départements. Séance du 27 mars 1822. *Archives parlementaires*, XXXV, 663, 665. *Discours* (1827-1828), II, 131-137.

1822/03/29   *Incipit*: 'On raconte qu'un soldat', *Le Courrier français*, n° 88, 29 mars 1822, p.6. *Checklist* D314.

1822/03/29   Chambre des Députés. Sur le budget des dépenses de l'exercice 1822. Ministère de la guerre. Séance du 29 mars 1822. *Archives parlementaires*, XXXV, 748, 768-769.

1822/03/30   Chambre des Députés. Sur le projet de loi relatif au budget des dépenses de l'exercice 1822. Ministère de la guerre. Chapitre X. (Frais de justice militaire). Séance du 30 mars 1822. *Archives parlementaires*, XXXVI, 3, 8.

1822/04/01   'Au rédacteur', *Le Courrier français*, n° 91, 1er avril 1822, p.2. *Checklist* D315.

1822/04/01   *Incipit*: '*L'Etoile* d'hier, 30 mars', *Le Courrier français*, n° 91, 1er avril 1822, p.2. *Checklist* D316.

1822/04/01   *Incipit*: 'La *Gazette de France* attaque un député', *Le Courrier français*, n° 91, 1er avril 1822, pp.2-3. *Checklist* D317.

1822/04/01   *Incipit*: 'La Quotidienne prétend', *Le Courrier français*, n° 91, 1er avril 1822, p.3. *Checklist* D318.

1822/04/01   *Incipit*: 'Les personnes qui connaissent les doctrines politiques que l'*Etoile* professe', *Le Courrier français*, n° 91, 1er avril 1822, p.4. *Checklist* D319.

1822/04/03   Chambre des Députés. Sur le budget des dépenses du budget de l'exercice 1822. Ministère de la Marine. Chapitre des colonies. Séance du 3 avril 1822. *Archives parlementaires*, XXXVI, 75-77. Edition: *Opinion ... sur le chapitre XI du budget du Ministère de la Marine*, [Paris]: impr. Hacquart, 1822. C.109a; *Checklist* B46. *Discours* (1827-1828), II, 137-144; Pléiade (1957), pp.1337-1341.

1822/04/04   *Incipit*: 'A qui en veut donc le *Drapeau Blanc*', *Le Courrier français*, n° 94, 4 avril 1822, p.1. *Checklist* D320.

1822/04/05   'A M. le Rédacteur', *Le Courrier français*, n° 95, 5 avril 1822, p.3. *Checklist* D321.

1822/04/06   Chambre des Députés. Sur la pétition du sieur Bourgeois, ancien militaire, à Amiens. Séance du 6 avril 1822. *Archives parlementaires*, XXXVI, 109.

1822/04/06   Chambre des Députés. Sur le budget des dépenses de de l'exercice 1822. Ministère des Finances. Chapitre IX. (Cour des comptes). Séance du 6 avril 1822. *Archives parlementaires*, XXXVI, 111-12.

1822/04/09   Chambre des Députés. Sur le budget des dépenses de l'exercice 1822. Ministère des finances, 3ᵉ partie. Chapitre II, (Douanes). Chapitre IV (Contributions indirectes). Séance du 9 avril 1822. *Archives parlementaires*, XXXVI, 172-173, 179, 180-181.

1822/04/10   Chambre des Députés. Sur la rédaction du procès-verbal. (Sur les destitutions des fonctionnaires). Séance du 10 avril 1822. *Archives parlementaires*, XXXVI, 188-189.

1822/04/10   Chambre des Députés. Sur le budget des dépenses de l'exercice 1822. Ministère des finances. 3ᵉ partie. Amendement de M. Benjamin Constant (Passeports). Séance du 10 avril 1822. *Archives parlementaires*, XXXVI, 202-203 (passeports); 204 (contre la clôture).

1822/04/11   Chambre des Députés. Sur le budget des recettes de l'exercice 1822. (Sur la clôture). Séance du 11 avril 1822. *Archives parlementaires*, XXXVI, 230.

1822/04/11   *Opinions prononcées dans la Chambre des Députés durant les sessions de 1818, 1819, 1821, par M. Benjamin Constant*, Paris: impr. Goetschy, 1822. (Prospectus). Dépôt légal: 11 April 1822. This projected edition never materialized. C.D4. *Checklist* E2.

1822/04/13   *Incipit*: 'Le Drapeau Blanc était hier plus naïf encore', *Le Courrier français*, nᵒ 103, 13 avril 1822, p.1. *Checklist* D322.

1822/04/13   Chambre des Députés. Sur le budget des recettes de l'exercice 1822. (Contre la clôture). Séance du 13 avril 1822. *Archives parlementaires*, XXXVI, 303.

1822/04/14   *Incipit*: 'Le Drapeau Blanc rapporte qu'un membre des Cortès', *Le Courrier français*, nᵒ 104, 14 avril 1822, p.1. *Checklist* D323.

1822/04/14   'Au rédacteur', *Le Courrier français*, nᵒ 104, 14 avril 1822, p.4. *Checklist* D324.

1822/04/19   Chambre des Députés. Sur l'ordre du jour. Séance du 19 avril 1822. *Archives parlementaires*, XXXVI, 449.

1822/04/23   'Au rédacteur', *Le Courrier français*, nᵒ 113, 23 avril 1822, pp.2-3. *Checklist* D325.

1822/04/29   '*Fastes civils de la France depuis l'ouverture de l'Assemblée des notables*, par MM. Dupont de l'Eure, Etienne, Manuel, Pagès, Tissot, Alex Goujon, Paris, 1822', *Le Courrier français*, nᵒ 119, 29 avril 1822, pp.3-4. *Checklist* D326.

1822/05/05   'Au Rédacteur', *Le Courrier français*, nᵒ 125, 5 mai 1822, pp.2-3. *Checklist* D327.

1822/05/07   *Incipit*: 'Le Drapeau Blanc consacre deux colonnes à prouver', *Le Courrier français*, nᵒ 127, 7 mai 1822, pp.1-2. *Checklist* D328.

1822/05/09   'Au rédacteur', *Le Courrier français*, nᵒ 129, 9 mai 1822, pp.1-2. *Checklist* D329.

1822/05/10   *Lettre adressée à M. le rédacteur du Courrier français*, [Paris]: impr. Constant-Chantpie, [1822]. *Signed*: 'Benjamin Constant'. Dépôt légal: 10 May 1822. C.52a. *Checklist* A52/1.

1822/05/13   *Incipit*: 'Sur les huit candidats', *Le Courrier français*, n° 133, 13 mai 1822, p.2. *Checklist* D330.

1822/05/16   'Portrait des électeurs payant 300 fr. (Extrait de la *Gazette de France* du 14 mai)', *Le Courrier français*, n° 136, 16 mai 1822, pp.4. *Checklist* D331.

1822/05/17   *Incipit*: 'Les journaux de l'aristocratie', *Le Courrier français*, n° 137, 17 mai 1822, p.3. *Checklist* D332.

1822/05/20   *Incipit*: 'Les élections de Paris sont terminées', *Le Courrier français*, n° 140, 20 mai 1822, pp.2-4. *Checklist* D333.

1822/05/26   *Incipit*: 'Nous lisons aujourd'hui, dans le *Journal des Débats*', *Le Courrier français*, n° 146, 26 mai 1822, p.2. *Checklist* D334.

1822/05/30   'Au Rédacteur', *Le Courrier français*, n° 150, 30 mai 1822, p.3. *Checklist* D335.

1822/05/31   *Incipit*: '*La Quotidienne* déclare aujourd'hui', *Le Courrier français*, n° 151, 31 mai 1822, pp.2-3. *Checklist* D336.

1822/06/05   'Au Rédacteur', *Le Courrier français*, n° 156, 5 juin 1822, p.3. *Checklist* D337.

1822/06/06   Chambre des Députés. Sur les élections du département de la Seine. Séance du 6 juin 1822. *Archives parlementaires*, XXXVI, 553-554.

1822/06/10   Chambre des Députés. Sur l'adoption d'une adresse au Roi. Comité secret du 10 juin 1822. *Archives parlementaires*, XXXVI, 584.

1822/06/22   Chambre des Députés. Sur la pétition du sieur Grand, étudiant en droit à Paris. Séance du 22 juin 1822. *Archives parlementaires*, XXXVI, 720-721.

1822/06/28   Chambre des Députés. Sur le projet de loi relatif aux douanes. Séance du 28 juin 1822. *Archives parlementaires*, XXXVII, 77.

1822/06/29   Chambre des Députés. Sur la pétition du sieur Lebeuf, à Longjumeau (demandant l'abolition de la peine de mort). Séance du 29 juin 1822. *Archives parlementaires*, XXXVII, 89-90.

1822/06/29   Chambre des Députés. Sur le projet de loi relatif aux douanes. Séance du 29 juin 1822. *Archives parlementaires*, XXXVII, 102.

1822/07/05   *Incipit*: 'Un journal s'étonnait hier', *Le Courrier français*, n° 186, 5 juillet 1822, p.2. *Checklist* D338.

1822/07/12   'Au rédacteur', *Le Courrier français*, n° 193, 12 juillet 1822, pp.2-3. *Checklist* D339.

1822/07/12   Chambre des Députés. Développement par M. Benjamin Constant d'une proposition relative aux pétitions. Séance du 12 juillet 1822. *Archives parlementaires*, XXXVII, 350-351. *Discours* (1827-1828), II, 145-152.

1822/07/19   Chambre des Députés. Sur le budget des dépenses de l'exercice 1823. Séance du 19 juillet 1822. *Archives parlementaires*, XXXVII, 489, 490.

1822/07/20   Chambre des Députés. Sur diverses pétitions. Séance du 20 juillet 1822. *Archives parlementaires*, XXXVII, 496-97, 498-99. *Discours* (1827-1828), II, 152-155.

1822/07/22   Chambre des Députés. Sur le procès-verbal (demande en rectification). Séance du 22 juillet 1822. *Archives parlementaires*, XXXVII, 523.

1822/07/22   Chambre des Députés. Sur le budget des dépenses de l'exercice 1823. Chapitre IV. Cours et tribunaux. Séance du 22 juillet 1822. *Archives parlementaires*,

XXXVII, 534-536. *Discours* (1827-1828), II, 155-163.

1822/07/25   Chambre des Députés. Sur le budget des dépenses de l'exercice 1823. Chapitre II. Etablissements de bienfaisance. Séance du 25 juillet 1822. *Archives parlementaires*, XXXVII, 649-51. *Discours* (1827-1828), II, 164-169.

1822/07/26   Chambre des Députés. Sur le budget des dépenses de l'exercice 1823. Chapitre V. Sciences, belles-lettres, beaux-arts, théâtres royaux. Dépenses variables des départements. Séance du 26 juillet 1822. *Archives parlementaires*, XXXVII, 661, 679-680.

1822/07/27   Chambre des Députés. Sur le budget des dépenses de l'exercice 1823. Ministère de l'intérieur. Chapitre XV. Dépenses de la police générale. Séance du 27 juillet 1823. *Archives parlementaires*, XXXVII, 686-688. *Discours* (1827-1828), II, 169-178.

1822/07/29   Chambre des Députés. Sur le budget des dépenses de l'exercice 1823. Ministère de la guerre. (Sur l'impression du discours de M. de Lameth). Séance du 29 juillet 1822. *Archives parlementaires*, XXXVII, 715.

1822/07/29   Chambre des Députés. Sur le budget des dépenses de l'exercice 1823. Ministère de la guerre. Chapitre X. Justice militaire. Séance du 29 juillet 1822. *Archives parlementaires*, XXXVII, 720-721.

1822/07/30   *Mémoires sur les Cent Jours, en forme de lettres, avec des notes et documens inédits, deuxième et dernière partie*, Paris: Béchet aîné; Rouen: Béchet fils, 1822. Dépôt légal: 30 July 1822. C.42c. *Checklist* A42/3.

1822/07/31   Chambre des Députés. Sur le budget des dépenses de l'exercice 1823. Ministère de la Marine. Chapitre XI. Colonies. Séance du 31 juillet 1822. *Archives parlementaires*, XXXVII, 773-775. *Discours* (1827-1828), II, 179-181.

1822/08/01   Chambre des Députés. Sur le budget des dépenses de l'exercice 1823. Ministère des finances. Chapitre V. Chambre des pairs. Séance du 1er août 1822. *Archives parlementaires*, XXXVIII, 12-13, 16. *Discours* (1827-1828), II, 182-187.

1822/08/03   Chambre des Députés. Sur la proposition de M. le général Lapoype concernant les pétitions. Séance du 3 août 1822. *Archives parlementaires*, XXXVIII, 74, 75. *Discours* (1827-1828), II, 188-190.

1822/08/06   Chambre des Députés. Sur le budget des recettes de l'exercice 1823. Sur l'amendement de M. Dequeux Saint-Hilaire sur la réduction des traitements. Séance du 6 août 1822. *Archives parlementaires*, XXXVIII, 124-25. Edition: *Opinion … sur l'amendement de M. Dequeux Saint-Hilaire, tendant à obtenir une réduction proportionnelle sur les traitemens*, [Paris]: impr. Hacquart, 1822. C.110a. *Checklist* B47. *Discours* (1872-1828), II, 190-196.

1822/08/07   Chambre des Députés. Sur le budget des recettes de l'exercice 1823. Journaux. Séance du 7 août 1822. *Archives parlementaires*, XXXVIII, 149-150. *Discours* (1827-1828), II, 197-202.

1822/09/15   'Au Rédacteur', *Le Courrier français*, n° 258, 15 septembre 1822, p.4. *Checklist* D340.

1822/09/16   *Lettre à Monsieur le procureur-général de la cour royale de Poitiers*, Paris: impr. Constant-Chantpie, 1822. Dépôt légal: 16 September 1822. C.53a-b. *Checklist* A53/1-2.

1822/[09]/-   *Lettre à Monsieur le procureur-général de la cour royale de Poitiers, deuxième édition*, Bruxelles: Lecharlier, Lacrosse, Remy, Wahlen, 1822. Probably published shortly after the first edition. C.53c. *Checklist* A53/3.

1822/09/22   '*Théorie des Cortès, ou Histoire des grandes assemblées nationales des royaumes de Castille et de Léon*, par don Fr. Martinez Marina, traduit de l'espagnol par P.F.L. Fleury',

Le Courrier français, n° 265, 22 septembre 1822, pp.2-4. *Checklist* D341.

1822/10/06   *Incipit*: '*De M. de Villèle*, tel est le titre', *Le Courrier français*, n° 279, 6 octobre 1822, pp.1-2. *Checklist* D342.

1822/10/21   *Incipit*: 'Dans un département qui doit renouveler', *Le Courrier français*, n° 294, 21 octobre 1822, pp.1-2. *Checklist* D343.

1822/10/22   'Des droits des présidens dans les collèges électoraux', *Le Courrier français*, n° 295, 22 octobre 1822, p.2. *Checklist* D344.

1822/10/22   *Avis aux électeurs de la seconde série*, [Paris]: impr. Constant-Chantpie, [1822]. Dépôt légal: 22 October 1822. C.54a. *Checklist* A54/1.

1822/10/28   *Incipit*: 'On a beaucoup écrit sur la sainte-alliance', *Le Courrier français*, n° 301, 28 octobre 1822, pp.2-3. *Checklist* D345.

1822/10/30   *A MM. les électeurs du département de la Sarthe*, [Paris]: impr. Constant-Chantpie, [1822]. *Signed*: 'Benjamin Constant'. Dépôt légal: 30 October 1822. C.55a. *Checklist* 55/1.

1822/11/06   *Seconde lettre à Messieurs les électeurs de la Sarthe*, [Paris]: impr. Constant-Chantpie, [1822]. *Signed*: 'Benjamin Constant' and dated 'Paris ce 3 novembre 1822'. Dépôt légal: 6 November 1822. C.56a. *Checklist* A56/1.

1822/11/13   *Extrait des minutes du Greffe du Tribunal de première instance du département de la Seine, séant au Palais de Justice, à Paris*, [Paris]: impr. Constant-Chantpie, [1822]. Dépôt légal: 13 November 1822. C.111a. *Checklist* B48.

1822/12/19   *Note sur la plainte en diffamation contre M. Mangin, procureur-général près la Cour royale de Poitiers*, [Paris]: impr. Constant-Chantpie, [1822]. *Signed*: 'Benjamin Constant'. Dépôt légal: 19 December 1822. C.57a. *Checklist* A57/1.

1822/12/19   *Incipit*: 'L'année 1822 a été remarquable', *Le Courrier français*, n° 353, 19 décembre 1822, p.3. *Checklist* D346.

1822/12/24   *Incipit*: 'Nous nous sommes arrêtés', *Le Courrier français*, n° 358, 24 décembre 1822, p.4. *Checklist* D347.

1822/-/-   *Mémoires sur les Cent Jours, en forme de lettres, avec des notes et documens inédits*, Paris: Béchet aîné, Rouen: Béchet fils, 1822. Reissue. C.42b(1). *Checklist* A42/2.

1822/-/-   *Biografia universale*, vols. I-III, Venezia: Missiaglia, 1822. C. B1b. *Checklist* C1/t1.

1823

1823/01/02   *Incipit*: 'Personne ne peut avoir oublié', *Le Courrier français*, n° 2, 2 janvier 1823, pp.3-4. *Checklist* D348.

1823/01/27   *Incipit*: 'Il y a des argumens de position', *Le Courrier français*, n° 27, 27 janvier 1823, p.2. *Checklist* D349.

1823/03/12   *Incipit*: '*La Quotidienne*' essayait hier le raisonnement', *Le Courrier français*, n° 71, 12 mars 1823, p.3. *Checklist* D350.

1823/03/15   'Au rédacteur', *Le Courrier français*, n° 74, 15 mars 1823, pp.2-3. *Checklist* D351.

1823/03/19   *Incipit*: 'La *Gazette de France* s'épuise en raisonnement', *Le Courrier français*, n° 78, 19 mars 1823, p.2. *Checklist* D352.

1823/04/25-1823/05/09   *Curso de política constitucional*, traducido al español, por D. Marcial Antonio López, segunda edicion, Burdeos: impr. Lawalle jóven, 1823. 3 vols. Dépôt légal: 25 April-9 May 1823. C.131e. *Checklist* E1/t4.

1823/06/02   *Incipit*: 'Il y a des naïvetés précieuses', *Le Courrier français*, n° 153, 2 juin 1823, p.3. *Checklist* D353.

1823/06/07   'Fragment d'un Catéchisme constitutionnel', *Le Courrier français*, n° 158, 7 juin 1823, p.4. *Checklist* D354.

1823/06/10   'Logique et arithmétique tirées de l'*Etoile* et du *Journal des débats*', *Le Courrier français*, n° 161, 10 juin 1823, p.3. *Checklist* D355.

1823/06/12   *Incipit*: 'Des officiers de la 10ᵉ division', *Le Courrier français*, n° 163, 12 juin 1823, pp.3-4. *Checklist* D356.

1823/07/01   *Juillet 1823. De la religion, considérée dans sa source, ses formes et ses développements ... Prospectus*, [Paris]: impr. Firmin Didot. Dépôt légal: 1 July 1823. C.58. *Checklist* A58.

1823/07/14   'Prix de littérature et de politique', *Le Courrier français*, n° 195, 14 juillet 1823, pp.2-3. *Checklist* D357.

1823/07/19   *Incipit*: 'Hier *La Quotidienne* insultait M. le duc de Larochefoucault-Liancourt', *Le Courrier français*, n° 200, 19 juillet 1823, p.2. *Checklist* D358.

1823/07/20   *Incipit*: 'Des journaux français ont rapporté que Bessières a écrit', *Le Courrier français*, n° 201, 20 juillet 1823, p.3. *Checklist* D359.

1823/07/23   *Incipit*: '*La Quotidienne* ne recule pas', *Le Courrier français*, n° 204, 23 juillet 1823, p.2. *Checklist* D360.

1823/09/15   'A M. le Rédacteur', *Le Courrier français*, n° 258, 15 septembre 1823, p.2. *Checklist* D361.

1823/10/04   *Incipit*: 'Balaam voulait maudire et il bénissait', *Le Courrier français*, n° 277, 4 octobre 1823, p.2. *Checklist* D362.

1823/12/31   *Incipit*: 'Depuis la loi du 29 juin 1820', *Le Courrier français*, n° 365, 31 décembre 1823, p.2. *Checklist* D363.

1823/-/-   *Biografia universale*, vols VIII-XIII, Venezia: Missiaglia, 1823. C. B1b. *Checklist* C1/t1.

1824

1824/01/05   'A M. le Rédacteur', *Le Courrier français*, n° 5, 5 janvier 1824, p.2. *Checklist* D364.

1824/03/27   Chambre des Députés. Sur l'élection de M. Benjamin Constant. Séance du 27 mars 1824. *Archives parlementaires*, XXXIX, 617-620.

1824/03/27   Chambre des Députés. Sur l'élection de M. Benjamin Constant. Renvoi de l'élection à une commission spéciale. Séance du 27 mars 1824. *Archives parlementaires*, XXXIX, 620-631. *Discours* (1827-1828), II, 203-215; Pléiade (1957), pp.1342-1350.

1824/03/30   *De la religion, considérée dans sa source, ses formes et ses développements*, vol. I, Paris: Bossange père, Bossange frères, Treuttel et Würtz, Rey et Gravier, Renouard, Ponthieu, 1824. Dépôt légal: 30 March 1824. C.58a(1). *Checklist* A58/1(1).

1824/04/17   Chambre des Députés. Lettre de Benjamin Constant au Président. Séance du 17 avril 1824. (Letter dated 16 avril 1824). *Archives parlementaires*, XL, 15.

1824/04/- 'Assemblées représentatives', *Encyclopédie moderne*, III (1824). *Checklist* D364a.

1824/[05]/[12] *Consultation pour M. Benjamin Constant*, [Paris]: Gaultier-Laguionie, [1824]. Printed *ca.*12 May 1824. C.112a. *Checklist* B49.

1824/05/15 Chambre des Députés. Rapport par M. de Martignac sur les titres d'éligibilité de M. Benjamin Constant. Séance du 15 mai 1824. *Archives parlementaires*, XL, 564-573.

1824/05/21 Chambre des Députés. Discussion des conditions d'éligibilité de M. Benjamin Constant. Séance du 21 mai 1824. *Archives parlementaires*, XL, 647-665.

1824/05/22 Chambre des Députés. Discussion des conditions d'éligibilité de M. Benjamin Constant. Séance du 22 mai 1824. *Archives parlementaires*, XL, 671-685 (with Constant's speech pp.678-684). *Discours* (1827-1828), II, 216-243; Pléiade (1957), pp.1350-1368.

1824/05/29 Chambre des Députés. Sur le projet de loi relatif à la septennalité. Séance du 29 mai 1824. *Archives parlementaires*, XLI, 73.

1824/06/08 Chambre des Députés. Sur le projet de loi relatif à la septennalité. Séance du 8 juin 1824. *Archives parlementaires*, XLI, 300-306. Edition: *Discours dans la discussion du projet de la septennalité*, [Paris]: impr. Agasse, 1820. C.113a. *Checklist* B50. *Discours* (1827-1828), II, 243-273.

1824/06/24 'A M. le Rédacteur', *Le Constitutionnel*, 24 juin 1824. *Checklist* D365.

1824/06/28 Chambre des Députés. Sur le projet de loi relatif aux crédits supplémentaires pour l'exercice 1823. Séance du 28 juin 1824. *Archives parlementaires*, XLI, 613-614. Edition: *Discours dans la discussion du projet de loi relatif aux crédits supplémentaires pour l'exercice 1823*, [Paris]: impr. Agasse, 1824. C.114a. *Checklist* B51.

1824/07/02 'A M. le Rédacteur', *Le Constitutionnel*, 2 juillet 1824. *Checklist* D366.

1824/07/08 Chambre des Députés. Sur le projet de budget de 1825. Séance du 8 juillet 1824. *Archives parlementaires*, XLII, 74-77. Edition: *Opinion sur le budget de 1825*, [Paris]: impr. Hacquart, 1824. C.115a. *Checklist* B52. *Discours* (1827-1828), II, 274-289.

1824/07/14 Chambre des Députés. Sur le budget de 1824. Chapitre V. Agriculture, etc. Séance du 14 juillet 1824. *Archives parlementaires*, XLII, 284-285. Edition: *Opinion improvisée* à *l'occasion du chapitre V du budget du Ministère de l'intérieur*, [Paris]: impr. Hacquart, 1824. C.116a. *Checklist* B53.

1824/07/15 Chambre des Députés. Sur le budget de 1825. Chapitre XI. Dépenses variables des départements. Séance du 15 juillet 1824. *Archives parlementaires*, XLII, 303.

1824/07/16 Chambre des Députés. Sur le budget 1825. Chapitre X. Justice militaire. Séance du 16 juillet 1824. *Archives parlementaires*, XLII, 331. Edition: *Opinion sur le chapitre X du budget du Ministère de la guerre*, [Paris]: impr. Hacquart, 1824. C.117a. *Checklist* B54.

1824/07/17 Chambre des Députés. Sur la pétition du sieur Charpentier, ancien militaire. Séance du 17 juillet 1824. *Archives parlementaires*, XLII, 352.

1824/07/17 Chambre des Députés. Sur le budget de 1825. Chapitre XI. Colonies. Séance du 17 juillet 1824. *Archives parlementaires*, XLII, 365-367, 368. *Discours* (1827-1828), II, 289-300; Pozzo di Borgo (1964), II, 65-74.

1824/07/22 Chambre des Députés. Sur le budget de 1825. Jeux de la ville de Paris. Séance du 22 juillet 1824. *Archives parlementaires*, XLII, 457. Edition: *Opinion ... sur l'article du budget des recettes relatif aux jeux de la ville de Paris*, [Paris]: impr. Hacquart, 1824. C.118a. *Checklist* B55.

1824/07/29   *Adolphe, anecdote trouvée dans les papiers d'un inconnu, troisième édition*, Paris: Brissot-Thivars, 1824. Dépôt légal: 29 July 1824. C.18f. *Checklist* A18/6.

1824/07/-   'M. B. Constant's Work on Religion. To the Director of the European Review', *European Review*, July 1824, pp.322-324. *Checklist* D367.

1824/08/16   *Commentaire sur l'ouvrage de Filangieri, deuxième partie*, Paris: Dufart, 1824. Dépôt légal: 16 August 1824. C.50a(2). *Checklist* A50/2.

1824/08/-   'De la religion, par M. Benjamin Constant', *Revue européenne*, août 1824, 306-308. *Checklist* D368.

1824/[09]/-   *De la religion, considérée dans sa source, ses formes et ses développements*, vol. I, Bruxelles: Mat, 1824. Unauthorized reprint. C.58b(1). *Checklist* A58/2(1).

1824/[09-12]/-   *De la religion, considérée dans sa source, ses formes et ses développements*, vol. I, Bruxelles: Tarlier, Voglet, 1824. Reprint. C.58c(1). *Checklist* A58/3(1).

1824/-/-   *Die Religion, nach ihrer Quelle, ihren Gestalten und ihren Entwickelungen* ... Deutsch herausgegeben von Dr. Philipp August Petri, Bd. I, Berlin: Reimer, 1824. C.58f(1). *Checklist* A58/t1.

1825

1825/01/01   Lettre au Président de la Chambre des Députés, 29 décembre 1824, *Le Moniteur universel*, 1er janvier 1825. *Checklist* D368a.

1825/01/08   Chambre des Députés. Sur la pétition de Me Isambert, avocat aux conseils, fondé de pouvoir des hommes de couleur de la Martinique, qui ont été déportés au Sénégal en 1824. Séance du 8 janvier 1825. *Archives parlementaires*, XLII, 651. *Discours* (1827-1828), II, 301-305.

1825/01/26   Chambre des Députés. Sur la pétition de M. Gambier. Séance du 26 janvier 1825. *Archives parlementaires*, XLII, 713-714. *Discours* (1827-1828), II, 305-309.

1825/02/08   Chambre des Députés. Sur le règlement. Séance du 8 février. *Archives parlementaires*, XLIII, 63-65.

1825/02/11   Chambre des Députés. Sur le projet de loi concernant l'indemnité à accorder aux émigrés. Séance du 11 février 1824. *Archives parlementaires*, XLIII, 122-124.

1825/02/14   Chambre des Députés. Sur l'élection de M. Lebeau. Séance du 14 février 1825. *Archives parlementaires*, XLIII, 164, 165, 166.

1825/02/22   Chambre des Députés. Sur le procès-verbal. Séance du 22 février 1825. *Archives parlementaires*, XLIII, 354, 355.

1825/02/22   Chambre des Députés. Sur le projet de loi d'indemnité à accorder aux émigrés. Séance du 22 février 1825. *Archives parlementaires*, XLIII, 374.

1825/02/23   Chambre des Députés. Sur le projet de loi d'indemnité à accorder aux émigrés. Séance du 23 février 1825. *Archives parlementaires*, XLIII, 389-394. Edition: *Discours sur le projet de loi d'indemnités*, [Paris]: impr. Firmin Didot, 1825; dépôt légal: 26 February 1825. C.119a. *Checklist* B56. *Discours* (1827-1828), II, 309-330; Pozzo do Borgo (1964), II, 97-116.

1825/03/04   Chambre des Députés. Sur le projet de loi d'indemnité à accorder aux émigrés. Article 2. Amendement de M. le général Foy. Séance du 4 mars 1825. *Archives parlementaires*, XLIII, 578-580.

1825/03/10   Chambre des Députés. Sur le projet de loi d'indemnité à accorder aux émigrés. Article 14. Amendement de M. Benjamin Constant. Séance du 10 mars 1825. *Archives parlementaires*, XLIII, 666-667.

1825/03/14   Chambre des Députés. Sur le projet de loi d'indemnité à accorder aux émigrés. Séance du 14 mars 1825 *Archives parlementaires*, XLIII, 743.

1825/03/15   Chambre des Députés. Sur l'amendement de M. Du Hamel renvoyé à la commission d'indemnité. Séance du 15 mars 1825. *Archives parlementaires*, XLIV, 6-7. *Discours* (1827-1828), II, 331-336.

1825/03/24   Chambre des Députés. Sur le projet de loi relatif à la dette publique et à l'amortissement. Article 3. Amendement de M. Benjamin Constant. Séance du 24 mars 1825. *Archives parlementaires*, XLIV, 248-251. *Discours* (1827-1828), II, 336-346.

1825/03/25   Chambre des Députés. Sur le projet de loi relatif à la dette publique et à l'amortissement. Articles 3 et 4. Amendements de M. Benjamin Constant et de M. Leroy. Séance du 25 mars 1825. *Archives parlementaires*, XLIV, 254-255, 264-265.

1825/03/26   Chambre des Députés. Sur la pétition du sieur Masson, charron, à Ponchard, Seine-et-Marne. Séance du 26 mars 1825. *Archives parlementaires*, XLIV, 267.

1825/03/26   Chambre des Députés. Sur diverses pétitions. (Contre la clôture). Séance du 26 mars 1825. *Archives parlementaires*, XLIV, 269.

1825/04/05   Chambre des Députés. Sur le projet de loi concernant la piraterie et la baraterie. Séance du 5 avril 1825. *Archives parlementaires*, XLIV, 422-426, 432-433.

1825/04/06   Chambre des Députés. Sur le projet de loi concernant les congrégations religieuses de femmes. Séance du 6 avril 1825. *Archives parlementaires*, XLIV, 465-466. Edition: *Opinion sur la loi relative au sacrilège*, [Paris]: impr. Béraud, 1825. C.120a. *Checklist* B57. *Discours*, (1827-1828), II, 347-365.

1825/04/08   Chambre des Députés. Sur la pétition de la dame Leskinakouska, Polonaise d'origine. Séance du 8 avril 1825. *Archives parlementaires*, XLIV, 481-482.

1825/04/14   Chambre des Députés. Sur le projet de loi sur le sacrilège. Séance du 14 avril 1825. *Archives parlementaires*, XLIV, 658-661, 661-663. Pozzo di Borgo (1964), II, 80-95.

1825/04/22   Chambre des Députés. Pétition du sieur Petit, à Paris, dépossédé d'un domaine national. Séance du 22 avril 1825. *Archives parlementaires*, XLV, 61.

1825/04/22   Chambre des Députés. Sur l'ouverture de la discussion des amendements de la Chambre des pairs au projet de loi relatif à l'indemnité des émigrés. Séance du 22 avril 1825. *Archives parlementaires*, XLV, 69-70.

1825/04/23   Chambre des Députés. Sur le projet de loi amendé par la Chambre des pairs concernant l'indemnité des émigrés. Séance du 23 avril 1825. *Archives parlementaires*, XLV, 78-79.

1825/04/26   *Extrait de l'Encyclopédie moderne. Christianisme, par M. Benjamin Constant*, [Paris]: impr. Moreau, [1825]. Dépôt légal: 26 April 1825. C.59a. *Checklist* A59/1, D369.

1825/04/28   Chambre des Députés. Sur le projet de loi portant règlement définitif du budget de 1823. Séance du 28 avril 1825. *Archives parlementaires*, XLV, 221-224. Edition: *Opinion sur le projet de loi portant règlement des crédits et des dépenses de l'exercice 1823*, [Paris]: Impr. royale, mai 1825. C.121a. *Checklist* B58. *Discours* (1827-1828), II, 366-382.

1825/05/03   Chambre des Députés. Sur la pétition du sieur Bordenave, capitaine au long cours, à La Rochelle. Séance du 3 mai 1825. *Archives parlementaires*, XLV, 312-313.

1825/05/06   *Comentario sobre la ciencia de la legislación de Filangieri*; traducido al castellano por D.J.C. Pages, 2 vols, Paris-Bruselas: Rosa, 1825. Dépôt légal: 6 May 1825. C.50b. *Checklist* A50/t1.

1825/05/07   'Christianisme. Causes humaines qui, indépendamment de sa source divine, ont concouru à son établissement', *Le Globe*, n° 104, 7 mai 1825, pp.521-523. *Checklist* D370.

1825/05/10   'Christianisme … Par M. Benjamin Constant. (IIe article)', *Le Globe*, n° 105, 10 mai 1825, pp.530-531. *Checklist* D371.

1825/05/10   Chambre des Députés. Sur le budget de 1826. Affaires étrangères. Chapitre 1er. Séance du 10 mai 1825. *Archives parlementaires*, XLV, 426-28. Edition: *Opinion … sur la discussion des articles du projet de loi relatif au budget de 1826*, [Paris]: Imprimerie royale, mai 1825. C.122a. *Checklist* B59.

1825/05/12   'Christianisme … Par M. Benjamin Constant (IIIe et dernier article)', *Le Globe*, n° 106, 12 mai 1825, pp.534-535. C.59.a. *Checklist* A59/1, D372.

1825/05/13   Chambre des Députés. Sur le budget de 1826. Ministère de l'intérieur. (Sur les censeurs dramatiques; sur les dépenses secrètes). Séance du 13 mai 1825. *Archives parlementaires*, XLV, 490-491.

1825/05/16   Chambre des Députés. Sur le budget de 1826. Ministère de la marine. Chapitre 1er. Administration centrale. Séance du 16 mai 1825. *Archives parlementaires*, XLV, 560-561; 563 (sur le parlement anglais).

1825/05/19   Chambre des Députés. Sur le budget de 1826. Sur l'article additionnel de M. Labbey de Pompierres. Séance du 19 mai 1825. *Archives parlementaires*, XLV, 610-611.

1825/08/21   'A M. le Rédacteur', *Le Courrier français*, n° 233, 21 août 1825, p.3. *Checklist* D373.

1825/09/03   *Curso de política constitucional*, traducido al castellano, por D.J.C. Pages, Paris: Parmantier; Mégico: Bossange, Antoran, 1825. 4 vols. Dépôt légal: 3 September 1825. C.131f. *Checklist* E1/t5.

1825/09/07   *Appel aux nations chrétiennes en faveur des Grecs, rédigé par M. Benjamin Constant; et adopté par le comité des Grecs de la Société de la morale chrétienne*, Paris: Treuttel et Würtz, 1825. Dépôt légal: 7 September 1825. C.60a. *Checklist* A60/1.

1825/09/13   *Extrait de l'Encyclopédie moderne. Christianisme. Par.* [*sic*] *M. Benjamin-Constant*, [Paris]: impr. Moreau, [1825]. Dépôt légal: 13 September 1825. C.59b. *Checklist* A59/2, D374.

1825/[09-12]/-   *Appel aux nations chrétiennes en faveur des Grecs, rédigé par M. Benjamin Constant; et adopté par le comité des Grecs de la Société de la morale chrétienne*, Paris: Treuttel et Würtz, 1825. Reprint. C.60b. *Checklist* A60/2.

1825/[09-12]/-   *Beroep op de Christen Natien, ten gunste der Grieken*, 's Gravenhage: Visser, 1825. C.60c. *Checklist* A60/t1.

1825/[09-12]/-   *Appell till de Christna Folken för Grekerna*, Stockholm: Nestius, 1825. C.60d. *Checklist* A60/t2.

1825/10/10   'A M. le Rédacteur', *Le Courrier français*, n° 283, 10 octobre 1825, p.2. *Checklist* D375.

1825/10/10   *De la religion, considérée dans sa source, ses formes et ses développements*, vol. II, Paris: Béchet aîné, 1825. Dépôt légal: 10 October 1825. C.58a(2). *Checklist* A58/1(2).

1825/[11-12]/-   *De la religion, considérée dans sa source, ses formes et ses développements*, vol. II, Bruxelles: Mat, 1825. C.58b(2). *Checklist* A58/2(2).

1825/[11-12]/-   *De la religion, considérée dans sa source, ses formes et ses développements*, vol. II, Bruxelles: Tarlier, Voglet, 1825. C.58c(2). *Checklist* A58/3(2).

1825/12/03   Discours prononcé dans la séance d'ouverture de l'Athénée royal de Paris, le 3 décembre 1825. See below under 23 December 1825.

1825/12/07   *Incipit*: 'Nous trouvons dans un journal littéraire la lettre suivante [de Benjamin Constant]', *Journal du Commerce*, n° 2172, 7 décembre 1825, p.2. *Checklist* D375a.

1825/12/23   *Coup d'œil sur la tendance générale des esprits dans le dix-neuvième siècle; extrait du discours prononcé par M. Benjamin Constant, dans la séance d'ouverture de l'Athénée royal de Paris, le 3 décembre 1825*, [Paris]: impr. Rignoux, [1825]. (*Revue encyclopédique*, 84ᵉ cahier, T. XXVIII). Dépôt légal: 23 December 1825. C.61a. *Checklist* A61/1, D376.

1826

1826/02/10   Chambre des Députés. Sur le projet d'adresse au Roi. Séance du 10 février 1826. *Archives parlementaires*, XLVI, 3, 4.

1826/02/20   Chambre des Députés. Sur la pétition du sieur Revol, ancien négociant à Orléans, demandant l'abolition de la peine de la marque. Séance du 20 février 1826. *Archives parlementaires*, XLVI, 62.

1826/02/20   Chambre des Députés. Sur la dénonciation par M. le comte de Salaberry d'un article du *Journal du Commerce*, offensant pour la Chambre. Séance du 20 février 1826. *Archives parlementaires*, XLVI, 68-69.

1826/02/21   Chambre des Députés. Sur la proposition de citer à la barre le *Journal du Commerce*. Séance du 21 février 1826. *Archives parlementaires*, XLVI, 91. *Discours* (1827-1828), II, 383-387.

1826/02/27   'A M. le Rédacteur,' *Le Courrier français*, n° 58, 27 février 1826, pp.1-2. *Checklist* D377.

1826/02/27   Chambre des Députés. Sur la procédure à suivre pour la comparution à la barre de l'éditeur du *Journal du Commerce*. Séance du 27 février 1826. *Archives parlementaires*, XLVI, 107-108.

1826/02/28   Chambre des Députés. Sur le procès-verbal. Séance du 28 février 1826. *Archives parlementaires*, XLVI, 109-110.

1826/02/-   '*L'Industrie et la morale considérées dans leur rapport avec la liberté*; par Charles-Barthélemi Dunoyer', *Revue encyclopédique*, XXIX (février 1826), pp.416-435. *Checklist* D377a.

1826/03/01   Chambre des Députés. Comparution à la barre de l'éditeur responsable du *Journal du Commerce*. Séance du 1ᵉʳ mars 1826. *Archives parlementaires*, XLVI, 143.

1826/03/06   Chambre des Députés. Sur la proposition de M. Boucher relative aux députés fonctionnaires. Comité secret du 6 mars 1826. *Archives parlementaires*, XLVI, 154.

1826/03/11   Chambre des Députés. Sur le droit de pétition. Séance du 11 mars 1826. *Archives parlementaires*, XLVI, 281-282.

1826/03/11   Chambre des Députés. Sur la pétition du sieur Marin, propriétaire à Paris, demandant la suppression des jeux et de la loterie. Séance du 11 mars 1826. *Archives parlementaires*, XLVI, 289-290.

1826/03/20   Chambre des Députés. Sur le projet de loi relatif à l'indemnité à accorder aux anciens colons de Saint-Domingue. Article 13. Amendement de M. Benjamin Constant. Séance du 20 mars 1826. *Archives parlementaires*, XLVI, 393-396, 405. Edition: *Discours ... dans la discussion des articles du projet de loi sur l'indemnité à accorder aux colons de Saint-Domingue*, [Paris]: impr. Agasse, 1826. C.123a. *Checklist* B60. *Discours* (1827-1828), II, 387-400.

1826/03/25   Chambre des Députés. Sur deux pétitions sollicitant une répression plus efficace de la traite des noirs. Séance du 25 mars 1826. *Archives parlementaires*, XLVI, 417-418.

1826/04/05   *De la religion, considérée dans sa source, ses formes et ses développements, deuxième édition*, vol. I, Paris: Leroux et Chantpie, Béchet aîné, 1826. Dépôt légal: 5 April 1826. C.58d(1). *Checklist* A58/4(1).

1826/04/08   Chambre des Députés. Sur la pétition des membres de la Société royale de médecine de Bordeaux concernant l'article 11 du projet de loi relatif aux écoles secondaires de médecine. Séance du 8 avril 1826. *Archives parlementaires*, XLVII, 29, 30.

1826/04/08   Chambre des Députés. Sur des pétitions relatives au droit d'aînesse. Séance du 8 avril 1826. *Archives parlementaires*, XLVII, 42, 46, 47.

1826/04/13   Chambre des Députés. Sur le projet de loi relatif aux douanes. Séance du 13 avril 1826. *Archives parlementaires*, XLVII, 126-127.

1826/04/15   Chambre des Députés. Sur le projet de loi relatif aux douanes. Séance du 15 avril 1826. *Archives parlementaires*, XLVII, 170.

1826/04/20   Chambre des Députés. Sur la proposition de M. de Cambon tendant à faire nommer une commission spéciale pour examiner les comptes relatifs à la guerre d'Espagne. Séance du 20 avril 1826. *Archives parlementaires*, XLVII, 294-96. *Discours* (1827-1828), II, 400-407.

1826/04/24   Chambre des Députés. Sur le projet de loi concernant le règlement définitif du budget de 1824. Séance du 24 avril 1826. *Archives parlementaires*, XLVII, 381-385. Edition: *Discours ... dans la discussion du projet de loi concernant le règlement définitif du budget de 1824*, [Paris]: impr. Agasse, 1826. C.124a. *Checklist* B61. *Discours* (1827-1828), II, 408-425.

1826/04/27   Chambre des Députés. Sur le projet de loi concernant le règlement définitif du budget de 1824. Séance du 27 avril 1826. *Archives parlementaires*, XLVII, 480-482. *Discours* (1827-1828), II, 426-432.

1826/04/28   Chambre des Députés. Sur le procès-verbal. Séance du 28 avril 1826. *Archives parlementaires*, XLVII, 491.

1826/04/29   Chambre des Députés. Sur le droit de pétition. Séance du 29 avril 1826. *Archives parlementaires*, XVLII, 520-522. *Discours* (1827-1828), II, 433-438.

1826/05/02   Chambre des Députés. Sur la proposition de M. Casimir Périer relative à l'amortissement. Séance du 2 mai 1826. *Archives parlementaires*, XLVII, 593-594.

1826/05/09   Chambre des Députés. Sur le projet de loi relatif aux substitutions. Séance du 9 mai 1826. *Archives parlementaires*, XLVII, 681-685. *Discours* (1827-1828), II, 438-462.

1826/05/12   Chambre des Députés. Sur la proposition de M. Casimir Périer relative à l'amortissement. Séance du 12 mai 1826. *Archives parlementaires*, XLVII, 761-762.

1826/05/13   Chambre des Députés. Sur la pétition de vingt-sept habitants de Paris relative à la répartition des fonds de l'amortissement. Séance du 13 mai 1826. *Archives parlementaires*, XLVIII, 6-8.

1826/05/17   Chambre des Députés. Sur le projet de loi de finances pour 1827. Séance du 17 mai 1826. *Archives parlementaires*, XLVIII, 105-108. Edition: *Discours ... dans la discussion générale du budget de 1827*, Paris: L'Huillier, 1826; dépôt légal: 23 May 1826. C.125a. *Checklist* B62. *Discours* (1827-1828), II, 462-474.

1826/05/22   'A M. le rédacteur ', *Le Constitutionnel*, 22 mai 1826, p.2. *Checklist* D378.

1826/05/23   Chambre des Députés. Sur le projet de loi de finances pour 1827. Article 2. Etat B. Ministère de la justice. Chapitre 3. Conseil d'Etat. Séance du 23 mai 1826. *Archives parlementaires*, XLVIII, 218-219. *Discours* (1827-1828), II, 475-480.

1826/05/24   Chambre des Députés. Sur le projet de loi de finances pour 1827. Article 2. Etat B. Ministère des affaires étrangères. Chapitre 1er. Dépenses fixes. Séance du 24 mai 1826. *Archives parlementaires*, XLVIII, 240-241, 245-246. *Discours* (1827-1828), II, 480-483.

1826/05/27   Chambre des Députés. Sur la pétition du sieur Marchand, avocat à Strasbourg, relative à la formation et à la composition du jury. Séance du 27 mai 1826. *Archives parlementaires*, XLVIII, 292.

1826/05/29   Chambre des Députés. Sur le projet de loi de finances pour 1827. Article 2. Etat B. Ministère de l'intérieur. Séance du 29 mai 1826. *Archives parlementaires*, XLVIII, 327-329. *Discours* (1827-1828), II, 483-489.

1826/06/03   Chambre des Députés. Sur le droit de pétition. Séance du 3 juin 1826. *Archives parlementaires*, XLVIII, 429, 430.

1826/06/03   Chambre des Députés. Sur le projet de loi de finances pour 1827. Art. 2. Etat B. Chapitre 10. Justice militaire. Séance du 3 juin 1826. *Archives parlementaires*, XLVIII, 433-436.

1826/06/05   Chambre des Députés. Sur le projet de loi de finances pour 1827. Art. 2. Etat B. Chapitre 18. Dépenses temporaires. Séance du 5 juin 1826. *Archives parlementaires*, XLVIII, 449, 450.

1826/06/05   Chambre des Députés. Proposition de M. Benjamin Constant relative à l'impression des discours sur les lois de finances. Comité secret du 5 juin 1826. *Archives parlementaires*, XLVIII, 453.

1826/06/06   Chambre des Députés. Sur le projet de loi de finances pour 1827. Art. 2. Etat B. Budget de la marine. Chapitre 1er. Séance du 6 juin 1826. *Archives parlementaires*, XLVIII, 470-472. *Discours* (1827-1828), II, 490-498.

1826/06/08   Chambre des Députés. Sur le projet de loi de finances pour 1827. Art. 2. Etat B. Budget du ministère des finances. Chapitre 7. Chambre des Pairs. Séance du 8 juin 1826. *Archives parlementaires*, XLVIII, 494-495.

1826/06/09   Chambre des Députés. Sur le projet de loi de finances pour 1827. Art. 2. Etat B. Chapitre 20. Loterie. Séance du 9 juin 1826. *Archives parlementaires*, XLVIII, 519. *Discours* (1827-1828), II, 499-501.

1826/06/10   Chambre des Députés. Sur le projet de loi de finances pour 1827. Article 3. Recettes. Impôts. Séance du 10 juin 1826. *Archives parlementaires*, XLVIII, 529-530. *Discours* (1827-1828), II, 501-509.

1826/06/15   Chambre des Députés. Sur diverses pétitions. Séance du 15 juin 1826. *Archives parlementaires*, XLVIII, 638, 639.

1826/06/26 *Encyclopédie progressive. Religion*, [Paris]: impr. Pinard, [1826]. Dépôt légal: 26 June 1826. C.62a. *Checklist* A62/1, D379.

1826/07/14 [Réponse aux électeurs], *Le Courrier français*, n° 195, 14 juillet 1826, pp.2-3. *Checklist* D380.

1826/08/08 *Incipit*: 'L'Etoile d'hier, 7 août', *Le Courrier français*, n° 220, 8 août 1826, p.2. *Checklist* D381.

1826/08/21 'De l'intervention de la France dans les affaires de Portugal', *Le Courrier français*, n° 233, 21 août 1826, p.2. *Checklist* D382.

1826/09/15 'A Monsieur le Rédacteur', *Le Courrier français*, n° 258, 15 septembre 1826, p.2. *Checklist* D383.

1826/12/22 Chambre des Députés. Sur la nomination de la commission de l'adresse. (Sur une demande de communication de pièces formulée par M. Casimir Périer). Séance du 22 décembre 1826. *Archives parlementaires*, XLIX, 41-42.

1826/12/28 Chambre des Députés. Sur l'adresse au Roi. Comité secret du 28 décembre 1826. *Archives parlementaires*, XLIX, 61-63. *Discours* (1827-1828), II, 510-518.

1826/-/- *Adolf*. Oversat af J.J. Østrup, Kjøbenhavn: Nissen, 1826. C.18m. *Checklist* A18/t5.

1826/-/- *Commentario alla scienza della legislazione di G. Filangieri; prima traduzione italiana*, Italia, 1826. C.50c. *Checklist* A50/t2.

1827

1827/01/31 Chambre des Députés. Sur diverses pétitions. Séance du 31 janvier 1827. *Archives parlementaires*, XLIX, 327-328.

1827/02/01 Chambre des Députés. Sur le projet de loi relatif au tarif des lettres. Séance du 1ᵉʳ février 1827. *Archives parlementaires*, XLIX, 343, 346-347. *Discours* (1827-1828), II, 519-530.

1827/02/03 Chambre des Députés. Sur le règlement. Séance du 3 février 1827. *Archives parlementaires*, XLIX, 392-393. *Discours* (1827-1828), II, 531-537.

1827/02/03 Chambre des Députés. Sur le projet de loi relatif à la taxe des lettres. Article 8. Séance du 3 février 1827. *Archives parlementaires*, XLIX, 404-406.

1827/02/12 Chambre des Députés. Sur la présentation du projet de loi primitif sur le jury avec les amendements votés par la Chambre des Pairs. Séance du 12 février 1827. *Archives parlementaires*, XLIX, 517.

1827/02/12 Chambre des Députés. Sur diverses pétitions. Séance du 12 février 1827. *Archives parlementaires*, XLIX, 519-520.

1827/02/13 Chambre des Députés. Sur le projet concernant la presse. Séance du 13 février 1827. *Archives parlementaires*, XLIX, 549-553. Edition: *Opinion sur le projet de loi relatif à la police de la presse*, [Paris]: Henry, 1827. C.126a. *Checklist* B63. *Discours* (1827-1828), II, 538-557; Laboulaye (1861, 1872), II, 25-40; Pléiade (1957), pp.1380-1393.

1827/02/14 Chambre des Députés. Sur le projet de loi concernant la presse. Séance du 14 février 1827. *Archives parlementaires*, XLIX, 558.

1827/02/16 Chambre des Députés. Sur le projet de loi concernant la presse. Séance du 16 février 1827. *Archives parlementaires*, XLIX, 615, 616-617.

1827/02/19   Chambre des Députés. Sur le projet de loi concernant la presse. Art. 1ᵉʳ. Amendement de M. de Saint-Chamans. Séance du 19 février 1827. *Archives parlementaires*, XLIX, 676.

1827/02/22   Chambre des Députés. Sur le projet de loi concernant la presse. Disposition additionelle de M. Benjamin Constant. Séance du 22 février 1827. *Archives parlementaires*, XLIX, 719-720, 722.

1827/02/23   Chambre des Députés. Sur le projet de loi concernant la presse. Séance du 23 février 1827. *Archives parlementaires*, XLIX, 731, 737-738.

1827/02/24   Chambre des Députés. Sur le projet de loi concernant la presse. Art. 3ᵉ. Sur l'amendement de M. Pardessus. Séance du 24 février 1827. *Archives parlementaires*, XLIX, 742-743.

1827/02/28   Chambre des Députés. Sur le projet de loi concernant la presse. Séance du 28 février 1827. *Archives parlementaires*, L, 18, 22, 24, 28-29.

1827/03/01   Chambre des Députés. Sur le projet de loi concernant la presse. Séance du 1ᵉʳ mars 1827. *Archives parlementaires*, L, 48-50.

1827/03/02   Chambre des Députés. Sur le projet de loi concernant la presse. Séance du 2 mars 1827. *Archives parlementaires*, L, 70, 71.

1827/03/03   Chambre des Députés. Sur le projet de loi concernant la presse. Article additionnel de M. Benjamin Constant. Séance du 3 mars 1827. *Archives parlementaires*, L, 79-80, 81.

1827/03/05   Chambre des Députés. Sur le procès-verbal. Séance du 5 mars 1827. *Archives parlementaires*, L, 88.

1827/03/05   Chambre des Députés. Sur le projet de loi concernant la presse. Séance du 5 mars 1827. *Archives parlementaires*, L, 90, 99-101, 106.

1827/03/07   Chambre des Députés. Sur le projet de loi concernant la presse. Séance du 7 mars 1827. *Archives parlementaires*, L, 134.

1827/03/10   Chambre des Députés. Sur le projet de loi concernant la presse. Séance du 10 mars 1827. *Archives parlementaires*, L, 197-200. *Discours* (1827-1828), II, 558-566; Laboulaye (1861, 1872), II, 41-48.

1827/03/12   Chambre des Députés. Sur le projet de loi concernant la presse. Séance du 12 mars 1827. *Archives parlementaires*, L, 271-273. *Discours* (1827-1828), II, 566-569.

1827/03/13   Chambre des Députés. Sur le projet de loi concernant la traite des noirs. Séance du 13 mars 1827. *Archives parlementaires*, L, 329-330. *Discours* (1827-1828), II, 569-573.

1827/03/15   Chambre des Députés. Sur une modification d'un règlement touchant le compte rendu des séances. Séance du 15 mars 1827. *Archives parlementaires*, L, 391-393. *Discours* (1827-1828), II, 574-582.

1827/03/27   Chambre des Députés. Sur le projet de code forestier. Bois et forêts du domaine de la couronne. Art. 86. Séance du 27 mars 1827. *Archives parlementaires*, L, 549-551.

1827/03/29   *Souscription pour l'impression de deux volumes contenant les Discours de M. Benjamin Constant à la Chambre des députés.* (Prospectus). Paris: impr. Everat, 1827. Dépôt légal: 29 March 1827. C.132. *Checklist* E2/1.

1827/03/31 Chambre des Députés. Sur diverses pétitions. Séance du 31 mars 1827. *Archives parlementaires*, L, 646.

1827/04/02 Chambre des Députés. Sur les obsèques du duc de La Rochefoucauld. Séance du 2 avril 1827. *Archives parlementaires*, L, 684, 685. *Discours* (1827-1828), II, 583-586.

1827/04/04 Chambre des Députés. Sur la proposition de M. La Boëssière, relative au règlement. Séance du 4 avril 1827. *Archives parlementaires*, L, 749-750.

1827/04/07 Chambre des Députés. Sur la pétition du sieur Lemonier, libraire à Lannion (Côtes-du-Nord) relative aux brevets de libraire. Séance du 7 avril 1827. *Archives parlementaires*, LI, 97.

1827/04/07 Chambre des Députés. Sur la pétition du sieur Martin, avocat à l'Orgues (département du Var) relative aux certificats de bonne conduite. Séance du 10 avril 1827. *Archives parlementaires*, LI, 148, 150.

1827/04/23 Chambre des Députés. Sur la proposition de M. de la Boëssière relative au règlement. Amendement de M. Benjamin Constant. Séance du 23 avril 1827. *Archives parlementaires*, LI, 411-414. *Discours* (1827-1828), II, 587-603.

1827/04/25 Chambre des Députés. Sur la pétition du sieur Jambard, à Paris, sur la loterie. Séance du 25 avril 1827. *Archives parlementaires*, LI, 471-472.

1827/04/26 Chambre des Députés. Sur le projet de loi concernant le règlement définitif du budget de 1825. Séance du 26 avril 1827. *Archives parlementaires*, LI, 476-479.

1827/04/27 Chambre des Députés. Sur le projet de loi concernant le règlement définitif du budget de 1825. (Sur le département des affaires étrangères). Séance du 27 avril 1827. *Archives parlementaires*, LI, 511-512.

1827/04/30 Chambre des Députés. Sur le projet de loi concernant les crédits supplémentaires pour 1826. Séance du 30 avril 1827. *Archives parlementaires*, LI, 563-565.

1827/05/01 Chambre des Députés. Sur la pétition du sieur Félix Mercier, suppléant destitué de la justice de paix à Rougemont (Doubs) relative aux pétitions contenant des accusations contre les ministres. Séance du 1er mai 1827. *Archives parlementaires*, LI, 566-567.

1827/05/03 Chambre des Députés. Sur la pétition du sieur de Piétri, de Sartine (Corse), réclamant la mise en vigueur dans ce département, de la loi sur le jury. Séance du 3 mai 1827. *Archives parlementaires*, LI, 597-598.

1827/05/08 Chambre des Députés. Sur le projet de budget pour 1828. Séance du 8 mai 1827. *Archives parlementaires*, LI, 660-664. *Discours* (1827-1828), II, 604-624.

1827/05/12 Chambre des Députés. Sur la pétition des propriétaires de terrains environnant les murs d'enceinte de la ville de Paris réclamant contre les actes arbitraires de l'administration municipale de Paris. Séance du 12 mai 1827. *Archives parlementaires*, LI, 745, 746.

1827/05/15 Chambre des Députés. Sur le projet de budget de 1828. Art. 2. Ministère de la justice. Chapitre 1er. Administration centrale. Séance du 15 mai 1827. *Archives parlementaires*, LII, 35-36.

1827/05/16 Chambre des Députés. Sur le projet de budget de 1828. Ministère de la Justice. Chapitre 8. Justice criminelle. Séance du 16 mai 1827. *Archives parlementaires*, LII, 61-62.

1827/05/18 Chambre des Députés. Sur le projet de budget de 1828. Ministère des affaires ecclésiastiques. Chapitre 10. Collèges et instruction primaire. Séance du 18 mai 1827. *Archives parlementaires*, LII, 129-135, 136. *Discours* (1827-1828), II, 624-634.

1827/05/26   Chambre des Députés. Sur les pétitions des sieurs Félix Mercier et du sieur Ricard, réclamant l'organisation de commissions de censure. Séance du 26 mai 1827. *Archives parlementaires*, LII, 291.

1827/05/29   [A un étudiant de médecine], *L'Indépendant*, n° 220, 29 mai 1827, p.3. *Checklist* D383a

1827/05/29   Chambre des Députés. Sur le projet de budget de 1828. Article 3. Recettes. Droits de timbre. Séance du 29 mai 1827. *Archives parlementaires*, LII, 327-28. *Discours* (1827-1828), II, 634-640.

1827/06/05   *Souscription aux discours de M. Benjamin Constant. (Prospectus)*. Paris: Dupont, Pinard, 1827. Dépôt légal: 5 June 1827. C.132. C. Suppl. Add. 5. *Checklist* E2/1

1827/06/09   *Souscription aux discours de M. Benjamin Constant* ... Paris: Dupont, Pinard, 1827. Dépôt légal: 9 June 1827. C.132. *Checklist* E2/1.

1827/06/30   'A M. le rédacteur', *Le Courrier français*, n° 181, 30 juin 1827, p.2. *Checklist* D384.

1827/07/10   *Discours de M. Benjamin Constant à la Chambre des Députés*, Tome premier, Paris: Dupont, 1827. Dépôt légal: 10 July 1827. C.132a(1). *Checklist* E2/1(1).

1827/08/13   *De la religion, considérée dans sa source, ses formes et ses développements*, vol. III, Paris: Béchet aîné, 1827. Dépôt légal: 13 August 1827. C.58b(3). *Checklist* A58/1(3).

1827/[09-12]/-   *De la religion, considérée dans sa source, ses formes et ses développements*, vol. III, Bruxelles: Mat, 1825 [=1827]. C.58b(3). *Checklist* A58/2(3).

1827/[09-12]/-   *De la religion, considérée dans sa source, ses formes et ses développements*, vol. III, Bruxelles: Tarlier, Voglet, 1827. C.58c(3). *Checklist* A58/3(3).

1827/11/11   Réponse de l'honorable M. Benjamin Constant au toast qui lui a été porté, au banquet qu'on lui a offert à son passage à Strasbourg, le 2 octobre dernier, *Courrier du Haut-Rhin*, 11 novembre 1827. *Checklist* D384a.

1827/11/13   Discours, Colmar, 16 octobre 1827, *Courrier du Haut-Rhin*, 13 novembre 1827. *Checklist* D384b.

1827/11/27   *Adolfo, anécdota hallada en los papeles de un desconocido, traduccíon castellana*, Paris: Belin, 1828 [=1827]. Dépôt légal: 27 November 1827. C.18n. *Checklist* A18/t6.

1827/12/04   Souscription. Recueil des discours de M. Benjamin Constant à la chambre des députés. *Le Courrier français*, n° 338, 4 décembre 1827, p.4. C.132. *Checklist* E2, D385.

1827/12/04   'A M. le rédacteur', *Le Courrier français*, n° 338, 4 décembre 1827, p.3. *Checklist* D386.

1827/-/-   *Die Religion, nach ihrer Quelle, ihren Gestalten und ihren Entwickelungen* ... Deutsch herausgegeben von Dr. Philipp Angust Petri, Bd. II, Berlin: Reimer, 1827. C.58f(2). *Checklist* A58/t1(2).

1827/-/-   *Ueber die Einführung des Christenthums*. In: *Religion und Philosophie in Frankreich* ... von F.W. Carové, Göttingen: Vandenhoeck und Ruprecht, 1827. C.59c. *Checklist* A59/t1.

1828

1828/02/11   Chambre des Députés. Vérification des pouvoirs. (Sur des élections). Séance du 11 février 1828. *Archives parlementaires*, LII, 600-601.

1828/02/15 Chambre des Députés. Vérification des pouvoirs. (Sur des élections). Séance du 15 février 1828. *Archives parlementaires*, LII, 664-665.

1828/02/20 Chambre des Députés. Vérification des pouvoirs. (Sur des élections). Séance du 20 février 1828. *Archives parlementaires*, LII, 710-713.

1828/02/21 Chambre des Députés. Vérification des pouvoirs. (Sur la situation des députés ajournés). Séance du 21 février 1828. *Archives parlementaires*, LII, 732-733.

1828/02/22 *Discours de M. Benjamin Constant à la Chambre des Députés*, Tome II, Paris: Dupont, 1828. Dépôt légal: 22 February 1828. C.132a(2). *Checklist* E2/1(2).

1828/02/28 Chambre des Députés. Scrutin pour l'élection de candidats à la questure. (Lettre de Benjamin Constant au Président de la Chambre). Séance du 28 février 1828. *Archives parlementaires*, LII, 736.

1828/03/06 Chambre des Députés. Sur le projet d'adresse au Roi. Comité secret du 6 mars 1828. *Archives parlementaires*, LII, 753-754.

1828/03/11 Chambre des Députés. Proposition de M. Benjamin Constant tendant à l'abrogation de l'article 4 de la loi du 17 mars 1822 concernant la censure. Comité secret du 11 mars 1828. *Archives parlementaires*, LIII, 31.

1828/03/11 Chambre des Députés. Proposition de M. Benjamin Constant tendant à mettre en harmonie avec la Charte les dispositions des lois du 21 octobre 1814 et du 25 mars 1822. Comité secret du 11 mars 1828. *Archives parlementaires*, LIII, 31-32.

1828/03/12 *Discours de M. Benjamin Constant à la Chambre des Députés*, Paris: Dupont, 1828. 2 vols. Dépôt légal: 12 March 1828. C.132b(1-2). *Checklist* E2/2.

1828/03/13 Chambre des Députés. Sur des propositions tendant à la suppression de la censure facultative. Comité secret du 13 mars 1828. *Archives parlementaires*, LIII, 65-67. Edition: *Développemens de la proposition ... tendante à supplier le Roi de proposer une loi qui abroge l'article 4 de la loi du 17 mars 1822 sur la censure facultative*, [Paris]: Imprimerie royale, mars 1828. C.127a. *Checklist* B64.

1828/03/14 Chambre des Députés. Développement par M. Benjamin Constant d'une proposition relative à l'imprimerie et à la librairie. Comité secret du 14 mars 1828. *Archives parlementaires*, LIII, 77-79.

1828/03/22 Chambre des Députés. Sur des élections. Séance du 22 mars 1828. *Archives parlementaires*, LIII, 143-144.

1828/03/25 Chambre des Députés. Sur des élections. Séance du 25 mars 1828. *Archives parlementaires*, LIII, 160-161.

1828/03/29 Chambre des Députés. Sur des pétitions relatives aux élections. Séance du 29 mars 1828. *Archives parlementaires*, LIII, 183-184.

1828/04/05 Chambre des Députés. Sur des pétitions relatives aux élections. Séance du 5 avril 1828. *Archives parlementaires*, LIII, 209-211. Edition (German translation): *Reden und Meinungen*, Strassburg: Schuler, 1828. C.133a. *Checklist* E2/t1.

1828/04/06 Chambre des Députés. Sur des propositions relatives au règlement. Séance du 6 avril 1828. *Archives parlementaires*, XXX, 607-612.

1828/04/19 Chambre des Députés. Sur la pétition du sieur Sarrat, à Paris, sur une question financière. Séance du 19 avril 1828. *Archives parlementaires*, LIII, 378. Edition (German translation): *Reden und Meinungen,* Strassburg: Schuler, 1828. C.133a. *Checklist* E2/t1.

1828/04/23   Chambre des Députés. Sur la proposition de M. de Conny relative aux députés fonctionnaires. Comité secret du 23 avril 1828. *Archives parlementaires*, LIII, 413.

1828/04/26   Chambre des Députés. Sur la pétition des sieurs Bissette, Volny et Fabien fils, à Paris, condamnés pour fait de tentatives séditieuses par la cour royale de la Martinique. Séance du 26 avril 1828. *Archives parlementaires*, LIII, 460-462, 463-464. Edition (German translation): *Reden und Meinungen*, Strassburg: Schuler, 1828. C.133a. *Checklist* E2/t1.

1828/04/28   Chambre des Députés. Sur le procès-verbal. Séance du 28 avril 1828. *Archives parlementaires*, LIII, 474-475. Edition (German translation): *Reden und Meinungen*, Strassburg: Schuler, 1828. C.133a. *Checklist* E2/t1.

1828/05/02   Chambre des Députés. Sur le projet de loi concernant la révision des listes électorales. Séance du 2 mai 1828. *Archives parlementaires*, LIII, 611, 614. Edition (German translation): *Reden und Meinungen*, Strassburg: Schuler, 1828. C.133a. *Checklist* E2/t1.

1828/05/03   Chambre des Députés. Sur la pétition du sieur Félix Mercier, suppléant destitué de la justice de paix de Rougemont (Doubs), demandant la révision des lois électorales qui rétablissent le double vote et la septennalité. Séance du 3 mai 1828. *Archives parlementaires*, LIII, 635. Edition (German translation): *Reden und Meinungen*, Strassburg: Schuler, 1828. C.133a. *Checklist* E2/t1.

1828/05/06   Chambre des Députés. Sur le projet de loi sur les listes électorales. Séance du 6 mai 1828. *Archives parlementaires*, LIII, 688-689. Edition (German translation): *Reden und Meinungen*, Strassburg: Schuler, 1828. C.133a. *Checklist* E2/t1.

1828/05/07   Chambre des Députés. Développement par M. Benjamin Constant d'une proposition relative à l'inscription au procès-verbal du nom des membres manquant aux appels nominaux. Séance du 7 mai 1828. *Archives parlementaires*, LIII, 702-704. Edition: *Développement de la proposition ... tendant à ce que les noms des députés qui n'auront pas répondu à l'appel, ni au réappel, sans être absens par congé ou pour cause de maladie, soient inscrits au procès-verbal*, [Paris]: Imprimerie royale, mai 1828. C.128a. *Checklist* B65. Edition (German translation): *Reden und Meinungen*, Strassburg: Schuler, 1828. C.133a. *Checklist* E2/t1.

1828/05/12   Chambre des Députés. Sur le projet de loi relatif aux listes électorales. Séance du 12 mai 1828. *Archives parlementaires*, LIII, 763, 765. Edition (German translation): *Reden und Meinungen*, Strassburg: Schuler, 1828. C.133a. *Checklist* E2/t1.

1828/05/14   Chambre des Députés. Sur le projet de loi relatif à l'émission de 4 millions de rentes. Séance du 14 mai 1828. *Archives parlementaires*, LIV, 57-59. Edition (German translation): *Reden und Meinungen*, Strassburg: Schuler, 1828. C.133a. *Checklist* E2/t1.

1828/05/17   Chambre des Députés. Sur la pétition des habitants de Sesseinheim (Bas-Rhin) demandant la destitution du maire de cette commune. Séance du 17 mai 1828. *Archives parlementaires*, LIV, 98-99. Edition (German translation): *Reden und Meinungen*, Strassburg: Schuler, 1828. C.133a. *Checklist* E2/t1.

1828/05/17   Chambre des Députés. Sur la pétition du sieur Pierre Grand, avocat à la Cour royale de Paris relative à la situation de la Basse-Bretagne (pétition présentée et distribuée à la Chambre par M. Benjamin Constant). Séance du 17 mai 1828. *Archives parlementaires*, LIV, 114, 116-117. Edition (German translation): *Reden und Meinungen*, Strassburg: Schuler, 1828. C.133a. *Checklist* E2/t1.

1828/05/20   Chambre des Députés. Sur le projet de loi relatif à la création de quatre millions de rentes. Séance du 20 mai 1828. *Archives parlementaires*, LIV, 153.

1828/05/21   Chambre des Députés. Sur le procès-verbal. Séance du 21 mai 1828. *Archives parlementaires*, LIV, 170-171, 172.

1828/05/24 Chambre des Députés. Sur la pétition du sieur Guillard, agrégé à Paris, demandant que les veuves des fonctionnaires de l'Université aient droit à une pension. Séance du 24 mai 1828. *Archives parlementaires*, LIV, 256. Edition (German translation): *Reden und Meinungen*, Strassburg: Schuler, 1828. C.133a. *Checklist* E2/t1.

1828/05/30 Chambre des Députés. Sur le projet de loi relatif à la presse périodique. Séance du 30 mai 1828. *Archives parlementaires*, LVI, 403-409. Editions: (German translation): *Reden und Meinungen*, Strassburg: Schuler, 1828; Pozzo di Borgo (1965), pp.164-184. C.133a. *Checklist* E2/t1.

1828/05/31 Chambre des Députés. Sur la pétition du sieur Marchand, avocat à Strasbourg, demandant l'abrogation du privilège exclusif du transport des lettres dont jouit l'administration des postes. Séance du 31 mai 1828. *Archives parlementaires*, LIV, 444-445. Edition (German translation): *Reden und Meinungen*, Strassburg: Schuler, 1828. C.133a. *Checklist* E2/t1.

1828/06/02 Chambre des Députés. Sur le projet de loi relatif à la presse périodique. Séance du 2 juin 1828. *Archives parlementaires*, LIV, 456-458. Edition (German translation): *Reden und Meinungen*, Strassburg: Schuler, 1828. C.133a. *Checklist* E2/t1.

1828/06/04 Chambre des Députés. Sur le projet de loi relatif à la presse périodique. Séance du 4 juin 1828. *Archives parlementaires*, LIV, 531-533. Edition (German translation): *Reden und Meinungen*, Strassburg: Schuler, 1828. C.133a. *Checklist* E2/t1.

1828/06/06 Chambre des Députés. Sur des élections. Séance du 6 juin 1828. *Archives parlementaires*, LIV, 549.

1828/06/09 Chambre des Députés. Sur le projet de loi relatif à la presse périodique. Séance du 9 juin 1828. *Archives parlementaires*, LIV, 605.

1828/06/10 Chambre des Députés. Sur le projet de loi relatif à la presse périodique. Séance du 10 juin 1828. *Archives parlementaires*, LIV, 622.

1828/06/11 Chambre des Députés. Sur le projet de loi relatif à la presse périodique. Séance du 11 juin 1828. *Archives parlementaires*, LIV, 656, 659. Edition (German translation): *Reden und Meinungen*, Strassburg: Schuler, 1828. C.133a. *Checklist* E2/t1.

1828/06/12 Chambre des Députés. Sur le projet de loi relatif à la presse périodique. Séance du 12 juin 1828. *Archives parlementaires*, LIV, 679, 681-682, 688-689. Edition (German translation): *Reden und Meinungen*, Strassburg: Schuler, 1828. C.133a. *Checklist* E2/t1.

1828/06/13 Chambre des Députés. Sur le projet de loi relatif à la presse périodique. Séance du 13 juin 1828. *Archives parlementaires*, LIV, 708-709. Edition (German translation): *Reden und Meinungen*, Strassburg: Schuler, 1828. C.133a. *Checklist* E2/t1.

1828/06/14 Chambre des Députés. Sur la mise en accusation des anciens ministres. Séance du 14 juin 1828. *Archives parlementaires*, LIV, 725-726.

1828/06/23 'A M. le rédacteur', *Le Courrier français*, n° 175, 23 juin 1828, p.2. *Checklist* D387.

1828/06/30 Chambre des Députés. Sur le budget des dépenses de de 1829. Séance du 30 juin 1828. *Archives parlementaires*, LV, 435-440. Edition (German translation): *Reden und Meinungen*, Strassburg: Schuler, 1828. C.133a. *Checklist* E2/t1.

1828/07/12 Chambre des Députés. Sur diverses pétitions. Séance du 12 juillet 1828. *Archives parlementaires*. LVI, 78. Edition (German translation): *Reden und Meinungen*, Strassburg: Schuler, 1828. C.133a. *Checklist* E2/t1.

1828/07/15   Chambre des Députés. Sur le budget des dépenses pour 1829. Ministère de l'intérieur. Encouragement aux lettres. Séance du 15 juillet 1828. *Archives parlementaires*, LVI, 135-136, 137. Edition (German translation): *Reden und Meinungen*, Strassburg: Schuler, 1828. C.133a. *Checklist* E2/t1.

1828/07/18   'A M. le Rédacteur', *Le Courrier français*, n° 200, 18 juillet 1828, p.2. *Checklist* D388.

1828/07/19   Chambre des Députés. Sur la pétition de M.Hue-Sallé, négociant à Orléans concernant l'administration des postes. Séance du 19 juillet 1828. *Archives parlementaires*, LVI, 241-243. Edition (German translation): *Reden und Meinungen*, Strassburg: Schuler, 1828. C.133a. *Checklist* E2/t1.

1828/07/25   Chambre des Députés. Sur le budget des dépenses de 1829. Ministère des finances. Séance du 25 juillet 1828. *Archives parlementaires*, LVI, 417-421. Edition (German translation): *Reden und Meinungen*, Strassburg: Schuler, 1828. C.133a. *Checklist* E2/t1.

1828/07/28   Chambre des Députés. Sur le budget des dépenses de 1829. Contributions indirectes. Séance du 28 juillet 1828. *Archives parlementaires*, LVI, 477.

1828/07/29   'Vote important dans la séance de ce jour', *Le Courrier français*, n° 211, 29 juillet 1828, p.1. *Checklist* D389.

1828/07/29   Chambre des Députés. Sur le budget des dépenses pour 1829. Postes. Séance du 29 juillet 1828. *Archives parlementaires*, LVI, 503.

1828/08/02   Chambre des Députés. Sur le budget des recettes pour 1829. Article additionnel de M. Dumeilet sur la publicité des dépenses départementales. Séance du 2 août 1828. *Archives parlementaires*, LVI, 627-628.

1828/08/11   'A M. le rédacteur', *Le Courrier français*, n° 224, 11 août 1828, p.2. *Checklist* D390.

1828/10/-   *Mémoires inédites*. Coulmann, *Réminiscences* (1869), III, 44-56. *Checklist* A65/1.

1828/12/13   *Adolphe, anecdote trouvée dans les papiers d'un inconnu, quatrième édition*, Paris: Dauthereau, 1828. Dépôt légal: 13 December 1828. C.18g. *Checklist* A18/7.

1828/12/26-27   'A M. le Rédacteur', *Le Courrier français*, n°ˢ 361-362, 26-27 décembre 1828, pp.1-2. *Checklist* D391.

1828/12/31   'A M. le Rédacteur', *Le Courrier français*, n° 366, 31 décembre 1828, pp.1-2. *Checklist* D392.

1828/-/-   'Une victoire sur la conscience. Fragment', *Annales romantiques*, 1827-1828, 1828, pp.209-210. *Checklist* D392a.

1828/-/-   *Reden und Meinungen der Deputirten des Niederrheinischen Departements. Session vom Jahr 1828*. Strassburg: Schuler, [1828]. C.133a. *Checklist* E2/t1.

1828/-/-   *Comento sulla scienza della legislazione di G. Filangieri; prima traduzione italiana, seconda edizione*, Italia, 1828. C.50d. *Checklist* A50/t3.

1829

1829/01/01   'A M. le Rédacteur', *Le Courrier français*, n° 1, 1ᵉʳ janvier 1829, pp.2-3. *Checklist* D393.

1829/01/01   'A M. le Rédacteur', *Le Courrier français*, n° 1, 1ᵉʳ janvier 1829, pp.3-4. *Checklist* D394.

1829/01/05   'A M. le Rédacteur', *Le Courrier français*, n° 5, 5 janvier 1829, pp.1-2. *Checklist* D395.

1829/01/11   'A M. le Rédacteur', *Le Courrier français* n° 11, 11 janvier 1829, p.2. *Checklist* D396.

1829/01/15   'A M. le Rédacteur', *Le Courrier français*, n° 15, 15 janvier 1829, pp.1-2. *Checklist* D397.

1829/01/17   'A M. le Rédacteur', *Le Courrier français*, n° 17, 17 janvier 1829, pp.2-3. *Checklist* D398.

1829/01/20   'A M. le Rédacteur', *Le Courrier français*, n° 20, 20 janvier 1829, pp.1-2. *Checklist* D399.

1829/01/27   'Comment le ministère aura-t-il la majorité dans la Chambre des députés?', *Le Courrier français*, n° 27, 27 janvier 1829, pp.1-2. *Checklist* D400.

1829/01/31   'De la répartition des voix part dans la Chambre', *Le Courrier français*, n° 31, 31 janvier 1829, pp.1-2. *Checklist* D401.

1829/02/02   'A M. le Rédacteur', *Le Courrier français*, n° 33, 2 février 1829, p.2. *Checklist* D402.

1829/02/06   'Réponse à la *Quotidienne* sur M. Daunou', *Le Courrier français*, n° 37, 6 février 1829, p.2. *Checklist* D403.

1829/02/08   'A M. Kératry, député de la Vendée', *Le Courrier français*, n° 39, 8 février 1829, p.3. *Checklist* D404.

1829/02/09   'De *la Quotidienne* et du général Saldanha', *Le Courrier français*, n° 40, 9 février 1829, pp.1-2. *Checklist* D405.

1829/02/15   'A M. le Rédacteur', *Le Courrier français*, n° 46, 15 février 1829, p.3. *Checklist* D406.

1829/02/19   Chambre des Députés. Sur l'ajournement de la proposition de M. Labbey de Pompierres relative à la mise en accusation de l'ancien ministère Séance du 19 février 1829. *Archives parlementaires*, LVII, 166.

1829/02/23   *Incipit*: 'Un correspondant de la *Gazette de France*', *Le Courrier français*, n° 54, 23 février 1829, pp.1-2. *Checklist* D407.

1829/02/26   'De la prétendue scission dont les journaux parlent', *Le Courrier français*, n° 57, 26 février 1829, pp.1-2. *Checklist* D408.

1829/03/05   'De la liberté de la presse suivant les journaux ministériels', *Le Courrier français*, n° 64, 5 mars 1829, p.1. *Checklist* D409.

1829/03/09   Chambre des Députés. Sur une proposition du général Demarçay relative à la commission du budget. Séance du 9 mars 1829. *Archives parlementaires*, LVII, 306-308.

1829/03/12   'A M. le Rédacteur', *Le Courrier français*, n° 71, 12 mars 1829, p.1. *Checklist* D410.

1829/03/18   *Mémoires sur les Cent Jours, en forme de lettres, avec des notes et documens inédits; nouvelle édition, augmentée d'une introduction*, Paris: Pichon et Didier, 1829. Dépôt légal: 18 March 1829. C.42d(1-2). *Checklist* A42/4.

1829/03/18   Chambre des Députés. Sur le projet de loi concernant le monopole du tabac. Séance du 18 mars 1829. *Archives parlementaires*, LVII, 469-478. Edition: *Opinion sur le projet de loi relatif à la fabrication et à la vente exclusive du tabac*, [Paris]: impr. Henry, 1829. C.129a. *Checklist* B66.

1829/03/18   Chambre des Députés. Sur l'examen préparatoire du budget. Séance du 18 mars 1829. *Archives parlementaires*, LVII, 489.

1829/03/20   'De la Séance de ce jour [19 mars 1829]', *Le Courrier français*, n° 79, 20 mars 1829, p.1. *Checklist* D411.

1829/03/20   Chambre des Députés. Sur le projet de loi relatif au monopole du tabac. Séance du 20 mars 1829. *Archives parlementaires*, LVII, 655-656, 662, 663.

1829/03/21   Chambre des Députés. Sur le procès-verbal. Séance du 21 mars 1829. *Archives parlementaires*, LVII, 675-77.

1829/03/25   'Déclaration de guerre du ministère contre la majorité de la Chambre', *Le Courrier français*, n° 84, 25 mars 1829, pp.1-2. *Checklist* D412.

1829/03/28   Chambre des Députés. Sur la pétition du sieur André, de Nanteuil (département de l'Oise) qui se plaint d'avoir été dépouillé du droit qu'il avait sur une étude de notaire. Séance du 28 mars 1829. *Archives parlementaires*, LVII, 715.

1829/03/28   Chambre des Députés. Sur une pétition. Séance du 28 mars 1829. *Archives parlementaires*, LVII, 721.

1829/04/06   Chambre des Députés. Sur le projet de loi sur l'organisation départementale. Séance du 6 avril 1829. *Archives parlementaires*, LVIII, 188-193. Pozzo di Borgo (1964), II, 125-144.

1829/04/06   'Des pétitions', *Le Courrier français*, n° 96, 6 avril 1829, p.1. *Checklist* D413.

1829/04/13   'A M. le Rédacteur', *Le Courrier français*, n° 103, 13 avril 1829, pp.1-2. *Checklist* D414.

1829/04/15   'Douleurs de certains journaux à l'occasion de la loi des postes', *Le Courrier français*, n° 105, 15 avril 1829, p.1. *Checklist* D415.

1829/04/18   Chambre des Députés. Sur la pétition des propriétaires de vignobles. Séance du 18 avril 1829. *Archives parlementaires*, LVIII, 427.

1829/04/21   Chambre des Députés. Sur le projet de loi relatif à la dotation de la Chambre des Pairs. Séance du 21 avril 1829. *Archives parlementaires*, LVIII, 482.

1829/04/22   Chambre des Députés. Sur le projet de loi relatif à la dotation de la Chambre des Pairs. Séance du 22 avril 1829. *Archives parlementaires*, LVIII, 517, 520.

1829/04/22   'Du déficit sur les produits du trimestre', *Le Courrier français*, n° 112, 22 avril 1829, pp.1-2. *Checklist* D416.

1829/04/23   'De l'extension de l'amendement de M. Sappey aux pensions au second et au troisième degré', *Le Courrier français*, n° 113, 23 avril 1829, p.1. *Checklist* D417.

1829/04/25   Chambre des Députés. Sur une pétition des anciens employés de l'administration des contributions indirectes relative à l'ordonnance du 21 janvier 1825. Séance du 25 avril 1829. *Archives parlementaires*, LVIII, 597.

1829/04/27   'A M. le Rédacteur', *Le Courrier français*, n° 117, 27 avril 1829, p.1. *Checklist* D418.

1829/04/29   'De la terreur qu'inspire aux journaux contre-révolutionnaires la possibilité d'une dissolution de la Chambre', *Le Courrier français*, n° 119, 29 avril 1829, pp.1-2. *Checklist* D419.

1829/05/01   *Incipit*: 'Les feuilles de la faction continuent leurs clameurs: continuons nos réponses', *Le Courrier français*, n° 121, 1ᵉʳ mai 1829, p.1. *Checklist* D420.

1829/05/02   Chambre des Députés. Sur la pétition du sieur de Parron, ex-percepteur des contributions à Clermont-Ferrand relative à une décision du Conseil d'Etat. Séance du 2 mai 1829. *Archives parlementaires*, LVIII, 693.

1829/05/02   *Incipit*: 'La commission du budget a nommé aujourd'hui', *Le Courrier français*, n° 122, 2 mai 1829, p.2. *Checklist* D421.

1829/05/04   Chambre des Députés. Sur des projets de loi relatifs aux crédits supplémentaires pour 1828. Séance du 4 mai 1829. *Archives parlementaires*, LVIII, 749-750.

1829/05/06   Chambre des Députés. Sur des projets de loi relatifs aux crédits supplémentaires. Séance du 6 mai 1829. *Archives parlementaires*, LIX, 27-28.

1829/05/07   'Coup d'œil sur la position actuelle', *Le Courrier français*, n° 127, 7 mai 1829, pp.1-2. *Checklist* D422.

1829/05/07   Chambre des Députés. Sur le projet de loi relatif aux crédits supplémentaires de la guerre. Séance du 7 mai 1829. *Archives parlementaires*, LIX, 43-44.

1829/05/08   'A M. le Rédacteur', *Le Courrier français*, n° 128, 8 mai 1829, p.1. *Checklist* D423.

1829/05/09   'A M. le Rédacteur', *Le Courrier français*, n° 129, 9 mai 1829, pp.1-2. *Checklist* D424.

1829/05/13   'De la responsabilité des ministres relativement aux lois adoptées', *Le Courrier français*, n° 133, 13 mai 1829, p.2. *Checklist* D425.

1829/05/15   'A M. le Rédacteur', *Le Courrier français*, n° 135, 15 mai 1829, p.1. *Checklist* D426.

1829/05/15   Chambre des Députés. Sur la pétition du sieur de Maubreuil, détenu à Poissy, demandant la révision de son affaire. Séance du 15 mai 1829. *Archives parlementaires*, LIX, 217-218.

1829/05/18   Chambre des Députés. Sur le projet de loi portant règlement définitif du budget de 1827. Séance du 18 mai 1829. *Archives parlementaires*, LIX, 272-275.

1829/05/19   Chambre des Députés. Sur le projet de loi portant règlement définitif du budget de 1827. Séance du 19 mai 1829. *Archives parlementaires*, LIX, 308-309.

1829/05/19   'A M. le Rédacteur', *Le Courrier français*, n° 139, 19 mai 1829, p.1. *Checklist* D427.

1829/05/20   Chambre des Députés. Sur le projet de loi portant règlement définitif du budget de 1827. Séance du 20 mai 1829. *Archives parlementaires*, LIX, 358-360.

1829/05/21   *Incipit*: '*Le Messager des Chambres* se plaint', *Le Courrier français*, n° 141, 21 mai 1829, p.1. *Checklist* D428.

1829/05/22   Chambre des Députés. Appel au règlement. Séance du 22 mai 1829. *Archives parlementaires*, LIX, 402.

1829/05/22   Chambre des Députés. Sur la pétition du sieur Lacroze, épicier à Raimbœuf, demandant la suppression du monopole du tabac. Séance du 22 mai 1829. *Archives parlementaires*, LIX, 408-409.

1829/05/23   *Incipit*: 'Le journal ministériel continue', *Le Courrier français*, n° 143, 23 mai 1829, p.1. *Checklist* D429.

1829/05/25   Chambre des Députés. Sur la proposition de M. Mauguin relative à la procédure pour la mise en accusation d'un ministre. Comité secret du 25 mai 1829. *Archives parlementaires*, LIX, 483-484.

1829/05/26   Chambre des Députés. Sur la proposition de M. Mauguin relative à la procédure pour la mise en accusation d'un ministre. Comité secret du 26 mai 1829. *Archives parlementaires*, LIX, 491-492.

1829/05/27   Chambre des Députés. Développement d'une proposition de M. Benjamin Constant relative au règlement. Séance du 27 mai 1829. *Archives parlementaires*, LIX, 513-514.

1829/05/29   'A M. le Rédacteur', *Le Courrier français*, n° 149, 29 mai 1829, p.1. *Checklist* D430.

1829/06/01   [Two letters by 'le Comte d' ...'], *Le Courrier français*, n° 152, 1er juin 1829, pp.1-2. *Checklist* D431.

1829/06/02   Chambre des Députés. Sur le budget des dépenses de l'exercice 1830. Séance du 2 juin 1829. *Archives parlementaires*, LIX, 693-705.

1829/06/06   Chambre des Députés. Sur la pétition du sieur Sachot, propriétaire à Gurey, département de Seine-et-Marne, demandant que les communes nomment leur maire et leurs conseils municipaux. Séance du 6 juin 1829. *Archives parlementaires*, LX, 83.

1829/06/07   'A M. le Rédacteur', *Le Courrier français*, n° 158, 7 juin 1829, p.1. *Checklist* D432.

1829/06/10   'A M. le Rédacteur', *Le Courrier français*, n° 161, 10 juin 1829, p.1. *Checklist* D433.

1829/06/12   Chambre des Députés. Sur le budget de 1830. Ministère de l'intérieur. Séance du 12 juin 1829. *Archives parlementaires*, LX, 269-273.

1829/06/13   Chambre des Députés. Sur la pétition du sieur Franque, avocat à Paris, demandant que les ministres soient obligés de s'expliquer, dans le délai d'un mois, sur les pétitions qu'on leur renvoie. Séance du 13 juin 1829. *Archives parlementaires*, LX, 301, 302-303.

1829/06/15   'A M. le Rédacteur', *Le Courrier français*, n° 166, 15 juin 1829, p.1. *Checklist* D434.

1829/06/16   Chambre des Députés. Sur le budget des dépenses de 1830. Ministère de l'intérieur. Bibliothèque du roi, Beaux-Arts, etc. Séance du 16 juin 1829. *Archives parlementaires*, LX, 386-387, 388, 392-393.

1829/06/17   Chambre des Députés. Sur le budget des dépenses de 1830. Ministère de l'intérieur. Dépenses secrètes. Séance du 17 juin 1829. *Archives parlementaires*, LX, 447, 449-450.

1829/06/18   Chambre des Députés. Sur le budget des dépenses de l'exercice 1830. Ministère de l'intérieur. Sur l'extradition des réfugiés. Séance du 18 juin 1829. *Archives parlementaires*, LX, 462-463.

1829/06/18   'Inconvéniens d'une éloquence facile', *Le Courrier français*, n° 169, 18 juin 1829, p.1. *Checklist* D435.

1829/06/20   Chambre des Députés. Sur la pétition du sieur Raynaud, instituteur protestant, demandant d'être réintégré dans son école, ou qu'on lui donnât une indemnité proportionnée au préjudice qu'il a éprouvé. Séance du 20 juin 1829. *Archives parlementaires*, LX, 529.

1829/06/22   *Mélanges de littérature et de politique*, Paris: Pichon et Didier, 1829. Dépôt légal: 22 June 1829. C.134a. *Checklist* E3/1.

1829/06/22   'A M. le Rédacteur', *Le Courrier français*, n° 173, 22 juin 1829, p.2. *Checklist* D436.

1829/06/24   'Sur la séance de ce jour, [23 juin 1829]', *Le Courrier français*, n° 175, 24 juin 1829, pp.1-2. *Checklist* D437.

1829/06/27   Chambre des Députés. Sur des pétitions. Séance du 27 juin 1829. *Archives parlementaires*, LX, 680.

1829/07/01   Chambre des Députés. Sur le budget des dépenses de l'exercice 1830. Ministère de la marine. Séance du 1er juillet 1829. *Archives parlementaires*, LXI, 10-14.

1829/07/04   Chambre des Députés. Sur la pétition des négociants de Lille demandant la suppression du monopole du tabac. Séance du 4 juillet 1829. *Archives parlementaires*, LXI, 74.

1829/07/05   'A M. le Rédacteur', *Le Courrier français*, n° 186, 5 juillet 1829, pp.1-2. *Checklist* D438.

1829/07/06   'Des attaques nouvelles qui se préparent contre le gouvernement représentatif', *Le Courrier français*, n° 187, 6 juillet 1829, pp.1-2. *Checklist* D439.

1829/07/07   Chambre des Députés. Sur le budget des dépenses de l'exercice 1830. Ministère des finances. Administration dans les départements. Forêts. Séance du 7 juillet 1829. *Archives parlementaires*, LXI, 159-160, 162, 163, 165.

1829/07/08   Chambre des Députés. Sur le budget des dépenses de l'exercice 1830. Ministère des finances. Article additionnel au budget des dépenses. Séance du 8 juillet 1829. *Archives parlementaires*, LXI, 177-178.

1829/07/08   'La Quotidienne grand seigneur', *Le Courrier français*, n° 189, 8 juillet 1829, p.1. *Checklist* D440.

1829/07/09   Chambre des Députés. Sur le projet de loi relatif à l'ouverture d'un crédit éventuel de 25 millions sur l'exercice de 1829. Séance du 9 juillet 1829. *Archives parlementaires*, LXI, 198-200, 200-201.

1829/07/11   Chambre des Députés. Sur la pétition du sieur Dufrezchède de Surzur (département du Morbihan), demandant qu'il soit pris des mesures pour améliorer le sort des esclaves dans les colonies. Séance du 11 juillet 1829. *Archives parlementaires*, LXI, 267, 268.

1829/07/13   'A M. le Rédacteur', *Le Courrier français*, n° 194, 13 juillet 1829, p.1. *Checklist* D441.

1829/07/14   Chambre des Députés. Sur le budget des recettes de 1830. Bourses de commerce. Séance du 14 juillet 1829. *Archives parlementaires*, LXI, 339.

1829/07/16   Chambre des Députés. Sur la pétition de divers marchands de Béziers réclamant contre les abus du colportage. Sur la pétition d'hommes de couleur de la Martinique et de la Guadeloupe demandant qu'une loi fixe leurs droits civils et politiques. Séance du 16 juillet 1829. *Archives parlementaires*, LXI, 404, 407.

1829/07/17 'A M. le Rédacteur', *Le Courrier français*, n° 198, 17 juillet 1829, pp.1-2. *Checklist* D442.

1829/07/22 *Incipit*: 'Je lis dans la *Gazette de France* ...', *Le Courrier français*, n° 203, 22 juillet 1829, p.2. *Checklist* D443.

1829/07/27 'A M. le Rédacteur', *Le Courrier français*, n° 208, 27 juillet 1829, pp.1-2. *Checklist* D444.

1829/07/28 'Des excès dans les luttes politiques', *Le Courrier français*, n° 209, 28 juillet 1829, p.1. *Checklist* D445.

1829/07/31 [Au rédacteur], *Le Courrier français*, n° 212, 31 juillet 1829, p.2. *Checklist* D446.

1829/08/07 'A M. le Rédacteur', *Le Courrier français*, n° 219, 7 août 1829, pp.1-2. *Checklist* D447.

1829/10/06 'A M. le Rédacteur', *Le Courrier français*, n° 279, 6 octobre 1829, p.3. *Checklist* D448.

1829/10/24 'A M. le Rédacteur', *Le Courrier français*, n° 279, 24 octobre 1829, pp.1-2. *Checklist* D449.

1829/10/- 'Réflexions sur la tragédie à l'occasion d'une tragédie allemande de M. Robert, intitulée *Du pouvoir des préjugés*, premier article', *Revue de Paris*, VII (octobre 1829), pp.5-21. *Checklist* D450.

1829/10/- 'Réflexions sur la tragédie ... deuxième et dernier article', *Revue de Paris*, VII (octobre 1829), pp.126-140. *Checklist* D451.

1829/11/05 'A. M. le Rédacteur', *Le Courrier français*, n° 309, 5 novembre 1829, pp.1-2. *Checklist* D452.

1829/12/21 'La Quotidienne prêchant pour les jeux', *Le Courrier français*, n° 355, 21 décembre 1829, p.1. *Checklist* D453.

1829/12/23 'A M. le Rédacteur', *Le Courrier français*, n° 357, 23 décembre 1829, p.1. *Checklist* D454.

1829/12/26-27 'Quelle conduite doit tenir la Chambre à la prochaine session?', *Le Courrier français*, n°ˢ 360-361, 26-27 décembre 1829, p.1. *Checklist* D455.

1829/12/29 'Quelle conduite doit tenir la Chambre à la prochaine session?', *Le Courrier français*, n° 363, 29 décembre 1829, pp.1-2. *Checklist* D456.

1829/-/- *Mélanges de littérature et de politique*, Bruxelles-Londres: Impr. Librairie Romantique, 1829. 2 vols. C.134b. *Checklist* E3/2.

1829/-/- *Œuvres diverses sur la politique constitutionnelle*, Paris: Aillaud, 1829. 2 vols. C.135a. *Checklist* E4/1.

1829/-/- *Die Religion, nach ihrer Quelle, ihren Gestalten und ihren Entwickelungen* ... Deutsch herausgegeben von Dr. Philipp August Petri, Bd. III, Berlin: Reimer, 1829. C.58f(3). *Checklist* A58/t1(3).

1830

1830/01/01 'A M. le Rédacteur', *Le Courrier français*, n° 1, 1ᵉʳ janvier 1830, pp.1-2. *Checklist* D457.

1830/01/05 'Un dernier mot sur le refus du budget', *Le Courrier français*, n° 5, 5 janvier 1830, pp.1-2. *Checklist* D458.

1830/01/07 'A M. le Rédacteur', *Le Courrier français*, n° 7, 7 janvier 1830, p.2. *Checklist* D459.

1830/01/12 'Vertige des journaux ministériels', *Le Courrier français*, n° 12, 12 janvier 1830, pp.2-3. *Checklist* D460.

1830/01/15 'De la prérogative royale', *Le Courrier français*, n° 15, 15 janvier 1830, p.2. *Checklist* D461.

1830/01/16 'Nouveaux axiomes de politique ministérielle', *Le Courrier français*, n° 16, 16 janvier 1830, p.1. *Checklist* D462.

1830/01/16 *Incipit*: 'En annonçant la correspondance de Garrick', *Le Courrier français*, n° 16, 16 janvier 1830, p.2. *Checklist* D463.

1830/01/18 'Seconde lettre sur la prérogative royale', *Le Courrier français*, n° 18, 18 janvier 1830, pp.1-2. *Checklist* D464.

1830/01/21 'De l'art. 14 et de la fausse interprétation qu'on lui a donnée', *Le Courrier français*, n° 21, 21 janvier 1830, pp.1-2. *Checklist* D465.

1830/01/31 'De la prérogative royale suivant la Charte', *Le Courrier français*, n° 31, 31 janvier 1830, p.2. *Checklist* D466.

1830/02/13 'Dernière lettre sur la prérogative suivant la Charte et sur l'inviolabilité du serment des rois', *Le Courrier français*, n° 44, 13 février 1830, p.2. *Checklist* D467.

1830/02/17 'A M. le Rédacteur', *Le Courrier français*, n° 48, 17 février 1830, pp.2-3. *Checklist* D468.

1830/02/21 'A M. le Rédacteur', *Le Courrier français*, n° 52, 21 février 1830, p.2. *Checklist* D469.

1830/02/22 'Prévisions prouvées par la *Quotidienne*', *Le Courrier français*, n° 55, 22 février 1830, p.2. *Checklist* D470.

1830/02/- 'Souvenirs historiques à l'occasion de l'ouvrage de M. Bignon. Première lettre', *Revue de Paris*, XI (février 1830), pp.115-125. *Checklist* D471.

1830/03/07 'Appels à la dictature inspirés par le ministère', *Le Courrier français*, n° 66, 7 mars 1830, p.2. *Checklist* D472.

1830/03/15 Chambre des Députés. Sur l'adresse au roi. Comité secret du 15 mars 1830. *Archives parlementaires*, LXI, 580. Pozzo di Borgo (1964), II, 151-154.

1830/03/19 'A M. le Rédacteur', *Le Courrier français*, n° 78, 19 mars 1830, pp.2-3. *Checklist* D473.

1830/03/22 'A M. le Rédacteur', *Le Courrier français*, n° 81, 22 mars 1830, pp.1-2. *Checklist* D474.

1830/03/23 'A M. le Rédacteur', *Le Courrier français*, n° 82, 23 mars 1830, p.2. *Checklist* D475.

1830/03/25 'Bruits répandus par la faction des absolutistes', *Le Courrier français*, n° 84, 25 mars 1830, pp.1-2. *Checklist* D476.

1830/03/- 'Aristophane', *Revue des Paris*, XV (mars 1830), pp.239-246. *Checklist* D476a.

1830/04/05 'Jugement de la *Gazette* sur le jugement prononcé contre elle', *Le Courrier français*, n° 95, 5 avril 1830, pp.1-2. *Checklist* D477.

1830/04/11 'Nécessité de connaître les députés qui ont voté l'adresse', *Le Courrier français*, n° 101, 11 avril 1830, pp.1-2. *Checklist* D478.

1830/04/14 'Aptitude des royalistes, suivant la *Quotidienne*', *Le Courrier français*, n° 104, 14 avril 1830, p.2. *Checklist* D479.

1830/04/16 'Plan du ministère en cas de conservation de la Chambre actuelle', *Le Courrier français*, n° 106, 16 avril 1830, p.2. *Checklist* D480.

1830/04/18 'Isolement progressif du ministère', *Le Courrier français*, n° 108, 18 avril 1830, p.2. *Checklist* D481.

1830/04/22 'De la liberté des élections suivant le ministère', *Le Courrier français*, n° 112, 22 avril 1830, p.2. *Checklist* D482.

1830/04/24 'Fausse interprétation de l'arrêt de la Chambre des mises en accusation de la Cour royale', *Le Courrier français*, n° 114, 24 avril 1830, p.1. *Checklist* D483.

1830/04/25 'A M. le Rédacteur', *Le Courrier français*, n° 115, 25 avril 1830, p.2. *Checklist* D484.

1830/05/01 'A M. le rédacteur', *Le Courrier français*, n° 121, 1er mai 1830. *Checklist* D485.

1830/05/07 'A M. le rédacteur', *Le Courrier français*, n° 127, 7 mai 1830, pp.1-2. *Checklist* D486.

1830/05/13 'De la palinodie de la *Gazette*', *Le Courrier français*, n° 133, 13 mai 1830, pp.1-2. *Checklist* D487.

1830/05/17 'A M. le Rédacteur', *Le Courrier français*, n° 137, 17 mai 1830, pp.1-2. *Checklist* D488.

1830/05/29 'A M. le rédacteur', *Le Courrier français*, n° 149, 29 mai 1830, p.3. *Checklist* D489.

1830/05/30 'A M. le Rédacteur', *Le Courrier français*, n° 150, 30 mai 1830, p.2. *Checklist* D490.

1830/06/07 'Titres d'un candidat ministériel', *Le Courrier français*, n° 158, 7 juin 1830, p.2. *Checklist* D491.

1830/06/09 'De la prétendue conspiration d'Orléans', *Le Courrier français*, n° 160, 9 juin 1830, pp.1-2. *Checklist* D492.

1830/06/13 'Des bulletins ouverts ou fermés suivant la *Gazette de France*', *Le Courrier français*, n° 164, 13 juin 1830, p.1. *Checklist* D493.

1830/06/16 'Manœuvres électorales', *Le Courrier français*, n° 167, 16 juin 1830, p.1. *Checklist* D494.

1830/06/18 'De la circulaire de M. Peyronnet', *Le Courrier français*, n° 169, 18 juin 1830, p.1. *Checklist* D495.

1830/06/19 *Incipit*: 'La Quotidienne recherche avec curiosité', *Le Courrier français*, n° 170, 19 juin 1830, p.2. *Checklist* D496.

1830/06/20 'A M. le rédacteur', *Le Courrier français*, n° 171, 20 juin 1830, pp.3-4. *Checklist* D497.

1830/06/29   'Des doctrines opposées du Journal Villèle et du journal Peyronnet, et de l'embarras de ce dernier', *Le Courrier français*, n° 180, 29 juin 1830, pp.2-3. *Checklist* D498.

1830/07/05   'Encore un mot sur les événemens de Montauban', *Le Courrier français*, n° 186, 5 juillet 1830, pp.1-2. *Checklist* D499.

1830/07/10   'Nouvelles propositions des journaux ministériels pour le changement de la loi des élections', *Le Courrier français* n°191, 10 juillet 1830, pp.1-2. *Checklist* D500.

1830/07/15   'De l'intervention populaire', *Le Courrier français*, n° 196, 15 juillet 1830, p.2. *Checklist* D501.

1830/07/16   'Des procès de tendance redemandés par l'*Universel*', *Le Courrier français*, n° 197, 16 juillet 1830, p.2. *Checklist* D502.

1830/07/18   'Du silence de l'*Universel*', *Le Courrier français*, n° 199, 18 juillet 1830, p.2. *Checklist* D503.

1830/07/20   'Nouvelle imposture de l'*Universel*', *Le Courrier français*, n° 201, 20 juillet 1830, *Checklist* D504.

1830/07/21   *Incipit*: 'Il y a des falsifications', *Le Courrier français*, n° 202, 21 juillet 1830, p.2. *Checklist* D505.

1830/07/24   'Des causes assignées au résultat des élections', *Le Courrier français*, n° 205, 24 juillet 1830, pp.1-2. *Checklist* D506.

1830/07/-   'Souvenirs historiques. Deuxième lettre', *Revue de Paris*, XVI (juillet 1830), pp.102-112. *Checklist* D507.

1830/07/-   'Souvenirs historiques. Troisième lettre', *Revue de Paris*, XVI (juillet 1830), pp.221-233. *Checklist* D508.

1830/08/05   Chambre des Députés. Vérification des pouvoirs. (Sur une élection). Séance du du 5 août 1830. *Archives parlementaires*, LXIII, 43.

1830/08/05   Chambre des Députés. Sur la nomination du Président de la Chambre. Séance du 5 août 1830. *Archives parlementaires*, LXIII, 47.

1830/08/06   Chambre des Députés. Sur la proposition de M. Bérard tendant à modifier la Charte. Séance du 6 août 1830. *Archives parlementaires*, LXIII, 59.

1830/08/07   Chambre des Députés. Sur la proposition de M. Bérard tendant à modifier la Charte. Séance du 7 août 1830. *Archives parlementaires*, LXIII, 62-63, 69, 74, 76.

1830/08/07   'A M. le Rédacteur', *Le Courrier français*, n° 219, 7 août 1830, p.4. *Checklist* D509.

1830/08/14   Chambre des Députés. Sur le projet de loi relatif à la revision des listes électorales et du jury. Séance du 14 août 1830. *Archives parlementaires*, LXIII, 128.

1830/08/19   Chambre des Députés. Vérification des pouvoirs. (Sur l'élection de M. de Murat dans l'arrondissement d'Hazebrouck). Séance du 19 août 1830. *Archives parlementaires*, LXIII, 177.

1830/08/19   Chambre des Députés. Vérification des pouvoirs. Sur la proposition relative au serment des fonctionnaires. Séance du 19 août 1830. *Archives parlementaires*, LXIII, 182.

1830/08/23   Chambre des Députés. Sur la proposition relative aux modifications à apporter au règlement. Séance du 23 août 1830. *Archives parlementaires*, LXIII, 220, 224, 225.

1830/08/25   Chambre des Députés. Sur le projet de loi relatif à la réélection des députés appelés à des fonctions publiques. Séance du 25 août 1830. *Archives parlementaires*, LXIII, 247-248.

1830/08/27   Chambre des Députés. Sur le projet de loi relatif à la réélection des députés promus à des fonctions publiques. Séance du 27 août 1830. *Archives parlementaires*, LXIII, 282, 284.

1830/08/30   Chambre des Députés. Sur le projet de loi ayant pour objet de pourvoir aux élections vacantes. Séance du 30 août 1830. *Archives parlementaires*, LXIII, 308.

1830/09/06   Chambre des Députés. Sur la prise en considération d'une proposition relative à une loi communale. Séance du 6 septembre 1830. *Archives parlementaires*, LXIII, 400-401.

1830/09/09   Chambre des Députés. Proposition de M. Benjamin Constant relative à l'exercice de la profession d'imprimeur et de libraire. Séance du 9 septembre 1830. *Archives parlementaires*, LXIII, 427.

1830/09/11   Chambre des Députés. Proposition de M. Benjamin Constant relative à l'exercice de la profession d'imprimeur et de libraire. Séance du 11 septembre 1830. *Archives parlementaires*, LXIII, 445-446.

1830/09/11   Chambre des Députés. Sur une pétition des sieurs Fabien et Bissette, hommes de couleur libres de la Martinique, demandant la mise en accusation des anciens ministres de Peyronnet, de Clermont-Tonnerre, et de Chabrol. Séance du 11 septembre 1830. *Archives parlementaires*, LXIII, 452.

1830/09/13   Chambre des Députés. Développement et prise en considération d'une proposition de M. Benjamin Constant relative à l'exercice de la profession d'imprimeur et de libraire. Séance du 13 septembre 1830. *Archives parlementaires*, LXIII, 484-485. Editon: *Développemens de la proposition de M. Benjamin Constant, sur la libre profession d'imprimeur et de libraire*, [Paris]: Imprimerie royale, septembre 1830. C.130a. *Checklist* B67.

1830/09/23   Chambre des Députés. Sur l'ordre du jour. Séance du 23 septembre 1830. *Archives parlementaires*, LXIII, 658.

1830/09/25   Chambre des Députés. Sur une pétition des commissaires-priseurs. (Sur la situation intérieure de la France). Séance du 25 septembre 1830. *Archives parlementaires*, LXIII, 667, 672-673.

1830/09/30   Chambre des Députés. Sur la proposition de M. Mauguin concernant la situation de la France. Séance du 30 septembre 1830. *Archives parlementaires*, LXIII, 741-742.

1830/10/04   Chambre des Députés. Sur le projet de loi adopté par la Chambre des Pairs déférant au jury les délits de presse et les délits politiques. Séance du 4 octobre 1830. *Archives parlementaires*, LXIV, 39.

1830/10/19   'Sur deux arrestations de la *Quotidienne*', *Le Courrier français*, n° 292, 19 octobre 1830, p.1. *Checklist* D510.

1830/10/22   'Avis à la *Quotidienne* et aux Carlistes', *Le Courrier français*, n° 295, 22 octobre 1830, pp.1-2. *Checklist* D511.

1830/10/22   'A M. le Rédacteur', *Le Courrier français*, n° 295, 22 octobre 1830. *Checklist* D512.

1830/11/05   Chambre des Députés. Sur l'élection du Président de la Chambre. Séance du 5 novembre 1830. *Archives parlementaires*, LXIV, 214.

1830/11/06   Chambre des Députés. Sur la proposition de M. Bavoux relative aux journaux. Séance du 6 novembre 1830. *Archives parlementaires*, LXIV, 271-273.

1830/11/09   Chambre des Députés. Sur la proposition de M. Bavoux relative aux journaux et écrits périodiques. Séance du 9 novembre 1830. *Archives parlementaires*, LXIV, 310-311.

1830/11/10   Chambre des Députés. Sur la proposition de M. Bavoux relative aux journaux et écrits périodiques. Séance du 10 novembre 1830. *Archives parlementaires*, LXIV, 324, 325.

1830/11/10   Chambre des Députés. Sur une citation signifiée au comte de Lameth. Séance du 10 novembre 1830. *Archives parlementaires*, LXIV, 334-335. Pozzo di Borgo (1964), II, 161-169.

1830/11/12   Chambre des Députés. Sur le projet de loi sur les récompenses nationales. (Sur les combattants de juillet). Séance du 12 novembre 1830. *Archives parlementaires*, LXIV, 352, 353.

1830/11/17   Chambre des Députés. Sur la proposition de M. Benjamin Constant, tendant à rendre libres les professions d'imprimeur et de libraire. Séance du 17 novembre 1830. *Archives parlementaires*, LXIV, 454.

1830/11/19   Chambre des Députés. Sur le projet de résolution relatif à l'affaire de M. Lameth. Séance du 19 novembre 1830. *Archives parlementaires*, LXIV, 493-494.

1830/11/20   Chambre des Députés. Sur la pétition du sieur Pibon, courtier à Bordeaux, demandant une loi qui abolisse les droits réunis. Séance du 20 novembre 1830. *Archives parlementaires*, LXIV, 510.

1830/11/20   Chambre des Députés. Sur la pétition du sieur Jullias de Nîmes, demandant qu'une loi rende l'instruction primaire gratuite dans toute la France, et que chaque commune en acquitte la dépense en ce qui la regarde. Séance du 20 novembre 1830. *Archives parlementaires*, LXIV, 515.

1830/11/25   Chambre des Députés. Sur le projet de loi sur la répression des délits de la presse. (Sur la répression des attaques contre la royauté). Séance du 25 novembre 1830. *Archives parlementaires*, LXIV, 638.

1830/11/26   Chambre des Députés. Sur une pétition du sieur Beyler et cinq autres habitants de Colmar, demandant l'intervention de la Chambre auprès du gouvernement pour faire rendre compte au sieur Scherb, maire de la commune de Niedermarschevikz, de sa gestion depuis 26 ans qu'il exerce des fonctions de maire. Séance du 26 novembre 1830. *Archives parlementaires*, LXIV, 670.

1830/12/09   Chambre des Députés. Lettre du 9 décembre 1830 de Charlotte de Constant au Président de la Chambre annonçant la mort de Benjamin Constant le 8 décembre 1830. *Archives parlementaires*, LXV, 396.

1830/12/12   'Funérailles de Benjamin Constant', *Le Courrier français*, n° 346, 12 décembre 1830, pp.2-3. *Checklist* D513.

1830/-/-   *Adolphe, anecdote trouvée dans les papiers d'un inconnu, cinquième édition*, Bruxelles: Hauman, 1830. C.18h. *Checklist* A18/8.

1830/-/-   *De la religion, considérée dans sa source, ses formes et ses développements*, vol. I, Paris: Pichon et Didier, 1830 Reissue. C.58e(1). *Checklist* A58/5(1).

1830/-/-   *De la religion, considérée dans sa source, ses formes et ses développements*, vol. II, Paris:

Pichon et Didier. Reprint. C.58e(2). *Checklist* A58/5(2).

1830/-/-   *De la religion, considérée dans sa source, ses formes et ses développements*, vol. III, Paris: Pichon et Didier, 1830. Reissue. C.58e(3). *Checklist* A58/5(3).

1830/-/-   *Mélanges de littérature et de politique*, Louvain: Michel, 1830. 2 vols. C.134c. *Checklist* E3/3.

1831/04/06   *De la religion, considérée dans sa source, ses formes et ses développements*, vols IV-V, Paris: Pichon et Didier, 1831. Prepared for the press before Constant's death in December 1830. Dépôt légal: 6 April 1831. C.58a(4-5). *Checklist* A58/1(4-5).

1833/04/10   *Du polythéisme romain*, ouvrage posthume de Benjamin Constant, précédé d'une introduction de M. J. Matter, Paris: Béchet aîné, 1833. 2 vols. Published from Constant's manuscripts on religion. C.63a. Dépôt légal: 10 April 1833. *Checklist* A63/1.

Appendix 1
Classified list of translations

Translations of correspondence (items F/t1-4) are not included in this list.

Arabic

1948 *Adolphe*, tr. Shams al-Dīn al-Ghuriyānī, Cairo: Maṭbaʿat Rīwāyāt al-Jayb. A18/t84a

Bulgarian

1903 *Adolphe*, tr. Iv. D. Stoynov, Sofia: Biblioteka. A18/t26
1921 *Adolphe*, tr. G. D. Yurukov, Sofia: Mozaika. A18/t45

Catalan

1912 *Adolphe*, tr. A. Esclasans, Barcelona-Badalona: Proa. A18/t32
1928 *Adolphe*, tr. A. Esclasans, Barcelona-Badalona: Proa. A18/t32
1982 *Adolphe*, tr. A. Esclasans, Barcelona-Badalona: Proa. A18/t32

Chinese

1958 *Adolphe*, tr. Tu Êrh Fu, Taipei: Hsin Hsing. A18/t98

Czech

1903 *Adolphe*, tr. R. Traub, Prague: Otty. A18/t23
1957 *Adolphe*, tr. J. Pospíšil, Prague: SNKL. A18/t96

Danish

1826 *Adolphe*, tr. J. J. Østrup, Copenhagen: Steen. A18/t5
[1907] *Adolphe*. A18/t27
1929 *Adolphe*, tr. K. Engel, Copenhagen: Woel. A18/t57
1946 *Adolphe*, tr. K. N. Christensen, [Copenhagen]: Andersen. A18/t79

Dutch

1799 *Des réactions politiques*, tr. J. G. H. Hahn, The Hague: van Cleff. A3/t2
1825 *Appel aux nations chrétiennes*, The Hague: Visser. A60/t1
1837 'De la liberté religieuse', Arnhem: Thieme. E1/t7
1877 *Adolphe*, tr. Busken Huet, Amsterdam: Funke. A18/t14
1888 *Adolphe*, tr. Busken Huet, Haarlem: Tjeenk Willinck. A18/t14
1911 *Adolphe*, tr. Busken Huet, Amsterdam: Wereldbibliotheek. A18/t29
1944 *Adolphe*, tr. H. van Tichelen, Hoogstraten: Modern Uitgeverij. A18/t74
1951 *Adolphe*, tr. Busken Huet, Amsterdam-Antwerp: Wereldbibliotheek. A18/t87
1954 *Adolphe, Cécile*, tr. Busken Huet and C. Serrurier, Amsterdam: Veen; Brussels: Reinaert. A18/t93
   Cécile, tr. C. Serrurier, Amsterdam-Antwerp: Wereldbibliotheek. A70/t6
1957 *Cécile*, tr. C. Serrurier, Amsterdam-Antwerp: Wereldbibliotheek. A70/t6

1960 *Adolphe*, tr. Plemp van Duiveland, Amsterdam-Antwerp: Contact. A18/t105
1961 *Adolphe*, tr. J. van Velde, Utrecht: Bruna. A18/t108
1962 *Adolphe*, tr. Plemp van Duiveland, Amsterdam-Antwerp: Contact. A18/t105
1967 *Adolphe, Cécile*, tr. Busken Huet and C. Serrurier, Amsterdam: Veen; Brussels: Reinaert. A18/t93
    Adolphe, tr. Plemp van Duiveland, Amsterdam-Antwerp: Contact. A18/t105
1969 *Adolphe, Cécile*, tr. Plemp van Duiveland and J. Fredric, Amsterdam: Contact. A18/t120
1978 *Adolphe*, tr. G. Pape, Wijnegem: Spectrum. A18/t127

English

1797 *De la force* ..., tr. J. Losh, London: Robinson. A2/t3
1815 *De la liberté des brochures*, London: *The Pamphleteer*. A12/t1
    De la responsabilité des ministres, London: *The Pamphleteer*. A14/t1
1816 *Adolphe*, tr. A. Walker, London: Colburn. A18/t1
1817 *Adolphe*, tr. A. Walker, Philadelphia: Carey. A18/t2
    De la doctrine politique, tr. T. E. Darby, London: Ridgway. A19/t1
181[7] 'Notice sur Mme de Staël'. C2/t1
1819 *Eloge de Sir Samuel Romilly*, tr. Sir T. C. Morgan, London: Colburn. A36/t1
1821 *De la dissolution de la Chambre des Députés*, London: *The Pamphleteer*. A46/t1
1838 *Mélanges* (extracts), tr. G. Ripley, Boston: Hilliard, Gray. E3/t1
[185-] *Christianisme*, tr. W. Maccall, Glasgow: Robertson. A59/t2
1867 *Eloge de Sir Samuel Romilly*, tr. W. H. Bennet, London: Routledge. A36/t2
1924 *Adolphe*, tr. P. Hookham, London: Philpot. A18/t51
1925 *Adolphe*, tr. J. Lewis May, London: Paul; Philadephia: McKay. A18/t54
    Adolphe, tr. P. Hookham, New York: Knopf. A18/t55
1933 *Adolphe*, tr. W. Lalor Barrett, New York: MacVeagh. A18/t64
1941 *De l'esprit de conquête*, tr. H.B. Lippmann, New York: Reynal and Hitchcock. A10/t3
1948 *Adolphe, Cahier rouge*, tr. C. Wildman and N. Cameron, London: Hamilton. A18/t82
    Adolphe, Cahier rouge (reissue of the preceding item), New York: Pantheon. A18/t83
1951 *Adolphe*, tr. J. M. Murry, London-New York: Nevill. A18/t88
1952 *Cécile*, tr. N. Cameron, London: Lehmann. A70/t2
1953 *Cécile*, tr. N. Cameron, Norfolk: Laughlin. A70/t4
1959 *Adolphe, Cahier rouge*, tr. C. Wildman and N. Cameron, Indianapolis: Bobbs-Merill. A18/t99
    Adolphe, Cahier rouge, (as preceding item), London: Hamilton. A18/t100
    Adolphe, Cahier rouge, (as preceding item), New York: New American Library. A18/t101
1964 *Adolphe*, tr. L. W. Tancock, London: Penguin. A18/t114
1980 *Adolphe*, tr. L. W. Tancock, London: Penguin. A18/t114

Finnish

1920 *Adolphe*, tr. L. Onerva, Helsinki: Karlsson & Jantunen. A18/t44

German

1796 *De la force* ..., tr. P. Usteri, Leipzig: *Klio*. A2/t1
    De la force ..., Lübeck: *Frankreich*. A2/t2
    Aux Citoyens représentans du peuple, Lübeck: *Frankreich*. B1/t1
1797 *Des réactions politiques*, Lübeck: *Frankreich*. A3/t1
    Des effets de la terreur, Lübeck: *Frankreich*. A4/t1
1798 *Discours au Cercle constitutionnel*, Lübeck: *Frankreich*. A6/t1.

1800 *Sur les victoires de l'armée d'Italie*, Lübeck: *Frankreich*. B8/t1
1814 *De l'esprit de conquête*, tr. J. J. Stolz, Hanover: Hahn. A10/t1
 Réflexions sur les constitutions, tr. J. J. Stolz, Bremen: Heyse. A11/t1
1816 *Adolphe*, Tübingen: *Morgenblatt*. A18/t1a
1817 *Adolphe*, Pest: Hartleben. A18/t3
1824 *De la religion*, vol. I, tr. P.A. Petri, Berlin: Reimer. A58/t1
1827 *De la religion*, vol. II. A58/t1
 Christianisme, tr. F.W. Carové, Göttingen: Vandenhoeck und Ruprecht. A59/t1
1828 *Reden und Meinungen*, tr. E. Stöber, Strasbourg: Schuler. E2/t1
1829 *De la religion*, vol. III. A58/t1
1831 *De la responsabilité des ministres*, tr. D. G. v. Ekendahl, Neustadt a.d. Orla: Wagner.
 A14/t2
1834-35 *Sämmtliche politischen Werke*, tr. F. J. Buß, Freiburg: Wagner. E4/t1
1836 *Réflexions sur les constitutions*, tr. F. J. Buß, Freiburg: Wagner. A11/t2
1839 *Adolphe*, tr. H. Künzel, Frankfurt am Main: Sauerländer. A18/t10
1844 *Du triomphe inévitable ...*, tr. A. Heller, Mannheim: Basserman. A49/t1
[1898] *Adolphe*, tr. J. Ettlinger, Halle: Hendel. A18/t21
1910 *Adolphe*, tr. O. Flake, Munich and Leipzig: Müller. A18/t28
1917 *Adolphe*, tr. O. Hauser, Weimar: Duncker. A18/t35
1919 *Adolphe*, tr. E. Schellenberg, Leipzig: Insel. A18/t39
 Journaux intimes, tr. F. Schwarz, Potsdam: Kiepenheuer. A66/t1
1942 *De l'esprit de conquête*, tr. H. Zbinden, Bern: Lang. A10/t4
1944 *Adolphe*, tr. W. J. Guggenheim, Zurich: Pegasus. A10/t75
1946 *De l'esprit de conquête*, tr. J. Ziwutschka, Vienna: Amandus. A10/t10-11
 Über die Freiheit, tr. W. Lüthi, Klosterberg, Basel: Schwabe. A4/t4
1947 *De l'esprit de conquête*, tr. H. H. Haußer, Heidelberg: Rausch. A10/t12
 Adolphe, tr. J. Ziwutschka, Vienna: Amandus. A18/t80
1948 *De l'esprit de conquête*, tr. H. Zbinden, Stuttgart: Reclam. A10/t13
1949 *Adolphe*, tr. L. Roth-Schlenk, Bühl/Baden: Roland. A18/t85
1955 *Cécile*, tr. H. Helbling, Zurich-Stuttgart: Fretz und Wasmuth. A70/t7
1956 *Adolphe*, tr. M. Voigt and R. Kilbel, Leipzig: Dieterich. A18/t95
1962 *Adolphe*, tr. W. J. Guggenheim, Munich: Goldmann. A18/t110
1963 *Adolphe, Cécile*, tr. M. Hölzer and H. Helbling, Frankfurt am Main: Insel. A18/t112
1965 *Adolphe*, tr. M. Voigt and R. Kilbel, Leipzig: Dieterich. A18/t95
1970 *Werke*, Bd. I-II, tr. E. Rechel-Mertens, Berlin: Propyläen. E4/t7
1972 *Werke*, Bd. III-IV. E4/t7
1982 *Adolphe*, (reprint of 1817 German translation), Munich: Winkler. A18/t130

Greek

1953 *Adolphe*, tr. P. Vovolinis, Athens: Kerameus. A18/t89

Hebrew

1970 *Adolphe*, tr. Ada Zemah, Tel Aviv: Dvir. A18/t122

Hungarian

1845 *Des réactions politiques*, tr. S. Halimbai [Perlaky], Pest: Trattner-Károlyi Betüivel.
 A3/t4
1862 *Cours de politique constitutionnelle*, tr. Sándor Perlaky, Pest: Trattner-Károlyinál.
 E1/t11
1886 *Adolphe*, tr. M.G. Béri, Budapest: Franklin-Társulat. A18/t16
1920 *Adolphe*, tr. Béla Zolnai, Budapest: Athenaeum. A18/t43

1943 *Adolphe*, tr. László Bóka, Budapest: Franklin-Társulat. A18/t73
1958 *Adolphe*, tr. László Bóka, Budapest: Európa. A18/t97
1979 *Adolphe*, tr. László Bóka, Budapest: Szépirodalmi. A18/t128

Italian

1820 *Entretien d'un électeur avec lui-même*, Lecce: Balsamo. A24/t1
     Cours de politique, tr. L.G.C., Naples: Nobile. E1/t2
1822 *Biographie universelle*. C1/t1
1823 *Biographie universelle*. C1/t1
1826 *Commentaire sur l'ouvrage de Filangieri*, Italia. A50/t2
1828 *Commentaire sur l'ouvrage de Filangieri*, Italia. A50/t3
1833 *Commentaire sur l'ouvrage de Filangieri*, Capolago: Elvetica. A50/t4
1835 *Adolphe*, tr. C. Bini[?], Leghorn: Vignozzi. A18/t9
     Portraits et souvenirs ... Venice: Il Gondolieri. C8/t1.
1838 *Commentaire sur l'ouvrage de Filangieri*, Capolago: Elvetica. A50/t6
1840-42 *Biographie universelle*. C1/t2
1841 *Commentaire sur l'ouvrage de Filangieri*, Brussels: Società belgica. A50/t7
1848 *Principes de politique*, Palermo: Muratori. A17/t1
1849 *Cours de politique*, tr. Galeffi, Florence: Monni. E1/t8
1850-51 *Cours de politique*, tr. Galeffi, Florence: Monni. E1/t9-10
1855-56 *Commentaire sur l'ouvrage de Filangieri*, Milan: Borroni e Scotti. A50/t8
1890 *Adolphe*, Naples: Pietrocola. A18/t17
     'De la liberté des anciens', tr. P. Fea, Turin: Unione Tipografico-Editrice. E1/t12
1903 *Adolphe*, tr. A. Polastri, Milan: Sonzogno. A18/t24
     Adolphe, Milan: Fratelli Treves. A18/t25
1914 *Adolphe*, Florence: Quattrini. A18/t34
1917 *Adolphe*, tr. L. Mazzucchetti, Milan: Istituto Editoriale Italiano. A18/t36
1923 *Adolphe*, tr. M. Bontempelli, Milan: Casa Editrice Milano. A18/t47
     Adolphe, tr. M. Bontempelli, Milan: Casa Editrice Imperia. A18/t48
     Adolphe, tr. M. Bontempelli, Milan: Bietti. A18/49
     Adolphe, tr. M. Ortiz, Florence: Sansoni. A18/t50
     Journaux intimes, tr. G. Gallavresi, Milan: Facchi. A66/t2
     'Lettre sur Julie', etc., tr. M. Ortiz, Florence: Sansoni. C8/t2
1928 *Adolphe*, Florence: Quattrini. A18/t56
1930 *Adolphe*, tr. F. Carbonara, Brussels: Psiche. A18/t59
1932 *Adolphe, Cahier rouge*, tr. F. Flora, Milan-Rome: Treves-Treccani-Tumminelli. A18/t62
1933 *Adolphe, Journaux intimes*, tr. G. Gerace, Turin: Unione Tipografico-Editrice Torinese. A18/t65
1934 *Scritti politici*, tr. S. Valitutti, Bologna: Cappelli. E4/t3
1941 *Adolphe, Journaux intimes*, tr. G. Gerace, Turin: Unione Tipografico-Editrice Torinese. A18/t65
[1943] *Cahier rouge*, tr. E. Emanuelli, Milan: Bompiani. A68/t2
1944 *De l'esprit de conquête*, tr. C. Botti, Turin: Einaudi. A10/t5
     Adolphe, tr. E. Emanuelli, Rome: Colombo. A18/t76
     Adolphe, Journaux intimes, tr. G. Gerace, Turin: Unione Tipografico-Editrice Torinese. A18/t65
     Mémoires sur les Cent Jours, tr. E. Emanuelli, Milan: Gentile. A42/t1
1945 *De l'esprit de conquête*, tr. E. Lecci, Milan: Denti. A10/t6
     De l'esprit de conquête, tr. S. Annino, Venice: Miuccio. A10/t7
     De l'esprit de conquête, tr. U. Ortolani, Rome: Atlantica. A10/t8
     De l'esprit de conquête, tr. A. Visconti, Milan: Ambrosiana. A10/t9
     Mémoires sur les Cent Jours, tr. E. Emanuelli, Milan: Gentile. A42/t1

1948 *Cours de politique*, tr. T. Mascitelli, Naples: Porcelli. E1/t14
1949 *Adolphe*, tr. M. Ortiz, Florence: Sansoni. A18/t50
1950 *Des réactions politiques*, tr. M. Fiore, Naples: Edizioni scientifiche italiane. A3/t5
1951 *Adolphe, Journaux intimes*, tr. G. Gerace, Turin: Unione Tipografico-Editrice Torinese. A18/t65
       Journaux intimes, Rome: Capriotti. A66/t3
1953 *Adolphe, Cahier rouge, Cécile*, tr. P. Bianconi, Milan: Rizzoli. A18/t90
1954 *Discorso sulla libertà*, tr. L. Nutrimento, Treviso: Canova. E4/t5
1956 *Adolphe, Journaux intimes*, tr. G. Gerace, Turin: Unione Tipografico-Editrice Torinese. A18/t65
1961 *De l'esprit de conquête*, tr. A. Donaudy, Milan: Rizzoli. A10/t14
1962 *Antologia*, tr. G. Zanfarino-Bonacci, Bologna: Il Mulino. E4/t6
1963 *Adolphe, Journaux intimes*, tr. S. de Simone, Turin: Unione Tipografico-Editrice Torinese. A18/t111
       Adolphe, tr. L.G. Tenconi, Milan: Leda. A18/t113
1965 *Principes de politique*, tr. U. Cerroni, Rome: Samonà e Savelli. A17/t3
1968 *Adolphe*, tr. O. Del Buono, Milan: A18/t118
1969 *Journaux intimes*, tr. P. Serini, Turin: Einaudi. A66/t4
1970 *Principes de politique*, tr. U. Cerroni, Rome: Editori riuniti. A17/t4
1977 *Adolphe, Cahier rouge, Cécile*, tr. L. Tullio, Milan: Curcio. A18/t126
1979 *Adolphe*, tr. T. Cremisi, Milan: Garzanti. A18/t129.
1983 *De l'esprit de conquête*, tr. C. Botti, Turin: Einaudi. A10/t5

Japanese

1934 *Adolphe*, tr. Kasho Shinjo, Tokyo: Shunyodo. A18/t66
1935 *Adolphe*, tr. Yukio Otsuka, Tokyo: Iwanami Shoten. A18/t67
1948 *Adolphe*, tr. Yukio Otsuka, Tokyo: Tancho Shobo. A18/t67
       Adolphe, tr. Kenichiro Hayashi, Tokyo: Sekai Bungakusha. A18/t84
1951 *Cécile*, Tokyo: Prou. A70/t1
1953 *Cécile*, tr. Keisaku Kubota, Tokyo: Shinchosha. A70/t3
1954 *Adolphe*, tr. Kasho Shinjo, Tokyo: Shinchosha. A18/t94
1960 *Adolphe*, tr. Takeshi Takemura, Tokyo: Kadokawa Shoten. A18/t106
       Adolphe, tr. Isamu Kurita, Tokyo: Tozai Gogatsusha. A18/t107
1964 *Adolphe*, tr. Toyota Ichihara, Tokyo: Chikuma Shobo. A18/t117
1965 *Adolphe*, tr. Yukio Otsuka, Tokyo: Iwanami Shoten. A18/t67
1969 *Adolphe*, tr. Fumihiko Takita, Tokyo: Chuo Koronsha. A18/t121
       Adolphe, tr. Toyoto Ichihara, Tokyo: *Sekai Bungaku Zenshu*. A18/t117
       Adolphe, tr. Toyoto Ichihara, Tokyo: *Chikuma Sekai Bungaku*. A18/t117
1975 *Adolphe*, tr. Motoo Ando, Tokyo: Shueisha. A18/t125

Norwegian

1894 *Adolphe*, tr. H. Christensen, Kristiania: Aschehoug. A18/t20

Polish

1831 *Cours de politique*, tr. W. Niemoiowski, Warsaw: Kuryer Polski. E1/t6
1917 *Adolphe*, Cracow: Gebethner; Warsaw: Gebethner & Wolff. A18/t37
1922 *Adolphe*, (revised edition of the preceding item). A18/t37
1930 *Adolphe*, Warsaw: Bibl. Boya. A18/t61
1932 *Cahier rouge*, tr. Tadeusz Żeleński (Boy), Warsaw: Bibl. Boya. A68/t1
1948 *Adolphe*, Warsaw: Wiedza. A18/t61
1957 *Adolphe*, Warsaw: Państwowy Instytut Wydawniczy. A18/t61

1980 *Journaux intimes*, tr. J. Guze, Warsaw: Czytelnik. A66/t5

Portuguese

1937 *Adolphe*, tr. Campos Lima, Lisbon: Guimarães. A18/t69
1947 *Adolphe*, tr. A. de Mesquita, Rio de Janeiro: Pongetti. A18/t81a
1968 *Adolphe, Cécile*, tr. M.J. Marinho, Lisbon: Portugália. A18/t119

Romanian

1858 *Adolphe*, tr. E. Drăghici, Jaşii. A18/t13
1898 *Adolphe*, tr. B. Marian, Craiova: Samitca. A18/t22
[1913] *Adolphe*, tr. S. Georgescu, Bucharest: Cartea românească. A18/t33
[1922] *Adolphe*, tr. T. Teodorescu-Branişte, Bucharest: Cultura natională. A18/t46
1924 *Adolphe*, tr. B. Marian, Bucharest: Alcalay. A18/t52
[1924] *Adolphe*, tr. Paul Ionescu, Bucharest: Lumina. A18/t53
1936 *Adolphe* tr. B. Marian, Bucharest: Alcalay. A18/t52
1945 *Adolphe*, tr. P. Rozopol, Bucharest: Enciclopedia Fotografică. A18/t78
1964 *Adolphe*, tr. T. Teodorescu-Branişte, Bucharest: Editura pentru literatura univer-
    sală. A18/t116
1973 *Adolphe*, Bucharest: Eminescu. A18/t124

Russian

1818 *Adolphe*, Orel: Provincial Press. A18/t4
1831 *Adolphe*, tr. N. A. Polevoy, *Moscow Telegraph*. A18/t7
    Adolphe, tr. P. A. Vyazemsky, St Petersburg. A18/t8
1886 *Adolphe*, tr. P. A. Vyazemsky, St Petersburg: Stasyulevich. A18/t15
1932 *Adolphe*, Moscow: Zhurn.-gaz. ob''ed. A18/t63
1959 *Adolphe*, tr. A. S. Kulisher, Moscow: Goslitizdat. A18/t104

Serbo-Croat

1883 *Principes de politique*, etc., tr. Dj. S. Simić, Belgrade: Royal Serbian State Press.
    E4/t2
1930 *Adolphe*, tr. I. Hergešić, Zagreb: Zaklade. A18/t60
1953 *Adolphe*, tr. I. Hergešić, Zagreb: Zora. A18/t91
    Adolphe, tr. N. Trajković, Belgrade: Novo pokolenje. A18/t92
1964 *Adolphe, Cécile*, tr. N. Trajković and C. Kotevska, Belgrade: Rad. A18/t115

Spanish

1820 *Cours de politique*, tr. M. A. López, Madrid: Sigüenza y Vera. E1/t1
1821 *Cours de politique*, tr. M. A. López, Bordeaux: Lawalle. E1/t3
1823 *Cours de politique*, tr. M. A. López, Bordeaux: Lawalle. E1/t4
1825 *Cours de politique*, tr. J. C. Pages, Paris-Mexico. E1/t5
    Commentaire sur l'ouvrage de Filangieri, tr. J. C. Pages, Paris-Brussels: Rosa. A50/t1
1828 *Adolphe*, Paris: Belin. A18/t6
1836 *Commentaire sur l'ouvrage de Filangieri*, tr. J. C. Pages, Paris: Librería Americana.
    A50/t5
1844 *Des réactions politiques*, Barcelona. A3/t3
1845 *Adolphe*, tr. P. Vidal, Barcelona: Borrás. A18/t11
1854 *Adolphe*, Madrid: 'Las Novedades'. A18/t12
1890-91 *Principes de politique*, tr. A. Zozaya, Madrid: Rodríguez. A17/t2

1892 *Adolphe*, tr. P. Vidal, Salamanca. A18/t18
1893 *Adolphe*, Madrid. A18/t19
1912 *Adolphe*, tr. R. Leval, Barcelona: López. A18/t30
    Adolphe, tr. R. Leval, Paris: Michaud. A18/t31
1918 *Adolphe*, tr. V. Clavel, Barcelona: Cervantes. A18/t38
1919 *Adolphe*, tr. P. Pérez, Madrid: Calleja. A18/t40
    Adolphe, tr. A. Espino, Madrid: Calpe. A18/t41
    Adolphe, tr. M. Abril, Madrid: Estrella. A18/t42
1924 *Adolphe*, tr. A. Espino, Madrid: Calpe. A18/t41
1929 *Adolphe*, Madrid: *Revista literaria*. A18/t58
1942 *Adolphe*, tr. F. Gutiérrez, Barcelona: Gráficas Marco. A18/t70
    Adolphe, tr. J. Z. Barragán, Barcelona: Maucci. A18/t71
1943 *Adolphe*, tr. L. Valle, Buenos Aires: Editorial Nova. A18/t72
    Cours de politique, tr. A. Zozaya, Buenos Aires: Americalee. E1/t13
1944 *Adolphe*, tr. A. S. Barbudo, Mexico: Leyenda. A18/t77a
1947 *Adolphe*, tr. J. B. Olivares, Buenos Aires: Sopena Argentina. A18/t81
1950 *Adolphe*, tr. A. Espina, Buenos Aires-Mexico: Espasa-Calpe Argentina. A18/t86
1953 *Cécile*, tr. S. Bullrich, Buenos Aires: Emecé. A70/t5
1961 *Adolphe*, Barcelona: Exito. A18/t109
1968 *Cours de politique*, tr. F. L. de Yturbe, Madrid: Taurus. E1/t15
1970 *Principes de politique*, tr. J. H. Alfonso, Madrid: Aguilar. A17/t5
1976 'Réflexions sur le théâtre allemand', Buenos Aires: Hachette. E3/t2

Swedish

1815 *De l'esprit de conquête*, tr. L. A. Mannerheim, Stockholm: Gadelius. A10/t2
1825 *Appel aux nations chrétiennes*, Stockholm: Nestius. A60/t2
1944 *Adolphe*, tr. C. I. Sandström, Stockholm: Natur och Kultur. A18/t77
1959 *Adolphe*, tr. C. I. Sandström, Stockholm: Natur och Kultur. A18/t102

Turkish

1935 *Adolphe*, tr. A. Kâmi Akyüz, Istanbul: Hilmi Kitapevi. A18/t68
1949 *Cahier rouge*, tr. Sona Tatlıcan, Istanbul: Millî Eğitim Basımevi. A68/t3
1959 *Adolphe*, tr. Samih Tiryakioğlu, Istanbul: Varlık Yayınevi. A18/t103
1973 *Adolphe*, tr. Samih Tiryakioğlu, Istanbul: Hayat Neşriyat Anonim Şirketi. A18/t123

Appendix 2
Bibliographical writings on Benjamin Constant:
a select list

See also items A18/42, A18/85, A18/101, A18/113 and A18/127.

Quérard, J.-M., *La France littéraire, ou dictionnaire bibliographique*, II, Paris: Firmin Didot, 1828, pp.274-276. See also continuation by Ch. Louandre et Félix Bourquelot, *La littérature française contemporaine, 1827-1844*, III, Paris: Félix Daguin, 1848, pp.57-58.

Rudler, Gustave, *Bibliographique critique des œuvres de Benjamin Constant*, Paris: Armand Colin, 1909.

Lanson, Gustave, *Manuel bibliographique de la littérature française moderne*, Paris: Hachette, 1913, pp.1000-1002. (Nouvelle édition, 1921).

Léon, Paul L., *Benjamin Constant*, Paris: Rieder, 1930, (Maîtres des littératures, 6). Bibliography, pp.91-93.

Talvart, H., et Place, J., *Bibliographie des auteurs modernes de langue française*, III, Paris: Editions de la Chronique des lettres françaises, 1931, pp.213-229.

Thieme, Hugo P., *Bibliographie de la littérature française de 1800 à 1930*, I, Paris: Droz, 1933, pp.477-481. See also continuations: S. Dreher et M. Rolli, *Bibliographie de la littérature française, 1930-1939*, Lille: Giard; Genève: Droz, 1948, p.101; Marguerite L. Drevet, *Bibliographie de la littérature française, 1940-1949*, Genève: Droz; Lille: Giard, 1954, pp.156-157.

Cordié, Carlo, *Gli scritti politici giovanili di Benjamin Constant (1796-97)*, Como: Carlo Marzorati, 1944. (Testimonia: Raccolta di testi e documenti per l'Insegnamento Superiore). Bibliography, pp.xxxiii-liv.

Cordié, Carlo, *Benjamin Constant*, Milano: Ulrico Hoepli, 1946. (I Propilei: Guide storico-letterarie a autori, scuole, movimenti culturali, 1). 'Bibliografia generale', pp.14-35; also includes bibliographical sections on individual works.

Roulin, Alfred [& Roth, Charles], (ed.), Benjamin Constant, *Œuvres*, Paris: Gallimard, 1957. (Bibliothèque de la Pléiade, 123). Bibliography, pp.25-32.

Pozzo di Borgo, O. (ed.), *Ecrits et discours politiques par Benjamin Constant*, Paris: Jean-Jacques Pauvert, 1964, 2 vols. Bibliography, vol. I, xix-xxx.

Cordié. Carlo Cordié, 'Contributo bibliografico sul gruppo di Coppet', *Annali della Scuola Normale Superiore di Pisa. Lettere, storia e filosofia*, Ser. 2, XXXIII (1964), 257-350; 'Secundo contributo', *Annali ...* XXXVI (1967), 103-135; 'Terzo contributo', *Annali ...* XXXVIII (1969), 129-148; 'Quarto contributo', *Annali ... Classe di lettere e filosofia*, Ser. 3, I (1971), 439-453; 'Quinto contributo' *Annali ...* VI (1976), 1017-1050.

Cordié, Carlo, 'La collaborazione di Benjamin Constant alla "Biographie universelle"', *Atti della Accademia della Scienze di Torino, Classe di scienze morali, storiche e filologiche*, CI (1966-1967), 411-457.

Cioranescu, Alexandre, *Bibliographie de la littérature française du dix-huitième siècle*, I, Paris: Editions du Centre national de la recherche scientifique, 1969, pp.580-589.

Constant, Benjamin, *Recueil d'articles: Le Mercure, La Minerve et La Renommée*. Introduction, notes et commentaires par Ephraïm Harpaz, Genève: Droz, 1972, 2 vols. (Travaux d'histoire éthico-politique, 22).

Constant, Benjamin, *Recueil d'articles 1795-1817*. Introduction, notes et commentaires par Ephraïm Harpaz, Genève: Droz, 1978. (Travaux d'histoire éthico-politique, 32).

Lowe, David K., *Benjamin Constant; an annotated bibliography of critical editions and studies, 1946-1978*, London: Grant and Cutler, 1979. (Research Bibliographies & Checklists, 26).

Hofmann, Etienne, *Bibliographie analytique des écrits sur Benjamin Constant (1796-1980)*, réalisée par Brigitte Waridel, Jean-François Tiercy, Norbert Furrer et Anne-Marie Amoos, sous la direction d'Etienne Hofmann, Lausanne: Institut Benjamin-Constant; Oxford: The Voltaire Foundation, 1980.

Courtney, C.P., *A bibliography of editions of the writings of Benjamin Constant to 1833*, London: Modern Humanities Research Association, 1981. (Publications of the Modern Humanities Research Association, 10).

Constant, Benjamin, *Recueil d'articles 1820-1824*. Introduction, notes et commentaires par Ephraïm Harpaz, Genève: Droz, 1981. (Travaux d'histoire éthico-politique, 35).

Courtney, C.P., *A bibliography of editions of the writings of Benjamin Constant to 1833. A supplement*, Cambridge: privately printed, 1984; second edition, revised, 1985.

Chronological index of editions

This index does not include items in sections D and F of the checklist.

General index

The index does not include the titles of Constant's speeches, which are listed in chronological order in section B of the checklist (see also E2/1-3) and in the chronology. The names of printers and publishers, and place of publication, are not listed for items in sections D and F. Items in the chronology are indexed only when they are not listed in the checklist.

Abbreviations: A = *Artist or engraver*; R = *Review or Reviewer*; T = *Translation or Translator*

Tiercy, Jean-François, p.293

Tiryakioğlu, Samih (T), A18/t103, A18/t123

Tissot, Pierre-François, *Fastes civils de la France*, D326(R); letter from Constant, F7

'Titres d'un candidat ministériel', D491

Tjeenk, H. D. Willink, publisher (Haarlem), A18/t14

Toccagni, Giuseppe, A50/t8

Toesca, Maurice, A18/129

Tokyo, A18/t66-67, A18/t84, A18/t94, A18/t106-107, A18/t117, A18/t121, A18/t125, A70/t1, A70/t3

Toronto, A18/39

Touquet, éditeur, Paris, petition of, p.249

Tozai Gogatsusha, publisher (Tokyo), A18/t107

Tradition, La, publisher (Paris), A18/73

Trajković, Nikola (T), A18/92, A18/t115

Transfuge Benjamin de Constant, Le, A15/1

Trattner-Károlyi, publisher (Pest), A3/t4, E1/t11

Traub, R. (T), A18/t23

Traynier, Jean (A), A18/79

Traz, Robert de, A18/43, A18/81(R)

Trésor des Lettres françaises, Le, publisher (Paris), A18/117

Treuttel et Würtz, publishers (Paris), A18/1-3, A58/1(1), A60/1-2

Treves, Fratelli, publisher (Milan), A18/t25

Treves-Treccani-Tumminelli, publishers (Milan and Rome), A18/t62

Treviso, E4/t5

Trognon, Alphonse, C6/1

Trois règnes de l'histoire d'Angleterre, by Sauquaire-Souligné, D184(R)

Troisième lettre à MM. les habitans du département de la Sarthe, A43/1, D256, E1/5

'Troisième lettre à un Député à la Convention', D3

Trompeo, P. P., A18/102

Tröttel, *see* Treuttel

Tu Êrh Fu (T), A18/t98

Tübingen, A18/t1a

Tullio, Lisa (T), A18/t126

Turin, A10/t5, A18/t65, A18/t111, A66/t4, E1/t12

Turnell, Martin, A18/t88(R)

Tyrrell, E. P., p.ix

Unione Tipografico-Editrice Torinese, A18/t65, A18/t111, E1/t12

Universel, L', D502-D505

Usteri, Paul (T), A2/t1

Utrecht, A18/t108

Valitutti, Salvatore (T), E4/t3

Valle, Luis (T), A18/t72

Valpy, A. J., publisher (London), A12/t1, A14/t1, A46/t1

Vandenhoeck und Ruprecht, publishers (Göttingen), A59/t1

Vandérem, Fernand, F188

Var (département), elections, D512

Varlık Yayınevi, publisher (Istanbul), A18/t103

Varnier, Alphonse, letter to Constant, F185

Vaucluse, protestants, D137

Vaulchier Du Deschaux, Louis-René-Simon, marquis de, letter from Constant, F298

Vauthier, Gabriel, F182

Veen, L. J., publisher (Amsterdam), A18/t93

Veillées littéraires illustrées, Les, A18/12

Velde, Jacoba van (T), A18/t108

Venice, A10/t7, C1/t1

Venturi, Franco, A10/t5

Verbe, Editions du, (Geneva), A68/5

Vercruysse, Jerôme, F292

Verly, letter from Constant, F192a

Véron, Louis, letters from Constant, F183, F304

Versailles, A74/3

'Vertige des journaux ministériels', D460

Vianey, Joseph, F209

Vibert, P.-E. (A), A18/35

'Victoire sur la conscience, Une', D392a

Vidal, P. (T), A18/t11, A18/t18

Vie de Mauvillon, p.209

Vienna, A10/t10-11, A18/4, A18/5, A18/t80

Viénot, John, C9/1

Vignozzi, Tipografia (Leghorn), A18/t9

Villèle, Jean-Baptiste-Guillaume-Joseph, comte de, D342(R), D498, E2/3; letter from Constant, D498, E2/1(2), E2/2(2), F233, F236, F279, F308

Villemain, Abel-François, C6/1

Villers, Charles de, letters from Constant, F2, F127, F164

Villet, Ch., publisher (Paris), C5/1

Vinaver, Eugène, A18/70

Vinogradov, V., A18/t63